THE ROLE OF CUSTOMARY LAW IN SUSTAINABLE DEVELOPMENT

For many nations, a key challenge is how to achieve sustainable development without a return to centralized planning. Using case studies from Greenland, Hawaii and Northern Norway, this book examines whether 'bottom-up' systems such as customary law can play a critical role in achieving viable systems for managing natural resources. Customary law consists of underlying social norms that may become the acknowledged law of the land. The key to determining whether a custom constitutes customary law is whether the public acts as if the observance of the custom is legally obligated. While the use of customary law does not always produce sustainability, the study of customary methods of resource management can produce valuable insights into methods of managing resources in a sustainable way.

PETER ØREBECH is a Research Scholar at the European Law Research Center, Harvard Law School.

FRED BOSSELMAN is Professor of Law Emeritus at the Chicago-Kent College of Law.

JES BJARUP is Professor of Law Emeritus at the University of Stockholm.

DAVID CALLIES is Benjamin A. Kudo Professor of Law at the University of Hawai'i at Manoa.

MARTIN CHANOCK is Professor of Law at La Trobe University, Melbourne.

HANNE PETERSEN is Professor of Greenlandic Sociology of Law at the University of Copenhagen.

THE ROLE OF CUSTOMARY LAW IN SUSTAINABLE DEVELOPMENT

PETER ØREBECH, FRED BOSSELMAN, JES BJARUP,
DAVID CALLIES, MARTIN CHANOCK
AND HANNE PETERSEN

CAMBRIDGE
UNIVERSITY PRESS

CAMBRIDGE UNIVERSITY PRESS
Cambridge, New York, Melbourne, Madrid, Cape Town, Singapore, São Paulo

Cambridge University Press
The Edinburgh Building, Cambridge CB2 2RU, UK

Published in the United States of America by Cambridge University Press, New York

www.cambridge.org
Information on this title: www.cambridge.org/9780521859257

First published 2005

Printed in the United Kingdom at the University Press, Cambridge

A catalogue record for this book is available from the British Library

ISBN-13 978-0-521-85925-7 hardback
ISBN-10 0-521-85925-5 hardback

To Vincent Ostrom

CONTENTS

PREFACE

Duncan A. French, in his book on the role of the state and sustainable development (2002), wrote: "For many developed States a key challenge is how to achieve sustainable development without a return to centralized planning, an anathema to most States with developed market economies." In this volume we propose that "bottom-up systems" like customary law play a role in the achievement of viable social systems.

This book is a compilation of contributions that was first debated during the Working Group meeting at Rockefeller Foundation Study and Conference Center in Bellagio (1999) on "The role of customary Law in a local self-governing sustainable development model." The group met in 2000 at Richardson School of Law, Honolulu and in 2002 at University of Tromsø, Norway for discussions on the prospects of customary law establishing sustainable societies.

Most of the chapters are the sole responsibility of one or two contributors. Jes Bjarup undertook the studies presented in Chapter 3; Fred Bosselman has written Chapters 1, 6, 11, and Section 10.1 as well as the introduction and the conclusion. David Callies is the author of Section 2.1 and Chapter 4; Martin Chanock the author of Chapter 8 and Section 9.8; Hanne Petersen of Sections 2.3 and 10.3; and Peter Ørebech of Chapters 1, 5, 7 and Sections 2.2, 9.1–9.7, 9.9, 10.2, and the introduction and conclusion.

Despite the many authors and their sole responsibility for their contributions, the chapters are in many ways linked together. Hopefully the reader will find at least one "red thread"!

ACKNOWLEDGEMENTS

Collaborators have contributed greatly to this project: first of all, Vincent Ostrom, who planted the seeds of self governing entities' production of normative structure as viable structures of resources management. He recommended that the Rockefeller Foundation provide research facilities at the Study and Conference Center in Bellagio (1999). Alan Berolzheimer and Juli Campagna provided very helpful editing assistance, and Jayne Hoffman and Juli Campagna helped out with the registries. The Chicago Kent College of Law's Cassandra Mehlum and Vince Rivera worked out textual discrepancies and shaped up the manuscript design.

Our gratitude goes to Rockefeller Foundation for support and offering great localities at Bellagio and The Norwegian Research Council for travels funding. Thanks also to the Norwegian College of Fisheries Science and University of Tromsø for sponsoring the 2002 event and to Chicago Kent College of Law for excellent working conditions. David Callies thanks his research assistant Emily Henderson, then a Ph.D. candidate, for her tireless research in the stacks of the Squire Law Library; Dr. Malcolm Grant, CBE, President and Provost of University College London but then Head of Department, Land Economy, for encouragement, advice and office space; David Wills, Dirctor, and Peter Zawada, Deputy Director, of the Squire Law Library for faculty privileges and research space; Professor John Baker, Fellow of St. Catharine's College for counsel and advice, and Clare Hall for meals, accommodation and fellowship, all during the two terms spent at Cambridge University in 1999 as a Visiting Fellow, preparing my contribution on customary law, and to Peter Ørebech for organizing the seminar at Villa Serbolini in Bellagio in early 1999 where our project commenced. Thank you all!

Peter Ørebech & Fred Bosselman

TABLE OF CASES

Bount v. Layard, Ch. 4.
Bourke v. Davis, 44 Ch. D. 110 (1889). Ch. 4
Marquis of **Breadalbane** v. McGregor, (1848) VII Bell 43. Ch. 4
Broadbent v. Wilkes, 125 Eng. Rep. 1214 (1742). Ch. 4
Brocklebank v. Thompson, 2 Ch. D. 344 (1903). Ch. 4
Bryant v. Foot, L.R.-3 Q.B. 497 (1868). Ch. 4
Byrd v. Wilford, 78 Eng. Rep. 717 (1596). Ch. 4

C

Chafin v. Betsworth, 83 Eng. Rep. 644 (1618). Ch. 4
Champneys v. Buchan, 62 Eng. Rep. 41 (1857). Ch. 4
The King v. Nicholas of **Chanceux**, 97 Selden Soc. 61 (1329). Ch. 4
Chassagnou & Others v. France, 7 BHRC 151 (1999). Ch. 4
Lord **Chesterfield** v. Harris, 2 Ch. 397 (1908). Ch. 4
Cole v. Hawkins, (1713) 10 Mod. 251. Ch. 4
Rt. 1985 s. 247 (Common Fisheries in Kaafjord). Ch. 2 (n. 129)
RG 1962 s. 262 (Common Grazing Case). Ch. 5
Concord Mfg. Co. v. Robertson, 25 A. 718, 721 (1889). Ch. 4
Continental Shelf (Tunis v. Libya), 1982 I.C.J. (Feb. 24). Ch. 7
Coote v. Ford 83 L.T.R. 482 (1900). Ch. 4
Corbin-Dykes Elec. Co. v. Burr, 500 P.2d 632, 634 (1972). Ch. 1
Coriton & Harvey v. Lithby, 86 Eng. Rep. 114 (1670). Ch. 4
Cort v. Birbeck, 99 Eng. Rep. 143 (1779). Ch. 4
State v. **Cozzens**, 2 R.I. 561 (1850). Ch. 4

D

Davis v. Trehane, 6 App. Cas. 460 (1881). Ch. 4
Day v. Savadge, 80 Eng. Rep. 235 (1614). Ch. 4
City of **Daytona Beach** v. Tona-Rama, Inc., 294 So.2d 73, 78 (1974). Ch. 4
Denn v. Sprey, 99 Eng. Rep. 1201 (1786). Ch. 4
Derry v. Sanders, 1 K.B. 223 (1919). Ch. 4
Devered v. Ratcliffe, 78 Eng. Rep. 442 (1590). Ch. 4
Devonald v. Rosser, 2 K.B. 728 (C.A. 1906). Ch. 4.
Drake v. Wigglesworth, 125 Eng. Rep. 1369 (1752). Ch. 4
Dyce v. Hay, 2 Ch. 538, 581 (1905). Ch. 4
Dyce v. Lady James Jay, (1852) 1 Macqueen 305; 19 Digest (Repl.) 15. Ch. 4

E

F

G

H

Parton v. Mason, 73 Eng. Rep. 440 (1561). Ch. 4
Payne v. Ecclesiastical Comm'r & Landon, 30 T.L.R. 167 (1913). Ch. 4
Payne v. Providence Gas Co., 77 A. 2d 145 (1910). Ch. 4
Pele Def. Fund v. Paty, 837 P.2d 1247 (1992). Ch. 2
In re **Porter**, 890 P.2d 1377, 1386 (1995). Ch. 4
Pub. Access Shoreline Hawaii v. Hawaii County Planning Comm'n, 903 P.2d 1246 (1995). Ch. 2

R

Rice v. Cayetano, 528 U.S. 495 (2000) (7-2 decision) (Stevens, J. & Ginsburg, J. dissenting). Ch. 2 & 10
Richards v. Dovey, 125 Eng. Rep. 1352 (1746). Ch. 4
Case Concerning the **Right of Passage** over Indian Territory (Port. v India), 1960 I.C.J. 6 (Apr. 12). Ch. 9
Roe v. Parker, 5 Term. Rep. 26 (1792). Ch. 4
Rogers v. Brenton, 10 Q.B. 26 (1847). Ch. 4
Rogers v. Pedro, 642 P.2d 549 (1982). Ch. 2
Rollesley v. Toft, (1495) 102 Selden Soc. 31. Ch. 4
Rowles v. Mason, 123 Eng. Rep. 829, 892 (1611). Ch. 4

S

Salforde's Case, 3 Dyer 357b (1577). Ch. 4
Scales v. Key, 113 Eng. Rep. 625 (1840). Ch. 4
Rt. 1896 s. 500 (Seaweed Sheds Case). Ch. 5
Selby v. Robinson, 2 Term. Rep. 758 (1788). Ch. 4
Simpson v. Bithwood, 83 Eng. Rep. 703 (1691). Ch. 4
Simpson v. Wells, 7 Q.B. 214 (1872). Ch. 4
Smith v. Archibald. Ch. 4 (n. 207)
Smith v. State of Md., 59 U.S. 71, 74–75 (1855). Ch. 2
Idaho v. **Southern Refrigerated Transp**., Inc., 1992 U.S. Dist. LEXIS 1869 (D. Idaho, 1991). Ch. 7
Sowerby v. Coleman, L.R.-2 Ex. 96 (1867). Ch. 4
Rt. 1972 s. 77 (Sperillen Case). Ch. 5
Steel v. Houghton, 126 Eng. Rep. 32 (1788). Ch. 4
Stevens v. City of Cannon Beach, 510 U.S. 1207 (1994) (7-2 decision) (Scalia, J. dissenting). Ch. 1
Swift v. Gifford, 23 F. Cas. 558 (D. Mass. 1872) (No. 13, 696). Ch. 1

T

Tanistry Case, 80 Eng. Rep. 639 (1608). Ch. 4
NJA 1981 p.357 (Taxed Mountain Case). Ch. 5
Taylor v. Devey & Graham. Ch. 4
Tennessee Valley Authority v. Hill, 437 U.S. 153 (1978) (6-3 decision) (Powell, J. and Rehnquist, J. dissenting). Ch. 5 (nn. 37 & 38)
State ex rel. **Thornton** v. Hay, 462 P.2d 671 (1969). Ch. 4
Traherne v. Gardner, 119 Eng. Rep. 721 (1856). Ch. 4
Rt. 1888 s. 682 (Trondheimfjord Mussels Case). Ch. 5 & 10
Rt. 1918 II s. 261 (Trysil Firewood Case). Ch. 5

U

Case 68/86 U.K. v. Council, 1988 E.C.R. 855 para. 24. Ch. 7

V

R. v. **Van Der Peet**, 1996 (137) D.L.R. 289. Ch. 8
City of London v. **Vanacre**, 12 Mod. 270, 271 (1699). Ch. 4
Rt. 1983 s. 569 (Vansjö Lake Case). Ch. 5 & 10
Vinkestone v. Ebden, (1698) 1 Ld Raym 384. Ch. 2 (n. 34)

W

Wake v. Hall, 8 L.R.-A.C. 195 (1883). Ch. 4
Wakefield v. Duke of Buccleuch, L.R.-4 Eq. 613 (1866). Ch. 4
Walmesly v. Marshall, 56 Eng. Rep. 647 (1628). Ch. 4
Warrick v. Queens Coll., Oxford, 10 L.R. Eq. 105 (1870). Ch. 4
RG 1967 s. 351 (Waste Dumping Case). Ch. 7
Weekly v. Wildman, 91 Eng. Rep. 1169 (1698). Ch. 4
Wilkes v. Broadbent, 93 Eng. Rep. 1146 (1745). Ch. 4
Lady Wilson v. Willes, 7 East 121 (1806). Ch. 4
Wolstanton, Ltd. v. Newcastle-under-Lyme Borough Council, 3 All E.R. 101 (1940). Ch. 4
Wyld v. Silver, 3 W.L.R. 841 (1962). Ch. 4

Y

Commonwealth v. Yarmirr, HCA 56, 2001 AUST HIGHCT LEXIS 48. Ch. 10
Yarmirr v. N.T. Austl., 1998 AUST FEDCT LEXIS 500 (AUST FEDCT, 1998). Ch. 10
Yielding v. Fay, Cro. Eliz. 569 (1594). Ch. 4

LIST OF INTERNATIONAL CONVENTIONS

A

Agenda 21 Programme of Action for Sustainable Development

Agreement for the Implementation of the Provisions of the UN Convention on the Law of the Sea of 10 December 1982 relating to the Conservation and Management of Straddling Fish Stocks and Highly Migratory Fish Stocks (MHLC)

Agreement on the Application of Sanitary and Phytosanitary Measures, Annex 1A to the Agreement Establishing the World Trade Organization (SPS Agreement)

B

Bamako Convention on the Ban of the Import into Africa and the control of Transboundary Movement and Management of Hazardous Wastes within Africa 1990

C

Cartagena Protocol on Biosafety to the Convention on Biological Diversity

Convention Concerning Indigenous and Tribal Peoples in Independent Countries (ILO No. 169)

Convention for the Prevention of Marine Pollution by Dumping from Ships and Aircraft

Convention for the Protection of Human Rights and Fundamental Freedoms (European Convention on Human Rights)

Convention on Civil Liability for Oil Pollution Damage

Convention on Long-Range Transboundary Air Pollution on Further Reduction of Sulphur Emissions 1979, 1994 Protocol thereto

Convention on the Protection and Use of Transboundary Watercourses and International Lakes (Helsinki Water Convention)

Copenhagen Declaration on Social Development

Convention on the Conservation and Management of Fisheries Resources in the South-East Atlantic Ocean 2000 (CC AMFR)

Convention on Conservation & Management of Highly Migratory Fish Stock in the Western & Central Pacific (MHCC)

D

Draft Articles on Responsibility of States for Intentionally Wrongful Acts

G

General Agreement on Tariffs and Trade 1994 (GATT)

I

ILA New Delhi Declaration on Principles of International Law Relating to Sustainable Development

International Convention for the Prevention of Pollution from Ships 1973

International Covenant on Civil and Political Rights 1966

J

Johannesburg Summit 2002

K

Kyoto Emission Control Provisions 1997 [Protocol to the UN Framework Convention on Climate Change]

N

North Atlantic Fisheries Convention 1980 (NEAFC)

R

Rio Declaration on Environment and Development 1992

U

United Nations Convention on the Law of the Sea (UNCLOS)

United Nations Draft Declaration on the Rights of Indigenous Peoples

United Nations Framework Convention on Climate Change

United Nations General Assembly World Charter for Nature

INTRODUCTION

FRED BOSSELMAN AND PETER ØREBECH

When the authors of this book told people that we were working on a book about customary law and sustainable development, we often encountered puzzled looks. A few people said, "What's sustainable development?" Many more asked, "What's customary law?" Others wondered how two such disparate topics could be related?

Chapter 1 begins by briefly discussing the meaning of each of the two phrases, and suggests the nature of the linkage between them. Here we raise the question of whether and under what conditions customary law might be looked to as a way of developing natural resources in a sustainable and precautionary manner. Recent research by Elinor Ostrom and others has called attention to the key role that common-pool resources play in sustainable solutions to natural resource management . Many customary law systems employ an intricate mix of public, private and common property concepts. Sometimes such a mix can better achieve sustainability in situations where a system that adamantly relied on private or public property alone may have failed.

Chapter 2 discusses three illustrative instances of the use of customary law in natural resource management in three different areas of the world: Hawaii, Northern Norway and Greenland. By putting the case studies up front, it is our intention not only to describe the conflicts briefly, but also to get in just "enough" law so that readers can proceed to the more detailed chapters of their choice. In each of these regions, the indigenous people established customary laws that regulated the use of natural resources. In later chapters, we will return to examine how those laws have interacted with modern civil or common law systems, and how that interaction has affected the sustainability of those resources.

Before Europeans came to Hawaii, the Polynesian people had developed a complex culture based on customary law. The islands were divided into pie-shaped territories ("ahupua'a") running from the center of the island to the sea. Each territory was under the jurisdiction of an ali'i, or a noble. Within each territory, the residents engaged in agriculture, raising products such as taro and yams. Hawaiian customary law allowed each resident of an ahupua'a to travel throughout the territory to engage in gathering activities. These activities included picking fruit, fishing, and hunting wild pigs. They also involved finding plants for medicinal or ceremonial purposes, and collecting firewood, thatching and house timbers.

Anyone engaged in legitimate gathering activities was allowed access to private land to the extent necessary to carry out the gathering activity. The king enforced rules, however, that limited both the types and the locations of certain gathering activities. These rules varied over time, but were apparently designed to conserve resources. Thus fishing might be restricted in certain seasons, and certain types of scarce plants were designated as forbidden ("kapu").

As Hawaii was absorbed into modern culture, the old gathering practices faded away. Today the State of Hawaii operates under a legal system similar to the other American states. The descendants of the Polynesians have not, however, been willing to give up their rights to engage in traditional gathering practices, and their demand to retain the rights of access to private property that prevailed under customary law is one of the main tenets of a movement to preserve Native Hawaiian culture. The conflict between this movement and the expectations of private landowners is being played out in the courts and legislature of Hawaii.

In Norway, the country's famous fjords heavily indent the coast. The Saami occupied and fished in the northernmost coastal areas once known as Lappland. Icy temperatures and typically rough seas discouraged extensive trips to distant fishing grounds. While Saami people most often settled near the fjord-bottom, Norse settlers used to dominate headlands and outer parts of islands and peninsulas. As the fish straddled deep into the fjords close to the shore, the Saami obtained much of their food from fishing in the fjords and nearby coastal waters. This system was protected under law until terminated by the new District Fisheries Act of Finmarken in 1830.

Over time, the Saami adopted improved techniques. They moved from oars to motors, from open to sheltered boats, from single hooks to long-line, gill nets and purse seines. Some also switched to trawling. They treated the ocean as a common pool, open to all who used the common fishing techniques. Newcomers were welcomed, and even given directions to good fishing areas, as long as they used typical fishing methods. No individual or group had a pre-emptive right to any particular fishing area, at least not after 1728. Over the centuries, these native fisheries never threatened stocks.

The development of larger-scale fishing technology created a conflict with Saami customary laws. Large trawlers with modern gear could take far more fish than was possible using traditional methods. In 1990, in order to protect the supply of fish, the Norwegian government introduced regulations limiting access to the common pool. These regulations, however, also governed traditional fishing. Saami fishermen have been unable to function effectively in this regulatory environment. They are dependent on subsistence fishing, and have not been able to meet the minimum catch requirement established by the fishing authorities as prerequisites for further fishing rights. Consequently many small-scale fishers are now denied full cod fishing rights by the government rules. The conflict between the Saami fishermen and the large-scale fishing interests has led Norwegian institutions to examine the appropriate role of customary law in Norway today. The Ministry of Justice recently published a report on this subject.[1]

Southern Greenland is at the same latitude as Norway. Greenland, unfortunately, does not enjoy the warming effects of the Gulf Stream. The vast majority of this huge island is covered by a massive ice cap, confining human occupation to the coast. Inuit people, closely related to the Inuits living in Canada and Alaska, have traditionally occupied these coastal areas. Living in a climate hostile to agriculture,[2] the Inuit developed an economy based on hunting. Whales, seals and caribou provided food, oil and skins for clothing, and bone for tools. Hunting these animals was an arduous activity most efficiently undertaken by groups. Large extended families traveled around the country to hunt different animals at different seasons. Under customary law, most forms of property were communal, shared by all members of the extended family, including foster children. The roles of men and women in traditional Inuit society were sharply delineated. Men did the hunting, which required great physical strength and endurance. Women prepared the products of the hunt; produced food and clothing; and collected water and fuel. Some of the women's responsibilities, such as cleaning and preparing sealskins, were viewed as quite unpleasant work.

As in Norway and Hawaii, globalization in Greenland has led to a decline in traditional practices. Fishing, originally a low status activity in the Inuit culture, has become economically attractive now that a number of fish processing plants have been built. Most of the employees of these plants are women, who often supply the only cash income in their household. Traditional hunting practices persist to some degree, especially in the more remote areas of Northern Greenland, but hunting has been impacted by international pressure to reduce the taking of whales and seals. Greenland obtained home rule from Denmark in 1979, so the Greenlanders themselves have dealt with the conflict between traditional customs and modern legislation. Their ambivalence toward retaining traditional rules reflects the distinct effects modernization has had on men as opposed to women.

In Chapter 3, Jes Bjarup emphasizes the key role of Thomas Reid, the leader of the "common sense" school of Scottish philosophy, in developing an intellectual foundation for customary law. Reid viewed knowledge as a communal enterprise among human beings actively engaged in the pursuit of understanding their common world. Other animals, said Reid, "cannot lay down a rule to themselves, which they are not to transgress, though prompted by appetite or ruffled by passion."[3] But humans have the cognitive capacity to introduce customs of conduct that can serve as legal rules, and to recognize that all members of society have some common interests that induce them to regulate their conduct by certain rules.

The formation of customary law is possible because humans have the capacity to engage in the intentional activity of making rules concerning the appropriateness of human conduct using customary beliefs of what is right or wrong. Reid's interpersonal approach recognizes that humans are rational and responsible individuals facing the task of developing structures to serve human ends. One way of doing this is for humans to act both rationally and communally to create valid rules of customary law that regulate the conduct of both themselves and others. This interpersonal perspective makes room for customary law as a separate and distinct procedure alongside legislation for the making of valid legal rules.

Chapter 4 explains the customary law prerequisites as elucidated in the Anglo-American legal systems. These prerequisites determine whether any disputed custom qualifies as customary law. In England's common law system, the courts long ago established specific rules for determining the validity of local customs. These rules were concisely summarized by William Blackstone, the widely read eighteenth-century treatise writer, and are often referred to as the "Blackstonian rules."[4] New research by David Callies detailed in this chapter shows that Blackstone's analysis accurately represented the court decisions of his time, and that the English courts continue to rely on a flexible version of the Blackstonian rules.

Some historians have assumed that because the original English rules required proof that a custom had existed since time immemorial, the idea of customary law must be obsolete in England. But modern English courts are more likely just to require solid proof of "long usage"[5] that has not been interrupted by any purposeful abandonment of the customary right. The modern English courts also continue to exercise the discretion to declare invalid any "unreasonable" custom or any custom that is so indefinite that it lacks certainty or consistency. Some American courts have also relied on the Blackstonian rules to uphold customary law, although their interpretation of the rules has sometimes been hard to square with either the original or the current English version.

In Norway, like many civil law jurisdictions, jurists and scholars recognize a number of legal sources,[6] including customary law, as pointed out in Chapter 5.[7] The Norwegian judicial rules for validating a custom as law are quite similar to the Blackstonian rules. They operate, however, in a rather different context from the Anglo-American one. Norway has a long tradition of codification and centralization, pursuant to which the government might simply confirm the legality of social norms without relying on any judicial input. This is accomplished either through legislation or by administrative rule. Some civil law countries, including Norway, have confirmed the superiority of customary law by expressly not overturning ancient customary law when writing new legislation.

Courts have occasion to evaluate the validity of customary laws only if they are disputed. Both civil and common law judges have needed rules for deciding whether particular customs qualified as "customary law," and they have applied the rules with a degree of flexibility through general criteria such as "reasonableness." The judges appear to be using an instrumental approach in evaluating particular customs;[8] that is, they attempt to predict the result of applying the customary rule, and then determine whether that result would be satisfactory.

Chapter 6 argues that all societies must react to the need for rapid legal change, especially as relates to environmental planning in communities under stress. Modern scholarship in law, management, economics and ecology emphasizes the need for resiliency and adaptability in resource management systems in the face of unpredictable future technological, environmental and cultural change.

In recent years there have been many case studies of particular examples of the use of customary law in natural resources management. In reviewing an extensive sample of these studies, Fred Bosselman concludes that a customary law process must meet five criteria if it is to have the resiliency to manage resources sustainably: (1) it must have recorded a history of successful adaptation; (2) it must provide a vehicle for making changes efficiently; (3) it must provide feedback mechanisms; (4) it must use fine-grained rules that are easily adjusted; and (5) it must create a balance of rights and responsibilities.

In Chapter 7, Peter Ørebech discusses the relationship of customary law to "bottom-up" democracy. In a democracy, rules should be transparent, predictable, determinate, coherent and consistent. He demonstrates that customary law meets all of these requirements. It embodies the democratic ideal in that it requires continuous public affirmation; if that fails, the traditional customary system is illegitimate and will not survive. New generations may opt for traditional solutions or may explicitly or tacitly reject them.[9]

In countries with a civil law tradition, a more positivist legal philosophy has often prevailed. Civil law countries have typically endeavoured to codify all legal rules. Such countries might be expected to be less receptive to laws based on custom than common law countries, where the gradual evolution of case law was a dominant element. Under the dominant paradigm of legal positivism, the status of legal authority granted to customary law was assigned little weight as a low priority source.[10] Sweden has clearly operated within this paradigm.[11] Other civil law countries that had originally been unreceptive to considering customary law as a primary principal source of legal authority have started to recognize its advantages.[12] Some of the legal arguments used to overcome medieval superstition demonstrate the lingering doubts held by legal positivists toward customary law. These arguments cleared the way for contractualism and exclusive state autonomy. Clearly a withering of the state would have perilous side effects. Concern over such an unlikely prospect, however, should not obscure an objective evaluation of customary law in the context of resource utilization and management strategies.[13]

Peter Ørebech compares the instrument of customary law with regulatory and market solutions. To what extent can we evaluate the effectiveness of such customary laws in comparison to distributive plurality decisions? A confident answer depends upon the conceptual design and the sustainability position within decision-making procedures. Generally it may be said that the substantive content of the customary law is not indifferent to the sustainability outcome. How people adapt to elements like internalization of externalities, personal responsibility and restoration are vital components in the process of obtaining viable resources.

In Chapter 8, Martin Chanock shows how international law and international commerce provide both opportunities and challenges for customary law in large parts of the third world. Colonial powers had delegated much of the legal administration of affairs among natives to local interlocutors. The justification for this delegation was the fiction that these backward people were applying only a static form of primitive law comparable to the ancient customs of tribal Europe. So to comply with this fiction the interlocutors had to create law that was adapted to new conditions while claiming to be old.

In the post-colonial era, the new nations often tried to use their customary law as a means of strengthening national identity. But because national boundaries reflected compromises among the colonial powers more than actual cultural unity, the new nations were usually faced with the problem of dealing with a multiplicity of groups with differing customs. Meanwhile, given the new opportunity to control the exploitation of their natural resources, many of these new nations opted for centralized control and became mired in corruption and lawlessness. In this context, the claims of local groups to rights under customary law became one of the few vehicles by which such groups could contest state power. Their customary law was not static; it used local customary processes to adapt customary law to changing conditions.

As many developing nations sought to maximize current income, at least for their elites, many groups within these countries became aware of the unsustainability of the exploitation of the country's resources. Tens of thousands of grass-roots agencies throughout the world, often working in cooperation with large Northern-based non-governmental organizations (NGOs), used the language of both custom and sustainable development in an attempt to decentralize control over natural resource management. Their objective was not to return to pre-market forms of social organization but to adapt customary processes to the new conditions of growing populations, globalizing markets, depleting resources and changing technologies.

Once customary law is seen as a process of indigenous natural resources management that embodies adaptive responses, and not merely inflexible traditions, its possibilities as a vehicle for sustainable management begin to seem more realistic. This does not suggest that customary law systems are inherently conservation- oriented. Instead, it suggests that in those countries where the sole alternatives are failing bureaucratic – or kleptocratic – states and rapacious international markets, the chances of a sustainable customary alternative may well be worth considering.

Chanock emphasizes that customary law will not be able to cope with today's world if it is viewed as the diametric opposite of the modern economy. Unlike Henry Maine's vision of custom as a pre-contractual exaltation of status, Chanock argues that customary law incorporates contract and always has. Contracts are formed in the context of custom, however. Institutional arrangements, which combine contract and custom, can provide both an individual basis for consent and responsibility and a cultural basis for determining the acceptability of measures to deal with new situations.

The concept of custom has always had a specialized usage in international law. Chapter 9 examines two ways in which international law is evolving in ways that strengthen the positions of both customary law and sustainable development.

First, international institutions are increasingly relying on international organizations and NGOs to establish and administer rules for natural resource management. Many of these international agreements incorporate sustainability objectives and precautionary principles, such as those found in the agreements relating to fisheries management. The 2002 Johannesburg Summit provides a basis for hope that these goals can be incorporated into agreements with broader applicability in the future.

Secondly, the international community has started to give greater recognition to the rights of indigenous peoples to create and employ their own rules for the territory that they occupy. Canada, New Zealand and Australia have been world leaders in recognizing the importance of lending validity to the customary laws of indigenous peoples. It remains to be seen whether other countries will follow suit.

Chapter 10 returns to the three case studies outlined in Chapter 2. Hawaii, Norway and Greenland illustrate three different ways in which modern governments can react to customary laws that relate to natural resources: retention, rejection and modification. Unlike the failing states discussed in Chapter 8, each of the case studies involves the integration of customary law into a sophisticated legal system of a democratic government – a context that provides some basis for optimism. Nevertheless, the wide-ranging differences among customary law systems, and among the governments that are affected by them, suggest the need for a continuing program of research into customary law.[14]

Chapter 11 compares the many and varied reasons why policy makers decide to implement customary law. Chief amongst these are empowerment, cooperation, innovation and data collection. Indigenous and other local knowledge-source groups are much more likely to cooperate and share their wisdom with resource managers if their practices are integrated into conservation projects and when they participate in the environmental law-making and law-interpreting process.

Chapter 11 further emphasizes a key point discussed throughout the book. Customary law is not a panacea. This chapter argues against some of the flawed reasoning behind customary law choices that can actually have adverse effects on sustainable development. Both nostalgia and privatization appeal to a sense that modern life and government control have gotten out of hand. Appeals to customary law systems must be based on rational analysis, and not on ideological sentiment. Those who wish to dominate or exclude other ethnic or user groups sometimes seek to bolster their claims with customary law arguments. Inequities based in custom, however, are no different from those imposed by positive law – injustice in search of legitimization.

Finally, Chapter 12 offers the authors' conclusions and suggestions for further research. The study of customary law's potential for improving the sustainability of development is in its infancy. It deserves careful attention from objective observers who can analyze why it often works and often does not.

We intend to take up the challenge of construing alternatives to "governmental control and command." Duncan A. French said: "For many developed States a key challenge is how to achieve sustainable development without a return to centralized planning, an anathema to most States with developed market economies."[15] This book proposes that "bottom-up systems" – practices that develop customary law systems – play a critical role in achieving viable social systems. It is all about local practices serving as examples of conduct that meet our obligations toward future generations.

Charles E. Larmore states that "Examples, it is urged, have the task of persuading us to do our duty. They excite the imagination and the passions in a way in which, supposedly, moral rules and reason in general are less able to do; and since most of us are not motivated most of the time by rules and reason alone, examples serve an indispensable function."[16] People rely on examples when deciding how to act. Examples play a considerable role in moral deliberation.[17] Only good practices, however, become acknowledged customary law. We believe that Joseph L. Sax is right to assert that still valid, ancient usage reflects "a scientific, knowledge-based recognition of the importance of estuaries and wildlife, of diversity and biological productivity, and of the possibilities for sustainable development."[18] Science is constantly revealing new truths about the web of life through validated ecological findings. These discoveries often confirm the ancient practices embodied in customary law.

It should be said that the chapters can be read alone or in any sequence that might interest the reader. Our intent is that the chapters be more connected than just some collection of short stories; our hope is that they contribute constructively to each other. On the other hand, any single chapter may stand alone as well. They are all critical links in the chain that is being forged between the legal institution of customary law and the political norm of sustainability.

Endnotes

1. NOU Peter Ørebech, *Sedvanerett i fisket. Sjøsamene i Finnmark* [*Fisheries Customary Law. The Coastal Saami*] (Statens forvaltningstjeneste, Oslo, 2001), p. 34.
2. The Norse settlers in Greenland grew barley during the fourteenth century, but when temperatures dropped sometime around the sixteenth century, this population vanished.
3. Thomas Reid, *Essays on the Active Powers of Man*, in *The Works of Thomas Reid* (ed. by Sir William Hamilton, reprint with intro. by Harry M. Bracken, Georg Olms Verlag, Hildesheim, 1983), Essay III, Part III, Ch. VIII, p. 596b.
4. Sir William Blackstone, *Commentaries on the Laws of England* (London, John Murray, 1857), vol. 1.
5. See e.g., *New Windsor Corp. v. Mellor*, [1974] 2 All ER 510, 511. See discussion at pp. 166–170 below.
6. Paul Ricoeur, "The Plurality of Sources of Law" (1994) *Ratio Juris* vol. 7, no. 3, pp. 272–286.
7. "Customary law is among these sources. Law and custom interact, but neither can be fully reduced to the other." Ekkehart Schlicht, *On Custom in the Economy* (Clarendon Press, Oxford, 1998), p. 191.
8. "An instrumentalist judge will see himself or herself as an officer of government charged with contributing to the good society according to his or her conception of what that is." Dale Nance, *Law & Justice* (1st edn., Carolina Academic Press, Durham, 1994), p. 88.
9. For example, Papua New Guinea adopted a constitution that provides that the courts should treat local custom as law in preference to imported common law, while the neighboring Solomon Islands have made proof of custom quite difficult. Jennifer Corrin Care and Jean G. Zorn, "Statutory Developments in Melanesian Customary Law" (2001) *Journal of Legal Pluralism*, vol. 46, p. 50. See also Manfred O. Hinz, "The Conflict between the Constitution and Customary Law – Conflicts between System and Concepts," in Karin Fisher-Buder (ed.), *Human Rights and Democracy in Southern Africa* (New Namibia Books, Windhoek, 1998), p. 168 ("Both the customary law and the common law of Namibia in force on the date of Independence shall remain valid . . .").

10. See pages 224–230 and 289–296 below.
11. Bertil Bengtsson, "Epilog," in Birgitta Jahreskog (ed.), *The Saami National Minority in Sweden* (Rättsfonden, Stockholm, 1982), p. 250.
12. See pages 305–306 below.
13. Leon Sheleff, *The Future of Tradition. Customary Law, Common Law, and Legal Pluralism* (Frank Cass, London, 2000), pp. 55–75.
14. We extend the legal historical approach taken by Peter Karsten, *Between Law and Custom* (Cambridge University Press, Cambridge, 2002) into the societies of today, within as well as without areas of British influence.
15. Duncan A. French, "The Role of the State and International Organizations in Reconciling Sustainable Development and Globalization" (2002) *International Environmental Agreements: Politics, Law and Economics* 135, at 141.
16. Charles E. Larmore, *Patterns of Moral Complexity* (Cambridge University Press, Cambridge, 1987), p. 1.
17. This is what Charles E. Larmore, above note 16, at pp. 5–14 describes as "the centrality of judgment."
18. Joseph L. Sax, "The Limits of Private Rights in Public Waters" (1989) *Environmental Law* vol. 19, 473, at 476.

1

The linkage between sustainable development and customary law

PETER ØREBECH AND FRED BOSSELMAN

The authors of this book believe that the role customary law plays in the sustainable development of natural resources deserves more study than it has received. Too often, customary law has been dismissed as an ancient body of doctrine that is of interest only to legal historians, but customary law *lives.*[1] This book looks at both the potential benefits and the potential risks that customary law may pose for sustainable development.

Because neither "customary law" nor "sustainable development" is a term so familiar to most readers that it needs no definition, we will begin by defining each of these terms and explaining how they relate to each other.

1.1 Sustainable development

Implicit in most of western, public environmental goals for the management of natural resources is the idea that the current generation wants future generations to be able to benefit from such resources in much the same way that we have. The goal is to develop our natural resources, but to do so in a way that does not permanently destroy them. Responsible governments hope to utilize our resources in a manner that can be continued indefinitely without making future generations suffer from lack of soil, water, energy and other vital resources. This idea of "conservation" has a long history, but the use of the terms "sustainable development" and "precautionary principle" to describe it is quite new. These concepts address a key question for environmental managers: how should policies be decided in the face of scientific uncertainty?

In this chapter the task is to investigate sustainable development as a political goal, and the precautionary principle as a legal instrument towards that goal. From mere ideas and notions, political and juridical norms are developing. We have concentrated our efforts on considering how these concepts developed from their early days of pure ideal existence through a phase of political norms, into their present legal position.

The sustainable and precautionary terminology arose out of the desire to harmonize the objectives of the early environmental movement of the 1970s with the aspirations of third world nations that were seeking to improve their economies. These countries often listened suspiciously to the rhetoric of environmental groups and thought they heard the elite of the prosperous countries trying to keep the developing countries from catching up by denying them a role in the industrialization that caused that prosperity.

The huge differences in the standard of living among the various countries gave credence to that argument. The United States and the major nations of Europe symbolized to many in the developing world the kind of rich country that they hoped to someday become. European and American exhortations about the importance of environmental protection were particularly resented by those who thought that developed countries could far more easily forego a measure of economic advancement than could poorer countries.[2] Thus the inequality of the current distribution of resources weakened the effect of the environmental argument.

On the other hand, analysts from developing countries recognized that intergenerational distribution arguments applied as effectively to poor nations as to rich nations. If Zambia uses up its resources today, what will its children have tomorrow? Diplomats sought to combine the developing countries' desire for progress with their recognition of the risks of over-development.

A United Nations commission chaired by former Prime Minister Brundtland of Norway issued a report that identified the concept of sustainable development as one that would be acceptable to both the developed and developing nations. The report emphasized that economic growth was good, as long as it was done in a way that did not lead to deprivation for future generations. The Commission defined sustainable development as "development that meets the needs of the present without compromising the ability of future generations to meet their own needs."[3] Despite the rather imprecise nature of this objective, the mainstream environmental organizations lent their support, and sustainable development soon became a widely accepted objective for the management of natural resources.[4]

Sustainability "requires that the system of law must be transformed into an open and flexible system in continual communication with societal development."[5] Some would say that sustainability is a *paradigm* elucidated through practice. Consequently this paradigm "relies less on what is said about it by way of verbal definition than what is done on its behalf by way of alternative practices."[6] In terms of management theory it is a question of "adaptive management ethics."[7]

Clearly the concept has changed during the years, making it possible to cite a "gallery of definitions."[8] The notion of "sustainable development has the function of a 'meta-fix' that will unite everybody."[9] As members of the United Nations argue, most states of the world are obliged, at least politically, to adopt systems of resources management that do not initiate over-exploitation and disastrous climate changes. In our sense "sustainability" is implemented either through the amplification of principles or by experimental adaptation to practical solutions.

The Brundtland Commission certified sustainable development as the main platform of global politics. In fact, Brundtland framed the growth versus environment debate, noting that sustainability is vital "to meet the needs of the present without compromising the ability of future generations to meet their own needs."[10] The basic ideas of the Brundtland Commission were later confirmed by the 1992 Rio Declaration, Article 8 of which promotes the idea of sustainable development, and Article 15, the principle of precaution.

Despite the fact that the Commission's concept is general and fails to specify the appropriate means to achieve sustainability, politicians and research groups have suggested some principles for implementing it. The International Institute for Sustainable Development says that the first task is to establish a vision of sustainable development and clear goals that provide a practical definition of that vision in terms that are meaningful for the decision-making unit. The second task is to deal with the content of any assessment and the need to merge a sense of the overall system with a practical focus on current priority issues. Third are the key issues of the process of assessment and finally the necessity for establishing a continuing capacity for monitoring steps in relation to resources exploitation.[11]

The broad definition of the Brundtland text provides opportunities for diverse solutions, and the appropriate interpretation is delegated to each participating state. For instance, in 1996 the US President's Council for Sustainable Development concluded that in order to meet the Brundtland definition,

> The United States must change by moving from conflict to collaboration and adopting stewardship and individual responsibility as tenets by which to live . . . A sustainable United States will have a growing economy that

> provides equitable opportunities for satisfying livelihoods and a safe, healthy, high quality of life for current and future generations. Our nation will protect its environment, its natural resource base, and the functions and viability of natural systems on which all life depends.[12]

The idea of sustainable development includes a conservative attitude toward risk assessment known as the "precautionary principle."[13] "This emerging international environmental norm,[14] which is grounded in the public law of both United States and Germany, posits that states have the power, if not the duty, to prevent uncertain environmental harm, if there is evidence of significant environmental risks, even if our understanding of the magnitude of these risks is incomplete."[15] A similar situation is emerging in the European Union.[16] Unfortunately, this principle is also frequently disregarded by those who benefit in the short run from assuming away long-term risks.

By its nature, the goal of sustainable development is not static. Technology and culture are constantly changing, and we can only predict the wants and needs of future generations in a very generalized way. Since we do not know for sure the impacts of human activity, we need an instrument that forecasts dangerous threats or unpleasant consequences to viable societies. The precautionary principle is a technique that reduces risks and uncertainties by making room in decision-making processes for consideration of the future consequences of human actions.

Though sustainable development is a widely accepted objective, achievement of that objective is proving difficult. The immediate financial gains from rapid resource development are tempting for both the private and public sectors. Some rationalize their greed by arguing that something new will always come along to replace the depleted resources. Others simply grab the money and ignore the needs of future generations. A generation is a long time in the context of human planning capabilities.[17] Moreover, because sustainability is an instrumental objective, its achievement can only be determined by examining the consequences of its application many years into the future.[18] How can we predict the consequences of any system of resource management over such a long period of time?[19] Is there anything about customary law that suggests that it might facilitate such forecasts?

1.2 Customary law

The primary focus of this book is on the use of customary law for natural resource management because the management of natural resources is an essential component of sustainable development.[20] The major purpose of this book is to ascertain the extent to which customary law institutions may be able to achieve the goal of sustainable resource management, and to understand how such systems fit into the overall pattern of jurisprudence and political institutions.[21]

Throughout the world, the exploration of systems of customary law for managing natural resources has become a major research interest for political scientists, anthropologists, economists and geographers. The University of Indiana political scientist Elinor Ostrom has been one of the pioneers of modern research into systems of natural resource management. Dr. Ostrom points out that "The rich case-study literature illustrates a diversity of settings in which appropriators dependent on common-pool resources have organized themselves to achieve much higher outcomes than is predicted by the conventional theory [or] under government operation."[22] This has led some students of customary rules, like University of Pittsburgh historian Peter Karsten, to observe that "Rules adopted by ordinary people 'work'; those they don't accept, those forced upon them by 'pig-headed' legislators, often don't work."[23] This coincides with the observation made by the Danish-Norwegian King Christian IV in 1604 when he refused to let the Norwegian General Code of Law replace customary laws, and allowed it to replace only existing codified laws, instead.[24]

Karsten agrees, as do we, that not all popular norms should remain unchanged. Our hypothesis is that in many instances "custom thus suggests a route by which a 'commons' may be managed."[25] Customs are adopted routines, which through the experience of life have often proven competitively successful. As Oliver Wendell Holmes, Jr. observed in a famous comment, "The life of the law has not been logic: it has been experience."[26]

Today, viable customary law systems are dynamic and adjustable.[27] For many years, anthropologists tended to underestimate the sophistication of customary law. Tel Aviv University sociologist Leon Sheleff suggests that

> anthropologists are partly to blame for the inaccuracies that often attach to the customary law. Often even when stressing the nature of custom as law, they would tend to describe it as an inflexible framework basically as it was at the time of the research. Very few anthropologists probed to determine how the customs have developed over time.[28]

Customary law is a popular normative pattern that reflects the common understanding of valid, compulsory rights and obligations. These underlying social norms may become the acknowledged law of the land. For definitional purposes, we need to identify the point at which a custom attains the status of customary law, an issue that has been the source of some disagreement.[29]

For a custom to acquire the status of law it must carry a popular perception of valid legal obligation (*opinio necessitatis sive obligationis*). The key to determining whether a custom constitutes customary law is whether the public acts as if the observance of the custom is legally obligated. As Frances Wharton put it,

> The ground of customary law . . . is not the will of the people to create the law, nor is it the conviction that the law already exists, but it is the popular consciousness that *so the law must be*. Customary law does not rest on the power of the people over the law, but on the power of the law over the people.[30]

Not all customs meet that test. Philosophers in the tradition of Hume have used the term "custom" to define all human behavior patterns.[31] A baby's decision to walk by putting one foot in front of another is a custom, but no one would think of such a custom as customary law.[32] In Chapter 3, Jes Bjarup demonstrates that Thomas Reid's concept of a custom as an interactive behavior pattern among humans is the philosophical basis for the idea of customary law, and not Hume's broadly defined concept of custom.[33] Reid's view is grounded in the social operations of the mind that lead humans to conceptualize legal rules as normative propositions that are binding or mandatory since they are supported by sanctions, not in the sense of physical force, but in the sense of recognition that authorizes the rule as a legal rule.[34]

If people disagree about a custom, they may appeal to the courts to make the ultimate decision on the interpretation and validity of the custom. Customary law enjoys extra-judicial existence,[35] and no court may refuse to apply customary law that is acknowledged by its subjects and meets customary law prerequisites.[36] As customs become more complex, their interpretation is likely to be challenged before arbitrators or judges. Their decisions may then become precedents, especially in legal systems that follow the common law tradition, but such step-by-step adjudication has also been used in civil law systems.[37] The court's function is to determine whether the custom meets the legal prerequisites of customary law. As discussed in Chapters 4 and 5, the court has a degree of discretion in deciding the reasonableness of the custom,[38] but if a custom is not unreasonable and meets the prerequisites, the court is bound to apply it as law. This was also the position held both by ancient Roman law[39] and throughout post-Roman Europe.[40]

Some commentators take the position that customary law does not exist until recognized by courts. When confirming the existence of customary law, there are those who argue as follows: the decisions of the courts are the vital element needed to avoid "fictitious" customary law. Law must either be initiated by the legislators or interpreted by the courts. The institution of customary law is only an ex *post facto* rationalization of some metaphysical belief. Dennis Lloyd argues that we know whether a *de facto* practice and usage is the manifestation of a customary law rule only if a court tells us so.[41] It is court adjudication that converts local practices into customary law.

Our position, on the other hand, is that customary law exists extra-judicially; the court's function is limited to applying the law to the case in dispute.[42] But if people have actually recognized the customs' binding legal obligation, then the customs existed as law whether or not a court ever considered them. The legal norm is obeyed and, if not acknowledged, is at least tacitly applied.[43]

The courts' power to decide "that so the law must be" depends upon the courts being asked to do so. In cases of undisputed customs, they are not asked to decide. These customs are legally valid without court recognition, simply by social approval. Their binding force is based upon popular recognition, not the courts' subsequent adjudication.[44]

English courts recognize the limited nature of their role in making customary law decisions. As one court said: "We find that the law to have been accepted as stated for a great length of time, and I apprehend that it is not now within our province to overturn it."[45] John W. Salmond made the point succinctly: "Custom is law not because it *has been* recognised by the courts, but because it *will be* so recognised, in accordance with fixed rules of law, if the occasion arises . . ."[46] No doubt courts play an important role, and in many areas, local customs would have been forgotten if not for the court's confirmation, but if customs are generally applied without controversy, no court decision is needed.[47]

During the colonial period, British colonial administrators analogized many of the customs of the conquered nations to the peculiar local customs found in obscure corners of the British Isles. They granted recognition to these local customs in the same way that the Kings' courts had originally accepted local English customs, pretending that they were inflexible, unchanging and unchangeable, and applicable only to people who lived in primitive and unchanging conditions. Such customary law was law applicable to, and to be administered by, people seen to be racially and culturally inferior. Thus was created a whole new concept of customary law appropriate only for those non-European societies that the British viewed as static, ignoring the fact that the customs actually applied by the local people were responsive to changing conditions, thus complicating the role of custom in post-colonial nations.[48]

In modern nations with centralized governments and written constitutions, some legal scholars may fear that customary law presents a challenge to state sovereignty.[49] But constitutionalism, and the idea of a constitution, can incorporate customary law as part of its fabric. The idea of an "ancient constitution" embodies, as Carol Rose suggests, all kinds of long-established practices, customs and local privileges that create the identity of the body politic.[50] One may say that "law" is created by normative decisions that are "born" in the depths of people's souls, accepted *inter partes* and finally authorized by *tacitus consensus*, which may be a more or less reluctant acceptance of what seems like inevitable obligations.

How should we measure the popular understanding of such an obligation? Extended patterns of observed behavior are an expression of an underlying normative structure that in some instances is elevated into the spheres of customary law. But one simply cannot observe the *opinio necessitatis sive obligationis*. Empirical study is often needed to determine to what extent a particular custom creates this sense of valid legal obligation. In that case the character of the general acknowledgement might be found through polls, interviews or the systematic observation of participants.[51]

Another way that a body of customary law builds up is when legal scholars write it down in an effort to bring coherence to an increasingly complex pattern of custom.[52] For example, an itinerant English judge wrote down the various customs used by the inhabitants of the fens in a document called the Code of Romney Marsh,[53] which then became treated as a "customal" – what we would today call a "restatement" of the customary law,[54] which in turn was used by the courts to resolve wetland disputes in other regions.[55] In Norway, codification has traditionally and historically been based upon customary law examination.[56]

The most famous scholarly analyst of customary law was William Blackstone, the eighteenth-century English lawyer whose treatise was very influential in the development of the common law both in Britain and in its colonies and former colonies. Blackstone analyzed and published the rules that the English courts had been using in deciding whether a particular custom was customary law. As the path-breaking research by

David Callies in Chapter 4 shows, Blackstone was not inventing his own theory of customary law, but was faithfully reporting the ways by which the English courts had used the common law decision-making process to decide which customs qualified as customary law.[57]

Common law countries still follow the rules that Blackstone found. Norway and Denmark also have long customary law traditions, built on a Blackstonian-like system of prerequisites, and their jurists debate about which customary laws fit into their civil law traditions.[58] And today, as discussed in Chapter 9, many countries must face the claims of indigenous people that international norms of customary law require the recognition of their local customary laws.[59]

1.3 The linkage

Neither customary law nor sustainable development are merely metaphysical concepts. In the real world, customary law and sustainable development *do exist.* These norms are neither "hard facts" of natural sciences, nor socio-material artifacts (human installations), but *institutional facts.* Customary law is a legal instrument, while sustainability is a political norm that is increasingly being transformed into legal rules. Customary law is initiated and developed by interactions among individuals[60] as they adapt their institutions to changing conditions of life.

Successful adaptations reflect those patterns of behavior that proved effective in the struggle for survival – a struggle in which the human race has been remarkably successful. As Smithsonian anthropologist Rick Potts has shown, from the earliest days of *homo sapiens*, the species needed to adapt to the "shifting, unforeshadowed settings of the Pleistocene;" the uncertainties of nature's perturbations "favored faculties sensitive to environmental change and capable of stabilizing human needs."[61]

Human beings were able to successfully adapt, and thus survive, because they were able to do what earlier hominids could not. Human beings were able to develop and broaden their aptitudes and abilities and to apply this amazing array of evolved capacities to their evolving surroundings. Human beings rely upon symbolic thought, mental creativity, imagination, complex cultural institutions, home-based behaviors, intricate social reciprocity and long-distance exchange of resources in their struggles to adapt.[62] Members of groups such as trades, tribes, families, societies and other informal structures of social life were the first to recognize the need for and to participate in necessary adaptive behaviors.

In the eighteenth century, the Scottish philosopher Thomas Reid noted that this kind of socially generated adaptation is what distinguishes humans from animals. As Reid put it, animals

> are not capable of self-government, and when they act according to the passions or habit which is strongest at the time, they act according to the nature that God has given them, and no more can be required of them. They cannot lay down a rule to themselves, which they are not to transgress, though prompted by appetite, or ruffled by passion. We see no reason to think that they can form the conception of a general rule, or of obligation to adhere to it.[63]

Self-imposed cultural limitations on the exploitation of common-pool resources allowed human groups to adapt and survive. Human beings recognized that environmental change was both probable and unpredictable. As a result, they needed to practice precaution and to sacrifice present, immediate gratification to future uncertainty. In some cases, interpersonal consensus determined the constraints placed upon common-pool resource exploitation. In others, shamans constrained exploitation through taboos[64] or superstitious beliefs.[65] We know from social anthropology that informal interpersonal norms, whatever their source, are often vital in applying the precautionary principle and achieving sustainability.[66]

Since the earliest times, self-imposed or group-imposed restrictions such as these have undoubtedly been met with resistance by those individuals wishing and willing to take greater risks. In recent years however, ideas such as rationalism, privatization, short-range economics and globalization have severely challenged and exerted great pressure on these types of culturally rooted restrictions. Examining those customary limitations on the exploitation of common-pool resources that have nonetheless withstood and survived such extraordinary demands may lead to valuable information about potential systems for managing resources sustainably in the future.

In what philosophers call the pyramid of policy-means-ends hierarchy,[67] customary law and sustainable development are interdependent. In this pyramidal means-end model, sustainable development is the meta-goal, while customary precautionary principles are *instruments* to provide good solutions towards that end. Statutes may also be instruments designed to achieve sustainable development, but bureaucratic implementation often diverts legal results from the statute's intentions.[68] On the other hand, customary law that is not intentionally created to satisfy any political goal may, by the very nature of its continuing tacit success among user groups, promote sustainable effects.

If customary law is to be helpful in promoting sustainable development it must retain the resilient qualities that enable it to adapt to environmental change.[69] For example, Hanne Petersen emphasizes in Chapter 10 that few Inuit in Greenland wish to be locked into rigid codification of past customs that might inhibit their ability to survive in world markets, even though they may cherish customs that serve as an inspiration for adapting to the changing circumstances of the world.[70] Customs can be traditional, in the sense of time-tested and wise, without being inflexible. They may embody a concept of "sustainable development" of resources as experienced by life, i.e., a case-by-case, day-to-day adaptation to natural changing conditions. Learning from practical life requires consideration of traditions, practices and customs.[71]

Some observers have assumed that the Blackstonian idea of customary law is useless in most of the world because they believe it still requires proof that the custom existed since "time out of mind."[72] But as Plucknett said over a century ago, "the remarkable feature of custom was its flexibility and adaptability. In modern times we hear a lot too much of the phrase 'immemorial custom.' In so far as this phrase implies that custom is or ought to be immemorially old it is historically inaccurate."[73]

Today, English courts continue to recognize that customary law need not be stagnant. And so do the Norwegian courts, adopting Blackstone-similar criteria.[74] Under the Blackstonian rules, a custom must have been accepted by the people as long as the memory of living people extended, but that did not mean that the custom itself could not include internal systems for adaptation to changing conditions. For example, in *Fitch v. Rawling*[75] the parishioners had proven a long-established custom of playing games on the common land. The court held that they were not forbidden from playing cricket there merely because the game of cricket was a relatively recent invention.[76]

The *Fitch* case exemplifies the idea that customary law is a process – a recognized way of initiating and implementing authoritative rules – rather than the fixed content of the rules themselves. Customary law may involve secondary rules used to modify primary rules, as Jes Bjarup explains in Chapter 3. In such cases, the customary law is the procedure that is used to make and declare a valid rule having normative force as reason for belief and action.[77] The secondary rules are always mandatory rules since they provide people with the authority to introduce primary rules as well as the criteria of validity for the making of legal rules.

In this sense, customary law may be a process. In Chapter 8, Martin Chanock describes the use of customary law as "a language in which claims are made, and images of equity evoked, rather than a set of rules belonging to and observed by a community."[78] To recognize customary law as a process does not reject the need to show that the process has had longevity. The longevity requirement is a means to document popular confirmation of the process, but it is not a requirement that the process have been rigid and inflexible.[79]

Blackstone's emphasis on the longevity of any customary law process as a basis of its legitimacy has had an indirect advantage insofar as sustainability is concerned. It has created an incentive for the supporters of customary processes to retain historical records.[80] This means that it may be possible to study empirically the history of customary law systems to determine whether they have promoted sustainability in the past, and to predict how they would react to future changes in the surrounding environment in ways that would be supportive of sustainable development and the precautionary principle.[81]

Unfortunately, however, American courts have not always applied customary law in a manner that promotes sustainable development. As David Callies points out in Chapter 4, in some instances they have revived old customs that seem irrelevant in the light of changes in the social, physical and technological environment.[82] It is not axiomatic that customary law will lead to sustainable development just because it is customary.

Systems of customary law for resource management differ from each other in a wide variety of ways, making it difficult to generalize meaningfully about "customary law" as a single category.[83] Instead, the large and growing number of empirical studies of particular customary law systems for resource management provide source material from which we will seek to discern factors that describe those customary law systems that appear to enhance sustainability.[84] Many of these studies have taken place in the context of the growing interest in common-pool resources.

1.4 What has common property to do with customary law?

Many customary law systems have evolved as means for turning common-pool resources into what Carol Rose has defined as "limited common property"; i.e. property that is commonly owned but not subject to open access. These "fluid, emergent forms" of property may be particularly useful for managing natural resources whose "constituent features may be roughly known but not completely specifiable in advance."[85] In places where the general public can manage itself and prevent wasteful overuse of a resource, customary law "can tame and moderate the dread rule of capture that supposedly tends to turn every common into a waste."[86]

Modern recognition of the value of common property rights began when empirical research demonstrated that many customary law systems were preventing the overuse of common property. Common property management systems tend to be bottom-up developed institutional facts designed to accommodate the delicate balance between predators, human influence and natural cycles and changes over the years. Long-term trial and error has shaped social norms adaptable to the ever-changing living fabric of life.

This research suggested that neither privatization nor centralized planning were the only means of overcoming the "tragedy of the commons." Discussions about the tragedy of the commons have been a staple of the academic debate about resource management for the past three decades. To understand the confusion about the commons one must go back to the original essay that gave life to the concept of the tragedy of the commons. In 1968, California ecologist Garrett Hardin wrote "perhaps the most influential article ever written in the environmental field"[87] – a short essay about world population growth entitled "The Tragedy of the Commons."[88] He analogized the problem to the "inevitable" failure of peasants to prevent overgrazing of common lands. Because each individual peasant would stand to benefit by grazing one more cow, even though that cow would contribute to the overall malnutrition of the herd, depletion of the resource was sure to follow:

> Picture a pasture open to all. It is to be expected that each herdsman will try to keep as many cattle as possible on the commons. . . . Explicitly or implicitly, more or less consciously, he asks, "What is the utility to *me* of adding one more animal to my herd?" This utility has one negative and one positive component.[89]

The positive component is one additional animal. The negative component is that all of his animals are a bit weaker. But since "the effects of overgrazing are shared by all the herdsmen," the negative component is overshadowed by the positive benefits of an additional animal. Therein is the tragedy, Hardin wrote. Each man is locked into a system that compels him to increase his herd without limit – in a world that is limited. Ruin is the destination toward which all men rush, each pursuing his own best interest in a society that believes in the freedom of the commons. Freedom in a commons brings ruin to all.[90] From his parable, Hardin drew the conclusion that we must "explicitly exorcise" the "invisible hand" when dealing with problems involving commons. For commons that could not be privatized[91] he favored "coercion."[92]

Hardin proceeds from an atomistic view of human beings as rational egoists proceeding from the solitary operations of the mind to make choices to maximize their own preferences. This conception of human nature leads to the view that economics is the only respectable social science. This is surely important in relation to natural resources utilization since the economic view conceives of human interaction in terms of Hume's naturalistic account of causal relations between human beings. This view then leads to a society of agents pursuing exclusively their private interests in the use of natural resources.[93] The result may be ruin for them as well as for the environment.

The facts cited by Hardin to support his thesis have been challenged by recent studies suggesting that management of common lands in medieval England may have been much more efficient than previously believed.[94] It has also been shown that the "common" pasture of medieval England was actually open only to a limited number of people who (1) resided in the area, (2) had a legal right to use it, and (3) had a practical ability to take advantage of it. Such land might better be called "limited common property," as Carol Rose suggests,[95] to make it apparent that Hardin's logic applies only if the resource is a commons open to all users (i.e., lacks excludability).[96] Hardin himself pointed out in a 1994 essay that commons was a metaphorical one, and that his argument was not intended to apply to a "managed commons."[97] He would probably agree that "perhaps in the changed perception of the commons lies a remedy for ruin."[98]

Many customary law systems utilize a mixture of both private property and a type of common property that is available to a limited group of users.[99] A recognition of the usefulness of limited common property is not intended to challenge the importance of private property, which is dominant throughout Western society and in many non-Western ones as well.[100] But such systems should not ignore the Roman law categories of *res communes omnium* and *res nullius*, i.e. the two main categories of public property rights.[101] Public property rights are still used for fisheries[102] and to some extent for pasturelands.[103] We hope that this book will help to fill the conceptual gap in our understanding of potential systems for governing resource exploitation created by the "educated or miseducated [jurists] with two thousand years of theoretical elaboration centered solely on individual property."[104]

Extensive research has been undertaken into the operation of common property systems since the mid 1980s.[105] Much of the work has been supported by the international development agencies that are building projects in countries where common property systems are often being used.[106] The research suggests that one should not treat private rights and common rights as opposing alternatives, but as tools to be used to solve those problems for which each may be best suited.[107] Many individual case studies of common-pool resources have been conducted. Some tentative conclusions are that over-utilization of common-pool resources is less likely if the following conditions exist: (1) the resources are private or limited common property rather than open commons,[108] (2) a cohesive user group[109] whose members communicate well among themselves manages the resources,[110] (3) the resource can be "stored," thus giving users more flexibility as to time of use and making it easier to devise allocation rules that are perceived as fair,[111] (4) well-defined geographical limits bound the area in which the resources are located,[112] and (5) institutions exist that facilitate ongoing communication among users to enable adaptation of the rules to changing conditions.[113]

We should emphasize that most of this research into common-pool resource management has searched for principles that would be applicable to all rule-making systems, whether statutory, administrative or customary. But if any generalization can safely be made on the basis of studies to date, it is that replacing locally derived rules with outside forces is the most common threat to the efficient management of common property resources.[114] Social norms that tend to evolve into customary laws often develop geographic and material delimitation; sometimes participation is limited by lack of knowledge or proximity.[115] Customary law that incorporates elements of both private, limited common and public property rights can produce what Elinor Ostrom calls the "drama of the commons."[116]

In Norway, several studies of fishing practices, both among indigenous peoples (the Saami)[117] and Norwegians,[118] found that social norm-directed practices never caused the extinction of fisheries.[119] Overexploitation was introduced by hi-tech fishing (trawling and Danish seines) at the end of the 1980s. Other studies have also noted similar success of some local self-governing institutions.[120] Although the high seas, "that great and still remaining common of mankind," are by nature difficult to manage, some trades have created their own social structures, as in the 1872 case of whale hunting (*Swift v. Gifford*),[121] which confirmed the existence of customary law among citizens from the state of Massachusetts.[122]

Such trade-related customary laws have become increasingly important in the management of ocean fisheries.[123] The latest development in high sea management is the initiation of Regional Fisheries Organizations (RFO) that have "made a common by compact."[124] The RFO enjoys legal personality, legislative competency and discretionary power. In the lacunae, however, custom may occur. The conclusion from a 1998 Straddling Fish Study is that neither "the state command and control system" nor the "privatization scheme" is the answer to the Hardin challenge.[125] The special role of custom in international law is discussed in more detail in Chapter 9.

We recognize, however, that where new rules are imposed in the guise of old rules, they may have a negative impact on resource protection, as David Callies points out in Chapter 4. He cites the example of a Californian court decision that opened all of the resources of the state's sandy shorelines to the use of the entire public without limitation. The reaction to that decision was truly a "drama," the final act of which was legislative action reversing the court's decision.[126] As this case illustrates, it is necessary to be aware that greed can operate under the cover of custom, and may work to diminish the property rights of others in ways that may raise constitutional issues in modern societies.[127]

There is an obvious need to investigate the underlying social structures that promote sustainable development solutions in viable self-governing societies. The viability is important to the notion of "free states," because free states traditionally have been defined by their capacity for self-government.[128] But as Martin Chanock points out in Chapter 8, even in failing states characterized by lawlessness and corruption, customary law may be able to carve out a unique role that protects the sustainability of local ways of life in the face of bleak national conditions.

So it can be seen that the notion of a "common pool" mandates neither a tragic nor a comic common. In some instances, customary law is the only possible ruling instrument for a common pool if the legislature refrains from codification. In other instances legislation turns out to be inefficient because of bureaucratic deviation from clear legal rules or lack of perceived legitimacy. Each instance must be scanned separately, and even well-functioning customary law regimes may need some support from public regulation. Our hypothesis is that social structures that tend to become customary laws should be analyzed to see if they are well equipped to meet the challenges of the changing fabric of life.

1.5 Some terminology distinctions

The word "custom" can be used in many ways in a legal context. As a means of clarifying the scope of this work it is important to distinguish between "customary law" as used herein and (1) the customs of lawyers and judges, (2) the common law's use of precedent, and (3) illegal customs.

First, judges and lawyers use various customs in their decision-making processes. A distinction should be made between customs as legal rules, and customs as filters to use during the process of judicial interpretation of statutes. The interpretive stance toward elements of usage, practice, and custom that dominates among lawyers and the judiciary will influence the textual analysis they make. Interpretive solutions that oppose the prevailing legal understanding among leading jurists are usually condemned to failure.[129] The contributors to this book do not reject this kind of customary influence in the legal process. But our topic addresses the place of custom as law and not as a process of adjudication. We have no intention of discussing customs that prevail among judges.[130]

A second distinction should be made between a system of customary law and a system based on judicial precedents, or one could say between customary law and common law. Some authors consider "common law as a system of customary law."[131] Courts' knowledge of law is often derived from "experience and study – of the judicial decisions of their predecessors – the principal and most authoritative evidence, that can be given, of the existence of such a custom as shall form a part of the common law."[132] The evidence of legal principles embodied in judicial precedent should not, however, be confused with the assertion of customary law.[133]

While judicial precedents have always been of great importance in common law systems,[134] our focus is upon "bottom-up," popularly initiated practices that generate customary law from the experience of people's usage, practice, customs or manner as evidenced by life. Judicial precedents may become useful in promoting the awareness of customary law, but a lack of such precedents does not deny the existence of customary law. Judges are not the only people who are beginning to reason instrumentally in deciding whether to approve particular legal rules. Legislators, administrators and lobbyists all try to evaluate whether particular rules will work satisfactorily to achieve public policy objectives. As the empirical studies discussed in Chapter 6 have shown, many legislative and administrative bodies have chosen to implement customary law rules for resource management, not because they are forced to, but because they think the customary rules and processes may work.

A third distinction should be made between customary law and governmental practices that develop into customs. The Magna Carta is illustrative: "All evil customs concerning forests and warrens – shall within forty days after the inquisition be completely and irrevocably abolished."[135] This rule confirms that illegitimate governmental practices that lack public acknowledgement do not obtain the force of customary law.[136] Nor does the law of the conquering power introduced without consent of the legal subjects qualify as customary law.[137]

One final distinction: the production of customary law under international law is atypical, since the subjects of international law are states and international organizations, but the substantive content of many international customary law systems does concern or affect natural resource management.[138] Consequently, we discuss the international customary law of resource management separately.[139]

Endnotes

1. As opposed to the assertions made by rationalists (Rational Choice theorists), the emergence of cooperation and norm is not problematic. On the contrary, cooperating and norm building are central to our nature as human beings. Once in place, rule systems organize ongoing normative deliberations that seek to define and redefine the nature of the community. "How do people alter rules that others would like them to live by when those rules no longer appear to be compatible with the new conditions or surroundings" (Peter Karsten, *Between Law and Custom* (Cambridge University Press, Cambridge, 2002), p. 1). The authors of this book concur with this programmatic statement. Customary laws and traditional rights are not metaphysical beliefs, but are instead institutional facts that can be studied empirically. We do not adhere to the "epistemological idealism" of Scandinavian Legal Realism and its "anti-empiricist view" that "knowledge is a relation to propositions rather than to objects." Legal norms grounded in rational calculus, which are said not to be present in extralegal norms (see above), are effective customs even before the customs are transformed into customary laws. For philosophical and theoretical perspectives, see Jes Bjarup in Chapter 3.
2. This accusation is taken seriously and is expressed in many modern treaties distinguishing rights and obligations between developing and industrialized states. See, for instance, the 1997 Kyoto Protocol on Climate Change and the Pacific Highly Migratory Fish Stock Convention (MLHC) of September 9, 2000, Part VII.
3. World Commission on Environment and Development, *Our Common Future* (United Nations and Oxford University Press, New York, 1987), p. 43.

4. Reference to sustainability is made in several treaties (see Chapter 9). In some instances sustainable development is used. In others the viability requirement is formulated as sustainable yields, or even maximum sustainable yields. See the 1982 Law of the Sea Convention Articles 63, 68 and 118. Some commentators have suggested that the reason that the concept of sustainable development is popular is because it is capable of being interpreted in so many different ways that almost any interest group can argue that its position is consistent with sustainability. Sanford E. Gaines, "Rethinking Environmental Protection, Competitiveness and International Trade" (1997) *U. of Chicago Legal Forum* 231–232; Julie L. Davidson "Sustainable Development: Business as Usual or a New Way of Living?" (2000) *Environmental Ethics*, vol. 22, p. 25. Not every environmental theorist supports the concept. Advocates of "deep ecology" think that it is too accommodating to development. Some people in the extractive industries, on the other hand, consider it too restrictive.
5. See the moral and ethical deliberations in Paul H. Gobster and R. Bruce Hull (eds.), *Restoring Nature: Perspectives from the Social Sciences and Humanities* (Island Press, Washington DC, 2000). See also Peter Ørebech, "Sustainable Development by Means of Market Distribution Mechanism," in Andrea Baranzini and Fabrizio Carlevaro (eds.), *Econometrics of Environment and Transdisciplinarity* (AEA List, International Conference, Lisbon, 1996), p. 906.
6. Peter Bautista Payoyo, "Cries of the Sea," in Payoyo, *World Inequality, Sustainable Development and the Common Heritage of Humanity* (Martinus Nijhoff Publishers, Dordrecht, Boston, Lancaster, 1997), p. 161, note 8.
7. See pp. 245–248 below.
8. See D. W. Pearce et al., *Blueprint for a Green Economy* (Earthscan, London, 1989), pp. 173–85.
9. S. Lele, *Sustainable Development: A Critical Review* (World Development, Montreal, 1996), p. 607, at p. 613.
10. The World Commission on Environment and Development, *Our Common Future*, p. 43.
11. See, for instance, the International Institute for Sustainable Development, *Assessing Sustainable Development* (IISD, Winnipeg, 1997). This group has also conducted studies at the Rockefeller Foundation Bellagio Study Center in Italy. Nevertheless, it is difficult to establish workable principles that employ deductive methods in a means-end model in order to deal with aspects of assessing progress toward sustainable development. See Arne Naess, "Økologi og filosofi." ["Ecology and Philosophy"] (Universitetsforlaget, Oslo, 1972).
12. Sustainable America: A New Consensus for Prosperity, Opportunity, and a Healthy Environment for the Future, February 1996. Executive Order No. 12852, 29 June 1993, amended 19 July 1993, 42 U.S.C. 4321.

13. The application of the precautionary principle suggests caution in the absence of "improved techniques for dealing with risk and uncertainty." See, e.g., 1995 Straddling Fish Stock Agreement Article 6(2).
14. See Chapter 9.
15. A. Dan Tarlock, "Who Owns Science?" (2002) *Pennsylvania State Envtl Review*, vol. 10, pp. 135, 141 (citations omitted).
16. See Commission of the European Communities. Communication from the Commission on the precautionary principle, Brussels, 2.2.2000 COM(2000) 1 final. This political program has been implemented in several regulations, for some illustrations see Chapter 9. The Inter-Departmental Liaison Group on Risk Assessment, "The Precautionary Principle: Policy and Application," has looked at the situation in the United Kingdom (30 September 2002).
17. A generation is usually defined as the typical period between the birth of parents and the birth of offspring. For humans, this has often been roughly assumed to be thirty years. *Random House Dictionary of the American Language*, Unabridged (2nd ed., New York, 1987), p. 795.
18. The term "instrumentalism" is usually associated with the work of John Dewey, who advocated that "policies and proposals for social action should be treated as working hypotheses, not as programs to be rightly adhered to and executed. They will be experimental in the sense that they will be entertained subject to constant and well-equipped observation of the consequences they entail when acted upon, and subject to ready and flexible revision in the light of observed consequences." John Dewey, *The Public and Its Problems* (Henry Holt & Co., New York, 1927), pp. 202–3.
19. See generally, John C. Dernbach, "Sustainable Development as a Framework for National Governance" (1998) *Case W. Res. L. Rev.*, vol. 49, p. 1. For an interesting study of the way the term "sustainability" is being interpreted in practice, see Environmental Law Institute, *Sustainability in Practice* (Environmental Law Institute, Washington DC, 1999).
20. Of course, customs that flourish under commercial law also contribute to the understanding of customs as instruments of law, but they have no central role in this book. Theodore F. T. Plucknett, *A Concise History of the Common Law* (5th ed., Little Brown, Boston, 1956), p. 314. For a recent discussion of customary commercial practices in former British colonies, see Peter Karsten, *Between Law and Custom* (Cambridge University Press, Cambridge, 2002), pp. 269–362.
21. The *scientific* position taken in this work – which we call "Legal Culturalism" – is that the dichotomy between "extralegal" and legal norms as separate spheres is false. See the (now deceased) Norwegian legal scientist Nils Kristian Sundby, *Om normer* [*On norms*] (Universitetsforlaget, Oslo, 1976). For an opposing view, see another Norwegian, Jon Elster, *The Cement of Society: A Study of Social Order* (Cambridge University Press, Cambridge, 1989), p. 101. Our position

stems from the observation that neither non-written nor written laws enjoy *a priori existence*, that acknowledgement is basic to ethical, moral or legal norms and that all normative categories may be empirically studied. Irrespective of its classification, normative validity is measured on the basis of dyadic, triadic and multiadic recognition. The latter category creates customary laws.

22. Elinor Ostrom, "Reformulating the Commons," in Joanna Burger et al. (eds.), *Protecting the Commons: A Framework for Resource Management in the Americas* (Island Press, Washington DC, 2001), pp. 170, 20–21. This is a question of procedural rather than substantive advantages, because both written and unwritten law may express any kind of right and obligation.
23. Karsten, *Between Law and Custom*, p. 539.
24. See pp. 283–284 below.
25. Carol Rose, "Property & Persuasion," in Rose, *Essays on the History, Theory and Rhetoric of Ownership* (Westview Press, Boulder, 1994), p. 124.
26. Oliver W. Holmes, Jr., *The Common Law* (Little, Brown & Company, Boston, 1881). As Alfred Marshall noted, "Custom exerts a deep and controlling influence over the history of the world." Alfred Marshall, *Principles of Economics* (Macmillan, London, 1890), p. 465.
27. See pp. 282–300 below. See also United Kingdom supreme court judge Lord Lloyd of Hampstead, as quoted in Torstein Eckhoff and Nils Kristian Sundby, *Rettssystemer* [*Legal Systems*] (Universitetsforlaget, Oslo, 1991) ("A legal system is not an abstract collection of bloodless categories but a living fabric in a constant state of movement").
28. Leon Sheleff, *The Future of Tradition. Customary Law, Common Law and Legal Pluralism* (Frank Cass, London, 2000), p. 85.
29. Although these semantic issues may seem pedantic, some scholars have debated them quite heatedly. One could say that the definition of customary law is more about words and concepts than about realities. Moreover, arguments as to what needs to be clarified as customary law are also flexible. "There is nothing to pre vent jurists, any more than other systematizers, from delimiting, defining, or classifying their subject-matter in whatever way they please." Dennis Lloyd, *The Idea of Law* (Penguin Books, London, 1991), p. 226. A definition may be "a living system, defined and modified by constant use." Julie Stewart, "Untying the Gordian Knot! *Murisa v. Murisa* S-41–92, a Little More Than a Case Note" (1992) *Legal Forum*, vol. 4, p. 13. Customary law is the carrier of "living law." Eugen Ehrlich, *Fundamental Principles of the Sociology of Law* (Harvard University Press, Cambridge, MA, 1936).
30. Francis Wharton, *Commentaries on Law* (Kay & Brother, Philadelphia, 1884), pp. 20–21 (italics added).
31. See pp. 93–102 below.
32. The German economist Ekkehart Schlicht provides the following suggestive description: "Custom is ubiquitous in all spheres of life. It shapes habits and

convictions, sways emotion and cognition, and influences motivation and action. Through all these channels, custom pervades social and economic interaction." Ekkehart Schlicht, *On Custom in the Economy* (Clarendon Press, Oxford, 1998), p. 1.

33. See pp. 102–107 below.
34. See Chapter 3 at pp. 108–114.
35. This might be argued *de sententia ferenda* as well as *de lege lata. Lex non-scripta* is a valid norm *ex tunc.*
36. As Paolo Grossi stated, "It was indeed a rich patrimony that spilled out before the eyes of all, but it was waiting for someone who could recognize it." Paolo Grossi, *An Alternative to Private Property* (University of Chicago Press, Chicago, 1981), p. 16. The recognition that Professor Grossi portrays is the analytic discovery of the common pool system of villages and regions as described by anthropologists or other scientists. People well acquainted with local cultures clearly experienced their substance and function. The "missing link" described was the lack of scientific analysis.
37. See the discussion of the development of common pool concepts in Norway in Chapter 5.
38. As Professor Callies points out at pp. 207–213, a legal realist may sometimes be skeptical that the judges are using custom to implement new doctrines. See also J. Scalia, dissenting from the Supreme Court's denial of *certiorari* in *Stevens v. City of Cannon Beach*, 510 U.S. 1207 (1994).
39. "A well conceived custom is valid law, and this is what is called customary law. Because legislation obliges us by no other reason than because the people decided it, legal rules acknowledged by the people by unanimous consent, without any written statement, must, as well, reasonably bind all men; because what difference does it make if the people announce their will by decisions or by tacit consent of living life? Therefore, one can clearly suggest that legislation is not only terminated by the political decisions of the legislator, but it also becomes outdated through unanimous tacit consent." Emperor Julian's Digestae, I. 32 § 1, cited from Holger Federspiel, *Romerske Retskilder* (Nyt Nordisk Forlag, Copenhager, 1930), pp. 2–3. The citation is translated from Danish by the co-author of this chapter (Peter Ørebech). In a time like ours, so heavily inflicted with positivistic thought, it is peculiar to note that in ancient times no statute was considered valid law before it was confirmed by custom. Legislation that suffered from lack of popular acknowledgement was not law. Cf. the Canon law (*Decretum Gratiani* 1, IVc.3): "The law is established when published, its confirmation is due to public *de facto* tacit approbation. Like some legislation today which is terminated by contradictory public customs, the confirmation of statutes is dependent upon these customs."
40. Maxim M. Kovalevski, who in reference to the oral traditions of medieval society, states: "How can one ask of illiterate peasants of the later Middle Ages

inventories of their holdings, inventories that probably never were drawn up, since the word of the elders sufficed to recognize the existence of the custom?" Maxim M. Kovalevski: "Le passage historique de la propriété collective à la propriété individuelle," in *Annales de l'institut international de sociologie* (Paris, 1896), vol. 2, pp. 207–208 quoted in Grossi, *Alternative to Private Property*, p. 115, note 51.

41. Lloyd, *The Idea of Law*, p. 246 ("the fact that the court retains the power to declare that any custom is invalid as being unreasonable shows plainly enough, not only the subordinate role of the custom, but also that, whatever the theory, no custom can be regarded as authoritative in itself unless the court has set its judicial seal upon it"). In relation to historic explanations of facts, see Quentin Skinner, *Liberty before Liberalism* (Cambridge University Press, Cambridge, 1998), p. 104.
42. J. G. A. Pocock, *The Ancient Constitution and the Feudal Law: A Study of English Historical Thought in the Seventeenth Century* (Norton, New York, 1967), p. 30 ("local customs, like those of Kent, survived only because the king's courts recognized them").
43. Hans Kelsen, "On the Pure Theory of Law" (1966) *Israel Law Review* vol. 1, p. 2.
44. Francis Hagerup, *Retsencyclopædi* (Aschehoug, Kristiania, 1919), p. 12 ("The validity of customary law is not derived from a tacit legislative acceptance. The basic ground of both binding forces [formal and informal law] is to be found in the people's recognition") (translated from Norwegian).
45. *Fookes v. Beer*, 9 A.C. 630. This view is part of an ancient tradition. Since the time of Justinian the Emperor, customary law has obtained the status of positive law, *consesu utentium*. The Digest of Roman Law I. 3,32.
46. John Salmond, *Jurisprudence* (Sweet & Maxwell, London, 1924), p. 229. He goes on to say that the Austinian theory forgets that the operation of custom is determined by fixed legal principles.
47. See the definition of "custom and usage" in a leading American legal dictionary: "Custom and Usage: A usage or practice of the people, which, by common adoption and acquiescence, and by long and unvarying habit, has become compulsory, and has acquired the force of a law with respect to the place or subject-matter to which it relates. It results from a long series of actions, constantly repeated, which have, by such repetition and by uninterrupted acquiescence, acquired the force of a tacit and common consent. *Louisville & N. R. Co. v. Reverman*, 243 Ky. 702, 706, 49 S. W. 2d 558, 560 (1932). An habitual or customary practice more or less widespread, which prevails within a geographical or sociological area; usage is a course of conduct based on a series of actual occurrences. *Corbin-Dykes Elec. Co. v Burr*, 18 Ariz. App. 101, 103, 500 P.2d 632, 634 (1972)." Associate Justice Joseph R. Nolan et al. (eds.), *Black's Law Dictionary* (6th edn, West Publishing Co, St. Paul MN), p. 385. Norwegian courts also

unconditionally respect and concur with Parliamentary (Storting) legislation, but the validity of unanimous customary law developed by the people is not questioned, but presumed (see Chapter 5).

48. This issue is developed in more depth by Martin Chanock in Chapter 8 at pp. 339–344.
49. See generally Chapter 7.
50. Rose, "Property & Persuasion," pp. 73–74. See the discussion in Chapter 8 at pp. 344–346.
51. Peter Ørebech's study of Saami customary law (NOU 2001:31 – Ministry of Justice), cited in Chapters 2 and 10, is based on interviews interpreted by knowledgeable Saami research associates.
52. Customs expounded by anthropologists, judges or scholars neither gain nor lose the status of customary law merely because they have been written down. If the customs retain the popular perception of valid legal obligation (*opinio necessitatis sive obligationis*) they remain valid customary law, but if they lose that perception because of obsolescence, environmental change, or whatever reason, the pre-existing precedents should be assumed to have lost their validity. Whether written or not is not decisive. Plucknett, *Concise History of the Common Law*, pp. 313–314.
53. William Holloway, *The History of Romney Marsh* (John Russell Smith, London, 1849), p. 73.
54. Albert Kiralfy, "Custom in Medieval English Law" (1988) *Journal of Legal History*, vol. 1, pp. 26, 26–27, 36.
55. Fred P. Bosselman, "Limitations Inherent in the Title to Wetlands at Common Law" (1996) *Stanford Environmental Law Journal*, vol. 15, pp. 247, 283.
56. See Chapter 5.
57. See pp. 159–160 below.
58. See pp. 229–230 below. Sweden, on the other hand, has rejected customary law.
59. See pp. 405–406 below.
60. This explains why the metaphysics of Karl Olivecrona is wrong: "[I]t is impossible to find any fact that corresponds to the idea of a right. The right eludes every attempt to pin it down and place it among the facts of social life." Karl Olivecrona, *Law as Fact* (Stevens, London, 1939), p. 89. In the same vein, see Axel Hägerström, "Begreppet viljeförklaring på privaträttens område" (1935 *Theoria*), vol. I, pp. 32 ff. For an opposing view, see Nils Kristian Sundby, "Legal Right in Scandinavian Analyses," *Natural Law Forum* (Notre Dame University, 1969), pp. 72 ff. at p. 106.
61. Rick Potts, *Humanity's Descent: The Consequences of Ecological Instability* (William Marrow and Company, New York, 1996), p. 243.
62. *Ibid.*, p. 249.
63. Reid, *Active Powers*, Essay I, Ch. V, p. 523. See a more extensive discussion by Jes Bjarup in Chapter 3, pp. 102–107.

64. Johan Colding and Carl Folke, "The Taboo System: Lessons Learned About Informal Institutions for Nature Management" (2000) 12 *Georgetown Int'l Envtl L. Rev.* 413, 430–431.
65. See the Saami fisheries rights study as discussed in Section 2.2, Chapter 5 and Chapter 10. Cf. the function of customs that absorb superstitious beliefs that would otherwise have vanished and that are resurrected due to courts' confirmation.
66. See the very important documentation brought to light by Anita Maurstad, *Sjarkfiske og ressursforvaltning* [*Low-tech Fishing and Resource Management*] (University of Tromsø, Tromsø, 1997).
67. See Naess, *Økologi og filosofi.*
68. Which is documented in P. Ørebech: "Tvers igjennom lov til seier!" Om torskeresolusjonen av 1989, den skjulte agenda og ranet av Fiskeriallmenningen [Overruling the Law. About the Cod Resolution of 1989, the Hidden Agenda and the Robbery of the Commons]. *Report to The Power & Democracy Studies* (Unipub as, Oslo, 2003).
69. See Chapter 6 at pp. 246–252 below.
70. See Chapter 10 at pp. 422–428.
71. "We often hear about business standards and principles, but perhaps a better idea for the restorative economy is *practices.* I am drawn to the word not only for its practical sense, but because it implies that there is something *to be learned*, and that through *consistent* and *applied practice*, one improves one's ability, gets better at a skill, strives for understanding. Practice seems a more humble word than principle, a word behind which it is easy to hide, and which often leads to some sort of failure. You can betray a principle, but you can always keep on practicing." Paul Hawken, *The Ecology of Commerce: A Declaration of Sustainability* (Harper Collins Business, New York, 1994). (italics added).
72. Karsten, *Between Law and Custom*, p. 32.
73. During Coke's time, the increasingly powerful monarchy had insisted that a right rooted in custom and rendered independent of the sovereign's interference had to be shown immemorial in the full sense of traceable to no original act of foundation, but it was always a fiction. The practice of adding new principles of law disguised as the oral traditions of the ancients was common in these times. Henry Sumner Maine, *Dissertations on Early Law and Custom* (John Murray, London, 1883) pp. 169–70. See also Susan J. B. Cox, "No Tragedy on the Commons" (1985) *Environmental Ethics*, vol. 7, p. 49 (fictional events often gradually became accepted as truth). Similarly, Norway's "ancient time prerequisite" results in a time-out-of-mind standard that is limited to living persons. See Chapter 5, pp. 233–234.
74. See Chapter 5.
75. (1795) 2 Hy Bl 393; [1775–1802] All ER 571; 126 ER 614.
76. See generally Chapter 4 for more detailed analysis.

77. See pp. 149–151 below. The idea of primary and secondary rules originated in the work of H. L. A. Hart, *The Concept of Law* (Oxford University Press, Oxford, 1961), pp. 77ff.
78. See pp. 346–356 below.
79. See Chapter 6 at pp. 254–257.
80. See pp. 253–254 below.
81. See pp. 257–258 below. Of course, other systems of law have long histories as well, and there is no intent to suggest that only customary law systems deserve such analysis.
82. See the discussion of customary law as applied by the Hawaiian courts in Chapters 2 and 11, pp. 46–54 and 411–413.
83. As chapters 4 and 5 demonstrate, there are some common patterns among European and North American ideas of customary law, and various theories have been propounded to try to establish a clear distinction between "indigenous" thought patterns and "Western" thought patterns, but there is no agreement in the scientific community upon any basis for such a distinction. Arun Agrawal, "Dismantling the Divide Between Indigenous and Scientific Knowledge" (1995) *Development and Change*, vol. 26, pp. 413, 427–31.
84. See pp. 252–265 below.
85. Carol M. Rose, "The Several Futures of Property: Of Cyberspace and Folk Tales, Emission Trades and Ecosystems" (1998) *Minnesota Law Review*, vol. 83, p. 129, 180.
86. Rose, "Property & Persuasion", pp. 125–127. Several instances of Norwegian legal history discussed in Section 2.2, 4 are also illustrative.
87. William H. Rodgers, Jr., *Environmental Law* (2nd edn. West Publishing Co, St. Paul MN, 1994), p. 39.
88. Garrett L. Hardin, "The Tragedy of the Commons" (1968) *Science*, vol. 162, p. 1243.
89. *Ibid.*
90. *Ibid.* at 1244.
91. Classical economic theory advocates the privatization of common property as a means of avoiding the kind of problems that Hardin describes. See, e.g., Rose, *Property & Persuasion*, pp. 105–108.
92. Hardin, "Tragedy of the Commons" at 1246–1247. Hardin recommended that the coercion be achieved by democratic processes: It was to be "mutually agreed upon by the majority of people affected." *Ibid.* at 1247.
93. See Chapter 3, pp. 147–148.
94. Robert C. Allen, "The Efficiency and Distributional Consequences of Eighteenth Century Enclosures" (1982) *The Economics Journal*, vol. 92, p. 937; Bennett Baack, "Testing the Impact of Exclusive Property Rights: The Case of Enclosing Common Fields," in Roger L. Ransom, Richard Sutch and Gary M. Walton (eds.) *Explorations in the New Economic History: Essays in Honor of*

Douglass C. North (Academic Press, New York, 1982); Susan J. B. Cox, "No Tragedy on the Commons" (1985) 7 *Envtl Ethics* 49; Carl J. Dahlman, *The Open Field System and Beyond: A Property Rights Analysis of an Economic Institution* (Cambridge University Press, New York and Cambridge, 1980); J. M. Neeson, *Commoners: Common Right, Enclosure and Social Change in England, 1700–1820* (Cambridge University Press, New York, 1993); J. A. Yelling, *Common Field and Enclosure in England* 1450–1850 (Archon Books, Hamden Conn., 1977). For modeling exercises reaching similar results, see Bruce A. Larson and Daniel W. Bromley, "Property Rights, Externalities, and Resource Degradation: Locating the Tragedy" (1990) *Journal of Development Economics*, vol. 33, p. 235; Carlisle Ford Runge, "Common Property Externalities: Isolation, Assurance, and Resource Depletion in a Traditional Grazing Context" (1981) *American Journal of Agricultural Economics*, vol. 63, p. 595. See also Brian R. Binger and Elizabeth Hoffman, "Institutional Persistence and Change: The Question of Efficiency" (1989) *Journal of Institutional and Theoretical Economics*, vol. 145, p. 67.

95. Rose, "Several Futures of Property", at p. 180.
96. Firket Berkes et al., "The Benefits of the Commons" (1989) 340 *Nature* 91, 93; Dahlman, *Open Field System and Beyond*, pp. 100–102; Piers Blaikie and Harold Brookfield, *Land Degradation and Society* (Methuen, New York, 1987), p. 186.
97. Garrett Hardin, "The Tragedy of the Unmanaged Commons" (1994) *Trends in Ecology and Evolution*, vol. 9, no. 5, p. 199 ("ecologists have failed to see subtle signs of management in traditional societies. Such a managed commons presents no problem to the theory of unmanaged commons").
98. Cox, "No Tragedy on the Commons", p. 49.
99. Not every customary law is a focus of our interest. Our topic is property law. The resources we investigate typically involve common or public property rights (*res communes omnium* or *res nullius*). In Norway this division is illustrated by the concept of "allmenningsrett" (common property rights) versus allemannsrett (public property rights) – the latter being the concept of the open common without input restrictions.
100. Grossi, *Alternative to Private Property*.
101. *Ibid.*
102. Peter Ørebech, "Sedvanereet som gunnlag for bærekraftig forvaltning av fiske i de 'ytre almenninger,'" ["Customary Law as a Foundation for Sustainable Fishing Management"] in Bjørn Sagdahl (ed.), *Fjordressurser og Reguleringspolitikk* (Kommuneforlaget, Oslo, 1998) pp. 141 ff. Nevertheless, the neoclassical economists continue to encourage the privatization of ocean and fisheries resources. See R. Quentin Grafton, Dale Squires and Kevin J. Fox, "Private Property and Economic Efficiency: A Study of a Common-Pool Resource"

(2000) *Journal of Law & Economics* 679. See the criticism of their position in P. Ørebech, "What Restoration Schemes Can Do? Or, Getting It Right Without Fisheries Transferable Quotas," (2005) *Ocean Development and International Law*, vol. 36, pp. 159–178.

103. Robert C. Ellickson, *Order Without Law. How Neighbours Settle Disputes* (Harvard University Press, Cambridge, Mass., 1991). See also Elinor Ostrom, *Governing the Commons: The Evolution of Institutions for Collective Action* (Cambridge University Press, Cambridge, 1990).
104. Grossi, *Alternative to Private Property*, p. 5.
105. National Research Council, Proceedings of the Conference on Common Property Resource Management (1986), vii–viii.
106. The World Bank has been actively encouraging the participation of local groups in project design and management in order to avoid some of the problems created when traditional control mechanisms are ignored. See World Bank Participation Source Book (Environment Department, World Bank, February 1996); The World Bank and Participation (Operations Policy Department, The World Bank, September 1994).
107. Ostrom, "Reformulating the Commons", p. 17.
108. Berkes et al., *Benefits of the Commons*, at p. 93.
109. Shui Yan Tang, *Institutions and Collective Action: Self-Governance in Irrigation* (ICS Press, San Francisco, Calif., 1992), pp. 130–131; Ostrom, *Governing the Commons*, p. 206; Berkes et al., *Benefits of the Commons*, at p. 93.
110. Elinor Ostrom et al., *Rules Games and Common-Pool Resources* (University of Michigan Press, Ann Arbor, 1994), p. 144; Ellickson, *Order Without Law*, pp. 167–168, 178–181; Bruce Campbell and Ricardo A. Godoy, *Commonfield Agriculture: The Andes and Medieval England Compared* (Proceedings of the Conference on Common Property Resource Management, National Research Council, 1986), pp. 323, 339–342.
111. Ostrom et al., *Rules Games and Common-Pool Resources*, pp. 312–315.
112. *Ibid.*, pp. 308–312.
113. *Ibid.*, p. 149.
114. Blaikie and Brookfield, *Land Degradation and Society*, pp. 192–193; Jeffrey A. McNeely, "Common Property Resource Management or Government Ownership: Improving the Conservation of Biological Resources" (1991) 10 *International Relations* 211; Tang, *Institutions and Collective Action*, pp. 132–138.
115. A study of ancient English commons of the wetlands by Fred Bosselman found that the "fen people" used a limited common property system of property rights sustainable for centuries. The study notes four distinctions that merit discussion. First, Hardin's 1968 hypothetical commons were not similar to the commons of the wetlands. While the latter institution carried

a limited common pool right, Hardin's tragic common was completely open. Second, the latter institution overlooked the importance of communicative interrelationship. The third distinction is "the critical difference between the grazing land resource used in Hardin's paradigm and the wetlands resource in medieval England," because the latter enjoyed the storage capacity lacking in Hardin's model. Fourth, while the Hardin resources were fairly homogeneous in resource allocation among members, wetlands contained mobile and varied resources distributed disproportionately in particular sub-areas. Fred P. Bosselman, "Limitations Inherent in the Title to Wetlands at Common Law" (1996) 15 *Stanford Environmental Law Journal* 247, at 304–311.

116. Ostrom et al., (eds.), *The Drama of the Commons Committee on the Human Dimensions of Global Change* (National Research Council, National Academy Press, Washington DC, 2002).
117. NOU 2001: 34 (Ministry of Justice): Peter Ørebech, *Sedvanerett i fisket. Sjøsamene i Finnmark.*
118. Ørebech. "Sedvanerett som gunnlag for bærekaftig forvaltning av fiske i de 'ytre almenninger,'" pp. 141 ff.
119. See Maurstad, *Sjarkfiske og ressursforvaltning.*
120. See, for instance, Ostrom, *Governing the Commons*, p. 24; Robert McC. Netting, *Smallholders, Householders, Farm Families and the Ecology of Intensive, Sustainable Agriculture* (Stanford University Press, Stanford, Calif., 1993); William Blomquist, *Dividing the Waters, Governing Groundwater in Southern California* (ICS Press, San Francisco, CA, 1992).
121. 23 Fed. Cas. 558 (D. Mass. 1872) (No. 13, 696).
122. Robert C. Ellickson, "A Hypothesis of Wealth-Maximizing Norms: Evidence from the Whaling Industry" (1989) *Journal of Law, Economics and Organization*, vol. 5, no. 1, p. 83.
123. Peter Goodrich, *Reading the Law: A Critical Introduction* (Basil Blackwell, London, 1986), p. 64.
124. John Locke, *Second Treatise of Civil Government* (Basil Blackwell, Oxford, 1956), secs. 27–34.
125. P. Ørebech, K. Sigurjonsson and Ted L. McDorman, "The 1995 United Nations Straddling and Highly Migratory Fish Stocks Agreement: Management, Enforcement and Dispute Settlement," *The International Journal of Marine and Coastal Law* (No. 2, May 1998).
126. See Chapter 4 at pp. 207–213.
127. See Chapter 11 at pp. 439–441.
128. See e.g., Richard Price, *Two Tracts on Civil Liberty in Political Writings* (ed. by D. O. Thomas, Cambridge University Press, Cambridge 1991), p. 22. Thus, the discussion in Chapter 7 focuses on the core of the philosophical discussion of liberty and liberalism as well.

129. "As the law cannot be detached from law making and the settling of disputes, it cannot be detached from the customs prevailing in the lawyers' community. Any full discussion of law must build on custom, if only for this reason." Schlicht, *On Custom in the Economy*, p. 200.
130. While our work is mainly oriented toward *de sententia ferenda* ("the law as possibly developed in the near future") and *de lege ferenda* ("the law as it should be") arguments, Peter Ørebech also sets forth *de lege lata* ("the law as is") in his discussion of the international law of sustainable development in Chapter 9. David Callies and Peter Ørebech both discuss *de lege lata* when presenting the prerequisites for customary law in England and Norway in Chapters 4 and 5, respectively.
131. Brian Simpson, "The Common Law and Legal Theory," in William Twining (ed.), *Legal Theory and Common Law* (Basil Blackwell, Oxford, 1986), p. 18.
132. Sir William Blackstone, *Commentaries on the Laws of England* (John Murray, London, 1857), vol. I, p. 113.
133. Bridwell and Whitten point out that "In a customary law system, precedent and custom are distinct and treated as such. However, some civil law writers, operating under the influence of a positivist law theory of the common law, have a tendency to treat them as identical. It may be that some of their confusion is due to the apparent interaction of Blackstone's theory of precedent with the relatively mature common law system that existed by the late eighteenth and early nineteenth centuries." Randall Bridwell and Ralph Whitten, *The Constitution and Common Law* (Lexington Books, Lexington, MA, 1977), p. 17.
134. This reflects the practice of the "Kings Courts," (Plucknett, *Concise History of the Common Law*, p. 302), although much customary law consisted of folk practice as confirmed by manor courts, and later by "Popular Courts of Justice," (Maine, *Dissertations on Early Law and Custom*, p. 173) derived from a combination of landlords' decisions and informal norms generated from below. See Dahlman, *The Open-Field System and Beyond.*
135. Magna Carta clause 48. These "customs" were forced upon high and low by King John, mighty public servants, royal officials, justice administrators, petty officials, etc. A. E. Dick Howard, *Magna Carta: Text and Commentary* (The University Press of Virginia, Charlottesville VA, 1964), pp. 16–18.
136. See also clause 62: "We have also wholly remitted and pardoned all ill-will, wrath, and malice which has arisen between Us and Our subjects, both clergy and laymen, during the disputes, to and with all men."
137. For instance, the Deutsche Reichskammergericht law-reception of 1495, which introduced written and non-written Roman law into German law, was not "bottom-up" produced. Ole Fenger, *Romerret i Norden* [*Roman Law in the Nordic Countries*] (Berlingske forlag, Copenhager, 1977), p. 113, cf. 166.

138. The Regional Fisheries Organizations are examples of international bodies that develop the case-by-case-based practice that tends to become customary law. See pp. 307–311 below. These instances may have some similarities to local customary law.
139. See Chapter 9.

2

Three case studies from Hawaii, Norway and Greenland

DAVID CALLIES, PETER ØREBECH AND HANNE PETERSEN

2.1 Hawaiian customary rights

2.1.1 The native Hawaiians

Polynesians originally came to Hawaii during the eighth century AD, bringing Polynesian culture that included agricultural practices and domestic animals. Beginning with Captain Cook in 1778, numerous European explorers brought European artifacts – as well as diseases to which the Hawaiians had no immunity. Missionaries followed and began to convert the people to Christianity and to try to eliminate some aspects of Polynesian culture that they believed to be immoral.

Meanwhile, there had been a great deal of infighting among various groups of Polynesians on the various islands, which largely ended with the accession of Kamehaha I as the acknowledged King of the Hawaiian Islands. Mercantile interests from Europe and the United States began to use Hawaii as a trading base and vied with each other for control of the islands and domination of the local Polynesian culture and politics. Eventually, American interests persuaded the Hawaiian monarchy to cede control of the political structure of the islands to the United States, which annexed Hawaii as a territory.

The Polynesian economy, which had been based on small-scale agriculture and hunting and gathering, was replaced by plantation agriculture with sugar and pineapple as the dominant crops, and by international trade and military activity. Waves of immigrants from various Asian countries, other Pacific islands and the United States came to fill the jobs created in this economic expansion, bringing with them elements of their own cultures that blended with the earlier Polynesian and European elements into a uniquely Hawaiian culture.

Many of the descendants of the early Polynesians assimilated into this cosmopolitan society, achieving great success and often intermarrying with people of many different origins. Other Polynesian descendants opted out of integration, choosing to maintain elements of the traditional culture, primarily in more remote rural areas. One institution created by the last descendant of Kamehaha, the Bishop Estate, became the largest private landowner in Hawaii, exerting great political and economic power.

Some descendants of the Polynesians, resenting what they believed to be past discrimination against their ancestors, created a social and political movement to obtain reparations and greater political power. Other such descendants sought to preserve and cherish elements of the old Hawaiian culture without necessarily changing the political structure.

Gradually, the Native Hawaiian movement became an important force to be reckoned with, achieving legislative support at both the federal and state level. Government set aside lands for Hawaiian homesteads, and established health programs and other benefits for people who could demonstrate the requisite heritage from the original Polynesians. The state courts in Hawaii recognized the validity of native Hawaiian hunting and gathering rights in a variety of situations that led to conflict with private and public land development activities.

But administration of institutions for native Hawaiians was not without controversy. The Bishop Estate, which had been created to fund education for native Hawaiians, became involved in many corrupt activities that were of little benefit to the beneficiaries, and the scandal resulted in the ouster of the trustees. Resentment against the political aims of the Native Hawaiian movement stimulated litigation challenging the programs providing benefits for native Hawaiians, which culminated in the United States Supreme Court's decision in *Rice v. Cayetano*[1] holding that "Native Hawaiian" was an unconstitutional racial classification that did not qualify for the same special treatment as American Indians. Although *Rice* held only that native Hawaiians could not be given privileged voting status, it has raised questions about many other programs designed to benefit native Hawaiians, some of which are being contested in new litigation.

Some native Hawaiians have responded with increased militancy, seeking to restore the monarchy and secede from the United States, while others are seeking Congressional legislation to resolve the legitimacy of existing programs. In the midst of this turmoil, the Hawaiian state courts have been continuing to enforce Hawaiian customary law as the basis for rules governing the rights of native Hawaiians to exploit the natural resources of the islands. The interpretation of this customary law, and the analysis of the controversy it has created, provide a case study of the application of customary law to current conditions.

The customary rights of native Hawaiians in Hawaii derive from several sources, the most prominent of which are statutory and constitutional. Several important cases deal with both these sources and the rights they guarantee. Generally, the most important traditional and cultural rights are those to fish, hunt and gather. Applicable to all of these rights are what is usually called "ohana values," which traditionally govern the practice of these rights by native Hawaiians:

1. Only take what is needed for subsistence.
2. Do not waste the resource.
3. Allow the resource to replenish and reproduce.
4. Respect and protect the knowledge which has been passed down from one generation to the next.
5. Respect each others' areas.
6. Throughout an "expedition" focus on the goal for which you have set out to fish, hunt or gather.
7. Respect the spirits of the resources; do not become loud and boisterous.[2]

Customary law in Hawaii is primarily derived from several key common law cases from the Hawaii Supreme Court, together with the relatively recently (1978) added Article XII, section 7 of the Hawaii State Constitution, which provides that "the State shall protect all rights, customarily and traditionally exercised for subsistence, cultural and religious purposes and possessed by ahupua'a tenants who are descendants of native Hawaiians who inhabited the Hawaiian islands prior to 1778, subject to the right of the State to regulate such rights." As appears below, several cases have interpreted those parts of section 7 dealing with ahupua'a tenants, the terms traditional and cultural, and what limits, if any, there are on such rights. What follows is a summary of these rights and the present legal status of these rights following a series of important court decisions.

The most common and controversial of the rights exercised by native Hawaiians are those rights associated with gathering activities. This is because gathering activities depend critically upon access to that which may be gathered, and that access often depends upon rights to go upon land of another, often privately-held. Under the ancient Hawaiian gathering system, gathering was for three primary purposes: supplementing a subsistence lifestyle of tenant farmers with plants and animals otherwise not available to him; obtaining of products for communal purposes when required by a resident chief; and survival during times of famine and drought.[3]

Generally, the gathering rights of native Hawaiians were restricted to lands within their ahupua'a, the pie-shaped land division extending from the mountains or uplands to the sea, and generally governed by a noble or ali'i.[4] Both cultivated and non-cultivated materials were gathered, depending upon the nature of the ahupua'a. Some things were gathered for food, others for medicinal and ceremonial purposes. MacKenzie notes that among the cultivated plants in the uplands were taro, yams, pi'a, olena, 'ohe and 'awa. Others such as ohia lehua grew wild. Native Hawaiians also "gathered" fish from the streams and both coral reef and deep ocean areas, limu, opihi and other marine products along the sea coast, and hunted for feral pigs in the uplands and mountains.[5] Resources were conserved by means of various kapu (forbidding of certain practices by the chiefs or ali'i), which, for example, might forbid deep water fishing during spawning season.[6]

The first apparent codification of such traditional gathering rights appears to be an 1839 codification of practices then present in upland and ocean areas. Tenants were specifically authorized or permitted to exercise such rights within an ahupua'a subject to various restrictions. Thus, for example, restrictions were placed on the kind and quantity of trees that could be felled, as well as certain birds, which were reserved for the king. Any commoner could fish in the open sea, but only ahupua'a residents could fish between the shoreline and the reef. Entire species could be declared "off-limits" to commoners by chiefs and the king. Upland, sandalwood was so declared by the king in the 1839 laws, to protect his monopoly, for exportation to the orient.[7]

With the advent of plantation agriculture and ranching, both the small holdings of native Hawaiian tenants and gathering practices went into steep decline. Hawaii changed from a subsistence to a mercantile economy, and many gathering practices were forgotten and little-used. However, even in the third quarter of the nineteenth century, the Hawaii Supreme Court recognized such rights. In *In re Boundaries of Pulehunui*[8] the court specifically recognized the rights of both "chief and his people" to products not only of fisheries but the products of the highlands such as fuel, canoe timber, mountain birds and all the varied products of the intermediate land as might be suitable to the soil and climate of the different altitudes "and the right of way to the same."

However, customary rights generally took a substantial legal hit in *Oni v. Meek*[9] in which the court appeared to abolish customary and traditional rights of every kind. As appears below, this case was explained away in the famous *PASH* decision. Meanwhile, gathering rights generally were nicely set out, together with their legal basis, in the 1982 case of *Kalipi v. Hawaiian Trust Co.*[10] While the case is probably most famous for restricting the right of the plaintiff to gathering in his own ahupua'a (and as he did not reside where he was seeking to gather, the court held he lacked the right to so gather where he presently wished to do so) it is equally instructive with respect to what was being gathered and under what legal authority.

The first such source is statutory: HRS 1-1, which declares the common law of England to be the law of Hawaii "except . . . by . . . established Hawaiian usage." Such usage amounted to "native understandings and practices which did not unreasonably interfere with the spirit of the common law." The court held that such balancing of native usage and other recognized property interests would need to occur on a case-by-case basis.

Which practices were common is derived from that next part of the opinion dealing with HRS 7-1 (the old Kuleana Act), which sets out what a native tenant may gather within his ahupua'a: firewood, house timber, aho cord, thatch or ti-leaf. The court restricted the gathering of the above to tenants, living within the ahupua'a where the gathering would occur, on undeveloped land, and for the purpose of practicing native Hawaiian customs and traditions. These rights were substantially expanded by *Pele Defense Fund v. Paty* and *Public Access Shoreline Hawaii v. Hawaii County Planning Commission* (see below).

2.1.2 Access rights independent of gathering rights

Native Hawaiians exercised access rights in order to gather in a traditional and cultural fashion, as noted in the preceding section. They also enjoyed access to so-called kuleana parcels within an ahupua'a and to a network of trails for foot travel generally. Historically, the need for these trails was apparently conceived by the ali'i in charge of a particular district or ahupua'a, then laid out, designed and planned by the local land agent or konohiki, then actually constructed by the commoners.[11] The trails ran either from the mountains to the sea within an ahupua'a in order to give ahupua'a residents access to taro terraces and cultivated crops, and for hunting and gathering, or horizontally across ahupua'as from one district to another.[12]

Today, the right of access is generally divided into two categories, according to Paul Lucas: access rights to a kuleana parcel and access rights between two or more ahupua'a or districts. Early Hawaii Supreme Court cases generally recognized such access rights in the first or kuleana category under the common law concept of easement. Where none was expressly reserved or found, such easements were often declared by implied grant or by necessity.[13] Moreover, the Kuleana Act discussed in the preceding section provided native tenants a statutory right of access to their kuleanas. It is discussed in several later cases confirming such access rights based on both the statute and upon necessity and Hawaiian custom.[14]

Access between districts is somewhat more complicated. Gathering and tending crops within the ahupua'a does not readily form a basis for such rights. While there appears to be statutory authority for protecting access to and along trails on government property,[15] it is less clear with respect to private land. Again, *Oni v. Meek* would make such rights based solely on customary rights difficult to maintain except, of course, as modified by the *PASH* case. On the other hand, the Hawaii Supreme Court in an unpublished memorandum opinion did uphold a trial court decision in *Barbra v. Okuna* in which fishermen and other residents attempted to establish access to shoreline trails[16] across private land. The lower court found that such trails were used by Hawaiians in prehistoric times to move from place to place and that such use continued and was not inconsistent with Hawaii's existing property laws, and therefore that the fishermen and residents had demonstrated that a right-of-way over the Hawaiian trail was established by custom.[17]

In *Oni v. Meek*,[18] a pre-statehood case, the plaintiff claimed a statutory right to engage in the custom of pasturing horses on unused private land.[19] The court concluded that such a right, if it existed, was extinguished by the passage of an 1851 statute that granted "people on the lands" the right to take "firewood, housetimber, aho cord, thatch, or ki leaf drinking water, and running water."[20] In the court's view, the 1851 statute listed "all the specific rights of the [people] (excepting fishing rights) which should be held to prevail against the fee simple title" of private landowners.[21] Moreover, the court found that the asserted pasturage right was "so unreasonable, so uncertain, and so repugnant to the spirit of the present laws, that it ought not to be sustained by judicial authority."[22] It therefore rejected plaintiffs' attempt to assert the customary right of pasturage.[23]

In *Kalipi v. Hawaiian Trust Company, Ltd.*,[24] the Hawaii Supreme Court recognized the existence of a broad range of customary native Hawaiian rights, while establishing geographical and pragmatic limits on their exercise. In *Kalipi*, a native Hawaiian plaintiff claimed the right to gather on private land "natural products for certain traditional native Hawaiian practices."[25] More specifically, Kalipi sought to gather "ti leaf, bamboo, kukui nuts, kiawe and medicinal herbs and ferns" on undeveloped land adjacent to land upon which he owned a houselot. At trial, a jury concluded that Kalipi did not enjoy the gathering rights he asserted. On appeal to the Hawaii Supreme Court, Kalipi argued that native Hawaiian gathering rights were enshrined in, and protected by, statute and "custom and tradition."[26]

In considering the existence of native gathering rights, the court noted that, if allowed, such rights would conflict with the "exclusivity traditionally associated with fee simple ownership."[27] However, noting that it had an obligation under the state constitution to preserve and enforce native rights, the court concluded that the principle of exclusivity was not sufficient to preclude the exercise of native rights if found to exist. Turning to Kalipi's substantive claims, the court agreed that customary gathering rights flowed from HRS section 7-1, which granted those "on the land" the right to "take" numerous items from the land.[28]

Although it recognized that HRS section 7-1 granted numerous native rights, the court was clearly troubled by the fact that such rights were a "remnant of an economic and physical existence largely foreign to today's world."[29] It therefore viewed its task as one of conforming the native rights expressed in HRS section 7-1 to the "modern system of land tenure."[30] Accordingly, the court interpreted HRS section 7-1 "to assure that lawful occupants of an ahupua'a may, for the purposes of practicing native Hawaiian custom and traditions, enter undeveloped lands within the ahupua'a to gather those items enumerated in the statute."[31] In so doing, the court established two important limits on the exercise of statutory gathering rights. First, it established that such rights could only be exercised in an ahupua'a, a land division running from the mountains to the sea, by people who live in that same area. Second, even when otherwise properly exercised, the practice of gathering rights under HRS section 7-1 was allowed only on undeveloped land.[32] The Court subsequently determined that Kalipi could not legally exercise the gathering rights he claimed under HRS section 7-1 because he did not live in the ahupua'a in which he wished to gather.[33]

The court next considered whether Kalipi's asserted gathering rights were authorized by the following language in Hawaii Revised Statutes section 1-1:

> The common law of England, as ascertained by American and English decisions, is declared to be the common law of the State of Hawaii in all cases, except as otherwise expressly provided by the Constitution or laws of

> the United States, or by the laws of the State, or fixed by Hawaiian judicial precedent, or established by Hawaiian usage[.]
>
> [emphasis in original]

The court declared that the "Hawaiian usage" exception was "akin to the English doctrine of custom whereby practices and privileges unique to particular districts continued to apply to the residents of those districts in contravention of the common law."[34] Nevertheless, in the court's view, section 1-1 did not necessarily establish the legality of native Hawaiian customs. Rather, it determined that "retention of a Hawaiian tradition should in each case be determined by balancing the respective interests and harm once it is established that the custom has continued in a particular area."[35] Accordingly, the court read the reference to "Hawaiian usage" to protect Hawaiian practices on undeveloped land beyond those explicitly reserved by HRS section 7-1 as long as "no actual harm is done thereby."[36] The court noted that use of land for "spiritual and other purposes," and for the gathering of items "not delineated in section 7-1" was thus theoretically permissible.[37]

In concluding that native Hawaiians had the right to exercise traditions beyond those expressly reserved by HRS section 7-1, the court rejected the argument that *Oni v. Meek* established section 7-1 as the sole repository of Hawaiian customary rights. Although it conceded that Oni said that section 7-1 defined the scope of customary rights retained by native Hawaiians, the court concluded that the Oni was concerned only with the pasturage rights asserted, rather than with the viability of customary rights as a whole. Moreover, the *Kalipi* court viewed *Oni* as limited to the issue of whether certain customary rights were preserved by statute.[38] It therefore interpreted *Oni* to "stand for the proposition that section 7-1 expresses all commoners' rights statutorily insured at the time of the Mehele," (emphasis added). Viewed in this light, *Oni* did not preclude the recognition of rights under the broader doctrine of custom recognized in HRS section 1-1. The court subsequently noted that the nature and scope of customary rights would depend on factual circumstances not before it, and that there was "an insufficient basis to find that such rights would, or should accrue to persons who did not actually reside in the ahupua'a in which such rights are claimed."[39] Emphasizing that Kalipi did not reside in the ahupua'a in which he attempted to gather natural products, the court rejected his claims under section 1-1.[40]

In *Pele Defense Fund v. Paty*,[41] the Hawaii Supreme Court held that native Hawaiians could exercise customary rights in areas adjacent to their area of residency, if they could show that past native Hawaiians had traveled from one area to another in practicing the asserted customs. In *Paty*, the state of Hawaii granted certain public lands to a number of private companies in exchange for a near-equal amount of private land.[42] Pele Defense Fund (PDF) subsequently filed suit to enjoin the new owners of the once public land from excluding native Hawaiians who wished to engage in traditional practices. The trial court dismissed PDF's claim that the Hawaii Constitution protected the right of its members to enter private lands to exercise gathering rights even if they did not reside in the immediate area.[43] On appeal, the Hawaii Supreme Court considered whether PDF members had to show that they were residents of the private lands in which they desired to exercise customary rights in order to establish that such rights existed.[44] The court noted that *Kalipi* allowed native Hawaiians to exercise rights only in the area in which they resided and that, as in *Kalipi*, the plaintiffs in *Paty* did not live on the land where they wished to exercise traditional rights.[45] However, unlike *Kalipi*, PDF members asserted customary rights on the land on which they did not reside on the basis of "the traditional access and gathering patterns of native Hawaiians in the . . . region," not on the mere ownership of land in the area.[46] Finding that the drafters of Article XII, section 7 of the Hawaii Constitution intended to protect all customary rights, the court concluded that "[i]f as argued by PDF, the customary and traditional rights associated with tenancy in an ahupua'a extended beyond the boundaries of the ahupua'a, then Article XII, section 7 protects those rights as well."[47] The court recognized that PDF had presented evidence at trial "supporting the contention that the access and gathering patterns of tenants in Puna" did not conform to the idea that native Hawaiians exercised customary rights only in the area in which they lived.[48] The court therefore found genuine issues of material fact concerning PDF's claim that its members had a right to enter formerly public lands for customary purposes.[49] Accordingly, it remanded the issue back to the lower court.

In *Public Access Shoreline Hawaii v. Nansay*,[50] (*PASH*) the Hawaii Supreme Court finished the work it started in *Paty* by clearly and completely rejecting the limits *Kalipi* had placed on the exercise of native Hawaiian customary rights. In *PASH*, resort developers applied to the Hawaii Planning Commission for a special management area permit (SMAP) that would allow construction of a coastal resort on the Big Island of Hawaii.[51] Public Access Shoreline Hawaii, a group composed of native Hawaiians, sought and was denied a contested case hearing before the Hawaii Planning Commission. PASH appealed the denial to the Intermediate Court of Appeals, which held that the Planning Commission had impermissibly ignored its obligation to protect native Hawaiian rights when it denied PASH's standing to participate in the SMAP hearing.[52] In the view of the Intermediate Court of Appeals, the existence of customary native rights distinguished PASH's interests from that of the general public, and therefore gave it a right to participate in the hearing.[53]

On appeal, the Hawaii Supreme Court agreed that "as native Hawaiians who have exercised such rights as were customarily and traditionally exercised for subsistence, cultural and religious purposes on undeveloped land," PASH had an interest in the SMAP permit for resort development that was sufficiently distinguishable from that of the general public to give it standing.[54] On its own initiative, the court then considered whether the Hawaii Planning Commission had an obligation and authority to protect native rights on unoccupied, private land through imposition of SMAP conditions or otherwise.[55] Focusing on the Commission's obligations under Article XII, section 7 of the Hawaii Constitution, the court emphasized that Kalipi established that the Hawaii Constitution protected the exercise of native customary rights on undeveloped lands by native Hawaiians who resided within those lands.[56] However, the Court concluded that Kalipi "did not foreclose the possibility of establishing, in future cases, traditional Hawaiian gathering rights in one [area] that have been customarily held by residents of another [area]."[57] Further, the court found that *Kalipi* and *Paty* had not foreclosed modification of the requirement from *Kalipi* that customary rights be exercised only on undeveloped land and produce "no actual harm."[58] Finally, the court argued that, in focusing on native Hawaiian residency, the court in *Kalipi* had not properly addressed Kalipi's claim that broad native Hawaiian rights were protected by tradition as well as statute.[59]

Having narrowed *Kalipi* to its facts, the court formulated its own interpretation of the scope of customary native Hawaiian rights. The court first explained that HRS section 1-1 codified a modified version of the Blackstonian doctrine of custom and thereby established that native Hawaiian traditions could continue to exist even if not explicitly recognized by statute. The court emphasized that, unlike English customary law, Hawaiian customary law did not require practices to exist from "time immemorial" to qualify for legal protection in Hawaii. Instead, the court concluded that the 1892 passage of HRS section 1-1, which codified the doctrine of custom, established that Hawaiian practices need only have been established by 1892.[60] Further, the court concluded that "the common law rights ordinarily associated with tenancy do not limit customary rights existing under the laws of this state."[61] It thus declined to limit the customary rights of native Hawaiians to the area in which they lived. Further, the court held that customary rights could be exercised by all native Hawaiians who were descendants of those who inhabited the islands prior to Captain Cook's arrival in 1778.[62]

Recognizing that its recognition of broad and pervasive customary rights would conflict with current understandings of property, the court reviewed the development of private property in Hawaii and concluded that "the western concept of exclusivity is not universally applicable in Hawaii."[63] Moreover, the court refused to "place undue emphasis on non-Hawaiian principles of land ownership" by following the suggestion in *Kalipi* that the exercise of traditional rights would be permissible only on undeveloped land. Indeed, the court reversed the limitations in *Kalipi* by holding that the exercise of native customary rights "may" be inconsistent on land that is fully developed.[64] Although the court realized that allowing any native Hawaiian to enter partly developed land at will could lead to "disruption," the court explained that the state could regulate the exercise of native rights to avoid harm and that "the non-confrontational aspects of traditional Hawaiian culture should minimize potential disturbances."[65] The court therefore concluded that the Hawaii Planning Commission had an obligation to protect the native Hawaiian rights established in *PASH* to the extent "feasible." In what can only be described as a postscript, the court rejected the contention that the state-sanctioned entry of native Hawaiians onto private property would constitute a taking of private property in violation of the Fifth Amendment to the U.S. Constitution.[66]

In *State of Hawaii v. Hanapi*,[67] the Hawaii Supreme Court retreated from the sweeping pronouncements in *PASH* by holding that it was always "inconsistent" to permit the exercise of native Hawaiian rights on improved residential lands. In *Hanapi*, a native Hawaiian was arrested and charged with trespassing after entering and remaining on private property to view the restoration of a small pond. At trial, Hanapi asserted that he had entered the property to practice "religious and traditional ceremonies of healing the land," and that these and other practices were protected customary rights that allowed him to lawfully enter the property.[68]

Although it recognized customary right as a legitimate defense to a trespassing charge, the Hanapi court concluded that the burden was on the defendant to "demonstrate that the right is protected."[69] The court explained that a person carries such a burden by showing that he is qualified as a native Hawaiian in the sense of being a descendant of those Hawaiians who inhabited the island prior to 1778, that the asserted right is protected as a customary right, and that the right was exercised on undeveloped land.[70] The court recognized that it had previously held in *PASH* that the practice of customary rights "may" be inconsistent on land that has reached "full development."[71] Such statements were intended, the court explained, to limit conflict between native rights and "modern reality." Consistent with that purpose, the court in *Hanapi* clarified the geographical scope of native customary right by holding that "if property is deemed 'full developed,' i.e., lands zoned and used for residential purposes with existing dwellings, improvements and infrastructure, it is always 'inconsistent' to permit the practice of traditional and customary native Hawaiian rights on such property."[72] Further, the court noted that property other than that which is zoned residential may be developed to a point where it would be "inconsistent" to allow native practices.[73]

Turning to the asserted right in *Hanapi* to enter private property for religious healing, the court determined the establishment of a customary practice requires "an adequate foundation in the record connecting the claimed right to a firmly rooted tradition or customary native Hawaiian practice."[74] The court noted that such a foundation could be established by expert or local witness testimony.[75] However the court found that *Hanapi* "did not offer any explanation of the history or origin of the claimed right. Nor was there a description of the 'ceremonies' involved in the healing process." Accordingly, the court held that the lower court had properly rejected Hanapi's claim of privilege and thus, that substantial evidence existed to support his conviction.[76]

Finally, in 2001 the Hawaii Supreme Court created a framework for performing an impact analysis of the effect of development on traditional and customary rights, and held that in order to protect Hawaiian rights, government agencies had an obligation to perform such an analysis before making land use decisions.[77]

2.1.3 Conclusion

Essentially, the law on native Hawaiian custom in Hawaii today permits native Hawaiians of any blood quantum to go on private or public lands to exercise traditional or cultural rights, provided the land is not developed. A residentially zoned and occupied lot is conclusively developed and therefore not subject to native Hawaiian customary rights. It is also the obligation of all governmental regulatory and permitting agencies to investigate the effect of any proposed development on traditional and customary Hawaiian rights and to take steps to ameliorate any adverse effects which such development might have. However, the burden is on those claiming native Hawaiian rights to prove that the custom is both native Hawaiian and that the claimants are entitled to exercise the right. The impact of these rights and obligations will be summarized in Chapter 10.

2.2 Saami fisheries customary law

> Fisheries are among the trades, not only the most important, but also the only clearly important or vital ones. With the exception of the Mountain Saami and the miners of Kaafjord, who are not dependent upon fisheries exploitation, fisheries are indirectly or directly the basis for the common existence of the coastal population.
>
> Fredrik Rode[78]

2.2.1 Introduction

In this section we will develop the modern indigenous view of Saami not as ethnically or geographically distinct from Norse or Norwegian inhabitants, but as integrated parts of local societies. The fight for ethnically based special fishing rights has turned into a demand for local customary rights. As indicated, the Saami struggle for local rights has failed due to strong pressure from nationally based interests advocated by the Norwegian Fishermen's Association and the Ministry of Fisheries. At present local customary law fisheries regimes have survived, but such regimes have not yet been recognized. These regimes (see Section 2.2.4) illustrate that local self-management may prevent wasteful overuse of a resource (see Chapter 6).

Nonetheless, the Saami and other inhabitants in the northernmost counties of Norway have to live under the general fisheries regulations. In practice Saami and small-scale fishermen are denied participation rights because of the termination of open access fishing in 1990. This practice is contrary to both manifest customary law (Chapter 5) and international law obligations towards indigenous peoples (Chapter 9).

2.2.2 The Saami legal and political framework[79]

The Saami are the indigenous people of northern Scandinavia who settled in Sápmi or Saami dnan (Saami land). Norse settlers (Norwegians along the coast and Finns and Swedes in inland areas) gradually conquered the Saami land. During this period Norse settlers colonized much of the reindeer grazing land and the state enforced strict tax regulations. In Finnmark, the Northernmost County of Norway, Norwegian policy promoted assimilation of the Saami into Norwegian culture up until World War II.[80] At present almost 80,000 Saami people live in Norway, Finland, Russia and Sweden. Some 20,000 live in Sweden, 45,000 in Norway, 10,000 in Finland and 2,000 in Russia. The Saami people share mainly language, means of livelihood and culture. The Saami language belongs to the Finno-Ugric language family. The closest related languages are Finnish and Estonian. The Saami were hunters and food-gatherers, who later became fishers and reindeer herders. These occupations remain fundamental to the Saami culture today.

Over time, the Saami living in the interior developed quite a different economic base from the coastal Saami. The inland Saami rounded up the wild reindeer and became herdsmen.[81] Norwegian law reserved the right to control reindeer to people of Saami ethnicity,[82] and this helped solidify Saami identity. Along the coast, however, the Saami depended on fishing, an occupation they have shared with the Norse immigrants to Finnmark since the early thirteenth century. Saami fishing practices have been based on customary law, a normative system that is built upon an "equal footing doctrine."[83] Members of society, whether Saami or Norse, were equally allowed to benefit from the available resources. The reliability of the fish harvest encouraged the coastal Saami to establish permanent settlements much earlier than the inland Saami. The coastal groups

> Share a number of features, which are not only quite different from those of the more familiar hunter-gatherers, but many of them would be more readily acceptable as characteristic of food producing societies. They [Saami hunter-fishers] are less mobile, in many instances sedentary, with settlements supporting larger aggregations of people.[84]

The size and permanency of the coastal settlements reflected the ecological adaptability of Saami social entities – their ability to produce and consume without exhausting local resources. Among the many important elements in ecologically efficient fishing was the capacity of storing fish – the flake (hjelle) for drying fish that was commonly used in all coastal Saami societies – which made delayed consumption possible.[85] The harvest took place when the resources of the sea were abundant, but spared resources during lean periods, which kept the fjord with a minimum stock of diverse resources. Since the fish was not only consumed, but also sold on the local or regional markets, Saami societies have participated "in the world economy for a long time."[86] Thus one cannot say that the Saami existed on subsistence fishing in the past, unlike today, when they participate in the fishing trade. The successful and viable Saami harvesting methodology resulted in a more rapid increase in the Saami than in the Norwegian population through the period of 1750 to 1800.[87]

In the eighteenth century, Norway acknowledged Saami customary law. The 1751 Norway–Sweden Boundary Treaty (Lapp Codicil) § 10 states that Saami reindeer herders may "according to ancient custom" migrate across the border.[88] The Codicil's recognition converted Saami traditional customs into customary law; "ancient Saami customs that the Codicil reflects . . . therefore achieve the status of customary law."[89] Similar implications follow from the 1604 King Christian IV and 1687 King Christian V General Codices that repealed ancient statutes only,[90] but that verified the validity of ancient customs.[91] Accordingly Saami customary laws are historic.[92] By prohibiting Swedish Saami from settling at the sea front or from exploiting fisheries or seal hunting (Lapp Codicil § 13), the customary rights of the indigenous coastal Saami were protected. Accordingly, fjord inhabitants enjoyed legal protection against other Saami intruders to the area. Similarly, the Trade Statutes of 20 August 1778 § 32 codified protection for all fjord inhabitants, without regard to ethnicity, as against any non-local fishermen.

The coast of Finnmark was traditionally divided into fishing districts called "Sii'das."[93] "The ancient legal understanding . . . was that coastal fishery rights were held by those villages closest to the fishing field. Complying with that custom was fairly easy. Because of the small sized boats, fishermen did not journey any farther from their local fishing districts than they could return on the same day."[94] This situation was codified by King's Statute of 20 August 1778 § 32:

> Besides, the inhabitants of the Northern districts shall without interruption, enjoy fisheries on the outer skerries of Finmarken according to ancient custom, where appropriate, and conduct their trade, however not stay at fjord bottoms or place gill nets critic to inhabitants long lines.

The Saami exclusive right to fishing grounds was terminated by the Act of Finmarken of 13 September 1830. Since the coastline extended out so far, the fishermen only rarely left their neighborhood.[95] The fishermen who came from far-away areas and spread into the fjords subsequent to the 1830 Act not only seized Saami economic rights but also changed local fisheries into a trans-ethnic trade. Consequently, the Saami exclusivity lapsed.[96]

> You know that some times the big purse seines came along . . . and it was no good. Because local people used only small boats . . . At the time, people kicked up a loud fuss and shouted, of course. It really was of no use to shout at them, however, because they [small-scale fishermen] were totally powerless.[97]

As the 1830 Act of Finmarken took resource rights away from the local population, outsiders plunged into fisheries. The mutual fisheries participation rights gave members of all society equally enlarged fisheries areas. The enlarged geographic area was consequently the only difference between the pre-Sii'da and the post-Sii'da fishing rights. The "equal footing doctrine" is a remnant of the ancient Saami customary law.

By ignoring ancient fisheries patterns, hi-tech fishers that exploited Saami fishing fields often ruined local resources. Since lack of continual support is detrimental to the success of customary law, "paradigmatic shifts" are especially critical. Hi-tech fishing participation severed from ancient customs overran traditional normative structures and captured resources. As a result, customary fishery norms deteriorated.

Even though the Saami and Norse legal regimes were totally unified from 1830 on, Norwegian legislation applied territorial restrictions to resolve fisheries conflicts, which in principle protected Saami and Norse local fishing grounds. The 1938 and 1951 Trawl Acts restricted trawlers to areas more than four miles from shore. And during the last half century, lots of local regulations implemented by the Ministry of Fisheries were imposed on the locations where purse-seiners and shrimp trawlers could operate.[98] Legislators also began to regulate the number of people who could participate in the fishing industry. For the sake of closing up the modern hi-tech fishery, the Fisheries Participation Act of June 16, 1972 # 57 (now the Act of March 15, 1999 # 26) was introduced. Its purpose was to eliminate the heavy pressure on fisheries stocks caused by the introduction of modern purse seine technology.

Saami small-scale fisheries were dealt a blow by the 1990 Ministry of Fisheries regulation. The agency reacted to declining stocks of cod by closing up the commons and introducing partly tradable fishing quotas that replaced the open access low technology small-scale fishing.[99] As a result of this permit system based on transferable quota rights, the Saami common pool fisheries have effectively been closed up. Newcomers are not permitted to fish, and traditional Saami villages have been emptied.

These regulations raise a very basic issue: can administratively adopted rules trump long-standing customary laws of open access? Norwegian courts recognize the validity of customary law (see Chapter 5). If Saami rules of open access fishery are based on customary law, the termination clearly requires a Parliamentary (Storting) decision. Since the *lex superior* principle rules in Norway and the Storting has not privatized the outer commons, the key issue is whether these social norms qualify as customary law. The Saami people, since ancient times, have never excluded other ethnic groups from fishing, and they have adhered to a rule of open access fisheries rights. But the Ministry's regulations, instead of discriminating *for the benefit of* Saami fishing, as recommended by the former chairman to the Saami Law Committee,[100] severely restricted the Saami fishing possibilities. The introduction of individual vessel quotas in 1990 meant that "because of economies of scale in the fleet, there was a development toward fewer, larger vessels."[101] Since the small-scale Saami fishermen proved economically efficient they were not priced out of the market. Consequently, Ministry intervention became a tangling "must" for the hi-tech advocates.

Since Saami fishermen are afforded no particular protection, the legal situation of the Saami fishermen is thus identical to the general fisheries law system along the coasts of Norway. In Section 2.2.3 the main principles of this fisheries regulation system are explained. Section 2.2.4 looks at some possible lines of development in the years to come.

2.2.3 Ethnic customary law, local or general customary law?

Unlike many other indigenous peoples, the coastal Saami have not claimed rights to special customary laws limited to people of Saami ethnicity. Instead, they have sought to enforce customary laws applicable to all the residents of Finnmark, whether Saami or Norse. This poses the legal issue of whether customary law based on geography has the same weight as customary law based on ethnicity.

The Saami never took the position that the customary law applied exclusively to people of Saami ethnicity. Their law was based on an "equal footing" principle, that welcomed outsiders to use their fishing grounds with gear identical to Saami fishers. They even showed outsiders the best places to fish. Consequently, many Norse people integrated into the Saami fishing communities. A Saami made this remark:

> The fact that Snefjord and not Havøysund [two close villages in the same municipality] is part of the Saami fishing zone really is some damned inequality. Since all people fish in the same fishing fields, there should

> be equal rights. I oppose that zone division. It is confusing whether people should sign into the Saami People's Register or whatever . . . Do those who conduct hand-line fishing enjoy special advantages and extra subsidies because of their Snefjord address? That is racism. It circumvents the municipal as well as the central democratic system.[102]

Even though the traditional Saami fishermen's life is on the eve of destruction,[103] those Saami who see fisheries as a modern way of living believe the "equal footing" principles of common pools should remain. The customary laws of Saami fisheries reflect open access rights that have been perpetuated throughout the years of the adjustment to the practice of competing Norwegian fisheries.[104] Saami fishing practices do not differ from those of the other ethnic groups of the County of Finnmark. The fisheries are really ruled by valid, *local* customs of Finnmark that protect "coastal or fjord people's rights" and not Saami people's independent way of living and practices,[105] thus providing special treatment to fjord-societies that have traditionally been inhabited by Saami people.[106] In other words, the issue becomes a question of *lex loci*, not the *lex peregrines*.

Norway is a relatively homogenous country. There is no understanding among the non-Saami inhabitants of Finnmark that some of their neighbors, based solely on their ethnicity, enjoy superior legal protection and rights.[107] Like the Saami, the Norse inhabitants of Finnmark believe that people living in the same areas and conducting the same trade should enjoy (or suffer from) the same normative system. There simply should be one system of equal rights. Ethnic diversity as a basis for legal rights might be accepted in the reindeer trade, which is conducted solely by the Saami. As regards the coastal Saami, however, centuries of ethnic intermarriage have led to a society where one simply cannot identify some coastal inhabitants as ethnic Saami while defining others as ethnic Norwegians or Finnish (or Kvæn). The following statement by an inhabitant of Snefjord in Western Finnmark (Municipality of Måsøy) makes this point:

> Some of my ancestors came from Ibestad [southern part of the county of Troms, mixed Norse and Saami area]. One branch was from Tana [Saami nuclear area of the county of Finnmark] and, yes, on my mother's side they came from Northern Sweden, Pajala-area and Haparanda [Kvæn – a Finnish people]. Another branch came from Tröonderlag, [Norse inhabitants mainly] . . . So, it is a remarkable mixture.[108]

Fishery practices of people living in Saami nuclear-areas are not distinct from Norwegian fishing practices in other districts. It is impossible to separate Saami and Norwegian fisheries on the basis of Saami s*pecific identity* or Saami *specific practice.* Saami and Norse fishers alike observe "the principle of equality" or "the equal footing doctrine,"[109] which means that one person's right is just as good as another's.[110]

Unlike the United States, Norway does not treat its indigenous people as separate nations.[111] Most of the Indians found in the United States were granted *some* protection through a non-integration US policy that created Indian reservations solely for native people. Treaties embedded legal protection for Indian rights based on tribal soil. Positive discrimination for the benefit of indigenous people has been upheld in the United States based on the geographical dimension to these special rights. Nevertheless, the argument of Indian ethnicity is increasingly difficult to maintain. "It is plain that the principle, or the pretense, that blood should be a central defining fact of being Indian will soon become untenable. How much blending can occur before Indians finally cease to be Indians?"[112]

Saami coastal people, on the other hand, were subject to heavy pressure to integrate, lacked "territory" and – with the exception of the 1751 Lapp Codicil – lacked legal instruments constituting specific Saami rights. The rather indistinct rights for the benefit of the Saami are anchored in vague customary law only. According to a Saami Law Committee mandate and a Nordic Saami Institute report,[113] the basic justification of Saami rights should be their *special ethnic position.* The coastal Saami, however, are a distinct ethnic group whose way of life differs from that of the reindeer herders of the inner Finnmark.[114] Few similarities exist between these two different Saami ways of life. Conversely, the non-nomadic Saami coastal people have adapted to Norse ways of living. "The coastal Saami are increasingly denationalized. They refrain from using traditional attire and language. Their way of life is similar to Norwegian settlers."[115] Rights are tied to social identities.[116]

Components of cultural identity include practices, occupations, social roles, joint behavior, perception, opinions, symbols and language.[117] The Saami Law Commission maintains that Saami culture is dynamic and not tied to an ancient way of living, but rather to the identified Saami material and spiritual cultural characteristics.[118] But what if the coastal Saami culture and the general coastal Norwegian culture are merging into a common culture? One Saami spokesman said: "Our culture of living by the sea is compound. It is impossible to speak of Saami culture since Norwegian and Finnish elements are present. We are not introduced to a specific Saami culture. Our people live by the sea, we belong to the coastal culture, but we are Saami."[119] The critical point here, however, is not occupational trades or ways of living, but rather whether people see themselves as Saami.

The explanation for Saami and Norse ethnic delimitation has been based upon natural adaptation and ecology. Early Norwegian social anthropologists object to such an understanding, pointing to the fact that ethnicity is more or less a symbolic, cognitive fact, not a functional aspect of race. Elements such as different language, historicity, religion and "Weltanschauung" mark this ethnic boundary.[120] It is a question of self-definition and acknowledgement. When the link between rights and identity breaks, the ethnic-related customary laws fail. The Swedish Saami population does not satisfy the identity requirement. "The old generation of Saami settlers lost their identity long ago and became a part of the Swedish population. In this way, much of the Saami taxed land was lost as an expression of the right of the Saami to that land."[121]

Norwegian anthropologist Kolsrud suggests that a similar blending of cultures has occurred among the coastal Saami of Norway, but not among those who live inland:

> Coastal Saami people have lost their foothold in the inherited way of living because of incredibly stronger outer cultural pressure, compared with the mountain Saami. From the economic perspective, there has been almost no difference between the Saami and the other ethnic group, and the Saami have consequently not had the possibility of avoiding the competition. They did not enjoy advantages of a symbiotic trade like reindeer herding and were soon left behind in economic development.[122]

Nevertheless, the Saami Law Commission states that the "Saami people are obviously ethnic groups that qualify for cultural protection under [the 1966 UN-covenant on civil and political rights] Article 27."[123] It seems that the reindeer-trading Saami populations fulfill the criteria of an ethnic group, whereas the coastal Saami do not. Instead, the coastal Saami happened to end up with a "tragedy-of-the-commons-like"[124] public property right solution. The question is whether this social norm has evolved into a legal norm.

2.2.4 *Commons in a cold climate*[125] *– a fisheries law perspective*[126]

Having found no trace of any specific ethnically oriented fishery rules because ethnic bonds have disappeared due to assimilation, the bottom line is: how is the local fishery management system characterized under the present Norwegian regime, legally speaking? What "lebensraum" are Saami nuclear-area fishermen accorded?

The Saami question is no longer a racial or genetic issue. It has become a question of functionality and subjective attitudes: "I used to be a Saami, but now I am a Norwegian."[127] What we have are areas of the coast that habitually had Saami inhabitants. Since fishing resources are defined "to belong to the Norwegian people in common,"[128] Saami nuclear-area fishermen are scrutinized under the *general legal* system of fishery rights in Norway. To understand the present situation, we need to pick up the thread from the past and follow how current fishery regulations were adopted. The purpose of this section is to discuss the outer fisheries common and the common's fisherman's legal protection of his rights. Saami fishermen enjoy the exact same protection as the common's fisherman. Because statutory law is lacking in this field, it is necessary to place the present customary law situation in the context of legal history.

Fishing along the coasts and on the high seas has traditionally been classified as a public property right in Norway[129] as well as in the United States.[130] While "the Public Trust" is the name given to marine fisheries in the Anglo-American system, the "outer commons" – "den ytre allmenningen" is the Norse (Icelandic-Norwegian) label for the same institution.[131]

Due to the fisheries customary law basis, there is some doubt as to whether fisheries rights are protected against state intervention. Some would classify Saami rights as reflecting a lack of public regulations;[132] i.e. in "eine rechtliche Reflexwirkung."[133] This view is popular among Nordic legal scientists.[134] As documented in Chapter 5, however, legal sources seem to point to rather well-preserved legal fishery rights.

The present legal situation results from over a thousand years of customary law development that is not set forth here.[135] Generally it can be said that the customary law of fishing rights for the local fishermen has been challenged from time to time by national level regulations that abolish the fishing rights belonging to the coastal population as such. But each and every time, the customary law of open access fisheries has won out in the end. This time, however, the battle seems more relentless than ever (see Section 2.2.5).

For the last three decades, several attacks against the open access fisheries have taken place. First there was the Ministry of Fisheries privatization policy, which demolished public property rights by establishing tradable licenses and tradable quotas. Second, were the new statutes (since 1990) excluding groups of fishermen from full participation rights. This has struck mightily upon fjord-fisheries and small villages along the coast. Will this inevitably lead to the silent death of Saami culture and villages? Or is another scenario possible?

2.2.5 *The Saami seek their rights*

At the request of a research committee chaired by a Swedish anthropology professor, Tom G. Svenson, and the Norwegian Research Council, the author [Peter Ørebech] agreed to gather and analyze background material on Saami fishing law for the Ministry of Justice and the Saami Law Committee. The report containing this material (for some main points see Chapter 5) was published in 2001/02.[136]

The report showed that the Saami believe that Ministry regulations that privatized the commons by distributing transferable quotas to individual fishermen are inconsistent with local customary law: "The word(s) 'equally-entitled' . . . are here . . . used to characterize . . . a particular right that is shared equally by a certain number of people."[137] The equal rights of fishery participation related to all parts of the investigation areas, the fjords and the coastal areas of Finnmark. Fishing activity was geographically limited only by practical reason. Why should the Saami nuclear district fishermen participate in external fisheries when the local resources were more than abundant?[138]

Saami and Norse fished without restrictions, and new participants could engage in fishing wherever appropriate. Not only relatives, but also elders in general introduced recruits to fishing sites and revealed ancient knowledge to them. There was simply no limited entry scheme whatsoever. No fisherman possessed his own fishing fields during a given year or from one year to another: all the informants interviewed acknowledged a system of equal participation rights.[139]

The participants use varying terminology in trying to identify the source of their common practices. Some called upon extra legal normative systems ("just"), others upon general customary laws of the districts (local custom), and still others upon public property rights. However, as stated by the Supreme Court in the 1995 *Balsfjord Case*, no customary law prerequisite requires that all persons involved unanimously adhere to identical titles. To the question of whether any local or foreign fisherman may reserve a fishing field, all the answers were negative.

The Saami argue that because local customary law ranks as formal law, changes in open access fisheries require a parliamentary decision. Local customary laws of Finnmark enjoy the rank of formal laws; therefore, any changes in the open access system of fisheries would be unlawful in the absence of a parliamentary decision. No such decision was taken in the case of the exclusionary quota scheme introduced by the Norwegian Ministry of Fisheries.

Whether the Saami arguments are likely to succeed may depend on how the courts of Norway interpret the legal status of customary law, an issue discussed in Chapter 5. In addition, the Saami could achieve their goals through action at the national legislative level. A summary of the current status of the Saami arguments is found in Chapter 10.

Since customary laws based upon purely ethnic rights are now out of the picture, the Saami nuclear areas fully depend upon the general legal situation in local fisheries, as outlined in Section 2.3 of this chapter. However, a new international road seems to chart a new and prosperous area for the future of Saami coastal societies (see Chapter 10).

2.3 Customs and law under home rule in Greenland

2.3.1 Customs under colonialism

Until 1953 Greenland was a Danish colony. The indigenous population lived in settlements – "colonies" – of varying size along the coast, primarily on the southern part of the West coast, where living conditions are superior as the sea does not freeze during winter. Hunting especially of sea mammals, had been the main way to gain a living in the earliest part of the century, but due to climatic changes, seals gradually disappeared around 1920, and fishing became more important, although initially it did not have a high status to be a fisherman.

In 1948–49 the Danish Government sent a Judicial Expedition to Greenland to examine whether Greenland could become an integrated part of the Danish Realm juridically – thus becoming subject to Danish state legislation on par with the rest of Denmark. The reports of this expedition (JUREX) were quite comprehensive, but their conclusions were rather ambivalent, and not clearly in favour of a monocentric state legislation covering all of the Danish Realm. This may be one of the reasons why they were never published contrary to a number of other reports on the modernization programme, which was to take place in Greenland during the 1950s.[140]

The JUREX report described a number of areas especially marriage and family life, property and tort, contracts, inheritance, criminal offences and sanctions. It concluded reluctantly that legal unity might be obtained – with the necessary interpretational modifications – in most areas except criminal sanctions, where a specific law and judicial system for Greenland was later established and is still in force. A Reform Commission has been working on adjustments of the system since 1994. It was expected to finalize a report by 1998, but the report did not appear until 2004.[141]

2.3.2 *Customs and Danish state law in Greenland*

From 1953 until Greenland obtained home rule in 1979, it was legally an equal part of the Danish Realm. Practically this was a period of what has been termed "Danization" in the educational system and in the social ideals about what a modern welfare system should look like. Health and social conditions in Greenland had been appalling compared to Danish standards after World War II. Confrontation with Western consumer society during the American occupation under World War II and aims at modernizing Greenlandic society among important Greenlandic political figures supported the interest in this development. It mainly introduced a social democratic, modernized, industrial way of life as both a political, economic and also legal model.[142]

Fishing plants were established and offered waged work mainly to Greenlandic women. Earlier social norms and customs were destroyed or changed quite rapidly, although a cultural "backlog" has been in existence long after. In practice the smallest settlements were closed down. Infrastructure, such as schools, shops and other public service were closed, and thus people had to move from the settlements.

In the first part of the century, customs in Greenland concerned both ways of living within the extended family – often including foster-children, sharing of food hunted, caught or collected by men and women in the family – and organization of communal activities such as hunting, construction of temporary or permanent habitation and joint travels.

With the changing living and social conditions, much of the basis for these customs was destroyed or became obsolete especially in the most populated southwestern part of Greenland. Remnants of these customs are still stronger today in North[143] and East Greenland.[144] The introduction of economic, social and legal modernization from 1953 had a lot of unwanted side effects such as social disruption, alcoholism, increased suicide rates and severe social, cultural and individual crisis, loss of identity and language.

In 1972 a referendum was held in Denmark and Greenland about membership of the European Union. A majority of Greenlandic voters voted against membership, but due to their legal status in the Danish Realm they were forced to join, whereas the Faroe Islands, which had home rule since 1948, stayed outside. This contributed to the already existing political demand for increased self-determination, which finally found its legal form with the introduction of home rule in 1979.

2.3.3 Customary law and home rule legislation in Greenland after 1979

The act on Home Rule in Greenland prescribes the establishment of a home rule parliament and a home rule government. The judiciary stayed as a competence under the joint Danish Realm – mostly because, since the beginning of the 1950s, it had already been organized according to local conditions and staffed by local lay judges on the magistrate court level.

The new parliament and government was now to take over the legislative and administrative power, which so far had been performed by the Danish Parliament and the Danish government especially in the Ministry of Greenland. This was a tremendous task, which could not be carried out without several compromises. The Parliament consisted of 100 per cent indigenous politicians. However, the administration, and especially the "central" home rule administration from the beginning to the present, has been heavily dependent upon and influenced by imported academic staff, mainly from Denmark.

The formal educational level in Greenland had been much lower than in other Nordic countries, and it is only gradually increasing. The number of university students grew from 20 in 1974 to 357 in 1994, 75 of whom studied at Ilisimatusarfik, University of Greenland. The total population grew from 49,468 in 1972 to 55,419 in 1994. About 15 per cent of the population are non-Inuit.[145]

Danish law was still influential in a number of areas. In the period after home rule its influence has probably been strengthened due to both strategic considerations and Euro-centrism of both politicians and staff and less due to direct pressure or suppression. Even with the establishment of home rule in Greenland, the model and the yardstick of comparison stayed the Western – and not least the Nordic – model. In the area of law and legislation, this has, to my view, led to a period of "imitation,"[146] where both the Greenlandic parliament and government have been strongly guided by outside models and counselors.

The Danish anthropologist and now director of the International Work Group for Indigenous Affairs (IWGIA), Jens Dahl, has written extensively on the historical process behind home rule.[147] In his last book, *Saqqaq. An Inuit Hunting Community in the Modern World*, he writes that: "It could be said to be ironic that although the Greenlanders wanted self-government to create a 'Greenland on Greenlandic conditions', this has to some extent been experienced as a centralization and a blow against local customs in exactly those communities that symbolize the Greenlandic culture."[148] His new book deals specifically with how, today, there is less room for local management of hunting and fishing compared to only a decade ago. He underlines however that

> The emergence of Greenland as a national society is seen by most Greenlanders as a legitimate development, and the laws, rules and ordinances issued by the central authorities in Nuuk are generally supported by people along the coast. The outcome, however, can be conflicts among levels of customs, customary knowledge, and management procedures. Such conflicts do not necessarily indicate that procedures belonging to one level are more legitimate than those of another level. Management decisions taken by Home Rule might be considered quite as legitimate as those customary rules and management practices that have developed in small communities. This will be reflected in the development of new customs and new knowledge regimes, which gradually will replace other customs and knowledge regime.[149]

In relation to consideration of customs and customary law, it is my impression that the practice of imitation of modern legislative regulation has led to a process of neglect of both local and Greenlandic customary law especially in the home rule government and in the administration. Anyway, knowledge of custom is quite limited both due to the strong foreign and transient elements in the administration and to the strongly local character of many customs.[150]

Dahl writes that "the character of the Home Rule 'state', its power, its scope, and its area of function are primarily products of the Danish presence in the country for more than 250 years and not a product of a national economic and social development."[151] With the change to a parliament and a government with indigenous representatives and leaders, I suspect that the legitimizing role of culture and (some) customs, which has been strong among other Inuit in the Arctic (Alaska and Canada) and among indigenous peoples in other parts of the world, has been weakened considerably in Greenland. Especially in the early years of home rule, the mere fact that representatives were Greenlandic, endowed them with a strong legitimacy, which probably did not need a strong underpinning through explicit and formal consideration of customs in home rule regulations. The background of the representatives in itself provided a guarantee that Greenlandic considerations would be taken. This has been the case in the judiciary, and here it has seemingly worked rather well.

Another reason for the neglect and/or amnesia in relation to customs is perhaps also that, contrary to some rhetoric among parts of the urbanized, modernized, educated Greenlandic elite especially in the most left-wing party IA, there is probably great ambivalence about the past among great parts of the population, especially the younger ones, and not least among young women. Dahl writes that among younger women there is an increasing awareness of and opposition to the dominance traditionally associated with the hunter role. Young women are especially opposed to beating, which is common in many families.[152] Young women also dislike the traditional female role, which was an integrated part of customary life of a hunter's wife, of scraping and cleaning sealskins.[153]

Elders are not regarded as highly in Greenland as among Canadian and Alaskan Inuit, since authority in home-ruled Greenland is vested in modern roles and institutions that often require formal education. Although it is seldom explicitly expressed today, one gets the impression that for some people customs may be considered a hindrance for economic and social development of society, even though for others their cultural and ideological importance may be considerable. What is sought for is rather what is often described as "the best of both worlds."[154]

But it is important to remember that customs are not static, and that one of the most important characteristics of a hunting community and mode of production seems to be its flexibility, "flexibility permeates all or most aspects of social life."[155] What remains to be seen according to Dahl is: "what kind of customs will develop within this new 'community' and how a new kind of legitimacy corresponding to this level will develop. We might see what could be interpreted as a hierarchy or as 'levels of legitimacy."[156]

2.3.4 Local customs and the world market

The process and period of what I will call a parallel actual and structural neglect of local customs and practical imitation of mainly Danish law was still going on in several areas in the 1990s. The reasons for this are not only Eurocentrism among administrative staff, or image-cultivation on behalf of the Greenlandic home rule on the international scene, but also Greenland's strong integration into the world market, and the gradual creation of a world community where ecological concerns and ideology plays an important role. Greenland's economy is strongly export-oriented, and Greenland receives large annual block grants from Denmark. This means that Greenlandic politicians are very keen on presenting an image to the international world as a modern, highly developed society, and as a trade partner that is reliable, responsible and trustworthy – in short "a society worth visiting, investing in and listening to."[157]

There seems to be a process of mixed influence going on around the end of the twentieth century. On the one hand, there is no doubt that the influence of the world market is becoming stronger. Everybody in even the smallest Greenlandic settlement today knows that it is necessary to adapt to the world market in some way or another, through tourism, mining, export and in education.[158]

Home rule as an administrative and political domain has removed control from the communities to other non-territorial based levels, and it has for instance established an administrative and geographically defined hunting territory, which is no longer based on social control, customary knowledge or traditions.[159] On the other hand, the days of almost automatic legitimacy of the home rule parliament and government and their activities seem to be gone, and a hidden and direct critique of home rule institutions and home rule policy creeps up. A few Greenlandic academics are obtaining important positions in the home rule administration and consulting research institutions (for fisheries) and are thus gradually and slowly contributing to a change of practice and communication among citizens and administration. The Ministry of Fisheries and Hunting is staffed by mainly Greenlandic personnel and is headed by an indigenous, academically trained woman. This creates conditions for much greater attentiveness to local concerns and demands.

The first examples below are mainly related to the male-dominated sphere of hunting. The second set of examples consider changes of customs and external and internal factors of importance related to gender roles and the female-dominated spheres of life. Complementary gender roles in Inuit society are of considerable importance today.[160] Since hunting as a way of life and mode of production is strongly dependent upon the household and the gender division in the household, changes in the division of labor between men and women, and changes in the structure of authority, will influence the viability of at least some of the customs underpinning this way of life.

2.3.5 *Hunting examples*

2.3.5.1 Seal and sealskin

During the 1970s, international animal rights groups focused strongly upon seal hunting methods in the Canadian Arctic – especially hunting of so-called "baby seals" or pups.[161] One of the legal outcomes of this campaign was the European Council's Directive 83/129/EEC about the import into member states of certain kinds of seal pelts and goods fashioned thereof. The Directive directly prohibits import and trade in the European Common Market of fur from white coats and bluebacks – pups of harp and hooded seals.[162]

Baby seals were never hunted in Greenland. But the economic outcome was that prices on all kinds of sealskins dropped dramatically in the world market from the end of the 1970s. The home rule Government decided to subsidize hunters who were selling sealskins. Thus the individual hunter was not directly hit economically by the fall in world market prices, but the home rule Government had increasing social expenditures and decreasing sales from the seal skin factory it owned in Great Greenland.[163]

Greenpeace, Brigitte Bardot and animal rights organizations became very unpopular among Inuit in the Arctic for a very long period, and Great Greenland struggled to improve its international image. By now it seems to have succeeded through a campaign combining indigenous and perhaps postmodern approaches, as its recent flashy catalogues demonstrate.

In Greenland these animal rights campaigns were understood as directed against and undermining a traditional and customary way of living. In Greenlandic self-understanding, hunting was seen as a sustainable activity, and considerable energy was spent on educating international opinion on how a customary way of life that involved killing of animals could also be sustainable.[164]

Having become integrated into the world, it becomes clear that traditional rules are insufficient to cope with the globalization of the small hunting settlements in Greenland. The ecological setting of today is a global setting, where outside global actors have a say and may influence local customs and home rule regulation. But globalization of hunting regulations and resource exploitation will tend to institutionalize authority, and thus undermine the informal authority which was the basis of customary and communal hunting.[165]

2.3.5.2 Whalehunting

The International Whaling Commission (IWC) does not have a very good name in Greenland either. Greenland entered the IWC when Denmark signed the Whaling Convention in 1946. The IWC has led a very restrictive policy against whaling, thus reducing the possibilities of expanding the export options for Inuit in Greenland and Canada. To avoid these restrictions Greenland entered into an agreement with Canada in 1989 to cooperate formally in the safeguarding and management of the narwhal and beluga.

Hunters in Greenland were somewhat dissatisfied with the restrictions that grew out of this agreement, but Greenlandic (and non-Greenlandic) biologists feel that their counselling about conservation of the narwhal and beluga populations are perhaps taken more seriously by the home rule Government due to the international pressure from world opinion and the agreement.

The Greenlandic biologist Aqqaluk Rosing has indicated that Greenlandic hunters are more willing to accept limitations in their customarily free access to living resources in this area where the resource is "internationally mobile" and to be shared with neighbouring populations. Due to the mobility of whales it is also difficult for hunters to argue against estimates about populations by biologists, even though there are considerable differences.

Whale hunting and especially beluga hunting is described as a communal complex, as an important public activity and a "decisive forum for securing a cohesive and legitimate authority structure for the community." In relation to this activity, traditions of sharing of equipment and gifts of meat foster alliances and relationships. Hunting beluga and other game secures the role of the hunter as the provider of essential cultural and identity-carrying goods.[166]

2.3.6 *Hunting and quotas*

2.3.6.1 Caribou

In relation to the population of caribou in Greenland, there is a great difference in the estimations of hunters and biologists. According to Greenlandic biologist, Aqqaluk Rosing, the caribou populations are very local, breed quickly, and accurate scientific estimations seem to be very costly and difficult to carry out.[167]

A few years ago it was, however, feared that the whole caribou population would die out, and in 1995 quotas were introduced for the first time. This led to strong popular resistance and probably a lot of actual transgression of laws. People were not willing to give up their customary rights to free access to living resources and especially to hunt caribou and discussions about quotas and criteria for distribution of quotas have been very emotional and lengthy. In this area politicians have yielded somewhat to popular pressure and disregarded scientific advice more.

Caribou hunting is not an issue that attracts international attention; it is not important for Greenlandic national economy, although it may have some importance for subsistence economy, which is still significant in Greenland. But like all forms of hunting it has a cultural and political prominence which is not to be neglected. This is be related to (earlier) practices of sharing game with the community and also of consuming food together. Today caribou is mostly shared and consumed within the extended family.

2.3.7 Customs, sustainable knowledge and gender

These examples also raise the issue of the importance of traditional/local knowledge versus euro-scientific knowledge, which seems to be discussed much more in Greenlandic society today than the controversy between customs and legislation. But as these discussions are clearly linked they should perhaps be considered together.[168]

The controversy between customs and legislation is a controversy between citizens and lawmakers, where lawmakers may overrule the practices and norms of local people in their attempt to create a uniform system of law with (more) international/global legitimacy. The controversy between traditional or local knowledge and euro-scientific knowledge is rather a controversy between economic agents or experienced performers of certain activities or occupations – especially fishermen and hunters, who are also voters, on the one hand, and "expert knowers" on the other, especially formally trained biologists and natural scientists, who act as consultants for legislators in their preparation of regulations. This is clearly a controversy with political implications as the examples demonstrate.

My own observations and the work of Dahl indicate that customs do not have an absolute legitimacy in contemporary Greenland. They coexist with Greenlandic, Danish and international regulation and they are influenced by these other levels of regulation. It is also my impression that customs are not considered to be better guarantees of a sustainable way of life in the "hunting mode of production" than are other types of norms. Dahl claims that it is the hunting mode of production as such that relies on sustainable use of nature and of resources:

> Low population density, frequent movement between communities, and a number of cultural harvesting habits have always safeguarded the reproduction of the renewable resources . . . It is important to understand clearly that it is not the actions of each individual that are guided by

> sustainability . . , but ensuring sustainability takes place at the level of the functioning of the mode of production. One of the means of providing for this is traditional knowledge, which includes religious and non-religious practices and ways of dealing with the game animals. Traditional knowledge is orally transmitted, based on observed behavior, and essential for a hunter's control of the process of production. Today, new means such as quotas and various types of hunting restrictions have been adopted; they ameliorate the potential deleterious effects of the disappearance of the old control mechanisms and the adoption of new technology. Notwithstanding these new means, sustainability continues to be a pillar of the hunting mode of production.[169]

2.3.8 Gendered customs – a brief historical reflection

Descriptions of life in Greenland in the eighteenth and nineteenth centuries shows that seal hunting was an important way of securing human survival, and that it was regulated by a complicated pattern of customs concerning hunting, sharing and use. It is also clear that gender divisions were very strong and important, and that hunting that required considerable physical strength and perseverance was almost exclusively carried out by men – who were often related by family ties.[170] The family comprised married children as well as foster children. Joint ownership of boats and summer tents and common labor in obtaining means of support and maintenance was usual. Every family usually had more than one (male) provider, and widows and unmarried women rarely set up housekeeping by themselves, but were generally provided for by housemates or kindred. When a man died, the oldest son inherited the boat and tent along with the duties incumbent on the provider. Inheritance represented a question of obligations and burdens rather than of personal gain for Greenlanders.[171]

According to Henrik Rink it might be considered a law that every man, as far as he was able to do it, should practice the trade of a hunter on the sea, until he was either disabled by old age or had a son to succeed him. If he neglected this duty he brought upon himself reprehensions both of members of his own family as well as of the wider community. He was also bound to bring up his sons to become hunters from their early childhood.[172]

In his chapter on "Social Order, Customs and Laws" from 1875, the former Royal Inspector of South Greenland (from 1858–68), Henrik Rink, writes very little about customs governing women's lives. It is, however, clear from other sources that women would take care of and prepare the products of hunting and fishing, and that they would take care of household duties, cooking, washing, cleaning, maintaining and producing clothes. Collecting water and fuel was also women's work. Girls were educated by adult women, and neither boys nor girls could receive differentiated forms of training or education.[173]

Life in the settlement was based on a strong gendered division of labor but also upon a necessity of cooperation between men and women as well as between generations. As far as ownership of or influence on (limited) property was concerned, however, the household or family was dominated by the father and husband.[174]

Traditionally there were strict rules according to which meat was shared among participants in a hunt. The custom of giving meat gifts has not completely disappeared. Today a hunter's wife will take care of the sharing procedure, and decide how the meat hunted by the men is shared with other members of closer or more distant communities.[175]

The change from hunting towards fisheries, which became both more important for large parts of the population and gradually also more industrialized in the beginning of the twentieth century meant that the fish also had to be processed in a more industrialized way. This required a labor force, which was often recruited amongst unmarried and also amongst married women. Performing waged labor meant that both the divorced woman and the unmarried woman became less dependent upon male maintenance and did not necessarily have to be trained in the duties and work of their mothers (or fathers).[176] The change from hunting to fishing was also due to a reduction in the seal stock, and to concerns about means for survival as well as concerns about efficiency in fisheries.[177]

In her 1968 study Agnete Weis Bentzon reflects upon the implications of a more industrialized economy with more jobs to offer for the authority of parents and for an increased independence of the younger generation. She mentions especially the importance of these changes for women and for their ability to accept paid work.[178] The gender division of labor in families is characterized by the fact that possibilities for paid work are bigger in cities and lowest in the settlements.[179]

Hunting traditions and customs deal with relations between humans and nature, but as the examples show, they are interrelated with and dependent upon gender relations and upon specific and historical forms of gendered division of labor, which also take the form of traditions and customs.

This interrelationship indicates that considerations about a securing of sustainability by means of (certain) customs must reflect on change in gendered relations and divisions of labor, which may influence the viability and even sustainability of such customs. An understanding of sustainability must reflect upon the complexity of (other) relations that influence and change customs and norms related to humans and nature.

2.3.9 Contemporary examples related to the female life sphere

In the long-term perspective, the most significant factor in undermining traditional authority might prove to be the rise of women to more and more positions of institutional authority.[180] Modernization has changed the customary lifestyle of women even more than that of men. Sons are more important to the viability of the traditional hunting household than are adult daughters, and sons and daughters receive dissimilar socialization in relation to modern society and to learning traditional activities.[181] The formal educational level for women has been growing more quickly than is the case for men, and their income-generating activities have increased more than men's. The hard life of a hunter's wife is no longer very attractive to a young contemporary Greenlandic woman. There is thus a surplus of men in many of the traditional hunting communities and settlements, where the number of women has for a long time been decreasing. Now there seems to be a somewhat reverse trend, where women are returning to some settlements to take up the salaried jobs there – sometimes being married to local hunters.

> The increased availability of salaried jobs has de facto made women the provider of the main cash income in many households. This is appreciated by the men, because the income enhances their opportunities to continue in a hunting way of life. So, in a way, the new status of women can be used for them to persist in asserting the ideology of "man the provider."[182]

Women are the most mobile part of the Greenlandic population today. They seem to be adapting to and to be attracted by modern lifestyle more than men. Loss of (some) customs could seem less of a loss for women than for men. The gendered division of labor has changed, and women's contribution to processing of hunting products continues to decrease, and is becoming almost superfluous.[183]

Responsibility for intergenerational relations in the home has been lying mainly with women. Children have been and are highly valued, and are often still brought up both by the parent and the grandparent generation. Other relatives are also contributing to the care, thus making it possible for young mothers, for instance, to complete formal educations or perform paid work. Foster children are also still quite common. The number of single mothers seems to be growing, but there are no statistics covering this field so far. Young girls are said to bear children to please the wish of their mothers for a grandchild – but also as a source of monetary income, since maintenance in the first place is paid by the municipality. Greenlandic municipalities have thus accumulated large outstanding debts from fathers who do not pay the maintenance for their children with whom they no longer live. A small municipality like Kangaatsiaq with a population of 1,518 persons had thus accumulated an outstanding debt of 4,4 million DKr in 1999 related to unpaid maintenance contributions.[184]

There are indications that this unwillingness of fathers to pay for their children may be due to a custom, where mothers took primary care for maintaining children within the framework of a subsistence economy based upon, amongst other customs, the sharing and giving of food resources, where often it would be the hunter's wife who would be in charge of giving meat gifts. If this could be an element of an explanation, however, it is one which demonstrates that customary arrangements about family life have great economic consequences for the establishment of a modern, welfare-state type of home rule in a society where income sources are rather limited.

Social expenditures are very large for Greenlandic society. Changes – or continued existence of customs in this area – may be of even greater economic and practical importance for society than changes or continuity of customs related to male occupations, although they are rarely considered in the public debate to the same degree. This may be due to the fact that in the Greenlandic identity debate, identity questions and identity markers seem to have been strongly connected to male lifestyle. Customary male behavior and male pride thus may be at odds with the behavior implicitly expected to lie behind a "modern" welfare regulation of maintenance by fathers.

2.3.10 Gendered customs and gendered political life

Recent developments may perhaps change this connection between traditional identity and masculinity in a modern, often male-dominated, public debate and allow room for "modernized" or perhaps even "post-modernized" gendered identities drawing upon gendered customs under change. Whether these new emerging customs will contribute to a more sustainable lifestyle in general in Greenlandic society remains to be seen. But at least on paper the discussion and rhetoric of sustainability is having some impact on the discussions about gendered politics.

On November 6, 1999, a group of women mainly from Nuuk, the capital of Greenland, founded Arnat Partiaat, a nationwide women's party. The initiative to the establishment of the party was taken by a Greenlandic woman, who was trained at a Danish university, and was then working at the Greenlandic Institute of Nature. In an article in one of the two national bilingual Greenlandic newspapers in August 1999, she criticized the male-dominated parties for not considering the so-called "soft values" in political life.[185] She was herself for many years the partner of the former head of the Greenlandic Home Rule Government, who since 1997 has been a director in Royal Greenland (the home-rule-owned fishing company). His mother was the most prominent female politician in Greenland before home rule.

The newspaper article sparked a lively debate in Greenlandic society in both the printed press, television and radio. In practice the women's party also opened up opportunities for much greater involvement of ethnic Danish women. So far Danes have hardly been involved in Greenlandic politics even though they make up about 15 per cent of the population, and a great number have lived in Greenland for many years. To my knowledge this ethnic cooperation has not given rise to criticism, rather it may have released a considerable amount of political energy among groups that so far have not been very actively involved in politics.

There was, however, some criticism of the idea of a gender-segregated party. At an initial meeting about the idea on September 20, a large number of women from the old parties were present. The conclusion after the meeting was not to establish a party. But the meeting had already sparked off considerable self-reflection in the male-dominated governing party, Siumut, which decided to hold a women's caucus in order to increase female representation. Later public debates revealed that there was still considerable interest in the idea, and on November 6 the party was established. The establishment of the party, the public discussions about it and its statutes can be interpreted as a reflection upon the customs of gender complementarity in Greenlandic social life. Women are not seen as competing with men, as is often the case in Euro-American societies, and the initiative is not seen as divisive or exclusive as far as can be judged from newspaper coverage and personal communications.

It should also be remembered that in April 1999, Nunavut was established in Canada, introducing a Canadian equivalent to Greenland's home rule. The development of Nunavut has been followed with great interest in Greenland during the past years. One of the founding mothers of the Greenlandic women's party followed the referendum in Nunavut in May

1997, which turned down the proposal of gender parity in the Nunavut legislative assembly. This proposal was suggested by the male-dominated Nunavut Implementation Commission. The Commission referred both to the very weak representation of women in most Western parliaments, and to the custom of joint decision-making in Inuit societies. Even if the proposal did not come through, the discussion has probably had an impact in certain parts of Greenlandic society, which has as its other neighbor Iceland. Iceland has for many years had a women's party in parliament. The initiative was thus not understood as something alien and subversive, but rather as a much needed revitalization and innovation of contemporary Greenlandic political life. It is seen as giving priority to areas, which are acknowledged by many people to have been neglected too much.

A few quotes from the party statutes may give an idea about the tone of the new party and its implicit recognition of traditional gendered customs, which are combined with a post-modern rhetoric and self-understanding:

> §2 Founding ideas behind Arnat Partiaat
>
> We envisage a society, where women and men support each other, where the human being is at the centre, and where all citizens take joint responsibility. Keywords are solidarity, trust, openness, and ecological sustainability. Children are active participants in the development of society, and grown ups must secure that the physical and psychological development has highest priority.
>
> §3 The Background for the Establishment of a Women's Party
>
> * Women and men think differently.
>
> * Men and women have equal worth and are equally important when good and balanced decisions are to be taken.
>
> * Decisions today are primarily taken by men. Therefore women must be included in decision-making processes at all levels.
>
> * Women's experience with care for the family and organization of work is an important asset for society.
>
> * In the women's party we will support each other and establish networks by women. We will work to secure that it becomes easier for family life, leisure, education, work and political activities to coexist.
>
> * We as women proclaim that we are ready to take upon us real joint responsibility.

It is difficult to predict whether the ambitions of the Women's Party to combine gendered customs with modern party politics aiming at creating, amongst other objectives ecological sustainability, will be successful. In the first place these changes may not be seen in the modern laws produced by the home rule parliament, but they have contributed somewhat to a change of political climate and discussion.

It can be seen that Greenlanders are actively adapting their traditional customs to meet the needs of a changing environment. In Chapter 10 we will summarize some consequences of this adaptation.

Endnotes

1. 528 U.S. 495 (2000).
2. D. McGregor, Masters Thesis on File, University of Hawaii.
3. Melody Kapilialoha McKenzie, *Native Hawaiian Rights Handbook* (Native Hawaiian Legal Corp., Honolulu, 1991), at p. 223.
4. *Ibid.*
5. *Ibid.*, p. 223.
6. *Ibid.*, p. 224.
7. *Ibid.*, p. 225.
8. 4 Haw. 239 (1879).
9. 2 Haw. 87 (1858).
10. 656 P.2d 745 (1982).
11. McKenzie, *Native Hawaiian Rights Handbook*, p. 211.
12. *Ibid.*, p. 212.
13. See, e.g., *Kalaukoa v. Keawe*, 9 Haw. 191 (1893) and *Henry v. Ahlo*, 9 Haw. 490) (1894), McKenzie, *Native Hawaiian Rights Handbook*, pp. 213 and 214.
14. See, e.g., *Palama v. Sheehan* 440 P.2d 95 (1968), *Haiku Plantations Ass'n v. Lono* 618 P.2d 312 (1980), and *Rogers v. Pedro*, 642 P.2d 549 (1982), discussed at McKenzie, *Native Hawaiian Rights Handbook*, p. 215.
15. HRS 171-26 et. seq. 15 No. 8160., mem (Dec. 1982).
16. No. 8160, mem. (Dec. 1982).
17. See discussion by Paul Lucas in McKenzie, *Native Hawaiian Rights Handbook*, p. 217 from which much of this discussion is taken.
18. 2 Haw. 87 (1858).
19. *Ibid.*, p. 91.
20. Hawaii Revised Statutes (HRS) section 7-1 (1976).
21. *Oni*, 2 Haw. at 91. (emphasis added).
22. *Ibid.*, p. 90.
23. See *ibid.*
24. 656 P.2d 745 (1982).
25. *Ibid.*, p. 747.
26. *Ibid.*
27. *Ibid.*, p. 748.
28. *Ibid.*

29. *Ibid.*, p. 749.
30. *Ibid.*
31. *Ibid.*
32. See *ibid.*, pp. 749–750.
33. See *ibid.*, p. 750.
34. *Ibid.*, p. 751 (citing Sir William Blackstone, *Commentaries on the Laws of England*).
35. *Ibid.*
36. *Ibid.*
37. *Ibid.*, note 4.
38. See *ibid.* (emphasis added).
39. *Ibid.*, p. 752.
40. *Ibid.*
41. 73 Haw. 578, 837 P.2d 1247 (1992).
42. *Ibid.*
43. See *ibid.*, p. 616.
44. See *ibid.*
45. See *ibid.*, p. 618.
46. See *ibid.*, p. 619.
47. See *ibid.*, pp. 619–620.
48. *Ibid.*, p. 620.
49. See *ibid.*, p. 621.
50. *Pub. Access Shoreline Hawaii v. Hawaii County Planning Comm'n*, 903 P.2d 1246 (1995).
51. See *ibid.*, p. 1250.
52. See *ibid.*, p. 1251.
53. See *ibid.*
54. See *ibid.*, pp. 1255–1256.
55. See *ibid.*, p. 1256.
56. See *ibid.*, pp. 1259–1261.
57. *Ibid.*, p. 1260.
58. See *ibid.*, pp. 1260–1261.
59. See *ibid.*
60. See *ibid.*, p. 1268.
61. *Ibid.*
62. See *ibid.*, pp. 1269–1270.
63. *Ibid.*, p. 1267.
64. See *ibid.*, p. 1272 (emphasis added).
65. *Ibid.*, p. 1268.
66. See *ibid.*, pp. 1272–1273.
67. 970 P.2d 485 (1998).
68. See *ibid.*, pp. 488–89.

69. *Ibid.*, p. 492.
70. See *ibid.*, p. 494.
71. See *ibid.* (quoting *PASH*, 903 P.2d at 1271).
72. *Ibid.*, pp. 494–95 (quoting *PASH*, 903 P.2d at 1271) (emphasis added).
73. See *ibid.*, note 10.
74. *Ibid.*, p. 495.
75. See *ibid.*, note 12.
76. See *ibid.*
77. *Ka Pa'Akai O Ka'Aina v. Land Use Comm'n*, 7 P.3d 1068 (2000).
78. Fredrik Rode, *Optegnelser fra Finmarken, samlede i Aarene 1826–1834: og senere udgivne som et Bidrag til Finmarkens Statistik* [*Notes from Finmarken, assembled in the Years 1826–1834*] (Skien, 1842). This and all subsequent translations from Norwegian are by the author.
79. See also Section 2.2.3 in this chapter.
80. Trond Thuen, *Quest for Equity. Norway and the Saami Challenge* (ISER, St. Johns, Newfoundland, 1995), p. 29.
81. Robert Paine, *Herds of the Tundra* (Smithsonian Institution Press, London, 1994).
82. Reindeer Industry Act of 1978.
83. See Peter Ørebech: "Sedvanerett som grunnlag for bærekraftig forvaltning av fiske i de 'ytre almenninger'" ["Customary Law as a Foundation for Sustainable Fishing Management"], in Bjørn Sagdahl (ed.), *Fjordressurser og Reguleringspolitikk* (Kommuneforlaget, Oslo, 1998), pp. 148–150.
84. M. A. P. Renouf, *Prehistoric Coastal Economy in Varangerfjord, North Norway* (University of Cambridge, 1981, unpublished Ph.D. thesis).
85. Knut Odner, *The Varanger Saami* (Scandinavian University Press, Oslo, 1992).
86. *Ibid.*, p. 182.
87. Einar Niemi, *Vadsøs historie* (Universitetsforlaget, Oslo, 1983), bd. I, pp. 409–410.
88. Hurst Hannum, *Autonomy, Sovereignty, and Self-Determination* (University of Pennsylvania Press, Philadelphia PA, 1990), pp. 249–251.
89. NOU 1984:18 *Om samenes rettsstilling* [*About the Saami rights and obligations*] (Statens Forvaltningstjeneste, Oslo), p. 190.
90. Christian V Norwegian Law, the preamble.
91. Oscar Platou, *Forelæsninger over Retskildernes Theori* [*Lectures in the Theory of Legal Sources*] (T. O. Brøgger, Kristiania, 1915), p. 56.
92. *Ibid.*, p. 192.
93. A. Ræstad, *Kongens Strømme. Historiske og folkerettslige undersøkelser angaaende sjøterritoriet* [*Kings Streams. Historical and International Law Investigations Regarding the Territorial Sea*] (Doctoral Thesis, Kristiania, 1912), p. 117.

94. Sverre Tønnesen, *Retten til jorden i Finnmark. Rettsreglene om den såkalte "statens umatrikulerte grunn" – en undersøkelse med særlig sikte på samenes rettigheter* [*The Possessory Right to Finnmark. The Rules of the Public Land – with the emphasis on Saami Legal Rights*] (Universitetsforlaget, Oslo, 1979), p. 93.
95. Ræstad, *Kongens Strømme*, p. 117.
96. Peter Ørebech, *Om allemannsrettigheter Saerlig med henblikk på rettsvernet for fiske ved igangsetting og utøving av petroleumsvirksomhet* [*Public Property Rights. With a Special Emphasis on the Conflict between the Fishing and Petroleum Industries*] (Osmundsson, Oslo, 1991), p. 310.
97. Interview no. 5 (Kokelv). The Einar Eythorson and Stein R. Mathisen Man and Biosphere (MAB)-project "Local knowledge in relation to the management of renewable common pool resources," p. 3. For a synthesis of observations drawn from the same project, see these authors in Svein Jentoft (ed.), *Commons in a Cold Climate. Coastal Fisheries and Reindeer Pastoralism in North Norway: The Co-Management Approach* (Man and the Biosphere Series No. 22, Parthenon, New York, 1998), pp. 206 ff.
98. Peter Ørebech, *Reguleringer i Fisket* [Fisheries Regulations] (Marinjuss, Tromsø, 1986).
99. Anita Maurstad, *Sjarkfiske og ressursforvaltning* [*Low-tech Fishery and Resources Management*] (University of Tromsø, Tromsø, 1997).
100. Carsten Smith: "Rettslige forpliktelser myndighetene er bundet av overfor den Saamiske befolkningen ved regulering av fiske," ["The Governmental Agencies' Legal Obligations toward Saami Fisheries Rights"] *Legal Report for Ministry of Fisheries*, 1990.
101. National Resource Council, *Sharing the Fish, Toward a National Policy on Individual Fishing Quotas* (National Academy Press, Washington DC: 1999), pp. 101, 121–122.
102. Peder Mathisen presents a similar opinion in an unpublished 1994 interview, conducted by Tore Nesheim, p. 18.
103. See the interview in the newspaper *Finnmark Dagblad* February 27, 1993 with Dagny Larsen, the last Saame-woman in Porsanger municipality to participate in the traditional coastal Saami trade for a living.
104. Knut Kolsrud, *Sjøfinnane i Rognsund* [*The Coastal Saami People of Rognsund*] (Studia Septentrionalia vol. 6, Oslo, 1955), p. 81, at p. 123.
105. Gudmund Sandvik, *Om oppfatningar av retten til og broken av land og vatn I Finnmark fram mot lutten av 1960-ara* [*About the legal opinions regarding Finnmark onshore and offshore utilization during the period up to the end of the 1960s*] in NOU 1997:4 (Statens Forvaltningstjeneste, Oslo), annex 1, p. 578, at p. 591.
106. This is the perspective of Tor Arne Lillevoll, "Open Common for Fjord Fishery in Coastal Saami Areas," in Svein Jentoft (ed.), *Commons in a Cold*

Climate. Coastal Fisheries and Reindeer Pastoralism in North Norway: The Co-Management Approach (Man and the Biosphere Series No. 22, Parthenon, New York, 1998), pp. 121 ff.

107. Bjørn Olav Megard, "Om å forstå 'de lite samevennlige' i Finnmark og om forslaget til 'Samisk grunnforvaltning'" ["To Understand the 'Saami Critical' Inhabitants of Finnmark and the Saami Land Resources Management Scheme"] *Kritisk Juss* (Oslo, 1999), p. 43 with further references.
108. MAB interview 1996 Snefjord (Eythorsson & Mathisen), p. 4. Part of the UNESCO Man & Biosphere Project 1996–99.
109. *Martin v. Waddel*, 41 U.S. (3 How.) 212 (1845).
110. Frederic Brandt, *Tingsretten fremstillet efter den norske Lovgivning* [*Property Law as displayed in Norwegian Provisions*] (Kristiania, 1867), p. 181.
111. As pointed out earlier, the one group of indigenous people in the United States whose special nationality was not recognized is the native Hawaiians.
112. Fergus Bordewick. *Killing the White Man's Indian: Reinventing Native Americans at the End of the Twentieth Century* (Doubleday, New York, 1996), pp. 329–330.
113. See NOU 1984:18 *Om samenes rettsstilling* [*About the Saami Rights and Obligations*], p. 114.
114. Tom G. Svensson, *Ethnicity and Mobilization in Saami Politics* (Stockholm Studies in Social Anthropology, Stockholm, 1976).
115. Erik Solem, *Lappiske rettsstudier* [*Saami Legal Studies*] (Universitetsforlaget, Oslo, 1970), p. 33.
116. Tom G. Svensson, "Local Communities in the South Saami Region," in Birgitta Jahreskog (ed.), *The Saami National Minority in Sweden* (The Legal Rights Foundation, Stockholm, 1982), p. 102.
117. Tor Arne Lillevoll, "Åpen allmenning for fjordfiske i sjøsamiske områder?" ["A Still Open Outer Common for the Fishermen in the Coastal Saami Areas"], in Bjørn Sagdahl (ed.), *Fjordressurser og Reguleringspolitikk* (Kommuneforlaget, Oslo, 1998).
118. See NOU 1984:18 *Om samenes rettsstilling*, p. 382.
119. Interview in Ságat, October, 30, 1993, p. 10 with Hermann Kåven from the district of Brenna in the Municipality of Porsanger.
120. Bjørn Hebba Helberg, *Fiskeriteknologi som uttrykk for sosial tilhørighet. En studie av nordnorsk fiske i perioden 400–1700 e.Kr.* [*Social Membership as Expressed by Fishery Technology. A North-Norwegian Fishery Study from the Period of 400–1700* AD] (Stensilserie B no. 38, University of Tromsø, Tromsø, 1993), p. 220.
121. See Israel Ruong, "Saami Usage and Customs," in Birgitta Jahreskog (ed.), *The Saami National Minority in Sweden* (The Legal Rights Foundation, Stockholm, 1982), p. 33.

122. Knut Kolsrud, *Sjøfinnane i Rognsund* [*The Coastal Saami of Rognsund*] (Studia Septentrionalia, vol. 6, Oslo, 1955), p. 81, at p. 123.
123. See NOU 1984:18 *Om samenes rettsstilling*, p. 309.
124. See Garrett Hardin, "The Tragedy of the Commons" (1968) 162 *Science* 1242–1248 and Garrett Hardin: "The Tragedy of the Unmanaged Commons" (1994) vol. 9, no. 5, *Trends in Ecology and Evolution*, p. 199.
125. For a sociological and social-anthropological study see Svein Jentoft (ed.), *Commons in a Cold Climate. Coastal Fisheries and Reindeer Pastoralism in North Norway: The Co-Management Approach* (Man and the Biosphere Series No. 22, Parthenon, New York, 1998).
126. Peter Ørebech has written extensively upon this topic, see *Konsesjoner i fiskerirett* [*Fisheries Licencing System*] (TANO, Oslo, 1982), Norsk fiskerirett [Norwegian Fisheries Law] (Universitetsforlaget, Oslo, 1984), *Reguleringer i fisket* [*Fisheries Regulations*] (Marinjoss, Tromsø, 1986), *Norsk havbruksrett* [*Norwegian Ocean Ranching Law*] (Grøndahl, Oslo, 1988) and Peter Ørebech: "Sedvanerett som grunnlag for bærekraftig forvaltning av fiske i de 'ytre almenninger'" ["Customary Law as a Foundation for Sustainable Fishing Management"], in Bjørn Sagdahl (ed.), *Fjordressurser og Reguleringspolitikk* [*Fjord-resources and Regulation Policies*] (Kommuneforlaget, Oslo, 1998).
127. Einar Eythorson and Stein R. Mathisen, "Changing Understandings of Coastal Saami Local Knowledge," in Svein Jentoft (ed.), *Commons in a Cold Climate. Coastal Fisheries and Reindeer Pastoralism in North Norway: The Co-Management Approach* (Man and the Biosphere Series No. 22, Parthenon, New York, 1998), pp. 211–212.
128. Norwegian Storting [the Parliament]: Innst.O. nr. 38 (1998–1999). Innstilling fra næringskomiteen om lov om retten til å delta i fiske og fangst (deltakerloven) s. 5 sp. 1[Proposal on a New Act of Fishery Participation Rights], confirmed Innst.O. nr. 73 (2000–2001).
129. In Norwegian "allemannsrettigheter," see e.g., Norwegian Supreme Court Decisions – Norsk Retstidende (Rt.), Rt. 1985 s. 247 (Common Fisheries in Kaafjord). More generally, see Ørebech, *Om allemannsrettigheter* [*Public Property Rights*].
130. See e.g. *Smith v. State of Maryland*, 59 U.S. 71, 74–75 (1855): ". . . the enjoyment of certain public rights, among which is the common liberty of taking fish" (Curtis, J.).
131. Because only very few places are under the scheme of private fishing rights, I fully exclude instances of "several fisheries." For the distinction, see *Arnold v. Mundy* 6 N.J.L. 1, 22–26 (N.J., 1821).
132. The property right perspective is confirmed in *McCready v. Virginia*, 94 U.S. 391 (1876).
133. Rudolph Ihering, *Geist des römischen Rechts, auf den verschiedenen Stufen seiner Entwichlung* (Leipzig, 1871), III s. 339: "eine rechtliche Reflexwirkung."

134. Peter Wetterstein, "Damage from International Disasters in the Light of Tort and Insurance Law," General Reports to the 8 World Congress on Insurance Law, The World Commission on Environment and Development, *Our Common Future 1987* (United Nations, 1990), p. 78, note 18. In the same direction, Steffan Westerlund. *Rätt och miljö* [*Law and Environment*] (Carlssons, Stockholm, 1988), p. 177. See also Lorents Rynning, *Allemandsret og særret. Belyst ved forskjellige arter av raadighet over fremmed grund, som ikke gaar ind under de almindelige bruksrettigheter* [*Public Property Right and Possessory Rights*] (Oslo, 1928) and C. A. Fleischer, *Petroleumsrett* [*Petroleum law*] (Universitetsforlaget, Oslo, 1983), p. 585.
135. Peter Ørebech, "Norwegian Fisheries Regulations in Historical Retrospect" Paper presented to the Man & Biosphere UNESCO conference in Svolvaer, Norway 1993.
136. NOU 2001: 34 (Ministry of Justice): Peter Ørebech, *Sedvanerett i fisket. Sjøsamene i Finnmark* [*Fisheries Customary Law. The Coastal Saami*].
137. Solnørdal, O: *Den trønderske almenningsretten i gamalnorsk tid.* [*The Ancient Trøndelag (law district of Mid Norway) Common Pool Legislation*] TfR 1933, Appendix p. 53.
138. See, e.g., the unpublished interview of September 23, 1998 with Håkon Skogen (Børselv, 74 years of age) by Hilmar Nilsen and Harry Pettersen.
139. For a similar conclusion, see Eythorson and Mathisen, "Changing Understandings of Coastal Saami Local Knowledge", p. 208.
140. See Hanne Petersen, "50 år efter Den Juridiske Ekspedition – Spredte refleksioner over kolonier, køn og ret," in Blume and Ketscher (eds.), *Ret og skønsomhed i en overgangstid. Festskrift til Agnete Weis Bentzon* (Akademisk Forlag, Copenhagen, 1998).
141. See Per Walsøe and Kirsten Trolle, "Det grønlandske retsvæsen indsigter og udsigter," in Hanne Petersen and Jacob Janussen (eds.), *Retsforhold og samfund i Grønland* (Atuagkat, Nuuk, 1998), pp. 85–94 and Per Walsøe, "Grønlands kredsretter," in Blume and Ketscher (eds.), *Ret og skønsomhed i en overgangstid. Festskrift til Agnete Weis Bentzon* (Akademisk Forlag, Copenhagen, 1998).
142. See Jes Adolphsen and Tom Greiffenberg, "Social Democratism and the Development of Greenland," in Hanne Petersen and Birger Poppel (eds.), *Dependency, Autonomy, Sustainability in the Arctic* (Ashgate, 1999), pp. 147–154.
143. About the North-west coast habits and traditions, see Gretel Erlich, *This Cold Heaven. Seven Seasons in Greenland* (Pantheon Books, New York, 2001).
144. See Grete Hovelsrud-Broda, "Sharing of local produce – sharing of imports and cash. A study of differential distribution patterns," (Paper presented at the 11th Inuit Studies Conference, September 1998, Nuuk).
145. See Statistical Yearbook Greenland 1997, Statistics Greenland.
146. See Hanne Petersen, "Lovgivningsvirksomhed under hjemmestyre," in Hanne Petersen and Jakob Janussen (eds.), *Retsforhold og samfund i Grønland*

(Atuagkat, Nuuk, (1998), pp. 129–148, and Hanne Petersen, "'The Best of Two Worlds' – Pluralism or Ambivalence in Norms and Values." (Paper presented for the 11th Inuit Studies Conference, September 1998, Nuuk (unpublished).)

147. See Jens Dahl, "Arktisk selvstyre. København, Akademisk Forlag, and Greenland: Political Structure of Self-government" *Arctic Anthropology*, vol. 23 (1–2), pp. 315–324.
148. See Jens Dahl, *Saqqaq. An Inuit Hunting Community in the Modern World* (University of Toronto Press, Toronto, Buffalo, London, 2000), p. 17.
149. *Ibid.*, p. 17.
150. *Ibid.*, p. 98.
151. *Ibid.*, p. 20.
152. *Ibid.*, p. 199.
153. *Ibid.*, p. 188.
154. See Petersen, "'The Best of Two Worlds' – Pluralism or ambivalence in norms and values."
155. See Dahl, *Saqqaq*, p. 213.
156. *Ibid.*, p. 259.
157. See Udenrigspolitisk Redegørelse fra Grønlands Landsstyre, 1993.
158. See Dahl, *Saqqaq*, p. 28.
159. *Ibid.*, p. 259.
160. See Lise Lennert, *Kvinder i Grønland – sammen og hver for sig.* (Atuakkiorfik, Nuuk, 1991).
161. See Finn Lynge, *Arctic Wars. Animal Rights, Endangered Peoples* (Dartmouth, New England, 1992).
162. See Finn Lynge, *Arctic Wars*, p. 103.
163. See Parnûna Heilmann, "Sælskindet – spændt ud af dilemmaer." Final thesis for MA at Ilisimatusarfik (unpublished, 1997).
164. See Finn Lynge, "Nature Management: Kill and Care. Reflections on the Origins of a Controversy," in Hanne Petersen and Birger Poppel (eds.), *Dependency, Autonomy, Sustainability in the Arctic* (Ashgate, Aldershot, Brookfield USA, Singapore, Sydney, 1998).
165. See Dahl, *Saqqaq*, pp. 92 f.
166. *Ibid.*, p. 213.
167. Interview with Aqqaluk Rosing Asved, Grønlands Naturinstitut, January 1999.
168. See *Voices from the Bay. Traditional Ecological Knowledge of Inuit and Cree in the Hudson Bay Bioregion.* Compiled by Miriam McDonald, Lucassie Arragutainaq, Zack Novalinga (Canadian Arctic Resources Committee. Environmental Committee of Municipality of Sanikiluaq, 1997).
169. See Dahl, *Saqqaq*, pp. 213 f.
170. See Henrik Rink, *Tales and Traditions of the Eskimo* (C. Hurst & Company, London; Arnold Busck International Booksellers, Copenhagen, 1875/1974), pp. 22 f.

171. *Ibid.*, p. 25.
172. *Ibid.*, pp. 31–32.
173. See Agnete Weis Bentzon, *Familiens organisation i de grønlandske samfund* (Nyt fra Samfundsvidenskaberne nr. 10, Copenhagen, 1968), p. 18.
174. See Agnete Weis Bentzon, *Familiens økonomiske administration og ejendelenes tilhørsforhold i de Vestgrønlandske samfund* (Nyt fra Samfundsvidenskaberne nr. 11, 1968), p. 47.
175. See Ole Hertz, *Økologi og levevilkår i Arktis. Uummannamiut* (Christian Ejlers Forlag, Mellemfolkeligt Samvirke, 1995), p. 140.
176. See Bentzon, *Familiens organisation*, p. 20.
177. *Ibid.*, p. 21.
178. *Ibid.*, p. 20.
179. See Bentzon, *Familiens økonomiske*, p. 36.
180. See Dahl, *Saqqaq*, p. 58.
181. *Ibid.*, p. 196.
182. *Ibid.*, p. 207.
183. *Ibid.*, pp. 130 and 186.
184. Interview with consultant Niels Holm, Kanukoka (Association of Greenlandic Municipalities), January 1999.
185. See the Internet site: www.arnat.gl (Women's Party site), p. 23 and Newspaper articles from Sermitsiak, and AG from August to November 1999. The Women's Party ran for election in 2001 with 7 candidates, but was not voted in, and dissolved itself gradually during 2003.

3

Social interaction: the foundation of customary law

JES BJARUP

3.1 Knowledge, law and custom

This chapter is concerned with knowledge, law and custom. Custom and law are ways to regulate the behavior or conduct of human beings that raise the practical question for the individual what to do that in turn is related to the epistemological question what to believe. Action depends upon belief, and I shall begin with the epistemological question to be illustrated by reference to the naturalistic view advanced by David Hume and the criticism put forward by Thomas Reid. Hume sets out to destroy the received view of knowledge grounded in reason based upon the conception of man as born in god's image and to replace it with the naturalistic view of knowledge grounded in experience based upon the conception of man as an intelligent animal, to be presented in Section 3.2. The former conception of man has been advanced to support the personal perspective of the epistemic authority of the individual knower grounded in rational insight into the nature of things that is rejected by Hume in favour of the naturalistic view that grounds knowledge in experience based upon custom.[1] However, Hume's naturalistic view is still committed to the personal perspective of knowledge as an individual achievement since Hume only relies upon his own experience as a judicious spectator of the world. Hume's naturalistic view has been influential in the scientific pursuit of knowledge since it supports the epistemic authority of scientists as impartial and disinterested spectators of the world. It has also been challenged by Reid and I consider his criticism in Section 3.3. For Reid, Hume is right that it is important to consider human nature but Hume overlooks that human beings are not only animals but also persons having intellectual powers of understanding and active powers of the mind.[2] This leads Reid to reject the personal perspective in favour of the interpersonal perspective of knowledge as a communal enterprise between autonomous persons. Hume's naturalistic view supports a naturalistic account of social interaction as causal relations between human beings in terms of causes of beliefs and feelings and uniformities of behavior. This is challenged by Reid's rationalistic account in terms of intellectual or communicative relations between persons relying upon common sense and human testimony with respect to what there is reason to believe, to do and to feel, to be considered (see Section 3.4). I then apply these perspectives with respect to Hume's account of moral relations between human beings grounded in feelings and Reid's account based upon reason, in Section 3.5. I consider Hume's account of human relations to the use of natural resources grounded in the invention of laws of justice and Reid's criticism grounded in reason and natural rights, in Section 3.6. I then use these perspectives to consider statutory law and customary law as sources of law by reference to the analytical and historical approach, to use the distinction introduced by Sir Henry Maine, in Section 3.7.[3] I also present the analytical approach advanced by Jeremy Bentham and John Austin in terms of the imperative theory of law that holds that the source of law is found in the authoritative will of the sovereign as expressed in commands that only leave room for custom as a legal source of law if accepted by the sovereign.[4] The historical approach put forward by Maine and Friedrich Carl von Savigny who hold that the analytical approach ignores the historical development of the law and its origin in the consciousness of a people as manifested in customary law.[5] I argue that there is a place for customary law as a legal procedure that turns rules into valid legal rules and reject the view put forward by H. L. A. Hart who holds that custom is not a very important source of law in the modern world.[6] I then present the view advanced by Lon L. Fuller that it is important to understand that customary law has its origin in interaction.[7] This is true but he subscribes to the naturalistic account as opposed to the rationalistic account of social interaction that is important for the place of customary law as a legal procedure to introduce valid legal rules.

3.2 Hume's naturalistic view: the personal perspective

Hume is concerned to provide the proper foundation for the pursuit of knowledge within the various sciences based upon the view that "the science of man is the only solid foundation for the other science," but it is also the case that this science "yet has been hitherto the most neglected."[8] Hume sets out to provide the remedy and "proposes to anatomize human nature in a regular manner, and promises to draw no conclusions but where he is authorized by experience." This is Hume's naturalistic view based upon experience and the use of the experimental method of reasoning that provides the foundation for the scientific pursuit of knowledge of man's place in nature and society. Hume's naturalistic view has been influential within science in relation to reasoning from causes to effect, within moral philosophy in relation to reasoning from is to ought, and within legal philosophy in relation to reasoning about justice and property. As Gerald Postema puts it, "Hume, in fact, is pivotal in the development of British legal theory."[9] If so, there is a case for considering Hume's view in its philosophical context. Postema also holds that according to Hume, "one's sense of self and the sense of one's worth is not epistemologically privileged." This seems to me to be mistaken since one's self in the sense of personal experience is epistemologically privileged by Hume as manifested in his position as a judicious spectator of the operations of his own mind. Thus Hume endorses the personal perspective in terms of the epistemic authority of the individual who only relies upon his own experience in the pursuit of knowledge, or so I shall argue.

Hume's naturalistic view signals a departure from the traditional philosophical view advanced by philosophers such as Rene Descartes, George Berkeley, Benedict Spinoza, Gottfried Wilhelm Leibniz and John Locke based upon the conception of man as born in god's image.[10] Thus man is conceived as a "miniature god" endowed with reason and will to engage in the rational inquiry into the working of nature that leads to the epistemological ideal of knowledge in terms of rational insight and the related ontological view of the world as an intelligible order or system of necessitating causes and effects.[11] The foundation is that god is the omnipotent creator of the world and his divine activity is to act as the supreme legislator in relation to the physical government of nature and the moral government of man. I shall consider the former in this section and return to the latter in Section 3.5. Considering the government of nature, god commands the physical world to operate according to fixed laws that necessarily and eternally regulate the way things are. The corollary is that the physical world exists as an appropriate area for man to study based upon the use of reason as the divine element that separates man as a rational animal from the brutes. This is the insight ideal of knowledge grounded in the infallibility and certainty of human reason that demonstrates the validity of logical and mathematical reasoning and the truth of the principle of causal universality that holds that everything that exists necessarily has a cause, the principle of causal necessity that holds that every particular cause necessarily has a particular effect; and the principle of causal similarity that holds that like causes have like effects. These principles are used in scientific thinking to discover the validity and efficacy of the laws of nature as manifested in the distinction between science that relies upon reason and theology that relies upon revelation or between cognitive beliefs as expressed in scientific statements and religious faith as expressed in religious articles. However, there is a theological foundation for scientific thinking since the concept of a scientific law is introduced and defined in terms of god's commands.[12]

Thus the physical world of nature is conceptualized as an intelligible order or system governed by laws in terms of god's commands that can be known by human beings by means of the use of infallible reason as expressed in scientific judgements. This is also the position endorsed by Sir William Blackstone as manifested in his definition of law.

> Law in its most general and comprehensive sense, signifies a rule of action; and it is applied indiscriminately to all kinds of action, whether animate or inanimate, rational or irrational. Thus we say, the Laws of motion, of gravitation, of optics or mechanics, as well as the Laws of nature and of nations. And it is that rule of action, which is prescribed by some superior, and which the inferior is bound to obey.[13]

Blackstone also holds that man is "the noblest of all sublunary beings, a creature endowed with both reason and will" and "commanded to make use of those faculties in the general regulation of his behaviour." This is to endorse the conception of man as born in god's image that serves as the foundation for Blackstone's scientific approach to the law grounded in rational insight.

The implication of the insight ideal is the rejection of the Aristotelian conception of nature as a purposive and organic order in favour of the Newtonian conception of nature as a mechanical system of inanimate things and animate bodies. The physical nature is conceptualized as clockwork created and made to operate according to the laws passed by god. This is also Blackstone's view, writing

> when the supreme formed the universe, and created matter out of nothing, he impressed certain principles upon that matter, from which it can never depart, and without which it would cease to be. When he put that matter into motion, he established certain laws of motion, to which all moveable bodies must conform. And to descend from the greatest operations to the smallest, when a workman forms a clock, or other piece of mechanism he established at his own pleasure certain arbitrary laws for its direction; as that the hand shall describe a given space in given time; to which law as long as the work conforms, so long it continues in perfection, and answers the end of its formation.

Blackstone conceives god as the supreme workman working at his will or pleasure in passing his laws, but then there is a problem. If the laws made and given by god are expressions of his arbitrary will then the application of the principle of causal similarity results in arbitrary laws and this puts the belief in the uniformity of nature in jeopardy. The problem may be solved by invoking the distinction between god's absolute power to create laws at his will or pleasure and his ordained power to maintain the laws he has freely chosen to make. This distinction makes it possible to underline the contingency of the natural order and at the same time to affirm its stability and uniformity.[14] Thus the physical world of nature is complicated but not unintelligible since what there is operates according to fixed laws as manifested in the uniformity of nature. However, the will of god in the sense of his purpose with making his laws is inscrutable for human beings and this implies that there is no cognitive access to god's purpose with his creation of the laws that govern the behaviour of bodies. The corollary is that there is no scientific place for qualitative descriptions stating the essential form and matter of bodies or things or any purposive or teleological explanations in terms of final causes. The world of nature is a mechanical order devoid of any values and meaning and this confines the scientific approach to present quantitative descriptions of the structure of things in terms of size and shape and to provide mechanical explanations of their movement in terms of efficient causes and their inevitable effects. Human beings are created in god's image and have the cognitive and volitional capacity to discover the laws that govern the physical world due to the divine element of godlike reason. This makes it possible for human beings to demonstrate the perfection of human knowledge as manifested in the study of nature by Sir Isaac Newton and his theories of the laws of the motion of bodies that can be stated in mathematical formulas. This is the theoretical aspect of scientific knowledge concerning the real and lawful necessities among objects and events that make it possible to explain and predict them. But there is also the practical aspect since this makes it possible to apply scientific knowledge to control and dominate nature and thus contribute to improve the quality of life for human beings. This raises the question of the government of man, and the answer is that god also passes the moral laws or natural laws in terms of his commands for the moral conduct of human beings as moral agents who have the capacity to know and follow god's commands and thus establish moral and social order among human beings on the one hand and the proper use of natural resources on the other. I shall return to this in Section 3.5.

Hume rejects the appeal to the insight ideal based upon reason in favour of the appeal to experience based upon the conception of man as an intelligent animal alongside other animals within the world that can be known by human efforts alone.[15] For Hume, "men are necessarily born in a family-society, at least; and are trained by their parents to some rule of conduct and behaviour."[16] Thus the sociality of human beings is not a godlike but a purely biological fact since a human being is placed in social interaction with other human beings within the conditions set by the physical and social environment. Postema holds that the family is the "ur-society" for Hume, but Hume holds the modern view and presents the family not as an entity but as a collection of individuals.[17] Thus the unit of society is the individual faced with the epistemological task of seeking true beliefs in order to survive and also with the moral and social task to establish various behavioral patterns in relation not only to other members of the family but also to members within the larger society concerning the distribution of resources in order to live and enjoy the goods of life. In order to pursue these tasks there is also the philosophical task to provide the proper foundation for these beliefs and behavioral patterns that is Hume's concern based upon an examination of human nature. Hume proceeds upon the naturalistic view concerned with the "mental geography, or delineation of the distinct parts and powers of the mind" based upon observation.[18] The result of this observation is that human reason is not a divine spark of rational insight but solely a mundane element of thinking that is shared with other animals. As Hume puts it, "no truth appears to me more evident, than the beasts are endow'd with thought and reason as well as men." Although they share a common nature there are also crucial differences since human beings surpass the beasts with respect to demonstrative reasoning and the use of testimony.

Hume divides the objects of reason into relations of ideas and matters of fact. The relation of ideas is about the logical relations between ideas as manifested in logical and mathematical reasoning by human beings. Only human beings use this demonstrative reasoning but it is limited to the use of ideas "without dependence on what is anywhere existent in the universe." This reasoning enables them to arrive at true conclusions within the world of ideas, but it has nothing to contribute with respect to matters of fact. This is the task of reason in the sense of causal reasoning that is crucial for the finding of ideas with respect to what to believe, to do and to feel. The use of causal reasoning is related to the faculty of understanding as a natural instinct of inferences that is found among all sensitive animals, be they beasts or humans, alongside the other instincts related to the faculties of the senses that operate to form impressions about things and their relations. The use of causal reasoning is based upon the belief that there are inherent causal necessities between matters of facts as manifested in the uniformity of nature, and this requires a philosophical examination in order to establish its proper foundation.

According to the insight ideal, the foundation is based upon the use of human reason as godlike reason into the necessary relations between matters of fact. Hume rejects this view in favour of the naturalistic view based upon experience to arrive at the belief that there is no necessity but only regularity to be observed between relations of facts. Hume makes his point by the example of a billiard ball lying on the table that is struck by another ball.[19] As Hume writes, "this is as perfect an instance of the relation of cause and effect as any which we know, either by sensation or reflection. Let us therefore examine it." This examination leads Hume to hold that "every object like the cause produces always some object like the effect. Beyond these three circumstances of contiguity, priority, and constant conjunction, I can discover nothing in the cause." The task of reflection is to consider the relations between ideas by means of reason in the sense of demonstrative reasoning and Hume introduces Adam "created in the full vigour of understanding, without experience." This is, of course, a reference to the conception of man as born in god's image endorsed by the insight ideal that holds that reason can reveal the inherent necessities between the movements of the billiard balls. By contrast, Hume holds the opposite view, claiming that Adam "would never be able to infer the motion in the second ball from the motion and impulse of the first. It is not anything that reason sees in the cause, which makes us infer the effect." The inference is based upon the idea that there are necessary relations between ideas but Hume's rejoinder is that there is no contradiction in holding the idea that when one billiard ball encounters another on the table then the second ball flies immediately up into the air rather than moving the second ball. For Hume, Adam "with all his science, would never have been able to demonstrate that the course of nature must continue uniformly the same, and that the future must be conformable to the past." Thus Hume rejects that demonstrative reasoning can reveal the existence of any inherent necessities in events.

There is still reason in the sense of causal reasoning concerning matters of fact or the relation between natural events, but this reasoning is of no avail since it can never demonstrate that this relation is a matter of necessity without presupposing the idea that there are necessary relations between the events. What experience teaches Adam and every other animal is the impact of the surrounding objects or events that excite and forcefully strike the mind and produce sensory impressions that correspond to simple ideas that are worked upon the faculty of understanding to form complex ideas or to draw causal inferences. It is manifest to experience that one event is followed by another event but not that the events are bound to occur with any necessity. Thus there is no inherent necessity in the events since what can be observed are only constant regularities between events. The corollary is that the world is a contingent world related to the working of the mind. This may seem to lead Hume to endorse the skeptical view that nothing can be known. But Hume's philosophical skepticism is put forward to destroy the ideal of rational insight and vindicate the naturalistic view and the possibility of knowledge based upon experience. Thus human beings are placed on a par with animals with respect to observation and experience of causal relations among events. It is also the case that human beings are inventive animals having the capacity to use the faculty of imagination that operates by means of the principles of association concerning the resemblance, contiguity and constant conjunction among present impressions to produce the natural idea that there are necessary relations among events. Thus the world is intelligible in terms of the uniformity and necessity between events, but the important fact is that the necessity and uniformity are located within the world of ideas of the mind as opposed to being located in the events in the world of facts. For Hume, causation is only concerned with relations between events or objects as a matter for scientific investigation based upon the principles of universality, necessity and similarity used in causal reasoning. The task is to provide the proper foundation for these principles and it cannot be reason and this leads Hume to hold that it is custom.

As Hume puts it,

> it is custom alone, which engages animals, from every object, that strikes their senses, to infer its usual attendant, and carries their imagination, from the appearance of the one, to conceive the other, in that particular manner, which we denominate *belief*. No other explication can be given for this operation, in all the higher, as well as lower classes of sensitive beings, which fall under our notice and observation.[20]

For Hume, belief is not a matter of the rational attitude based upon cognition but rather a matter of the natural attitude based upon impressions in relation to the use of the experimental method of reasoning. As Hume puts it,

> the experimental reasoning itself, which we possess in common with beasts, and on which the whole conduct of life depends, is nothing but a species of instinct or mechanical power, that acts in us unknown to ourselves; and in its chief operations, is not directed by any such relations or comparisons of ideas, as are the proper objects of our intellectual faculties.[21]

Animals and human beings share the same faculties and engage in interaction with the surrounding world using the experimental or inductive method of reasoning to move from impressions of what has happened to ideas of what will happen. This is Hume's naturalistic account of social interaction between human beings and objects in terms of causal relations that enable them to learn to arrive at natural beliefs concerning the working of nature in terms of constant regularities among objects and events as manifested in the uniformity of the physical nature and constant regularities of behavioral patterns as manifested in the uniformity of human nature. It goes without saying that the use of the method of inductive reasoning is important for human beings in order to sustain life and happiness within their physical and social surroundings. However, inductive reasoning cannot be conceptualized as a rational procedure for the formation of rational beliefs based upon reason as advanced within the insight ideal of knowledge. According to Hume's naturalistic view, inductive reasoning is a mundane mechanism that mechanically produces causal attitudes of natural ideas or impressions based upon the impact of objects upon the mind. The implication is that inductive reasoning is conceptualized as a non-rational or mechanical procedure for the formation of natural beliefs grounded in observations of the repeated conjunctions between events. Hence the emphasis upon time to sustain the impact of causal experiences upon the mind as manifested in customs. Thus custom

> is the great guide of human life. It is that principle alone which renders our experience useful to us, and makes us to expect, for the future, a similar train of events with those which have appeared in the past. Without the influence of custom, we should be entirely ignorant of every matter of fact beyond what is immediately present to the memory and senses. We should never know how to adjust means to ends, or to employ our natural powers in the production of any effect. There would be an end at once of all action, as well as of the chief part of speculation.

Surely there may be good or bad customs and this raises the question how to decide between them. Hume provides the answer by reference to Newton's use of the experimental method to explain the working of nature in terms of physical laws that can be stated in mathematical formulae, although Hume does not discuss the use of mathematics. For Hume, Newton is "the greatest and rarest genius that ever arose for the ornament and instruction of the species." Newton proceeds upon the personal perspective of the insight ideal that is rejected by Hume in favor of the naturalistic view. However, Hume's naturalistic view is also a personal perspective since it is based upon the perspective of the individual and his passive experience of the impact of objects that cannot be mistaken since "consciousness never deceives." Hume's epistemic authority is based upon his personal experience as a "judicious spectator" of the impact of objects upon his mind as expressed in his judgements but then he also relies upon the words of other beings as manifested in their testimonies. For Hume, human testimony constitutes an important difference between the brute animals and human animals. As Hume puts it, "after we have acquired a confidence in human testimony, books and conversations enlarge much more the sphere of one man's experience and thought than those of another."[22]

Hume is right to emphasize the importance of human testimony since human beings, in contrast to animals, have the capacity to use language to tell stories and convey information by means of testimony.[23] Human testimony has been ignored within the insight ideal based upon the cognitive authority of the rational insight of the knower. Hume rejects this position in favor of the naturalistic approach grounded in his personal experience. Hume's reference to the importance of human testimony may suggest that he abandons the personal perspective in favor of an interpersonal perspective that holds that human knowledge is not solely an individual affair but rather a communal enterprise between human beings based upon human testimony. This makes human testimony important not only as a means to facilitate information and coordination among human beings but also as an independent source of knowledge. The importance of the latter as a source of knowledge is manifested in the fact that I can only learn and know my own name by trusting the authoritative words of other persons. I shall return to the importance of human testimony in Section 3.4. In this section I shall consider Hume's approach to human testimony in order to decide if Postema is right that Hume does not privilege his own experience.

Hume puts great store by human testimony. As he puts it,

> there is no species of reasoning more common, more useful, and even necessary to human life, than that which is derived from the testimony of men, and the reports of eye-witnesses and spectators. This species of reasoning, perhaps, one may deny to be founded on the relation of cause and effect. I shall not dispute about a word. It will be sufficient to observe that our assurance in any argument of this kind is derived from no other principle than our observation of the veracity of human testimony, and of the usual conformity of facts to the reports of witnesses. It being a general maxim, that no objects have any discoverable connection together, and that all the inferences which we can draw from one to another, are founded merely on our own experience of their constant and regular conjunction; it is evident that we ought not to make an exception to this maxim in favour of human testimony, whose connection with any event seems, in itself, as little necessary as any other.[24]

Hume relies upon his own experience of nature that cannot be mistaken but it is otherwise with the reliance upon human testimony since this raises questions whether to trust the reliability of other people and the veracity of their accounts.

Hume provides the answer in terms of the operation of custom upon the human mind to arrive at beliefs about the world. As Hume puts it, "custom, to which I attribute all belief and reasoning, may operate upon the mind in invigorating an idea after two several ways."[25] One way is Hume's account of the formation of natural beliefs based upon causal reasoning as described above. The other way is belief grounded in the use of mere ideas since "the frequent repetition of any idea infixes it in the imagination." Hume's discussion of the reliance upon human testimony is carried out within the contest of miracles and the remarkable propensity of people to believe whatever is reported without considering the conformity between what is reported and the way things are in reality. For Hume, the explanation is the inherent weakness in human nature of "credulity, or a too easy faith in the testimony of others." Hume does not succumb to this "credulity," and relies upon human testimony but only if it passes the standard of human experience since "it is experience only, which gives authority to human testimony; and it is the same experience, which assures us of the laws of nature."[26] The laws of nature are based upon experience and, as Coady has shown, Hume uses the term "experience" to refer ambiguously to common experience among people and to his own experience.[27] This is also manifested in Hume's account of testimony that requires him to isolate the testimony made by other people about the world for comparison with his own experience of the world in order to decide what it is reasonable to believe. In this respect Hume only relies upon human testimony to the extent that it fits with his own experience. Hume considers the reliability of human testimony in relation to miracles and his argument is advanced to undermine "the foundation of a system of religion" to arrive at the view that religion "is founded upon Faith, not reason."[28] However, Hume's naturalistic view is in no better position since the pursuit of scientific knowledge is not founded upon reason but upon animal faith in the use of inductive reasoning based upon personal experience as a judicious spectator. Thus Hume's reference to testimony does not imply that he endorses the interpersonal perspective but is rather a vindication of the personal perspective.[29] It follows that Postema is mistaken since Hume privileges his own experience to support the epistemic authority of the knower as the passive but judicious spectator of the working of nature and its impact upon his mind.

Hume's epistemology is advanced to support the naturalistic view that knowledge is grounded in scientific observations in relation to the experimental method of inductive reasoning. Thus inductive reasoning is the only proper scientific method not only with respect to the study of nature but also to the study of morality, law and politics. For Hume, the naturalistic view is based upon the personal perspective of the epistemic authority of the knower in terms of the scientist who only relies upon his own experience to the exclusion of the reliance upon human testimony as an independent source of knowledge. This has been the position within the natural sciences where scientists emerge as impartial and independent spectators of what there is in the world that in turn can be recorded in scientific judgements concerned with the description of events as the foundation for formulation of scientific laws of nature. These laws can be stated using the mathematical language to explain and predict what there is in the world. In this way natural science serves as the model for the scientific approach within the social sciences aiming at the formulation of scientific laws of social and human behavior as manifested within economics based upon the conception of human beings as solitary and rational agents motivated by self-interest to engage in social interaction with other people in the pursuit of the satisfaction of various preferences.

Within the law, Maine adopts the naturalistic approach dedicated to "submitting the subject of jurisprudence to scientific treatment" in a similar way as the inquiries "in physics and physiology" by reference to observations as opposed to conjectures.[30] What matters is to adopt the historical and comparative method in order to observe the origin of legal ideas in primitive societies and trace their developments into modern societies. As Maine puts it, "if by any means we can determine the early forms of jural conceptions, they will be invaluable to us. These rudimentary ideas are to the jurist what the primary crusts of the earth are to the geologist. They contain, potentially, all the forms in which law has subsequently exhibited itself." Maine's scientific "research into the primitive history of society and law" is not a research of the existence of law in primitive societies that relies upon oral testimonies and personal observations. Maine's research into the law in ancient societies is based upon human testimonies as presented in written poems and codes in order to formulate the laws of development of legal ideas. In this respect Maine follows Hume and only relies upon human testimonies if they pass his assumption that "the constitution of ancient society" is a matter of "patriarchal despotism." This implies that the life of man is "practically controlled in all his actions by a regimen not of law but of caprice" since the authoritative statement of what is right is "a judicial sentence after the facts, not one presupposing a law which has been violated, but one which is breathed for the first time by a higher power into the judge's mind at the moment of adjudication." This leads Maine to hold that there is a movement from this stage to the stage of customary law that is followed by the stage of codes as manifested in Roman law. This development also suggests the existence of "a law of progress" that holds that "the movement of the progressive societies has hitherto been a movement *from Status to Contract.*" This law is not only of theoretical interest but has practical implications for the scientific treatment of the problems of social life since what matters is freedom of contract as manifested in "the Ricardian economic man as the goal of progress."[31]

Maine introduces the inductive method into the study of law in order to present an account in terms of scientific laws concerning the development of legal ideas. Sir Frederick Pollock adopts this method in his approach to account for the making and application of the law by the courts. Pollock holds that "the ultimate object of natural science is to predict events – to say with approximate accuracy what will happen under given conditions."[32] It follows that the object of legal science "is likewise to predict events. The particular kind of event it seeks to predict is the decisions of courts of justice." The natural sciences proceed upon the fundamental assumption that nature is uniform in order to make reliable predictions. Legal science must be based upon a similar assumption of the uniformity of law in the sense "that the same decision is always given on the same facts." We cannot make nature uniform but it is possible to make law uniform. This is so since human beings make law and this ensures the possibility that the same decision will be given on similar facts. This possibility can be realized since it is grounded in "an ideal standard of scientific fitness and harmony" that is found in "the legal habit of the mind itself" as manifested in "the collective opinion of legal experts." The personal perspective of the insight ideal endorsed by Blackstone is replaced with the personal perspective of the legal expert based upon naturalistic view advanced by Hume. Thus Postema is right that Hume "is pivotal in the development of British legal theory." However, Hume's naturalistic view has been criticized by Reid.

3.3 Reid's commonsense view: the interpersonal perspective

Like Hume, Reid holds that an inquiry into the operations of the mind is fundamental in order to account for the extent and justification of human knowledge. The starting point for Reid is an examination of the use of language since "the language of mankind is expressive of their thoughts, and of the various operations of their minds."[33] This implies that there is a natural language of common sense having a common conceptual structure that shows that human beings are born as social and intelligent beings within the common and independently existing material world. The conceptual structure of the language of common sense serves as the foundation for the various specific languages that are used by human beings to engage in various linguistic actions to express attitudes of beliefs and feelings in relation to the nature of external objects and the standards of proper conduct as well as to reflect upon the operations of the mind. This reflection reveals that there is a distinction between the social and solitary operations of the mind that has "a real foundation in nature." As Reid puts it, "the Author of our being intended us to be social beings, and has, for that end, given us social intellectual powers, as well as social affections. Both are original parts of our constitution, and the exertions of both no less natural than the exertions of those powers that are solitary and selfish." Reid endorses the conception of man as born in god's image but it does not follow that he subscribes to the personal perspective put forward within the insight ideal. On the contrary Reid rejects this perspective since it is grounded in the solitary operations of the mind in favor of the interpersonal perspective grounded in the social operations of the mind. This is the important distinction between the solitary and social operations of the mind that has been ignored by philosophers.

As Reid explains the distinction, the social operations are

> such operations as necessarily suppose an intercourse with some other intelligent being. A man may understand and will; he may apprehend, and judge, and reason, though he should know of no intelligent being in the universe besides himself. But, when he asks information, or receives it; when he hears testimony, or receives the testimony of another; when he asks a favour, or accepts one; when he gives a command to his servant, or receives one from a superior; when he plights his faith in a promise or contract these are acts of social intercourse between intelligent beings, and can have no place in solitude. They suppose understanding and will; but they suppose something more, which is neither understanding nor will; that is society with other intelligent beings. They may be called intellectual, because they can only be in intelligent beings.[34]

The speech acts of questioning, testifying, promising and commanding necessarily require the use of language as expressed grammatically "by the second person of the verbs." Hence these speech acts are also necessarily social actions between a speaker and the linguistic expression of his attitude and a listener and his attitude of understanding. By contrast, the use of language is only a contingent feature of the solitary operations of the mind as expressed grammatically in the first person in terms of judgements and feelings. There is no contradiction in a tacit belief or a tacit feeling, but a tacit question or a tacit command is a contradiction. To be sure, the solitary operations may depend upon the use of language but the crucial point is that this presupposes the social operations since the human capacity to use language has to be taught and learnt in social interaction with other people. It follows that the social operations are ontologically and epistemologically prior to the solitary operations. As Reid puts it,

> if nature had not made man capable of such social operations of the mind, and furnished him with a language to express them, he might think, and reason, and deliberate, and will; he might have desires and aversions, joy and sorrow, in a word, he might exert all those operations of the mind, which the writers in logic and pneumatology have so copiously described, but, at the same time, he would still be a solitary being, even when in a crowd; it would be impossible for him to put a question, or give a command, to ask a favour, or testify a fact, to make a promise or a bargain.

The priority of the social operations implies that human reason is a social rather than a solitary capacity that leads Reid to advance the rational account of social interaction in terms of communicative relations between human beings as persons as opposed to the naturalistic account put forward by Hume in terms of causal relations between human beings. It also leads him to reject the personal perspective of knowledge as a solitary enterprise between the knowing subject and the object known in favor of the interpersonal perspective of knowledge as a communal enterprise among persons actively engaged in the pursuit of knowledge of a common world.

Reid uses the distinction between the social and solitary operations in his attack upon the individualist camp of philosophers, or "the egoists" as Reid calls them, mentioning Descartes and Berkeley, who "disbelieve the existence of every creature in the universe but themselves and their own ideas."[35] The foundation for this position is the personal perspective of the insight ideal that conceptualizes the human mind in terms of self-consciousness that makes it possible for human beings to reflect upon the ideas within the mind. This leads to the view that what is immediately present to the mind is not any external object in the world but solely the idea of objects within the mind that can be recorded by means of the solitary use of language in terms of judgements or propositions. Locke also endorses the personal perspective since he holds that "all the immediate objects of human knowledge are ideas in the mind." Berkeley goes further and denies the existence of the material world of objects in favor of the spiritual world of ideas based upon the personal perspective of the solitary being and his godlike knowledge. Although Hume rejects the insight ideal in favour of the naturalistic view he follows suit and conceptualizes the mind in terms of its solitary operations. This leads Hume to claim that "for my part, when I enter most intimately into what I call *myself*, I always stumble on some particular perception or other, of heat or cold, light or shade, love or hatred, pain and pleasure. I can never catch *myself* at any time without a perception, and never can observe any thing but the perception."[36] Hume's search for the idea of the self cannot be based upon man as born in god's image since Hume rejects this in favor of the conception of man as an intelligent animal using the philosophical theory of ideas. As Reid puts it, Hume "adopts the theory of ideas in its full extent; and in consequence, shews that there is neither matter nor mind in the universe; nothing but impressions and ideas. What we call a *body*, is only a bundle of sensations; and what we call the *mind* is only a bundle of thoughts, passions, and emotions, without any subject."[37] If Hume's account is true then the concept of a person can only be used to refer to a pattern of overlapping experiences without any discernible bond to unite them. For Reid this is an affront to common sense grounded in the theory of ideas that has led Berkeley and Hume astray, "one, to disbelieve the existence of matter, and the other, to disbelieve the existence of both matter and mind." Berkeley and Hume are led astray because they ignore the social operations of the mind or reduce them to the solitary operations of the mind in relation to the use of the philosophical theory of ideas. The use of the social operations of the mind that makes it obvious that human beings are not trapped within the circle of their own perceptions of ideas in the mind makes it necessary for them "to find arguments to prove the existence of external objects, which the vulgar believe upon the bare authority of their senses."

For Reid, the senses or more generally the human faculties are directed by principles of truths that regulate human beliefs and actions. It is a principle of truth that there are human beings situated within a common world. Another principle of truth is that the perception of an object implies a distinction between "the mind that perceives, the operation of that mind, which is called perception, and the object perceived."[38] The existence of these three distinct things is acknowledged in the structure in all languages, but in addition philosophers have introduced "a fourth thing in this process, which they call the idea of the object, which is supposed to be an image, or representative of the object, and is said to be the immediate object." Reid rejects the philosophical theory of ideas as mistaken since it confounds the idea of an object with the object and overlooks that it is "by means of the material world that we have any correspondence with thinking beings, or any knowledge of their existence." He also rejects the personal view of the insight ideal aiming at the perfection of human knowledge since "seeking to become wise, and to be as gods, we shall become foolish, and being unsatisfied with the lot of humanity, we shall throw off common sense." This is also exemplified in Hume's naturalistic view.

Hume's naturalistic view is committed to the possibility of knowledge grounded upon an appeal to custom. Reid shares Hume's view that custom is important since

> man would never acquire the use of reason if he were not brought up in the society of reasonable creatures. The benefit he receives from society, is derived partly from imitation of what he sees others do, partly from the instruction and information of what they communicate to him, without which he could neither be preserved from destruction, nor acquire the use of his rational powers.[39]

Reid also shares Hume's view that human beings and animals are sensitive creatures having consciousness and capable of feeling pain and pleasure that have principles of behavior in common in order to preserve and sustain life. Thus there are mechanical and animal principles that operate without any use of thought to produce patterns of regular behavior as manifested in individual habits and common customs. This is regularian behavior that is important since it is prior to learning to engage in the intentional activity of using language for the formation of rational beliefs and rational conduct that is brought about by means of intellectual principles and the use of the social operations of the mind. The faculty of the senses provides animals, including humans, with experience of the world, but the use of the intellectual principles provides human beings with a public language of concepts to understand the world. The behavior of animals is governed by animal principles to produce various determinate modes of life as manifested in animal customs. The life of human beings depends upon the use of the intellectual principles to regulate beliefs and actions to arrive at indeterminate modes of life as manifested in human customs. It follows that the term "custom" can be used in different senses. There are the customs of animal behavior that can be recorded in laws of nature. And there are the customs of human conduct that are introduced by human beings having the cognitive capacity to think and act according to laws of their own making. Hume's failure is to overlook the social operations of the mind that account for the crucial difference between animals and human beings.

As Reid puts it,

> there are two operations of the social kind, of which the brute animals seem altogether incapable. They can neither plight their veracity by testimony, nor their fidelity by any engagement or promise. If nature had made them capable of these operations, they would have had a language to express them by, as man has. But of this we see no appearance.

It is the prerogative of human beings that they can communicate by means of language and talk in meaningful ways about man's place in nature and society. It is also the human predicament that we have to rely upon the authority of persons and the veracity of what they report in their testimonies as rational grounds of beliefs. Reid adopts the interpersonal perspective based upon the social operations of the mind and holds that human beings are so constituted that we naturally tend to rely upon "the testimony of nature given by the senses, as well as in human testimony given by language."[40] The testimony of nature is based upon the use of the human faculties in conjunction with intellectual principles of truths. A first principle of truth holds "that the natural faculties, by which we distinguish truth from error, are not fallacious."[41] This is an epistemological principle that cannot be demonstrated or proved since "to judge of a demonstration, a man must trust his faculties, and take for granted the very thing in question." Thus Reid holds that we must trust our faculties "and this we must do implicitly, until God give us new faculties to sit in judgement."

For Reid, man is born in god's image and this may lead to the view that the human trust in the use of our faculties ultimately is provided by god. It is held that Reid subscribes to what is called "providential naturalism."[42] This is not the place to enter into a discussion but I believe that it is possible to hold that the epistemological principle provides its own evidence as suggested by Reid by reference to Aristotle "that every proposition to which we give a rational assent, must either have its evidence in itself, or derive from some antecedent proposition. As, therefore, we cannot go back to antecedent propositions without end, the evidence must at last rest upon propositions, one or more, which have their evidence in themselves – that is upon, first principles."[43] Thus human beings are "born under a necessity of trusting to our reasoning and judging powers; and a real belief of their being fallacious cannot be maintained for any considerable time by the greatest skeptic, because it is doing violence to our constitution." It follows that the epistemological principle that the human faculties are trustworthy depends upon the human constitution. What matters in this respect is not that man is born in god's image but that human beings are born with the intellectual and volitional capacity to become rational persons and responsible agents.[44] This is the interpersonal perspective that conceptualizes the human mind in terms of rationality in relation to the use of the social operations of the mind. This implies that the rational capacities are learned capacities among human beings as intelligent persons based upon social interaction in terms of communicative relations between human beings as persons that appeal to "first principles, which are really the dictates of common sense, and directly opposed to absurdities in opinion, [and] will always, from the constitution of human nature, support themselves, and gain rather than lose ground among mankind." Thus Reid's naturalistic view is based upon the interpersonal perspective and the social operations of the mind in contrast to Hume's naturalistic view based upon the personal perspective and the solitary operations of the mind.

3.4 Human testimonies and social interaction

Reid's interpersonal perspective also makes an appeal to human testimony. In contrast to Hume, Reid holds that human beings are so constituted that they rely upon human testimony as an independent source of knowledge. For Reid, the trust in testimony is based upon the principles of veracity and credulity. The former principle states that there is a propensity for persons to tell the truth by using language to convey true beliefs and sincere feelings. The principle of credulity states that there is a disposition to confide in the veracity of others and thus to believe what is told. These principles are implanted in human nature to tally with each other as the foundation for learning and reasoning in society with other people in order to arrive at rational beliefs about the world. As Reid points out, "it is evident, that, in the matter of testimony, the balance of human judgement is by nature inclined to the side of belief; and turns to that side of itself, when there is nothing put into the opposite scale. If it was not so, no proposition that is uttered in discourse would be believed, until it was examined and tried by reason; and most men would be unable to find reasons for believing the thousandth part of what is told them. Such distrust and incredulity would deprive us of the greatest benefits of society, and place us in a worse condition than that of savages."[45] Thus Reid rejects Hume's account of testimony based upon the personal perspective in favor of the interpersonal perspective and the reliance upon human testimony as an independent and important source of knowledge. This is related to the difference between Reid's rationalist account and Hume's naturalistic account of social interaction that can be illustrated by reference to learning to speak a language.

According to Hume, animals and human beings are talking animals and engaged in social interaction with other animals by means of using language in the sense of noises to inform and bring about the appropriate behavior. There is a difference, however, rooted in "a principle of human nature" that "men are mightily addicted to *general* rules" based upon "a general sense of common interests; which sense all the members of the society express to one another, and which induces them to regulate their conduct by certain rules."[46] The use of language is not an intellectual but mechanical operation of the mind related to the impressions of objects received through the senses. This is Hume's naturalistic account that holds that the unit of meaning is the individual word and its meaning depends upon impressions produced by causal relations with objects. In this way rules are developed in terms of behavioral patterns that turn animal noises into meaningful words as manifested in the distinction between simple and complex ideas. Hume's account implies that any idea that cannot be correlated to an impression must be discarded as a meaningless word or noise. Human beings have an interest to exchange messages by means of using the appropriate words to express and evoke the appropriate ideas concerning the appropriate behavior and engage in social interaction as causal interaction between a speaker and his words that must be decoded by the listener in order to produce the appropriate understanding of the ideas and the related behavioral response. The use of the appropriate vocabulary enables human beings to engage in social interaction in order to sustain cooperation and coordination based upon "stable interactional expectancies," to use Fuller's phrase.[47] This is the personal perspective of social interaction based upon the solitary operations of the mind that has been so influential.[48]

By contrast, Reid endorses the interpersonal perspective that holds that it is the intellectual activity of the mind that confers meaning upon use of words in sentences as manifested in the language of common sense intertwined with modes of conduct. This implies that the unit of meaning is not the individual word but the sentence used in communicative relations between human beings as persons to convey what to believe, to do and to feel. The meaning of the use of language is not a matter of behavioral rules or conventions based upon causal impressions of objects but a matter of social rules or conventions as normative requirements for the appropriate use of words in sentences. Reid rejects Hume's view that human beings think in ideas or images, but if we grant this, then it is thinking that confers meaning upon the ideas or images and not the other way round. The understanding of the linguistic meaning is not a mental process but a mental capacity that is acquired by human beings when they enter into various communicative relations with other people. Thus children have to learn the correct and incorrect application of the use of the public language by trusting the authority of their parents and teachers and the veracity of their accounts of the social conventions. In this way children acquire the capacity to understand the linguistic meaning of words and sentences and master the correct use of language. This implies that the understanding of what is said or written about a given topic is prior to and independent of an interpretation. There is only need for an interpretation if what is said or written is obscure or ambiguous and this presupposes some understanding in order to provide the proper explanation of the disputed phrase. Thus the understanding of language is not the decoding of patterns of sounds or noises but the ability to perform various linguistic actions based upon beliefs and feelings about the social and physical environment.

Human testimony is also important for the understanding of what persons mean when they use meaningful sentences to express their attitudes about a given topic. This is to address the question of social interaction in relation to what persons are doing when they use language. Hume advances the naturalistic account of social interaction between the personal perspectives of human beings using words or sentences as a stimulus to influence and produce the appropriate behavioural responses. This fits with his account of human beings as situated within various causal chains of natural and social events. It also fits with his account of causation in terms of regularities between events. For Hume, human beings are intelligent animals that observe these regularities in order to react and behave properly. However, it is tantamount to denying the existence of human beings as persons. As John Yolton puts it, "in a world of events only, there could be no persons."[49] This is also Reid's objection that Hume ignores that causation is not only a matter of relations between events but also a matter to bring something about by human agency. Hume confines causation to be event causation concerning regularities between objects and their impact upon the mind to the exclusion of human agency concerned with causation in relation to the power to bring something about by acting. The different forms of causation are manifest to common sense as expressed linguistically in the distinction between what happens to human beings and what human beings can do. Hume rejects agency causation because it presupposes the meaning of cause as an active power to do something but there is no impression of this power upon the mind, hence it follows that the word is meaningless and the concept of active power must be discarded. Reid rejects Hume's account of meaning and holds that the concept of power is not acquired through the use of the senses but through the understanding of the nature of human beings. Thus Locke is surely correct that "the only clear notion or idea we have of active power, is taken from the power which we find in ourselves to give certain motions to our bodies, or a certain direction to our thoughts."[50]

The use of the concept of power is also manifested in the use of language in relation to animals and human beings. Animals as well as human beings have to learn to move their limbs in order to walk, but only human beings can act and go for a walk. The former is a matter of movements of one's limbs which can be learnt and exercised in solitude but the latter requires the concept of being the cause of an action that only can be learnt by means of the social operations of the mind. Animals and human beings behave according to mechanical and animal principles of behavior but only human beings have the capacity to become authors of their own actions and govern themselves. As Reid puts it, animals

> are not capable of self-government, and when they act according to the passion or habit which is strongest at the time, they act according to the nature that God has given them, and no more can be required of them. They cannot lay down a rule to themselves, which they are not to transgress, though prompted by appetite, or ruffled by passion. We see no reason to think that they can form the conception of a general rule, or of obligation to adhere to it.[51]

Animals behave according to causes in relation to the operation of the mechanical and animal principles to produce determinate modes of behavior that can be accounted for in terms of causal laws. This is event causation in contrast to agency causation in relation to human beings having the capacity to become authors or causes of their own actions. This capacity is acquired through communicative relations based upon the social operations of the mind that makes it possible for children to take steps to become rational persons and responsible agents to bring about indeterminate modes of conduct in relation to various ends. The various modes of human conduct are in turn subject to human regulation in terms of various rules as manifested in human customs, moral standards and customary and statutory laws.

Reid's account of human agency is related to the interpersonal perspective since it makes it possible for persons to engage in the intentional activity of using sentences to express various linguistic acts and enter into meaningful discourses with other persons governed by the principles of veracity and truth. Thus human beings can learn "how to do things with words," to use J. L. Austin's phrase, or engage in various kinds of linguistic actions that relate the propositional contents expressed in sentences to an independently existing reality, to use the terminology of John Searle.[52] It is the human capacity to think that makes it possible to use concepts in order to describe and classify what there is, or ought to be, in the world as well as to describe and classify human activity in terms of conduct based upon reasons as opposed to bodily movements or behavior based upon causes. This is in turn important for the pursuit of knowledge of the world. For the personal perspective, the knower is conceptualized as the passive and detached spectator reflecting upon what happens to the mind in order to arrive at beliefs about the working of nature and society as expressed in scientific judgements. Reid endorses the interpersonal perspective that conceptualizes the knower as an actor and participant engaged in physical interaction with things and events and in communicative interaction with other persons with respect to what there is reason to believe, to do and to feel. In this respect, human beings rely upon experience and the use of the inductive method of reasoning in order to understand "the grammar of nature," as Reid puts it by reference to Newton's theories of the operations of various laws of nature. Like Hume, Reid endorses Newton's use of the principles of causality but he rejects Hume's view that they are grounded in custom in favor of "an instinctive prescience of the operations of nature, very like to that prescience of human actions which makes us rely upon the testimony of our fellow-creatures."[53] For Reid, the causal principles are based upon reason in terms of contingent principles of truth, and this implies that inductive reasoning is a rational procedure for the formation of rational beliefs in contrast to Hume's view that inductive reasoning is a non-rational procedure for the formation of natural beliefs. As noticed above Reid's naturalistic view is committed to the epistemological principle "that the natural faculties, by which we distinguish truth from error, are not fallacious." It follows that the natural faculties can be trustworthy without being infallible and this underlies the interpersonal perspective and the reliance upon the testimonies of other people.

Thus another important source for the formation of rational beliefs is the reliance upon human testimony grounded in the principles of veracity and credulity. In this respect, human testimony is an independent and important source of knowledge since the greatest part of knowledge is received through trusting the authority of human testimony from "our fellow-creatures." This is the case even within mathematics, "a science, in which, of all sciences, the authority is acknowledged to have the least weight."[54] Reid illustrates this by the example of a mathematician, who has made an important discovery and carefully confirmed it by his own reasoning but still anxious about its validity and "commits his demonstration to the examination of a mathematical friend, whom he esteems a competent judge, and waits with impatience the issue of his judgement." Reid then puts the question,

> whether the verdict of his friend, according as it is favourable or unfavourable, will not greatly increase or diminish his confidence in his own judgement? Most certainly it will, and ought. If the judgement of his friend agree with his own, especially if it be confirmed by two or three able judges, he rests secure of his discovery without farther examination; but,

> if it be unfavourable, he is brought back into a kind of suspense, until the part that is suspected undergoes a new and a more rigorous examination.

The same sort of thing happens in perceptual matters within the natural sciences where research depends upon trusting not only one's personal experience but also the testimonies of one's colleagues. The implication is that knowers are not to be seen as solitary but as communal agents engaged in the common pursuit of what there is reason to believe. Testimony is also important within the area of the law in order to establish the existence of particular customary rules; that is the subject of Blackstone's account considered in Chapter 4. Human testimony is also important in relation to witnesses and the verdicts of jurors and judges to decide cases. In this respect it is interesting to see the development of the institution of the jury from being composed of persons being informed about the facts to being composed of persons altogether uninformed about the facts in order to decide the issues.[55]

The interpersonal perspective stresses the social and political conditions of knowledge based upon communication and freedom of thought. Freedom of thought is not only a solitary operation of having thoughts but also involves the social operation to express these thoughts. Thus there is a conceptual relation between thinking and expression. As Immanuel Kant puts it,

> how much and how correctly would we *think* if we did not think as it were in community with others to whom we *communicate* our thoughts, and who communicate theirs with us! Thus one can very well say that this external power which wrenches away people's freedom publicly to *communicate* their thoughts also takes from the freedom to *think* – that single gem remaining to us in the midst of all the burdens of civil life, through which alone we can devise means of overcoming all the evils of our condition.[56]

This community consists of communicative relations related to teaching and learning that accustom human beings to become rational persons and responsible agents, having the capacity to use the intellectual powers of understanding and the active powers of the will to arrive at what there is reason to believe and to do. The starting point is the common-sense distinction between what is settled or established as the area of knowledge as opposed to what is not settled and thus within the area of belief. This is not to say that the boundaries between these areas are fixed and unalterable. On the contrary this is a matter for debate in relation to public justifications. It is not to say that judgements of common sense always state the truth but it is to say that these judgements must be taken into consideration before we try to doubt them. The interpersonal perspective stresses the social character of human thinking and acting but this does not rule out the ideal of the autonomous person. As Reid puts it, men and women have "the natural, the unalienable right of judging for themselves."[57] But the autonomous person is not conceptualized as the solitary knower working everything out for her or himself. This is to endorse the personal perspective of the epistemic authority of the individual advanced within the insight ideal by reference to reason and within Hume's naturalistic approach by reference to experience. By contrast, the interpersonal perspective holds that the autonomous person is the communal knower engaged in communicative relations with other persons based upon the critical use of reason that makes it possible to examine the credentials of the authority of established habits of thinking and customary rules of conduct. As Reid puts it, "arguments, whatever be the degree of their strength, diminish not a man's liberty; they may produce a cool conviction of what we ought to, and they can do no more."[58] The critical attitude accepts that custom is a guide but the great guide is human reason in the pursuit of knowledge that can be used to improve human life. The interpersonal perspective is also important for the government of human beings since it implies that human societies and political communities are communicatively constituted by human beings as rational persons and responsible agents having the capacity to perform various linguistic actions for guidance and measure of persons and their conduct.

3.5 Law, morality and social interaction

According to the insight ideal, god not only passes the physical laws of nature for the behavior of bodies but also the moral law of nature in terms of eternally valid commands to be observed by man created as a social being endowed with reason and will, see above Section 3.2. This implies that the sociality of man is a god-given fact and also that man is a person having the intellectual capacity to arrive at knowledge of the moral law by means of reason as opposed to revelation as well as the volitional capacity to follow the moral law. The moral law is valid since it is passed by god and endowed with normative force for human conduct in the sense that it must be obeyed. This implies that the moral law can be transgressed by human beings in contrast to the physical laws that determine the movement of inanimate things and animal behavior. However, the transgressions are subject to god's punishment that sustains the validity and normativity of the moral law and ensures that it is in force for human conduct. Hence the importance that human beings are endowed with reason to understand that the moral law is there to be obeyed and with the volitional capacity to act accordingly on pain of being punished. The moral law in terms of god's commands may provide the framework for a personal morality in interaction within other people within the social and physical environment. It can also provide the framework for a public morality of human government since the moral law or natural law serves as the foundation for the making of valid law by the appropriate human authorities. The role of god has certainly been important for human thinking in terms of theories of natural law and natural right. Suffice it to mention that Locke subscribes to the insight ideal and holds that god governs the world and his theory of natural law is presented within a theistic framework of mankind as the workmanship of god.[59] The moral government of man is grounded in a constitutional government based upon the fundamental law of nature that enjoins that mankind must be preserved. The law of nature empowers the political authority to pass human or positive laws to further the public good, but it also constrains the exercise of political authority to make laws that conform to the natural law and respect the natural rights to life, liberty and property endowed to men.

Blackstone also subscribes to the insight ideal and restricts his inquiry into "laws in their more refined sense" that is to say the laws of nature denoting a rule of action "prescribed by some superior, and which the inferior is bound to obey."[60] The superior is, of course, god and the inferior human beings having the intellectual capacity to understand and obey the laws of nature passed by the will of god in terms of "those relations of justice that existed in the nature of things antecedent to any positive precept." For Blackstone, god's will is determined by his wisdom hence "the Creator himself, in all his dispensations, conforms to the eternal immutable laws of good and evil." God is endowed with infinite goodness and this is important since god passes the law of nature that "is binding over all the globe, in all countries, and at all times: no human laws are of any validity, if contrary to this; and such of them as are valid derive all their force and all their authority mediately or immediately from the original." The validity of the law of nature implies that it has normative force for human beings in the sense that it must be obeyed and god "has graciously reduced the rule of obedience to this one paternal precept that man should pursue his own true and substantial happiness." This is the province of personal morality but the law of nature is also important for the province of public morality since it serves as the foundation for the validity of municipal or positive law passed by the sovereign parliament. This is manifested in the written law of enacted law or Acts of Parliament and the unwritten law that is divided into the common law as the expression of the customs of the realm and local customs that only concern the people of particular areas. This constitutes the positive law that is Blackstone's concern to present as

> a rational science which distinguishes the criteria of right and wrong; which teaches to establish the one and prevent, punish, or redress the other; which employs in its theory the noblest faculty of the soul and exerts in its practice the cardinal virtues of the heart; a science which is universal in its use and extent, accommodated to each individual yet comprehending the whole community.

Blackstone is committed to the insight ideal dedicated to "examining the great outlines of the English law, and tracing them up to their principles."[61] These principles are grounded in the authority of reason as manifested in the principle of human liberty in conjunction with the principles of justice set out in the code of Justinian "that we should live honestly, should hurt nobody, and should render to every one his due."

Hume is firmly opposed to any theory of natural law or natural right based upon the existence of an objective and rational moral order as the foundation for the government of man by means of the positive law. For Hume, the physical world of nature is devoid of any meaning or value and if this is the case it is evident that nature cannot serve as a standard for human conduct. This leads to the insistence upon the separation between natural facts and moral values and the appeal to experience to account for the existence of moral values. In this respect, experience shows that animals lack morality, not because they lack reason since reason is nothing but an animal instinct, but because "animals have little or no sense of virtue or vice; they quickly lose sight of the relations of blood; and are incapable of that of right and property."[62] Hence morality is solely a human affair grounded in human nature and the circumstances of life. As noticed above, Hume holds that the sociality of man is a natural and biological fact since children are born into a family and "trained by their parents to some rule of conduct and behaviour." This raises the question concerning the understanding of the training of children within the family as well as the question concerning the proper rules of conduct. Maine provides an answer in terms of the patriarchal family as a coercive institution governed by the absolute authority of the father. As he puts it, "law is the parent's words" and "law" is conceptualized in terms of "a despotic father's commands."[63] This is a morality of obedience to commands based upon the principle of coercion to ensure compliance within the family that serves as the basis for Maine's explanation of the development of law. Hume rejects the morality of commands based upon the principle of coercion in favor of a morality based upon the principle of persuasion. Thus the family is not a coercive institution but rather the custodian of social and filial affections between parents and children in relation to the moral inculcation of the proper sentiments to other people in terms of virtues and vices on the one hand and the proper sentiments with respect to human behavior to external things or objects in terms of the virtue of justice on the other. One reason for this position may be Hume's own upbringing by his mother that leads Hume to hold that parents do not educate their children as despots but rather as loving and caring human beings. Another reason may be Hume's rejection of the insight ideal that is related to religion and natural law grounded in divine commands that is the foundation for the division between duties to self, to others and to god that is ignored by Hume in his account of morality.

Hume restricts morality to be concerned with the moral character of human beings in terms of virtues and vices as manifested in human actions based upon "the undoubted maxim that no action can be virtuous, or morally good, unless there be in human nature some motive to produce it, distinct from the sense of morality."[64] Hume is concerned with the epistemological question concerning the foundation for the proper principles of approval of human character and his answer parallels his account of the foundation of the non-moral standard of natural beliefs. The answer cannot be found by observation of the physical nature since it is devoid of any meaning of value. Hence the answer can only be found within human nature, and Hume holds that "the minds of all men are similar in their feelings and operations." Thus human nature is uniform and it follows that Hume only has to look within his own mind to find the appropriate motives for the appraisal of human actions. For Hume, "'Tis evident, that when we praise any actions, we regard only the motives that produced them, and consider the actions as signs or indications of certain principles in the mind and temper. The external performance has no merit. We must look within to find the moral quality." Hume adopts the personal perspective of a judicious spectator concerned with the observation of his solitary operations of his mind in order to find the appropriate motives. It cannot be reason since reason is solely concerned with the logical relations between ideas within the mind without any regard to matters of fact. Besides "morals excite passions, and produce or prevent actions. Reason of itself is utterly impotent in this particular. The rules of morality, therefore, are not conclusions of our reason." When Hume looks within his own mind the motives to actions are based upon the impressions of pain and pleasure produced by "the very view and contemplation of certain characters and passions." The impressions of pain and pleasure account for the causal origin of moral ideas and also supply the standard of approval or disapproval concerning the moral character of human beings since these sentiments "are not only inseparable from vice and virtue, but constitute their very nature and essence." The foundation of morality is grounded in sentiments of feelings of pleasure and pain that account for the causes of virtue and vice and consequently account for their effects as expressed in behavior or by means of the use of words that refer to feelings of praise or blame related to the circumstances of utility. It follows that morality is "more properly felt than judg'd of" as expressed in moral judgements concerning the merit or demerit of human actions as signs of the moral character of human beings. Hume rejects the cognitive view that moral judgements express moral beliefs that can be true or false in favor of the non-cognitive view that moral judgements only express moral sentiments of sympathy and antisympathy of the human character in terms of the standard of utility related to virtues and vices.

Hume proceeds upon the naturalistic account of social interaction to account for the socialization of human animals based upon the use of the moral vocabulary to express and evoke sentiments of praise and blame concerning the proper human character and related behavior. As Hume puts it, "to have the sense of virtue, is nothing but to *feel* a satisfaction of a particular kind from the contemplation of a character. The very *feeling* constitutes our praise or admiration." The feeling of satisfaction is sympathy that is rooted in what is useful or agreeable for human beings as manifested in the natural virtues of personal merit as opposed to the demerit of vices. Thus "personal merit consists altogether in the possession of mental qualities, *useful* or *agreeable* to the *person himself* or to *others*" as manifested in love, benevolence and humanity.[65] By contrast, Hume puts "celibacy, fasting, penance, mortification, self-denial, humility, silence, solitude, and the whole train of monkish virtues" within the catalogue of the vices since they "neither advance a man's fortune in the world, nor render him a more valuable member of society; neither qualify him for the entertainment of company, nor increase his power of self-enjoyment." What matters for individuals is to advance their fortunes by means of work and keep the reward of their labors in order to live a respectable and profitable life. This requires the socialization of human beings and they engage in moral discourses in terms of feelings based upon the solitary operations of the mind to produce the appropriate attitudes concerning the moral character of human beings in terms of virtues and vices. The moral relations are causal relations between facts in the world that are the subject matter for the scientific study of morality from the personal perspective of the judicious spectator using the inductive method of reasoning to formulate the laws of moral character grounded in the principle of utility that can be used to explain and evaluate human behavior.

Reid challenges Hume's view by holding that he overlooks the social operations of the mind related to the use of rational principles of truths and moral principles of human goods. Morality is grounded in "the moral faculty of conscience" or practical reason as "an intellectual and active power of the mind" that is manifested in "the conceptions of right and wrong in human conduct, of merit and demerit, of duty and moral obligation, and our other moral conceptions; and that, by the same faculty, we perceive some things in human conduct to be right, and others to be wrong; that the first principles of moral are dictates of this faculty; and that we have the same reason to rely upon those dictates, as upon the determinations of our senses, or our other natural faculties."[66] Reid rejects Hume's maxim and holds that actions to be moral actions must be grounded in moral motives. It is also the case that the normative concepts are "too simple to admit of a logical definition" and thus "cannot be resolved into that of interest, or what is most for our happiness." In a similar way, the moral concepts of what is good or bad are not a matter of feelings but "the offspring of reason and can only be in beings endowed with reason." The normative and moral concepts express rational principles of human actions and serve as moral motives for the actions performed by human beings as rational agents. Thus morality is related to human agency. This is Reid's rationalistic account of the socialization of human beings in relation to the social operations of the mind as manifested in moral discourses as communicative relations that turn human beings into rational persons and responsible agents by means of the expression of beliefs concerning the moral character of persons as well as the merit or demerit of their actions grounded in rational principles. Thus Reid subscribes to the cognitive view that moral judgements express beliefs that can be true or false. To be sure, there is also room for moral discourse as an exchange of moral expressives grounded in feelings of love and hatred. This is Hume's account of moral discourse based upon the solitary operations of the mind that reduces judgements of moral beliefs to be expressives of moral feelings. This is a distortion of moral discourse since it overlooks the primacy of the social operations of the mind as manifested in the interpersonal perspective among persons and their expressions of what there is reason to believe, to do and to feel based upon the principles of veracity and credulity. As Reid puts it,

> This doctrine, therefore, that moral approbation is merely a feeling without judgement, necessarily carries along with it this consequence, that a form of speech, upon one of the most common topics of discourse, which either has no meaning, or a meaning irreconcilable to all rules of grammar and rhetoric, is found to be of common and familiar in all languages, and in all ages of the world, while every man knows how to express the meaning, if it have any in plain and proper language. Such a consequence I think sufficient to sink any philosophical opinion on which it hangs.

Hume buttresses his account of morality and moral reasoning by reference to the capital difference between reasoning in terms of "propositions, is, and is not" and reasoning in terms of propositions with "an ought, or an ought not" that has been overlooked "in every system of morality."[67] To be sure, Hume is right that it is impossible to derive ought propositions from is propositions, but this is solely a matter of logic. It does not follow that ought propositions are expressions of sentiments nor that the use of the inductive method of reasoning is the only scientific method that turns morality into a scientific subject as Hume invites us to believe. For Reid, morality is grounded in the use of practical reason that implies that moral reasoning is a matter of using moral principles to arrive at what there is moral reasons to believe, to do and to feel with respect to persons and their conduct.

3.6 Justice, law and social interaction

Hume next considers human beings and their relations to external objects or property based upon his naturalistic view that is advanced as an attack upon the theories of natural law or natural rights relying upon the fiction of "the state of nature, or that imaginary state, which preceded society."[68] The fiction can be used to refer either to the state of "men in their savage and solitary condition" or to the state "like that of the golden age, which poets have invented; only with this difference, that the former is describ'd as full of war, violence and injustice; whereas the latter is painted out to us, as the most charming and peaceable condition, that can possibly be imagin'd." The common feature of these fictitious states is that "there was no such thing as property; and consequently cou'd be no such thing as justice or injustice" and the same holds "with regard to promises." However, the state of nature is "a mere philosophical fiction, which never had, and never cou'd have any reality" since it is based upon the conception that "all society and intercourse (are) cut off between man and man." This is to endorse Jean-Jacques Rousseau's view that human beings in the state of nature "maintained no kind of intercourse with one another, and were consequently strangers to vanity, deference, esteem, and contempt; they had not the least idea of *meum* and *tuum*, and no true conception of justice; they look upon every violence to which they were subjected, rather as an injury that might easily be repaired than as a crime that ought to be punished; and they never thought of taking revenge, unless perhaps mechanically and on the spot, as a dog will sometimes bite the stone which is thrown at him."[69] Hume proceeds upon Rousseau's account and holds that "it seems evident, that so solitary being would be as much incapable of justice, as of social discourse and conversation." For Hume, even the savage condition that precedes society "may justly be esteem'd social" since human beings are necessarily born and socialized within a family. Thomas Hobbes does not deny this in his account of the state of nature. Rousseau's account that human beings are not sociable in the state of nature is rejected by Hobbes since human beings engage in social interaction.[70] For Hobbes, the state of nature is the social condition that human beings are in when there is no government and this is not a mere philosophical fiction but an empirical reality that has some historical support as manifested in the life among Indians in America and among present sovereign nation states. Hume also holds that "the state of society without government is one of the most natural states of men," although it is "impossible they shou'd maintain a society of any kind without justice."[71] For Hobbes, the state of nature is the natural condition of human beings as rational persons engaged in social interaction based upon the natural right to self-preservation that is related to the fundamental law of nature "that every man, ought to endeavour Peace, as farre as he has hope of obtaining it; and when he cannot obtain it, that he may seek, and use, all helps, and advantages of Warre."[72] It follows that the state of nature is not opposed to a state of social conditions but to a state of organized civil conditions that is brought about by human beings as rational agents as manifested in a commonwealth. It is interesting to notice that Kant endorses Hobbes's conception of the state of nature. As Kant puts it, "a state of nature is not opposed to a social but to a civil condition, since there can certainly be society in a state of nature, but no civil society (which secures what is mine or yours by public laws)."[73]

For Hobbes, the natural right to self-preservation is an end that implies the natural right to use the appropriate means to pursue this end and it is this situation that is a cause of conflict that creates war. However, Hume overlooks that war is not grounded in "men's untamed selfishness and barbarity" but in conflicting passions of honour and power. For Hobbes, the state of nature has an epistemic character since every individual is a rational agent and judge of what seems to be right or wrong to do, and this leads to war since there is no common standard of what is right or wrong or any common authority to decide conflicts among human beings. As rational agents they also share the end to endeavour to establish peace enjoined by the law of nature. This is the natural condition among human beings that raises the epistemological question how to establish the authoritative meaning of the normative vocabulary to be used to control and regulate human conduct in order to achieve the common good of peace. Hobbes provides the answer by reference to covenants among individuals to introduce the human institution of the sovereign that turns the state of nature into a civil state or commonwealth. The political authority of the sovereign is grounded in the consent of the people that makes the sovereign the epistemic authority to determine the meaning of the normative vocabulary of what is right or wrong, just or unjust. The sovereign is also authorized to act as the supreme legal authority to make, apply and enforce the law to secure the end of coordination and peace among competing individuals. The law is the positive law that is grounded in the will of the sovereign as expressed in his commands to his subjects that are bound to observe them. The authority of the sovereign accounts for the validity and normativity of the law that can be enforced, if necessary by means of the use of coercive sanctions. This is so since the sovereign is also endowed with the supreme physical power to enforce the law and this accounts for the efficacy of the law. In this way

> every man may know, what Goods he may enjoy, and what actions he may doe, without being molested by any of his fellow subjects: And this is it men call Propriety. For before constitution of Sovereign Power all men had right to all things; which necessarily causeth Warre: and therefore this Proprietie, being necessary to Peace, and depending on Sovereign Power, is the Act of that Power, in order to the publique peace.[74]

Since the sovereign makes the law, "the law is the public conscience" that brings an end to the conflict between human beings since they have undertaken to submit to "the publique reason" of the law instead of following "our own Private Reason." It is the law that determines the conceptual meaning of what is right or wrong and this implies that "no law can be unjust" since the positive law is the standard of justice. It does not follow that there can be no wrong law. The positive law can be put to the test in terms of what is good or bad in relation to the standard of utility.

Hume rejects the state of nature as a fiction in favor of the savage state of society as the reality that precedes the state of human society and government. He also rejects that human beings have any natural rights, even the right to self-preservation since self-preservation is solely a biological fact that determines individuals to live together in relationships to sustain and preserve life within the scarce resources provided by the physical environment. The savage state of society is composed of competing individuals engaged in social interaction with objects in order to satisfy their needs and wants. Hume applies his naturalistic account of social interaction as causal interaction among human beings and their natural propensities that lead to conflicts "which proceed from the concurrence of certain *qualities* of the human mind with the *situation* of external objects. The qualities of the mind are *selfishness* and *limited generosity*: And the situation of external objects is their *easy change*, join'd to their *scarcity* in comparison of the wants and desires of men."[75] From the personal perspective of social interaction, human beings are engaged in the pursuit of objects not only in order to satisfy their desires to survive but also to satisfy their wants grounded in avarice.

> This avidity alone, of acquiring goods and possessions for ourselves and our nearest friends, is insatiable, perpetual, universal, and directly destructive of society. There scarce is any one, who is not actuated by it; and there is no one, who has not reason to fear from it, when it acts without any restraint, and gives way to its first and most natural movements.

It follows that the savage state of society has an epistemic character since human beings are possessive animals in pursuit of objects without any common standard or authority to settle conflicts. Thus Hume faces the epistemological question to establish the existence of a common standard concerning the meaning of the normative vocabulary that can be used to decide conflicts and provides the answer by reference to the nature and situation of human beings.

For Hume, property "may be look'd upon as a species of causation; whether we consider the liberty it gives the proprietor to operate as he please upon the object, or the advantages, which he reaps from it."[76]

Causation is involved not only in the relation between the proprietor and the object but also in relations between proprietors. The question is to present an account of these relations. Hume applies his naturalistic account of the causal relation between natural events to present a naturalistic account of the relations between the proprietor and his operations upon the object that produces various effects. With respect to causal relations between events Hume holds that reason cannot reveal any inherent necessity between causes and effects. Thus the necessity is located within the human mind based upon the use of human imagination and the impact of custom. With respect to the relation between human beings and external objects, reason cannot discover any natural relations and Hume rejects that justice "is founded on reason, or on the discovery of certain connexions and relations of ideas, which are eternal, immutable and universally obligatory."[77] This fits with Hume's view that the physical nature is devoid of any meaning or values and the corollary is the rejection of the appeal to "the reason of the thing" advanced within theories of natural law and natural rights. It also follows that the relation cannot be natural but is a moral relation since "the property of an object, when taken for something real, without any reference to morality, or the sentiments of the mind, is a quality perfectly insensible, and even inconceivable." This fits with Hume's view that the meaning of the normative vocabulary can only be found within the human mind but the meaning is not grounded in reason but in sentiments of pain and pleasures in relation to human artifice based upon utility. This implies the rejection of the theories of natural law and natural rights that hold that morality is based upon reason as manifested in the universal and natural right to self-preservation. For Hume, morality is solely a matter of desires or sentiments and in this respect, "'tis certain we can naturally no more change our own sentiments, than the motions of the heavens." However, human beings are intelligent and inventive animals and introduce the virtue of justice as a useful device that makes it possible to curb and control the vice of avidity that is a threat to the existence of society among possessive individuals. Justice is an artificial virtue since it is invented by human beings in contrast to the natural virtue of benevolence inherent in human nature. In another sense the virtue of justice is natural virtue or sentiment that can be used to control and direct sentiments with respect to the possession of objects as manifested in "the laws of society; that is by the laws of justice."

Like Hobbes, Hume holds that it is the law that is crucial for the existence of civilized conditions among human beings and the foundation is found in "a convention enter'd into by all the members of society to bestow stability on the possession of those external goods, and leave every one in the peaceable enjoyment of what he may acquire by his fortune and industry."[78] Hume is adamant that this convention "is not of the nature of promise" since promises only arise from human conventions. For Hobbes, it is possible for human beings to promise and enter into contracts in the state of nature but this is ruled out by Hume since fidelity is not a natural virtue nor is there any natural obligation to keep promises among "rude and savage men" living in the state of society that precedes the state of human society and government produced by conventions. These conventions are based upon the solitary operations of the mind as expressed in the exchange of sentiments concerning the proper behavior with respect to objects. Thus

> I observe, that it will be for my interest to leave another in the possession of his goods, *provided* he will act in the same manner with regard to me. He is sensible of a like interest in the regulation of his conduct. When this common sense of interest is mutually express'd, and is known to both, it produces a suitable resolution and behaviour.

There are conflicting interests among human beings with respect to the possession of external objects but Hume holds that there is "a sense of interest suppos'd to be common to all." The sense of common interest is grounded in the solitary operations of the mind as manifested in behavioral patterns in relation to other people. As Hume puts it, "I see evidently, that when any man imposes on himself general inflexible rules in his conduct with others, he considers certain objects as their property, which he supposes to be sacred and inviolable." The fact that an individual has imposed a rule for his own behavior leads to the expectation that other individuals will regulate their behavior in a similar way and this is the foundation for social interaction among human beings that lead to them producing conventions that mould the behavior of individuals to the interests of other individuals with the result "that every one has acquir'd a stability in his possessions." However, this convention is not self-enforcing among acquisitive beings since the expectation that something will happen does not give assurance that the expectation will be satisfied until a common authority is found to guard and protect it. This is the common perspective that is provided by the existence of government and the laws of justice that constitute the crucial difference between the savage condition and the human condition since "without justice, society must immediately dissolve, and every one must fall into that savage and solitary condition, which is infinitely worse than the worst situation that can possibly be suppos'd in society."[79]

For Hume, the laws of justice are solely based upon the principle of utility that provides the foundation for the authoritative meaning of the normative vocabulary concerning the relations between human beings and objects as well as the relations between human beings. In this way the laws can be used to change the situation of human beings by transforming their impressions that these relations are natural and contingent relations into impressions that they are moral and stable relations. The stability is supported by the use of the law that turns the moral relations into legal and uniform relations. This accounts for the validity and normativity of the law but what is more important is the efficacy of the law as a causal impact upon the minds of human beings. The maintenance of the laws of justice is the cause that produces the effect upon the minds. The result of the operation of the laws of justice is that "there immediately arise the ideas of justice and injustice; and also those of property, right and obligation. The latter are altogether unintelligible without first understanding the former. Our property is nothing but those goods, whose constant possession is establish'd by the laws of society; that is by the laws of justice."[80] As Hume also puts it "nor is the expression improper to call them *laws of nature*; if by natural we understand what is common to any species, or even if we confine it to mean what is inseparable from the species." The conceptual meaning of the normative vocabulary is rooted in human feelings or sentiments of pleasure and pain as manifested in the laws of nature. Blackstone also refers to human feelings of pain and pleasure by reference to god's will and wisdom to pass the laws of nature. Hume appeals to human nature and the good of mankind that is served by the principle of utility related to the human invention of the laws of nature. For Hume, there are "three fundamental laws of nature, that of the stability of possession, of its transference by consent and of the performance of promises. "'Tis on the strict observance of those three laws, that the peace and security of human society entirely depend, nor is there any possibility of establishing a good correspondence among men, where these are neglected. Society is absolutely necessary for the well-being of men; and these are as necessary to the support of society." These laws are human contrivances that are invented to work upon the human mind in order to harness the natural passions and channel them to work in appropriate ways in the pursuit of objects that satisfy human wants and needs. In this way the laws operate not only to secure the subsistence and well being of the individual but also to serve the common good concerning the security of life and property of possessive individuals in the pursuit of happiness. This calls for sympathy that is assisted and maintained by "custom and education" since parents are "induc'd to inculcate on their children, from their earliest infancy, the principles of probity, and teach them to regard the observance of those rules, by which society is maintain'd, as worthy and honourable, and their violation as base and infamous." Thus the operation of the virtue of justice is primarily related to the character of human beings informed by the laws of justice to behave appropriately in relation to other people and their property. What is distinctive about a just human being is that the mind is influenced by "the sentiments of honour," that is the sentiment of self-interest to honor the rules governing possessions that is extended to include a sentiment of public interest that it is to the mutual advantage of human beings to follow the rules concerning property and contract.

In this way Hume's account can also be adduced to support "a common law conventionalism," to use Postema's expression.[81] Hume's account supports a theory of institutions of property and contract grounded in the idea that "public utility is the *sole* origin of justice" as manifested in "the *particular* laws, by which justice is directed, and property determined" within a political society.[82] The existence of a political or civilized society is necessary for the preservation of life among human beings and this makes it a matter of concern to have rules that determine issues of conflict among self-seeking individuals engaged in the pursuit of external goods. Thus the conceptual meaning of the legal vocabulary of what is right and wrong, just and unjust is imposed by human beings grounded in the principle of utility as manifested in "statutes, customs, precedents, analogies and a hundred other circumstances." This accounts for the validity of the law and its normative force to regulate and coordinate human behavior and secure the stability of property and contract among human beings. Human beings have a fundamental desire to improve their lives and the existence of law functions as a cause that determines the behavior of people as the effect. This requires that the law has a causal impact upon the minds of people in order to produce the effect of regularities of behavior. What matters is therefore the efficacy of the law that is brought about by the enforcement of the law by the courts. The strict enforcement of the law enables human beings to engage in causal reasoning with respect to what happens in society since the laws are applied to work upon the mind and this makes it possible to predict the outcomes that the courts will have for a particular conflict. The regular enforcement of the law will have an impact in advance upon the behaviour of the parties and this is of mutual advantage for human beings as acquisitive and possessive individuals concerned with the satisfaction of their wants and needs. Thus it matters enormously that the existing laws of property and contract are maintained in order to support social interaction among individual agents and coordinate their behavior to work in the appropriate ways and secure and protect the fruits of their labors. This is in turn related to legal science having the task to provide information about the working of the law from the personal perspective of a judicious spectator.

Hume's naturalistic view has been influential and leads Bentham to see "that *utility* was the test and measure of all virtue."[83] The principle of utility is not only the fundamental principle for the evaluation of the law, it is also the fundamental principle for decision making within the law related to expectations regarding beliefs concerning the conduct of public officials and private persons. This leads Bentham to reject custom and the common law in favour of the project "to frame for each nation a complete new code in point of substance as well as form." Hume's naturalistic view has also informed Hart's influential account of the "minimum content of natural law."[84] It has also been challenged by Reid.

Like Hume, Reid holds that it is important to consider the nature and situation of human beings but Hume's account is grounded in the solitary operations and ignores the social operations of the mind. It is the social operations of the mind that make it possible for human beings to become rational persons and responsible agents having the capacity to be governed by laws of their own making or invention. The invention of rules is based upon the use of the faculty of conscience or practical reason that determines the conceptual meaning of the moral vocabulary of what is right or wrong or just and unjust in relation to what there is reason to believe and do. The existence of reason is the crucial difference between animals and human beings since animals lack reason due to the lack of the social operations of the mind and are only governed by the mechanical and animal principles that produce and coordinate various modes of natural behavior to serve fixed ends. Animals can also be trained artificially to produce learned behavior to certain ends by discipline but "they are not capable of self-government" in the sense of being governed by conceptions of rules of conduct and the obligation to obey them.[85] Only human beings have the capacity to govern themselves as free agents and authors of their own actions to pursue ends governed by the use of reason. A free agent is a being whose behavior counts as his own actions since they are brought about by the exercise of the will informed by reason to pursue ends set by him. As an author of the action, the agent is in control of the exercise of his intellectual and active powers to make decisions about what to do or not to do. Hence it follows that the agent can be held accountable for his commissives as well as for his omissives. This is manifested in communicative relations between persons as agents since they have the linguistic capacity to present an answer for their conduct in relation to the social environment of other people and the physical environment of objects and events. This is causation in relation to human agency in terms of reasons for action as opposed to causation in relation to objects or events in terms of causes of behavior.

Hume's account of justice is based upon causation in relation to human beings and the possession of objects as regulated by laws of justice within the state of a civilized society. For Reid, the implication is that "in the state of nature, there can be no distinction of property" and he arrives at the conclusion that "Mr Hume's state of nature is the same with that of Mr. Hobbes."[86] For Hobbes and Hume, there is no property in the state of nature because there is no stability of possessions, but there is also a crucial difference. Hobbes proceeds upon the conception of human beings as rational persons having the natural right to self-preservation and the capacity to perform actions dictated by the fundamental law of nature as a rule of reason that enjoins them to seek peace. Hume rejects the existence of the natural right to self-preservation in favor of the natural desire to possess shared by all human beings that is controlled and regulated by "the laws of nature" to establish peace. But Hume's use of the phrase differs from Hobbes. For Hobbes, a law of nature is a rule of reason, that is, it is constituted by reason concerning human conduct and the rule can be found by the use of reason. By contrast, Hume's laws of nature are invented by human beings in relation to the solitary operations of the feelings and this invention "proceeds immediately from original principles, without the intervention of thought or reflexion."[87] The original principles are the mechanical and animal principles of desires and will that produce regularian behavior that can be observed and accounted for in the same way as mechanical regularities between billiard balls can be observed and accounted for in terms of natural laws of movement. This is causation between events as opposed to causation in relation to human beings having the capacity to be authors of their own actions. For Hume, human beings are not acting but acted upon or moved to follow the prevailing laws of justice within the political society. This is conducive for social cooperation and coordination among individuals and useful for the maintenance of peace. Human beings can behave securely based upon the expectations that there are natural uniformities between natural events. In a similar way human beings can behave securely based upon the expectations that there are social uniformities between social events. But in both cases, the expectations are based upon event causation about what will happen to a human being as opposed to the expectation of what is due to a person that is crucial for agency causation. Hume rejects agency causation in favor of event causation and this fits with his view that human beings are intelligent animals that behave according to the physical laws of nature as well as the laws of justice. Human beings cannot change the former and the implication is that this also holds for the human laws of nature. Hume's naturalistic view of justice cannot be said to advance a natural law theory but it can be used to reinforce a common law conventionalism.

Reid rejects Hume's view that public utility is the only foundation for the law since this is to ignore that there is "a natural principle in the constitution of man, by which justice is approved, and injustice is disapproved and condemned."[88] This implies that justice is not an artificial but a natural virtue related to the use of practical reason and moral principles to inform the form and content of laws within the political society. Among these principles is the principle of utility to procure what is good and bad either to us or to society that is invoked by Hume to account for the virtue of justice. If Hume is right then "justice can have no merit beyond its utility to procure utility." However, Hume is wrong since he ignores that there is "an intrinsic worth in justice, and demerit in injustice" grounded in reason that can be discerned by every human being as a rational person and moral agent. This is manifested in use of language to express rules of conduct in terms of the concept of injury that is related to the concepts of moral obligation and justice. Animals cannot be moral or virtuous and Hume explains this by reference to the lack of the appropriate feelings related to virtues and vices. By contrast, Reid considers that animals cannot act as moral agents since they lack reason and the use of language that makes it possible to distinguish between being hurt and being injured. Animals can be hurt but only human beings can be injured. As Reid puts it,

> every man, capable of reflection, perceives, that an injury implies more than being hurt. If I be hurt by a stone falling out of the wall, or by a flash of lightning, or by a convulsive and involuntary motion of another man's arm, no injury is done, no resentment raised in a man that has reason. In this, as in all moral actions, there must be the will and intention of the agent to do the hurt.

Perhaps this is a slip for the term "injury" that is used by persons to refer to the rational motive of resentment or indignation that entitles a person to respond as expressed in judgements of condemnation related to justice in contrast to being hurt that only leaves room for judgements of disapproval.

There are various ways in which a human being can be injured that is related to the morality of justice that serves as the foundation for the existence of natural rights. Every man has the natural right to self-preservation that implies a right to the necessary means of life. "And that justice which forbids the taking away the life of an innocent man, forbids no less the taking away from him the necessary means of life. He has the same right to defend the one as the other; and nature inspires him with the same resentment of the one injury as of the other."[89] Every man also has the natural right of liberty, and this "implies a right to such innocent labour as a man chooses, and to the fruit of that labour. To hinder another man's innocent labour, or to deprive him of the fruit of it, is an injustice of the same kind, and has the same effect as to put him in fetters or in prison, and is equally a just object of resentment." These rights are related to "that some kind, or some degree, of property must exist wherever men exist, and that the right to such property is the necessary consequence of the natural right of men to life and liberty." These rights exist in the state of nature in which

> every man's property was solely at his own disposal, because he had no superior. In civil society it must be subject to the laws of that society. He gives up to the public part of that right, which he had in the state of nature, as the price of that protection and security which he receives from civil society. In the state of nature, he was the sole judge in his own case, and had right to defend his property, his liberty, and life, as far as his power reached. In the state of civil society, he must submit to the judgment of the society, and acquiesce in its sentence, though he should conceive it to be unjust.

Hume's account of justice ignores the existence of natural rights to life and liberty and is restricted to a narrow account concerning property and contract. As Reid puts it, Hume "seems to have taken up a confined notion of justice, and to have restricted it to a regard to property and fidelity in contracts. As to other branches he is silent. He nowhere says, that it is not naturally criminal to rob an innocent man of his life, of his children, of his liberty, or of his reputation."[90] Even Hume's confined account of justice is mistaken since it is based upon the solitary operations of the mind. Thus Hume holds that justice is rendered useless "if every man has a tender regard for another, or if nature supplied abundantly all our wants and desires."[91] Hume refers to the poetical account of the state of nature composed of solitary individuals but this overlooks the social operations of the mind used in communicative relations between persons. Even within a state of abundance a person may injure another person and thus perform an unjust action and even if persons are benevolent, justice is required between persons. In the opposite case of the state of nature in terms of the "extreme want of all common necessaries," the strict laws of justice are not suspended but required as manifested in the equal distribution of food. The same applies in cases of war since justice authorizes the use of force for self-defence and for the reparation of intolerable injuries. In criminal cases in which a person is convicted, it is not the case that "the ordinary rules of justice are, with regard to him, suspended for a moment," since justice requires that a person be convicted according to the laws of justice.

Hume presents the action of "willful murder" in order to examine it

> to see if you can find that matter of fact, or real existence, which you call *vice*. In which-ever way you take it, you only find certain passions, motives, volitions and thoughts. There is no other matter of fact in this case. The vice entirely escapes you, as long as you consider the object. You never can find it, till you turn your reflexion into your own breast, and find a sentiment of disapprobation, which arises in you, towards his action. Here is a matter of fact; but 'tis the object of feeling, not of reason. It lies in yourself, not in the object. So that when you pronounce any action or character to be vicious, you mean nothing, but that from the constitution of your nature you have a feeling or sentiment of blame from the contemplation of it.[92]

This is Hume's account of moral motivation that holds moral motivation is not only a matter of beliefs or reasons but also requires that the person has the appropriate feelings or preferences in order to perform an action. As Reid points out, the implication for the office of a judge is that "mankind have very absurdly called him a *judge;* he ought to be called a *feeler*."[93] For Reid, beliefs alone can serve as motivating reasons for actions as well as provide the reasons that justify the actions. Thus after the circumstances of the case are known to the judge, the judge has to make a decision whether the person is guilty or not, and this decision is motivated and justified by reference to the law as reasons for belief and action as manifested in his judgment.

Hume's account of promises as "mere artificial contrivances for the convenience and advantage of society" is also false since it overlooks that a promise is not a solitary act of the will expressed in words but a social act of the mind that is expressed by means of propositions accompanied with understanding and will to become bound to perform an obligation in relation to another person, accepting the promise. Hume also confounds the intention to become bound that is a social act of the mind in relation to another person with the intention to perform that is a solitary act of the mind that neither constitutes nor dissolves the obligation of being bound. Hume reduces the institution of promises to be a legal institution and this overlooks that promises exist prior to and independently of the positive law as a moral and human institution based upon the social operations of the mind and grounded in the principles of truth and veracity that are decisive for trust among human beings. Hume concurs that trust is important but his account of promises implies that there can be no promises in the state of nature. For Hume, government is not grounded in promises but in conventions based upon utilitarian considerations. In this way trust can be maintained by means of the maintenance of the law. By contrast, Reid holds that contract is the foundation for the government having the task to secure the natural rights to life, liberty and property by means of laws prescribing the proper procedures that turn rules into legal rules or valid laws that direct and regulate the natural rights. The natural rights are prior to the making of positive laws and provide the moral standard that inform the content of the valid law on the one hand and provide the standard for the evaluation of the law on the other. Reid rejects Hume's view that justice is founded upon utility. It is rather the other way round that "honest citizens, though subject to no laws but their own making, far from making utility the standard of justice, made justice to be the standard of utility."[94] As noticed above, Reid holds that the human faculties are trustworthy but also fallible and this may lead to mistakes concerning what is true as well as what is right. As Reid puts it, "as all the works of men are imperfect, human laws may be unjust; which could never be, if justice had the origin from the law, as the author (i.e. Hume) seems here to insinuate." Reid refers to Hume's account that the laws of justice are recorded in propositions concerning human behavior in relation to property and the conceptual meaning of the legal vocabulary is based upon feelings of what is just or unjust. It follows that the law embodies justice and the corollary is that the moral standard for the evaluation of law cannot be natural rights and justice based upon reason. The only standard is utility to produce what is of advantage or disadvantage to human beings in terms of happiness based upon feelings of pleasure and pain. This is the foundation for the law that can be enforced, if necessary by means of use of coercive sanctions. By contrast, Reid holds that the proper standard is not utility grounded in sentiments but justice grounded in reason that respects "the true dignity of our nature" as rational persons and responsible agents. This implies that the normative force of the law is grounded in sanctions in the sense of acceptance and respect for the law as reasons for belief and action. To be sure, the law can be enforced by the use of coercive sanctions but this concerns the question of the efficacy of the law that is distinct from the question of the validity and normative of law to secure the legal conditions for persons to live a life as autonomous agents.

Hume holds that contract and property are legal institutions established by the positive laws of justice that secure the conditions that make it possible for human beings to live a happy life. In this respect "it appears evident that the ultimate ends of human actions can never, in any case, be accounted for by reason, but recommend themselves entirely to the sentiments and affections of mankind, without any dependence on the intellectual faculties."[95] Hume's naturalistic account leads the instrumental account of reason that holds that human beings are rational and acquisitive agents that are driven by self-interest to operate within the existing legal structure in order to satisfy their needs and wants in the pursuit of happiness. The laws of justice are solely grounded in human conventions in terms of the utility of circumstances and this implies that they can in principle be altered and even abolished without any affront to principles of corrective and distributive justice. The adherents of the common law block this implication by reference to the settled laws that are the foundation for social interaction among human beings in terms of the stability of expectations that is the requisite for the peace and interest of society. The common expectation of the appropriate effects of the working of the law is a matter of public utility that strongly suggests that it is neither useful nor beneficial to change the law by legislation. However, as Pollock puts it, "Acts of Parliament might at first sight be likened to catastrophic events which cannot be predicted; but it is easily seen that this would be a hasty and imperfect simile. For their actual operation is not to produce catastrophic results, but to introduce new sets of conditions which must be taken into account in future predictions."[96] It follows that human beings can use the principle of utility as the decision principle in relation to the social conditions brought about by the use of statutory law. The language of natural rights is replaced with the language of security of expectations.

As Bentham puts it, "instead of rights, talk of expectations" as the rational foundation for belief and action. In a similar way, the talk of natural rights against the government must be replaced with the language of "securities against misrule."[97] Thus the law can be justified by human preferences based upon the principle of utility to serve the aim of organizing and facilitating social interaction in terms of causal relations between human beings as rational and solitary agents engaged in the pursuit of happiness. For Reid, the law is rather justified by reference to reason informed by the intellectual and moral principles of justice that enable human beings to engage in social interaction in terms of communicative relations between rational and communal agents with respect to what there is reason to believe and to do. In this respect, reason can be used not only in a substantive way to deliberate about the ends but also in an instrumental way to deliberate about the appropriate means to achieve human ends by means of the law grounded in the respect of the dignity of human beings as rational persons and responsible agents.

3.7 Jurisprudence, law and custom

As Reid points out, custom and law are examples of the social operations of the mind that involve social interaction between an author and his utterance on the one hand and the auditor and his attitude on the other. This raises the jurisprudential question concerning the understanding of this relation that is addressed by the analytical approach advanced by Bentham and Austin. This is the imperative theory of law that holds that the author can only be the sovereign who regulated the conduct of the auditors or subjects by means of his commands that can be enforced, if necessary, by the use of coercive sanctions. As Austin puts it, "every law is a command that is laid down for the guidance of an intelligent being by an intelligent being having power over him."[98] The intelligent beings are human beings of sovereign and subjects and this raises the question how they are identified. Bentham and Austin follow Hume and reject the appeal to natural law and social contracts in favor of the appeal that they are to be identified by reference to social facts. As Bentham puts it, "the ultimate efficient cause of all power of imperation over persons is a disposition on the part of those persons to obey: the efficient cause then of the power of the sovereign is neither more nor less than the disposition to obedience on the part of the people."[99] It follows that customary ways of conduct among people are important for the position of the sovereign as "the constituent cause" that brings about the law as a human and social institution to regulate the social condition among people as rational agents. The identification and institution of the sovereign is the foundation for the distinction between the source of law in the legal sense based upon the agency of the sovereign as manifested in the rules of positive law as opposed to the source of law in the moral sense based upon the agency of individuals as manifested in the rules of positive morality. The sovereign may be influenced by the rules of positive morality but the validity of the legal rules depends solely upon the will of the sovereign.

As Bentham points out there are different kinds of laws, there is the ordinary class of laws prescribing what people shall do or "laws *in subditos* or *in populum*" and there is the "transcendent class of laws" prescribing to the sovereign what he shall do when making the law or "laws *in principem*."[100] Bentham's distinction is akin to Hart's distinction between primary rules and secondary rules and it is the secondary rules that matter for the making of law since they are concerned with the ontological requirements that turn rules into valid legal rules and the epistemological requirements concerning the identification of the persons having the authority to make the law by means of the appropriate procedures. This raises the question of the status of the secondary rules that is answered by Austin in terms of positive morality and by Bentham in terms of constitutional law. In both cases, the validity of the law demarcates the area governed by legal rules in contrast to the area governed by non-legal rules in terms of morality, prudence, customs and fashions that may have an influence upon the content of the law. This raises the question of the content of the secondary rules since they may not only refer to formal requirements but also to substantive requirements in terms of moral principles for the making of the law as reasons for belief and action. Bentham's imperative theory confines the content of the constitutional rules to be concerned with the formal requirements with respect to persons and their actions. What seems to me to be important to stress is that the legislator is both law-maker and law-giver at the same time since the law is made according to the constitutional or secondary rules that are mentioned and used simultaneously as guides and measures for the making and declaration of valid legal rules in terms of laws *in populum* or primary rules. In this respect, legislation is an acknowledged procedure that authorizes persons to act as legislators for the making of valid law in terms of statutory laws. It may also be the case that customary law serves as an independent and separate procedure based upon secondary rules that authorize people to act as legislators for the making of valid law in terms of customary law. The valid legal rules have normative force as binding reasons for belief and action since the legal rules can be enforced by the sovereign by means of the sue of coercive sanctions. The question of the validity and normativity of the law is related to but distinct from the question of the efficacy of the law that is concerned with the impact of the law upon the minds of rational agents to secure social interaction.

Austin and Bentham only recognize legislation as a procedure to make the law in terms of commands that are manifested either directly in the legislative mode in terms of statutes or indirectly in the judicial mode in terms of judiciary law. The imperative theory is advanced as an attack upon customary law as an independent procedure for the making of law that is put forward by the classical Roman jurists in general and Blackstone in particular. These jurists "fancy that a rule of law made by judicial decision on a pre-existing custom, exists as *positive law*, apart from the legislator or judge, by the institution of the private persons who observed it in its customary state."[101] Austin and Bentham do not deny that custom may be a source of law in the moral sense of positive morality based upon the beliefs held by people that may have an influence upon the content of the laws but only the authority of the sovereign can put the stamp of validity upon positive morality and turn it into positive law. Thus Austin holds that customary law is not a distinct kind of law but merely rules of positive morality among people until "the legislator or judge impress them with the character of law." The individual members of the society may establish rules of conduct in terms of customary rules but as "*positive law*, it comes from the sovereign or subordinate judges who transmute the moral and imperfect into legal and perfect rules." These rules constitute the province of jurisprudence as an expository science about what the positive law is as opposed to what the positive law ought to be that is the province of jurisprudence as a censorial science of legislation grounded in the principle of utility.

For Maine, the merit of the analytical approach is the endeavor to "construct a system of jurisprudence by strict scientific process and to found it, not on *a priori* assumption, but on observation, comparison and analysis of the various legal conceptions."[102] The demerit is the practical implication of Austin's theory that the sovereign has "the power of compelling the other members of the community to do exactly as it pleases." For Maine, this is tantamount to despotism since it implies that the relation between the sovereign and his subjects is a matter of brute force. The sovereign is not bound by any moral standards when making the law as an expression of his will that binds his subjects in virtue of his superior force. Maine's objection raises the question concerning the understanding of social interaction and it seems to me that Maine proceeds upon the naturalistic account concerning the relations between the sovereign and his subjects. In this case the sovereign passes the commands as causes that have an impact upon the behavior of his subjects as effects. This is social interaction as causal relations to produce the appropriate behavior by means of the use of coercive sanctions.[103] The rejoinder is that the will of the sovereign is not necessarily an arbitrary will based upon the principle of caprice but rather an informed will based upon the principle of utility as the standard that determines the conceptual content of the law. Maine also overlooks the rationalistic account of social interaction that holds that the relations between sovereign and citizens are intellectual or communicative relations concerning the proper rules of conduct as reasons for belief and action based upon the principle of utility and these rules are maintained by the use of coercive sanctions in order to secure the life and property of the members of society. Both accounts of social interaction rely upon the principle of utility in order to establish a common measure of what is right or wrong conduct that informs the making of the law by the sovereign. Thus the imperative theory is related to the morality of utilitarianism. Maine's rejoinder is that "the jurist, properly so called, has nothing to do with any ideal standard of law or morals." This is tantamount to endorsing the naturalistic view based upon the personal perspective of the scientist as neutral observer of the facts in order to establish the laws of social development.

The jurist, properly, so called, has the task to study and present the law as an integral part of the development of society based upon the historical and comparative method. This is another demerit of the analytical approach since it is based upon an abstraction that ignores "the entire mass of its historical antecedents, which in each community determines how the Sovereign shall exercise or forbear from exercising his irresistible coercive power."[104] Maine provides the remedy by his historical approach that leads him to hold that there is "a law of development" grounded in the uniformity of human nature concerning the government of the Indo-European races. In the first phase, the behavior of people is governed by oral commands that are inspired by divine agencies. This gives way to the second phase of regulation by unwritten law or customary laws that are only known to and applied by an aristocratic class. This is in turn replaced with the phase of written law where people are governed by public rules set out in codes, like the twelve tables of ancient Rome.

Maine's account raises the question of concerning the procedures for the making of the law in terms of legislation and customary law that are recognized as separate procedures in Roman law based upon a statement in the Digest, that

> immemorial custom is observed as a statute, not unreasonably; and this is what is called the law established by usage. Indeed, inasmuch as statutes themselves are binding for no other reason than because they are accepted by the judgement of the people, so anything whatever which the people show their approval of, even where there is no written rule, ought properly to be equally binding on all; what difference does it make whether the people declare their will by their votes, or by positive acts and conduct.[105]

This passage concerns the authority to create positive law as an intentional human activity that is regulated by different procedures of secondary rules of law. There is the centralized procedure of legislation to create valid legal rules as manifested *in ius scriptum* or statutory law and there is the decentralized procedure of customary law to create valid legal rules as manifested *in ius non scriptum* or customary law. The written law of statutory law refers to the procedure of legislation and the unwritten law of customary law refers to the procedure of customary law although it is grammatically written down and recorded. Thus the feudal law is recorded in writing and added to the Corpus Juris Civilis.[106] The grammatical distinction refers only to the mode of the expression of the rule, that is to say whether the rule exists in writing or not. Rules can exist without being expressed in writing and the lack of writing makes a difference in relation to the procedures to create legal rules, their content and how they are conveyed and made known among people. It seems to me that Maine's account of the history of ancient law overlooks that judicial sentences in primitive societies may be controlled by a procedure of oral law grounded in customary law. These procedures can be written down but this does not change their status as secondary rules for the creation of primary rules. The grammatical distinction can also be used to make a distinction between *lex scripta* or statutory law and *lex non scripta* or customary law in relation to the sources of knowledge of the law. As Maine points out, "the law, thus known exclusively to a privileged minority, whether a caste, an aristocracy, a priestly tribe, or a sacerdotal college, is true unwritten law. Except this, there is no such thing as unwritten law in the world."[107] Thus English case law is clearly written down as recorded in cases but it is unwritten law in the sense that knowledge about the law is confined to the privileged class of the lawyers. This is Bentham's objection that people lack direct access to the law and have to rely upon the testimonies of lawyers and this makes knowledge about the law difficult and expensive. The remedy is to reject the customary procedure in favor of the legislative procedure for the making of a codification that provides the public information and framework for social interaction in terms of the proper standards of conduct based upon the principle of utility.

The imperative theory rejects the customary procedure in favor of the legislative procedure as the only proper procedure for the making of the law by the legislator and Maine follows suit. This invites a comparison with the historical approach advanced by Savigny. Savigny's approach is based upon the personal perspective of insight into the nature of law grounded in feelings of truth in relation to the impact of visible objects upon the mind.[108] Thus the scientist is a spectator confronted with the reality of law as a positive fact and his task is to understand the development of the law in terms of "the organic connection of law with the being and character of the people" that is manifested "in the progress of times."[109] The development of the law is grounded in a "law of inward necessity" as manifested in the common consciousness of the people that is replaced with the consciousness of jurists representing the community and concerned with the scientific treatment of the law. Thus law "is first developed by custom and popular faith, next by jurisprudence, – everywhere, therefore, by internal silently-operating powers, not by the arbitrary will of a law-giver." Savigny's historical approach is dedicated to a systematic inquiry into Roman law in order to purify it from foreign elements, especially due to the work of medieval jurists, in order to unravel the underlying principles that regulate social interaction among people. In this respect, the origin of the law is found in the organic relation between the consciousness of people in terms of inner instincts and feelings and the law as manifested in the customary law that represents the national unity of a people like its language and manners. For Maine customary law is the despotism of usage that is blindly followed and replaced by codes as signs of liberations. Thus Justinian's code is the starting point for Maine's distinction between the stationary societies and progressive societies. Some societies, like those of India, cease to develop new forms, whereas the progressive societies, like the Romans and English, proceed to develop the code by means of fictions, equity and legislation.

By contrast, a code for Savigny is a sign of despotism since it is based upon the arbitrary will of the legislator. The target of Savigny's critique is Kant's theory of the natural right to freedom that implies that persons have the capacity to exercise the rational will to create laws of their own making. Another target is Bentham's imperative theory and the call for codification based upon the will informed by the principle of utility. Both theories appeal to the will as the foundation for the activity of the legislator to create the positive law. Savigny's critique proceeds upon the assumption that the legislative activity based upon the will is an arbitrary will and this implies contingency. Savigny applies the principle of causal similarity to arrive at the result that positive law is arbitrary law. What is arbitrary is not intelligible and this implies that positive law is not intelligible either. This calls for Savigny to provide the proper remedy that shows that the law is not created by any will at all but found in the consciousness of the people as manifested in customary law that in turn is developed and refined by legal scholars. This is Hume's point that custom is the great guide in human life. The existence of customary law is a matter of fact and Savigny applies the principle of causal necessity to hold that customary law exists therefore necessarily has a cause. The cause cannot be the human will but rather found in an invisible element within the mind that is externally manifested in the visible effect of customary law. Hence it follows that customary law is not the origin of the law but only evidence of the law as it exists in the spirit of the people. What is intelligible is the existence of customary law as positive facts that have an impact upon the mind of people as manifested in social interaction among human beings in terms of their legal relations. Savigny follows Hume's naturalistic account of social interaction and conflates the distinction between custom as behavioral uniformities and customs of human conduct. Savigny's theory implies that human beings cannot be conceived as agents having the capacity to act as legislators using legislative or customary procedures for the making of valid law. It follows that the legal authority is neither the legislator nor the judge but the epistemic authority of the jurist or legal scholar having a chair in the university. Like Maine, Savigny holds that "the jurist, properly so called, has nothing to do with any ideal standard of law and morals." Thus Savigny rejects the scientific character of censorial jurisprudence advanced by Bentham and Austin and restricts the province of jurisprudence to be concerned with the systematization and interpretation of positive law and the elaboration of legal concepts for the benefit of legislation by the king and the administration of justice by the courts. The jurist occupies the position as a neutral and impartial spectator of the law whose testimonies about the law can be trusted by everyone. Savigny occupies the position as the legal scholar dedicated to present the scientific view of law from the personal perspective of a cognitive sovereign. This is in turn important for social interaction within society since it contributes to sustain the existing conditions that are important for the security of life and property.

It seems to me that Savigny's position based upon the personal perspective should be replaced with the interpersonal perspective of knowledge. The interpersonal perspective also makes room for customary law as a separate and distinct procedure alongside legislation for the making of valid legal rules. These methods are based upon social interaction in terms of communicative relations among persons as communal agents engaged in the intentional and intellectual activity of making valid rules by means of the exercise of the rational will or practical reason. Hart has questioned the importance of custom, holding that "custom is not a very important 'source' of law in modern societies."[110] A similar position is held within recent Scandinavian jurisprudence.[111] It may be the case that custom is not a source of law in the moral sense that influences the content of statutory law. Still it may be the case that custom is a source of law in the legal sense of constituting a procedure for the creation of positive law. It seems to me that Hart fails to notice this as manifested in his account of a primitive society in which people live according to a set of primary rules and only the introduction of secondary rules is considered to turn these rules into a legal system based upon the creation of secondary rules. This is, as Hart puts it, "a step from the pre-legal into the legal world." Hart overlooks that there may be customary procedures that serve as secondary rules for the creation and application of primary rules even within a primitive society. This procedure is, historically, a primitive procedure, hence its defects of slowness and uncertainty of ascertainment. But custom as a procedure to create customary law can change or abolish existing rules as well as create new rules. For Hart, the only proper procedure to create valid legal rules in the modern world is the method of legislation. In this respect he follows Austin and Bentham who also reject the customary procedure in favor of the legislative procedure. The rejoinder to this position is that the customary procedure of creating positive law is not only the older but also the hierarchically higher procedure of creating legal rules as manifested in the rules of international law. But Hart characteristically endorses the Austinian view that international law is "not a system but a set of rules."

By contrast, Fuller has advanced the thesis that "we cannot understand 'ordinary law' (that is officially declared or enacted law) unless we first obtain an understanding of what is called customary law."[112] The target of Fuller's approach is the influential account put forward by T. E. Holland.[113] According to Holland, custom

> is a long and generally observed course of conduct. No one was ever consciously present at the commencement of such a course of conduct, but

> we can hardly doubt that it originated generally in the conscious choice of the more convenient of two acts, though sometimes doubtless in the accidental adoption of one of two indifferent alternatives; the choice in either case having been either deliberately or accidentally repeated till it ripened into habit. The best illustration of the formation of such habitual courses of action is the mode in which a path is formed across a common. One man crosses the common, in the direction in which is suggested either by the purpose he has in view, or by mere accident. If others follow in the same track, which they are likely to do after it once has been trodden, a path is made. Before a custom is formed there is no juristic reason for its taking one direction rather than another, though doubtless there was some ground of expediency, of religious scruple, or of accidental suggestion. A habitual course of action once formed gathers strength and sanctity every year. It is a course of action which every one is accustomed to see followed: it is generally believed to be salutary, and any deviation from it is felt to be abnormal, immoral. It has never been adjoined by the organized authority of the state, but it has unquestioningly been obeyed by the individuals of which the state is composed.

Fuller describes customary law as "a language of interaction" and claims that this is overlooked in Holland's account since there is "no hint that customary law originates in interaction or that it serves the purpose of organizing and facilitating interaction." To be sure, Fuller is right that customary law is the language of interaction but this is also recognized by Holland. However, both subscribe to Hume's naturalistic account of social interaction that should be replaced with Reid's rationalistic account, or so I shall argue.

Holland's account of custom illustrates the personal perspective advanced by Hume in his epistemological approach to what happens in the world. Holland places his individual in a radically first-personal situation within the commons, making a choice to bring about his purpose of making a path. This requires that he must have his body at his disposal to execute his choice of making a path as manifested in his behavior that leads to regular behavior that is common among animals and human beings. This is Hume's account of custom in terms of uniformities of behavior among human beings that is vital for social coordination and cooperation. However, Hume's account ignores the difference between custom in the sense of regular behavior and custom in the sense of human action brought about by the intentional activity of persons. It is only human beings as agents that have the capacity to engage in the intentional activity of performing actions and making rules for their own conduct based upon representations of what to do in specific situations. This capacity implies that the individual understands the surrounding world through concepts and knows what he is doing by walking, that is to say that he is engaged in making a path or rule for his future conduct as opposed to moving his body across a common. What is important for Holland's individual is not his understanding of his bodily movements but his understanding of what he is doing, that is to say making a path as manifested in his non-linguistic action that also can be expressed in a linguistic action in terms of a sentence concerning his action and its objective. Thus Holland's individual has the capacity to transform his bodily behavior into an action by means of understanding the corresponding linguistic representation of what he is doing, that is to say acting as opposed to being acted upon by the environment.

Holland's individual is the author of his own actions and creates a rule for his future conduct. The validity of the rule is grounded in his own consent and its normative force is manifested in his conduct since it represents a reason for action. It seems to me that there is no contradiction involved in accepting the validity of the rule but denying its normativity. Surely I may endorse my rule of conduct as a reason for action but there may be other reasons that override this reason in some circumstances. If so, then the rule is still a valid rule. To be sure, the normativity of the rule must manifest itself in my conduct. I must follow the rule I have enacted and the interesting element in this respect is not the attitude of habitual obedience but rather my attitude to non-obedience.[114] Holland stresses the attitude of habitual obedience since he suggests that the action or rule "gathers strength and sanctity every year." The attitude of habitual obedience is also manifested in cases of regular behavior or personal habits where I do something as a rule, say go for a walk in the morning. If I do not go for a walk then this may call for an explanation. By contrast, if I do not honor my rule of conduct then I am accountable and must provide a justification for my omission. Holland hints at this when he writes that deviation from the rule "is felt to be abnormal, immoral." Thus what is important is that the individual establishes a custom of conduct as opposed to a habit of regular behavior. Customs of conduct serve as rules of normative requirements that in turn may lead to the performance of actions being executed more or less automatically. This implies that the agent does not have to reflect upon his actions in relation to his custom and thus can enter into other activities. It should be added that it is always possible for the agent to reconsider the merit or de-merit of his rules of conduct. Holland does not mention this aspect, although it is important. Surely there may be good as well as bad customs.

If I create a rule for my own conduct then this may serve as a guide for other people. Hence customary rules of conduct are an important feature of social life among humans. Holland suggests this when he writes, "if others follow in the same track, which they are likely to do after it has been trodden, a path is made." What Holland's example illustrates, however, is that the individual alone can establish the path. Once the path is there other human beings may follow suit. This is Hume's naturalistic account of social interaction in terms of causal relations between social but solitary individuals that produce regularities of behavior that are endorsed by Holland. Thus the individual is concerned with his causal relations to the physical environment on the one hand and to other individuals on the other. Fuller also subscribes to Hume's account of social interaction since Fuller's language of interaction is used by humans to exchange sentiments to produce the appropriate responses. For Fuller,

> to interact meaningfully men require a social setting in which the moves of the participating players will fall generally within some predictable pattern. To engage in effective social behaviour men need the support of intermeshing anticipations that will lead them to know what their opposite numbers will do, or that will at least enable them to gauge the general scope of the repertory from which responses to their actions will be drawn.[115]

There is no hint in Fuller's account that human beings engage in social interaction in terms of communicative relations as communal agents engaged in the pursuit of their ends to be justified by means of reasons.

Holland assumes that it is a good thing for his individual to make a decision to form a path across the commons. Thus he implies that his individual is an agent who makes decisions based upon reason. As I see it, Holland's account suggests he endorses the Humean view of rationality that holds that the task of reason is confined to inform the individual about the surrounding environment of objects in order to pursue the attainment of his ends set by his desires or preferences. Thus Holland's individual only considers the relation between his own activity and its object that is to say to establish a path through the commons, to the exclusion of other agents. For Holland, a customary rule is only considered in terms of a dyadic relation between an agent and the object. This is also a common way of representing property as a dyadic relation between the owner of an object (A) and what is owned as object (O). This representation is related to the personal perspective of agents as social but individual agents engaged in social interaction. By contrast the interpersonal perspective conceives the agent as a communal agent involved in establishing rules for human conduct with respect to objects and actions in relation to other persons. Thus the customary rule is considered and represented in terms of a triadic relation between the agents (A), other human agents (B) with respect to a range of objects or actions (O). This is in turn important for the understanding of the commons. If the concept of the commons is conceptualized as a negative community that belongs to no one, then it is capable of being appropriated without violating anybody's rights. Hence Holland's individual commits no injustice to other people by making his path. This is Holland's understanding since he holds that there is "no juristic reason" involved in the decision making. By contrast, if the concept is conceptualized as a positive community then it belongs to everyone in the same manner. It is still open for all to appropriate provided that the appropriation is limited to a person's due in terms of what is necessary to support and sustain one's life. The conceptual question what is a person's due is precisely to take a "juristic reason" into consideration in terms of justice as the standard of right action when a person makes up his mind what to do and chooses a course of conduct. This consideration is ruled out by Holland's individual. He may have acquired the concept of justice but then he does not use the concept when he makes up his mind what to do and executes his decision by making a rule for his own conduct.

For Holland's individual this rule is "sacrosanct" since "any deviation from it is felt to be abnormal, immoral." This may be the case for Holland's individual as a rational agent. It is quite otherwise for other humans. As rational agents they have to consider whether or not to endorse this rule for their actions. Holland assumes that they just follow suit. But this is not necessarily the case. Holland's individual may have the intention to create a rule for his own conduct in terms of the path. He may also have the intention to exclude other people from using the path he has made, and thus leave other humans to exercise their own powers and honest toil to make their own paths. Fuller holds that Holland does not consider this possibility and thus ignores social interaction among people. This is not the case since Holland subscribes to Hume's account of social interaction in relation to instrumental reasoning. Thus the task of reason is confined to inform the social but individual agent about objects and actions that are necessary for the attainment of his ends set by his desires or preferences. Holland holds that this is the common understanding of rationality among human beings. Fuller also shares this instrumental view of reason that enables human beings to produce stable interactional expectancies. As he puts it, "stable interactional expectancies can arise with reference to roles and functions as well as to specific acts; a language of interaction will contain not only a vocabulary of deeds but also a basic grammar that will organize deeds into meaningful patterns."[116] If this is so then this may produce what Garrett Hardin has called "the tragedy of the commons."[117] Hardin holds that "a rational being seeks to maximize his gain." Thus Hardin subscribes to the instrumental understanding of reason to be used in social interaction with other people in relation to the environment. Thus social interaction is only a matter of causal relations among human beings as social but individual agents in pursuit of their goals based upon the attitude of "help yourself." The tragedy is produced by the acceptance of the personal perspective of social interaction based upon the instrumental understanding of reason. The tragedy may be avoided by adopting the interpersonal perspective of social interaction among communal agents engaged in the exchange of beliefs in relation to helping themselves as well as other people based upon the substantive understanding of reason concerned not only with the means but also the ends to be pursued.

The interpersonal perspective makes room for the use of customary law as a procedure for the creation of customary rules as normative requirements for human conduct in relation to the environment. This raises the question concerning the legal status of customary rules. This implies the use of "juristic reason" that Holland excludes in his account. I am certainly entitled to be my own legislator concerning my own rules of conduct. It does not follow that I can create any kind of rule since this involves "juristic reason" taking other people into consideration. In this respect custom is also a procedure for the creation of legal rules in terms of customary law by human agents. This procedure involves juristic reason and Holland's denial implies that he fails to consider custom as a procedure that transforms customary rules into customary law. This vitiates his account of custom and this is perhaps what Fuller's criticism is about. Fuller considers custom as a procedure to create man-made rules in terms of the conditions of *opinio juris* and usage by reference to Article 38 of the Statute of the International Court of Justice.[118] This article is concerned with customary law as a source of law in the legal sense of secondary rules for the making of customary law as primary rules of conduct since it directs the court to apply "international custom, as evidence of a general practice accepted as law." It has been held that the foundation for this article is Savigny's understanding of customary law that has led to a considerable amount of discussion. I shall confine myself to some remarks concerning Savigny's understanding of the element of *opinio juris*. For Savigny, customary law is only a proof of the existence of a pre-existing law in the human mind. This implies that custom cannot serve as a legal procedure for the human creation of valid legal rules. Savigny rejects that human beings are agents having the capacity to engage in the intentional activity of creating valid rules that serve as normative reasons for human conduct. For Savigny, human beings are determined to act according to feelings of right. These feelings reside in the spirit of the people and produce by necessity regularities of behavior as manifested in customary law. Savigny's view implies that human beings are conscious instruments and the crucial distinction is between human beings as mere instruments and human beings as knowing instruments. The former category comprises ordinary people, the latter category the scholars like Savigny as the impartial and judicious spectator faced with the task of presenting a scientific account of the customary law in terms of uniformities of behavior. In this respect the condition of *opinio juris* is of paramount importance since uniformities of behavior are common to all human beings as a matter of necessity as manifested in various manners in different countries. The only way to account for the difference between customary manners and customary law is to apply the concept of *opinio juris* that is conceptualized in terms of inner feelings and sentiments of what is right or wrong that is externally manifested in the appropriate legal relations between people. This raises the question concerning the understanding of the relation between the internal operations of the mind and its external manifestations in human behavior. There is a vast literature addressing this question and I only wish to claim that Savigny understands the relation to be a causal relation between events from the inside out. Thus the invisible mental event of *opinio juris* necessarily causes the visible event of the appropriate act of customary behavior. This accounts for the existence of customary law that is followed by people. Savigny's position is related to Hume's account of causation and social interaction. But Savigny holds that the origin of customary law is a matter of necessity whereas Hume holds that it is a matter of human invention.

Savigny's critics also subscribe to the view that the relation is a causal relation between events. But for the critics the relation is rather the other way round. It is the existence of customary law as an external event that causes the internal event of having the appropriate feeling of *opinio juris*. Thus the relation is from the outside in. It follows that it is the external behavior that matters in terms of uniformities of behaviour and that there is no need for the mental element of *opinio juris*. This seems to be Fuller's position as well. This position is also related to Hume's naturalistic account of social interaction in terms of uniformities of behavior that provide the framework for social cooperation and coordination among human beings in terms of "stable interactional expectancies," to use Fuller's phrase.

Thus there is some common ground between Savigny and his critics. They both endorse that the relation is a causal relation. But then they differ concerning the scientific understanding of this relation. For Savigny, the relation is found in human nature as manifested as a necessary relation between mental events and external events of behavior. This position may lead to holding that customary laws are necessary laws that cannot be changed. Hence the rejection of the procedure of legislation to create statutory law. Savigny also denies the existence of custom as a procedure to create customary laws. What is left is Savigny's scientific approach based upon historical insight as a guide for the legal behavior of human beings. By contrast the critics hold that this causal relation is only a contingent relation between external events that have an impact upon the human mind. Thus customary law is there to observe as a positive fact of human behavior but it is possible that this can be changed by human beings as rational agents. Hence the importance of the naturalistic approach to provide the proper scientific information in relation to the content of customary law. Another approach is to replace the legal procedure of custom with the legal procedure of legislation to produce statutory laws or a codification. Although there are differences between the historical and the naturalistic approach they share a common element since they both subscribe to the personal perspective concerning the pursuit of knowledge to be used in social interaction among people to sustain the social conditions of life within society.

I wish to claim that the element of *opinio juris* cannot be understood in the way suggested by Savigny and his critics. Savigny's position stresses the importance of the concept of *opinio juris* but rejects that human beings are agents having the capacity to act. By contrast, the critics hold that human beings are rational agents having the capacity to act but then they reject the importance of the concept of *opinio juris*. This is the personal perspective of social interaction as causal relations between human beings as rational but solitary agents. This perspective should be replaced with the interpersonal of social interaction among human beings as rational but communal agents using the method of customary law to create valid legal rules in terms of customary laws. This perspective conceptualizes the concept of *opinio juris* in relation to human agency based upon beliefs that there is reason to believe and do. Thus the relation between the internal operations of the mind and the external action is a conceptual relation that implies that the agent has the capacity to perform actions that fall under a description that the agent understands and endorses. Hence the agent is engaged in the intentional activity of establishing a rule for his own conduct with the further intention that this rule also should be valid for other agents. In this intentional activity the agent cannot be separated from his action since the agent has to understand what kind of action or rule he has in mind to enact. The intentional activity may be a creative activity concerned with introducing a new rule as a customary law. In this case the making of a new rule is based upon the understanding of the secondary rules of validity that governs the customary procedure to create a customary law. The person is both law-maker and law-giver at the same time since the law is made according to the secondary rules that are mentioned and used simultaneously as guidance and measures for the making and declaration of valid legal rules in terms of primary rules. Thus customary law is the procedure that is mentioned and used to make and declare a valid rule of customary law having normative force as reason for belief and action.

It is a manifest fact that an action is external to the agent insofar as the action is performed. If the action is the announcement of a rule of conduct then it is possible to make a distinction between the state of mind of the agent and the actions done by the agent. The former is concerned with questions concerning the doing of agents in terms of his beliefs and intentions as reasons for actions. The latter is concerned with questions of what it is permissible or non-permissible for agents to do. Savigny discusses the former question by reference to error in relation to the *opinio juris.* Since Savigny subscribes to the view that *opinio juris* is a matter of internal feelings it cannot possibly be mistaken. This view can be questioned since what seems to be the right thing to do on the basis of feelings is one thing; what is the right thing to do is another. Savigny's answer that the right thing to do is to follow the rules of customary law invites the rejoinder that these rules may be wrong. Savigny's mistake is that he conceptualizes the concept of *opinio juris* in terms of feelings since the concept is to be conceptualized in terms of beliefs. If this is done, then the represented action in the rule is accompanied by the belief that it is permissible to perform the action according to the rule. This belief may be mistaken but this is a matter for rational discussion. This raises the question concerning the kind of actions that are permissible to perform by an agent. In this respect there is also a place for *opinio juris* in relation to rules concerning the normative powers of persons to engage in legal relations with other persons. This is the use of custom as a procedure that both enables but also constrains agents to create valid rules of customary law. The formation of customary law depends upon the fact that human beings are agents having the capacity to engage in the intentional activity of making rules concerning the appropriate human conduct using the method of custom based upon beliefs of what is right or wrong. What is important is that we are not bound to follow the rules of customary law as passive spectators. Human beings as rational persons and responsible agents face the task to develop structures to achieve human ends. One method is to use the peaceful procedure of customary law to create valid rules of customary laws to serve human ends based upon social interaction as communicative relations between persons as communal agents engaged in the exchange of views with respect to what there is reason to believe and to do.

In this chapter I have tried to present the idea of custom and its importance. By way of conclusion, I would like to quote Francis Bacon: "since custom is the principal magistrate of man's life, let men by all means endeavour to obtain good customs."[119] One way to establish good customs is to adopt the personal perspective advanced by Hume and his modern followers based upon the view that human beings are rational but solitary agents. Another way is to adopt the interpersonal perspective advanced by Reid that holds that human beings are rational and communal agents having the capacity to engage in the exchange of beliefs concerning what there is reason to believe and to do using the method of customary law to create valid rules of their own making based upon the exercise of practical reason that legislates universally in relation to human ends. I would like to see this perspective adopted as a common practice in relation to the enactment of rules of customary law by means of the method of customary law.

Endnotes

1. David Hume, *A Treatise of Human Nature: Being an Attempt to Introduce the Experimental Method of Reasoning into Moral Subjects* (P. H. Nidditch (ed.), 2nd edn., including "An Abstract of a Book", Clarendon Press, Oxford 1978). David Hume, *Enquiries Concerning Human Understanding and Concerning the Principles of Morals* (P. H. Nidditch (ed.), 3rd edn., Clarendon Press, Oxford, 1975).
2. *The Works of Thomas Reid* (ed. by Sir William Hamilton, reprint with intro. by Harry M. Bracken, Georg Olms Verlag, Hildesheim, 1983). The *Works* include: *Essays on the Intellectual Powers of Man*, pp. 213 ff. and *Essays on the Active*

Powers of Man, pp. 511 ff. See also Thomas Reid, *Practical Ethics* (ed. by Knud Haakonssen, Princeton University Press, Princeton, 1990).

3. Henry Sumner Maine, *Lectures on the Early History of Institutions* (7th edn., John Murray, London 1897), p. 434. See also Henry Sumner Maine, *Ancient Law: Its Connection with the Early History of Society, and its Relation to Modern Ideas* (London 1861, Theommes Press, reprint Bristol 1996), p. 7.
4. Jeremy Bentham, *A Comment of the Commentaries and a Fragment of Government* (ed. by J. H. Burns and H. L. A. Hart, The Athlone Press, London, 1977), and Jeremy Bentham, *Of Laws in General* (ed. by H. L. A. Hart, The Athlone Press, London, 1970). John Austin, *Lectures on Jurisprudence or the Philosophy of Positive Law* (4th edn., ed. by Robert Campbell, Thoemmes Press, Reprint Bristol, 1996).
5. Carl Friedrich von Savigny, *Von Beruf unserer Zeit für Gesetzgebung und Rechtswissenschaft* (Heidelberg, 1814) transl. by Adam Hayward as *Of the Vocation of our Age for Legislation and Jurisprudence* (Littlewood & Co., London, 1831). See also Savigny, *Geschichte des Römischen Recht im Mittelalter* (J. C. B. Mohr, Heidelberg, 1834). Savigny, *System des heutigen Römischen Recht* (Weit und Comp., Berlin, 1840), transl. by W. Holloway as *System of Modern Roman Law* (J. Higginbottom, Madras, 1867).
6. H. L. A. Hart, *The Concept of Law* (2nd edn., Oxford University Press, Oxford, 1994), p. 45.
7. Lon L. Fuller, "Human Interaction and the Law" (1969) *American Journal of Jurisprudence*, vol. 14, pp. 1 ff.
8. Hume, *Treatise*, Preface, p. xvi and Book I, Part IV, Sec. VII, p. 273, Abstract, p. 646.
9. Gerald J. Postema, *Bentham and The Common Law Tradition* (Clarendon Press, Oxford 1986), p. 81 and p. 95.
10. See Edward Craig, *The Mind of God and the Works of Man* (Clarendon Press, Oxford 1987), Ch. 1. See also Reid, *Active Powers*, Essay IV, Ch. 5, p. 615b and Ch. 10, p. 629.
11. Walton H. Hamilton, "Property – according to Locke" (1931–1932) *Yale Law Journal*, vol. 41, pp. 864 ff, at p. 878 for the term "a miniature god." Leibniz also uses the term, see Craig, *Mind of God*, p. 51.
12. See Francis Oakley, "Christian Theology and the Newtonian Science: The Rise of the Concept of the Laws of Nature" (1961) *Church History*, vol. 30, pp. 433 ff. This raises the issue whether the laws passed by god express his will or his reason, see the articles by M. B. Foster, "The Christian Doctrine of Creation and the Rise of Modern Natural Science" (1934) *Mind*, vol. 43, pp. 446 ff and Foster, "Christian Theology and Modern Science of Nature" (1936) *Mind*, vol. 45, pp. 1 ff.
13. William Blackstone, *Commentaries on the Laws of England* (1st edn. 1765–69, see The Avalon Project at Yale Law School), vol. 1, p. 38. For a sustained attack upon Blackstone's view of law see Bentham, *Comment and Fragment*,

and Austin, *Lectures*, for the division of law into the proper sense in terms of the commands passed by god and the human sovereign and the improper or metaphorical sense of natural laws concerning the causal relations between inanimate and animate bodies.

14. Oakley, "Christian Theology," p. 447. As Oakley stresses, this distinction also has political and legal implications. See J. W. Tubbs, "Custom, Time and Reason: Early Seventeenth-Century Conceptions of the Common Law," in (1998) *History of Political Thought*, vol. 19, pp. 363 ff.
15. See Craig, *The Mind of God*, Ch. 2 for Hume's rejection of the insight ideal.
16. Hume, *Enquiries*, II, Sec. III, Part I, p. 190.
17. Postema, *Bentham*, p. 101, cf. p. 92. See Maine, *Ancient Law*, Ch. V, p. 126 for the distinction between ancient and modern society.
18. Hume, *Enquiries*, I, Sec. I, p. 13, and *Treatise*, Book I, Part III, Sec. XVI, p. 176.
19. Hume, *Treatise*, *Abstract*, pp. 649 f.
20. Hume, *Enquiries*, I, Sec. IX, p. 106, Hume's italics. See also *Treatise*, Book I, Part IV, Sec. I, p. 183, "all our reasoning's concerning causes and effects are deriv'd from nothing but custom, and that belief is more properly an act of the sensitive, than of the cogitative part of our natures."
21. Hume, *Enquiries*, I, Sec. IX p. 108, Sec. V, Part I, pp. 44 f., Sec. VII, Part I, p. 66.
22. Hume, *Enquiries*, I, Sec. IX, p. 107.
23. C. A. J. Coady, *Testimony. A Philosophical Study* (Clarendon Press, Oxford, 1992). See also Leslie Stevenson, "Why Believe What People Say?" (1993) *Synthese*, vol. 94, pp. 429 ff.
24. Hume, *Enquiries*, I, Sec. X, p. 111.
25. Hume, *Treatise*, Book I, Part III, Sec. IX, p. 115. I am indebted to Stevenson's article for this reference.
26. Hume, *Enquiries*, I, Sec. X, Part II, p. 127.
27. Coady, *Testimony*, pp. 79 ff.
28. Hume, *Enquiries*, I, Sec. X, Part II, p. 130.
29. Hume uses, of course, the term "we," but the term is used either to denote Hume himself as an instructor of mankind suggesting that the persons addressed agree with him, or to secure an impersonal style and tone, or both.
30. Maine, *Ancient Law*, Ch. V, p. 113, Ch. I, p. 3, and p. 8, Ch. V, p. 170, Maine's italics.
31. K. B. Smellie, "Sir Henry Maine" (1922) *Economica*, vol. 8, pp. 64 ff, at p. 77.
32. Sir Frederick Pollock, "The Science of Case Law," in Pollock, *Essays in Jurisprudence and Ethics* (Macmillan & Co., London, 1882) reprinted in Pollock, *Jurisprudence and Legal Essays*, ed. by A. L. Goodhart, Macmillan & Co., London, 1961), p. 170 and p. 179. This is, of course, also the definition of law put forward by Oliver Wendell Holmes, "The prophecies of what the courts will do in fact, and nothing more pretentious, are what I mean by then law," "The Path of Law" (1897) *Harvard Law Review*, vol. 10, pp. 457 ff., at p. 461. A similar position is advanced within Scandinavian legal realism. See Jes Bjarup

"Authority and Roles," in Werner Krawietz, Robert S. Summers, Ota Weinberger, Georg Henrik von Wright (eds.), *The Reasonable as Rational? Festschrift for Aulis Aarnio* (Duncker & Humblot, Berlin, 2000), pp. 197 ff.

33. Reid, *Intellectual Powers*, Essay I, Ch. V, p. 238b, Ch. VIII, p. 244.
34. Reid, *Active Powers*, Essay V, Ch. VI, p. 663a, cf. *Intellectual Powers*, Essay I, Ch. VIII, p. 245a, *Active Powers*, Essay V, Ch. VI, p. 664a.
35. Reid, *Intellectual Powers*, Essay II, Ch. VIII, p. 269a, Ch. X, p. 286a, and Essay VI, Ch. VI, p. 455a, Ch. V, p. 445a, p. 447.
36. Hume, *Treatise*, Book I, Part IV, Sec. VI, p. 252 (emphasis in original).
37. Reid, *Intellectual Powers*, Essay II, Ch. XII, p. 293a, Reid's italics.
38. Reid, *Intellectual Powers*, Essay II, Ch. XII, p. 293b, cf. Essay I, Ch. I, p. 226. Essay VI, Ch. VI, p. 455.
39. Reid, *Active Powers*, Essay III, Ch. II, p. 549a and Essay V, Ch. VI, p. 665b.
40. Reid, *Inquiry into the Human Mind*, Ch. 6, Sec. XXIV, p. 194. See Coady, *Testimony*, Ch. 3 and Ch. 7 for a critical exposition of Reid's account of testimony.
41. Reid, *Intellectual Powers*, Essay VI, Ch. V, p. 447, Ch. IV, p. 439.
42. See Reid, *Practical Ethics*, Haakonssen's introduction p. 38, cf. pp. 7f.
43. Reid, *Intellectual Powers*, Essay VI, Ch. VII, p. 466, Ch. V, p. 448. Moral principles are also valid without reference to god, see Reid, *Practical Ethics*, p. 145.
44. A similar position is held by Kant, "the original right of human reason, which recognizes no other judge than universal reason itself, in which everyone has a voice; and since all improvement of which our condition is capable must come from this, such a right is holy, and must not be curtailed," *Critique of Pure Reason* (transl. and ed. by Paul Guyer and Allen W. Wood, Cambridge University Press, Cambridge, 1997), A752/B780, p. 650.
45. Reid, *Inquiry into the Human Mind*, Ch. 6, Sec. XXIV, p. 197.
46. Hume, *Treatise*, Book III, Part II, Sec. IX p. 551, Hume's italics, and Book III, Part II, Sec. II, p. 490 for the next quotation.
47. Fuller, "Human Interaction," p. 24.
48. See P. M. S. Hacker, "Davidson on First-Person Authority" (1997) *The Philosophical Quarterly*, vol. 47, pp. 285 ff. and Claudine Verheggen, "Davidson's Second Person" ibid. pp. 361 ff.
49. John Yolton, "Action: Metaphysics and Modality" (1973) *American Philosophical Quarterly*, vol. 10, pp. 71 ff., at p. 84.
50. Reid, *Active Powers*, Essay I, Ch. V, p. 523a.
51. Reid, *Active Powers*, Essay III, Part III, Ch. VIII, p. 596b.
52. See John R. Searle, "Contemporary Philosophy in the United States," in Nicholas Bunnin and E. P. Tsui-James (eds.), *The Blackwell Companion to Philosophy* (Blackwells, Oxford, 1996), pp. 1 ff. and the reference to J. L. Austin, *How to do Things with Words* (ed. by J. O. Urmson, Clarendon Press, Oxford, 1962).
53. Reid, *Inquiry into the Human Mind*, Ch. VI, Sec. XXIV, p. 199.
54. Reid, *Intellectual Powers*, Essay VI, Ch. IV, p. 440.

55. See Theodore Waldman, "Origins of the Legal Doctrine of Reasonable Doubt" (1959) *Journal of the History of Ideas*, vol. 20, pp. 299 ff. This practice was not adopted until around 1816, citing James Bradley Thayer's *A Preliminary Treatise on Evidence* (Little, Brown & Co., Boston, 1896), at p. 308.
56. Immanuel Kant, *What Does it Mean to Orient Oneself in Thinking, in Religion and Rational Theology* (transl. and ed. by Allen W. Wood and George di Giovanni, Cambridge University Press, Cambridge, 1996), p. 16 (8:144), Kant's italics.
57. Reid, *Intellectual Powers*, Essay VI, Ch. IV, p. 440a. See also Coady, *Testimony*, pp. 99 f.
58. Reid, *Active Powers*, Essay II, Ch. II, p. 536b.
59. John Locke, *Two Treatises of Government* (ed. by Peter Lasslett, The New American Library, London, 1963). This raises the issue between voluntarism and intellectualism within the natural law tradition, see Francis Oakley, "Locke, Natural Law and God – Again" (1997) *History of Political Thought*, vol. 18, pp. 624 ff.
60. Blackstone, *Commentaries*, vol. 1, p. 40, p. 41 and p. 27.
61. Blackstone, *Commentaries* vol. 4, p. 5, quoted from Postema, *Bentham*, p. 34. It seems to me that Postema overlooks that Blackstone is committed to the insight ideal.
62. Hume, *Treatise*, Book II, Part I, Sec. XII, p. 326.
63. Maine, *Ancient Law*, Ch. V, p 125.
64. Hume, *Treatise*, Book III, Part II, Sec. I, p. 477 cf. Part III, Sec. I, p. 575, Part I, Sec. I, p. 457, Book II, Part I, Sec. VII, p. 296, Book III, Part I, Sec. II, p. 470.
65. Hume, *Enquiries* II, Sec. IX, Part I, pp. 268 and 270 (emphasis in original).
66. Reid, *Active Powers*, Essay III, Part III, Ch. VI, p. 592, Ch. V, p. 587, Ch. II, p. 581, Ch. VII, p. 598, Essay V, Ch. VII, p. 673.
67. Hume, *Treatise*, Book III, Part I, Sec. I, p. 469.
68. Hume, *Treatise*, Book III, Part II, Sec. II, p. 500, p. 502, and p. 493. *Enquiries* II, Sec. III, Part I, p. 189, p. 191. See also Postema, *Bentham* pp. 92 ff.
69. Jean Jacques Rousseau, *A Discourse on the Origin of Equality* (transl. G. D. H. Cole, J. M. Dent & Sons Ltd, London, 1913), p. 185.
70. Richard Tuck, *The Rights of War and Peace. Political Thought and the International Order from Grotius to Kant* (Oxford University Press, Oxford, 1999), pp. 6 f, cf. p. 199.
71. Hume, *Treatise*, Book III, Part II, Sec. VIII, p. 541.
72. Thomas Hobbes, *Leviathan, or The Matter, Forme, & Power of a Commonwealth, Ecclesiasticall and Civill* (ed. by Richard Tuck, Cambridge, 1991), Ch. 14, p. 92.
73. Kant holds a similar view, see Immanuel Kant, "The Metaphysics of Morals," in Kant, *Practical Philosophy* (transl. and ed. by Mary J. Gregor, Cambridge University Press, Cambridge, 1996), p. 397 (6:242).

74. Hobbes, *Leviathan*, Ch. 18, p. 125, Ch. 29, p. 223 and Ch. 37, p. 306.
75. Hume, *Treatise*, Book III, Part II, Sec. II, p. 494, Hume's italics, and p. 491.
76. Hume, *Treatise*, Book II, Part I, Sec. X, p. 310, and Book III, Part II, Sec. III, p. 506. Cf. Blackstone's definition of the right of property as "that sole and despotic dominion which one man claims and exercises over the external things of the world, in total exclusion of the right of any other individual in the universe," *Commentaries*, vol. 2, p. 2.
77. Hume, *Treatise*, Book III, Part II, Sec. II, p. 496, Part II, Sec. IV, p. 515, Sec. II, p. 495, p. 497.
78. Hume, *Treatise*, Book III, Part II, Sec. II, p. 489, and pp. 488, 490.
79. Hume, *Treatise*, Book III, Part II, Sec. II, p. 491 and p. 497.
80. Hume, *Treatise*, Book III, Part II, Sec. II, p. 490. and Sec. I, p. 484, Hume's italics, Part II, Sec. VI, p. 526, Sec. II, p. 500.
81. Postema, *Bentham*, Ch. 4: Hume's Jurisprudence: Common Law Conventionalism, pp. 110 ff.
82. Hume, *Enquiries* II, Sec. III, Part I, p. 192, and p. 182, Hume's italics.
83. Bentham, *Fragment*, p. 441, his italics. *Laws in General*, Ch. XIX, p. 244. See Postema, *Bentham* for an account of Bentham's project.
84. Hart, *Concept of Law*, pp. 193 ff.
85. Reid, *Active Powers*, Essay III, Part III, Ch. VIII, p. 596.
86. Reid, *Active Powers*, Essay V, Ch. V, p. 661.
87. Hume, *Treatise*, Book III, Part II, Sec. I, p. 484.
88. Reid, *Active Powers*, Essay V, Ch. V, p. 656, cf. p. 654.
89. Reid, *Active Powers*, Essay V, Ch. V, p. 658.
90. Reid, *Active Powers*, Essay V, Ch. V, p. 657.
91. Hume, *Treatise*, Book III, Part II, Sec. II, p. 494, *Enquiries* II, Sec. III, Part I, pp. 184 ff, *Treatise*, Part II, Sec. V, p. 525.
92. Hume, *Treatise*, Book III, Part I, Sec. I, p. 468, Hume's italics.
93. Reid, *Active Powers*, Essay V, Ch. VII, p. 677, Reid's italics.
94. Reid, *Active Powers*, Essay V, Ch. V, p. 661.
95. Hume, *Enquiries* II, App. I, p. 293.
96. Pollock, "The Science of Case Law," p. 184.
97. Postema, *Bentham*, p. 321, cf. p. 154 for the quotations from Bentham.
98. Austin, *Lectures*, Lec. I, p. 88, and Lec. VI, p. 226. Bentham, *Laws in General*, Ch. 1, p. 1, p. 18., Ch. XI, p. 139. See Bentham, *Introduction*, p. 283 for the quote. p. 94, and Lec. VI, p. 226.
99. Austin, *Lectures*, Lec. VI, p. 226, Bentham, *Laws*, Ch. 1, p. 18, Ch. XI, p. 139.
100. Bentham, *Laws*, Ch. VI, p. 64.
101. Austin, *Lectures*, Outline, p. 38, Austin's italics, Lecture XXX, p. 555.
102. Maine, *Lectures*, p. 343, p. 348, p. 370.
103. See Hart, *Concept of Law*, p. 20 for a similar criticism of Austin in terms of "gunman situation."

104. Maine, *Lectures*, p. 343, p. 360, p. 349 and p. 370.
105. *The Digest of Justinian* (transl. Charles Henry Monro, Cambridge University Press, Cambridge 1904), D. 1.3.32.21. See also *Justinian's Institutes* (transl. and intro. by Peter Birks and Grant McLeod, Duckworth, London, 1987), I.2, pp. 37 f.
106. Walter Ullman, "Bartolus on Customary Law" (1940) *The Juridical Review*, vol. 52, pp. 265 ff., p. 268.
107. Maine, *Ancient Law*, Ch. 1, p. 13.
108. Craig, *Mind of God*, Ch. 3, The Metaphysics of The Romantic Area, and Ch. 4 on Hegel.
109. Savigny, *Vocation of Our Age*, p. 290.
110. Hart, *Concept of Law*, p. 45, cf. p. 294 with reference to Sir John Salmond, *Jurisprudence* (11th. edn., Sweet & Maxwell, London 1957), Ch. 5, and p. 91, cf. p. 231.
111. See for Norway, Torstein Eckhoff, *Rettskildelāre* (ed. by Janttelgesen, 5th edn., Universitetsforlaget, Oslo, 2001), pp. 229 ff., Jan Fridthjof Bernt and David R. Doublet, *Juss, Samfunn og Rettsanvendelse* (Ad Notam Gyldendal, Oslo 1996), pp. 193 ff., for Sweden, Jan Hellner, *Rättsteori* (2nd edn., Juristförlaget, Stockholm 1994), pp. 112 f., Stig Strömholm, *Rätt, Rättskällor och Rättstillämpning* (5th edn., Norstedts Juridik, Stockholm, 1996) pp. 234 f., for Denmark, Alf Ross, *Om Ret og Retfärdighed* (Nyt Nordisk Forlag Arnold Busck, Copenhagen, 1953), pp. 197 ff. (transl. into English as *On Law and Justice* (Steven and Sons Ltd, London, 1958), pp. 91 ff.), Jens Ewald, *Retskilderne og den juridiske metode* (2nd edn., Jurist-og Økonomforbundets Forlag, Copenhagen, 2000), pp. 42 ff.
112. Fuller, "Human Interaction," p. 2.
113. T. E. Holland, *The Elements of Jurisprudence*, (9th edn., Clarendon Press, London, 1900), p. 54. Holland's account has been very influential as manifested in the reference by Charles Sumner Lobingier in the entry on Customary Law, Edwin R. A. Seligman (ed.), *Encyclopaedia of the Social Sciences* (Macmillan Company, New York, 1930), vol. 4, p. 662.
114. See A. D. Woozley, "The Existence of Rules" (1967) *Nous*, vol. 1, pp. 63 ff.
115. Fuller, "Human Interaction," p. 2, and see p. 6 and p. 15 for interaction in terms of stimulus and response.
116. Fuller, "Human Interaction," p. 33.
117. Garrett Hardin, "The Tragedy of the Commons" (1968) *Science*, vol. 162, pp. 1243 ff., 1244. See also Garrett Hardin, "The Tragedy of the Commons Revisited" (1999) *Environment*, vol. 41, issue 2, pp. 4 f.
118. Fuller, "Human Interaction," p. 16 and p. 19.
119. Francis Bacon, *Essays* (ed. by Michael J. Hawkins, K. M. Dent & Sons Ltd), London 1972, p. 120.

4

How custom becomes law in England[1]

DAVID CALLIES

This court will upon a writ of error take judicial notice of all private customs in private places; for they below are as much bound to proceed upon their customs as the Judges here upon the common law. Case 104. Anonymous 11 Mod 68

How that which may be claimed by all the inhabitants of England can be the subject of a custom, I cannot conceive. Customs must in their nature be confined to individuals of a particular description, and what is common to all mankind, can never be claimed as a custom.

Fitch v. Rawling, 2 H.Bl. 393 (1795) at 398;[1775–1802 All ER 571, 574; 126 ER 614, 616

[A]ll customs which are against the common law of England, ought to be taken strictly, nay very strictly, even stricter than any Act of Parliament that alters the common law. It is a general rule, that customs are not to be enlarged beyond the usage; because it is the usage and practice that makes the law in such cases, and not the reason of the thing, for it cannot be said that a custom is founded on reason, though an unreasonable custom is void; for no reason, even the highest whatsoever, would make a custom or law; so it is no particular reason that makes any custom law, but the usage and practice itself, without regard had to any reason of such usage; and therefore you cannot enlarge such custom by any parity of reason, since reason has no part in the making of such custom . . . but the law allows usage in particular places to supersede the common law, and is the local law, which is never to be extended further than the usage and practice, which is the only thing that makes it law.

Arthur v. Bockenham, 11 Mod. 148 (1707) at 160–161

4.1 An introduction to Blackstonian custom: why we should care about Blackstone?

Customary law is in derogation of that greatest of English gifts to the regulation of human behavior, the common law. Extolled on at least three continents as the epitome of fairness and consistency, common law permits the changing of law to reflect common social beliefs and attitudes by accretion rather than by avulsion. Although there is the occasional overruling of precedent, the norm is gradual change through multiple judicial decisions.

It is the common law that formed the basis of legal jurisprudence in the American colonies in the seventeenth century, and in the new United States in the eighteenth century. Reception statutes passed in the various states resulted in the formal adoption of English common law as the basis for legal process. The source for that common law tradition was William Blackstone's *Commentaries on the Laws of England.* Although there are at least sixteen editions of the *Commentaries*, the first edition of 1765–1769 was the most influential in the colonies, arriving on the eve of their revolutionary war.

As the law of custom increasingly finds its way into a variety of modern contracts, it is well worth examining what Blackstone meant by "special custom" and what developments in the law preceded and followed his criteria, for at least three reasons:

1. First, as indicated above, we must define custom somehow. Blackstone is one of the few commentators to have attempted to do so – and based on a substantial body of case law, at that.
2. Second, Blackstone is generally cited as the primary authority in most discussions of custom, both in commentary and case law.
3. Third, English cases before and after provide one of the richest sources of customary law, certainly within a common law tradition, demonstrating the reasons for Blackstone's seven criteria, and their evolution in comparatively modern English law.

Blackstone recognized three forms of customary law: common law ("general custom") by which he presumably meant common law as we view it today, court (procedural) custom of particular tribunals or courts, and "particular customs" practiced by and affecting the inhabitants of a defined geographical area. It is this third, or "particular" custom that Blackstone took care to carefully define and delimit, perhaps because it constitutes a threat to the common law tradition that he espoused and for which he argues in the *Commentaries.* He set out seven criteria that a customary right or practice must meet if it is to be a "good" custom, that is, one that is enforceable against a common law principle or tradition, for example, of exclusive possession of private land.

Although he cited comparatively few cases in the *Commentaries*, Blackstone drew these seven criteria from the case law as it had developed by the middle of the eighteenth century (and indeed, well into the nineteenth century). To be valid, to be enforceable, to result in an exercisable right of an individual despite common law principles to the contrary, a custom had to be immemorial, continuous, peaceable, reasonable, certain, compulsory and consistent. Even today, the law of custom is hedged by requirements, most of which derive directly from Blackstone's seven criteria. Thus, for example, a recent volume of *Halsbury's Laws of England*[2] describes the essential attributes of custom as follows:

> To be valid, a custom must have four essential attributes (1) it must be immemorial; (2) it must be reasonable; (3) it must be certain in its terms and in respect both of the locality where it is alleged to obtain and of the persons whom it is alleged to affect; (4) it must have continued as of right and without interruption since its immemorial origin. These characteristics serve a practical purpose as rules of evidence when the existence of a custom is to be established or refuted.[3]

Even so practical a source as a standard reference book of law for local government councillors has the following entry:

> Custom: If a right is given to or an obligation imposed upon all the Queen's subjects, it must be established by authority of the general law. A local custom can therefore never be general and a customary claim in the name of the general public will fail. Similarly a custom must be capable of definition, and so the courts will not uphold a claim on behalf of a class whose membership cannot be ascertained.[4]

4.2 The sources of custom

The sources of customary law are many and diverse.[5] They also vary in reliability both in terms of accuracy of description and their enforceability.[6] It is for these reasons that we have chosen to rely principally on reported cases for the best indication of what the law pertaining to custom was during the time of Blackstone, as well as before and after. Nevertheless, the other sources provide a far richer picture of the kinds of customs one might expect to find during a particular period, beyond those that were litigated in courts of record.

Among the most common sources are the custumals that describe those customs that were prevalent in medieval English manors and boroughs. In her two volumes on Borough Customs for the Selden Society,[7] Mary Bateson observes that there is difficulty in establishing the texts of custumals in part because of the diverse sources:

> The customary laws of the boroughs are recorded in many ways, in documents of more or less legal authority. Some borough customs – notably certain London customs – are among the statutes of the realm; some have the authority of Domesday Book; some are recorded in the borough charter; some are recorded on the borough court-roll, either because they have been pleaded in court, or because a single roll serves as register for all the records of the borough . . . Some customs are set on record because they have been subjected to reform, and the reformed usage is then generally stated in the form of a borough ordinance or bylaw. The penning of a custumal or code of customs was generally the work of a town clerk or other borough officer of unusually methodical habits . . . His manuscript, being entered into or kept with the official books, gradually acquired the force of law, although the method of compilation and the ultimate sanction are usually hidden from view. Sometimes the clerk adduces as his authority a similar collection of earlier date, which is rarely to be found now in existence; sometimes he gives clear indication that he has collected his facts from various official sources such as those we have named above, or he may give his own impression as a lawyer of the most approved practice of the borough court . . . In a few cases, the code is declared to be drafted and issued as a whole under the sanction of the governing body of the town.[8]

Obviously the problems of sources and their accuracy, let alone any notion of completeness, are enormous.[9] As Bateson notes, much probably remains buried in chests of borough archives despite the efforts of scholars such as Bateson. Then there is the problem of translation, since most of the older documents are in some form of French or Latin.[10] Bateson provides a number of sources nevertheless in the introduction to her two-volume collection.[11] These are arranged alphabetically by town, city or village. Thus for Ipswich:

> The custumal dated 1291 was issued by the authority of the officers and commonality, to replace an old "Domesday," which had been stolen; it has been printed by Sir Travers Twiss in the "Black Book of the Admiralty," ii. 1–207, from the fourteenth-Century (British Museum) Add. MS. 25012. He gives also an English rendering from the fifteenth-Century Add. MS. 25011. Sir Travers Twiss's French text has been used here. There is another fourteenth-Century copy of the French in Egerton MS. 2788, f.16, made for Paul le Roos, town clerk, 1343–4. It has not been collated, as its variants do not appear to be important.[12]

A few examples give the flavor of what one may find in and among these diverse sources, lending both colorful background and credibility to the case materials in the following section. Thus, from the Waterford rolls, an ancient nuisance-cum-building code, from about 1300:

> Of the oppression of houses. Furthermore, if it chances that one house lies up against another, and the wall-course of one neighbor is placed where the house on the other side ought to be, the neighbor ought to move his wall-course until such time as his neighbor has put up the frame of his house, without strife or dispute.[13]

From Northampton, another nuisance regulation from about 1190:

> Of a dispute concerning a building or a wall. If a dispute arises between neighbors concerning a wall, or a building, or a gutter, the bailiffs and good men of the pleas ought to view that tenement by lawful men of the neighborhood, and what they say concerning the matter ought to stand firm and established, without essoin and delay.[14]

From Waterford, a fascinating explanation of the hue and cry, what it is, when one was entitled to raise it, and the penalties for failure to respond, or to raise it improvidently:

> Furthermore if hue and cry be raised by day or by night, every neighbor who does not come at the cry, as reason demands, shall be amerced [fined] 6s 8d by the law of the city. And he who raises the hue and cry shall be brought to the prison, and shall be replevied out of prison: and this unless his life was in danger or his house broken into, or other injury was threatened whereby he was forced to raise the hue and cry, and provided the neighbors round about can bear witness for him before the bailiffs. And if he makes hue and cry where there is no need, he shall go to prison, and if he has any friend who will replevy him, he very well may be replevied and the amercement is 10s. And if he has nothing whereon the 10s can be levied, he shall stay in prison forty days. And if he wishes to go on living in the city, he shall find good security that no harm or mischief or hue or cry shall in any way arise again through him or any of his people. And if he cannot do this, he shall leave the town for ever and shall never come back.[15]

Custumals are often lengthy recitations of the relationship between lord and tenant or copyholder, framed primarily in the negative with only passing reference to rights and privileges. Thus, for example, from the Manor of Cockerham in Lancaster:

> It was ordered that the tenants and [blank] shall not dig more turves than they can conveniently and sufficiently use for burning, and the fuel from the holdings shall not be provided for strangers under pain of half a mark. And the tenants of each Crymbyill [Great Crimbles and Little Crimbles] shall maintain the dikes of the mill pond so that the pond does not burst for lack of them. And no tenant shall go to other mills. And the tenants of the marsh shall maintain the sea dikes each of them at his own place under payment of half a mark.[16]

Another fruitful source of custom besides the custumals are cases from the manorial courts. One respected source describes these courts as follows:

> The manorial courts were the courts baron, with civil jurisdiction, whose suitors were the free tenants of the manor, and the customary court, whose suitors were copyholders and customary tenants of the manor . . . These courts are incident to every manor as of common right. Neither the court baron nor the customary court was normally of record.[17]

The record offices of the various counties are excellent sources for these, though the counties which were the more popular for building manor houses – such as Buckinghamshire and Oxfordshire – are more likely to repay a visit than, say, Cambridgeshire, the fens by comparison not being a particularly attractive place to construct such manors.[18] The indexes to the collected manor rolls, court and otherwise, are organized in identical fashion by year of accession in each county record office, which makes that part of the research that much easier. However, the indexes are numbered, volume by volume, in the order that someone carted in the records from a particular manor.[19]

Thus, for example, in the volume of the index for Cambridgeshire, there appears a reference to a 1737 trial in the Manor of Great Abington. The records collection for that manor yielded handwritten jury verdict setting out "The Verdict of y Jurors & homages att a Court Baron held for y Ab. Mannor on Monday on y second day of August, Anno Dom 1737" with what appears to be a settlement and listing of certain customs of the manor, including:

> We find & present that every Copyholder of this Manor according to y ancient Custom & Usage may for every two acres of Common field Copyhold land whereof he is seized hath agoing for One sheep in y Lord flock to be kept there to be paid to y Lord of y Manor Horgvery shoop;

* * *

> We order that no person or persons Inhabitants of this parish shall putt or keep any horse or Guilding upon Broad Meadow save from Lammas Day.

The Selden Society has published a selection of decisions of such manorial courts concerning property and family law between 1250 and 1550 compiled by two American scholars in 1998.[20] As the authors point out in their introduction, the manorial courts were not above creating custom on the spot rather than slavishly following what purported to be established custom.[21] But this source is likely to be far less accurate a reflection of established, immemorial custom than the courts of record. Nevertheless, the manorial court roll excerpts which the authors have painstakingly collected and translated add a further dimension to the subject, even though precious few involve customs pertaining to the use of land.

Thus, for example, it is recorded at Flixton Priory Manor, in South Elmham (Suffolk) on January 16, 1316:

> William de Fenne surrendered into the lady's hands the entire tenement which he held of the lady without any reservation, for the benefit of Edmund Hermel and his heirs forever, to hold in villeinage at the lady's will, performing the customs, etc., saving the right, etc. And the said Edmund gives the lord a fine to have entry. Pledge, the hayward. For which same render the said Edmund will give to the said William each year for the term of his life two quarters of corn, namely four bushels of wheat one quarter of barley and four bushels of peas, namely the barley at Michaelmas and the other half at Easter in equal portions.[22]

And from the court rolls of the Manor of Dernford Sawston in Cambridge between 1336 and 1360:

> William Baret took the lord's water-mill with the fishing in the mill pool for one year from Christmas until the following Christmas, and pays for rent 10 quarters of wheat for the said mill. And the lord shall find all necessaries contingent on working the mill And if necessary the farmer to have a new grindstone and the said William should place it in position at his own expense and for such expense he will have the old grindstone which is insufficient for the mill.[23]

Nearer to Blackstone's time is the following 1609 order from a baronial court or commission resulting apparently from a complaint concerning the insufficient number of working horses allowed to be fed on the local common:

> First it is ordered by the sayd Commissioners that the sayd inhabitants within the towne of Stretham or the precincts thereof haueing anie auncient

> commonable messuage or Tenements shall and may, by right of his or hir sayd messuage or Tenement, yearlie depasture in the sayd Commons iue workeing horses or mares with their foales, soe they bee of his or hir owne proper goods and at such times of the yeer onelie as hee or shee of right beefore this order might haue done, for the bringing home of fother and turffs for his or hir provision.[24]

Lastly, there are the remaining records of those great estates still intact and in possession of their records. Even when the records themselves have been transferred to county record offices for safekeeping and cataloging as described above, often there are people connected with the estates – such as a resident land agent or the estate's solicitors – who will know something of the estate's old – and sometimes still existing – practices, which may rise to the level of a custom. Thus, for example, a "Dole" from the Englefield Estate, Theale, Reading, dating from 1581, setting out that each parishioner of Ufton should annually receive: "Ten bushels of wheat, to be made into good household bread; Twelve and a half ells of canvas for shirts and smocks; and Twelve and a half yards of narrow bluecloth for coats and cassocks."[25]

According to the Estate Manager, the wheat has become loaves of freshly baked bread and the canvas and bluecloth converted to sheets and duvets. The distribution is still announced and takes place annually each spring.[26]

However, for sheer serendipity, it is hard to beat the custom for allocation of grazing rights in Bishop's Caundle, Dorset. In an auction conducted by the chairman of the parish council, a candle is lit and the bidding starts, and the last bid received before the candle goes out, wins![27]

There is, of course, good reason to have at least a glance at the manorial rolls: sometimes the courts rely on them as the basis for discovering what the alleged custom is, which stands at the heart of a current dispute. This was certainly true in Blackstone's time, as evident from the 1792 inheritance case of *Roe v. Parker*.[28] There, the court specifically noted that proof of manorial custom was usually found by searching out precedent in court rolls. To the same effect is the nineteenth-century case of *Rogers v. Brenton*[29] and the early twentieth-century case of *Coote v. Ford*.[30] However, courts have also been critical of reliance on manorial courts and custumals, principally because they were not courts of record and therefore subject to the problems noted above. This was the view in the 1786 case of *Denn v. Sprey*[31] where the court held that rolls and custumals were not legally conclusive because they did not represent the proceedings of a court of record.

4.3 Blackstone's criteria

According to Blackstone, all special customs are broadly subject to three sets of rules: existence, legality when proved to exist and method of allowance. Existence and method of allowance have generally to do with categorizations and issues that are of only marginal relevance to this present study. It is the seven rules or criteria applicable to special custom (not common law, not special court rules, but land rights in derogation of common law particular to a defined and limited jurisdiction and exercised by a small and definite population). It is this special custom that courts have dealt with and which forms the basis still for English discussion and categorization of customary law.[32] The following discussion takes them in the order in which Blackstone presents them.

4.3.1 Immemoriality

> That it have been used so long, that the memory of man runneth not to the contrary. So that if any one can shew the beginning of it, it is no good custom. For which reason no custom can prevail against an express act of parliament, since the statute itself is a proof of a time when such a custom did not exist.
>
> (Blackstone, *Commentaries on the Laws of England*, 1st edition, at 76–77)

The use of a custom "so long that the memory of man runneth not to the contrary" is a criterion honored as much in the breach in current English cases as in its ancient purity. However, for centuries, "time out of memory" had a fixed, well-defined and accepted meaning. The phrase is a common one in setting up a custom as a defense against what would otherwise be an unlawful act (usually trespass). Thus, in the fourteenth-century case of *Hamstede v. Abbot of Abington,*[33] the plaintiff brought "replevin against the abbot . . . in respect of a reckoning-board wrongfully seized". The Abbot's defense? That the seizure was for failure to pay a one-penny brewing fee – the Tolcester Penny – "of which penny, i.e. the Tolcester Penny, the abbot and his predecessors have been seised from a time beyond memory, and whenever the penny has been in arrear, i.e. the Tolcester Penny, the abbot and his predecessors have destrained throughout the said time." The report of the case continues to describe that the defendant refused to pay the toll, and so the abbot's representative took the reckoning-board in lieu thereof. Again in the 1628 case of *Walmesly v. Marshall,*[34] a dispute over corn grinding, the plea set down in the report of the case emphasizes over and over again the importance of immemoriality:

> that by antient custome, time out of mynde of man, used within the said manor, and within the town of Selbye aforesaid, being an antient towne tyme out of mind of man, all and singular the tenants, inhabitants, residents and dwellers within the said manor, lordshippe and towne of Selbye, for all the time whereof the memory of man is not to the contrary, have used and been accustomed to grinde all theire corne and graine . . .[35]

The notion of immemoriality was not only taken seriously by the courts in Blackstone's time, but the definition of immemoriality was clear and unequivocal. Nothing demonstrates this rigid attachment better than the 1769 case of *Millar v. Taylor*,[36] an old copyright case that turned on the immemoriality of an alleged custom of a company to have sole rights to publish a book once registered with it. The custom was held to be bad because "Very certainly, it could not be immemorial: for, the art of printing was not known in this kingdom till the reign of Ed.4."[37] A note following the case indicates that, so far as the court knew, "The first work that is known to have a date to it, was the Psalter published in Mentz, in 1457."[38] Why is this dispositive? Because by accepted legal definition of immemoriality a custom had to be traceable back to the coronation of Richard I in 1189! In short, immemoriality must be provable, as empirical fact, not simply as assertion.

However, courts were not always so careful, even in Blackstone's time, about the niceties of how such an immemorial custom might be practiced. In the 1795 case of *Fitch v. Rawling*,[39] the court had no difficulty in finding that parishioners could play cricket under a custom for "all the inhabitants of a parish to play at all kinds of lawful games, sports and pastimes in the close of A. at all seasonable times of the year at their free will and pleasure."[40] Clearly there was no cricket in 1189. One of the judges simply observed that "The lord might have granted such a privilege, as is claimed by the first custom, before the time of memory."[41]

An example of such a showing is the strange 1495 case of *Rollesley v. Toft*,[42] in which a known and admitted felon complained of being dragged out of a house of refuge to stand trial, because:

> [T]his same man had on such a day and year taken refuge in a house which was in old times the land of the Templars, and he showed how all the Templars' lands were given to the Hospitallers in the time of Edward II, in the [seventeenth] year, and it had been used time out of mind that every house [of theirs was a sanctuary] and so he prayed to be restored.[43]
>
> . . . and the same master of that military order, and all his predecessors, as masters of the same order from time then beyond memory, had and were accustomed to have in the aforesaid house or messuage (and the ambit

> thereof) and in all their other houses or messuages and cottages (and their ambit) which were part of the possessions then being in the hands of the aforesaid templars or within their fee, the following immunities, liberties and privileges: that is to say, that anyone who should flee to any house or messuage (or the ambit thereof) which was . . . held from them and was within their fees, for any felony or murder committed by them, claiming there the liberties, immunities and privileges of that house or messuage, could throughout the time aforesaid have protection and safeguard in such houses or messuages or their ambits and could remain within the same houses or messuages and their ambits for all their lives at their pleasure without any kind of interference, denial or withdrawal.[44]

As to the manner of proving the custom, the 1786 case of *Denn v. Spray*[45] is instructive. There the issue was proper descent of title, there being alleged a custom in a particular manner that lands descend to an elder sister, when there is neither son nor daughter of the deceased. The court held: "A customary of a manor, appearing to be of great antiquity, and delivered down with the court rolls from steward to steward, although not signed by any person, is good evidence to prove the course of descent within the manor."[46]

Such was the law with respect to the criterion of immemoriality in Blackstone's time. However, it is also clear that as the coronation of Richard I faded ever deeper in the history of England, it was harder and harder to show that a custom dated from 1189 – or anything like. Therefore by the mid-nineteenth century, this criterion of immemoriality was reduced to a presumption that, once established, shifted the burden to the one attacking the custom to show by evidence that it was not immemorial. This shift is clearly apparent in a number of nineteenth-century cases.

Thus, in the 1837 case of *Bastard v. Smith*,[47] an action for trespass for breaking and entering certain closes and trenching through a lawn in order to divert water to a tin mine, to the claim that the custom could not be proved to be immemorial, Tindal, C. J., observed in summing up to a jury (at p. 136):

> Then, as to the proof of the custom, you cannot, indeed, reasonably expect to have it proved before you, that such a custom did in fact exist before time of legal memory, that is, before the first year of the reign of Richard I; for if you did, it would in effect destroy the validity of almost all customs: but you are to require proof, as far back as living memory goes, of a continuous, peaceable, and uninterrupted user of the custom: and then you should inquire whether any document, or memorial, of more ancient times, is

produced, tending to disprove the existence of the custom at that early period to which the law looks back.

On the other hand, although reversed on a pleading technicality two years later, the 1863 case of *Mounsey v. Ismay*[48] nevertheless continues to place emphasis on the need for traditional immemoriality:

> A custom to be good must have existed from the time of legal memory, that is, the reign of Richard the First, and whether the land which is subject to the custom was then pasture or arable, it is now impossible to ascertain; and I think the circumstance of the land being pasture or arable at the time when the alleged trespass was committed is immaterial in considering whether the custom is good.[49]

The custom alleged was for the freemen of the town of Carlisle to hold horse races on a particular close in a nearby hamlet.

Nevertheless, the extent of the presumption of immemoriality today is clear from the 1974 case of *New Windsor Corporation v. Mellor*,[50] in which the inhabitants of a borough claimed a right acquired by custom to indulge in lawful sports and pastimes on the New Windsor village green. The court held:

> Once it had been established that there had been long usage of the land for lawful sports and pastimes, that such usage had been as of right and that it was capable of subsisting as a custom, the court would be astute to find the origin from time immemorial and the Commissioner had been right to do so.[51]

The evidence before the court included a lease from 1691 referring to the custom. The court distinguished a statute from the reign of Henry VIII, which the borough claimed established the custom. If successful, this would have negated the presumption that the custom dated back to 1189, several hundred years before the reign of the Tudor monarchs.

This is not to say, however, that the presumption was automatic. Several cases turned on the inability of those claiming the custom to plead such presumptive immemoriality. Thus, in the eighteenth-century case of *Cole v. Hawkins*,[52] the court refused to find in favor of an alleged custom because "... it ought to have been averred, that they have from time out of mind repaired, &c., ..." and so there was a failure to plead a necessary element to establish a custom.

Equally as fatal to a claim of customary rights – and less curable – is a failure of proof. An example of relatively strict construction of this requirement of proof comes from the 1845 case of *Lockwood v. Wood*,[53] an action for non-payment of stallage fees for setting up stalls in a rural market. To the claim that inhabitants of Easingwold were exempt from such fees by immemorial custom, the court responded that in absence of proof that there was a market at the locus in question prior to 1639, the presumption of immemoriality must fail. Similarly in the 1872 case of *Simpson v. Wells*,[54] the court failed to find a custom for lack of immemoriality. There, appellant was charged with obstructing a public footpath by erecting a stall for the sale of refreshments at a statute sessions for the hiring of servants. The defendant claimed that such a right by custom was the same as at a fair. However, the court noted that such statute sessions commenced by statute during the reign of Edward III, well after 1189 and therefore "these meetings were not from time immemorial; and there is no more reason for saying it is a legal custom to put up stalls of refreshments on the highway at these meetings than at the assizes or quarter sessions, which usually cause an assemblage of people. Therefore there could not be such a custom, as there could not be any legal origin of it."[55]

Often, claims of custom failed when the court claimed the original showing of ancient usage was successfully rebutted by those with an interest in the affected land. In *Payne v. Ecclesiastical Commissioners and Landon*,[56] the tenants on copy-hold land in a manor showed that they had since 1599 asserted a custom to fish in certain waters within the manor, and that parole evidence supported their claim. However, the court found that much of the exercise had been over the protests of the lord of the manor and that a 1599 document showed conclusively that there was no such custom at that time. Therefore, the court "had come to the conclusion that the plaintiff had failed to prove the existence of an immemorial usage."[57] Again in a 1907 case, *Lord Fitzhardinge v. Purcell*,[58] the court found against alleged trespassers who claimed the right to go upon certain foreshores for the purpose of shooting wild ducks under a custom of the manor because, although there was evidence of a custom in some parts of the river to fish under certain conditions, ". . . the evidence as to the places where the custom prevailed was vague, and there was no proof of the exercise of the custom after the reign of James I."[59]

4.3.2 Continuity

> It must have been continued. Any interruption would cause a temporary ceasing: the revival gives it a new beginning, which will be within time of memory, and thereupon the custom will be void. But this must be understood with regard to an interruption of the right; for an interruption of the possession only, for ten or twenty years, will not destroy the custom.

> As if I have a right of way by custom over another's field, the custom is not destroyed, though I do not pass over it for ten years; it only becomes more difficult to prove: but if the right be any how discontinued for a day, the custom is quite at an end.
>
> (Blackstone, *Commentaries*, at 77)

This is perhaps one of the more difficult of Blackstone's criteria to establish from the cases, particularly of Blackstone's time, because it does not appear to have arisen apart from the extensive previous discussion of immemoriality. Nevertheless, it does appear that the continuity to which Blackstone refers, much like the law of easements, is one of right and not of usage. Certainly this is so by the twentieth century, as the discussion that follows demonstrates.

Though Blackstone cites no cases in his *Commentaries* for this criterion, it was established at least a century and a half before he wrote, that continuity was a requirement in the 1608 *Tanistry* case.[60] Continuity could be broken by a number of means. Thus, in the 1819 case of *Duke of Norfolk v. Myers*,[61] the question was whether a custom to grind corn at certain mills was sufficiently interrupted in continuity by a change to steam and other mechanical means, from water and horse mills, to void the custom and so excuse the defendant from bringing his corn to the mills of the Duke. While it appeared there were no cases so holding, the chancellor decided the question was one of law and so he sent the parties on their way. Earlier in the 1752 case of *Drake v. Wigglesworth*,[62] another corn-grinding mill case, the court decided that, while unity of possession (the land of the grinder and the land of the mill) might destroy a custom, there could be no such unity in this case. This principle is set out more clearly in the 1918 case of *Derry v. Sanders*[63] in which the defendant was charged with trespass for crossing the plaintiff's land, to which he defended that he was using a customary access way or path, and that such right of way had been used for over eighty years. While the judge indicated that "I regret the result,"[64] nevertheless the decision by Scrutton, LJ, found against the defendant and the customary right of way. Among the bases for the court's finding no customary right of way was end of continuity:

> a right of way by long usage between tenements part of a manor cannot be claimed by prescription, but must be claimed by custom of the manor, and if rights claimed by the custom of the manor are extinguished by enfranchisement unless expressly reserved or regranted, it will follow that the deed of enfranchisement in this case, whether the parties intended it or not, extinguished the customary right of way.[65]

In this case, the lord of the manor destroyed the copyhold tenure and created a freehold tenure by regrant, though in effect only releasing his rights as lord. Nevertheless, the manorial relationship upon which the right of way by custom depended was severed, the custom interrupted, and unless part of the regrant, it was destroyed.

Less arcane and perhaps more compelling of the older cases is the 1865 case of *Gavi v. Martyn.*[66] Here, tin miners had artificially brought water to the surface of certain lands for the purpose of "streaming" their tin. Plaintiff claimed the same water by prescription. The court held that whereas it was possible to obtain such a right by prescription, there was not a sufficient claim "of right" as the rights of the tin miners were established by custom of the county of Cornwall "and the miners had not permanently abandoned their right of control over the water in the stream when the plaintiff diverted it by the upper launder to his works."[67]

This matter of purposeful abandonment is particularly significant. Indeed, one of the more fascinating of the cases dealing with customary rights turns to a large extent on abandonment of a customary right, or the lack thereof. In the 1870 case of *Warrick v. Queens College, Oxford,*[68] freehold tenants of certain manors held by Queens College sued to restrain the college from enclosing certain nearby open space, leasing it to the government for artillery practice, and the building of buildings thereon. The basis of the suit for injunctive relief was the collection of common rights the plaintiffs claimed in the open space of that portion of the manors (the three common areas being Shoulder of Mutton Green, Plumstead Common and Bostal Heath) particularly to pasture cattle levant and couchant, feed geese and ducks, cut wood, hay and turf, and walk, drive and ride upon the commons for exercise and recreation. While the court found substantial evidence that several commoners, due to persuasion, threat and other means, had ceased exercising their common rights, it also found that where the lord has attempted to stop the user of a common, the fact that some of the tenants have yielded to such attempts was not an interruption of the right within the meaning of statutes defining interruption. As a consequence, what customary rights remained were sufficiently continuous to be upheld. Therefore the plaintiff commoners were entitled to their injunction.[69]

The relatively modern 1962 case of *Wyld v. Silver*[70] illustrates most conclusively the Blackstonian doctrine on this point: interruption of use does not equate with interruption of the right, which would end the custom. Based on custom, plaintiffs sought a declaration that as inhabitants of a parish, they were entitled to hold an annual fair on a plot of land acquired by defendant, and that the defendant was not entitled to disturb the soil or erect any building on it, ordering the defendant to remove what buildings and structures he had erected. Holding that the plaintiffs had shown their rights still existed, the court granted the injunction against the defendants. To the claim that the rights had long since been abandoned, Lord Denning, MR, held:

> True it is that no fair or wake has been held there within living memory. But no matter. They have a right, they say, to hold it on this piece of land . . . Needless to say, after so long a period of disuse, the inhabitants must establish their right with clearness and certainty, but I must say they have done it . . . [their proof] clearly show the right of the inhabitants, and there is no reason to suppose they have lost it. I know of no way in which the inhabitants of a parish can lose a right of this kind once they have acquired it except by Act of Parliament. Mere disuse will not do. And I do not see how they can waive it or abandon it. No one or more of the inhabitants can waive or abandon it on behalf of the others. Nor can all the present inhabitants waive or abandon it on behalf of future generations. . . . In my judgment, therefore, the inhabitants of Wraysbury still have the right to hold a fair or wake on this piece of land on the Friday in Whitsun week.[71]

Indeed, as the court above suggests, the issue of proof is often the most difficult in establishing continuity, as it once was in establishing immemorial usage. However, once the obstacle is overcome, courts have on occasion been generous in finding customary rights. Thus, in the 1840 case of *Scales v. Key*,[72] a custom found to exist in 1689 was held good, even though it had not been exercised for 150 years. On the other hand, the court in *Hammerton v. Honey*[73] found a strong presumption against custom when an alleged custom is unexercised for many years, and that lack of use is acquiesced in by those alleged to be entitled to that exercise.

The use of customary rights like the above to prevent use and development of the freehold is an increasingly common pattern, as we shall see in the sections which follow. As is apparent from the preceding discussion, English courts are willing to enforce such customary rights, but demand strict proof that they exist.

4.3.3 Peacefulness

> It must have been peaceable, and acquiesced in; not subject to contention and dispute. For as customs owe their origin to common consent, their

> being immemorially disputed either at law or otherwise is a proof that such consent was wanting.
>
> (Blackstone, *Commentaries*, at 77)

The criterion of peacefulness, like continuity, arises less often than the other criteria in reported cases. Blackstone cites none whatsoever in his discussion, though he does cite Coke on Littleton as with virtually all of the criteria.[74] Indeed, the issue of peacefulness appears most often to arise in the negative. Thus, in the 1913 case of *Payne v. the Ecclesiastical Commissioners and Landon*,[75] tenants of a manor asserted a customary right to fish in a particular area or messuage. After noting that the tenants had to establish, *inter alia*, that they had enjoyed the custom from time immemorial and that the usage was reasonable, the court noted "the continual protest by the lord or the farmer when the tenants asserted the custom."[76] The court held ("not without regret") that the custom failed for want of immemoriality as well, apparently, as peaceability.

On the other hand, the court in the 1863 case of *Wake v. Hall*[77] upheld mining customs, even though expanded to reflect modern machinery usage, in part because the "alleged ancient right, springs from unquestioned immemorial customs . . . [and] does not appear to have ever, before the present occasion, been the subject of controversy or litigation."[78] Again in *Warrick v. Queen's College, Oxford*[79] discussed in the previous section, in noting the recent attempts by the landowner to keep tenants from asserting their commoner rights, the court said: "But these are not sufficient to invalidate what appear to be the continued and uncontested rights of the freehold tenants . . . which, as I have said, I never find to have been contested until the year 1860."[80]

4.3.4 *Reasonableness*

> Customs must be reasonable; or rather, taken negatively, they must not be unreasonable. Which is not always, as Sir Edward Coke says, to be understood of every unlearned man's reason, but of artificial and legal reason, warranted by authority of a law. Upon which account a custom may be good, though the particular reason of it cannot be assigned; for it sufficeth, if no good legal reason can be assigned against it. Thus, a custom in a parish, that no man shall put his beasts into the common till the third of October, would be good; and yet it would be hard to shew the reason why that day in particular is fixed upon, rather than the day before or after. But a custom that no cattle shall be put in till the lord of the manor has first put in his, is

> unreasonable, and therefore bad: for peradventure the lord will never put in his; and then the tenants will lose all their profits.
>
> (Blackstone, *Commentaries*, at 77)

The criterion of reasonableness arises nearly as often as immemoriality and certainty. Indeed, the issue of reasonableness sometimes arose in the manorial courts in the fourteenth century. Thus in the Littleport Court Leet held on December 11, 1325,[81] Henry Sweetgroom mowed quite a lot of sedge beyond the "appointed quantity" in violation of the following custom, resulting in forfeit of the price of the sedge to the lord of the manor:

> whereas by the custom of the vill every tenant of a full-land and every freeholder holding as much as a full-land may mow in the fen for his sustenance to the amount of 6,000 of sedge, but so nevertheless that neither free nor bond can nor ought to give or sell of this without first obtaining the lord's leave or making fine to the lord, and if any free or bond man of the vill shall mow beyond this fixed and established number he shall give for each thousand 32d. to the lord and to the men of the vill for the repair of the church, so they say, in equal portions [i.e. one such portion to the lord, one to the men]. And for that neither free nor bond have any specialty from the lord, nor show any record by reason whereof the custom which they allege ought to be allowed them, therefore all the sedge which has been mown beyond the fixed and established quantity and which [superfluous amount] is presented below, shall remain to the lord as forfeited until etc.[82]

It is also the most difficult of the criteria to consistently establish in the reported cases. Its critical importance is best set out in *Arthur v. Bockenham*,[83] a dispute over an alleged custom permitting the devise of certain property acquired after the making of a will. With respect to reasonableness, the court set out the basis for sharply restricting custom, even more than acts of parliament, because of their detrimental effect on common law:

> all customs, which are against the common law of England, ought to be taken strictly, nay very strictly, even stricter than any Act of Parliament that alters the common law. It is a general rule, that customs are not to be enlarged beyond the usage; because it is the usage and practice that makes the law in such cases, and not the reason of the thing, for it cannot be said that a custom is founded on reason, though an unreasonable custom is void; for no reason, even the highest whatsoever, would make a custom or law; so it is no particular reason that makes any custom law, but the usage and practice itself, without regard had to any reason of such usage; and therefore

> you cannot enlarge such custom by any parity of reason, since reason has no part in the making of such custom. Now in the construction of Acts of Parliament it is otherwise, and there is a greater latitude allowed in them; and the reason that induced the law-makers to make such Acts to take away the common law, may be and is usually urged in making construction of them. There in doubtful cases we may enlarge the construction of Acts of Parliament according to the reason and sense of the law-makers expressed in other parts of the Act, or guessed, by considering the frame and design of the whole. But it is not so in the case of a custom, because not founded on any particular reason.[84]

Certainly, as both Coke and Blackstone suggest, reasonableness cannot depend solely on whether it appears reasonable to the freeholder or owner whose land is burdened with the exercise of a customary right, say, of common or passage, to have such a burden on his land, though there are cases that clearly hold that too much interference with that land will make the alleged custom void for unreasonableness. Certainly, reasonableness also means reasonable as a matter of law. But there are many variants in between, as appears below.

The criterion of reasonableness is not only one of the most common ones raised in cases dealing with custom,[85] but it is one of the earliest. Well before Blackstone wrote his commentaries, English courts were struggling with the concept and declaring customs bad because unreasonable. The earliest of these appears to be the 1401 yearbook case of *Miles v. Benet*,[86] which is almost certainly the source of Blackstone's example in his *Commentaries*. The alleged custom, that tenants should not put beasts into the common before the lord of the manor, was held void because the lord might not put in his beasts at all and thereby bar the commoners' rights for all time. This helped establish the principle that a custom that subjects a multitude to the whim of an individual is bad and unreasonable.[87]

Another often-cited case is the 1577 *Salforde's Case*[88] declaring a custom that a tenant in fee may only lease for six years was bad: ". . . this custom is void because against common reason, and the freedom of the estate of one who hath the fee simple."[89]

Again in 1590, in *Devered v. Ratcliffe*,[90] a custom that was contrary to established judicial procedure in a criminal matter was declared "not good, and the custom unreasonable."[91] To the same effect is the 1599 case of *Paramour v. Verall & Auters*,[92] in which an outrageous supposed custom of the City of London to arrest any citizen of the City for the debt of any particular citizen was held unreasonable and void. Equally outrageous was the custom of the manor in the 1599 case of *Parker v. Combleford*,[93] in which the lord took the horse of a stranger who died within the manor as heriot. While willing to uphold the custom as applied to those living on the manor, the court held that to apply it to a stranger amounted to a forfeiture of goods without reasonable compensation. On the other hand, in the 1594 case of *Jackman v. Hoddeston*,[94] the court found a custom to be reasonable under which the lord of the manor seized the lands of those who owed fines until such fines were paid, though the custom eventually failed for want of immemoriality. Likewise in the 1594 case of *Yielding v. Fay*,[95] the court upheld as "good and reasonable" a quaint custom requiring the rector of the parish to keep a bull and a boar "for the common use of the kine and sows of the parishioners at any time . . . for the increase of calves and pigs within the said parish,"[96] apparently on the ground that it was supported by parishioner tithes.

As indicated in the introduction to this section, Coke had quite a lot to say about reasonableness as a criterion for good custom, for which Blackstone cited him. Coke early on established that reasonableness of custom is a question of law, for the court, and not a question of fact, for a jury, in the 1612 case of *Rowles v. Mason*.[97] There, the custom alleged was that a copyhold tenant may cut down all the trees on his land and sell them. After distinguishing custom from prescriptive rights, Coke declared the custom "against common reason, incongruent and against common law, that a copy-holder for life may cut and sell the trees and custom ought to have reason and congruence."[98] There follow several examples of customs that would be bad because contrary to the law of estates as, for example, turbury attached to land rather than to a house.

Certainly one of Coke's more fulsome explanations of reasonableness comes in the 1614 case of *Hix v. Gardiner*.[99] The custom challenged was one of mill-suit, requiring inhabitants of a manor to use the lord's mill alone for the grinding of their grain. One of the grounds for the challenge was that the reason for the custom had not been pleaded, nor was it in evidence. Coke responded: "if no reason can be given, for the beginning of this, or of any other custom, yet *non sequitur*, this custom to be for this cause unreasonable, and against reason in the beginning of it, for that for some things no reason can be given."[100] As Coke observed earlier in the opinion, the inheritance customs of borough English and gavelkinde, both contrary to the common law principle of male primogenitor (oldest son inherits) "are no reasonable customs, the reason to be shewed of the beginning of them is impossible"[101] and yet they are upheld. Clearly Coke was of the opinion that the original reason for the custom was, other things equal, irrelevant.

Not so with respect to the reasonableness of the custom as applied, a distinction which Blackstone also makes. In the same year, 1614, Coke decided *Hill v. Hanks*,[102] an action for trover and conversion, in which the bell-man (town crier) by custom claimed the right to take a certain toll on grain, which the owner, challenging his right, now sought to reclaim. Observing that the case would be decided on the strength of the validity of the custom, "if the custome here be good, he may then take, and covert where he [bell-man] will"[103] Coke then observed that "they which do repair bridges, and cawsweys, may have toll by prescription; and so for murage, and pontage, the King may grant by his letters patents, to have a charge and imposition laid, but this ought to be *pro bono publico*, and also proportionable and so is 3E.3 if for murage, or pontage, to have an imposition, assessed upon the subjects, because they have the benefit of it."[104] Based on these examples, the reciprocity and public good demonstrated here, Coke then declared:

> I am very clear of the opinion, that the custome here is good, and it is also the more reasonable, because it is here in his plea expressed, that he [the bell-man] had paved the streets, and if the custom is good, then the taking is good, and if the taking here be good, then by this the property [the grain toll] is in him, and not in the plaintiff, and so no trover to be brought by him [the plaintiff].[105]

Several cases from the late seventeenth century follow Coke's lead with respect to reasonableness, particularly with respect to what is good for the public and also providing a reciprocity of advantage. Thus, for example, in the 1691 case of *Simpson v. Bithwood*,[106] a custom for the lord of the manor to take anchor and cable of ships cast on his land, in consideration for burying the dead and caring for survivors, was held good: "so the custom here is for the encouragement and safety of navigation; and although it be a charity, yet it is not unreasonable to have a recompense for a man's charity and charge."[107]

Again in the 1698 case of *Weekly v. Wildman*[108] the custom of all inhabitants of a town to have common for all commonable cattle was held unreasonable and so bad, because there was no limit to the number of cattle that could be turned loose on the land in question and the plaintiff had not given any reason why such a surcharge of the common would be good. The case came up in an interesting fashion. The defendant "had erected an engine by which he cast the water upon the said fen, more than could be carried off by the drains of the said fen, whereby the said fen was drowned, so that the plaintiff could not enjoy his common in so full and beneficial a manner as he ought."[109] Finally the 1690 case of *Pain v. Patrick*[110] follows the Coke analysis with respect to reasonableness and lawful beginnings in upholding a right-of-way by custom.

4.3.4.1 Unreasonable effect on land over which alleged custom is practiced

Although the older cases discussed above often dealt with such as tolls, inheritance and criminal procedures, it is under this criterion of reasonableness that the courts came to grips most often with the adverse effect on private property that the exercise of customary rights will likely have. This is particularly true of the cases that arose during Blackstone's time (middle of the eighteenth century), and shortly thereafter. Although the case turned as much on the issue of certainty (discussed in the next section) the 1742 mining case of *Broadbent v. Wilks*[111] is an excellent example of a Blackstone-era case in which the court could not abide the unreasonableness of the custom. The custom alleged:

> where the customary tenant of a manor has coal mines lying under the freehold lands of other customary tenants, within and parcel of the manor, he may sink pits in those lands to get the coals &c., may lay the coals when got and the earth and rubbish &c. on the land near to such pits, such lands being customary tenements and parcel of the manor, there to remain and continue (not saying how long, or for a convenient time), may lay and continue wood there for the necessary use of the pits, may take away carts and waggons part (not saying how much) of the coals, and burn and make into cinders the other parts there at his will and pleasure.[112]

The court declared this to be an unreasonable and void custom:

> And certainly no custom can be more unreasonable than the present. It may deprive the tenant of the whole profits of the land; for the lord or his tenants may dig coal-pits when and as often as they please, and may in such case lay their coals &c. on any part of the tenant's land, if near to such coal-pits, at what time of the year they please, and may let them there as long as they please . . . So that they may be laid on the tenant's land and continue there forever . . . which is absurd and unreasonable. The objection that this custom is only beneficial to the lord and greatly prejudicial to the tenants is, we think, of no weight, for it might have a reasonable commencement notwithstanding, for the lord might take less for the land on the account of this disadvantage to his tenant. But the true objections to this custom are, that it is uncertain and likewise unreasonable, as it may deprive the tenant of the whole benefit of the land, and it cannot be presumed that the tenant at first would come into such an agreement.[113]

The decision was sustained in 1745 in *Wilkes v. Broadbent*,[114] with particular emphasis on the great burden on private land without any noticeable public or private consideration.

The burdening of private lands with custom continued to be a fertile ground for litigation shortly after the last editions of Blackstone were published. In the 1818 case of *R v. Inhabitants of Ecclesfield*,[115] the alleged custom was for parishioners to repair a road in another parish. Citing both Blackstone and Coke, Lord Ellenborough held the custom to be unreasonable in part because "There cannot be a custom in one place to do something in another. The land in a particular place, and the inhabitants in respect thereof, may be charged by custom, for matters within the place; but custom will not apply to matters out of it" (citing Coke's *Gatewards Case* decision).[116]

Finally, another case of Blackstone's time, the 1752 case of *Drake v. Wigglesworth*,[117] picks up the theme of mutuality of consideration in yet another corn grinding dispute. The alleged custom was that all householders of the parish should grind all their corn used by them, within the parish, paying to the grinder a reasonable toll. Citing Coke and mutuality of consideration, the court found the custom good.

The unusually burdensome effect on the land over or on which it is exercised continued to be a ground for overturning customary rights into the nineteenth century. In the 1837 case of *Bastard v. Smith*[118] discussed earlier under immemoriality, Chief Justice Tindal instructed the jury as follows, with respect to the Devonshire custom for tin miners to direct water into their mines:

> . . . touching the unreasonableness of the custom, though you are not called on to say whether this be a reasonable custom or not (for that is a matter of law, not submitted by the present pleadings to your decision), still you may properly thus far look to the nature of the custom that, if you find it greatly affecting the rights of private property, you may fairly expect and require that it should be supported by evidence proportionably strong and convincing. You are not to come to the conclusion that inhabitants of a large district, like that over which the supposed custom extends, surrendered their rights over their own soil, unless you find repeated acts of exercise of the custom on the one hand, and of acquiescence on the other.[119]

The early twentieth century case of *Mercer v. Denne*[120] upheld the custom of the inhabitants of a parish (fishermen) to use a piece of land covered with shingle to spread and dry their nets as in favor of navigation.

The court permitted the exercise of the custom to change with the times so long as the burden on the landowner was not unreasonable:

> The tanning, cutching or oiling of nets [new] belonging to fishermen tend to preserve the nets and make them useful for a longer period, and the subsequent drying of nets seems to me to fall within the reasons thus assigned for the custom. It is laid down by Holt, J. in City of London v. Vanacre [a late seventeenth-century case][121] that "general customs may be extended to new things which are within the reason of those customs." There is not, in my opinion, evidence from which it ought to be inferred that the practice of tanning or cutching has arisen within the time of legal memory. But it was said that, so far as related to the drying after oiling, the use has extended over a period of from twenty-five to thirty-five years only, and, moreover, that this user was more burdensome than the old user for drying after tanning or cutching. I think, however, that the law as laid down by Lord St. Leonards in *Dyce v. Hay* cited by Farwell J., applies, and that those who are entitled to the benefit of a custom ought not to be deprived of that benefit simply because they take advantage of modern inventions or new operations so long as they do not thereby throw an unreasonable burden on the landowner.[122]

Again, "It must not be forgotten that the persons claiming under the custom are bound to exercise their rights reasonably and with due regard to the interest of the owner of the soil."[123] According to Falwell, J., in the court below (1904) reasonableness is determined at the inception of a custom and it is no objection that it may at times have been used in an unreasonable manner.[124] His opinion represents a good early-twentieth-century view of the limitations and requirements of custom.[125]

Perhaps there is no better example of language requiring the protection of underlying property rights than the 1847 case of *Rogers v. Brenton.*[126] Cornish tin miners claimed by custom to be able to renew their claims by renewing boundary posts, without actually working the tin mine. Although the court appeared to hold the renewal unreasonable without actual working of the mine, Lord Denman held tin bounding generally reasonable, only because there was a benefit to the public:

> Customs, especially where they derogate from the general rights of property, must be construed strictly; and above all things they must be reasonable. Bounding is a direct interference with the common law rights of property. It takes from the owner of land, who is unable or unwilling at a particular moment to dig for tin under his waste land, the right to do so, it may be

> forever, and vests it in a stranger, making only a customary render in return: it empowers the stranger not only to extract the mineral from beneath the surface but to enter on the surface and cumber it with the machinery, buildings and refuse stuff which the operations below occasion; and all this without the least regard to the convenience or interests of the owner. The only things which make this reasonable are the render of the toll tin to the owner and the benefit to the public secured thereby in the extraction of the mineral from the bowels of the earth. Both of these are not only lost, but the latter, it may be, positively prevented, if the bounder may decline to work, and yet retain the right to exclude the owner.[127]

Often the issue of customary rights and protection of land arose with respect to support of the surface of the earth. Thus, in the 1862 case of *Blackett v. Bradley & Others*,[128] "from time immemorial . . . the lord and his assigns had been used and accustomed as of right to search for, win and work the mines under the commons without leaving any support for the lands under which the mines were situate, and without making any satisfaction for any injury caused by such working."[129] The custom was held void as unreasonable on the strength of a previous case.[130]

The same line of reasoning is apparent in the 1867 case of *Wakefield v. Duke of Buccleuch*.[131] Here, the alleged custom was to let down the surface in mining operations without paying compensation to the surface owner. The court declared the custom unreasonable in light of the common law right of support, citing several enclosure cases.

In the 1881 case of *Davis v. Trehane*,[132] the court struck down an alleged custom to work mines in such a manner as to "let down" or otherwise injure the surface. To the argument that this was mining "in the usual and most approved way" in Glamorgan, the court said:

> But what does that mean? It refers simply to the mode of carrying on the underground works in the mine; which cannot by possibility, either in the county of Glamorgan, or anywhere, be a custom, or manner, of working, without regard to the rights of other persons . . . [these words] have no reference to the rights of other persons, which there could not possibly be any local custom in such a district as a county to disregard, and which must be respected in carrying out these works.[133]

This line of reasoning is repeated in the twentieth century in *Wolstanton, Ltd. v. Newcastle-Under-Lyme Borough Council*.[134] An alleged custom of mining, which caused subsidence and damage to neighboring land and buildings, was held unreasonable, again citing *Hilton v. Earl of Granville*.[135]

After setting out requirements for a custom (a lot about immemoriality here):

> I find it very difficult, if not impossible, to hold that a custom for the lord to get minerals beneath the surface of copyhold or customary freehold lands without making compensation for subsidence and damage to buildings is a reasonable custom while accepting the view that a custom for the lord and his tenants of collieries to lay rubbish in heaps on the copyhold land near the pits [citing Broadbent, above] is unreasonable. In either case, the lands of a copyholder might be made practically useless, although they would still be liable . . . to pay their rents and perform their stipulated services to the lord.[136]

4.3.4.2 Unreasonable contrary to major common law principle/natural justice

Reasonableness also arises as a basis for finding a custom "bad" because it contravenes some basic principle of law often expressed as a great common law principle. This is not easy to reconcile with the basic proposition respecting custom, that a custom is by nature in derogation of some common law principle: often the right of the landowner or holder of superior rights in land to exclude others, the case often arising on an action for trespass. Not surprisingly, the cases that find a custom bad on these grounds often involve inheritance, procedures or otherwise arise in some factual context other than the use of land.

Thus, for example, in the fourteenth-century case of *R v. City of London*[137] the court held that the mayor and aldermen of London could not by custom of the city declare persons outlaws, because this was the prerogative of the King or, by special mandate, his justices. Not only was there evidence that the mayor and citizens were not following their own procedures, but also "such a custom is contrary to the law and custom of the realm."[138] Eight years later, the court in *The King v. Nicholas of Chanceux*[139] declared certain customary tolls and franchises unreasonable as benefiting an individual to the prejudice of the multitude: "The law will not allow any usage that is to the common damage of the people. The longer such a usage has been maintained the greater the wrong, and the more you will be charged to the king for profits taken by reason of the usage."[140]

Again in the 1614 case of *Needler v. Bishop of Winchester*,[141] the court found bad a custom enabling a married woman to convey land without a separate examination because it deprived favoured persons in law of the kind of protection given them by the common law against the consequences of undue influence or folly.[142] In this vein, London trade customs were often found to be unreasonable as against great common law principles or principles of natural justice. In the 1596 case of *Byrd v. Wilford*,[143] a custom having to do with the holding of bonds was upheld as reasonable. But in the 1614 case of *Day v. Savadge*[144] a custom allowing a matter to proceed by jury certificate, rather than by jury in accordance with the customs of London, was held void as against principles of natural justice. Also in the later seventeenth-century case of *Lewis v. Masters*,[145] the court found a custom of London that permitted the creditor of an intestate to attach money in the hands of a debtor to the intestate before letters of administration were granted, to be bad: "[per Holt, C. J.] It is one thing if a custom be different from the law, and another thing if it be repugnant . . . there can be no custom to support this case; for customs that overthrow the principles of law, and which are unreasonable, are to be rejected."[146]

In Blackstone's time, such unreasonableness is apparently the reason for declaring a custom bad in the 1746 case of *Richards v. Dovey*.[147] There, an alleged custom for a parishioner who marries in a different parish to pay a fee to the rector of his home parish was held unreasonable and void. Again in the 1777 case of *Fisher v. Lane*[148] the court held a custom whereby in the case of an administrator, a debt due to the intestate could be attached by foreign attachment by custom of the city of London, unreasonable because:

> Customs of particular cities may deviate from the course of the common law, but a custom contrary to the first principles of justice can never be good; so this custom not to summon or give notice to a defendant in a suit commenced against him is contrary to the first principles of justice and (in my opinion as presently advised) cannot be good.[149]

Contrary to natural justice was the rationale of the court in striking down as unreasonable court process in the 1867 case of *London Corpn. v. Cox*.[150] Citing and quoting copiously from older opinions, the court noted repeatedly the unreasonableness of the custom. Finally in the 1908 case of *Johnson v. Clark*,[151] the court held bad a local custom permitting a married woman to dispose of real estate held in her name and with the consent of her husband, without her separate examination and acknowledgement (i.e., by signature only):

> It is quite clear that in the case of copyholds a custom for a married woman, with the concurrence of her husband, to surrender her interest, after

separate examination before the lord or the steward of the manor or his deputy, or even before two tenants of the manors, is a good custom . . . There appears, however, to be no authority in favour of a custom for a married woman to dispose of any interest in realty, even with her husband's concurrence, without some separate examination . . . On the other hand, there are two authorities which clearly contain an expression of judicial opinion against the validity of such a custom [citing *Needler v. Bishop of Winchester* and *George v. Jew*) . . . Looking at the matter apart from express authority, it is quite clear that for a custom to be good it must be reasonable or, at any rate, not unreasonable. [The court then discusses Coke's concept of reasonableness] . . . If this be so, it appears to follow that a custom to be valid must be such that, in the opinion of a trained lawyer, it is inconsistent, or, at any rate, not inconsistent, with those general principles which, quite apart from particular rules or maxims, lie at the root of our legal system. Thus a custom which is for the advantage of an industry or trade may be good, although it bear hardly on the individual; while, on the other hand, a custom which is for the advantage of an individual only and is prejudicial to the public, or a class of the public, is bad; for the common law, in principle, imposes obligations on the individual for the benefit of the public, and not on the public for the benefit of the individual . . . If I have correctly stated the test of reasonableness in connection with the doctrine that a custom to be valid must be reasonable, or, at any rate, not unreasonable, it is evident the test cannot be applied to the custom alleged without considering the principles underlying the common law so far as it relates to the capacity of married women. [The court then discusses the policies for protecting married women, whose husbands might otherwise take advantage of them]

. . . I have come to the conclusion, therefore, that the alleged custom cannot be upheld, because it is unreasonable, as conflicting with the general principle of the common law that an exercise of free will was essential to alienations and contracts, and that a married woman was not in a position to exercise such free will. Such a custom would, in other words, be against "common right."[152]

4.3.4.3 And all the rest

There are, of course, dozens of additional cases dealing with the reasonableness of a custom. What follows is a brief catalogue of situations in which the court found the custom unreasonable and so void, and in which courts have upheld customs against the claim that they were in some way unreasonable.

Disputes relating to common lands are a fruitful source of customary practices, and many of the results turn on reasonableness. In the 1620 case of *Barker v. Cocker*,[153] the court found that a local custom in Somerset, that the vicar of a parish could take every tenth lamb born in the parish, without regard to ownership, ". . . unreasonable, and against law, for by this means it might fall out, that some one might have but one lamb, and that might be taken for tythe, and he that had more should pay nothing at all."[154] Sometimes public benefit saves what might otherwise be a void custom. Thus, in the 1684 case of *Linn-Regis Corpn. v. Taylor*,[155] the custom of freemen and shipowners to dig gravel in the shore for ballast for their ships without paying the mayor of the city was held good: "But by the whole Court the custom here is good, it being for the maintenance of navigation, and so *pro bono publico*; and a custom is *lex loci*, and inherent in the soil whereto it is fixed for the service of every one that is qualified to use it."[156]

Unreasonableness in Blackstone's time is well-illustrated by the 1740 case of *Bell v. Wardell*.[157] A custom for all the inhabitants of a town, to walk and ride over a close of arable land at all seasonable times of the year, was held unreasonable because it was often exercised so as to trample corn planted there, even though the exercise was "seasonable" in one sense. In the corn-grinding 1616 case of *Harbin & Uxor v. Green*,[158] the court held unreasonable, and so bad, a custom of a bishopric that all inhabitants, resident of the city, must grind their corn at his mills, no matter how they acquired the corn:

> first, that the custom it self was unreasonable, for the reason and use of such a custom is, that the corn that a man doth grind, he should grind there, and not elsewhere . . . But the fault here is, that by this custom if a man buy corn, he cannot sell it again in corn in his house, for he must first grind it at these mills.[159]

In another of the corn-grinding cases, the court in the 1670 case of *Coriton and Harvey v. Lithby*[160] found an alleged custom for the tenants of a manor to grind all the corn spent in their houses was declared unreasonable, and so bad, "for a great deal of corn is used which is not proper to grind."[161]

Predictably, the question of reasonableness arose often in Blackstone's day, in a more general fashion than the categories discussed above. Thus in the 1779 case of *Cort v. Birbeck*,[162] yet another corn grindings case, the court upheld the following custom as reasonable:

> all the tenants, inhabitants, and residents, within the manor "ought to have ground, and still ought to grind, all their corn, grain and malt, which by them or any of them had been or should be used or spent ground within

the manor, at the plaintiff's mills, and not elsewhere, and to have paid and yielded, and to pay and yield to the plaintiff for the grinding thereof certain reasonable toll and multure!."[163]

Lord Mansfield, speaking for the court, upheld the custom on the ground that the tenants all agreed it applied only to corn grown within the manor:

When we heard this argued, a doubt arose on the extent of the custom, whether it goes only to corn growing in the manor, and ground there, or to all ground corn wherever it may grow, which is consumed within the manor. But it appears from the answers in the suit in the Exchequer (which his Lordship read,) that the defendants then insisted on the restrained sense, and that they were not bound to grind corn which grew out of the manor of Settle mills; and the decree established the custom to the extent now insisted upon, and proves it to be reasonable.[164]

Likewise the amount of the toll charged for such grinding was held a reasonable part of the custom in the 1817 case of *Gard v. Callard.*[165] All of the inhabitants of the borough of Modbury that brewed ale were by custom to grind at the plaintiff's mill and to pay him a certain toll. As to the amount of the toll the court held that under the circumstances and facts of the case, there was "cogent evidence that it was reasonable."[166]

Again in the 1755 case of *Fryer v. Johnson,*[167] the court found as unreasonable "a custom in the parish, time out of mind, that every parishioner has a right to bury his dead relations in the church-yard as near to their ancestors as possible, and the defendant refused to permit the plaintiff to bury a relation as near as possible to his ancestor."[168] The court held it both unreasonable and uncertain since the term was too vague as to nearness.

A twist on unreasonableness comes in the unreasonable exercise of a lawful custom in the 1797 case of *Fitch v. Fitch.*[169] There, the custom was for all the inhabitants of the parish of Steeple Bumstead to play at all times of the year, at all kinds of lawful games and pastimes on a certain close. While the court upheld the custom in a suit for trespass by some of the inhabitants, the court made an excellent statement about the reciprocal rights of the parties:

The custom appears to be established. The inhabitants had a right to take their amusement in a lawful way. It is supposed, that because they have such a right, the plaintiff should not allow the grass to grow. There is no foundation in law for such a position. The rights of both parties are distinct, and may exist together. If the inhabitants come in an unlawful way, or not

> fairly to exercise the right they claim of amusing themselves, or to use it in an improper way, they are not justified under the custom pleaded, which is a right to come to the close to use it in the exercise of any lawful games or pastimes, and are thereby trespassers. His Lordship therefore left it to the jury to say, whether the defendant had entered the close in the fair exercise of a right, or in an improper way.[170]

As the inhabitants had trampled on fresh-mown hay, threw it about and mixed gravel with it, the court found they had acted in an unlawful way, an unreasonable exercise of a lawful custom. Still, in the related case of *Fitch v. Rawlings*,[171] the court found the custom itself reasonable.

Finally, in the 1746 case of *Richards v. Dovey*,[172] the court held that a parish custom for every man inhabiting one parish who marries by license in another to pay a fee to the rector of the first parish is bad as unreasonable.

These principles carried forward into the nineteenth century. Some cases turn on how reasonable the present exercise of a custom might be today, particularly in terms of fees and payments. Thus, in the 1856 case of *Traherne v. Gardner*,[173] the court held certain fees payable by tenants for admission to their freeholds to be "monstrously excessive" and in derogation of copyhold law but was not prepared to say it could not be maintained if properly "made out," though it was not in this case.[174] However, the court had no such scruples about holding bad a similar custom in the 1868 case of *Bryant v. Foot*.[175] The court found that, considering the difference in the value of money in 1189 and 1868, an equivalent payment at this time would be unreasonable:

> In this case the question is whether 13s. is a legal fee or accustomed duty payable on the celebration of a marriage in the parish of Horton . . . it may be due if immemorially paid, that is to say, from the time of Richard I., and if a reasonable fee . . . That being so, I say unhesitatingly that I cannot find this is a reasonable fee now. It is a week's wages from an agricultural labourer, and it is not reasonable that such a sum should be demanded as of right from such a person for a duty which properly should be performed gratuitously.[176]

In the 1862 case of *Gibson v. Crick*,[177] the court held bad a commercial custom whereby an "introducing broker" was allegedly entitled to a share of a commission for chartering a vessel. The court held "preposterous" that an original broker should share in a commission if, for example, he recommended a second, who in turn recommended a third, who is then employed.

In the famous customary law case of 1875, *Hall v. Nottingham*,[178] the court upheld a custom for the inhabitants of a parish to enter upon certain land in the parish and erect a maypole and dance round and about it, and otherwise enjoy on the land "any lawful and innocent recreation at any times in the year."[179] The court believed the proper meaning of the word custom ". . . is something that has the effect of local law, but the general law puts a limit on that, and requires that it shall be reasonable and certain,"[180] and that the court entertained "some doubts" given it could take away from the owner of the freehold the whole use and enjoyment of his property, and that the previous authorities were in conflict. Nevertheless the court held that the custom was good.

The court came to a different conclusion in the 1867 case of *Sowerby v. Coleman.*[181] The alleged custom was for inhabitants of a parish to exercise and train horses at all seasonable times of the year, in a place beyond the limits of the parish. Aside from the problem of extra-parish customs discussed in the following section, it was argued:

> Secondly, this custom is unreasonable. It amounts to a claim of a profit à prendre, or is at least within the reason on which such a custom is disallowed, for it excludes the owner of the soil from any beneficial use of it, and that without compensation [citing *Gateward's Case*].[182]

The court agreed:

> Here all the inhabitants of the parish claim the right to go into the land of another person, and to use it for the purpose of exercising and training horses, at all "seasonable times" of the year; . . . Such a right, then, to exercise an indefinite number of horses, for an indefinite period of the year, would exclude the owner from the beneficial occupation of his property during probably the whole year.[183]

Finally, there is the "bridge" (to modern) 1900 case of *Coote v. Ford*,[184] upholding the custom, in theory, of commoners (residents) of a manor to take or destroy rabbits or game on the waste. Calling particular attention to certain presentments in court rolls of the manor in question, the court said:

> I would only add in regard to this part of the evidence that, if we were to read this part of the presentment as the presentment of a custom, I should have considerable hesitation in holding that it alleges a valid custom. It would be, according to its terms, a custom for any person not merely any copyholder, to kill rabbits on the manor without molestation. This appears to me to be on the face of it unreasonable . . . . But I see no reason why, as

> a matter of law, there might not be a good and valid custom or customary bye-law whereby the commoners might take or destroy the rabbits or other game.[185]

As the next section indicates, there is of course a measure of uncertainty that leads to unreasonableness, and the two are often related. This theme is the basis of the holding of unreasonableness in the modern 1964 case of *Fowley Marine Ltd. v. Gafford.*[186] There, a supposed custom for the world at large to moor boats was held to be too broad as well as unproven. To this issue of breadth and certainty (or lack thereof) we now turn.

4.3.5 *Certainty*

> Customs ought to be certain. A custom, that lands shall descend to the most worthy of the owner's blood, is void; for how shall this worth be determined? But a custom to descend to the next male of the blood, exclusive of females, is certain, and therefore good. A custom, to pay two pence an acre in lieu of tythes, is good; but to pay sometimes two pence and sometimes three pence, as the occupier of the land pleases, is bad for its uncertainty. Yet a custom, to pay a years improved value for a fine on a copyhold estate, is good: though the value is a thing uncertain. For the value may at any time be ascertained; and the maxim of the law is, id certum est, quod certum reddi potest.
>
> (Blackstone, *Commentaries*, at 78)

The matter of certainty is one of the most easily ascertainable of the seven criteria. As appears below, it is also the one about which courts before, during and after Blackstone's time have been the most clear. There are three aspects of certainty that English courts have identified: geographic area (usually small and well-defined), population (also usually small and well-defined), and practice.

4.3.5.1 Certainty of practice

Certainty of practice is that part of the criterion that requires the subject of the custom to be clearly defined and limited. Such was clearly the case in Blackstone's time. Thus, in the 1745 case of *Wilkes v. Broadbent*,[187] the custom was for the lord of the manor or his tenants, who were mining coal, "time out of mind to throw the earth, stones, coals &c. coming therefrom together in heaps upon the land near such pits . . ."[188] Not only did this totally deprive the other tenants of the value of their land, but "there being no restriction in time, and the word near was too vague and uncertain."[189] The opinion of the lower court[190] explains the nature of the uncertainty:

> If every uncertain custom be void, this cannot be good, for nothing can be more uncertain. The word "near" is not intelligible: but, to make it certain and intelligible, it should be "nearest" or "adjoining." Supposing many lands and of different persons lay within a small distance, some ten yards off, and some twenty &c; which of these lands must be said to be near within the meaning of this custom? The custom, that is laid, is to take away and carry away part of the coals placed there, and to burn and make into cinders the other parts thereof, not saying what part, nor how long it is to lie there. So in this respect the custom is likewise quite uncertain.[191]

Again, in the 1746 case of *Millechamp v. Johnson*,[192] an alleged custom for the inhabitants of a parish to play games on plaintiff's close was held bad for uncertainty: to play "any" rural games. Also in the 1788 case of *Steel v. Houghton*,[193] a custom for the poor and indigent in a parish to glean, although the principle problem was one of the indefiniteness of the class to which the custom applied the court also found that:

> Such a custom as will support the plea, must be universal, and everywhere the same, otherwise it is void for its uncertainty. If it exists only in particular counties or districts (such as the custom of being discharged from the payment of tithes of wood in some hundreds in the wilds of Kent and Sussex, or the custom of gavelkind), it is partial, and no part of the general customs of the realm. From the best inquiries I have been able to make, I find that this custom is not universal. In some counties it is exercised as a general right, in others, it prevails only in common fields, and not in inclosures, in others it is precarious, and at the will of the occupier. In the county where this action was brought, it never in practice extended to barley; nor is the time ascertained. In some counties the poor glean whilst the corn is on the ground; here the usage is laid to be after the crop is harvested.[194]

Again, "The practice also of gleaning is itself uncertain and changeable. In some counties it is entirely excluded, in others partially admitted, and in others modified with every possible variety."[195]

In the 1806 case of *Lady Wilson v. Willes*,[196] the alleged custom was that all the customary tenants of the manor having gardens have immemorially taken away, dug and carried away from the waste within the manor for the purpose of making and repairing grass-plots in the garden such turf covered with grass fit for the pasture of cattle, at all times of the year as often and in such quantity as the occasion required. Lord Ellenborough held:

a custom, however ancient, must not be indefinite and uncertain: and here it is not defined what sort of improvement the custom extends to: it is not stated to be in the way of agriculture or horticulture: it may mean all sorts of fanciful improvements: every part of the garden may be converted into grass-plots, and even mounds of earth raised and covered with turf from the common: there is nothing to restrain the tenants from taking the whole of the turbary of the custom and destroying the pasture altogether. A custom of this description ought to have some limit, but here is no limitation as laid, but caprice and fancy. Then this privilege is claimed to be exercised when occasion requires. What description can be more loose than that? It is not even confined to the occasions of the garden. It resolves itself, therefore, into the mere will and pleasure of the tenant, which is inconsistent with the rights of all the other commoners as well as of the lord. The third special plea is also vastly too indefinite: it goes to establish a right to take as much of the turf of the common as any tenant pleases for making banks and mounds on his estate: it is not even confined to purposes of agriculture. All the customs laid therefore are bad, as being too indefinite and uncertain.[197]

The trend of the law continued in this vein into the nineteenth and twentieth centuries. In the 1835 case of *Bluwett v. Tregonning*,[198] it was held uncertain, and so bad, for all the inhabitants of a parish to enter a particular close at all reasonable times of the year, to collect and carry away reasonable quantities of sand drifted onto the land by the sea. Indeed, one justice declared "The custom alleged is uncertain, indefinite and absurd. In point of fact there can be no rule for ascertaining, in a case like this, what is sand blown from the sea-shore and what is the original soil. And, in law, I do not see how there could be any such custom as this."[199]

One of the longest expositions on the issue of general certainty comes in the 1856 case of *Champneys v. Buchan*,[200] in which the court applies this criterion with a vengeance. The alleged custom was for the rector of a parish to collect certain sums from the occupants of houses within the parish for or in lieu of tithes, to which he was not otherwise entitled as a matter of law. The court found the custom invalid for want of certainty:

Now it is essential to the validity of any alleged custom that it should be certain. By this I understand not merely that the custom as alleged should point out clearly and certainly the principle or rule of the custom, but that the principle or rule so pointed out must be one which is definite and certain, so that by application of it to each particular case, it may be known with certainty what are the rights which the custom gives in that case. To apply this proposition to a custom rendering houses liable to payments as and for tithe, not only must the custom as alleged point out clearly and certainly the principle or rule by which the payments are regulated and determined . . . but the principle or rule so pointed out must be one which is definite and certain, so that by the application of it to the case of each particular house it may be known with certainty what the occupier of that house is liable to pay.

***

What then is the custom alleged by the plaintiff? The bill being silent on the subject, and the counsel for the plaintiff having argued the case on the footing of a special custom, I invited the learned counsel to state what he contended the custom to be. He frankly responded to that invitation and gave me this statement of the custom:

> "The occupiers of all houses and other buildings built or erected, and from time to time built or erected, within the parish of Whitechapel, shall pay to the rector of the said parish certain annual payment as tithes, or as rates for tithes, or in lieu and satisfaction of tithes; and the occupiers of houses and other buildings existing within the said parish shall pay such annual payments as have been usually paid from the building and occupation of the said houses, when the period of the erection thereof is known, and when the period of erection is unknown, such annual payments as have been anciently paid in respect of the said houses and other buildings; and the occupiers of houses newly built or erected shall pay such reasonable annual sums as shall be agreed upon between themselves and the rector, and, in default of such agreement, reasonable annual sums, to be ascertained by reference to the amounts payable by houses of a like description in the neighborhood."[201]

This the court found utterly to lack:

> what is essential to the validity of a custom, the quality of certainty. The principle or rule which it proposes for ascertaining what any newly-erected house is liable to pay is twofold: 1st, that the rector and the occupier should agree as to the annual amount which the house should be liable to pay; and, 2dly, where they cannot agree, the annual amount payable for the house or building is to be ascertained by reference to the amounts payable by other houses or buildings of a like description in the neighborhood thereof. With respect to the former, it is hardly necessary to say that a custom that a newly-erected house should be liable to pay such an annual amount as the occupier and the rector might agree upon would be void. With respect to the latter, it appears to me that such a custom would be equally void for uncertainty.

> I have searched in vain among the cases relating to customs for anything in the least approaching to such a principle or rule for ascertaining the amount payable as this of referring to the amounts payable by houses or buildings of the like description in the neighborhood. What is to be the test by which we are to try whether a certain house or building is of the like description with another house or building? Is the likeness to depend on annual value, or fee-simple value, or size, or form, or the materials used in the structure, or a combination of all or some of these considerations, or on what is it to depend? Who is to judge of the likeness? Is it to be tried by evidence of an array of architects, surveyors and builders, called as witnesses on the one side and the other? Besides, if we examine the rule or principle here proposed with every disposition to support it if possible, it is obvious that it assumes that there are, and always have been in this parish, houses and buildings of every possible description; otherwise, if a house or building should be erected, or should have been erected at any time during the six or seven centuries which have elapsed since the commencement of the time of legal memory, of a description different from that of any house or building then existing in the parish, it would be impossible to ascertain the amount which it ought to be liable to pay. Suppose a large hospital, or infirmary, or theatre, or hotel to be for the first time erected in the parish, where shall we find a building of the like description in the neighborhood, by reference to which it can be ascertained what ought to be paid for the newly-erected building? It assumes, moreover, that throughout the whole parish, all houses and buildings of the like description (by whatever test that similarity of description is to be tried) have always paid an equal annual amount, a fact which is neither alleged nor attempted to be proved, and which there are strong reasons for believing is entirely without foundation. And unless the fact be so, if there should be two or more houses or buildings of the like description in the neighbourhood paying different annual amounts, which of them is to govern the amount payable by the newly erected house? I might pursue this subject further and suggest other considerations to shew the impracticality of applying such a rule or principle as that which is proposed by the statement of the alleged custom. But I have said enough to illustrate the grounds upon which I am obliged to arrive at the conclusion, that such a custom as is suggested is void for uncertainty.[202]

On the other hand, "a custom for inhabitants of a parish to enter upon certain land in the parish, and erect a maypole thereon, and dance round and about it and otherwise enjoy on the land any lawful and innocent recreation at any times in the year" was upheld in the 1875 case of *Hall v. Nottingham.*[203] Noting that such local law is enforceable provided it is reasonable and certain, the court on appeal upheld the judgment below:

> Here, however, another objection is put forward, and we are to determine whether we are justified in saying this is so uncertain as to be bad. Looking to the nature and origin of such customs, it would be unreasonable to expect any precise certainty as to what could be enjoyed as a matter of right. If at the present time the inhabitants all met to discuss and determine such a matter, it would be unreasonable to expect them to be very precise as to the enjoyment which they are to have. I cannot myself see, independently of authority, that there is anything so uncertain in this alleged custom that we are bound to reject it. No doubt the case of *Millechamp v. Johnson* is to the effect that a custom to enjoy "any rural sports or games" was bad, as too general and uncertain; but in that case the words are very general . . .[204]

The more modern cases continue the trend toward requiring relatively strict certainty for a custom to be held good. Thus in the 1906 case of *Devonald v. Rosser*,[205] the court refused to approve a custom permitting owners of mines to temporarily shut down their works and suspend the employment of the workers whenever unable to obtain orders at remunerative prices:

> But here the closing of the works is a matter that depends entirely upon the will of the employer, upon the particular circumstances of the case, and upon the view that the employer takes of the prospect of trade, and as to whether it is worth his while to make plates for stock or not. Under those circumstances there can be no element of certainty about the alleged custom at all, and the defense of custom must fail.[206]

4.3.5.2 Certainty of locale

To be good, a custom needs to be confined to a particular place or locale, like a county, a shire, a hundred, a parish or a village.[207] Otherwise, it approaches the general application and usage that is the hallmark of the common law principle, to which a custom is usually opposed. This was true during and after Blackstone's time, and well before.

In the 1599 case of *Parker v. Combleford*,[208] the court declared a custom for the lord of the manor to take as heriot the best beast of any person dying within the manor, as bad in part because the custom was thus extended to those living outside the geographical area of the manor: "If this be a general custom which goes to the whole county, [presumably the court means common law as Blackstone would describe general custom in his *Commentaries* a century and a half later] it might be intended, and peradventure would be maintainable; but not as a private custom within the manor [meaning presumably special custom]."[209] In the 1648 case of *Chafin v. Betsworth*,[210] the defendant answered to a charge of trespass for the breaking of a close called the market place and erecting a stall there "by custom of the manor for all tenants to erect stalls there to sell their goods, and that the defendant being a tenant and a butcher, erected a stall to sell flesh."[211] The plaintiff tried to catch the defendant in a pleading error by pointing out that the plea did not say that the marketplace was within the manor, which it must to be considered a customary practice. The court reportedly held that "seeing it is said the custom of the manor is to erect stalls in pred' loco in quo, &c. this is a sufficient averment that the locus in quo is within the manor."[212] The case is typical in that the defendant is often accused of being a trespasser, which indeed he would be in most instances, unless he can justify his presence by means of some right in the land of the tenant or lord which permits him to enter without express permission. Custom was a common basis for defense, and locality of the custom was critical to proving the custom as above.

This was certainly true in and around Blackstone's time. Perhaps no stronger statement can be found than in the case of *Arthur v. Bockenham*,[213] dealing with a custom allegedly permitting after-acquired property to pass by devise after the making of a will. The court began by declaring why customs are to be strictly construed:

> because all customs which are against the common law of England, ought to be taken strictly, nay very strictly, even stricter than any Act of Parliament that alters the common law. It is a general rule, that customs are not to be enlarged beyond the usage; because it is the usage and practice that makes the law in such cases, and not the reason of the thing, for it cannot be said that a custom is founded on reason, though an unreasonable custom is void; for no reason, even the highest whatsoever, would make a custom law; so it is no particular reason that makes any custom law, but the usage and practice itself, without regard had to any reason of such usage, and therefore you cannot enlarge such custom by any parity of reason, since reason has no part in the making of such custom.[214]

The court then continued: "the law allows usage in particular places to supersede the common law, and is the local law, which is never to be extended further than the usage and practice, which is the only thing that makes it law."[215]

In the 1803 case of *Legh v. Hewitt*,[216] the defendant allegedly breached a duty to occupy a farm in a good and husband-like manner according to the custom of the country, by tilling half his farm at once, when no other farmer there tilled more than a third and many tilled only a fourth. The court refused to find such a custom because of the lack of a particular locale:

> . . . it is evident that the word custom, as here used, cannot mean a custom in the strict legal signification of the word; for that must be taken with reference to some defined limit or space which is essential to every custom properly so called. But no particular place is here assigned to it; nor is it capable here of being so applied.[217]

A few years later, in the 1828 case of *Gifford v. Lord Yarborough*,[218] the House of Lords found land formed by alluvion of the sea, imperceptibly, belongs to the owner of the adjoining demesne lands, and not to the crown, but not because of a special custom. Its rationale is instructive: "If there is custom regulating the right of the owners of all lands bordering on the sea, it is so general a custom as need not be set out in the pleadings, or proved by evidence, but will be taken notice of by the Judges as part of the common law."[219]

Indeed, alleged customs were often held bad for want of specific limitation to a given area of land. Thus, in a dispute over whether certain town officials could erect a barrier across an entrance to a walk, the court in the 1900 case of *Abercromby v. Fermoy Town Commissioners*[220] upheld customary rights of the inhabitants of a district to a right of way on foot, noting in passing that there could not be a custom in the king's subjects generally as this would be a general law and not a custom of a particular place, as required. To the same effect the 1913 case of *Anglo-Hellenic Steamship Company v. Louis Dreyfus and Co.*,[221] in which the question of charterers' liability for demurrage while a ship was waiting to load, turned on whether the common law of England or port custom prevailed. In the course of its opinion, the court defined custom with respect to place:

> A custom is a reasonable and universal rule of action in a locality, followed, not because it is believed to be the general law of the land or because the parties following it have made particular agreements to observe it, but because it "is in effect the common law within that place to which it extends, although contrary to the general law of the realm."[222]

Therefore, and perhaps obviously, to avail oneself of a customary right, one must both live in the district in which the custom is alleged, and practice the customary right in that same district. An interesting example of this type of custom is that of perambulating the boundaries of the parish by parishioners. Courts strictly construe the right, however, as is clear from the 1837 case of *Taylor v. Devey and Graham*[223] where the parishioners tried to exercise their customary rights of perambulation so as to enter and pass through plaintiff's house:

> The right to perambulate parochial boundaries, to enter private property for that purpose, and to remove obstructions that might prevent this from being done, cannot be disputed. It prevails, as a notorious custom, in all parts of England, is recorded by all our text writers, and has been confirmed by high judicial sanction. [The court cites *Goodday v. Michell*, noted at fn 696, where the court discussed perambulations but held against the exercise of the custom on pleading grounds] . . . Now it is obvious that the right to perambulate boundaries cannot confer a right to enter any house in the parish, however remote from the boundaries, and though not required to be entered for any purpose connected with the perambulation: and it seems to follow that a custom on that occasion to enter a particular house, which is neither upon the boundary line nor in any manner wanted in the course of the perambulation, cannot be supported. On principle, therefore, the custom laid is bad in law.[224]

The 1907 case of *Lord Fitzhardinge v. Purcell*[225] exemplifies these principles. In a typical action for trespass, the lord of certain manors brought the action against defendants who claimed customary rights to the foreshore and waters of a certain waterway for the purpose of hunting wildfowl. The court disallowed the defense:

> But whether or not the custom alleged be good law, I am of the opinion that the evidence in the present case is far short of what is required to prove any custom at all. The only evidence of any exercise of the alleged right by persons being wild-fowlers by trade is the evidence of an exercise of the right by the defendant and his father . . . It is not proved that any of these, with the exception of the defendant and his father, for some short period, lived in any part of the local area in which the alleged custom is said to prevail. It is proved that in exercising the alleged right none of them confined himself to shooting on the lands in question . . . the user proved, therefore, is more extensive than the custom alleged, and would only be partially explained by the custom if upheld.[226]

Compare this misuse of custom with the modern 1974 case of *New Windsor Corporation v. Mellor*,[227] in which the alleged custom was for the inhabitants of a certain borough to engage in lawful sports and pastimes on a village green. In upholding the custom, the court said: "The right claimed was one which was capable of existing as a custom since it was one which was confined to the inhabitants of a particular locality, i.e. the borough."[228]

Also (and maybe obviously also) a custom may not be extended from one locale to another. Thus, in the 1867 case of *Sowerby v. Coleman*,[229] the court held bad a custom for inhabitants of a parish to exercise and train horses at all seasonable times of the year, in a place beyond the limits of the parish, it having been alleged that the parish was both within and adjacent to the manor:

> But the ground on which I put my judgment, and which is, I think, conclusive of the question, is that this, being a custom of the nature above described, is claimed on behalf of all the inhabitants of one place, to be exercised and enjoyed in another and a different place . . . [the pleas show] the evil consequences which would flow from admitting the extension of such a right to inhabitants of another district. The claim tends to widen its extent, and, if held valid in the smaller division, might spread in the course of time to the neighboring hundred, or even to the neighboring county.[230]

Again, in the 1901 case of *Brocklebank v. Thompson*,[231] a dispute over an alleged custom for inhabitants of a parish to use a churchway through the demesne land of a manor, the court said:

> [T]here cannot be a custom in one place giving any right in another place . . . A custom claimed on behalf of the inhabitants of the manor of Snaton to have a right of way to church within the manor of Irton would not, I think, be a good manorial custom of either manor. But there might well be a lawful and valid custom of the parish of Irton for the inhabitants thereof to have a church-way or path through the demesne of Irton which is within the parish.[232]

Similarly, a custom may not be exercised in a number of parishes. In the 1895 case of *Edwards v. Jenkins*,[233] the court held a custom for the inhabitants of several adjoining or contiguous parishes to exercise the right of recreation over land situate in one of such parishes to be bad. Although the case turned principally on the question of indefinite numbers of people entitled to exercise the custom, the court also doubted whether a custom could be claimed in three parishes.[234]

4.3.5.3 Certainty of person

The requirement that there be certainty of persons was as important as certainty of place in order for a custom to be good. Thus, in the 1595 case of *Goodday v. Michell*,[235] the court suggested that a customary right of way might be enjoyed by all the members of the parish of Rudham in their annual perambulation, but they could not establish the same right by prescription ("they ought to allege a custom or usage within the parish").[236] Also in the 1665 case of *Abbot v. Weekly*,[237] the court upheld against a charge of trespass on a close, a custom for "all the inhabitants of the vill, time out of memory &c. had used to dance there at all times of the year at their free will, for their recreation."[238] It is worth noting that the land area, a close, was also certain.

This principle was well established in the time of Blackstone. This is evident from the 1788 case of *Selby v. Robinson*[239] in which there was an alleged "custom for poor and indigent householders living in A to cut away rotten boughs and branches in a chase of A."[240] Holding the defendants to be trespassers for breaking and entering plaintiff's closes, the court said: ". . . there is no limitation at all in this case; and it is impossible to ascertain who is entitled to this right under the custom as stated in the record; for the description of poor householders is too vague and uncertain."[241]

Again in 1788, in *Steel v. Houghton*,[242] the court struck down an alleged custom of gleaning on the ground that "the poor" was too uncertain and indefinite a class to exercise it:

> Next, the persons claiming this right, are vague and undefined. The term poor is merely relative. Before the statute of the 43rd of Eliz. there was no method of legally ascertaining who were of that description. Since that statute, justices and overseers are to determine what persons are of the number of the poor, to whom also must be added the qualifications of a settlement . . . They who claim this right then, are equally uncertain and precarious.[243]

The court was even more definite in the 1795 case of *Fitch v. Rawling*,[244] where the custom was for all the inhabitants of a parish to play at all kinds of lawful games at a particular close at all seasonable times of the year, including all persons for the time being in the same parish. As to the second part, the court said:

> But I hold the other custom to be as clearly bad, as the first is good. How that which may be claimed by all the inhabitants of England can be the subject of a custom, I cannot conceive. Customs must in their nature be confined to individuals of a particular description, and what is common to all mankind, can never be a custom.[245]

Again, forty years later in the 1828 case of *Gifford v. Yarborough*.[246] In holding that lands formed by accretion belonged to the owner of lands adjoining the sea, the court noted:

These are called special customs because they only apply to particular descriptions of persons, and do not affect all the subjects of the realm; but if they govern all persons belonging to the classes to which they relate, they are to be considered as public laws; . . . If there is a custom regulating the right of the owners of all lands bordering on the sea, it is so general a custom as need not be set out in the pleadings, or proved by evidence, but will be taken notice of by the Judges as part of the common law.[247]

And in a case involving the right of boatmen to carry their craft around a stretch of the Thames that was not navigable, the court observed in the 1889 case of *Bourke v. Davis*[248] that a right of recreation by custom upon the land of another cannot exist as a right in the public generally, but must be confined to the inhabitants of a particular district. To the same effect a fascinating case from Scotland, the 1848 case of *Marquis of Breadalbane v. McGregor*,[249] had drovers claiming the right to rest and refresh sheep on certain private lands along a way used for centuries to take them from Scotland to England for market. An owner of land upon which one of these "immemorial drove-stances" stood wished to move it too far from the way to be useful to the drovers. In the course of holding there was no right of resting attached to the public right-of-way that the drovers used, the court noted that the claim was far too broad, for the public generally,[250] to support it as a custom since it was not confined to a particular district.

Litigation over footpaths was a fruitful source of custom allegations in the eighteenth and nineteenth centuries. Thus, in the 1852 case of *Dyce v. Lady James Hay*,[251] a magistrate of Old Aberdeen brought an action against Lady James Hay alleging that he and other inhabitants of New Aberdeen, Old Aberdeen, the vicinity thereof, "and the public generally, had used and enjoyed from time immemorial a certain footpath running along the bank of the River Don, on the Defender's Estate" and that a particular strip "had been from time immemorial used and resorted to by the Purser and the other inhabitants of the places aforesaid 'for the purpose of recreation and taking air and exercise by walking over and through the same, and resting thereon as they saw proper.'"[252] While the court was quite willing to accept a custom for the use of unenclosed land for village sports and recreations,[253] it found the class too broad to sustain here:

What is insisted upon, therefore, is of this extensive nature, that the Pursuer claims as an inhabitant, but, in fact, on behalf of all the Queen's subjects, the right to go at all times upon the inclosed soil of a portion of the Appellant's property near the mansion-house, for the purpose of recreation just as they think proper. Now, that, I conceive is a claim so large as to be entirely inconsistent with the right of property; for no man can be considered to have a right of property, worth holding, in a soil over which the whole world has the privilege to walk and disport itself at pleasure.[254]

Churchways in the nineteenth century were also frequent sources of customary claims, and were upheld only if restricted to those who attended church so as not to be converted to public ways across the land of another, generally the lord of the manor. Thus, in the 1889 case of *Batten v. Gedye*,[255] the court recognized the existence of such a churchway in refusing to exercise jurisdiction where parishioners sought a mandatory injunction to restore steps allegedly part of it and removed by certain church officers:

> . . . on the grounds: (1) that the steps constituted a churchway, the right to use which was solely in the parishioners, and not a footway common to the public, and the Court would not exercise jurisdiction in respect of the interference with a churchway within the churchyard at the suit of a parishioner, a jurisdiction which was vested in the Ecclesiastical Court.[256]

Again in the 1901 trespass case of *Brocklebank v. Thompson*,[257] the disputed custom was

> that the inhabitants of the parish of Irton had by custom from time immemorial, or alternatively for the full period of forty years, or alternatively for the full period of twenty years next before the action brought, as of right and without interruption, at their own free will and pleasure, used, and were entitled to use, the disputed way as a churchway, for themselves, their families, guests, and servants, for passing on foot to and from the parish church of Irton.[258]

While the court did not think much of the custom as a manorial custom, since it would extend beyond the manor, nevertheless:

> [T]here might well be a lawful and valid custom of the parish of Irton for the inhabitants thereof to have a churchway or path through the demesne of Irton which is within the parish. Indeed, it is not easy to see how, in the absence of some such parochial custom, the inhabitants of Santon could formerly, having regard to the situation of that manor, get to their parish church at all. *Prima facie* a custom in reference to a way to a parish church would be a parochial custom for the parishioners, and, so far as I am aware, no mention is to be found in any reported case, or, in fact, in any law book, of a customary churchway not for the use and benefit of the parishioners at large . . . I hold that . . . the disputed way was and is by immemorial custom a churchway or path for the inhabitants generally of the parish of Irton.[259]

Such rights of way by custom were not, of course, limited to churchways, so long as there was a certain limitation to a particular class of persons capable of exercising the right of passage. Thus, in the 1900 case of *Abercromby v. Fermoy*,[260] the court upheld a public right of way over certain premises and forbade the town commissioners to erect a barrier across the entrance to the walk on the ground that: "our law has always recognized that the people of a district – a town, a parish or a hamlet – are capable of acquiring by dedication or custom, certain rights over land which cannot be gained by the general public."[261]

In another context, a case from the same period refused to find an alleged custom because the right seemed to extend to everyone. In the 1900 case of *Coote v. Ford*,[262] the alleged custom was for commoners of a manor to take or destroy rabbits or game on the waste. The court said:

> if we were to read this part of the presentment as the presentment of a custom, I should have considerable hesitation in holding that it alleges a valid custom. It would be, according to its terms, a custom for any person, not merely any copyholder, to kill the rabbits on the manor without molestation. This appears to me to be on the face of it unreasonable . . . The evidence in effect is that during the fifty years or so which preceded 1897 all sorts of people shot everything they could find to shoot on Martin Down. All this is excellent proof that until the year 1898 the plaintiff and his predecessors for many years let anyone who liked go in pursuit of game on Martin Down, and that Mr. Hodding and others who had copyhold interests in the manor believed that those interests gave them, their friends, and guests a right to shoot any sort of game there. But I cannot treat it as a proof of any value to the defendants in support of a customary right of the copyholders and their tenants to kill rabbits on the waste, and this is the custom which they have to prove.[263]

Of course, an alleged custom did not need to arguably extend to everyone for a court to find the class of people too large. In the 1895 case of *Edwards v. Jenkins*[264] discussed in the previous section on locality, the court found a custom for the inhabitants of several adjoining or contiguous parishes to exercise the right of recreation over land in one of such parishes bad not only for geographic reasons, but also because, "where a custom is asserted as regards the inhabitants of a particular parish, then, if the evidence goes to show that the privilege has been exercised by the inhabitants of other parishes, the proof is inconsistent with the allegation and the case fails on that ground."[265] The court went on to hold it could conceive of a custom over a larger area if properly pleaded and proved. Perhaps more directly on this point is the 1894 case of *Lancashire v. Hunt*,[266] in which an alleged custom to train unlimited numbers of race horses on the manorial common was held bad:

> the custom, so far as regarding training, was too wide, purporting as it did to show an exercise of an alleged right not limited to the inhabitants [of Stockbridge] at all, but quite as much for strangers and their horses as the inhabitants, which did not prove the custom alleged, but a different custom, which would be bad in law.[267]

This concern for certainty of class continued into the twentieth century. In the 1907 case of *Lord Fitzhardinge v. Purcell*,[268] the trespass case discussed in the previous section, the court found no custom to shoot wildfowl on land of certain manorial lords in part because besides the alleged trespassers:

> others not being wildfowlers by trade also exercised the alleged right. The user proved, therefore, is more extensive than the custom alleged, and would only be partially explained by the custom if upheld. I am of the opinion, under these circumstances, that the defendant cannot rely on the alleged custom as a justification of the acts complained of.[269]

Again in the 1908 case of *Lord Chesterfield v. Harris*,[270] in determining the validity of an alleged custom to fish with nets from boats on certain parts of a river, the court found no custom in part because:

> . . . the right thus claimed may be exercised by an indefinite number of persons, according as the freeholds in the five parishes are subdivided; and, further, that it is not in any way limited to getting fish for consumption on the property to which the right is appurtenant, but that it expressly contemplates fishing without stint with a view to sale at markets or fairs.[271]

So also, in the 1967 case of *Alfred F. Beckett Ltd. v. Lyons*, "the court found a custom to gather coal bad in part because of the large and indefinite group which could claim to exercise the right over private land."[272]

4.3.6 Compulsion

> Customs, though established by consent, must be (when established) compulsory; and not left to the option of every man, whether he will use them or not. Therefore a custom, that all the inhabitants shall be rated toward the maintenance of a bridge, will be good; but a custom, that every man is to contribute thereto at his own pleasure, is idle and absurd; and, indeed, no custom at all.
>
> (Blackstone, *Commentaries*, at 78)

The concept that a custom must be compulsory in order to be good is for the most part self-evident; a law is not a law if it is not obligatory on the parties. Most of the cases on custom pretty much assume that a custom is compulsory, so that the issue is rarely addressed separately. During Blackstone's time, the issue was phrased, if addressed at all, often by means of emphasizing the mutual obligations under certain customs. Thus, in the 1752 case of *Drake v. Wiglesworth*,[273] the court emphasized the obligations inherent in the custom that all householders of a parish grind their corn "which shall be used by them ground within the parish":[274] "I admit that there must be a mutual consideration; and in this case, to be sure, if a man is obliged to grind at a mill, the owner of the mill must keep it in order with all necessaries."[275] This mutuality of obligation is found in other cases as well, making it clear that those attempting to enforce rights under a customary law theory have obligations as well.

There are nevertheless a few cases that deal with the compulsory nature of a covenant much as Blackstone describes it. In the 1690 case of *Pain v. Patrick*,[276] the alleged custom was the upkeep of a right of way involving a bridge: "But as to the plea in bar, it is not good, because the erecting of a bridge is but laying out a way; it is a voluntary act, and no man by reason of his own act can be discharged of what he is to do, upon the interest he hath in the ferry."[277]

Later in the 1913 case of *Anglo-Hellenic Steamship Co. v. Louis Dreyfus and Co.*,[278] the demurrage case noted in a previous section, the court emphasized the binding nature of custom by comparing it to local common law: "A custom is a reasonable and universal rule of action in a locality, followed, not because it is believed to be the general law of the land or because the parties following it have made particular agreements to observe it, but because it is in effect the common law within that place to which it extends".[279]

4.3.7 Consistency

> Lastly, customs must be consistent with each other: one custom cannot be set up in opposition to another. For if both are really customs, then both are of equal antiquity, and both established by mutual consent: which to say of contradictory customs is absurd. Therefore, if one man prescribes that by custom he has a right to have windows looking into another's garden; the other cannot claim a right by custom to stop up or obstruct those windows: for these two contradictory customs cannot both be good, nor both stand together. He ought rather to deny the existence of the former custom.
>
> (Blackstone, *Commentaries*, at 78)

As with the previously discussed criterion, the criterion of consistency is largely self-evident and does not appear often in the cases on customary law. Of course, to agree with Blackstone that customs must be consistent, one with another, does not get us very far in deciding which customary right is entitled to precedence in the event of conflict.

One of the earlier disputes in which the issue of consistency arose appears to have been decided largely on the ground of which custom was the more reasonable. In the 1561 case of *Parton v. Mason*,[280] the court was faced with two conflicting customs in resolving a dispute over the seizure of an ox. According to the first custom: "the lord of the manor . . . was accustomed to have the best beast of every tenant dying seised of any messuage holden of the said manor upon that messuage after his death"[281] but: "there is another custom within the said manor, that if the best beast of the said tenant be cloigned before the seizure of it by the lord or his servant, that then the lord hath been accustomed to seize and take the best beast of any other being levant et couchant upon the said tenure."[282] The court held that the second custom "seems to be repugnant to the first custom, and is a several custom by itself."[283] It was also adjudged to be "void and unreasonable."[284]

Shortly after Blackstone wrote, the multiple disputes over the use of the close at Steeple Bumstead in Essex arose. In the 1795 case of *Fitch v. Rawling*,[285] the customs alleged were: for "all the inhabitants of a parish to play at all kinds of lawful games, sports and pastimes in the close of A at all seasonable times of the year at their free will and pleasure"[286] And "for all persons for the time being, being in the parish"[287] to do the same. The defendants were charged with trespass for playing cricket on the close belonging to plaintiff. One of the objections made was "that the customs, whether good or bad, are repugnant to each other, and, therefore, that the court cannot give judgment on either of the special pleas."[288] The court disagreed:

> It would be very strange if one Defendant should plead a good plea, and it were found for him, that he should not have judgment, according to the justice and truth of the case, though the other Defendant should plead a bad plea. But why are these customs inconsistent with each other? It might happen, that there might be at first a limited custom and afterwards a more extensive one, and I do not see why the second should root up the first, or why they might not both exist together, supposing the second to be a good one.[289]

As it turned out, as noted in an earlier section, the second was held bad as extending to too broad a class of persons, though the first was upheld.

In the 1818 case of *Badger v. Ford*,[290] the conflict was between "a custom for the lord to grant leases of the waste of the manor, without restriction"[291] and "by custom of the manor, all such tenements had a right of common."[292] When leases exercised under the first custom conflicted with the rights of commoners under the second, the court found the first "bad in point of law."[293] On the other hand, in the 1844 case of *Elwood v. Bullock*,[294] the court found customary rights to hold a fair consistent with customary rights to erect a booth on the highway during such a fair, provided there was still room for horses and carts to pass thereon.

4.4 Blackstonian custom in modern courts

American courts often relied on customary laws as the nation was established. There are a number of US court decisions confirming the customary law status of public property rights, although many of the decisions violated the fundamental Blackstonian criteria of certainty of place (too large) and certainty of persons (too many).

In *State v. Cozzens*,[295] the court referred to the Rhode Island Constitution, Article 1 and found that, "the people shall continue to enjoy and freely exercise all the rights of fishery and the privileges of the shore to which they have been heretofore entitled under the charter and usage of this state" (emphasis added). The court further stated that,

> the place where the said offense was alleged to have been committed is and has been freely enjoyed and used from the earliest settlement of this state to the time of the offense alleged in the indictment, as a common and public fishery, where the people of the state have been accustomed, under the charter and usages of the state, to fish for oysters and other shellfish (emphasis added).

The legal authority for fisheries rights was found to be rooted in accustomed usage as confirmed by the colonial charter of the state. The popular usage created the law and the written text of the colonial charter confirmed it. See also *Payne v. Providence Gas Co.*,[296] coming to the same conclusion.

The 1872 case of *Swift v. Gifford*,[297] which pertained to a whale-hunting dispute, confirms the existence of customary law in the state of Massachusetts.[298] Additionally, *Gough v. Bell*,[299] which involved net fishery issues in some of the navigable part of the River Delaware in New Jersey, found that the private property in these fisheries rests "in custom or local usage variant from the common law. Florida also adheres to the principle of customary law as a source of authority for public property rights."

> The general public may continue to use the dry sand area for their recreational activities, not because the public has any interest in the land itself, but because of a right gained through custom to use this particular area of the beach as they have without dispute and without interruption for many years.
>
> *City of Daytona Beach v. Tona-Rama Inc.*[300]

Some courts rejected the notion of customary law. One example is the Supreme Court of Connecticut in *Graham v. Walker.*[301] Another example is the Court of Appeals of New Jersey case of *Albright v. Cortright*,[302] stating that "a common law custom as distinguished from a usage of trade, must be immemorial; and this, in New Jersey, is impossible." The reason seems to be that none of the customs of the State of New Jersey clearly enough, enjoyed ancient usage, as defined since at least the first year of the reign of Richard I.

Today, custom is arising Phoenix-like from the ashes of Blackstone's limitations on the English common law that forms the basis of common law in the United States. As the Supreme Court of the State of Oregon put it in 1969, "Because so much of our law is the product of legislation, we sometimes lose sight of the importance of custom as a source of law in our society. It seems particularly appropriate in the case at the bar to look to an ancient and accepted custom in this state as the source of a rule of law."[303] It arises both from renewed interest in the rights of native Americans and from the "background principles of state property law" exception to the doctrine of regulatory taking.

In the first, custom can provide a means for guaranteeing certain rights of native peoples in lands owned (technically held in fee simple) by others. The argument that a true customary right survives transfer from one owner to another is strong, though, as the cases in the foregoing sections demonstrate, custom is always subject to control and destruction by legislative act. In the second, custom can provide a basis for a local, state or federal land use regulation that will survive constitutional challenge as a taking of property without compensation even if it leaves a landowner with no economically beneficial use of the land. Akin to its twin, nuisance exception, such a background principle of a state's law of property is not a part of the landowner's bundle of ownership sticks to begin with, so that its "taking by regulation" – like the perpetration of a nuisance – is not protected by the US Constitution's Fifth Amendment.

Property rights, however, and particularly private property rights, are hedged with restrictions governing such rights in land of another like easements, profits, licenses and covenants.

One with no right to enter the land of another is a trespasser, as is demonstrated by the majority of the land cases cited and quoted in the preceding sections where the action was almost always one in trespass against the intruder who pleaded custom and customary rights as a defense. This right to exclude is a critical part of American jurisprudence with respect to private property rights. As the American Law Institute notes in its *Restatement of the Law of Property*:

> A possessory interest in land exists in a person who has a physical relation to the land of a kind which gives a certain degree of physical control over the land, and an intent so to exercise such control as to exclude other members of society in general from any present occupation of the land.[304]

Another commentator describes the "notion of exclusive possession" as "implicit in the basic conception of private property."[305] By means of an unbroken line of decisions, the U.S. Supreme Court has held that the right to exclude is a fundamental right which is violated whenever government attempts to assert public rights over private land without declaring a public purpose and paying just compensation required by the Fifth Amendment. The right to exclude has a long and distinguished history as a fundamental private property right. As early as 1918, Justice Brandeis observed that, "[a]n essential element of individual property is the legal right to exclude others from enjoying it."[306]

Significantly, it makes no difference if the deprivation of the right to exclude costs the landowner nothing, as Professor Daniel Mandelker points out in his comprehensive treatise on land use.[307] Discussing some of the cases noted in the analysis below, he states:

> The court relied on its cases holding a deprivation of the right to exclude is a taking. It is significant in these cases that the access easement imposed little or no economic loss on the affected properties.[308]

Similarly, Professor Jan Laitos describes the right to exclude as one of those "rights valued so highly, that the abolishment will result in the offending law being declared unconstitutional."[309] More recent commentary follows this trend toward equating the right to exclude with property rights in land, sometimes in the context of common interest communities governed by homeowners' associations. Thus, Professor Tom Merrill in two thoughtful articles argues at length that "property means the right to exclude others from valued resources"[310] and "[t]hus, for all of these reasons [four discussed in his article] it appears sensible to embrace Justice Scalia's invocation of the right to exclude as the 'hallmark of property' – at least for the purposes of the Takings Clause."[311] In the same vein, Laura

Rahe summarizes the right to exclude others in the context of homeowners' associations in her article.[312] The U.S. Supreme Court has many times made the same point. Thus, in *Kaiser Aetna v. United States*:[313]

> In this case, we hold that the "right to exclude," so universally held to be a fundamental element of the property right, falls within this category of interests that the Government cannot take without compensation. This is not a case in which the Government is exercising its regulatory power in a manner that will cause an insubstantial devaluation of petitioners' private property; rather, the imposition of the . . . servitude . . . will result in an actual physical invasion of the privately owned marina. And even if the Government physically invades only an easement in the property, it must nonetheless pay just compensation.[314]

Again in *Loretto v. Teleprompter Manhattan CATV Corp.*:[315]

> Moreover, an owner suffers a special kind of injury when a stranger directly invades and occupies the owner's property. As [another part of the opinion] indicates, property law has long protected an owner's expectation that he will be relatively undisturbed at least in the possession of his property. To require, as well, that the owner permit another to exercise complete dominion literally adds insult to injury. Furthermore, such an occupation is qualitatively more severe than a regulation of the use of property, even a regulation that imposes affirmative duties on the owner, since the owner may have no control over the timing, extent or nature of the invasion.[316]

Nor does it make any difference if the "invasion" is less permanent or intrusive. As the Supreme Court noted in *Lucas v. South Carolina Coastal Council*,[317] in the event of regulations that compel the property owner to suffer a physical invasion, "no matter how minute the intrusion and no matter how weighty the public purpose behind it, we have required compensation."[318] This is true even if the law in question does no more than give strangers a permanent and continuous right to pass over private property, as the state of California attempted to do along the public beach but on private land in *Nollan v. California Coastal Commission*:[319]

> We think a "permanent physical occupation" has occurred, for purposes of that rule, where individuals are given a permanent and continuous right to pass to and fro, so that the real property may continuously be traversed, even though no particular individual is permitted to station himself permanently upon the premises.[320]

The Court reinforced these sentiments seven years later in holding another easement, this time for flood protection, an impermissible interference with the right to exclude in *Dolan v. City of Tigard.*[321] Seeing ". . . no reason why the Takings Clause of the Fifth Amendment, as much a part of the Bill of Rights as the First Amendment or Fourth Amendment, should be relegated to the status of a poor relation"[322] the Court held (clearly distinguishing an earlier decision permitting persons to distribute leaflets in a major private shopping center attracting thousands of patrons daily):

> By contrast, the city wants to impose a permanent recreational easement upon petitioner's property that borders Fanno Creek. Petitioner would lose all rights to regulate the time in which the public entered onto the greenway, regardless of any interference it might pose with her retail store. Her right to exclude would not be regulated, it would be eviscerated.[323]

Indeed, the right to exclude has achieved international status with the 1999 opinion of the European Court of Human Rights in the case of *Chassagnou and Others v. France.*[324] Before the court was the French Loi Verdeille,[325] which provides for the statutory pooling of hunting grounds. The effect on the plaintiffs – three farmers – was to force them to become members of a municipal hunters' association (ACCA) and to transfer hunting rights to the association, with the result that all members of the association may enter their property for the purpose of hunting.[326] The three farmers belonged to two anti-hunting, wildlife protection associations and strenuously objected to hunters on their property against their express wishes as landowners. In particular, they alleged the violation of Articles 9, 11 and 14 of the Convention for the Protection of Human Rights and Fundamental Freedoms together with Article 1 of its Protocol No. 1:

> Every natural or legal person is entitled to the peaceful enjoyment of his possessions. No one shall be deprived of his possessions except in the public interest and subject to the conditions provided for by law and by the general principles of international law.

The court framed the issues as follows:

> The applicants submit that the obligation for them to transfer hunting rights over their land to an ACCA, against their will and without compensation or consideration, constituted an abnormal deprivation of their right to use their property, firstly in that they were obliged to tolerate the presence of hunters on their land, whereas they were opposed to hunting for ethical reasons, and secondly in that they could not use the land they owned for the creation of nature reserves where hunting was prohibited.[327]

The government of France responded that the interference with the applicants' property rights was minor since they had not been deprived of the right to use their property and all they lost was the right to prevent other people from hunting on their land.

The court disagreed. The court began by noting that Article 1 of Protocol No. 1, quoted above, requires that any interference with individual property rights would further require a fair balance between the demands of the general community and the protection of individual fundamental rights.[328] The court also found that it was "undoubtedly in the general interest to avoid unregulated hunting and encourage the traditional management of game stocks,"[329] clearly the purpose of the Loi Verdeille. However, the court found the interference with the applicants' fundamental right to peaceful enjoyment of their land "disproportionate":

> [N]otwithstanding the legitimate aims of the Loi Verdeille when it was adopted, the Court considers that the result of the compulsory-transfer system which it lays down has been to place the applicants in a situation which upsets the fair balance to be struck between protection of the right of property and the requirements of the general interest. Compelling small landowners to transfer hunting rights over their land so that others can make use of them in a way which is totally incompatible with their beliefs imposes a disproportionate burden which is not justified under the second paragraph of Article 1 of Protocol No. 1. There has therefore been a violation of that provision.[330]

The court also found discrimination on the ground of property within the meaning of Article 14 of the Convention because only small landowners were required to transfer their hunting rights under the Loi Verdeille.[331] Concluding there was also a violation of Article 11 of the Convention, the court said:

> To compel a person by law to join an association such that it is fundamentally contrary to his own convictions to be a member of it, and to oblige him, on account of his membership of that association, to transfer his rights over the land he owns so that the association in question can attain objectives of which he disapproves, goes beyond what is necessary to ensure that a fair balance is struck between conflicting interests and cannot be considered proportionate to the aim pursued.[332]

Such obvious intrusions on private property, in particular the well-documented right to exclude, must comply with certain restrictions and criteria common to the concept of custom. Blackstone provides such criteria, and not only as a matter of reason, but as a matter of law, since he is almost always cited in the reported American cases on custom and customary law.[333] Unfortunately, they usually get it so wrong that the legitimate basis for custom must certainly fail. Without another basis for justifying such invasive intrusions on private property, those exercising such rights as trespassing, and governments that permit or require such trespasses, are taking private property without compensation contrary to the Fifth Amendment of the United States.

Of the seven criteria set out in the *Commentaries*, the most critical appear to be certainty, reasonableness, and continuity. Contrary to the language in the *Thornton Case* from Oregon,[334] reasonableness is not a matter of present use but of original legal unfairness at its inception. Customs that unduly burden property rights of the landowner, or that favor unduly one group or person over others, are unreasonable. If a custom is reasonable in these terms at its inception, then it is reasonable. Thus the court's statement that "reasonableness, is satisfied by the evidence that the public has always made use of the land, in a manner appropriate to the land and to the usages of the community," is beside the point, irrelevant and wrong.

The Blackstonian criterion of certainty goes to the clarity of the customary practice or right, the restrictive certainty as to locale (some legally recognized division like a county, a city, a town or a village) and certainty as to a class of persons or section of the public. The court's statement that "certainty, is satisfied by the visible boundaries of the dry sand area and by the character of the land, which limits the use thereof to recreation uses connected with the foreshore," is vague as to the first requirement, far too broad with respect to the second requirement, and altogether fails to deal with the third. As to continuity, the court says that a "customary right need not be exercised continuously, but it must be exercised without an interruption caused by anyone possessing a paramount right." True for the first part, false for the second part. As Blackstone and the cases make abundantly clear, it is the right of use that must be continuous. The use itself goes to evidence of that continuity of right, but the use itself is otherwise irrelevant.

To summarize, although Blackstone is often cited by American courts in support of customary rights, the courts have tended to interpret Blackstone's criteria in ways that are not supportable by the cases on which Blackstone relied. Their failure to follow the criteria strictly raises serious questions about the validity of their decisions under the Constitution of the United States.

Endnotes

1. For review and comment upon early drafts of this chapter, see note 16 *infra*; Dr. Gilbert Verbit, Life Member, Clare Hall; thanks to Mark Bailey, J.H. Baker, Charles Harpum, Fellow, Downing College; DeLloyd Guth, Faculty of Law, Univ. of Manitoba; Chris Jarman, Solicitor, Payne Hicks, London; Christopher Coombe, Partner, Linklaters and Alliance.
2. (4th edn reissue, Butterworths, London, 1998), vol. 12(1).
3. Paragraph 606, at 160. This entire section on custom is a superb explanation of custom today, prepared by one of the preeminent scholars in legal history, Professor J. H. Baker, Fellow of St. Catherine's College, Cambridge University.
4. Charles Arnold-Baker, *Local Council Administration* (4th edn., Butterworths, London, 1994), at p. 35.
5. See, for example, the summary of sources including many of those in the following text and notes, cited in Sir William Searle Holdsworth, *A History of English Law* (3rd edn., Methuenale, London, 1923), vol. II, at pp. 369–375.
6. Holdsworth, a *History of the English Law*, vol. II, at pp. 374–375.
7. *Borough Customs*, edited for the Selden Society by Mary Bateson, Fellow of Newnham College, Cambridge (Professional Books Ltd, London, 1972), in two volumes.
8. Bateson, *Borough Customs*, at Introduction, xv.
9. See Holdsworth, *History of the English Law*, vol. II, at pp. 374–375.
10. Bateson, *Borough Customs*, Introduction, at xvi.
11. See Bateson, *Borough Customs*, Introduction to vol. I, pp. xviii–lvi.
12. Bateson, *Borough Customs*, Introduction to vol. I, at p. xxxix.
13. Bateson, *Selden Society* vol. XVIII, 1972 edition, at 249–250.
14. Bateson, *Selden Society* vol. XVIII at 245.
15. Bateson, *Selden Society* vol. XVIII at 1–2.
16. From the 1326 Custumal of Cockerham, in the possession of Dr. D. M. Baily, former Domestic Bursar, Corpus Christi College, from R. Sharpe Franz, *Two Custumals of the Manor of Cockerham 1326 and 1483* a translation of the Lancaster and Cheshire Antiquaries Society (1954), vol. 64.
17. *Halsbury's Laws of England*, vol. 12(1), at para. 699, p. 249.
18. This according to Phillip Saunders, Deputy County Archivist at the County Record Office, Shire Hall, Cambridge, in a wide-ranging and most learned (his part, anyway) conversation on 18 May 1999.
19. Again, from Phillip Saunders, who reports that one such collection arrived in the open bed of a contractor's flatbed truck . . .
20. *Selected Cases in Manorial Courts 1250–1550* edited for the Selden Society by L. R. Poos and Lloyd Bonfield (Selden Society London, 1998).
21. *Ibid.*, at pp. xxxiv–xxxv.
22. *Ibid.*, at p. 50.
23. *The Court Rolls of the Manor of Dernford Sawston in the County of Cambridge for the Years 1336–1360*, expanded and translated by T. F. Tevesham, B.Sc., from

the original rolls at Sawston Hall, Sawston, 1965, copy given to the author by David Hall, solicitor and partner, Linklaters and Paynes, London, and Lord of the Manor of Littleport in June 1999.

24. Order Set Down the 28 of June 1609 by [various knights], etc. from W., Cunningham (ed), Common Rights at Cottenham & Stretham in Cambridgeshire, London, Offices of the Society, Gray's Inn, 1910.
25. From the will of Lady Marvyn of Ufton, as set out in an Englefield Estate information sheet. (See note 26 *infra.*)
26. Interview with K. R. McDiarmid, F.R.I.C.S., Resident Land Agent, The Englefield Estate, April 14, 1999, and correspondence and attachments dated May 11, 1999. I am grateful to Peter Stockwell of the firm of Payne Hicks Beach, Solicitors, for arranging for me to meet Mr. McDiarmid.
27. Interview with John Clark, London, May 20, 1999.
28. 5 Term Rep 26 (1792).
29. (1847) 10 QB 26, at extended note, p. 25.
30. (1900) 83 LT 482.
31. (1786) 1 Term Rep 466.
32. *Halsbury's Laws of England*, vol. 12(1).
33. (1319) 70 Selden Society 11, 13.
34. (1628) 4 Madd 105 fn. 1; 56 ER 647. See also, for carefully reciting the phrase, whereof the memory of man is not to the contrary, *Vinkestone v. Ebden*, (1698) 1 Ld Raym. 384.
35. *Ibid.*
36. (1769) 4 Burr 2303; 98 ER 201.
37. *Ibid.*, at 2368.
38. *Ibid.*, at 2417.
39. (1795) 2 Hy Bl 393; [1775–1802] All ER 571; 126 ER 614.
40. *Ibid.*
41. *Ibid.*, at 399; 574; 617.
42. (1495) 102 Selden Society 31.
43. *Ibid.*
44. *Ibid.*, at 33.
45. (1786) 1 TR 466; 99 ER 1201.
46. *Ibid.*, at 466.
47. (1837) 2 M & Rob 129; [1835–42] All ER 201.
48. (1863) 1 H&C 728.
49. *Ibid.*, at 735–736.
50. [1974] 2 All ER 510.
51. *Ibid.*, at 511.
52. (1713) 10 Mod. 251.
53. (1844) 6 QB 67.
54. (1872) 7 QB 214.
55. *Ibid.*, at 217–218.

56. (1913) 30 TLR 167.
57. *Ibid.*, at 168.
58. [1908] 2 Ch D 139.
59. *Ibid.*, at 141.
60. Davis 28; 80 ER 639.
61. (1819) 4 madd 83; 56 ER 639.
62. (1752) Willes 654; 125 ER 1369.
63. [1919] 1 KB 223.
64. *Ibid.*, at 243.
65. *Ibid.*, at 242–243.
66. (1865) 19 CB (NS) 732.
67. *Ibid.*, at 757.
68. (1870) 10 LR Eq 105.
69. "I regret much that the good understanding which seems to have prevailed between the college and the freehold tenants of the manor for centuries up to 1859 should ever have been disturbed, but the increased value for building purposes of the soil in these suburban commons has of late years created much litigation, stirring up antiquated questions of black-letter law – unfortunately at a great expense to the parties concerned, and with little profit to anyone who is not a member of the legal profession" (at pp. 129–130).
70. [1963] 1 Ch 243.
71. *Ibid.*, at 255–56.
72. (1840) 11 Ad. & El. 819; 113 ER 625.
73. (1876) 24 W.R. 603.
74. There is some variation in subsequent editions of the *Commentaries* in the footnotes to various parts of the discussion on custom, particularly with respect to the criteria. Thus, for example, the first edition appears to have no footnote j, which appears in the text and notes to several of the subsequent editions (at least in the second, fourth, fifth, seventh and eight) in the section on continuity. This and other minor variations in punctuation and capitalization does not appear to affect the substance of the text and references in any significant way. See original editions in the manuscripts collection of the Cambridge University Library, reviewed by the author in March of 1999.
75. (1913) 30 TLR 167.
76. *Ibid.*, at 168.
77. (1883) 8 LR AC 195.
78. *Ibid.*, at 215.
79. (1870) 10 LR Eq 105.
80. *Ibid.*, at 127, emphasis added.
81. As reported in volume IV of the Publications of the Selden Society for 1890, *The Court Baron*, edited by Frederick William Maitland and William Paley Baildon (Bernard Quaritch, London, 1890), at 145.
82. *Ibid.*, at 145.

83. 11 Mod 148, 6 Queen Anne.
84. *Ibid.*, at 160–162.
85. Occurring in nearly two-thirds of the roughly 200 cases of record reviewed by the author.
86. (1401) YB Trin 2 Hen, 4 f.24, pl.20.
87. See *Halsbury's Laws of England*, vol. 12(1).
88. (1577) 3 Dyer 357b.
89. *Ibid.*
90. (1590) Cro. Eliz 185; 78 ER 442.
91. *Ibid.*, at 186; 442.
92. (1599) Moore KB 603; 72 ER 786.
93. (1599) Cro. Eliz 725; 78 ER 959.
94. (1594) Cro. Eliz 351; 78 ER 599.
95. (1594) Cro Eliz 569.
96. *Ibid.*, at 569.
97. (1611) 2 Brown 192; 123 ER 829, 892.
98. *Ibid.*, at 199–200; 895.
99. (1614) 2 Bulst 195; 80 ER 1062.
100. *Ibid.*, at 196; 1064.
101. *Ibid.*, 1063.
102. (1614) 2 Bulst 201; 80 ER 1066.
103. *Ibid.*, at 203; 1068.
104. *Ibid.*
105. *Ibid.*, at 204; 1069.
106. (1691) 3 Lev. 307; 83 ER 703.
107. *Ibid.*, 308; 703.
108. (1698) 1 Ld. Raym 405; 91 ER 1169.
109. *Ibid.*
110. (1690) 3 Mod. Rep. 289; 87 ER 191.
111. (1742) Willes 360; 125 ER 1214.
112. *Ibid.*
113. *Ibid.*, at 363; 1216 (emphasis added).
114. (1745) 2 Stra 1224, 1 Wils 63; 93 ER 1146.
115. (1818) 1 B & Ald 348; 106 ER 128.
116. *Ibid.*, at 360; 133. *Gateward's Case* (1607) 6 Co. Rep. 596; 77 ER 344.
117. (1752) Willes 654; 125 ER 1369.
118. (1837) 2 M & Rob 126; [1835–42] All ER 201.
119. *Ibid.*, at 203.
120. [1904] 2 Ch 534; [1905] 2 Ch 538 (CA).
121. (1699) 12 Mod 270; 271.
122. [1905] 2 Ch 538; 581 (emphasis added).
123. *Ibid.*, at 584 (1905).
124. *Ibid.*, at 557 (1904).

125. *Ibid.*, at 551 (1904).
126. (1847) 10 QB 25.
127. *Ibid.*, at 58 (emphasis added).
128. (1862) 1 B&S 940; 121 ER 963.
129. *Ibid.*, at 940; 964.
130. *Hilton v. Earl Granville* 5 QB 701.
131. (1866) LR 4 Eq 613.
132. 6 App. Cas. 460.
133. *Ibid.*, at 464.
134. [1940] 3 All ER 101.
135. (1844) 5 QB 701.
136. *Wolstanton, Ltd v. New Castle-under-Lyme Borough Council* [1940] 3 All ER 101, at 111 (emphasis added).
137. (1321) 85 Selden Soc. 35.
138. *Ibid.*, at 37.
139. (1329) 97 Selden Soc. 61.
140. *Ibid.*, at 62.
141. (1614) Hob 220; 80 ER 367.
142. *Ibid.*, at 225–226.
143. (1596) Cro. Eliz. 464; 78 ER 717.
144. (1614) Hob 85; 80 ER 235.
145. (1695) 5 Mod Rep 75; 87 ER 528.
146. *Ibid.*, at 75–76; 528–29 (emphasis added).
147. (1746) Willes 622; 125 ER 1352.
148. (1777) 3 Wils 298; 95 ER 1065.
149. *Ibid.*, at 302–303; 1068 (emphasis added).
150. (1867) LR 2 HL 239.
151. [1908] 1 Ch 303.
152. *Ibid.*, at 309–318 (emphasis added).
153. (1620) Hob 329; 80 ER 471.
154. *Ibid.*
155. (1684) 3 Lev 160; 83 ER 629.
156. *Ibid.*, at 160; 629.
157. (1740) Willes 202; 125 ER 1131.
158. (1616) Hob 189; 80 ER 336.
159. *Ibid.*
160. (1670) 1 Vent 167; 86 ER 114.
161. *Ibid.*, at 168.
162. [1779] 1 Doug KB 218; 99 ER 143.
163. *Ibid.*, at 218–219; 143.
164. *Ibid.*, at 225; 146 (emphasis added).
165. (1817) 6 M & S 69; 105 ER 1169.
166. *Ibid.*, at 72; 1170.

167. (1755) 2 Wils 28; 95 ER 667.
168. *Ibid.*
169. (1797) 2 Esp. 543.
170. *Ibid.*, at 544–545.
171. (1795) [1775–1802] All ER 571; 2 HBL 394.
172. (1746) Willes 622; 125 ER 1352.
173. (1856) 5 E&B 913; 119 ER 721.
174. *Ibid.*, at 940–941.
175. (1868) LR 3 QB 497.
176. *Ibid.*, at 510.
177. (1862) 1 H&C 142; 158 ER 835.
178. [1875] 1 Ex D 1.
179. *Ibid.*, at 2.
180. *Ibid.*, at 3.
181. (1867) LR 2 Exch 96.
182. *Ibid.*, at 97.
183. *Ibid.*, at 99–100 (emphasis added).
184. 83 LT 482.
185. *Ibid.*, at 483 and 482.
186. [1967] 2 QB 808, [1967] 2 All ER 472.
187. (1745) 2 Stra 1224; 93 Er 1146.
188. *Ibid.*, at 1224; 1146 (emphasis added).
189. *Ibid.*, at 1225.
190. *Broadbent v. Wilkes* (1742) Willes 360; 125 ER 1214.
191. *Ibid.*, at 362.
192. (1746) Willes 205n(b).
193. (1788) 1 Hy Bl 51; 126 ER 32.
194. *Ibid.*, at 60.
195. *Ibid.*, at 62.
196. (1806) 7 East 121.
197. *Ibid.*, at 128 (emphasis added).
198. (1835) 3 Ad. & El. 554; 111 ER 524.
199. *Ibid.*, at 575–576.
200. (1857) 4 Drew 104; 62 ER 41.
201. *Ibid.*, at 116–117; 45–46.
202. *Ibid.*, at 117–119 (emphasis added).
203. (1875) 1 Ex D 1.
204. *Ibid.*, at 4.
205. [1906] 2 KB 728 (CA).
206. *Ibid.*, at 741.
207. For examples of customs limited to a particular area, but where there was no apparent dispute over such limitations, see *Drake v. Wigglesworth, Fitch v. Fitch, King v. Oswestry, King v. Joliffe*, and *Smith v. Archibald.*

208. (1599) Cro. Eliz. 725; 78 ER 959.
209. *Ibid.*, at 726.
210. 1 (1618) 3 Lev 190; 83 ER 644.
211. *Ibid.*, at 190.
212. *Ibid.*
213. 11 Mod 148, 6 Queen Anne.
214. *Ibid.*, at 160–161.
215. *Ibid.*, at 161 (emphasis added).
216. (1803) 4 East 154; 102 ER 789.
217. *Ibid.*, at 159. The court ordered a new trial, however, because it found evidence of bad farming which did not depend on custom, and a properly instructed jury might have found against the defendant.
218. (1828) 5 Bing 163; 130 ER 1028.
219. *Ibid.*, at 165, emphasis added.
220. [1900] 1 IR 302.
221. (1903) 108 LT 36.
222. *Ibid.*, at 37, citing the 1844 case of *Lockwood v. Wood.* emphasis added.
223. (1837) 7 Ad. & El. 409.
224. *Ibid.*, at 416.
225. [1908] 2 Ch D 139.
226. *Ibid.*, at 164 (emphasis added).
227. [1974] 2 All ER 510.
228. *Ibid.*, at 511 (emphasis added).
229. [1867] LR 2 Exch 96.
230. *Ibid.*, at 99–100 [more detail from another judge at p. 100].
231. [1903] 2 Ch D 344.
232. *Ibid.*, at 354.
233. [1896] 1 Ch 308.
234. *Ibid.*, at 312–313.
235. (1595) Cro. Eliz. 441.
236. *Ibid.*, at 441.
237. (1665) 1 Lev 176; 83 ER 357.
238. *Ibid.*, at 176.
239. 2 Term Rep. 758.
240. *Ibid.*, at 758.
241. *Ibid.*, at 759 (emphasis added).
242. 1 H Bl 51 (emphasis added).
243. *Ibid.*, at 62.
244. (1795) [1775–1892] All ER 571.
245. *Ibid.*, at 574.
246. (1828) 5 Bing 163; 130 ER 1023.
247. *Ibid.*, at 164; 1023–1024 (emphasis added). See also *Mounsey v. Ismay*, (1863) 1 H&C 729, where a custom for all the freemen of the City of Carlisle to enter

a close for the purpose of racing horses was raised as a defense against an action for trespass for entering the close, breaking down gates and fences and clearing mounds and thorns placed there by the owner. The court nevertheless held for the plaintiff landowner on other grounds (custom was a bad plea for an action brought as a claim to an easement under the Prescription Act). Also in *Grant v. Kearney* (1823) 12 Price 773, the court refused to recognize a custom of perambulation of inhabitants of a particular liberty to pass through the gardens of Lincoln's Inn, on the ground that they had failed to prove the custom applied to the liberty and had proved only such a custom with respect to a parish, the boundaries of which were not shown to be coterminous with the liberty. We can perhaps derive two lessons here: (1) the courts will often at this time make a great deal of the niceties of pleadings (see Dickens, *Bleak House*, and the notorious fictional case of *Jarndyce v. Jarndyce*) particularly where property rights are involved, and (2) it does not pay to mess with the barristers of Lincoln's Inn.

248. (1889) 44 Chanc Div 110.
249. VII Bell 43.
250. *Ibid.*, at 54.
251. (1852) I Macqueen 305; 19 Digest (Repl.) 15.
252. *Ibid.*, at 305; 300.
253. *Ibid.*, at 311; 302.
254. *Ibid.*, at 309; 301.
255. 41 Ch D 507.
256. *Ibid.*, at 508 (emphasis added).
257. [1903] 2 Ch 344.
258. *Ibid.*, at 345–36.
259. *Ibid.*, at 354–355.
260. [1900] 1 IR 302.
261. *Ibid.*, at 314.
262. (1900) 83 LT 482.
263. *Ibid.*, at 483 (emphasis added).
264. [1896] 1 Ch D 308.
265. *Ibid.*, at 313.
266. (1894)10 TLR 448.
267. *Ibid.*, at 448 (emphasis added).
268. [1908] 2 Ch D 397.
269. *Ibid.*, at 164–165.
270. [1908] 2 Ch D 397.
271. *Ibid.*, at 409 (emphasis added).
272. [1967] 1 Ch D 449.
273. (1752) Willes 654; 87 ER 191.
274. *Ibid.*
275. *Ibid.*, at 657; 1371.

276. (1690) 3 Mod Rep 289; 87 ER 191.
277. *Ibid.*, at 294; 194.
278. (1913) 108 LT 36.
279. *Ibid.*, at 37, emphasis added.
280. (1561) Dyer 199; 73 ER 440.
281. *Ibid.*
282. *Ibid.*
283. *Ibid.*, at 199–200; 441.
284. *Ibid.*, at 200; 441.
285. (1795) 2 H Bl 394; [1775–1802] All ER 571; 126 ER 614.
286. *Ibid.*, at 394; 571; 614.
287. *Ibid.*
288. *Ibid.*, at 397; 573; 616.
289. *Ibid.*, at 397–398; 573; 616.
290. (1819) 3 B & Ald 153; 106 ER 618.
291. *Ibid.*, at 153.
292. *Ibid.*, at 155.
293. *Ibid.*, at 153.
294. (1844) 6 QB 383.
295. 2 R.I. 561.
296. 77 A. 145 (1910).
297. Mass. Case No. 13,696, 23 Fed. Cas. P. 559.
298. Robert C. Ellickson, "A Hypothesis of Wealth-Maximizing Norms: Evidence from the Whaling Industry" *Journal of Law, Economics and Organization*, vol. 5, no. 1, p. 83.
299. 22 N.J. Law 441, 462.
300. 294 So2d 73, *Ibid.*, at p. 78.
301. 61 A. 98.
302. 45 A. 635.
303. *State of Oregon ex rel. Thornton v. Hay*, 462 P.2d 671 (1969).
304. Restatement of Property s. 7 (1936).
305. Richard A. Epstein, *Takings: Private Property and the Power of Eminent Domain* (Harvard University Press, Cambridge, MA, 1985), at p. 63.
306. *International News Service v. Associated Press*, 248 U.S. 215, 250 (1918) (Brandeis, J., dissenting).
307. Daniel R. Mandelker, Land Use Law (5th ed. 2003).
308. *Id.* at 2–26.
309. Jan G. Laitos, Law of Property Protection (1999) at Section 5.03[A]. For a summary of these and other sources, *see* Callies & Breemer, *supra*, n. 10.
310. Thomas W. Merrill, *Property and the Right to Exclude*, 77 Neb. L. Rev. 730, 754 (1998).

311. Thomas W. Merrill. *The Landscape of Constitutional Property*, 86 Va. L. Rev. 885, 974 (2000).
312. Laura T. Rahe, *The Right to Exclude: Preserving the Autonomy of the Homeowners' Associations*, 34 Urb. Law. 521 (Spring 2002).
313. 444 U.S. 164 (1979).
314. *Ibid.*, at 179–180.
315. 458 U.S. 419 (1982).
316. *Ibid.*, at 446. See David Callies, "Regulatory Takings and the Supreme Court: How Perspectives on Property Rights Have Changed from Penn Central to Dolan, and What State and Federal Courts are Doing about It," (1999) 28 *Stetson Law Review* 523, 526–529.
317. *See supra*, n. 3.
318. *Id.* at 1015.
319. 483 U.S. 825 (1987).
320. *Id.* at 832.
321. 512 U.S. 374 (1994).
322. *Id.* at 392.
323. *Id.* at 394.
324. 7 BHRC 151 (1999). Applications nos. 25088/94, 28331/95 and 28443/95, April 29, 1999.
325. Law No. 64–696 of 10 July 1964.
326. *Ibid.*, at para. 13.
327. *Ibid.*, at para. 72.
328. *Ibid.*, para. 75.
329. *Ibid.*, para. 79.
330. *Ibid.*, para. 85.
331. *Ibid.*, at paras. 92–95.
332. *Ibid.*, at para. 117.
333. Bederman, "Curious Resurrection of Custom", p. 1375; Paul Sullivan, "Customary Revolutions: The Law of Custom and the Conflict of Traditions in Hawaii" (1999) *University Hawaii Law Review*, vol. 20, p. 99; David Callies, "Custom and the Public Trust" (2000) *Environmental Law Reporter*, vol. 30, p. 100030.
334. *State of Oregon ex rel. Thornton v. Hay*, 462 P.2d 671 (Ore. 1969).

5

How custom becomes law in Norway

PETER ØREBECH

5.1 Customary law in Norway

Whether *inter partes* related customs are the positive law of the land is not just a factor distinguishing civil law societies from common law societies. The legal status of these customs also varies amongst different civil law countries. For example, Sweden terminated Saami customary laws in the mid-nineteenth century.[1] Norway, on the other hand, by the King Christian V General Codex of 1687 (Norske lov), abolished ancient statutes only.[2] Ancient customary laws were then tacitly recognized. Norway never followed in Sweden's footsteps, and as a result Norwegian customary laws are a valid legal source.[3]

Danish legal scholar Alf Ross asserts that customary law exists as norms derived from *de facto* customary ways of acting.[4] The place to find these norms is in the court decisions.[5] He seems to think that certain habits, which the general population both observes and recognizes, are validated by court decisions. These observable habits are the bearers of *opinio necessitatis sive obligationis* (a popular understanding of law), which is a feeling of being bound by and forced to adhere to a certain way of conduct (see Sections 7.1.2 and 7.1.3). Nevertheless, the fact that people acquiesce and conform their conduct can give a false sense that the practice followed also mirrors the required "common will."[6] Since the social facts of behavioral attitudes should not be confused with institutional facts,[7] one simply cannot draw any conclusions as to what people should do based upon what they actually do.[8]

It is not clear whether the attendant practices are based upon rational or superstitious beliefs. In the process of customary law, justification is a necessary criterion. Initial dyadic factors of delimitation eventually lead to pluralistic adherence, and human practice prevails. Through inquiries, interviews and participatory investigations into popular behavior, unanimous practice could be demonstrated. This anthropological method is applied in the Saami fishery rights study, discussed in Section 2.2 and Chapter 10.

The antagonists to this debate recognize that courts have a conserving function. Customs that would otherwise have vanished are resurrected because courts confirm them. For instance, in French law,[9] the positivist position is that only extra-legal normative structures are confirmed by the adjudication. The court's decision "gives life to" the custom. The customary law is binding *ex nunc* (from the date of the judgment). According to the a posteriori or "realistic school of jurisprudence," there are no customary laws before valid judgments are made.[10] This is a joint opinion under Norwegian jurisprudence.[11] There is no customary law until a third party mediator confirms it. This position is often combined with a view of custom as social fact that through repetition converts into institutional fact, due to an act of the sovereign. This is not exclusively a modern position. Some traces of this triadic (trilateral) legal understanding existed in the Middle Ages: "The Ruler's appropriation, therefore, is the constitutive element of the law character of social habits. Moreover Lucas holds, the tacit toleration of customs by the Ruler would not be sufficient: by his explicit consent he has to take an active part, as it were, in the creation of customary law."[12]

As opposed to giving too much credence to the enforcement criteria of Alf Ross, I support the Danish legal scientist Henrik Zahle[13] who defines "legal rules" as norms to which the public efficiently adapts.[14] The focus is dyadic; the law is explicitly or tacitly followed *inter partes*. The question of law is two-sided; it is based upon mutual understanding. From that point on, the rule is efficient. If challenged, the rule becomes inefficient. In that case triadic adjudication is the last resort. A judge must then decide what the law of the land is.

At the beginning of the nineteenth century and during the decline of the dominant position of the historic school of customary law, the prevailing theory still held that customary law does not rely upon any decisive action by the sovereign. Consequently, it seems that customary law and positive law are equivalent. Although apparently prohibited by legislation, customary law may terminate positive law. As the Norwegian Law Professor Oscar Platou commented, when he cited the Swiss Zivil Gesätsbuch (Civil Law Codex) § 1 ("the law is applicable to all legal questions . . . If no statute is available, then the justice is obliged to implement customary law"): "life is stronger than positive law."[15] Customary law was never relegated to an inferior position in Norway. In the Norwegian Civil Acts, the superior position of customary law is clearly stated. In the Danish trade law terminology of Henry Ussing (1886–1954), custom is the notion of tradition and usage that are so prevalent that they serve as an interpretive source.[16]

Whether a common property right is an institutional fact does not depend on whether people are aware of this fact. Apparently, legal institutions exist even though they may not be fully understood, recognized or taken advantage of.

Stating that a "custom is the basis of an unwritten rule – like customary law," the Norwegian legal scientists Bernt and Doublet argue that customary law is solely an oral source of law.[17] A Norwegian legal dictionary of the 1950s defines customary law as the body of legal rules that are not expressed in positive legislation, but are nevertheless followed by the legal community and implemented by the courts as binding rules.[18] This is clearly a Norwegian tradition since distinguished legal scientists like Per Augdahl unconditionally tie customary law to the unwritten sources of law: "Prior to the legislative tradition, a period ruled totally by customary law existed. And even under the reign of legislation, custom seems to have remained the dominant factor in developing law for quite a while given the legislators' lack of capability and practice."[19] Following the same school of thought, Oscar Platou states that: "The ancient Norwegian Codices of Frostating and Gulating were . . . codified customary law . . . Under the reign of natural law it was said that customary law was invalid until a legislator gave notice that it was law."[20] It follows that "customary law" is non-written and extra-statutory. For statutes that incorporate customary laws, the concept of "codified customary law" is used.

> In this country [Norway] legislation and custom are the vital sources of law. Several authors present these two sources as the only ones. Speaking of legislation, one does not incorporate the text only, but one includes the different factors that are observed during the interpretation of laws . . . And the notion of custom and customary law is partly used in its broadest sense covering all the other relevant elements.[21]

All "the other relevant elements" are non-textual. It seems clear that the dualism between legislation and customary law as implemented in Norwegian jurisprudence is identical to the division between written and unwritten law.

Focusing next on Danish jurisprudence we observe that Alf Ross argues that rules developed from a factual customary action constitute customary law.[22] What happens during the codifying process, however, is not clear.

Are these originally non-written norms still classified as "customary"? In "Statsforfatningsret" (Constitutional Law) Professor Ross proposes the following definition: "By non-written law we mean the law produced by custom or court practices."[23]

In most instances, the direction of the law has been from unwritten norms to codification. Even though the system of a huge, comprehensive codex – Bürgerlicher Gesätsbuch – seems passé, modern societies still place their trust in the superiority of written legislation.

Because their mission was too obscure, the Norwegian Parliament (Stortinget), in a remarkable 1992 decision, simply terminated the thousand-year-old outer commons statutes without promulgating any new laws in their place. The background for the termination was a peculiar Norwegian idea of "law-modernization."[24] According to this idea, old texts must continuously be replaced by new statute.[25] Contrary to the steadfast advice of the chairman of the expert committee,[26] who argued against termination, the Stortinget buried the millennium-old rules. Because new provisions were too complicated to write, the Stortinget further buried any attempt to (re-)codify them. The arguments that torpedoed any new codification are nicely illustrated by the famous British lawyer Sir John Davies (Chevalier):

> Davies wrote a defence of law French, admitting that it was wholly artificial language which had never been spoken outside the English courts, but arguing that centuries of use had invested its words with meanings so exactly appropriate to the legal terms and ideas they were expected to convey that it could not possibly be replaced by any other language without serious loss to the law's intelligibility.[27]

Davies described a situation identical to the Norwegian outer commons experience! The legislator simply gave up on the overwhelming task of formulating a text equivalent to the ancient practice(s) developed on the basis of Norwegian Law (NL) 3-12-1 of 1687 ("the outer and the upper commons joint use shall remain as in ancient times"). The Agency that had strongly advised the Stortinget to terminate the old texts was unable to further advise it on how to promulgate new ones.[28] The Ministry of Justice was not able to provide any advice, either, even though law-making procedures are the technical responsibility of its office. The Ministry stated that the termination of NL 3-12 would not disturb the legal position of common property rights. We anticipate that these provisions still may play a role as a legal source . . . Terminating the old provisions and codifying a new law of the commons seemed inadequate because in most questions of legal conflict the original texts would have to be consulted. The preparatory committee described the situation as follows:

> In case of termination, I do not see any reason for giving these provisions a new written form. The legal situation will then be that the legislator . . . has decided to tie the justification of common property rights conflicts to terminated provisions instead of formally valid rules. Accordingly, this is a non-favorable choice, which however does not change the legal situation in relation to the substantially valid legal sources.

Consequently, the termination of NL 3-12 does not change the legal situation. The written texts have been deleted, but the rules have not been. Accordingly, the legislature (Stortinget) was fully convinced that the terminated legislation as manifested in ancient traditions and implemented by court decisions and governmental practice reconciled the basic historic content and represented the continuity between ancient and newer provisions.

The law of the commons is a millennium-long implemented practice developed by people, courts and governments. What we see here is a rare event in the modern history of law. The law-maker deliberately decided that new codification of whatever content would fail to fill the gap created by the abandoned text. The complex legal situation that has developed simply could not be rewritten in any manner without causing "serious loss to the law's intelligibility," as stated by Professor Pocock.[29] Presented with such an overwhelming task, the legislator had to give up. In doing so, the legislator confirmed the superiority of the outer commons customary law.

Consequently a four-step ladder was used to arrive at the current situation: the initiation and establishment of a customary law from customs;[30] public confirmation by codification;[31] the re-confirmation in 1272,[32] 1604[33] and 1687;[34] and the unsuccessfully attempted codification and subsequent resurrection of customary law (1992).

Customary law is not the most important source of law. Nevertheless, it is said that custom is increasingly more important than what had previously been argued by the school of legal realists (also called Scandinavian Realists), "legal centrists," legal positivists and other fundamentalist directions, i.e. jurists that adhere to strict verbatim interpretation. The reason, as indicated by the Finnish legal scientist Hannu Tapani Klami, is that in many situations legislation does not "keep up" with the "living fabric of life." "The still dominant legalistic tradition . . . is considerably too positivistic to adapt to the requirements imposed by the rapidly changing conditions of society on legal science and legal analysis."[35]

That fact, however, does not turn customary law into the only resources management tool possible. Through individual adaptation and court interpretation, statutory law is dynamic and changeable. For instance, statutory loopholes require creative thinking and inventive solutions. If textual interpretation does not solve legal conflicts, then flexibility is achieved by the teleological interpretative method of the Scandinavian Realists.[36] When construing a principle, the courts take the legislature's intentions into consideration.[37] Since the court considers legislative intent, Scandinavian Realist adherents regard statutory interpretation as increasingly more democratic than the "quasi-governmental entity" customary law solution. Because some areas of law end up before the court only occasionally, however, one cannot rely on such flexible judicial development.

An apparently different interpretative method is to seek the solutions that satisfy the amalgam of "common sense and the public weal."[38] As stated by the Swedish Professor of Law, Anders Lundstedt,[39] it is the legal solution that mirrors "samhällsnyttans krav" – the need for social utility,[40] that gains support in the long run. This is often a true observation of the function of courts in the living fabric of life. The most highly disputed legal questions end up in the Supreme Courts. Legalistically speaking, one solution may be as good as another. Justices enjoy excessive discretion and are often free to pick the "right" solution.

Having studied the requirements of Anglo-American adjudication – the Blackstonian prerequisites (Section 4.1) – it is time to consider the Norwegian customary law requirements that rule Saami fisheries rights. Now that we have described the general preconditions, the time has come to apply these criteria to Saami area fisheries. For an ethnically based Saami fishery, see Chapter 2.

The question of customary law is important due to the fact that small-scale fisheries have successfully managed coastal fisheries for millennia without depletion of natural resources. Could that be credited to a viable system of customary participation rights?

While Denmark and Norway acknowledge non-codified rights, Sweden abolished non-codified property rights[41] via legislation in the 1850s. The Swedish legislation was then upheld by the so-called *Taxed Mountain Case*.[42] As discussed in Chapter 2, whether coastal Saami customary rights will prosper or perish depends on Norwegian customary law prerequisites. Should the customary law adjudication go against them, fisheries would then have legal rights based on tolerated (*precario*) usage or public law decrees. In that case, customary law would have no role to play.

In my fisheries rights research project, I documented that the fisheries trade is deeply rooted in customary law traditions.[43] Consequently, the assertion that traditional fishing rights are no more than the absence of state prohibitions or the result of lax owners according to *precario* usage, cannot stand. Let us therefore look more carefully into the general prerequisites of Norwegian adjudication.

5.2 Quasi-governmental entity law production

The position of the Norwegian Supreme Court is that the populace may initiate normative structures of a legal kind. Courts adhere to such norms, and confirm *ex post facto* their validity. Their binding force is based upon popular recognition, not the courts' subsequent adjudication. "The validity of customary law is not derived from tacit legislative acceptation. The basic ground of both binding forces [formal and informal law] is to be found in popular recognition."[44] Courts may either reject that particular social norm, or concur in it "as is." The "law" is created by normative decisions that are "born" in the depths of people's souls, accepted *inter partes*, and finally authorized by the courts. The theoretical implications are set forth in Chapter 7.

5.3 The diachronic perspective of validity

Customary law produced by quasi-governmental entities exists *ex ante* (from popular initiation on) and is validated by mutual tacit or express understanding. Some Nordic legal scholars, however, approach customary law rather differently. The Scandinavian "realistic school," led by the Danish legal philosopher Alf Ross,[45] opposes an *ex ante* understanding of law: For them, it is not a question of "having a right," it is a question of "getting a right." Law is intrinsic to the court's decision. Statements of law as in legal arguments preceding court decision are predictions only – *de sentencia ferenda* statements. The *de lege lata* situation is not clear before the adjudication. While Nordic jurists' basic concern is the court's reasoning, whereby popular practice is transformed into customary law, common law courts take a different approach. Under the common law system, popular practice is valid *ex tunc*, and can only be rejected by court if the customary law requirements are not satisfied. "Such a usage as by common consent and uniform practice has become the law of the place, or of the subject matter to which it relates."[46]

Common consent and uniform practice combined are implementing new customary law in Denmark and Norway. The court's task there is to confirm the well-established ancient customary law practice. Therefore, the subject matter to be decided is the law's consensus as clarified by uniform practice. The constitutive element is popular approval:

> For since (says Julianus,) the written law binds us for no other reason but because it is approved by the judgment of the people, therefore those laws which the people have approved without writing ought also to bind every body. For where is the difference, where the people declare their assent to a law by suffrage, or by a uniform course of acting accordingly.[47]

The principles of "spontaneous law" are valid without voting. It is a voluntary compact; i.e. a covenant.[48] If disputed, however, court authorization is necessary. The court's role is not only one of proving the custom, but also of establishing it forever:

> They have attached to the decision of the judge, on the question of law submitted to him by the parties, an authority higher than that which we recognize in a settled line of decisions, – comparable, indeed, to that won by the "*responsa prudentum*" at Rome.[49]

5.4 The factual exposure of norms or subtle legal considerations?

Before discussing the preconditions to recognized customary law, I would like to pose two basic questions. First of all, is the courts' reasoning related to "a practice or course of acting," or does it apply judges' legal understanding of the popular perception of legal norms? The second question is whether all persons bound by a custom must have knowledge of it in all details?

Clearly, the answer to the latter question is "no." According to Supreme Court decisions, the issue at stake is whether the overwhelming numbers of litigants agree that a certain principle is customary law. In the *Seaweed Case*[50] the Supreme Court confirmed that a "solid documentation of a general legal understanding on both sides" is required.[51] In this case the court found "It is however far from clear that such an understanding has been generally accepted."[52]

The first question is demonstrated by the *Bolstadfjord Case*.[53] Here the unanimous court adhered to a purely factual evaluation of "practice or course of acting" that took place at fjord fisheries. The participants' common understanding was not taken into consideration. Having examined the fishing and surveillance activities and the public's lack of reaction against the owners' restrictions on the open access fisheries, the Supreme Court stated: "from this I find evident that the landowners were fully confident of their own legal rights."[54] Similarly, the *Jölster-Lake Case*[55] emphasized the factual participant activity, thereby taking it for granted that "common practice" is an indisputable, visible sign of the subtle, underlying principle of law. If the factual situation clearly demonstrated a legal principle, further investigation into *opinio juris* would be superfluous.

If not, further investigation is needed: the *Fluberg Pasture Case*[56] based its decision upon the legal statements of eighty people inhabiting the area. Since the statements varied, the court found no evidence of customary law. The *Herring Fishery Case*[57] also explored "popular *opinio juris.*" Clearly the legal understanding among involved parties, and not the factual signs of such opinions, is "the real thing." The relevance of factual circumstances is purely evidentiary as supportive of legal opinions that are otherwise verified.

The next question is whether *opinio juris* requires consensus in all respects and in all details? The customary law finding in the *Herring Fishery Case* rejects the notion that diverging popular understanding is troublesome. "The slightly different answers to the questions of legal title, I do not take into consideration."[58] In the *Vansjö Case*,[59] after reviewing documents from the sixteenth and seventeenth centuries, the court reviewed witnesses' statements:

> In their testimony, each witness gave his or her own explanation for the behavior engaged in at the fisheries . . . Among the landowners the legal opinion confirm that all fisheries are private property . . . Among the fishers no unilateral legal opinion is present founding a basis for the proposed public property right . . . Consequently, I find no mutual understanding about rights and obligations that is necessary according to legal theory and court practice.[60]

Accordingly, the Supreme Court considered all three sources of evidence: old documents, practice conducted and legal arguments. None of the evidence was conclusive on its own.

In the *Balsfjord Case*,[61] the Supreme Court based its decision upon the perennial usage combined with the *opinio juris* of pasture as entitled in legal right. It is sufficient, the court held, that the activity be based upon "one or the other legal title"[62] and that the judges are convinced that the individuals bound knew of its compulsory character.[63]

In summary, action in the outer world mirrors individual legal "understanding." Notably, in recent decisions there is no indication of a common knowledge requirement that incorporates each element of customary law. Nevertheless, some mutual legal understanding must exist. As pointed out in the *Balsfjord Case*, "required mutual understanding" does not include a perception that is identical in all respects. Some minor discrepancies may exist without blurring the positive outcome of recognized customary law.

5.5 The customary law prerequisites – an outline

This section focuses on Norwegian customary law prerequisites, i.e. how the courts' reasoning transforms social norms into legal rules. (See Chapter 7 for arguments as to whether the Saami possess customary law rights under these rules.)

Court decisions set forth criteria obliging parties to honor bottom-up customs as "the law of the land." Non-contested customs, however, are acknowledged *inter partes*. Such customs are valid law between recognizing parties, whether the court criteria are satisfied or not. Here no court decisions are required. The legislator or public agent is also unaffected by court prerequisites since acknowledged social practice or usage may be considered customary law without regard to court prerequisites. In the following sections, only disputed customs are under consideration. Once contested, court prerequisites play a vital role in determining the validity of a custom as law.

Unlike the Blackstonian criteria[64] recognized by Anglo-American courts, the Norwegian customary law prerequisites vary in range from two (ancient usage and *opinio juris et necessitatis sive obligationis* custom) to six separate conditions (ancient usage, *opinio juris*, *rationem vincat* (morally well founded), public, justified and reasonable custom). Despite the formal differences, there are considerable similarities between the two sets of criteria, which I will address later. For now, what follows is an outline of the Norwegian prerequisites.

5.5.1 Prolonged practice

The *Balsfjord Case* (above) asserts that common grazing was ongoing for at least 150 years. The general requirement defined by legal scholars is that usage must be followed "since ancient times." In the *Trondheimsfjorden Mussels Case*,[65] the court states that the usage "has been customary since ancient times."[66] In the *Lågen Case*, the requirement is that people have engaged in shallow bank fishing since the first half of the last century.[67] The court stated, however, that the origin of fishing goes back even further than verified by the information.[68] The Eidsivating High Court takes a similar stance in the *Jessheim Common Grazing Case*: "as far back as the information is available."[69] A similar decision is made in the *Bolstadfjord Case*[70] even if the wording is different, "This right must have been practiced . . . for as long as the present generation can remember."[71] Compare also the *Jølster Lake Case*.[72] "In order to have this character [binding usage] . . . the usage must be so ancient that the oldest living people know nothing else."[73] In the *Vansjø Case*,[74] the practice "must disappear into the darkness of the past."[75]

Therefore, the criteria vary. Sometimes, the criterion is a relative concept, e.g. ancient times or "a very long period of time." Just as frequently the time span must be stated more concretely, e.g. "a score of years is far too short." Nevertheless, the Supreme Court has never clearly stated that the time must be at least "X" number of years. The reference to "the present generation" and the viewpoint that the remembrance go as far back as available information, points back a maximum of seven generations: the great-grandfather can remember what his great-grandfather told him. With no contradictory information, we assume that the present tradition equals the earlier tradition. In no case, however, does the Norwegian requirement of "prolonged practice" correspond to the formerly practiced British criterion of "ancient usage," which required continuous practice since the reign of King Richard the Lionheart, or September 3, 1189.[76]

5.5.2 Continuity

Another prerequisite is that the practice has been continuous. The *Mussels Case* (above) emphasizes that a group of undefined fishermen "have taken mussels in Sundstrømmen for many years,"[77] which indicates a continuous practice. In the *Lågen Case*[78] the court stressed that

> shallow bank fishing was conducted in direct view of the property owners, in fixed places over a delimited area and concentrated within a short period in the fall when the herring go up the river . . . Shallow bank fishermen have fished there every year . . . Shallow bank fishing . . . has gained great constancy and stability. A condition that has developed in this way and which is acknowledged to this extent should not and cannot now be disrupted.[79]

Shallow bank fishing is an enduring, annual event. Meanwhile, it will not take much for a break in this event to discontinue "the acknowledged practice." Compare the *Bolstadfjord Case* claiming that fishermen "put up with being turned away and, in particular, simply stopped fishing for several years when the fishing rights were rented out."[80] Clearly, if the pattern is broken for a certain period of time, we cannot speak of acknowledged consistent practice. Compare also the *Frosta Felling Rights Case*[81] where local usage was overruled due to lack of evidence because, among other things: "There has scarcely been any real talk of any definite, regular or independent use from the side of the crofter."[82]

In the *Vansjø Case*,[83] the court found insufficient public activity because the fishing, during the actual time period, "was pursued to a small extent;"[84] "was of low volume;"[85] "was of poor volume and importance;"[86] or was "fishing that was scattered and occasional."[87] Accordingly, recognition is related to intensive usage that is consistent and regular (not "scattered and occasional"), while acknowledged practice means that usage is consistently employed and pursued in the same way ("stable"). In most of the seasonal fisheries along the coast, it can easily be established that the practice has been repeated year in and year out. Thus, the practice is not scattered and occasional. It is unlikely that anyone will dispute this prerequisite.

5.5.3 *Opinio juris necessitatis*

Traditionally, a third customary law condition applies: the prolonged practice must be based on a common belief that a rule of law, and not just a social norm, was being followed. Three issues arise. First, is the creation of the rule. Above all, is the rule creation visible, and not hidden? Otherwise antagonists are defenseless against "creeping" legal norms. Second, have the parties to the dispute obtained a somewhat identical legal position? Third, should customary law be recognized despite the existence of minor material discrepancies? Clearly the proposed legal opinion should be held in good faith.

Practice conducted according to one valid legal entitlement does not develop customary law under another kind of entitlement.[88] That is, if agreed upon, practice cannot develop new law. *In concreto*, fisheries conducted pursuant to an agreement do not initiate valid customary rights that substitute for that agreement if terminated. See for instance the *Trysil Firewood Case*[89] stating that a new right cannot be established through the exercise of an already recognized right of access, since such practice is invisible to the owner and may not be contested. Accordingly, if tacit acceptance is founded in innocent right of use, the passivity of the lessor cannot create local customary law of a particular type. It must

> be assumed that no previous practice of intense independent cutting of dry [wood] and waste has taken place. Therefore, forest owners were not challenged to intervene when they, as understood by the parties, have certainly considered the existing practice an innocent right of use that represented no danger to the forest.[90]

Practice taking place under the cover of *precario* usage does not create customary law. Usage that develops into new legal entitlements should exceed or contradict the valid activity under law or the agreement between the parties. Despite this clear position, some instances of *precario* usage have developed into legal rights. The *Lake Vansjø Case*[91] is important in this regard because it demonstrates tacit approval of sporadic and occasional fishing:

> The usage developed in the shadow of the property owners' benevolent attitude. It is hardly in accordance with good customs and usage to deny people such lenient fishing. I refer to the *Lågen Case* at Rt. 1963 s. 370. In my opinion . . . a scattered and occasional usage . . . and without economic significance for the property owners or the users, is tolerated fishing. Subsequently, the conditions for acquisition of rights by ancient time usage do not exist. However, it follows from the *Lågen Case*, that tolerated fishing through the years is converted into a right. Whether such a development can be proven depends upon the individual circumstances.[92]

Tolerated usage may develop into an "acknowledged" right. It is important to describe the transfer mechanisms because they provide the criteria for the transition from non-customary law-based "contested right" to "established customary law right."

Since the practice is camouflaged, innocent usage does not give notice to antagonists who, consequently, refrain from any protest. The display of signs and public notice prevents trespassing. In the *Trondheimfjord Mussels Case* (also known as the *Sundstrømmen Case*), the mussel owners' "protection notice" prevented good faith fisheries from continuing.[93] The Supreme Court acquitted the defendants, who in accordance with ancient customary practice, had taken mussels in Sundstrømmen for years without any hindrances whatsoever until the mentioned [owners] put up a "protection notice" to prevent further fishing a few years earlier.[94] In this case the court recognized that the landowners had a reason to react because the mussel fishing was clearly visible. If the use was justified, the notice as such did not terminate the public property right.

On the other hand, timely presented objections are effective. See for instance the *Sperillen Case*,[95] in which the majority states: "Since the turn of the century, some have certainly fished to a broader extent and with looser association to the farms. Nevertheless, this has been contested in part, and permission to fish has been granted in part."[96] Consequently, the property owner barred fishing and did not remain passive. As the permission to fish suggests, the legal entitlement lay in the agreement, and not in *precario* usage.

One-sided recognition of custom is not enough. The antagonists must share the legal belief. In the *Trysil Firewood Case* (see above), the Supreme Court denied farmers' alleged right to trees belonging to others. The court reasoned that a right which had evolved to the detriment of the owner's rights, and for which no reciprocal legal rights or obligations were exchanged, had to be acknowledged by a joint understanding. The antagonist had to be a party to this understanding, and had to recognize that the exercise of the right had been lawful. In other words, the party surrendering user or ownership rights must recognize the existence of the right in the party assuming it.[97] This 1918 case did not satisfy the prerequisite of "shared legal opinion." The reciprocity requirement is confirmed by the *Jølster Case.*[98] "No one can create binding customs by behavior alone; in order to have this character, the use requires a reciprocal awareness of positive right and obligation."[99] The same viewpoints are presented in both the *Fluberg Pasture Case*[100] and the *Vansjø Case.*[101]

The reciprocal understanding should mirror the general opinion of the trade or district. The customary law should be generally recognized throughout the realm of the proposed rule, not only amongst those involved in the actual conflict. This is clearly stated in the holding of the *Seaweed Sheds Case.*[102] "The general opinion in the district, including the property owners, is that the latter may not forbid seaweed sheds on their beaches. That such an opinion has been commonly held, is, in my opinion, far from proven."[103] While the beneficiaries shared the legal conviction of open access seaweed sheds, the property owners' belief was slightly different. The owners thought they could only refrain from actually prohibiting the activity.

To what extent, however, should unanimous belief exist? In the *Fluberg Grazing Case,*[104] the High Court recognized twenty-two witnesses from different parts of the district, who,

> so to say, unanimously expressed the belief that they had a "duty" to fence off the home fields from outlying fields and roads. They also believed this to be the general opinion in the district . . . The observations the court made during inspection of the scene corroborate that it must have been the

> general opinion in the district that the duty to fence existed as stated . . . I hardly think that fences would have had been so well maintained [as they are] if the farmers did not believe that they were required to do so.[105]

To sum it up, the legal opinion should be held in good faith by both parties. The reciprocally held opinions need not be identical, however. Such a requirement is "impossible," due to the fact that if the parties involved fully agreed, no customary law would ever develop! No requirement claims that the antagonists share identical legal understanding in all respects. According to the *Common Grazing Case*[106] it is sufficient that opinions, at a general level, do not conflict, cf. the *Lågen Case* (see above):

> The fishermen continued shallow bank fishing believing that they had a right to do so. They were convinced that the property owners could not deny or interfere with that, nor could the owners get in the way of permanently positioned equipment. I cannot place much weight on the fact that they have provided reciprocally different answers when asked about the legal basis for their right in association with the case.[107]

> [i]f the property owners' opinion is that shallow bank fishing is dependent on their giving their permission, one would have expected them to express this concern in the appropriate situations . . .[108]

> The property owners' behavior . . . indicates that they have put up with the fishing, either because they assumed that they could not deny it, or because they were in doubt about their rights and therefore did not intervene. Shallow bank fishing by people without special fishing rights has developed because of the property owners' consistent passivity . . .[109]

Consequently, while the fishermen's implemented practice tends to document customary rights, the owners' input is limited to non-contesting. Despite the landowners' unclear *opinio juris*, a customary right similar to fisheries practice was upheld. The key is whether the qualifying groups advocate an adversarial understanding of the law. Their feeling of being obligated by the rule should be based on law, not on extra-legal principle.

5.5.4 Passivity

Tolerated uses and passivity are closely related because lack of reaction easily transforms innocent usage into a fixed right. Insufficient objection tacitly approves open access fishery. Obviously, passivity is of great importance. It proceeds from the *Lågen Case* that, depending on the circumstances, "the passivity of the property owners is important when adjudicating whether precario fishing has evolved into a right . . . . In the period after 1950 . . . the property owners did not stand by passively. In 1956, they formed their association whose objective was to protect the owners' interests."[110]

The importance of adequate reaction is shown in a long series of Supreme Court decisions. In the *Seaweed Sheds Case* (see above), the court emphasized that the seaweed shed in question was neither undisputed nor unchallenged, contrary to the finding of the lower courts.[111] In its *ratio decidendi* the court found that property owners had remained actively opposed to the public rights. Therefore, the court concluded that no unanimous legal opinion could be construed.

A comparable problem is taken up in the *Bolstadfjord Case* (see above). The plaintiffs alleged that salmon and trout fishing were reserved for the property owners on both sides of the fjord, and that the public had to ask for net fishery permission. This fishing was partly tolerated as long as it did not hamper the property owners. The Appellate Court concluded, and the Supreme Court upheld that:

> the public fishermen have not met their burden of proof . . . that fishing in Bolstadfjorden, under ancient times usage, is free for everybody and anybody, regardless of whether he is a property owner. In addition, it must be proven that this right has been practiced unchallenged, for as long as the present generation can remember. That is certainly not the case here.[112]

Clearly, the property owner that fails to protest against conflicting use will easily forfeit his alleged rights. The existence of a particular provocation is vital. Seen in context with the time requirement "unchallenged, for as long as the present generation can remember," one might say that the longer the period of time passed without any owner reaction, the greater the reason to allow passivity to terminate ownership rights. In that situation, *precario* usage may convert into legal rights. The distinction is far from clear. A good lead is found in the 1995 *Balsfjord Pasture Case*:[113]

> Traditionally the common pasture has been grazed without heavy burden to any landowner. The appellants claim that default reaction resulted in a *precario* usage only. Analyzing the situation, such a result seems erroneous, because . . . the common pasture has been of utmost importance to the farmers. The validity of *precario* usage depends upon whether each individual owner had the right to restrict further grazing on his land, even though the grazing did not harm him. The circumstances presented to the court fail to verify that this situation initiates such a right.[114]

The court adjudication is "contra-factual," meaning that if the grazing is *precario*, the landowner's exclusive right remains. Closure is then based upon the landowner's autonomous decision. None of the witnesses testified that any of the landowners, at any time, had implemented fencing rights on their land in order to force out "foreign cattle."

To summarize, Norwegian courts generally recognize a particular norm as customary law if (1) it has been in effect as long as living people can remember; (2) without significant interruption; (3) under a belief that the norm had legal status; and (4) without actively expressed opposition. In Chapter 10 we will see how these rules may be applied to the fishing practices of the Saami people.

Endnotes

1. Bertil Bengtsson, "Epilog," in Birgitta Jahreskog (ed.), *The Saami National Minority in Sweden* (Rättsfonden, Stockholm, 1982), p. 250.
2. King Christian V Codex, the preamble.
3. Oscar Platou, *Forelæsninger over Retskildernes Theori* [*Lectures in the Theory of Legal Sources*] (T. O. Brøgger, Kristiania, 1915), p. 56.
4. Alf Ross, *On Law and Justice* (Stevens, London, 1974), p. 109.
5. *Ibid.*, at 110.
6. N. Falck, *Juridische Encyclopädie* (Kiel, 1821) – all translations from Norwegian, Danish and German, here and in the following sections, are by P. Ørebech.
7. See especially Hans Kelsen, *Pure Theory of Law* (University of California Press, Berkley, Calif., 1967); and Neil McGormick, "Law as Institutional Fact" (1974) *Law Quarterly Review.*
8. Hans Kelsen, *Allegemeine Staatslehre* (Julis Springer, Berlin, 1925), pp. 16–21.
9. E. Lambert, *Etudes de droit législatif ou de droit civil comparé, I Série, B. 1. La fonction de droit civil comparé* (Paris, 1903).
10. Alf Ross, *Om ret og Retfärdighed* [*Law and Justice*] (Nyt Nordisk forlag, Copenhagen, 1953).
11. Arnold Ræstad, *Om gyldigheten av lokal sedvanerett efter norsk ret* [*About the Validity of Local Customary Law according to Norwegian Law*] (1913), p. 241.
12. Walter Ullmann, *The Medieval Idea of Law as Presented by Lucas de Pena. A Study in Fourteenth-Century Legal Scholarship* (London, 1946), p. 64.
13. Currently Danish Supreme Court Judge.
14. Henrik Zahle, *Dansk statsforfatningsret* [*Danish Constitutional Law*] (Christian Ejler's Forlag, Copenhagen, 1989), vol. 1, s. 26.
15. Platou, *Forelæsninger over Retskildernes Theori*, p. 87.
16. Henry Ussing, *Aftaler* [*Agreements*] (G.E.C. Gads, Copenhagen, 1955), p. 438.

17. Jan Fridthjof Bernt and David R. Doublet, *Vitenskapsfilosofi for jurister – en innføring* [*Philosophy of Science for Lawyers – An Introduction*] (Ad Notam Gyldendal, Bergen, 1998), p. 79.
18. Kr. Fr. Brøgger, *Lov og Rett* [*Law and Right*] (Aschehoug, Oslo, 1951), p. 903.
19. Per Augdahl, *Rettskilder* [*Sources of Law*] (Aschehoug, Oslo, 1973), p. 191.
20. Platou, *Forelæsninger over Retskildernes Theori*, p. 55.
21. Torstein Eckhoff, *Rettskildelære* [*Sources of Law*] (Universitetsforlaget, Oslo, 1980), p. 19.
22. Ross, *On Law and Justice*, p. 109.
23. Alf Ross, *Dansk Statsforfatningsret* [*Danish Constitutional Law*] (Nyt Nordisk forlag, Copenhagen, 1966), vol. 1, p. 155.
24. Under the supervision of The Legal Structure Committee, a sub-agency under the Ministry of Labor and Government Administration.
25. Decided by the Norwegian Storting by Law # 102 (1985), cf. Ot.prp. no. 1 (1985–86) pp. 1–2.
26. NOU 1985:32 *Revisjon av allmenningslovgivningen* [*Moderation of the Commons Legislation*].
27. J. G. A. Pocock, *The Ancient Constitution and the Feudal Law. English Historical Thought in the Seventeenth Century* (Norton, New York, 1967), p. 34.
28. See the letter of May 15, 1991 from the Ministry of Labor and Government Administration (j.no.91/01861) and the letter of October 29, 1991 from "The Legal Structure Committee": "The Committee strongly advised the Ministry of Agriculture to take the opportunity of transferring the provisions of NL 3-12 into new legislation."
29. Pocock, *Ancient Constitution and the Feudal Law*, p. 34.
30. May be even earlier than the establishment of the Kingdom of Norway, 872 AD.
31. Gulatingslagen and Frostatingslagen around 1000 AD.
32. King Magnus Lagaboete's Norwegian Rural Codex.
33. King Christian IV 1604 General Codex, http://www.hf.uio.no/PNH/chr4web/chr4innhold.html.
34. King Christian V 1687 General Codex, http://www.hf.uio.no/PNH/chr5web/chr5fortale.html.
35. Hannu Tapani Klami, "Om rättsdogmatisk forskning" ["About the Science of Legal Dogmatism"] (Åbo akademi, 1984), p. 12 – the translation is by the author of this chapter.
36. Per-Olof Ekelöf, *Är den juridiska doktrinen en teknik eller en vetenskap?* [*Is Legal Dogmatism a Matter of Mechanics, or a Science?*] (Gleerup, Lund, 1951), pp. 21 ff.
37. See for instance *Tennessee Valley Authority v. Hill*, 437 U.S. 153, 185 (1978) (Warren Burger majority opinion).
38. See the dissenting opinion of Lewis Powell, 437 U.S. at 196.

39. A. V. Lundstedt. *Grundlinjer i skadesståndsretten, senare delen bd II:2* [*Basic Structures in Tort Law*] (Almquist & Wiksell, Uppsala 1953), pp. 68–122.
40. See John Stuart Mill, *Utilitarianism* (Prometheus Books, New York 1987).
41. Bertil Bengtsson, "Postscript" in Birgitta Jahreskog (ed.), *The Saami National Minority in Sweden* (Rättsfonden, Stockholm, 1982), p. 250.
42. Of February 29, 1981.
43. Peter Ørebech, "Sedvanerett som grunnlag for bærekraftig forvaltning av fiske i de 'ytre almenninger' ["Customary Law as a Foundation for Sustainable Fishing Management"], in Bjørn Sagdahl (ed.), *Fjordressurser og Reguleringspolitikk* (Kommuneforlaget, Oslo, 1998), pp. 141 ff.
44. Francis Hagerup, *Retsencyclopædi* 12 (Aschehoug, Kristiania, 1919), p. 12.
45. Alf Ross, *On Law and Justice* (University of California Press, Berkley, CA, 1974).
46. Bouvier's *Law Dictionary and Concise Encyclopedia* (Rawle's third revision, Kansas City, 1914), p. 742.
47. William Blackstone, *Commentaries on the Laws of England* (John Murray, London, 1857), vol. I, p. 50.
48. Josiah Ober, *The Athenian Revolution. Essays on Ancient Greek Democracy and Political Theory* (Princeton University Press, Princeton NJ, 1996), p. 174.
49. Edouard Lambert, "Codified law and Case-law: Their Part in Shaping the Policies of Justice," in *Science of Legal Method. Selected Essays by Various Authors 257* (transl. by Ernest Bruncken and Layton B. Register, The Macmillan Company, New York, 1921).
50. Rt. (Norsk Retstidende – Norwegian Supreme Court Chronicle) 1896 s. 500. All translations from Norwegian literature and court records are by this author.
51. *Ibid.*, at 505.
52. *Ibid.*
53. Rt. 1912 s. 433.
54. *Ibid.*, at 436.
55. Rt. 1935 s. 838.
56. Rt. 1959 s. 1321.
57. Rt. 1963 s. 370.
58. *Ibid.*, at 376.
59. Rt. 1983 s. 569.
60. *Ibid.*, at 583–585.
61. Rt. 1995 s. 644.
62. *Ibid.*, at 648.
63. *Ibid.*
64. See Section 4.3.
65. Rt. 1888 s. 682.
66. *Ibid.*, at 684.
67. Rt. 1936 s. 370.

68. *Ibid.*, at 379.
69. RG 1962 s. 265 (Norwegian Journal of High Court and District Court Decisions).
70. Rt. 1912 s. 433.
71. *Ibid.*, at 443.
72. Rt. 1935 s. 838.
73. *Ibid.*, at 843.
74. Rt. 1983 s. 569.
75. *Ibid.*, at 579.
76. Michael T. Clanchy, *From Memory to Written Record* (Edward Arnold, London, 1979), p. 123.
77. Rt. 1888 at s. 684.
78. Rt. 1963 s. 370.
79. *Ibid.*, at 377–378.
80. Rt. 1912 s. 433.
81. Rt. 1931 s. 428.
82. *Ibid.*, at 430.
83. Rt. 1983 s. 569.
84. *Ibid.*, at 581.
85. *Ibid.*, at 583.
86. *Ibid.*, at 582.
87. *Ibid.*, at 583.
88. S. Brækhus and A. Hærem, *Norsk Tingsrett [Norwegian Property Law]* (Universitetsforlaget, Oslo, 1964), p. 612.
89. Rt. 1918 II s. 261.
90. *Ibid.*, at 265.
91. Rt. 1983 s. 569.
92. *Ibid.*, at 583.
93. Rt. 1888 s. 682.
94. *Ibid.*, at 684.
95. Rt. 1972 s. 77.
96. *Ibid.*, at 82.
97. Rt. 1918 II at s. 265.
98. Rt. 1935 s. 838.
99. *Ibid.*, at 843.
100. Rt. 1959 s. 1321.
101. Rt. 1983 s. 569.
102. Rt. 1896 s. 500.
103. *Ibid.*, at 505.
104. RG 1962 s. 261.
105. *Ibid.*, at 265.
106. RG 1962 s. 261.

107. Rt. 1963 at s. 376.
108. *Ibid.*, at 377.
109. *Ibid.*, at 378.
110. Rt. 1983 s. 569, at s. 583–84.
111. Rt. 1896 at s. 505.
112. Rt. 1912 at s. 443.
113. Rt. 1995 s. 644.
114. *Ibid.*, at 649.

6

Adaptive resource management through customary law

FRED BOSSELMAN

Some customary law systems work better than others. This chapter suggests that there are particular characteristics of certain customary law systems that indicate whether these systems are more likely to accomplish sustainable development objectives than other systems. The chapter focuses on a characteristic of complex systems that has received increasing attention in the literature of management, law, ecology and economics – resilience, defined as the system's ability to adapt to changing conditions.

Sustainable development requires management of resources in order to ensure that they can be adequately utilized both now and in the future. The customary law systems that are most relevant to that objective are those that deal with resource management. This chapter will evaluate systems of customary law for resource management from an instrumental perspective. How can we tell whether a particular system of customary law will succeed in managing resources in a way that produces sustainable development? In other words, will a given body of customary law work in a way that meets long-range objectives?

The first part of this chapter reviews the reasons why resource management systems need to be resilient. As we recognize the increased speed with which the earth's ecology, technology and social structure is changing, we recognize that any resource management system, whether or not customary in origin, needs to be capable of adaptation to a wide range of future changes in the surrounding environment if it is to operate in a sustainable manner.

The second part of the chapter looks at some of the many recent case studies of customary law systems to determine which systems seem to have demonstrated resilience. This review suggests that five characteristics of those systems may be good indicators of whether they will be able to adapt in sustainable ways: (1) Does the system have a good historical record, oral or written, of the way the system has worked in the past under different environmental conditions? (2) Is an effective procedural mechanism for making rule changes built into the system? (3) Does the system feed back the right information on current operations into the rule modification process? (4) Are the rules sufficiently finely detailed that they can be "tweaked" without wholesale revision? (5) Do the rules facilitate negotiation of modifications by providing for a balance of rights and responsibilities relating to a wide range of ecosystem functions?

6.1 Resilient customary law systems promote sustainable development

In the real world, the role of customary law in sustainable development is less likely to be determined by general principles relating to the role of custom in the legal system than by evaluations of specific customary law regimes to determine whether they are likely to produce desirable consequences. Simply put, some customary law systems seem to produce sustainable results and some do not.[1]

6.1.1 Resilience as a management strategy

One factor that is frequently used as a key test in determining whether any management system will be able to achieve sustainable development is its resilience. In modern terms, resilient systems of resource management are characterized as "adaptive management" systems.[2] They are capable of responding to what science increasingly sees as an unstable environment.[3] Recent literature in the fields of management, law, ecology and economics recognizes the need for such resilience.

In the business schools, management theorists are increasingly embracing adaptive planning methodologies. Earlier strategic planning theories emphasizing formulation of a grand plan dominated management theory in the 1980s. But managers found that information became useful to those planning processes only if it was packaged in a way to plug into the formula. If it was ambiguous or complex, or if it challenged the paradigm on which the planning was based, they tended to ignore it.

Empirical researchers found that firms that use strategic planning methods to "create intensive focus and unified cultures . . . do so at the expense of responsiveness. The singlemindedness that initially gives them an edge over competition and results in success, over time reduces internal diversity." Routines become rigid, non-core functions are cut, and "disconfirming information is neither sought nor fully entertained." Over time, the firm "ceases to pick up stimuli signaling fundamental changes in the environment and gradually reduces internal diversity until it is insufficient to respond to new demands from the environment."[4] "The economist's neoclassical model of the firm [as] a smoothly running machine in a world without secrets, without frictions or uncertainty, and without a temporal dimension," has in practice succumbed to "uncertainty, information asymmetry, bounded rationality, opportunism, and asset specificity."[5]

Many strategic planning theories have succumbed to these empirical studies that showed their ineffectiveness.[6] Faith in long-range and strategic planning failed to survive the economic turmoil that began with the oil embargo of 1973 and the floating exchange rates, high inflation and increasing international competition that followed; "organizations learned from practical experience that simple extrapolations of history and cadres of professional planners failed to lead to innovation, adaptation to change, or even survival."[7] Emphasis has shifted from the plan as document to the plan as a process through which new information is analyzed and communicated within the organization to enable decisions to be made promptly as the need arises.[8] As J. B. Ruhl puts it, if there is no incentive to experiment, any learning that has not yet materialized into tangible performance results is stultified.[9]

Modern management theory suggests that decision-making should be a "layered advice process" in which much information and many alternatives are discussed and analyzed.[10] These ideas have been significantly influenced by Japanese management theorists, who have emphasized a management structure based on a matrix in which communication takes place among all levels of the structure, rather than a pyramidal structure in which information is passed down from above.[11]

Some types of natural resource management have always been tied to objectives that require a long-range view.[12] Growing wood or preventing aquifer pollution, for example, cannot be evaluated meaningfully on a quarterly basis.[13] Canadian management professor Frances Westley has assessed natural resource management from the perspective of management theory. She advocates adaptive management as a way of managing an ecosystem that is "responsive to the variations, rhythms, and cycles of change natural in [the ecosystem and] able to react quickly with appropriate management techniques."

Westley points out that adaptive management has "an appeal that transcends the management of ecosystems. In the past decade – in response to radical shifts in world economies, resource bases, population dynamics, and competitive structures – private- and public-sector organizations in all domains have wrestled with similar challenges."[14] She describes adaptive management as a "learning-led" strategy. Learning introduces redundancies and inconsistencies into the organizational structure that "may modify the conclusive nature of existing ideologies." In learning-led strategies, consensus emerges through much discussion. But she warns that learning-led networks may not have a "foundation of action routines" on which to draw; i.e., they may be "relatively resource poor." Yet to the extent that mechanisms for sensing and responding to change "become rationalized and focused, the system may seem more efficient in the short run, but it may actually become more vulnerable."[15]

Stephen Haeckel characterizes this style of management as involving a four-stage "sense-and-respond" process. An adaptive organization first senses changes in its environment; then it incorporates the changes in light of its experience and objectives; then it decides how to respond; and finally it acts on that decision, meanwhile monitoring the results of its action and thus beginning the cycle again.[16]

Carl Walters argues that one of the most common faults of resource managers is using ignorance as an excuse for inaction. The "responses of resource systems to management can, in the end, only be learned through experience, so the common prescription to 'wait until we understand the system better' is based on a false presumption that extrapolation (to the conditions created by not waiting) will become possible even without experience."[17]

Variables, Walters argues, are inevitable. Profitability, risk, recent experience, the competitive scramble, erosion of biological stock and technological evolution; these will continue to be variables regardless of any management system, and will tend to prevent long-term maintenance of equilibrium. A manager who "tries to view his problem from any narrow perspective or disciplinary emphasis" will find that these variables will "come back to haunt" him.[18] We need to "embrace uncertainty, and admit that most resource management decisions are essentially gambles that we try to package by presenting reams of data and elaborate calculations.[19]

6.1.2 The need for resilient legal rules

Legal scholars have pointed to a number of legal issues that need to be addressed if resource management systems are to be managed adaptively. In particular, it may be important to reduce the law's traditional concern for predictability and certainty in favor of more flexibility to respond to changing conditions.[20]

Real estate law is a field in which the objective of certainty has understandably been emphasized. But William Rodgers advises that legal concepts of property in wildlife, water or oil may be more appropriate analogies for dealing with modern ecological theories of environmental change. These kinds of property are more fluid; they recognize the need to adapt to changes in the environment, while property rights in land have typically emphasized the value of finality.[21]

Dan Tarlock contends that the law of resource management should follow the science it seeks to implement. He emphasizes that "adaptive management is premised on the assumption that management strategies should change in response to new scientific information. All resource management is an ongoing experiment."[22] Other legal scholars have also suggested the need to abandon law's traditional preference for finality in the making of environmental rules.[23] Daniel Farber says that although scientists are constantly improving our environmental knowledge base, there is still a high degree of uncertainty. "Change has been a constant theme in environmental law," and he argues that we should treat that as an opportunity rather than a problem. We "need to be more experimental, trying a lot of different things and attempting to learn from the results."[24] J. B. Ruhl also argues that we still try to make too many permanent decisions about environmental policy even though we recognize that our old decisions are outmoded.[25]

6.1.3 Resilience in ecological systems

To ecologists, the key postulate of adaptive management is that environmental change is to be anticipated. The contemporary ecological paradigm, as described by one of its earliest proponents, Steward Pickett, is that ecosystems are open, can be regulated by external processes and are subject to natural disturbances. "Thus, rather than viewing ecosystems as being 'in balance', systems are seen as in flux . . ."[26]

University of Florida ecologist Crawford Holling argues that a feature of ecosystems is that the "environment is not constant. Environmental change is not continuous and gradual, but episodic." Ecosystems don't have a single equilibrium, they have multiple equilibria that define functionally different states, and movement between these states is a natural part of maintaining structure and diversity. Management policies that assume that existing conditions are the natural order of things "lead to systems that lack resilience and may break down from disturbances that were previously absorbed."[27]

Ecologists such as Holling and Pickett advocate management policies that use a dynamic model that treats ecological systems as constantly changing and open to outside processes.[28] Adaptive management systems based on such a model will "simultaneously retain and encourage the adaptive capabilities of people, of business enterprises, and of nature."[29] Holling says that sustainable development "requires flexible, diverse, and redundant regulation, early signals of error built into incentives for corrective action, and continuous experimental probing of the changes in the external world. Those are the features of adaptive environmental and resource management"[30] that can turn an unexpected event, such as drought, price change or market shift, into an opportunity rather than a crisis.[31] Sustainable development, he argues, "has embraced an adaptive management ethic . . ."[32]

Managers who use too short a time frame often fail to acknowledge that such disturbances as fire, flood and pestilence are part of natural ecological cycles.[33] Allen and Hoekstra point out that if viewed at an appropriate time scale "almost all processes that at first appear to be a linear progression will emerge as cyclical . . . Individual fires are directional and have a before and after; nevertheless, fires return in a fire cycle."[34] Resource managers are short-sighted if they treat each of these disturbances as one-time events, and focus on it exclusively, using techniques such as insecticides, fire suppression, rangeland management and fish hatcheries.[35] But these techniques slowly reduce spatial heterogeneity in favor of uniformity, which then enlarges the area at risk. For example, there are fewer breaks in the forest so fire or pestilence spreads more easily; in grasslands, exotics that outcompete drought-resistant grasses may spread more widely; in fisheries, wild species may be driven out by increased hatchery populations, leaving the industry dependent on hatcheries whose productivity declines with time.[36]

In many cases, the ability to recognize that a particular disturbance is part of a normal long-range cycle requires analysis over a long period of time.[37] Managers who are forced to operate on short time frames tend to consider short-term results more important than long-term objectives.[38] Robert Keiter argues that resource management proposals should be evaluated using an ecologically derived time scale.[39] In doing so, they need to recognize that change is a part of natural ecological processes.

However, some resource managers use the legitimacy of change as an excuse to speed up processes of change beyond the limits of the ecological system to absorb such changes without collapsing.[40] For example, ever since Aldo Leopold's pioneering works, we have been aware that the attempt to "wipe out" a predator or pestilence is likely to have a much more unanticipated impact than mere management measures.[41] Effective adaptive management requires continuous inputs from scientific research into the resilience of the natural environment.[42]

6.1.4 Ecology and economics

Economists Robert Costanza and Carl Folke analogize these anthropomorphic perturbations of ecological systems to destructive disease in humans:

> Since ecosystems experience succession as a result of changing climatic conditions and internal developmental changes, they have a limited (albeit fairly long) lifespan. The key is differentiating between changes due to normal lifespan limits and changes that cut short the lifespan of the system. Things that cut short the lifespan of humans are obviously contributors to poor health. Cancer, AIDS, and a host of other ailments do just this. Human-induced eutrophication in aquatic ecosystems causes a radical change in the nature of the system . . . since the lifespan of the first system was cut "unnaturally" short. It may have gone eutrophic eventually, but the anthropogenic stress caused this transition to occur prematurely.[43]

The relatively new field of "ecological economics" is also devoted to efforts to understand the "coevolutionary development of human beings and the natural world."[44] One issue that ecological economics has addressed is the need to include information about the resilience of ecosystems in economic decision-making processes:

> [One] useful index of environmental sustainability is ecosystem resilience, [which] is a measure of the magnitude of disturbances that can be absorbed before a system centered on one locally stable equilibrium flips to another. Economic activities are sustainable only if the life-support ecosystems on which they depend are resilient . . . The loss of ecosystem resilience is potentially important for at least three reasons. First, the discontinuous change in ecosystem functions as the system flips from one equilibrium to another could be associated with a sudden loss of biological productivity, and so to a reduced capacity to support human life. Second, it may imply an irreversible change in the set of options open both to present and future generations (examples include soil erosion, depletion of groundwater reservoirs, desertification, and loss of biodiversity). Third, discontinuous and irreversible changes from familiar to unfamiliar states increase the uncertainties associated with the environmental effects of economic activities.[45]

As the above discussion shows, people who have studied resource management from perspectives as different as management, law, ecology and economics have emphasized the need for resilient management systems. The rest of this chapter will review some of the empirical studies of customary law systems to try to identify criteria that will help determine whether the system can be expected to manage adaptively in the future.

6.2 Identifying resilient customary systems

Not all customary legal systems are characterized by resilience. As Shepard Krech observed in his extensive study of American Indian systems of resource management, some of these systems remained effective for centuries while others depleted the resource, forcing the tribes to move on.[46] Australian students of indigenous customs have made similar comments: "While it may not be popular in some quarters, we disagree with the view that indigenous peoples, including Aborigines, are necessarily conservationists at heart – that is, that they are innately conservation-inclined." There has been a great deal of "maladaptive retention of traditional beliefs in a changing world . . ."[47]

Some customary law systems may have worked well during relatively stable periods but collapsed when circumstances changed.[48] Charles Zerner studied fishing management practices in the Moluccas that had evolved over a century in ways that appeared to be sustainable. But when a new market developed for a different form of marine life, the failure of the traditional customs to manage the resource successfully suggested that the earlier appearance of sustainability was accidental.[49]

On the other hand, resilient management systems have often evolved where people recognized the likelihood of unpredictable environmental changes. Thus, for example, in Samoa the recognition that cyclones were a certain but unpredictable part of the environment may have contributed to customs of reliance on multiple crops that provided a better chance of withstanding damage from cyclones.[50]

How can we distinguish those existing systems of customary resource management that are likely to be sufficiently resilient to serve as models for the future?[51] Can ideal substantive resource management techniques be discerned from the observation of customary systems? Some observers have tried, but differences of opinion are frequent. For example, James Wilson and his colleagues suggest that in "more traditional societies, fisheries are managed by rules and practices limiting 'how' people fish rather than by attempting to regulate 'how much' of various species can be taken. The fact that such regulations are found so widely and have lasted for such a long time suggests that such rules are highly adaptive."[52] This particular view is directly contradicted by other observers, however, who argue that "input controls generally lead to inefficient outcomes" because they "lead to more variable yield than output controls."[53]

As the above example suggests, empirical investigators do not necessarily agree on substantive resource management principles that can be derived from a study of customary law systems. But there is greater agreement on some of the procedural and technical factors that make a customary law system operate in a sustainable manner. Based on a review of many of the published studies of these systems, five such factors seem to serve as useful indicators of the system's sustainability. We should ask about any system of customary resource management whether it (1) recognizes a history of adaptations that it has made in the past, (2) offers a vehicle for making changes in the rules effectively, (3) encourages "fine-grained" rules that facilitate modification, (4) provides meaningful feedback mechanisms, and (5) avoids unduly privatizing rights without privatizing responsibilities, and vice versa.

6.2.1 *Recording a history of adaptation*

The first question to ask about any customary law system is whether it is possible to review the history of the past experience of the system in responding to environmental change. A resilient system would be one that has already demonstrated a capability to respond to changing environmental conditions, and has recorded the history of that adaptation in a way that can educate future managers.[54]

In a study of local systems for fisheries management, a committee of the National Research Council emphasized that the amount of knowledge that is accumulated increases with the passage of time:

> Communities of fishing people that have developed long-standing, successful (legal and extralegal) arrangements for governing their use of fish stocks and fishing grounds share several general characteristics: . . . They have existed for long periods of time. Most likely, their families have fished in the areas for decades, and they want their children and grandchildren to have the opportunity to fish there in the future. They have extensive experience with their fishing grounds and the stocks they fish. They possess good information concerning the structure and functioning of their fishing grounds and variations over time.[55]

Scientists increasingly recognize that successful customary resource management systems often rely on very intricate patterns of knowledge developed over long periods of observation.[56] Studies of Australian Aboriginal resource management systems suggest that some "traditional environmental knowledge is rich with understanding of how their environment has changed over time." These include changes caused by cyclones, increased human populations, and new agricultural practices.[57] A study of Chinese agricultural practices also concluded that families with many generations of accumulated experience tended to utilize more sustainable practices than those with less experience.[58] Many customary systems have developed rules of thumb to enhance sustainability through comparison of levels of harvest of resources over time.[59]

Crises that the customary law system has confronted in the past may be an indicator of future success. Berkes suggests that a "resource crisis" may be a "necessary ingredient of social learning," and that a "conservation ethic may never develop if the group in question fails to experience a crisis or is unable to interpret it."[60] Of course some crises may be so disruptive that neither the ecological system nor the social system can recover, as suggested in studies of the *Exxon Valdez* oil spill[61] and the Everglades.[62] This suggests that the study of past patterns of changes in customary resource management systems may be particularly profitable.[63]

The value of a long history of practical experience may be particularly great where current scientific information is inadequate.

> The need to integrate the knowledge systems of science and local users seems greatest and most productive where (1) the predictive abilities of science are limited . . . and (2) practical knowledge can be obtained from communities with long (i.e., several generations and therefore, arguably, sustainable to some degree) traditions of natural resource use.[64]

This implies that resources for which good scientific data are hard to obtain, such as marine fisheries, may be particularly well served by customary law systems.

6.2.2 *Offering a vehicle for making changes*

To be resilient, a management system needs good procedural rules for changing the substantive rules, as Elinor Ostrom's work has demonstrated.[65] "Without the continuing capacity to match new rules to new circumstances," she suggests, resource managers will "face considerable difficulties in coping with the diverse environmental and strategic threats that arise in dynamic systems."[66] But Holly Doremus emphasizes that flexibility has its dangers, and that "we must develop institutions that combine the flexibility needed to allow appropriate responses to new information with sufficient constraints and oversight mechanisms to ensure that protective responses are in fact taken."[67]

Most customary law systems are dynamic, not static. Fikret Berkes asserts that "it is important to recognize indigenous resource management systems not as mere traditions but as adaptive responses that have evolved over time . . . in fits and starts."[68] "Traditional," says Berkes, "does not mean inflexible adherence to the past: it simply means time-tested and wise."[69]

Effective procedural rules depend on an attitude of open-mindedness among the rule-making group. A recent study by the World Bank of its natural resource management projects found that there was a strong correlation between successful projects and "stable, competent, flexible, and demand-responsive executing agencies that identify closely with project objectives."[70] Resource managers can use customary legal systems to build "resource management systems that are open to alternative ways of thinking, rather than being conceptually closed . . ."[71] Many viable systems of common property management have proved themselves capable of evolving quite rapidly to meet new conditions.[72]

Raymond MacCallum's proposal for a Canadian system of community-based fisheries management emphasizes that the "decision-making process must be participatory, enlisting knowledge input from all of its members, and receiving in return respect for the institutions and rules." If everyone believes that they have an ability to influence the rules, they should have a stake in the observance of those rules, thus creating a "community of interest" on objectives and methods that will give the management regime sufficient legitimacy to guarantee compliance with the rules.[73] Local governments can sometimes perform the function of modifying customary rules to meet changing economic or environmental conditions.[74]

The need to maintain a continuity of rule-making procedures is illustrated by Arun Agrawal's account of agricultural resource management in India. In the past, rules for managing the commons were enforced by an informal "panchayat," a self-selected council of elders with considerable social prestige. Today, the elected Village Council has "attempted to resurrect and create new rules for utilizing the commons" utilizing the help of the informal panchayat. The "traditional is less a dead and reified past, more a living history."[75]

The generation gap between older and younger leaders may need attention when rule-making procedures are addressed. A study of customary law in Australia suggests that the "control of knowledge" can become an issue within Aboriginal communities; "older people in positions of authority may wish to remain in control of knowledge so that younger people are obliged to seek it from them rather than being able to acquire it from written sources."[76] On the other hand, other studies of customary systems have found that younger generations respect elders' traditions but want to verify them through their own experience.[77] In former colonial societies, this generation gap may be aggravated by suspicion of the legitimacy of institutions initiated during colonial times.[78]

Where rules against the taking of particular species or invasion of particular habitats have religious origins they are often known as "taboos."[79] Although the religious nature of the restriction may strengthen its enforcement, it may also hinder its adaptability. Thus a permanent ban on the harvesting of certain species may increase the pressure on other species in ways that threaten to overturn the natural ecological processes.[80] In their study of taboos, however, John Colding and Carl Folke have found that some taboos vary over time. For example, they may be imposed by local chiefs in the Pacific Islands only in times of resource scarcity.[81]

Mutual trust among members of a community can reduce the need for formal rules and regulations.[82] Susan Hanna suggests that it is important to remember that rule-making procedures are "embedded" in the historical political and economic structure of a community. Resource management rules are part of the society's entire structure of norms, rules and enforcement procedures. "Embeddedness plays an important role in the success of resource management systems . . . The cost of ignoring the importance of embeddedness or of removing its functions is often the disruption of the resource management process."[83] For example, Bonnie McCay's historical study of oystering in New Jersey illustrates the difficulty of maintaining workable systems for managing those common resources that are particularly susceptible to environmental changes in the absence of accepted traditions for changing the rules.[84]

Community-level participation in the rule-making process often appears to be a key element in successful customary law systems.[85] In a study of rule-making in Maine fisheries, Susan Hanna concluded that the localized nature of customary rules facilitated their revision.

> Flexible local rule making allows revision of management decisions that do not lead to the desired outcome. Rules can be revised without the costly and time-consuming co-ordination process that would ensue from a more hierarchical decision process. Rapid response and continual monitoring are possible because action is local.[86]

Another study found that customary laws for resource management in the Pacific islands "are flexible in that there are constant negotiations at the community level regarding access and use" and the rules of tenure are being continually interpreted, transformed and redefined."[87] Berkes calls this "qualitative management," as distinguished from quantitative systems that focus only on a specific yield target.[88]

Local participation reduces centralized transaction costs. The small size of the communities and the cohesiveness of the population avoids many of the problems to which co-management is often vulnerable.[89] For example, a study of customary resource allocation in the South Pacific islands found a history of gradual change. Although the official recognition of *de facto* changes, and their acceptance, was often slow, yet "the fact that they are occurring shows how adaptable customary tenure can be in the face of new needs."[90] A series of Canadian studies of co-management in fisheries also concluded that local participation works best where the number of fishing groups is not so large as to prevent effective communication, thus making it possible to modify rules and practices with relatively low transaction costs.[91]

6.2.3 Providing feedback mechanisms

A mechanism for providing changes in rules will be successful only if information relevant to needed changes is available. A resilient system of adaptation to environmental change requires prompt and accurate feedback of information about the changes in environmental conditions into the decision-making process.[92] "Both indigenous knowledge and Adaptive Management focus on feedbacks and the maintenance of ecological resilience," according to Fikret Berkes.[93] "The key factor in successful adaptations may be the presence of appropriate feedback mechanisms which enable consequences of earlier decisions to influence the next set of decisions which make adaptation possible."[94]

There has been a growing movement to encourage cooperative management that views ecological systems from larger temporal and spatial scales with more extensive community involvement.[95] The idea of managing resources on a larger scale than typically practiced in the past has become known as "ecosystem management,"[96] a phrase with somewhat elusive content.[97] Fikret Berkes maintains that this type of large-scale ecological management is more common in customary systems than in conventional resource management.[98]

Perhaps ecologists' most consistent criticism of conventional resource managers relates to their failure to get feedback relating to factors other than the particular species that are intended for human consumption. Managers often fail to realize the extent to which the management of a few species has an indirect effect on the ecological systems that will create broader repercussions that, in turn, will impact the ability to manage the species of primary concern.[99] Ecosystem management, on the other hand, "involves preserving intrinsic values or natural conditions of the ecosystem; commodities are secondary by-products, much like interest on capital," according to Hanna Cortner and Margaret Moote. Ecosystem management does "not begin by enumerating outputs. The first priority is conserving ecological sustainability; levels of commodity and amenity outputs are adjusted to meet that goal. Science is viewed as highly uncertain, evolving, and multidisciplinary, with no claim on truth or best answers. Ecosystem management is necessarily flexible and adaptive, no longer following centralized protocols."[100]

Feedback on ecological conditions has been found to play a major role in many customary law systems. Temporal "taboos" in Oceania have promoted sustainability because they are based on "environmental feedback" about the condition of the resource.[101] Studies of the use of traditional ecological knowledge in New Guinea found that the local farmers were not simply following traditional recipes by rote but were constantly experimenting with new crops to discover their tolerances and requirements. They had "a genuine sense of enquiry and determination to learn from personal experience and the collective experience of others."[102] Indigenous Alaskans were willing to modify customary goose-hunting practices when they received feedback of flyway migration data and hunting restrictions in the lower forty-eight states.[103] And in southern Benin, feedback from results of planting new high-yielding varieties of oil palm led to a greater appreciation of traditional palm-oil cultivation practices.[104]

Management theory also emphasizes the benefits of deliberate "regenerative learning" as a feedback mechanism.[105] Although social systems go through cycles of creative destruction like ecosystems, "it is possible for actors within these systems to manage in such a way that the crises are minimally destructive and the rigidity is not excessive, while the regenerative learning and sense of direction remain strong." Finding the balance point requires continuous adjustment.[106]

Similar points have been made by legal scholars. Daniel Farber has spotlighted the importance of monitoring, feedback and evaluation to all environmental programs,[107] and Carol Rose has stressed that one of the biggest advantages of community-based common property regimes is that they are able to alter the rules rapidly in response to feedback regarding environmental changes.[108]

Feedback may also help modify the decision-making processes themselves. Becker and Ostrom have suggested that the choice of institutional arrangements for natural resource management may be an evolutionary process involving selection for more efficient institutions over time.[109] Adaptiveness and resilience develop both in ecological systems and social systems, but in ecological systems resilience is the result of evolutionary processes while social systems are guided by human intentions, so that we can create feedback mechanisms deliberately.[110]

6.2.4 *Encouraging fine-grained rules*

Feedback of information into the rule-making process will cause the rules to be changed only if the internal structure of the rules is adaptable to change. The technical aspect of rules that appears to correlate with their adaptability is "graininess."

Fine-grained rules can be changed more easily than coarse-grained rules. The term "grain" is widely used in science to describe the level of detail of scientific data, including ecological data.[111] Legal rules exhibit similar qualities of graininess.[112] A rule is fine-grained if it is capable of being modified in terms of small increments.[113] Thus for example, a rule that says that the speed limit is 55 mph is relatively fine-grained because it could be changed to 50 or 60 or even 56, while a rule that says you must stop on the red light and go on the green is coarse-grained and difficult to change except in dramatic fashion.

A wide range of graininess is found among legal rules for resource management. For example, a rule that says no logging may be undertaken in designated wilderness areas is coarse-grained. A rule that says no trees may be cut within 35 feet of a stream is fine-grained.

It is important to note that the difference between fine- and coarse-grained rules is not a matter of their relative precision. Both fine- and coarse-grained rules can be precise; not vague principles that are subject to varying interpretations.[114]

The advantage of fine-grained rules is that they can be tinkered with in small increments without demanding major policy reviews. Carol Rose has pointed out that one of the big advantages of most customary systems is that individual entitlements are defined in an adjustable way.[115] The complexity of these systems discourages the commodification of them, which may enhance sustainability of the resource.[116] And Berkes has observed that the use of flexible rules is one of the hallmarks of many customary systems.[117]

Fine-grained rules are important in resource management because of the complexity of the information that needs to be analyzed. Successful adaptive management requires, as J. B. Ruhl emphasizes, an "effort to translate biological diversity information into hard data on the value of nature to the goal of sustainable development."[118] Such ecological data are likely to be extremely complex and constantly changing, and attempts to analyze them on a coarse-grained basis are likely to suggest patterns that break down when the details become apparent.[119]

Where information is complex, negotiations to adjust the rights and responsibilities of various interests may be more successful if the rules are fine-grained.[120] As the property rights of Aboriginal Australians have become more clearly defined, they have felt more secure to negotiate changes in their detailed customs to meet changing conditions.[121] And a study of fishery management on the Klamath River concluded that effective negotiations were possible only after the courts defined Indian rights precisely, enabling the Indians to feel secure enough to negotiate agreements that modified their own rights as well as the rights of others.[122]

Graininess also fosters resilience. To the extent that resilience requires response to incremental changes in the environment, the fine-grained rules can be more easily "tweaked" in small increments.[123] For example, a study of fishing communities in the Dominican Republic found that a community that had successfully conserved the resources in its area was using very detailed customary practices that could be modified with changing weather and climate conditions.[124] The more that is learned about the conservation practices of Australian Aboriginals, the more complex and detailed their rules appear.[125]

The need for fine-grained rules can also be seen in the case studies reported in the National Research Council's book *Sharing the Fish*, in which the committee emphasized that successful fishing communities' rules are carefully matched to a situation or problem that community members have some control over and that they can resolve by incremental changes of actions or strategies.[126] Similarly, a review of Canadian experiments in co-management of fisheries suggested that tasks such as habitat restoration, which necessarily involve fine-grained management strategies, are often the most fruitful areas of local participation.[127] Colding and Folke suggest that this kind of "parametric management," as they call it, promotes resilience because the resource managers may adjust a wide range of fine-grained parameters such as area rotations, times for fishing, fishing methods and stages of the life cycle during which the fish may be taken.[128] Some studies of customary law suggest that fixed quotas or other coarse-grained rules[129] are difficult to implement because "they lack the flexibility of administration that comes with community based governance."[130]

Where rules vary in their graininess, the tendency to modify the fine-grained rules without changing the coarse-grained rules may skew the management process. In some cases, the resource managers may choose to tweak the only fine-grained rules over which they have control, even though they recognize that other factors outside their control may be more significant. A study of fisheries biologists in Texas noted that as the biologists watched the resource decline the only control they could exercise was to limit fishing because they were "powerless to control other variables such as pollution, freshwater inflow, or dredging."[131] Similarly, a study in Greenland found that fisheries biologists attempted to standardize procedures and use a limited number of measurable criteria in order to better be able to compare results over time, while local fishermen "used their knowledge the other way round . . . to adapt to an ever-changing environment" so that they would know what to do, however the conditions changed.[132]

In forestry management as well, scientific advances in resource management have been most effective when they have addressed operational applications of detailed management techniques, such as geographic information systems, damage sampling, and stand yield forecasting.[133] The carefully designed experimental ecology that is acceptable to the scientific literature is simply "noise" in the evolution of policy, one study suggests.[134] Many ecologists recognize the need for better communication of "knowledge of how the production of goods and services in specific ecosystems will respond to biophysical changes . . ."[135]

In comparing management of Swedish forests by local cooperatives and by state agencies, Lars Carlsson found that the cooperatives were able to adjust their management practices more flexibly than the state agencies and were better able to respond to changes in the environment.[136] Similar conclusions were reached by the National Research Council study of fishing quotas for Native Alaskan communities.[137] In their review of studies of African hunter-gatherers, Davidson-Hunt and Berkes concluded that in societies where unpredictable environmental conditions are the norm, customary rules tend to de-emphasize specialized occupational categories in favor of "generalist" behavior patterns; these maximize adaptability because people can make incremental changes in their role in society rather than being locked into particular specialties.[138]

Total bans on the use of certain resources may facilitate enforcement but they are difficult to amend if conditions change.[139] Australian Aborigines often used totemism in ways that produced sustainable results during periods of stability; certain areas were declared off limits for hunting and required ecologically sound management actions.[140] This type of coarse-grained, deeply embedded rule is among the most difficult to modify, and many such rules have been found to have had little relevance to conservation as an objective.[141] Similar concern has been expressed about statutory conservation covenants in New Zealand, and some attempts are being made to reduce their inflexibility.[142]

The use of transferable rights to harvest or destroy common resources has frequently been used as a way of adapting traditional rights to modern market conditions where liquidity is given a high value by most resource users.[143] Successful commodification depends on the reduction of as many variables that affect value as possible so that buyers can confidently value the product.[144] This puts great pressure on the designers of the system to remove the flexibility that may be needed to provide the necessary adaptability.[145] Finding an appropriate balance between the concreteness needed to attract buyers and the variability needed to promote adaptive management may require some sophisticated balancing of interests.[146]

6.2.5 Creating a balance of rights and responsibilities

Finally, the ability to achieve consensus on changes in customary rules often depends on whether the rules address a wide range of rights and responsibilities relating to all relevant aspects of the affected ecological systems. Where rules assign certain people or groups rights without responsibilities, or responsibilities without rights, their willingness to negotiate modifications in the rules is likely to be limited.

An appropriate mixture of rights and responsibilities can sometimes be achieved by the use of a mixture of private and limited common property that takes into account the working of the entire ecosystem process. Based on her extensive studies of a wide range of resource management systems,

Elinor Ostrom has cautioned against the use of privatization of rights without careful consideration of the responsibility for managing those parts of the system that cannot be privatized. In groundwater resource management, for example, the flow of water can be privatized but the basin itself must be managed jointly.[147]

Empirical studies of customary systems of resource management have frequently found that the successful legal systems employ an interrelated combination of private and common property.[148] Netting's pioneering study of customary law in the Swiss Alps found that "Communal property was not a survival from some ideal Gemeinschaft of primitive tribal brotherhood but a utilitarian mechanism for administering valuable but diffuse and relatively less productive alpine and forest resources. The commons existed contemporaneously and symbiotically with tight-fisted private rights in meadows and vineyards, cows and barns and houses."[149] As an example, Netting cited a

> regulation of alp rights in 1517 [that] laid down the principle that "no one is permitted to send more cows to the Alps than he can winter." This made the number of animals sent to the communal summer pasture directly dependent on the amount of hay and thus the meadow area possessed by each cattle owner. One could not merely put livestock on the alp and then sell them at the end of the season ... At one stroke this simple rule overturns the economic logic of the "tragedy of the commons" ...[150]

Other empirical studies have also noted the important role played by common property in resource management. In her study of clamming, Hanna found that "both informal local knowledge and the local production of scientific knowledge are enabled and enhanced by the particular structure of property rights that exist for the soft shell clam resource" because the law gave all residents of a town access to the tidal flats subject to the town's power to "appropriate them."[151] And a study of oil and gas development in Siberia's Yamal Peninsula concluded that sustainable development would be enhanced by increased recognition of the local reindeer herders' communal grazing rights.[152]

Customary systems of managing common property often confer both rights and responsibilities in a flexible fashion. As Carol Rose puts it, the ability to learn from "fluid, emergent forms of limited common property" may be a valuable opportunity for adaptive management, because all ecosystems have the dynamic character of works in progress and every "ecosystem is always in an emergent state, whose participants and constituent features may be roughly known but not completely specifiable in advance."[153] Inasmuch as the administrative costs of a customarily managed commons are low relative to an individual property system, property may sometimes be more valuable as a commons than as private property.[154] Since traditional communities' customary commons usages often apply to places where the general public can manage itself and prevent wasteful overuse of a resource, custom "can tame and moderate the dread rule of capture that supposedly tends to turn every common into a waste."[155]

To the extent that the management of resources benefits from a large number of independent participants who can monitor each others' activities and feed back information into the system, community management may be particularly appropriate for systems of common property.[156] As Carol Rose points out, an increase in participants is akin to the economies of scale that often apply in industrial production. As Adam Smith knew, commerce requires interaction among people, and common property can facilitate such interaction.[157] Rose cites the increasing use in many areas of environmental management of what she calls "Limited Common Property," meaning property that is open to a group but not to everyone. The scale of such use needs to be large enough to internalize some externalities of resource use but also "small enough to reduce bargaining costs among the participants, so that they can arrive at complex and nuanced norms to allocate mutual rights and responsibilities."[158]

Increasingly, analysts of resource management systems argue that the creation of partial property rights in resources may overemphasize the part of the system that is given property status at the expense of the rest of the ecosystem.[159] In forest, fishery and wildlife management, crises have driven home the point that individual resources can't be successfully managed except in the context of the full array of ecosystem components and processes.[160] For example, where only large fish have value in the marketplace, fishermen may simply toss out all but the biggest fish of the most desirable species.[161] A recent study of a system of Community Development Quotas for Native Alaskan communities warned of the need to ensure that the system of quotas did not discourage broader efforts toward environmental stewardship.[162]

In many instances, partial propertization can lead to distorted investment and conservation in the propertized resource, so that "conservation of *that* resource may be disproportionately great, while the use of non-propertized resources is simply spendthrift – an imbalance that can threaten a larger and intricately interrelated ecosystem."[163] Carol Rose notes that the owners of fish farms treat their own stock with care, but often harvest wild marine life indiscriminately as feed for their stock.[164] In Swaziland, small farmers conserve their arable land, to which they have individual title, but practice destructive cattle grazing on communal land, where they have the right to graze cattle but no responsibility for conservation.[165]

In other instances, partial privatization may cause unsustainable exploitation of the privatized resource if other resources are unavailable. In Ghana, the privatization of certain tracts of forest land freed those landowners from customary rules that had protected communal forests, with the result that the private land was harvested unsustainably.[166] This criticism has been made in relation to indigenous systems that appear to promote conservation by declaring the harvesting of certain species taboo, but in fact may cause overexploitation of other species.[167]

Property systems that grant property rights only in specific components of the ecosystem may make careful ecosystem management difficult. This criticism has often been leveled at the United States' Endangered Species Act,[168] which has the unusual effect of creating something very much like a property right in specific species that are endangered or threatened – a right that can be exercised by anyone who can legitimately claim to have a trustee-like interest in the species' protection.[169] This can lead to numerous instances in which the attempt to protect rights of one species conflicts with the rights of other equally threatened species.[170]

Resource management systems may be able to alleviate these incongruities by utilizing effectively the sustainable potential of both private property and common property concepts.[171] The fishing industry has been experimenting with various systems of transferable rights.[172] Many commentators have suggested that the allocation of quotas in terms of the amount of resource to be harvested, without allocating responsibilities in relation to harvesting methods, usually violates local norms and presents excessive enforcement costs.[173] In its recent report *Sharing the Fish*, the National Research Council undertook a comparison of the use of quotas in fisheries management with the use of quotas in regard to other forms of common pool resources. The report compares the extent to which the quotas are treated as property rights or not, and notes an increasing trend in the United States to deny allotments the status of private property.[174] As Allison Rieser has pointed out, this reflects an increasing concern with the ecological impact of selective privatization of rights to marine fish without associated private responsibilities.[175] Some tradeable permit programs however, have "evolved especially flexible management systems."[176]

Endnotes

1. See, e.g., Mauricio R. Bellon, "Farmers' Knowledge and Sustainable Agrosystem Management: An Operational Definition and an Example from Chiapas, Mexico" (1995) *Human Organization*, vol. 54, p. 263; R. F. Ellen, "Patterns of Indigenous Timber Extraction from Moluccan Rain Forest Fringes" (1985) 12 *Journal of Biogeography* 559.
2. For information on the experience of resource managers using adaptive management, an interesting source is the web site of the Adaptive Management Practitioners' Network at http://www.iatp.org/AEAM/index.html (accessed August 13, 2005).
3. P. Lal et al., "The Adaptive Decision-Making Process as a Tool for Integrated Natural Resource Management: Focus, Attitudes, and Approach" (2001) *Conservation Ecology*, vol. 5(2), p. 11. [online at http://www.consecol.org/vol5/iss2/art11]
4. Frances Westley, "Governing Design: The Management of Social Systems and Ecosystem Management," in Lance H. Gunderson et al. (eds.), *Barriers and Bridges to the Renewal of Ecosystems and Institutions* (Columbia University Press, New York, 1995), pp. 391, 396–397.
5. Richard P. Rumelt, Dan E. Schendel and David J. Teece, "Fundamental Issues in Strategy," 9, 26, in Richard P. Rumelt et al. (eds.), *Fundamental Issues in Strategy: A Research Agenda* (Harvard Business School Press, Cambridge MA, 1994), pp. 9, 26.
6. It would be presumptuous to suggest that adaptive management was a new idea. Machiavelli, for one, advised his prince to be prepared to change with the times, "for if one governs himself with caution and patience, and the times and affairs turn in such a way that his government is good, he comes out prosperous: but if the times and affairs change, he is ruined because he does not change his mode of proceeding, . . . whether because he cannot deviate from what nature inclines him or also because, when one has always flourished by walking on one path, he cannot be persuaded to depart from it." Niccolò Machiavelli, *The Prince* (transl. by Harvey C. Mansfield, Jr., University of Chicago Press, Chicago, 1985), p. 100.
7. Rumelt, et al., "Fundamental Issues in Strategy," pp. 9, 20.
8. J. C. Spender, *Industry Recipes: An Enquiry into the Nature and Sources of Managerial Judgement* (New York and Oxford, Basil Blackwell, 1989), pp. 66–67.
9. J. B. Ruhl, "Thinking of Environmental Law as a Complex Adaptive System: How to Clean up the Environment by Making a Mess of Environmental Law" (1997) *Houston Law Review*, vol. 34, pp. 933, 988.
10. Kathleen M. Eisenhardt, "Making Fast Strategic Decisions in High-Velocity Environments" (1989) *Academy of Management Journal*, vol. 32, p. 543.

11. Nobuo Takahashi, *Design of Adaptive Organizations* (Springer-Verlag, New York, 1987), pp. 65–74.
12. Having a long-term view is an obvious pre-condition for adaptive management. As Carl Walters notes, "there is no point in learning more about something you intend to destroy shortly." Carl Walters, *Adaptive Management of Renewable Resources* (Macmillan, 1986), p. 16.
13. Richard T. T. Forman, *Land Mosaics: The Ecology of Landscapes and Regions* (Cambridge University Press, Cambridge, 1995), pp. 476–477 ("Thinking long term is the hardest part of management").
14. Westley, "Governing Design", pp. 391, 394.
15. *Ibid.*, pp. 391, 401, 413, 417.
16. Stephan H. Haeckel, *Adaptive Enterprise: Creating and Leading Sense-and-Respond Organizations* (Harvard Business School Press, Cambridge MA, 1999), p. 14.
17. Walters, *Adaptive Management of Renewable Resources*, p. 194.
18. *Ibid.*, pp. 19–20.
19. *Ibid.*, p. 159.
20. "The idea that all management is an ongoing experiment poses a profound challenge to our legal system because it undermines a core principle of procedural and substantive fairness: finality . . . Once a decision is rendered, we expect parties to forever abide by the outcome. Finality takes many forms. Sometimes, it is represented by express doctrines and legislation, [and on] other occasions, finality is implicit. For example, the premise behind an environmental impact statement is that once environmental damage has been fully disclosed, a one-time decision can be made on the merits of the activity, and even if the activity will irrevocably alter the environment, the decision is legitimate and final." A. Dan Tarlock, "Environmental Law: Ethics or Science" (1996) *Duke Environmental Law & Policy Forum*, vol. 7, pp. 193, 206.
21. William H. Rodgers, Jr., "Adaptation of Environmental Law to the Ecologists' Discovery of Disequilibria" (1994) *Chicago-Kent Law Review*, vol. 69, p. 887 (discussing the need to broaden the variety of property rights needed for the protection of ecological values).
22. A. Dan Tarlock, "The Nonequilibrium Paradigm in Ecology and the Partial Unraveling of Environmental Law" (1994) *Loyola of Los Angeles Law Review*, vol. 27, p. 1121.
23. Some highly respected legal scholars, such as the University of California's Joseph Sax, would go even farther, taking the view that resource management laws cannot properly address ecological issues until we completely reorient our perspective of private property away from its penchant for hard and fast rules. He believes that modern property law facilitates transformation of resources without a full analysis of the resources' ecological values. As environmental conditions change, law will need to adapt to recognition of those changes. He

argues that we need to supplement our recognition of the transformative value of natural resources with an equivalent recognition of their ecological value: "Land is not a passive entity waiting to be transformed by its landowner. Nor is the world comprised of distinct tracts of land, separate pieces independent of each other. Rather, an ecological perspective views land as consisting of systems defined by their function, not by man-made boundaries. Land is already at work, performing important services in its unaltered state. For example, forests regulate the global climate, marshes sustain marine fisheries, and prairie grass holds the soil in place. Transformation diminishes the functioning of this economy and, in fact, is at odds with it." Joseph L. Sax, "Property Rights and the Economy of Nature: Understanding Lucas v. South Carolina Coastal Council" (1993) *Stanford Law Review*, vol. 45, pp. 1433, 1442. See also Joseph L. Sax, "Nature and Habitat Conservation and Protection in the United States" (1993) *Ecology Law Quarterly*, vol. 20, pp. 47, 50–51 (need to replace enclave system of conservation with approach based on ecosystems). Professor Eric Freyfogle has also emphasized the "promise of ecology." Eric Freyfogle, *Justice and the Earth* (The Free Press, 1995), pp. 128–132.

24. Daniel A. Farber, *Eco-pragmatism: Making Sensible Decisions in an Uncertain World* (University of Chicago Press, Chicago 1999), p. 179.
25. Ruhl, "Thinking of Environmental Law as a Complex Adaptive System", pp. 933, 996–1000.
26. V. T. Parker and S. T. A. Pickett, "Restoration as an Ecosystem Process: Implications of the Modern Ecological Paradigm," in Krystyna M. Urbanska et al. (eds.), *Restoration Ecology and Sustainable Development* (Cambridge University Press, Cambridge, 1997), pp. 17, 22.
27. Crawford S. Holling and Steven Sanderson, "Dynamics of (Dis)harmony in Ecological and Social Systems," in Susan S. Hanna et al. (eds.), *Rights to Nature: Ecological, Economic, Cultural, and Political Principles of Institutions for the Environment* (Island Press, Washington DC, 1996), pp. 57–61. Holling's views were originally set forth in C. S. Holling (ed.), *Adaptive Environmental Assessment and Management* (John Wiley and Sons, Washington DC, 1978).
28. Parker and Pickett, "Restoration as an Ecosystem Process," pp. 17, 24.
29. C. S. Holling, "New Science and New Investments for a Sustainable Biosphere," in AnnMari Jansson et al. (eds.), *Investing in Natural Capital: The Ecological Economics Approach to Sustainability* (Island Press, 1994), pp. 57, 72.
30. C. S. Holling, "Engineering Resilience versus Ecological Resilience," in Peter C. Schulze (ed.), *Engineering Within Ecological Constraints* (National Academy Press, Washington DC, 1996), pp. 31, 41.
31. Holling, "New Science and New Investments for a Sustainable Biosphere," at pp. 57, 72 ("Those adaptive capacities depend on those processes that permit renewal in society, economies, and ecosystems. For nature it is biosphere structure; for businesses and people it is usable knowledge; and for society as a whole it is trust.")

32. Holling and Steven Sanderson, "Dynamics of (Dis)harmony in Ecological and Social Systems," p. 57.
33. Giulio A. De Leo and Simon Levin, "The Multifaceted Aspects of Ecosystem Integrity" (1997) *Conservation Ecology*, vol. 1 (online journal) (attempts by resource managers to attain stability has led to a loss of resiliency that has produced worse crises than in unmanaged ecosystems).
34. Timothy F. H. Allen and Thomas W. Hoekstra, *Toward a Unified Ecology* (Columbia University Press, New York, 1992), p. 20.
35. "Conventional resource management is predisposed to block out disturbance, which may be efficient in a limited sense in the short term. But since disturbance is endogenous to the cyclic processes of ecosystem renewal, conventional resource management tends to increase the potential for larger-scale disturbances and even less predictable and less manageable feedbacks from the environment. These feedbacks, or surprises, can have devastating effects on ecosystems and on societies that depend on the resources that ecosystems generate. As the resilience of the buffering capacity of the system gradually declines, flexibility is lost, and the linked social-ecological system becomes more vulnerable to surprise and crisis." Carl Folke, Fikret Berkes and Johan Colding, "Ecological Practices and Social Mechanisms for Building Resilience and Sustainability," in Carl Folke and Fikret Berkes (eds.), *Linking Social and Ecological Systems: Management Practices and Social Mechanisms for Building Resilience* (Cambridge University Press, Cambridge, 1998), pp. 414, 415–416.
36. Holling, "New Science and New Investments for a Sustainable Biosphere," pp. 57, 67–68. Although catastrophic disturbance may be the most important variable affecting resource management, it is also the hardest one to predict successfully. Craig L. Shafer, "Terrestrial Nature Reserve Design at the Urban/Rural Interface," in Mark W. Schwartz (ed.), *Conservation in Highly Fragmented Landscapes* (Chapman & Hall, New York, 1997), pp. 345, 351.
37. Anthony W. King, "Hierarchy Theory: A Guide to System Structure for Wildlife Biologists," in John A. Bissonette (ed.), *Wildlife and Landscape Ecology: Effects of Pattern and Scale* (Springer, New York, 1997), pp. 185, 208.
38. See, e.g., Bryan Norton, "Change, Constancy and Creativity: The New Ecology and Some Old Problems" (1996) *Duke Environmental Law and Policy Forum*, vol. 7, pp. 49, 58–59; Ruhl, "Thinking of Environmental Law," pp. 933, 998–999.
39. Robert B. Keiter, "Beyond the Boundary Line: Constructing a Law of Ecosystem Management" (1994) *University of Colorado Law Review*, vol. 65, pp. 293, 302.
40. Judy L. Meyer, "The Dance of Nature: New Concepts in Ecology" (1994) *Chicago-Kent Law Review*, vol. 69, pp. 875, 882; Walters, *Adaptive Management of Renewable Resources*, p. 17.
41. Curt Meine, *Aldo Leopold: His Life and Work* (University of Wisconsin Press, Madison WI, 1988), pp. 468–469.

42. See generally William C. Clark, "Sustainable Science for a Sustainable Environment: A Transition Toward Sustainability" (2001) *Ecology Law Quarterly*, vol. 27, p. 1021.
43. Robert Costanza and Carl Folke, "The Structure and Function of Ecological Systems in Relation to Property Rights Regimes," Hanna et al. (eds.), in *Rights to Nature* (1996), pp. 13, 20.
44. Thomas Prugh, *Natural Capital and Human Economic Survival* (2nd edn., ISEE Press, Solomons MD, 1999), p. 21.
45. Kenneth Arrow et al., "Economic Growth, Carrying Capacity, and the Environment" (April 28, 1995) *Science*, vol. 268, p. 520.
46. Shepard Krech, *The Ecological Indian: Myth and History* (W. W. Norton & Co., New York, 1999), p. 212. See also Gordon G. Whitney, *From Coastal Wilderness to Fruited Plain: A History of Environmental Change in Temperate North America 1500 to the Present* (Cambridge University Press, Cambridge, 1994), pp. 98–120.
47. Neville White and Betty Meehan, "Traditional Ecological Knowledge: A Lens on Time," in Nancy M. Williams and Graham Baines (eds.), *Traditional Ecological Knowledge: Wisdom for Sustainable Development* (Centre for Resource and Environmental Studies, Australian National University, Canberra, 1993), pp. 31, 37–38. See also Robert A. Brightman, "Conservation and Resource Depletion: The Case of the Boreal Algonquins," in Bonnie J. McCay and James M. Acheson (eds.), *The Question of the Commons: The Culture and Ecology of Communal Resources* (University of Arizona Press, Tucson AZ, 1987), pp. 121, 137–139.
48. Iain J. Davidson-Hunt and Fikret Berkes, "Environment and Society through the Lens of Resilience: Toward a Human-in-Ecosystem Perspective," paper prepared for delivery at the International Association for the Study of Common Property Conference (Bloomington, Indiana, May–June, 2000), pp. 14–15.
49. Charles Zerner, "Tracking Sasi: the Transformation of a Central Moluccan Reef Management Institution in Indonesia," in Alan T. White et al. (eds.), *Collaborative and Community-Based Management of Coral Reefs: Lessons from Experience* (Kumarian Press, West Hartford CT, 1994), p. 19. See also Carol M. Rose, "Common Property, Regulatory Property, and Environmental Protection: Comparing Common Pool Resources to Tradable Environmental Allowances," paper prepared for delivery at the International Association for the Study of Common Property Resources (Bloomington, Indiana, May–June, 2000), pp. 12–13. (Decimation of particular resources is most likely to happen when traditional practices are confronted with sudden shifts in commercial demand from outsiders.)
50. Thomas Elmqvist, "Indigenous Institutions, Resilience and Failure of Co-management of Rain Forest Preserves in Samoa," paper delivered at the International Association for the Study of Common Property Conference (Indiana University, May–June, 2000).

51. Eugene Hunn, "What is Traditional Ecological Knowledge?" in Nancy M. Williams and Graham Baines (eds.), *Traditional Ecological Knowledge: Wisdom for Sustainable Development* (Australian National University Centre for Resource and Environmental Studies, Canberra, 1993), p. 13 (evaluating the sustainability of a customary system requires impartial and comprehensive analysis).
52. James A. Wilson et al., "Chaos, Complexity and Community Management of Fisheries" (1994) *Marine Policy*, vol. 18, pp. 291, 305. See also Johan Colding and Carl Folke, "The Taboo System: Lessons Learned About Informal Institutions for Nature Management" (2000) *Georgetown International Environmental Law Review*, vol. 12, pp. 413, 420 (systems that focus on how fishing is done rather than how much is harvested are more resilient).
53. National Research Council, *Sharing the Fish: Toward a National Policy on Individual Fishing Quotas* (National Academy Press, Washington DC, 1999), p. 115.
54. Fikret Berkes et al., "Rediscovery of Traditional Ecological Knowledge as Adaptive Management" (2000) *Ecological Applications*, vol. 10, pp. 1251, 1256–1257.
55. National Research Council, *Sharing the Fish*, p. 184.
56. Roman R. Pawluk, "The Role of Indigenous Soil Knowledge in Agricultural Development" (1992) *Soil and Water Conservation*, vol. 47, p. 298 (indigenous people often had intricate soil and water conservation systems based on observation of various soil types). On the other hand, where keeping of oral or written history has been poor, people may not be able to recall the effect of changing land use practices. O. T. Coomes and G. J. Burt, "Indigenous Market-Oriented Agroforestry: Dissecting Local Diversity in Western Amazonia" (1997) *Agroforestry Systems*, vol. 37, pp. 27, 31–32.
57. Richard Baker, "Traditional Aboriginal Land Use in the Borroloola Region," in Nancy M. Williams and Graham Baines (eds.), *Traditional Ecological Knowledge: Wisdom for Sustainable Development* (Australian National University Centre for Resource and Environmental Studies, Canberra, 1993), pp. 126, 134–136.
58. Paul Chandler, "Adaptive Ecology of Traditionally Derived Agroforestry in China" (1994) *Human Ecology*, vol. 22, pp. 415, 417.
59. Madhav Gadgil, "Prudence and Profligacy: A Human Ecological Perspective," in Timothy M. Swanson (ed.), *The Economics and Ecology of Biodiversity Decline: The Forces Driving Global Change* (Cambridge University Press, Cambridge, 1995), pp. 99, 102–103.
60. Fikret Berkes, *Sacred Ecology: Traditional Ecological Knowledge and Resource Management* (Philadelphia PA, Taylor & Francis, 1999), pp. 159–161.
61. The spill "weakened the social fabric of Cordova" by splitting those who accepted Exxon money from those who didn't. And the Chugach Alaska Native Corporation decided to clear-cut their land because of financial problems

incurred during the oil spill, a decision seen by others as a threat to the fishing industry. Duane A. Gill, "Environmental Disaster and Fishery Co-management in a Natural Resource Community: Impact of the Exxon Valdez Oil Spill," in Christopher L. Dyer and James R. McGoodwin (eds.), *Folk Management in the World's Fisheries* (University Press of Colorado, Niwot CO, 1994), pp. 207, 225.

62. Stephen S. Light et al., "The Everglades: Evolution of Management in a Turbulent Ecosystem," in Lance H. Gunderson et. al. (eds.), *Barriers and Bridges to the Renewal of Ecosystems and Institutions* (Columbia University Press, New York, 1995).
63. Colin Hunt, "Cooperative Approaches to Marine Resource Management in the South Pacific," in Peter Larmour (ed.), *The Governance of Common Property in the Pacific Region* (National Centre for Development Studies, Pacific Policy Paper 19, The Australian National University, Canberra, 1997). (Pointing out that the customary rules in most Pacific areas bear little relationship to those of two centuries ago.)
64. Curtis H. Freese, *Wild Species as Commodities: Managing Markets and Ecosystems for Sustainability* (Island Press, Washington DC, 1998), p. 133.
65. Elinor Ostrom, *Governing the Commons: The Evolution of Institutions for Collective Action* (Cambridge University Press, Cambridge, 1990), pp. 193–202.
66. Elinor Ostrom, *Crafting Institutions for Self-Governing Irrigation Systems* (ICS Press, San Francisco, CA, 1992), p. 63.
67. Holly Doremus, "Adaptive Management, the Endangered Species Act, and the Institutional Challenges of 'New Age' Environmental Protection" (2001) *Washburn Law Journal*, vol. 41, pp. 50, 56–57.
68. Berkes, *Sacred Ecology*, pp. 159–161.
69. Fikret Berkes, "Role and Significance of 'Tradition' in Indigenous Knowledge" (1999) *Indigenous Knowledge and Development Monitor*, vol. 7, p. 19.
70. Robert T. Watson et al., *Annual Review of Environment Matters at the World Bank* (World Bank Report No. 20104, 1999), p. 52.
71. Berkes, *Sacred Ecology*.
72. J. E. M. Arnold, "Management of Forest Resources as Common Property" (1993) *Commonwealth Forestry Review*, vol. 72, pp. 157, 160. For examples of case studies of rapidly adapting systems, see, e.g., Kibriaul Khaleque and Michael A. Gold, "Pineapple Agroforestry: An Indigenous System Among the Garo Community of Bangladesh" (1993) *Society and Natural Resources*, vol. 6, p. 71; Donald A. Messerschmidt, "Indigenous Environmental Management and Adaptation: An Introduction to Four Case Studies from Nepal" (1990) *Mountain Research and Development*, vol. 10, p. 3.
73. Raymond MacCallum, "The Community-Based Management of Fisheries in Atlantic Canada: A Legislative Proposal" (1998) *Dalhousie Law Journal*, vol. 21, pp. 49, 65–66.

74. Tomoya Akimichi, "Indigenous Resource Management and Sustainable Development: Case Studies from Papua New Guinea and Indonesia" (1995) 103 *Anthropological Science* 321 (Anthropological Society of Nippon); H. L. J. Spiertz, "The Transformation of Traditional Law: A Tale of People's Participation in Irrigation Management on Bali" (1991) *Landscape and Urban Planning*, vol. 20, p. 189.
75. Arun Agrawal, *Greener Pastures: Politics, Markets, and Community among a Migrant Pastoral People* (Duke University Press, Durham NC, 1999), pp. 49–50.
76. Deborah Bird Rose, "Reflections on Ecologies for the Twenty-first Century," in Nancy M. Williams and Graham Baines (eds.), *Traditional Ecological Knowledge: Wisdom for Sustainable Development* (Centre for Resource and Environmental Studies, Australian National University, Canberra, 1993), pp. 115, 117.
77. Graham Baines and Edvard Hviding, "Traditional Environmental Knowledge for Resource Management in Marovo, Solomon Islands," Nancy M. Williams and Graham Baines (eds.), in *Traditional Ecological Knowledge: Wisdom for Sustainable Development* (Australian National University Centre for Resource and Environmental Studies, Canberra, 1993). For a thorough depiction of intergenerational transfer of customary fishing knowledge in Oceania, see Kenneth Ruddle, "Local Knowledge in the Folk Management of Fisheries and Coastal Marine Environments," in Christopher L. Dyer and James R. McGoodwin (eds.), *Folk Management in the World's Fisheries: Lessons for Modern Fisheries Management* (University Press of Colorado, Niwot CO, 1994), p. 161.
78. Jesse C. Ribot, "Representation and Accountability in Decentralized Sahelian Forestry: Legal Instruments of Political-Administrative Control" (2000) 12 *Georgetown International Environmental Law Review* 447.
79. Colding and Folke, "The Taboo System," p. 413.
80. Ruddle, "Local Knowledge in the Folk Management of Fisheries and Coastal Marine Environments," pp. 161, 182–192.
81. Colding and Folke, "The Taboo System," pp. 413, 430–431.
82. Francis Fukuyama, *Trust: The Social Virtues and the Creation of Prosperity* (The Free Press, New York, 1995), pp. 26–27.
83. Susan Hanna and Svein Jentoft, "Human Use of the Natural Environment: An Overview of Social and Economic Dimensions," in Susan S. Hanna et al., (eds.), *Rights to Nature: Ecological, Economic, Cultural, and Political Principles of Institutions for the Environment* (Island Press, Washington DC, 1996), pp. 35, 47–48. For a discussion of the importance of community associations in the administration of Brazil's extractive reserves, see Environmental Law Institute, *Brazil's Extractive Reserves: Fundamental Aspects of Their Implementation* (ELI, Washington DC, 1995).

84. Bonnie J. McCay, *Oyster Wars and the Public Trust: Property, Law and Ecology in New Jersey History* (University of Arizona Press, Tucson AZ, 1998), pp. 183 ff.
85. Rose, "Common Property, Regulatory Property, and Environmental Protection," p. 3. (The "literature offers numerous examples in which larger government forays into resource management are distinctly inferior to community-based solutions, and indeed, government intervention may badly damage perfectly workable community systems.")
86. Hanna and Jentoft, "Human Use of the Natural Environment," pp. 35, 47–48. See also Carol M. Rose, "From Local to Global Commons: Private Property, Common Property, and Hybrid Property Regimes: Expanding the Choices for the Global Commons" (1999) *Duke Environmental Law and Policy Forum*, vol. 10, pp. 45, 64 (monitoring issues have feedback effects on the ways that individual entitlements are delineated, discouraging the definition of rights that cannot be monitored).
87. Hunt, "Cooperative Approaches to Marine Resource Management in the South Pacific," pp. 145, 152–153.
88. Berkes et al., "Rediscovery of Traditional Ecological Knowledge as Adaptive Management," pp. 1251, 1259.
89. Susan S. Hanna, "Managing for Human and Ecological Content in the Maine Soft Shell Clam Fishery," in Fikret Berkes and Carl Folke (eds.), *Linking Social and Ecological Systems: Management Practices and Social Mechanisms for Building Resilience* (Cambridge University Press, Cambridge 1998), pp. 190, 204–206.
90. R. Gerald Ward, "Changing Forms of Communal Tenure," in Peter Larmour (ed.), *The Governance of Common Property in the Pacific Region* (Australian National University National Centre for Development Studies, Canberra, 1997), pp. 19, 30 (suggesting that government should consider modifying customary systems as needed rather than replacing them).
91. Evelyn Pinkerton, "Attaining Better Fisheries Management through Co-management – Prospects, Problems, and Propositions," in Evelyn Pinkerton (ed.), *Co-operative Management of Local Fisheries* (University of British Columbia Press, Vancouver, 1989).
92. Norman L. Christensen et al., "The Report of the Ecological Society of America Committee on the Scientific Basis for Ecosystem Management" (1996) *Ecological Applications*, vol. 6, pp. 665, 670.
93. Berkes, *Sacred Ecology*, p. 30.
94. Fikret Berkes and Carl Folke, "Linking Social and Ecological Systems for Resilience and Sustainability," in Berkes and Folke (eds.), *Linking Social and Ecological Systems*, p. 19.
95. See, generally, The Keystone Center, *The Keystone National Policy Dialogue on Ecosystem Management: Final Report* (The Keystone Center, Washington DC, 1996).

96. Holly Doremus, "Patching the Ark: Improving Legal Protection of Biological Diversity" (1991) *Ecology Law Quarterly*, vol. 18, pp. 265, 318–324.
97. "Rarely has a term of public discourse gone so directly from obscurity to meaninglessness without any intervening period of coherence." Michael J. Bean, "A Policy Perspective on Biodiversity Protection and Ecosystem Management," in Steward Pickett et al., (eds.), *The Ecological Basis of Conservation: Heterogeneity, Ecosystems, and Biodiversity* (1997) (quoting from a similar comment by Robert Reich about the term "competitiveness").
98. Berkes et al., "Rediscovery of Traditional Ecological Knowledge as Adaptive Management," pp. 1251, 1253–1256.
99. Judy L. Meyer, "Conserving Ecosystem Function," in Steward Pickett et al. (eds.), *The Ecological Basis of Conservation: Heterogeneity, Ecosystems, and Biodiversity* (Chapman & Hall, New York, 1997), pp. 136, 139.
100. Hanna J. Cortner and Margaret A. Moote, *The Politics of Ecosystem Management* (Island Press, Washington DC, 1999), p. 37; for numerous examples, see Susan L. Cutter et al., *Exploitation, Conservation, Preservation: A Geographic Perspective on Natural Resource Use* (2nd edn., J. Wiley, New York, 1991), pp. 141–186.
101. Colding and Folke, "The Taboo System," pp. 413, 436.
102. Chris Healey and Eugene Hunn, "The Current Status of TEK: Papua New Guinea and North America," in Nancy M. Williams and Graham Baines (eds.), *Traditional Ecological Knowledge: Wisdom for Sustainable Development* (Australian National University Centre for Resource and Environmental Studies, Canberra, 1993), pp. 27, 28.
103. Erika Zavaleta, "The Emergence of Waterfowl Conservation Among Yup'ik Hunters in the Yukon-Kuskokwim Delta, Alaska" (1999) *Human Ecology*, vol. 27, p. 231.
104. Paolo Segalla, "The Oil Palms of Southern Benin: Indigenous Knowledge and Agroforestry Developments" (1999) *Agroforestry Today*, vol. 11, pp. 5, 6–7.
105. Tarlock, "Environmental Law: Ethics or Science," pp. 193, 206 (need for feedback loops has long been advocated but ignored in environmental law).
106. Westley, "Governing Design," pp. 391, 426. For suggestions for designing a feedback policy see Walters, *Adaptive Management of Renewable Resources*, pp. 231–256.
107. Farber, *Eco-pragmatism*, pp. 178–183.
108. Rose, "Common Property, Regulatory Property, and Environmental Protection," p. 13.
109. C. Dustin Becker and Elinor Ostrom, "Human Ecology and Resource Sustainability: The Importance of Institutional Diversity" (1995) *Annual Review of Ecological System*, vol. 26, pp. 113, 123.

110. Holling and Sanderson, "Dynamics of (Dis)harmony in Ecological and Social Systems," at pp. 57, 67, 74. ("In human systems, there is a substantial difference between passive adaptation and active learning. In natural systems, adaptation is the critical process, and cross-generational social learning (as opposed to adaptation) is unknown.")
111. Allen and Hoekstra, *Toward a Unified Ecology*, pp. 18–19; Forman, *Land Mosaics*, pp. 489–492. Another analogous scientific term is "resolution"; thus an optical instrument that was capable of distinguishing fine detail would be said to have a high resolving power. Michael Abercrombie et al. (eds.), *The New Penguin Dictionary of Biology* (8th edn, Penguin Books, New York, 1991), p. 361.
112. For a discussion of the importance of a thorough understanding of language in the interpretation of customary resource management rules, see Eugene Hunn, "The Ethnobiological Foundation for Traditional Ecological Knowledge," in Nancy M. Williams and Graham Baines (eds.), *Traditional Ecological Knowledge: Wisdom for Sustainable Development* (Australian National University Centre for Resource and Environmental Studies, Canberra, 1993), p. 16. For example, some of the languages of the Peruvian Andes use several hundred names for different varieties of the plant that other societies usually just call "potato." *Ibid.*, at 19.
113. Clayton Gillette uses the term "reversibility" to "refer to the capacity of decisionmakers to revisit the probabilistic connection between the factual predicates for a rule and its justification" and he intends to include within that definition "the capacity to revise, as well as reverse, prior formulations." Clayton P. Gillette, "Rules and Reversibility" (1997) *Notre Dame Law Review*, vol. 72, pp. 1415, 1417. The language of the rule can determine whether these revisions can easily be undertaken in small increments or whether it would be necessary to reverse the entire rule.
114. This distinction is quite different from the traditional rules/principles dichotomy, so aptly characterized by Carol Rose as "crystals" versus "mud." The distinction between rules and principles may not be particularly relevant to most systems of customary law because most customary law systems involve face-to face dealings among repeat players. Carol M. Rose, *Property and Persuasion: Essays on the History, Theory, and Rhetoric of Ownership* (Westview Press, Boulder, 1994), p. 225.
115. Rose, "Common Property, Regulatory Property, and Environmental Protection," p. 13.
116. Rose, "From Local to Global Commons," pp. 45, 65–66.
117. Berkes et al., "Rediscovery of Traditional Ecological Knowledge as Adaptive Management," pp. 1251, 1253, 1259.
118. Ruhl, "Thinking of Environmental Law as a Complex Adaptive System," pp. 933, 999.

119. James Gleick, *Faster: The Acceleration of Just About Everything* (Pantheon Books, New York, 1999), pp. 261–265, citing Richard K. Guy, "The Strong Law of Small Numbers" (1998) *American Mathematical Monthly*, vol. 95, p. 697.
120. I have suggested elsewhere that rules that outline detailed rights and responsibilities relating to endangered species are easier to modify as conditions change than rules that provide coarse-grained prohibition. Fred P. Bosselman, "The Statutory and Constitutional Mandate for a No Surprises Policy" (1997) *Ecology Law Quarterly*, vol. 24, pp. 707, 712–713.
121. Elizabeth Ganter, "Indigenous Participation in Coastal Management in the Northern Territory, Australia: Issues and Options" (1996) *Ocean and Coastal Management*, vol. 33, pp. 193, 207–210.
122. Danny Jordan, "Negotiating Salmon Management on the Klamath River," in Evelyn Pinkerton (ed.), *Co-operative Management of Local Fisheries* (University of British Columbia Press, Vancouver, 1989), pp. 73, 79.
123. Of course, people who don't trust the amendment process may quite logically seek rules that are as difficult to amend as possible. Oliver A. Houck, "On the Law of Biodiversity and Ecosystem Management" (1997) *Minnesota Law Review*, vol. 81, pp. 869, 879–880.
124. Brent W. Stoffle et al., "Folk Management and Conservation Ethics among Small-Scale fishers of Buen Hombre, Dominican Republic," in Christopher L. Dyer and James R. McGoodwin (eds.), *Folk Management in the World's Fisheries* (University Press of Colorado, Niwot CO, 1994), pp. 122–125.
125. Rosemary Hill et al., "Aborigines and Fire in the Wet Tropics of Queensland, Australia: Ecosystem Management Across Cultures" (1999) *Society and Natural Resources*, vol. 12, p. 205.
126. National Research Council, *Sharing the Fish*, p. 184.
127. Pinkerton, "Attaining Better Fisheries Management through Co-management," pp. 3, 7–12.
128. Colding and Folke, "The Taboo System," pp. 413, 420.
129. Where quotas are fixed for substantial periods of time through entitlements that are expensive to change they are coarse-grained even though they may be measured in small incremental units.
130. Wilson et al., "Chaos, Complexity and Community Management of Fisheries," pp. 291, 305. See also Grafton et al., "Private Property and Economic Efficiency," pp. 679, 682.
131. William Ward and Priscilla Weeks, "Resource Managers and Resource Users: Field Biologists and Stewardship," in Christopher L. Dyer and James R. McGoodwin (eds.), *Folk Management in the World's Fisheries* (University Press of Colorado, Niwot, CO, 1994), pp. 91, 106. (Their "focus on overfishing is legitimized through stories about fishers' values and inability to cooperate with one another, coupled with the notion that fishers know only how to find, catch, and sell oysters.")

132. Andreas Roepstorff, "Sustainability, Knowledge and Knowing What to Do," in Hanne Petersen and Birger Poppel (eds.), *Dependency, Autonomy, and Sustainability in the Arctic* (Ashgate Publishers, Aldershot and Burlington, 1999), pp. 259, 262–263.
133. John Gordon and Jane Coppock, "Ecosystem Management and Economic Development," in Marion R. Chertow and Daniel C. Esty (eds.), *Thinking Ecologically: The Next Generation of Environmental Policy* (Yale University Press, New Haven CT, 1997), pp. 37, 41.
134. Gordon L. Baskerville, "The Forestry Problem: Adaptive Lurches of Renewal," in Lance H. Gunderson et al. (eds.), *Barriers and Bridges to the Renewal of Ecosystems and Institutions* (Columbia University Press, New York, 1995), pp. 37, 100–101.
135. Edward Ayensu et al., "International Ecosystem Assessment" (October 22, 1999) 286 *Science* 685, 686.
136. Lars Carlsson, "Management, Resilience and the Strategy of the Commons," paper prepared for delivery at the International Association for the Study of Common Property conference (Bloomington, Indiana, May–June, 2000).
137. National Research Council, *The Community Development Quota Program in Alaska* (National Academy Press, Washington DC, 1999), pp. 139–140.
138. Davidson-Hunt and Berkes, "Environment and Society through the Lens of Resilience," pp. 10–11.
139. The classic anthropological study of the use of "taboos" as conservation measures is Roy Rappaport, *Pigs for the Ancestors* (2nd edn., Yale University Press, New Haven CT, 1984).
140. Deborah Bird Rose, "Common Property Regimes in Aboriginal Australia: Totemism Revisited," in Peter Larmour (ed.), *The Governance of Common Property in the Pacific Region* (National Centre for Development Studies, Pacific Policy Paper 19, The Australian National University, Canberra, 1997), pp. 127, 136–139.
141. Ruddle, "Local Knowledge in the Folk Management of Fisheries and Coastal Marine Environments," pp. 161, 189–191.
142. Victoria M. Edwards and Basil M. H. Sharp, "Institutional Arrangements for Conservation on Private Land in New Zealand" (1990) 31 *Journal of Environmental Management* 313, 321–322.
143. Rose, "Common Property, Regulatory Property, and Environmental Protection," pp. 9–12.
144. Davidson-Hunt and Berkes, "Environment and Society through the Lens of Resilience," pp. 16–17.
145. Sharon R. Siegel, "Applying the Habitat Conservation Model to Fisheries Management: A Proposal for a Modified Fisheries Planning Requirement" (2000) *Columbia Journal of Environmental Law*, vol. 32, pp. 141, 199–200.

146. Rose, "Common Property, Regulatory Property, and Environmental Protection," pp. 9–12 ("some ingenuity can no doubt help to create a practical balance between flexibility and security . . ."). For an example of an attempt to balance flexibility and security in the creation of resource depletion rights and responsibilities, see Bosselman, "The Statutory and Constitutional Mandate for a No Surprises Policy," p. 707.
147. C. Dustin Becker and Elinor Ostrom, "Human Ecology and Resource Sustainability: The Importance of Institutional Diversity" (1995) *Annual Review of Ecological Systems*, vol. 26, pp. 113, 122.
148. It is important to try to understand fully the property concepts of indigenous systems, which may be quite different than Western traditions. David P. Wilkins, "Linguistic Evidence in Support of a Holistic Approach to Traditional Ecological Knowledge," in Nancy M. Williams and Graham Baines (eds.), *Traditional Ecological Knowledge: Wisdom for Sustainable Development* (Australian National University Centre for Resource and Environmental Studies, Canberra, 1993), pp. 71, 72–75 (explaining ideas similar to "ownership" in certain Aboriginal languages in Australia).
149. Robert McC. Netting, *Balancing on an Alp: Ecological Change and Continuity in a Swiss Mountain Community* (Cambridge University Press, Cambridge, 1981), p. 228.
150. McC. Netting, *Balancing on an Alp*, p. 61.
151. Hanna, "Managing for Human and Ecological Content in the Maine Soft Shell Clam Fishery," pp. 190, 197.
152. Gail Osherenko, "Indigenous Political and Property Rights and Economic/Environmental Reform in Northwest Siberia" (1995) 36 *Post-Soviet Geography* 225. Such questions are common in former communist lands. Australian Aborigines are also debating the extent to which their property rights should remain communal and inalienable or become individualized and transferrable. Pam O'Connor, "Indigenous Policy, Native Title and the Rule of Law" (1998) *Agenda* (Australian National University), vol. 5, p. 501.
153. Carol M. Rose, "The Several Futures of Property: Of Cyberspace and Folk Tales, Emission Trades and Ecosystems" (1998) *Minnesota Law Review*, vol. 83, pp. 129, 180.
154. Margaret A. McKean, "Common-Property Regimes as a Solution to Problems of Scale and Linkage," in Susan S. Hanna et al. (eds.), *Rights to Nature: Ecological, Economic, Cultural, and Political Principles of Institutions for the Environment* (Island Press, 1996), pp. 223, 240 (Japanese common property system used to economize on enforcement costs).
155. Rose, *Property and Persuasion*: pp. 125–127.
156. Allison Rieser, "Property Rights and Ecosystem Management in U.S. Fisheries: Contracting for the Commons?" (1997) *Ecology Law Quarterly*, vol. 24, pp. 813, 827–829.

157. Rose, *Property and Persuasion*, pp. 141–143.
158. Rose, "The Several Futures of Property," pp. 129, 164–66, 176–180.
159. Hal Salwasser, "Ecosystem Management: A New Perspective for National Forests and Grasslands," in Jennifer Aley et al. (eds.), *Ecosystem Management: Adaptive Strategies for Natural Resources Organizations in the Twenty-First Century* (Taylor & Francis, Philadelphia PA, 1999), pp. 85, 91 ("Focusing only on outputs of products usually leads to simplified ecosystems"). See also Michael A. Heller, "The Boundaries of Private Property" (1999) *Yale Law Journal*, vol. 108, p. 1163 (courts encourage waste of resources by protecting "fragments" of property).
160. Norman L. Christensen et al., "The Report of the Ecological Society of America Committee on the Scientific Basis for Ecosystem Management" (1996) *Ecological Applications*, vol. 6, pp. 665, 669.
161. Carl Safina, *Song for the Blue Ocean* (Henry Holt & Co., New York, 1997), p. 30.
162. National Research Council, *The Community Development Quota Program in Alaska*, p. 142. For an economic analysis of the risks associated with the privatization of genetic resources, see Roger A. Sedjo and David Simpson, "Property Rights, Externalities and Biodiversity," in Timothy M. Swanson (ed.), *The Economics and Ecology of Biodiversity Decline: The Forces Driving Global Change* (Cambridge University Press, Cambridge, 1995), p. 79.
163. Rose, "The Several Futures of Property," pp. 129, 170–173.
164. Rose, "From Local to Global Commons," pp. 45, 61.
165. H. M. Mushala, "Soil Erosion and Indigenous Land Management: Some Socioeconomic Considerations" (1997) *Soil Technology*, vol. 11, pp. 301, 308–309. It is interesting to note that despite the vaunted political power of United States cattle producers, the right to graze cattle on public lands in the United States has not been treated as a property right. *Public Lands Council v. Babbitt*, 529 U.S. 728 (2000).
166. George Dei, "Indigenous African Knowledge Systems: Local Traditions of Sustainable Forestry" (1993) *Singapore Journal of Tropical Geography*, vol. 14, p. 28.
167. R. E. Johannes and Henry T. Lewis, "The Importance of Researchers' Expertise in Environmental Subjects," in Nancy M. Williams and Graham Baines (eds.), *Traditional Ecological Knowledge: Wisdom for Sustainable Development* (Australian National University Centre for Resource and Environmental Studies, Canberra, 1993), pp. 104, 107.
168. See Barton H. Thompson, Jr., "People or Prairie Chickens: The Uncertain Search for Optimal Biodiversity" (1999) *Stanford Law Review*, vol. 51, p. 1127.
169. See Alison Rieser, "Ecological Preservation as a Property Right: An Emerging Doctrine in Search of a Theory" (1991) *Harv. Envtl Law Review*, vol. 15, p. 393.
170. For a number of interesting examples, see Daniel Simberloff, "Flagships, Umbrellas, and Keystones: Is Single-Species Management Passé in the Landscape Era" (1998) 83 *Biological Conservation*, pp. 247, 250–251.

171. Alison Rieser, "Ecological Preservation as a Public Property Right," pp. 393, 401–403. For early examples of recognition of the importance of common property in resource management, see Julian C. Juergensmeyer and James B. Wadley, "The Common Lands Concept: A 'Commons' Solution to a Common Environmental Problem" (1974) 14 Nat. Res. J. 362; S. V. Ciriacy-Wantrup and Richard C. Bishop, "'Common Property' as a Concept in Natural Resources Policy" (1975) 15 *Natural Resources J.* 713.
172. For the history of the use of quota rights in fishing, see Anthony D. Scott, "Conceptual Origins of Rights-Based Fishing," in Philip A. Neher (ed.), *Rights-Based Fishing* 11 (Kluwer Academic Publishers, Boston MA, 1989).
173. Colding and Folke, "The Taboo System," pp. 413, 437–438.
174. National Research Council, *Sharing the Fish*, pp. 45–58.
175. Rieser, "Prescriptions for the Commons," pp. 393, 419–420.
176. Tom Tietenberg, "The Tradable Permits Approach to Protecting the Commons: What Have We Learned?" Paper prepared for delivery at the International Association for the Study of Common Property conference (Bloomington, Indiana, May–June, 2000), p. 20.

7

The place of customary law in democratic societies

PETER ØREBECH

7.1 Introduction

> By means of the idea of rights men have defined the nature of license and tyranny. Guided by its light, we can each of us be independent without arrogance and obedient without servility.
>
> Alexis de Tocqueville[1]

The necessary notification, visibility, vital firmness of mind, unity and harmony are built into the basic customary law instrument through pluralistic recognition and adherence. Customary law-making – as an instrument to command voluntary obedience[2] – is neither inimical to democratic thinking nor immature in relation to systems of parliamentary democracy. As Frederick A. Pollock said, the "only essential conditions for the existence of law are the existence of a political community, and the recognition by its members of settled rules binding upon them in that capacity."[3]

Alexis de Tocqueville defended areas of rights that belonged entirely to the "popular will" and that *no* parliament could overrule. The French historian Paul Janet makes this evident:

> What the Liberal school called the despotism of democracy was demagogic violence, the brutal and savage government of the masses. But de Tocqueville had in mind another kind of despotism, not that of militant democracy . . . No, he envisaged democracy at rest, successively leveling down and abasing all individuals, putting its fingers into all kinds of interests, imposing uniform and petty rules on every one, treating men as abstractions, subjecting society to a mechanical movement, and ending by responding itself in the absolute power of one man.[4]

7.1.1 "Bottom-up" democracy

While the compelling aristocratic position of the Middle Ages may have made customary law into a top-down, unjustified, lawless and illegitimate instrument of suppression, *inter partes* produced customary law in the hands of equal members of society now turns customary law into a "bottom-up" tool. I will argue that Pierre Bourdieu's agenda justifying popular norms, virtues, values and taste[5] is not as democracy-deviant as it may seem.[6]

Those political scientists who have no problem in accepting upstream procedural legitimacy back this position.[7] Customary laws are typically upstream and tend to adapt rather easily to "the living fabric of life."[8] Clearly customary law serves several important functions. Recent ethnological and sociological studies have described how bottom-up systems accumulate and launch knowledge and normative structures.[9]

Decisions in the arena of practice, custom and usage are – like markets – shaped by "distributive plurality"[10] and we have the problem of determining "popular will-realization." How do we know which customary law displays such will? Three issues need to be addressed. First, do *de lege lata* systems recognize customary law? Have the upper bodies of nation states made customary law part of their law? Second, what is the historic background for customary law systems? The third issue is the legislative concern: is customary law as democratic as top-down solutions?

First of all, constitutional limits on the power of governmental institutions complement the place and function of customary law in the legislative system of a state. "Private liberty is preserved because government is partially disabled . . . The constitution here is protecting democracy by taking certain issues off the agenda."[11] This institutional arrangement could "be understood as an effort to protect a private sphere from majority rule."[12] Or should we say, to protect a private sphere from top-down majority rule?

Disabling the legislature allows law-producing solitary or joint agents ("quasi-organs") to operate in the shadow of the constitutional concord. In the words of Cass R. Sunstein, the constitution – and, one may add – the customary or contract law solution that fills in these *lacunae*, "are protecting democracy." Customary law solutions will serve to overcome the "weakness of will" that parliamentary systems display. Thus a constitution that creates the top-down decision-making system itself has opted for either *solitary* or *communal* solutions as the best possible ones in a democratic sense, so that some areas of public life should be reserved to the *populace*. A similar illustration is found in the King Christian IV Norwegian Code and the still valid 1687 King Christian V Code that terminated all ancient written laws without touching customs. On the other hand, the general code did not recognize ancient customs. Since the *doctrine of continuity*[13] rules in Norway, and *not* the *doctrine of recognition*,[14] ancient customary laws are still valid. And even more important, a space is reserved for popular law-making. Thus customary laws are recognized not only by the people themselves, but also by intentional constitutional *restrictions on state action*, through which an arena of private will is purposefully left open for the public to rule by the means of contract, customary law and other private statements.

Second, history demonstrates the value of private "sacred areas" of law that no ruler should contravene. For example, in England "the need to make a case for an 'ancient constitution' against the king,"[15] and the 1604 House of Commons search for precedents that resulted in the "build up of alleged rights and privileges that were supposed to be immemorial, and this, coupled with the general and vigorous belief that England was ruled by law and that this law was itself immemorial."[16]

Inalienable and eternal rights were balanced against the "parliamentary sovereignty," comforting the needs of the times (as codified by, e.g., the Magna Carta).[17] The Parliament at Westminster was burdened with legal obligations created by "popular will" or "artificial reason" of generations.[18] Parliamentary power never displayed such excellence that customs, usage or tradition were thereby extinguished. The Magna Carta settled that fight in 1217 (at paragraph 48):

> All evil customs concerning forests and warrens [area on which game is preserved], forrests and warreners, sherrifs and their officers, or riverbanks and their conservators shall be immediately inquired into in each county by twelve sworn knights of such county, chosen by honest men of that county, and shall within forty days after the inquisition be completely and irrevocably abolished.

Some of the areas reserved for the English people are of special interest to viable resources management: "All fishweirs shall be entirely removed from the Thames and Medway, and throughout England, except upon the seacoast"[19] (at paragraph 33). "No banks shall henceforth be fenced, but such as were in defence in the time of our grandfather King Henry, by the same places and by the same bounds as they were accustomed in his time" (at paragraph 16). The "public trust doctrine," recognized in both England and the United States, grew out of the fact that the "question must be regarded as settled in England against the right of the king since Magna Carta to make such a grant" [i.e. of exclusive fishing rights].[20]

Third, in regard to the legislative issues of customary law, there are two basic topics to consider. First the political platform, which is mainly a question of legitimacy. Secondly, the legislative arguments for choosing customary law systems over parliamentary systems based on customary law's superiority. The arguments require me to compare the two systems.

To get a coherent answer to the legitimacy question, we need to know the sociological attributes of customary law. With minor alterations to Pierre Bourdieu's theory, one may say that customary law is a "bottom-up uprising" against the "top-down tyranny" over the judgement of right and wrong ("taste"), stressing the importance of upgrading popular culture and traditions ("popular taste") as the ultimate "legitimization" of cultural appearances (like "judgement of taste").[21] A solution well anchored in traditional knowledge clearly passes the legitimacy test. Such a solution may also furnish data of importance to viable resource management. The latter is, however, outside the scope of this paragraph.

Customary systems clearly result in improved acknowledgement of and increased respect for policies. Their impact is more widely felt than that, however. Customary systems can provide those persons who draft or implement political solutions and law, or who mediate conflicts, with culturally mature, collective knowledge. Drawing on this knowledge base also helps administrators to come up with solutions that meet popular approval (see Chapter 6). Administrators have an improved resource available to them in the form of popular knowledge as to the just allocation of the long-term return on resources rent. When they tap into this resource to solve administrative problems, their solutions are much more likely to meet with a satisfactory level of "legitimization."

The implication of acknowledging the bottom-up position, which rejects exclusive "parliamentary sovereignty,"[22] is that societies are burdened with legal obligations created by "popular will," or rather – as some critics say – "no one's will". This popular power is, however, not unknown throughout history. Sir Edward Coke (1552–1634) stated that individuals are legally bound by "artificial reason" or the accumulated wisdom of generations,[23] which points to the core problems of democracy.[24] The success of customary law should, like other consensus paradigms, be judged by its ability to promote valid majority decisions. We are likely to argue that the method of generating "public will" is of minor importance. The outcome of the process is more important. Vincent Ostrom suggests that a "person-to-person, citizen-to-citizen relationship" is the democratic paradigm in a nutshell.[25] If *inter partes* unanimity is the response to the democracy puzzle, customary law rules may also be as democratic as rules created by referenda where non-voters skip elections because their interests are not listened to. Since every top-down democratic system relies upon per capita assessment, a conflict between customary law and democracy should be measured by lack of popular influences. Decisions made by organs elected by voter turnouts of around 50 per cent are not that democratic.

In arguing that quasi-organ decision-making is consistent with democratic decisions, we are taking John Rawls' position. If each generation *refrains* from reserving the gains of culture and civilizations for its exclusive benefit, "[a]n ideally democratic decision will result, one that is fairly adjusted to the claims of each generation and therefore satisfying the precept that what touches all concerns all."[26] According to Rawls, there is no contradiction between the upholding of old traditions, customary law and democracy. Clearly new generations may opt for the traditional solutions. If explicitly or tacitly rejected, however, the traditional solution is overturned. Acknowledgement or lack thereof in a "person-to-person, citizen-to-citizen relationship" is what matters. The bottom-up system implies that popular traditions and judgement of *right and wrong* are transmitted not only from "the grassroots" but also from elder generations. This system is "ideally democratic" because of the continuous need for popular affirmation. If that fails, the traditional customary system is illegitimate, and will not survive.

Finally, a comparison of top-down and bottom-up democracy is needed to fully assess the benefits of customary law. Top-down proponents often overlook the disadvantageous aspects of the parliamentary decision-making processes. Although the executive branch may be indirectly democratic,[27] heavy lobbying and overly expansive delegation of enforcement power create opportunities for "groupthink," "[g]roup polarization,"[28] and corporate strongholds. Thus the "labyrinths" of executive branch implementation may easily corrupt political intentions,[29] as bureaucratic power, operating under the cover of discretionary "implementation," happens to deviate from initial legislative intent. Robert Michels suggests that "elitist" autocrats, making decisions based on their own knowledge and what they regard as "superb insight", will hinder genuine democracy from being realized."[30] John Milton[31] and others[32] believe that discretionary power on the part of those governing will invariably serve to reduce free nations to the status of slaves. The Bentham "logic of the will" paradigm, is, therefore, not what it seems. The ruling power is not the "pluralistic channel will," but the will of bureaucracy and strong corporate powers. Hence, we are far from "ideal democracy."

In actual politics, the alternative to direct democracy or bottom-up decisions may not be vigorous parliamentary power in the hands of directly elected politicians, but rather an executive branch tyranny brought into existence by the surrender of legislative responsibility to bureaucratic implementation by which user-inclusive rule-making replaces and compensates for the democratic deficiencies of executive legislation.

To the extent that decisions are considered democratic as long as participants are properly elected and the power of implementing organs is correctly delegated, top-down proponents overlook well-recognized objections. They blindly assume that electorates' control of delegated bureaucratic power means that administrative rules are *per se* democratic.[33] As the Austrian legal philosopher Hans Kelsen stated, most proponents of a "formal democracy line" take a rather fictitious "Volkssouveränität" perspective: "Die Fiktion der Repräsentation soll den Parlamentarismus vom Standpunkt der Volkssouveränität legitimiren." [Seen from the perspective of popular sovereignty, the fiction of representation just legitimates the parliamentary system.][34] Now consider whether parliaments do, in fact, represent the people and promote the "popular will." Pursuing Vincent Ostrom's thinking about bottom-up, self-organizing and self-governing capacities of local municipalities, this is far from obvious: "How people conduct themselves as they directly relate to one another in the ordinary exigencies of life is much more fundamental to a democratic way of life than the principle of one person, one vote, majority rule. Person-to-person, citizen-to-citizen relationships are what life in democratic societies is all about."[35] This quote focuses on pluralistic, contractual interaction (see Section 5.1). People take on mutual commitments by trading away liberties in exchange for future security. The state of real democracy is not to be measured solely in terms of the formal exercise of voting rights, but in terms of how knowledgeable, insightful society members acknowledge politics *and* politicians. According to Kelsen, "Bolschewismus und Faszismus" and "democracy" are contradictory concepts. Absolute monarchic decisions as well as the dictatorship of "state carrying parties," are contrary to "das ideal der Demokratie." The ultimate goal of popular free will is to create the "Willens im Staate."[36]

While the parliamentary system has a rather limited historical perspective, being the political ideal of eighteenth- and nineteenth-century constitutions, several bottom-up institutions have survived over the years. The consistent use of the jury under criminal procedure, for instance, illustrates the recognition of popular will. "The jury system is also considered an expression of democracy."[37] Similarly the two-*referenda* system, as developed from the *Forum Romanum*, the Greek *Polis* or Old Norse

Allthing, remains a stronghold of popular self-determination, whether codified or not. A good example of this is found in *City of Eastlake v. Forest City Enterprises*, in which the United States Supreme Court endorsed the position that a referendum "is far more than an expression of ambiguously founded neighborhood preference. It is the city itself legislating through its voters an exercise by the voters of their traditional right through direct legislation to override the views of their elected representatives as to what serves the public interest."[38]

Norway also illustrates how the non-codified system of referendum kept its position through heavy bottom-up pressures and became settled constitutional customary law.[39] The understanding of bottom-up democracy must take as its starting point ancient Greek democracy, a topic that "is an increasingly popular topic among historians."[40] Clearly a

> free state is a community in which the actions of the body politics are determined by the will of the members as a whole . . . if a state or commonwealth is to count as free, the laws that govern it – the rules that regulate its bodily movements – must be enacted with the consent of all its citizens, the members of the body politics as a whole.[41]

Presumably this objective is better formulated by local bottom-up procedures than by top-down decision-making procedures dominated by corporations and lobbyists.

Parliamentary democracies assume that judicial review[42] will provide "checks and balances" against "the tyranny of the majority."[43] This is a fallacy. Thomas Jefferson predicted that the "tyranny of the legislature is really the danger most to be feared," which would in turn be overrun by the "tyranny of the executive power [that] will come in its turn, but at a more distant period." Despite the laudable checks and balances built into the system, some opposition is raised because "change has been done by the courts, not by the democratic institutions of government."[44] Judges also express concern from time to time; see, e.g., Judge Vereshchetin, at the International Court of Justice, who declared that the court enjoyed "no right to judicial legislation."[45] While judicial review may be desirable, or at least bearable, executive review of legal failures is clearly condemned. Cass R. Sunstein's opposition to the "conventional nondelegation doctrine" does not envisage any executive branch review: "When Congress has spoken clearly, everyone agrees that agencies are bound by what Congress has said."[46] This is similarly stated by the European Court of Justice: a mere practice on the part of the Council cannot derogate from the rules laid down in the Treaty and therefore cannot create a precedent binding on the

Community institutions with regard to the correct legal basis.[47] While the legal situation is clear, the practical implications – as documented by the 1988 EU case – are often *contra legem*. Whenever bureaucracies renounce or at least redirect parliamentary decisions, democracy is at risk.[48] This is clearly seen in the case of the EU, where French is in fact and in principle the sole language of bureaucracy. Nonetheless, very few elected officials, whether from the European Parliament, the Commission or the Council levels speak fluent French. In a situation like this, courts' deviation based upon customary law, may in many instances reinstall "the popular will."

7.1.2 The positivists' opposition to customary law

By definition, parliamentary decision-making remains the primary law-producing public mechanism. This system evolved out of the 1648 *Constitutio Westphalia* axiom of sovereignty ("Landeshoheit") initiated by the "first truly European settlement in history."[49] Constitutions of European states and America rejected top-down aristocratic norm production as applied in England before King's Courts.[50]

In the aftermath of the *Constitutio Westphalia*, legal and political philosophies launched the idea of the "omnipotent state" that left little room for customary law. As follows from the famous John Austin statement, "laws properly so called" require not only a basic normative structure, but also a sovereign command and a rule of recognition.[51] A parliamentary decision enjoyed notoriety and provided sufficient notification. That idea brought everything before it long into the twentieth century. One logical deduction from the omnipotent state concept was that international law was not law at all.[52] The positivists' contemptuous view of customary law may be attributed to the view that popular practices obstruct "constitutional democracy."[53] According to Bentham, constitutional democracy was "the want of a system of adequate national representation, or rather the want of a representative democracy, in place of a more or less mitigated despotism: the want of the only form of government in which the greatest happiness of the greatest number is the end in view."[54]

In addition to the procedural questions, preliminary issues associated with the social function of legal institutions are raised.[55] Under this view, only democratic plurality or decisions based on "moral arithmetic" can defy medieval despotism. For instance, some feminist writers criticize customary law as hostile to women.[56] The positivist "liberal school" challenged "the despotism of democracy caused by demagogic violence, the brutal and savage government of the masses."[57] We see democracy as a bulwark against dark-age suspicion; nonetheless, the formal, parliamentary version of democracy is not necessarily the only vehicle for progress, science, humanity or toleration of dissent.[58] Such arguments made sense during the Middle Ages and even later,[59] but the decline of the aristocracy and upsurge in social equality have created an improved platform for bottom-up norm production. In a democracy, what matters is the fulfillment of legitimate claims for transparency, predictability, determinacy, coherency and consistency. Customary law does not necessarily contradict these substantial claims, simply because no "customs entrepreneur" may impose a usage or practice on others. Customary law consists of self-imposed norms that – in the beginning – are not intended for others, but which by their own persuasiveness tend to bring others "into line." For this very reason, comparing customary law adoption to parliamentary or executive branch legislation is inaccurate, simply because the pluralistic customary law more closely resembles contractual and international law structures.

Customary law is consistent with democratic values. In a democracy, rules should be transparent, predictable, determinate, coherent and consistent. Laws produced by the people themselves through bottom-up democracy can meet all of these tests.

Questions about the legitimacy of customary law are also a modern concern.[60] As in international law, the positivists raise issues in relation to transparency, predictability, determinacy, coherency and consistency. In general, they make six arguments based on (1) the superiority of public agencies, (2) the lack of identifiable customary institutions, (3) the need for uniformity, (4) the lack of flexibility, (5) the need for representative decision-makers, and (6) the risk of capture by special interests.

Their first argument suggests that the competency to impose civil and criminal law sanctions on people belongs exclusively to public agencies. Is this a false discrepancy, stemming from an overly formalistic notion of democracy or a perverted understanding of facts? Is Luhmann correct in stating that man for the first time in history has experienced the illuminating power of legal change by simple majority rule? One's response depends upon the *definition of democracy.* Clearly a formal, "one person, one vote, majority rule" concept would exclude all customary law systems. On the other hand, is direct and unrestricted popular participation in the making of laws basic to the "most thorough democracy?"[61]

Furthermore, if we speak of the *body politic* as the bearer of the popular will, defining the sum of all the many private interests as the public interest embodying the will,[62] we have to allow each individual an equal right to participate in law-making.[63] This clearly conjures up the ideal state of affairs. There are two possible approaches here. One is the direct democracy model. The second is the people's own participation, evolving new adaptive solutions *to the living fabric of life*, some of which may convert into customary law.

Wide-ranging constitutional abdication empowers owners, contractors or other private actors with too extensive a legislative power, critics insist. The all-powerful sovereign owes no obedience to others.[64] These objections are nevertheless fallacious since customary law is contractual in nature and lacks validity without popular acknowledgement.

An objection along the same line is that customary law solutions may turn out well, but we have no guarantees. As far as the environment is concerned, customary law often fails to find valid solutions.[65] But so do positive laws.

Secondly, it is argued that customary law has "no known person for its author, no known body of words for its substance."[66] By definition customary law, as the invention of quasi-organs, is not really "law." Jeremy Bentham belongs to this critical, anti-popular tradition initiated by Immanuel Kant: "Alle Regierungsformen nämlich, die nicht repräsentativ ist, ist eigentlich eine Unform" [Every system of Government that is not representative, is non-accurate].[67] From this Kant summarizes the implications for democracy: "dahingegen die Demokratische es unmöglich mach, weil alles da Herr sein will" [democracy makes this impossible, since all people are then made masters]. A customary law is nothing but a bottom-up despotism, executed by the populus – the idea that "der Volksgeist"[68] ["the spirit of the people"] produced "customary law is a fiction from beginning to end."[69] Replacing these metaphysical normative structures with written laws, Bentham argued, would clearly bring the modern era of rule of law and due process of law to the forefront.

A third alleged drawback is the law-abiding difficulty caused by ever-changing customary law. In the end, it is argued, this constant change may deflate national legal unity, and even worse, tear the nation state apart.[70] While Hart finds law to be the inheritor of customs,[71] Peter Goodrich argues that customs terminate state law, and consequently are destructive to public order.[72] John Salmond suggests the catastrophic results to which wide-open popular legislative power would lead:

> To hold . . . that the modern custom of merchants or of any class of the community possess any general authority to derogate from the common law . . . would be to establish a far-reaching and revolutionary principle of unknown extent and consequence, for which there is no sufficient justification in principle or authority, and which would be inconsistent with the permanence and uniformity of the established law of the land.[73]

Salmond's objections are clearly pertinent. Random and unilateral disobedience of legal obligations is irreparable under any system of law. But as Chapter 4 demonstrated, widespread and firm recognition is a prerequisite to the judicial enforcement of customary law.

Bentham criticized the anonymous, fictitious and non-textual character of customary law. Seemingly customary law lacks extra-judicial reconciliation possibilities because of its non-textual manifestation. Customary law is not beyond consideration, however, since "[t]he rule of law does not require that legal rules be carved in stone."[74] As the American jurist Joseph Story put it:

> Why, it is often asked, cannot the law of a country be reduced to a positive form? If it is a law it must be known, or ought to be known, so that every citizen may govern his conduct accordingly . . . They wear an air of plausibility, and therefore should be deliberately examined, and the errors to which it may lead, should be corrected by expounding the sources of them. It is very certain, that no nation, whose legal institutions are known to us, ever had a code of the nature above supposed, namely, one, which were comprehensive enough to embrace all the doctrines and details required for the private concerns and business of its whole population.[75]

Few legal conflicts are decided by strict legal interpretation. Adjudication at the appeals level results primarily from the fact that textual interpretation does *not* provide a ruling. The reason why the schism between written and non-written norms is of minor importance is probably due to the fact that legal conflicts are simply decided outside the courtroom, despite the existence of valid legal principles, on the basis of equity or other extra-legal principles:

> Of the innumerable questions which arise in any one age, or admit a forensic controversy and doubt, probably not . . . one in a thousand, ever comes before a court of justice to be there finally settled by adjudication. Many are settled by compromise; many by arbitration, or the intervention of friends; many are neglected or abandoned, from their comparatively slight importance, or poverty of the claimants, or their ignorance of, or indifference to, their rights, or from other causes tending to suppress litigation.[76]

Therefore, since no legal system abolishes people's freedom to opt for non-judicial solutions, all issues within a given conflict are open to negotiation and *bona fide* solutions. It is only if no such possibilities exist that people opt for adjudicated law.

A fourth objection relates to the dynamic status of life due to changing times. Since traditional Blackstonian customary laws include a principle of antiquity, positivists argue that such laws are out of sync with the terms of the time. However, as stated in Chapter 4, static ancient time usage was never an absolute binding prerequisite. Resilient systems of customary law adaptations, such as those advocated for future resource management, are quite consistent with a requirement that customary processes have a long tradition (Chapter 6). Even the most advanced code of law does not easily assimilate the "tales of the unexpected." New and unforeseen incidents constantly occur. In his commentary on the French Commercial Code, which he called the most "perfect specimen of legislation as ever have been," Joseph Story stated: "Such is the unavoidable imperfection of all human language, and such the shortsightedness of the most deliberate efforts of human wisdom!"[77] Not surprisingly, he concluded "that it is not possible to establish in any written code all the positive laws."[78] An identical conclusion was reached during the 1830s, when, after fifteen years of legislative endeavor, the "grand idea" of a Norwegian "Bürgerlicher Gesetzbuch" was dropped. The flexibility of ancient customs is at least as great as the "Grandes Codes."

A fifth objection relates to both Jean-Jacques Rousseau's idea of "The Social Contract,"[79] and to the original Athenian model of democracy. Here it is argued that the *populace* should rely on elections to transfer personal exclusive autonomy to representatives because "democracy must arise from the demos"[80] and that parliamentary representatives are bound by their electorate's mandates and act accordingly. Historical records indicate, however, that neither the American nor the French delegates to the constitutional assemblies of 1787 and 1789–91, respectively, followed their mandates. "The delegates to the Constituent Assembly decided to ignore their instructions altogether, and consider[ed] themselves the representatives of the nation rather than of their estates . . . The French delegates did not feel bound by their mandates, but accorded themselves the right to discuss whatever issue they wanted to take up."[81]

As Hans Kelsen has observed, representative democracy does not tie delegates to political programs:

> Diesem Zwecke dient die Fiktion der Repräsentation, der Gedanke, dass des Parlament nur Stellvertreter des Volkes sei, dass das Volk seinen Willen nur im Parlament, nur durch das Parlament äussern könne, obgleich das parlamentarische Prinzip in allen Verfassungen ausnahmslos mit der Bestimmung verbunden ist, dass die Abgeordneten von ihren Wählern keine bindenden Instruktionen anzunemen haben, dass somit das Parlament in seiner Funktion vom Volke rechtlich unabhängig ist.[82] [This purpose promotes the fiction of representation, the idea that the Parliament is a "step in" for the people, that the people's will is expressed in the Parliament only, even though the parliamentary principle of all constitutions lack provisions binding the member of Parliament to the voter's instructions, and subsequently the Parliament, in its functions, is legally unbound from its people.]

This brings up the core problem of "bootstrapping"[83] exclusive autonomy, as in Homer's classic problem. When sailing into areas of the Sirens' beautiful songs, Ulysses ordered his men to shackle him to the mast and to ignore his subsequent orders, knowing that their songs would overcome his weak will. The pluralistic channel democracies do not arrange for any such "bootstrapping," whether to pre-election position statements or to positions as expressed in political pamphlets or party programs.

A further contradiction is suggested by modern anthropological studies. Cases of political perversion of customary law are well documented. Powerful groups have maneuvered gracefully by means of more or less fictitious "customary law":

> Elders tended to appeal to "tradition" in order to defend their dominance of the rural means of production against the challenge by the young. Men tended to appeal to "tradition" in order to ensure that the increasing role which women played in production in the rural areas did not result in any diminution of male control over women as economic assets. Paramount chiefs and ruling aristocracies in politics which included numbers of ethnic and social groupings appealed to "tradition" in order to maintain or extend their control over their subjects. Indigenous populations appealed to "tradition" in order to ensure that the migrants who settled among them did not achieve political and economic rights.[84]

The argued misuse of customary law is indeed an historical fact and a regrettable use of power. Unfortunately customary law – like most legal codes – is and has been used to promote the egoistic interests of powerful groups. See the many illuminating examples presented in Chapter 6.

Asserting that positive law alone is the foundation of property rights, and that "extra-legal issues" are simply "imagination, with its favorite instrument, the word right,"[85] Bentham gave no place to customary law in his legal universe. Of course statutory law plays an important role in legal development, but legal rights derived from non-written sources are validated by legislation and adjudicative practices. It is understood that legal rights entitled by customary law *exist in the way of institutional facts* – also called "moral artifacts"[86] – as illustrated by a wide range of court decisions.[87] Unanimously accepted norms that by definition are "the popular will," cannot be measured against "human rationality." And even if they could be, it is hard to believe that irrational usage and practice, in the long run, would survive. Bentham deeply mistrusts the "anarchical fallacies,"[88] that he considers to be the product of "natural rights" doctrine:[89] "Rights are the fruits of the law and of the law alone; there are no rights without law – no rights contrary to law – no rights anterior to the law."[90] This is just a question of "which came first, the chicken or the egg?"[91] There is no "scientific" answer to that.[92] While philosophers like David Hume insist that rights are based upon law only, Thomas Reid argues that contractual rights come first, based upon reason and *inter partes* acceptance (see Chapter 3). These contractually based norms represent "the popular will" of the "distributive plurality."

Finally it could be said that this author is making "extravagant claims" of a democratic pedigree for customary law. Seemingly this objection is not trivial. I agree that customs sometimes result from rules imposed on a disenfranchised population by a group of elites. Although all members of a customary-law-governed society clearly do not play major roles, this does not mean that they are bereft of influence upon or power within it. Keep in mind that "inventing" customary laws is not identical to "inventing" standard contract documents. Societal members of lower status or position may initiate and contribute to the custom. Furthermore, the acknowledgement mechanisms of customary law are vital. In order to be successful, even the elite need backing for their proposed rules. As indicated by the Norwegian customary case law, all members of society need to adhere to the elites' rule. If they do not, even strong top-down pressure on disenfranchised people will not result in customary law.

On the other hand, elites are driven by bottom-up produced customary norms. Remember the two Norwegian kings who recognized customary law in 1604 and again in 1687. Furthermore, there are two factors that mitigate against the claim that customary law is not democratic. The first is the ability of the central legislature to pass supervening laws that restrict the power of customary law. Secondly, and critically, customary law must be legitimate or it will not be followed.

An additional and more formal rebuttal to the assertion of "extravagant claims" is that bottom-up produced norms meet the five criteria that provide them with democratic legitimacy. These criteria, as expressed by Rawls, are transparency, predictability, determinacy, coherency and consistency. Customary laws, as explained both in this chapter and in Chapter 1, are related to each one of these factors. In this chapter I argue for the bottom-up view and confirm three tests for the proof of "popular will realization." This theory is aligned with Rawl's on the coherence of traditions, customary law and democracy. As opposed to extravagant, it is my contention that these claims are restrained.

Method is at least as important as outcome in creating and legitimizing laws. This seemingly obvious fact is frequently overlooked. In this chapter I have tried to demonstrate the limits and falsehoods, or at least the polemics inherent to top-down democracy and the myopic interpretation of it when measured exclusively by suffrage. The tyranny of the executive branch, even in this age of extreme specialization, needs to be leashed by democratic controls. The critical role of acknowledgement and *opinio juris* in customary law cannot be overstated.

7.1.3 Customary law, common law and legislation

To the early positivists, the English common law was no more legitimate than customary law. Jeremy Bentham characterized the bottom-up realization of human wisdom as accidents of history that defied reason. "The yoke" of the obscure English Common law, the "trackless wilds of case law" were not law.[93] Bentham was advocating the logic of the public will, expressed in and recognized by the constitution of the state. "Whatever is given for law by the person or persons recognised as possessing the power of law, is *law*."[94] Only decisions made by authorized persons express the *acknowledged will* of the people. Consequently, norms produced outside the pluralistic channel are "extra-legal." For Bentham, common and customary law are equally invalid legal instruments. "*Common* law, as it styles itself in England, *judiciary* law, as it might more aptly be styled every where, that fictitious composition which has no known person for its author, no known assemblage of words for its substance, forms every where the main body of the legal fabric."[95] And as Bentham expressed:

> A customary law is not expressed in words . . . it has no parts . . . It is one single indivisible act, capable of all manner of constructions. Under the customary law there can scarcely be said to be a right or wrong in any case. How should there? Right is in conformity to a rule, wrong the deviation from it: but here there is no rule established, no measure to discern by, no standard to appeal to: all is uncertainty, darkness, and confusion.[96]

In summary, positivist legal science is eager to defeat metaphysical and non-positivist beliefs. The "real object" to be investigated is the manifestation of non-fictitious public texts of statutes, written on real paper. From that perspective, even the *most bureaucratic* and *unreasonable* norm is law. For the positivists, the element of social acceptability – the common popular will – of legal norms is quite irrelevant.

Leading common law proponents naturally disagreed with Bentham. Sir Edward Coke praised the law declared by judges, which he called "artificial reason." As J. P. A. Pocock stated, "the idea of judge-made laws [is] only a sophistication and extension of the idea of custom."[97] The law made manifest by court decisions embodies the wisdom of generations. It does not result from philosophical reflection, but from the accumulations and refinement of experience. What speaks through the judges is the distilled knowledge of many generations, each decision based on the experience of those who came before and tested by the experience of those living after. As Sir Edward Coke said,

> we are but of yesterday, (and therefore were in need of the wisdom of those who came before us) and had been ignorant (if we had not received light and knowledge from our forefathers) and our days upon the earth are but as a shadow in respect of the old ancient days and times past, wherein the law have been by the wisdom of the most excellent men.[98]

Customs carry the condensed wisdom of generations; embodied in the living fabric of life; valid because they are acknowledged.

The latest trend among political historians is to move from "the study of allegedly canonical texts" to "a more wide-ranging investigation into the changing political languages in which societies talk to themselves." The issue then is that "what it is possible to do in politics is limited by legitimization. However, what may be legitimized depends on what course of action can plausibly be arranged under existing normative principles."[99] Non-legitimate customs do not mirror anybody's "will" and should never be transformed into customary law. In the same way, courts sometimes feel free to derogate from legislation to obtain solutions they consider just![100]

Ancient customs may sometimes be wholly inconsistent with modern needs.[101] A mechanism for abolishing out-of-date customs is essential. But, as discussed in Chapters 2 and 5, existing legal standards legitimize customary law only as long as it retains popular support. The continuous adaptation of customary law to the living fabric of life protects against the positivist's fear of the grim grip of ancient, inflexible beliefs.

When focusing on customary law difficulties at variance with codified law, the gap portrayed is somewhat out of proportion. Thus, in comparing customary law *and* legislation, one finds more issues that bind them than divide them. First, popular recognition is the *sine qua non* for customary laws *as well as* for codified law (see Chapter 2). Second, the function of both is to bestow law and order. Both are driven by the fact that the sole purpose and function of law is to be obeyed. This assertion is based upon the law's recognition as "popular will." Not all will determinations should receive top ranking, as stated both by Jean-Jacques Rousseau in *The Social Contract*, and by Thomas Hill Green with "Will not Force is the basis of the State."[102] Consequently, "will" by consent is to be preferred to "will" by coercion.

This leads to the following conclusions, which are also defended by Jes Bjarup in Chapter 3. Firstly, pluralistic systems of bargaining, contracts and negotiations are superior to unilateral decision-making procedures. Secondly, norms forced upon people are less well received than rights and obligations that evolve out of multilateral agreements. Thirdly, laws created by "broad package deals" will more easily survive than solutions forced upon people which, by their very nature, give rise to suppression and coercive sanctions.

In most legal systems both codification and customary law have a place. Norway basically developed written law texts out of usage, custom and trade practices. There have been no objections to customary law *per se*, as a living instrument of law (see Section 2.2). When enacted, the King Christian IV Norwegian Code of 1604 declared that all ancient statutes, regulations and acts were terminated, and simultaneously acknowledged that the customary law remained valid law. In present-day Norwegian law, customs play an outstanding role in property law. Legislation[103] and the justification of a "double traced" system of law gives priority to customary law. In liability questions involving private law, unwritten customary rules may resolve the conflicts. This is the position of the Norwegian Private Law Committee, which conceded the difficulty of codifying the unwritten norms of the fisheries commons. "The draft [legislation] does not propose any provisions on the outer commons." Consequently, potential conflicts "should be tried before the Courts."[104]

The positivists do have substantial grounds for some of their criticism. Experience has shown that *medieval tradition* and *metaphysical beliefs* are detached from the urgent needs of societal change. As described in Chapter 5, customary law is extremely adaptive. We should not, therefore, be too concerned about "going backwards" at the present time. Clearly new customs soon reflect the necessary solutions for life. As indicated in the next chapter, customary law is still a strong, living entity that has a vital function to fulfill.

Some of its supposed shortcomings are simply based on gross exaggerations by antagonists who paint the issues all black and white. In their polarized opinion, customary law's salient characteristic is the grim grip of continuous, ancient, unproven beliefs, while pluralistic democracy exemplifies the valid legal instrument that adapts to the ever-changing social facts. This is not the case. Customary law is very flexible and adapts continuously to the "living fabric of life." Thus, there is no place for a custom dating back to Richard the Lionheart. What is required instead is an ancient norm relating to the custom. As we continue to discuss custom, we need to work from a non-static and flexible customary law context released from such past constraints as those imposed in Britain by the Richard the Lionheart requirement.

One important tool in the ongoing modernization project is the people's law-making capabilities. "[F]or the first time in universal history, legal changes by legislation became an immanent constituent of law itself" . . . "What is historically new and risky in the positivity of law is the *legislation of legal change*."[105] The excessive focus on pluralistic legislative decisions is neither astonishing nor strange. Historic customs seem antiquated and misplaced in modern times. Even Maine opposed old customs:

> It is a serious error to suppose that the non-feudal forms of property which characterised the cultivating communities had any real resemblance to the absolute property of our own day. The land was free only in the sense of being free from feudal services, but it was enslaved to custom. The facilitation of this process is the practical end of scientific jurisprudence.[106]

A mechanism for abolishing unfit customs is essential. In most instances, the "living fabric of life" is just such an elimination tool. Due to a lack of popular support, ancient customs deteriorate and vanish over time. Public decision-making organs may also put an end to obsolete customs. To make it clear, none of the authors of this book advocates that customs are insurmountable normative instruments. In some instances one must admit that customary law fails to find valid solutions.[107] Our point here is only this: one can not, as some scientists tend to do, presume that the customary law of the *commons* will ruin it all. In some instances the practices developed by popular will are best equipped to run a viable management system.

7.1.4 The burden of formal democracy

We have seen that "customary law [is] akin to the common law and the validity of custom [can] only be denied by ignoring the very nature of the Common Law itself."[108] Clearly, customary law also has a place within Anglo-American justice. When evaluating the pros and cons of customary law, we must keep in mind that the original notion of democracy is a material one that is assessed by the degree to which people adhere to it.[109] Customary law has an edge here. As noted, "public rights are exercised by the public, which in a democracy is the people."[110] People may choose to develop viable open access resources (public rights) in customary law systems, but not in formal pluralistic systems.

Currently there are no factual obstacles hindering self-governing societies from opting for direct democracy solutions. This can be attributed to the general reduction in the time spent working. If societies allow "everyone sufficient free time to take part in the general affairs of society – theoretical as well as practical . . . There are no politicians but at most people who engage in politics among other activities."[111] Considering what we know about the impossibilities of the democracy of Athens, however, statements like those are idealistic.

> Scholars will remember the vermilion-stained rope which was dragged along the streets of Athens to force the citizens to the place of the assembly . . . [and] noticed the effect which the burden of attendance on political duties had in throwing political privilege into a few hands and thus converting democracies into aristocracies.[112]

This is no isolated example. In England the compulsory duty to attend was considered burdensome, cf. the Magna Carta, which stated that no County Court shall meet more than once a month. Clearly, a scheme for democracy development ought to pursue realistic solutions. Decision-making systems with high transaction costs, such as the Athenian and the English ones, have obvious flaws. The referendum is appropriate for fundamental issues only. Since the meaning of democracy is to capture "the popular will," people's intense day-to-day involvement is what is valued. To achieve this, the democratic system should be constructed so that daily participation is easy and benevolent.

When measuring "democratic decisions," the basic legislative question is whether customary law captures "the popular will" more efficiently than statutory law, and then how to provide accurate legal protection to members of the society. Western societies today are no longer aristocratic. Instead, they are faulty bureaucratic decision-making systems, or even worse, bandit states.[113] Whatever their political structure, a strong likelihood exists that decisions are not made by the people. In relation to public property rights and the public trust doctrine, the question is whether extra-pluralistic channel decisions might initiate and develop legal protection for the benefit of the people.

Customary law may actually expand the powers and constraints imposed by constitutional law. Customary law has capacity and is simultaneously stable and amenable to change. This is overlooked by positivists like Karl Renner, who believe that only statutory law can achieve this task. This fundamental misconception underlies their claim that the primary appeal of law as an instrument for social change is "a mere platitude, a rather commonplace remark," [thereby refuting] that law can influence the economy to the point of changing the economy and having visible economic effects.[114] We claim that customary law can re-direct societies toward sustainable development every bit as well as statutes.

> Statutes and customary laws are, so to speak, only semi-manufactured products which are finished only through the judicial decision and its execution. The process through which law constantly creates itself anew goes from the general and abstract to the individual and concrete. It is a process of steadily increasing individualization and concretization.[115]

Consequently, legal rules implemented by customary law *as well as* legislation are continuously *formed* and *melted down* by the events of the living fabric of life.

> The body of persons to whose memory the customs are committed has probably always been a quasi-legislative as well as a quasi-judicial body, and has always added to the stock of usage by tacitly inventing new rules to apply to cases which are really new. When however, the customary law has once been reduced to writing and recorded by the process which I have described, it does not supply express rules or principles in nearly sufficient number to settle the disputes occasioned by the increased activity of life and

> the multiple wants which result from the peace and plenty due to British rule. The consequence is wholesale and indiscriminate borrowing from the English law."[116]

A proposition such as this suggests less flexibility and adaptability in the law than in fact exist. When a legal solution cannot be found, whether in written or unwritten sources, the actual reason for this failure is lack of "thorough study, laborious diligence, and a great variety of accessory knowledge."[117]

It is difficult to assess the types or amount of accessory knowledge that go into law-making. One advantage to a legal system comprised of written law is the simplicity in finding the law, making unnecessary the "very elaborate research into other books . . . and . . . the necessity of consulting an immense mass of learned collections and digests of antecedent decisions."[118] Such a straightforward view of the written law is adequate for cases where uncomplicated legal solutions suffice. For the more intricate questions that must be resolved by the courts, legal analysis requires a wide range of interpretative means.

The *instrumentation* and *implementation* of law are what matter, and not the *premature* semi-manufactured normative products.[119] Whether the written legislative system or the customary law system is best adjusted to the necessary process of maturation in ways that allow it to retain its flexibility is not easy to determine. When making this evaluation you have to know that formal rule production does not take place in elected, pluralistic organs like parliaments, but in bureaucracies without popular surveillance or control. Obviously the modern social democratic system of bureaucratically produced legislation is highly flexible. This systemic flexibility works to the detriment of democracy, however.[120]

When comparing the monolithic and strict pluralistic channel to diverse, popular norm production, one should keep in mind that law is "the felt necessities of the times."[121] Is customary law the best instrument of adjustment for the times? In answering this question, one ought to take "full-scale social experiences" into consideration. Events presently occurring in the former Soviet Union and India (see Chapter 3) shape our thoughts and provide knowledge for the road ahead. So does Martin Chanock's analysis in Chapter 8. Before examining the third world experience of customary law, we investigated alternative means of providing for sustainable development in Chapter 6. After that, we introduce the international law platform of sustainability and customary law (see Chapters 9 and 11).

Critics may say that these authors are overly optimistic about customary law's impact on resources viability. Is there any reason to believe that the local resource users who supposedly developed customary law were significantly concerned with protecting resources beyond those that their own communities needed to persist? Is it not a fact that the common property fisheries focus solely on the sustainable production of commodity resources for the fishers and are not at all concerned with other, non-commodity resource amenities that their fishing operations might harm? Nor are they at all concerned with the potential effects of local activities in other "jurisdictions." Clearly these authors agree that the utility of *domestic* customary laws is indeed limited to local trades and limited geographic areas. The multifaceted issues of actions, reactions and interactions are under no rational control and are not reflected by customs developed. However, through the living fabric of life, the experiences withstood or endured over time – the process of trial and error – bring to light quite complex relations that leave their mark on popular practices. An intuitive objection to new gear, participants, activity etc. is undeniably based upon experiences acquired from the living fabric of life. All new inventions need to be tried out in practical life, or "real life," before popular skepticism vanishes.

Clearly domestic customs suffer from local barriers. However, nothing in our writing proposes a universal rule of resource management based on Inuit rules or Saami norms. Our understanding is that international law (see Chapter 9) is a much easier row than domestic legal systems for native groups to hoe in terms of recognition and acknowledgement of their norms as law. International law becomes the "back door" for these groups to have domestic recognition. Fortunately, most states are parties to these documents. Then, it is also important that the applicable scientific community has recognized these groups' knowledge as "relevant and accurate" because the topic under discussion is the union of science and law. The central thrust of our message is that this is all work in progress. We have directed our efforts to setting forth the *tools* – chief amongst which is the precautionary principle – needed to *forge* the *transition* of sustainable development from a political stance to a legal norm.

7.1.5 "What are the alternatives: does customary law have a chance?"

The success of customary law does not depend solely upon the failure of advocates of formal democracy to critique it to death (see Chapter 5). Its success hinges on the achievement of alternative steering techniques. Does a good regulatory system exist?[122] Svein Jentoft states that we have lots of illustrations that "suggest that people in most fisheries-dependent districts should not hold great hopes that effective political steps will be taken toward more sustainable development."[123] Despite this pessimism about obtaining a political solution, some might still wonder whether bottom-up "distributive plurality decisions" are the way to go. At the same time, the cries of "foresight," "clairvoyance," "déjà vu" and "functional flexibility" seem to suggest that people are looking for a customary law attitude adaptable to the changing fabric of life.[124] So do empirical studies concluding that the "common understanding [of] traditional Norwegian fisheries were based on flexible adaptations to marine systems."[125]

Theoretical criticism of customary law solutions is debated in Chapter 9. Do *governmental command and control* or *market mechanism* face better odds? Clearly – as Martin Chanock states in Chapter 8 – where states do not function, custom competes not with "law" or with "the market" but with corruption. Then custom contends not with "law" or "the market," but with "bandit economies."

This chapter questions[126] the conclusions drawn from Garrett Hardin's famous "tragedy of the commons" metaphor,[127] and the common understanding that privatization or public regulation are the sole possible remedial instruments. A third option is found in Hardin's own "subtle signs" – i.e. underlying traces – of social norm systems in self-governing societies.[128] We focus on the law-making capacity of close-knit and even loose-knit groups of people, so-called "quasi organs" such as Indian Tribes – the "quasi-sovereign political entities."[129] The quandary lies in whether customary law comes up with solutions as advanced as the ones proposed by private markets or public control and command. Whether to go for the customary solution depends upon other advanced alternatives. One argument posits a rule-oriented solution by means of customary law as better than not having any norms at all. Random solutions by means of pure guesswork, or even worse, through organized kleptocracy with collapsing states and bandit economies are not workable in any social system.

To help solve our puzzle, we turn to game theory concepts. We do not take real world situations into consideration in the next section (see, however, Chanock in Chapter 8). Instead we compare the idealized, typical versions of "political command" and "market" when assessing the possible superiority of customary law in achieving sustainable development. If customary law is deemed inferior, public agencies may find reasons for opting out of it. The game theory findings are then ruled out by the illustration of the Straddling Fish Stock Agreement of 1995.

7.1.6 No other choice?

The working hypothesis of this book is that customs elaborated within non-governmental organs – also called "quasi-organs" (i.e. non-elected and self-instituted social entities) can sometimes accomplish more comprehensive sustainable systems than does statutory law. This is not self-evident, however, nor is it reflected in all or even many of the theoretical works on common pool self-governing systems.

In some instances customary law is the only ruling alternative. When presented with the difficult task of codification in the outer commons, the Norwegian Civil Law Commission took this position: "The draft legislation presented by the commission does not propose any provisions." The legal situation in the field "is considered a task for the Courts,"[130] which means that adjudication should take place on the basis of customary law. The Norwegian Parliament (Stortinget) took an identical position in 1992 when it terminated the 1687 codification of the outer commons, but failed to promulgate a new text. Thus, the ancient unwritten customary law was revived. As stated in Section 7.1.3, the Law Modernization Committee had no intention of terminating the *rule* of the outer commons. The customary outer common rules are still valid.

The Namibian Customary Courts share this belief.[131] Not only has the Namibian judiciary tacitly concurred in the informal legal system, but its government has actively recognized customary laws under the constitution and offered a special competent court to solve the problems of interpretation.

Furthermore, even the most intricate texts do not solve all future conflicts, leaving open at least some loopholes of law.[132] Comprehensive international treaties clearly suffer from loopholes. The 1982 UN Convention of the Law of the Sea, which was supplemented by seabed mining and the straddling fish stock rules in 1994 and 1995, neatly illustrates this. Despite fine-grained rules, even more specific solutions are under the discretion of the Seabed Authority and RFO practices. If closely followed, such practices may evolve into regional customary laws.

For loopholes of law and for complicated legal areas that fail to find their textual expression, there is but one solution – namely, customary law. Here the legislator has tacitly or expressly renounced the severe difficulties of getting things down on paper.

In the next section, some basic difficulties encountered by private markets or governmental control are considered in the framework of game theory. The success of customary law results not only from its own rich sources, but also stems from the failure of private markets and governmental regulations.

7.2 The means-end model

In this section I shall apply game theories as analytic tools to the analysis of an international agreement on straddling fisheries management. My hypothesis is that these theories may shed light on the process of customary law development.

7.2.1 A game theory point of departure

Customary law is a mechanism, like private markets and governmental command and control, that may contribute to sustainable development. These instruments had no place in the governmental command and control structure or "the pyramidal means-end model," that the philosopher Arne Naess targets for the purpose of achieving the meta-norm of sustainability.[133] Meta-norms should be deliberately put into place with instruments that are designed to support sustainability. A tool that is randomly chosen is unlikely to achieve selected goals. We will use this means-end model to evaluate the viability of customary law as a working tool.

In doing so we will figure out whether game theory rules out customary law as a realistic instrument of sustainability. We will test customary law under the "*prisoner's dilemma*" and "*cake theories.*" Do these theories single out customary law systems as non-viable resource allocation systems?

Before answering this question, we need to clarify game theory fundamentals. Because unilateral cheating leads to multi-party cheating, which in the long run ruins it for everyone, game theory predicts that the participants in these kinds of situations will pick "a tit for tat,"[134] or *BATNA* (best alternative that is unilaterally accessible) strategy.[135] The only way to overcome the failure predicted by game theory is through *cooperation*, that is to say, *not to defect from cooperative behavior.*[136] Some game theorists say that "grand packages that include tradeoffs,"[137] in other words, broad-based compromise deals, are the way to solve cheating and induce cooperation. These packaged deals seem identical to the social institutions that embrace customary law solutions. The hypothesis is that the same cooperation that solves game theory puzzles *also* helps form valid customary laws. To investigate that puzzle, let us check out the straddling fish stock situation.

7.2.2 The straddling fish stock illustration

The background story for this discussion is the early 1990s idealistic bilateral Arctic Cod Management Agreement between Russia and Norway. For reasons unknown, the distribution area of the cod expanded north into the high sea (Loophole). This led to Icelandic trawlers exploiting beyond the established TAC (total allowable catch). Iceland made an offer, a minor allocation of approximately 5,000 tons, but the Russian and Norwegian monopolists rejected it. As no cooperation was forthcoming, Iceland's only option was to continue fishing in the Loophole. After Iceland had continued its unilateral fishing activity for some five years, and after it had fished more than ten times the requested quota, Russia and Norway gave in and opened the fishery to Iceland. By that time, however, the distribution of the cod stock no longer covered the Loophole. This was not a tragedy, in any case, since Iceland's agreement opened up trawl fishing in the Norwegian exclusive economic zone (EEZ).

Exploiting straddling fisheries is originally a non-cooperative set up, i.e. a "prisoner's dilemma" game. On the high seas, one player's gain is another player's loss. Before the establishment of Regional Fisheries Bodies (RFO), there was no incentive to form coalitions. The situation presented a clear "prisoner's dilemma." "A cake" and "a dilemma" are both relevant to this game-theory classification.

With the establishment of RFOs, the international society of states now has a permanent forum for discussion and decisions. In a general way, this signals a will – but sometimes also indicates strong pressure through decision-making procedures[138] – not to defect from cooperation. Does this shift signal a departure from a "Prisoner's Dilemma Institution"[139] in favor of a "Repetitive Player's Game" (also called iterated prisoner's dilemma strategies)?[140] *Greed* and *fear* are vital features of the pre-RFO system of prisoner's dilemma. Have these traits been replaced by *mutual understanding* subsequent to the establishment of the RFO regimes? The distributive plurality decision dilemmas have been replaced by joint coordinated action within the framework of a conflict-solving mechanism, the RFO. Game theory depends on players being rational and not being carried away by unexamined feelings of greed and fear. When players are rational, game theory can predict patterns of decisions (which decisions, will be investigated in the next section). The question is how best *to renounce* distributive plurality decisions (see Section 7.2.4).

One possible objection to applying this analytical tool is that individual players should not be confused with states. Is the "prisoner's dilemma game" an appropriate paradigm? States do not feel greed or fear. Because players are physical persons, the "iterated prisoner's strategy" is a pattern of behavior, a personality. As "rulers" change, state policies and "state personalities" change. Consequently, one might say, the prisoner's dilemma scheme is oriented toward human beings, not cooperative organizations. However, since states, and let's not forget, states in the process of negotiation, are led by individuals, objections such as these cannot prevail. Thus game theories are also applicable to states' activity on the international plane. I first address the issue of the "cake," in paragraph (a) then I turn to the "dilemma" in paragraph (b).

(a) Traditionally there have been two cakes: the high seas and the EEZ. While there are highly productive local areas that lie beyond coastal states' jurisdictions, the majority of high seas production occurs immediately adjacent to EEZs. Much of the global harvested production is concentrated in relatively small areas with certain hydrographic and biological characteristics. Thus, the exploitable concentrations of marine resources are generally concentrated in certain well-defined areas for feeding and reproduction, rendering the stocks vulnerable to intense exploitation.[141] With modern technologies, stocks are becoming easy to locate.

Since the same species of fish straddle between zones, biologically there is only one "cake." The "two-cake" agenda was a political reality before the 1995 Straddling Fish Stock Agreement. To defect from cooperation now means to adhere to the pre-1995 agreement status of a single, isolated species that might be harvested without regard to the EEZ or high-sea fishing respectively. Setting up high-sea and EEZ joint management establishes a unity, i.e. one common pool resource.

(b) Vital to the dilemma classification is whether the prisoner's cumulative threshold of "fear" and "greed" is exceeded. If not, there is no prisoner's dilemma. In the era prior to the 1995 Straddling Stock Agreement, the thinking was simple and the dilemma was delightfully easy to solve. It went as follows. I *think* that some enemy will necessarily catch any fish that escapes my nets. I *fear* that the other person will defect from cooperation, disregard the exploitation rates or future generations, and take all available fish without further consideration. So, I take that fish, instead.

The prisoner's dilemma game reflects the communication that is missing between participant states or fishermen. And, what is important, there are no informal normative systems that keep participants from *greedy* options. But is this in fact the case? The presumption of this game overlooks Garret Hardin's 1994 revision of the tragedy syndrome, namely, that informal social norms ("subtle signs of normative structures") in many instances do manage the commons.[142] For the high seas, however, such customary normative structures are clearly missing.[143] Thus, we will not take informal normative structures into account for purposes of a high-seas illustration. In *this* situation, overlooking the informal social norms, to refrain from fishing, whether to benefit future generations, to promote sustainability or for whatever altruistic reason, is irrational. In *that* sense, I agree with John Nash's statement that rational players defect![144] *In casu* to cooperate (for i.e. High Seas and Coastal States to refrain from fishing, for instance, in the spawning season or at the spawning grounds) to benefit a future common resource optimization, is irrational. Since the players have not agreed to any mutual cooperation toward modest exploitation or sustainable resources development, any rational player will defect (i.e. take whatever fish are within range). A player who does not know whether the other player will cooperate in pursuit of that goal, is always better off defecting, no matter what his opponent does.

The fisherman's rationalization goes like this: since there is no fish exploitation agreement in place, the stock condition is probably not that critical. If *I* do not catch the fish, some *other* vessels most probably *will*. If I take the fish, I earn the money. If I do not, my opponents have it all. Even if "the others" do not catch it, my reluctance to do so doesn't serve my interests in any case since that particular fish will never cross my path again, and since in the long run, my modest fishing doesn't change anything either way! Therefore, I'll catch it!

Consequently, the *equilibrium point* is defection! There are some modifications to be made, however. Given that the two parties here have completely opposed interests, we cannot draw the conclusion that, under no circumstance is a reasonable settlement possible. Of course the rational solution is an equilibrium enforced by self-interest (personal greed) and mistrust (fear that the other may defect), a mistrust that is reasonable enough taking into consideration the antithetical goals of the players.

In many situations, however, the antagonists do not have completely opposed interests. Their conclusion simply presumes that high-sea fish are available. When faced with extinction, on the other hand, high-sea fishing nations' only rationale is cooperation. Using the model of "cake division," there are no longer two cakes, one within the EEZ and one beyond. The only cake left is internal to the EEZ. Then a rational, high-sea fishing nation's strategy is to reach an agreement for its own vessels to access previously closed EEZ. Does this represent the straddling fish stocks situation?

In other situations as well, high-sea fishing nations and coastal states have a common interest in viable resources utilization, which require access limitations and a scientific TAC system. By accepting the need for a common organizational framework and scientifically based exploitation, all parties have at least some common interests. John Nash showed that despite the anticipated *inter partes* "mutual defection," parties will cooperate *if* their joint action expands the common good.[145] This is exactly the straddling fish stock situation: rational high-sea fishing nations and coastal states cooperate in the goal of sustainable fish management in order to preserve an overall, long-term optimal outcome.

Under the 1995 agreement and the introduction of the RFOs, the straddling fish stock unilateral high-sea fishing nation and coastal state utilization, which starts out as a non-cooperative two-cake game, winds up incorporating bargain elements that enhance the possibility of achieving viable resource management solutions. Bargaining power, of course, does not come from the power of the word, but from material resources such as lobbying capacity, etc.[146] The solution, that is, the ensuing cooperation, is reached through political give and take, which does not necessarily deviate from logical arguments or from scientific, biological data.

In conclusion, the post-1995 agreement situation, supported by the RFO institution for joint action, the NEAFC arena management, is a cooperative game, and consequently, no "prisoner's dilemma" at all. The prisoner's dilemma was left behind in the period prior to the 1995 Straddling Fish Stock Agreement. Consequently, cooperation is the answer. The question is, how to justify it? How can you make players understand how to cooperate? Another vital question is whether any of the possible decision making schemes under the Straddling Fish Stock Agreement actually incorporate "equilibrium points." The important issue when establishing viable management schemes is, as pointed out by John Nash ("the Monday Morning Quarterback Game"),[147] that any outcome that makes players think – in retrospect – "I would have changed my strategy if I had known how the other guy would play," is, in fact, unstable. Under the Norwegian Arctic cod fisheries, the Norwegian and Russian defections vis-à-vis Iceland, which were transformed into cooperation some years later, are examples of unstable outcomes.

Since "rational choice" is measured by the outcome of the action,[148] unstable results come from "irrational choices." The viable straddling fish stock regime that all players should stick to, is a stable one. Is the top-down model the right answer? The crucial point then is which management system is stable enough to survive? Can the international society afford any more decades of trial and error?

In this connection, Nash's statement that rational players defect, seems wrong.[149] Rational people change strategies according to personal gains and losses. Having nothing to gain, but plenty to lose if he defects, no rational player will do so if the opportunity to cooperate comes along. The 1990 Norwegian and Russian defections (vis-à-vis Iceland) seemed rational at that time. In retrospect, however, it is easy to see that cooperation was the right answer even in the early 1990s. In terms of Nash's "*Monday Morning Quarterback,*" solutions are unstable if the players have nothing but regrets. Because of the Norwegian-Russian defection, Iceland first took full advantage of free fishing in the Loophole. Then, when the fish had dispersed, Iceland wisely acknowledged it would close the empty Loophole in exchange for access into Norway's and Russia's EEZ. Then, having nothing to gain from further defection, Iceland changed strategy in favor of cooperation, and gained quota rights in Russian and Norwegian waters.

This cooperation strategy embodies the fundamentals of customary law. Practices evolved under the framework of high seas and EEZ joint fishing strategies, within or without the RFO, may grow strong and govern the arena of fishermen and states. If practices become stable and are unanimously followed, because players are assured that the law, whether *jus cogens* or *jus dispositivum*, is obligatory, a "tit for tat" cooperative strategy may lead to cemented customary law structures.

7.2.3 Distributive plurality decisions[150]

One basic objection to environmental law solutions based on individualist approaches is expressed by the "tragedy of the commons" metaphor.[151] Privatization is the best solution under this view. While the process of reason forms statutory law, customary laws occur randomly by tacit acknowledgement. The question for debate is whether the institution of customary law is a distributive plurality regime or whether customary law is a case of "collective plurality decisions"?

This section focuses on the importance of customary law in managing open access resources as *in casu* fisheries rights. In considering the conduct of fishermen in the framework of self-governing societies, one question is whether chaotic distributive plurality decisions, geared toward personal egoistic benefit, may achieve sustainable development at all.[152] In our effort to come to grips with this puzzle, we should first do a side-step investigation of the game theory approaches *to uncoordinated decisions under private market solutions* (distributive plurality decisions).

Many people see the uncoordinated and unstructured behaviors of unorganized individuals as disastrous, cf. the game theory *second choice* "cake-sharing" example.[153] This seems to be the case with customary law since there are no explicit, initial agreements that precede cooperation. This is just a first-glance perception, however. Unilateral practices, once tried out, will be warmly or harshly received, rejected, changed, approved until – under a regime that acknowledges others as equally ranked and equally important – they ultimately converge toward a common platform. Then, due to the changing fabric of life, the platform will have to be adjusted and coordinated. Under the influence of a "tit for tat" ideology, the will of "us" and "them" merges into uniform practice. A custom that is not reasonable to other participants will vanish, and consequently fail to meet the customary law requirements.

Thus, when classifying customary law by type of decision, the "collective plurality decisions" classification is accurate. No social norm is unilaterally or exclusively made. The norm that finally gains acceptance is the product of the influence of many critical observers.

Peaceful social cooperation leaves open no other options but to invent and maintain unanimously acceptable solutions. The remaining problem is how to construct a platform for unanimous understanding. Should open access resource exploitation continue? Should resources be divided into few or many pieces? This is a question of economic efficiency. But not only – just distribution effects pervade economic analysis as well.[154]

So far, customary law is not excluded from the list of instruments to bring about sustainable development. Normative results occur in a collective plurality decision arena. The customary law option depends upon what the good workable alternatives are and whether customary law may avoid some of the most obvious clashes with the unfavorable consequences listed in the next section.

7.2.4 The problematic "economic man"

How should customary laws confront the "economic man" paradigm? An environmental concern is how to create "smart" regulation strategies in order to escape practices that ruin sustainable development.[155] Whereas most environmentalists are state interventionists, our interest lies in *bottom-up* created norms. Some stipulations have to be in place for customary law to succeed. One such stipulation is the philosophical rejection of the "economic man," the idea that individuals make rational choices based on their own self interest, and that the aggregate selfish actions will unintentionally provide for the common good. In the question of open access fisheries, neoclassic economists believe that privatization deficiency will result in continuous fishing until the marginal cost of taking one additional fish will exceed the marginal benefit; i.e. the problem of maximum sustainable yield and the "zero average product."[156] However, not "*all* people are *exclusively* pursuing their material self-interest . . . By now we have substantial evidence suggesting that motives of fairness affect the behavior of many people."[157] One side of this clash results from the conflict between economic efficiency and fairness of allocation, or redistribution equity.[158] Neoclassical economic thinking clearly does not take just distribution into consideration. Our intention here is to propose solutions that take fairness and equity elements into consideration. Something that happened in the Norwegian mackerel fisheries a few years ago is a brilliant illustration:

> The Ministry of Fisheries opened the fishery on August 8th. Mackerel was regulated by a Total Allowable Catch (TAC) and all vessels operated on a *first-come, first-served* basis. The Ministry said that once the TAC was reached, the fishery would be closed. Because the prices for mackerel were low at that time, "rush fishing" would have been a financial disaster for most fishermen. All attempts to have fisheries agencies move the starting date were unsuccessful.
>
> One of the fishermen, Mr. Dagfinn Alisøy, from Bulandet on the West Coast of Norway, acted like a Viking chief. He contacted the entire fleet by short wave radio and asked that nobody rush to the fishing fields until they received further orders (from him). At the date of "utror" – the starting date of fishing – no one went out. A remarkable solidarity set in that overcame the fishermen's frustration at the Ministry. The fishermen renounced the idea of grabbing to get the maximum possible mackerel catch. Nobody disobeyed. After two weeks, the mackerel quality and price improved, so a "go" was given and fishing commenced.[159]

The archetypal near-sighted "egocentric economic man" actually took "the others" into consideration. By not doing unto others what he would not like others to do unto him (for a version of the "golden rule," see Section 5.1), the leader anticipated the others' behavior, and came up with workable solutions. So, in considering his own self-interests, he also managed to gauge the best for others. While on the path of his own pursuits, he recognized "the others," and realized that these other participants would not just sit on the sidelines, doing nothing. The point is simple: fairness of allocation and redistribution equity are "a must." When deliberating, most common pool participants bear in mind the "golden rule." The traditional "economic man" will not dictate in the Norwegian fisheries trade.

7.2.5 Restoration for loss of externalities

To become environmentally successful, customary law must control externalities to obtain viable long-term resources exploitation. More specifically, the customary system must cope with transactional elements that suffer from a *lack of market value*, and, therefore, are not accounted for in transactions. Ronald Coase believes that the absence of transaction costs will create fair distribution of property rights.[160] However, since transaction costs are an unavoidable reality, socially optimal outcomes will not occur automatically. The situation worsens when elements until recently considered to be externalities, are internalized. The "real world transaction costs," therefore, become much higher than they were formerly.

Clearly one cannot trust all subjects to comply with good environmental practices. Sustainable trade requires that individuals be made liable for the harm they do. The internalization scheme emphasizes the implementation of the "Good Popular Rule" of personal liability for environmental harm caused. This requires restoration, which, unlike the "Good Governance" solution, gives market value to public property rights. It is a matter of "welfare maximization," and not "wealth maximization." As regards pasturage rights in California, Robert Ellickson found informal, close-knit group law production to be the most welfare maximizing. Could this finding be valid for fisheries resources as well?[161]

The basic question is whether these customary laws, however "invisible," could, under optimal conditions, direct societies toward the goal of sustainable development and just distribution of wealth? If all members of the close-knit group do not find that they benefit from the norms, such norms tend to be abolished.[162] Whether the outcome should include *restoration schemes*, is of course, an open question. What it should not do, as Cass R. Sunstein points out, is create aggregate willingness to pay:

> But there is a big difference between democratic judgments about social problems and aggregated willingness to pay. And in a democratic system, the democratic judgments ought to be preferred. This is especially the case if

> what ought to matter in environmental policy includes, as I think it should, the interest of future generations and if they will suffer, the interests of creatures who are not human.[163]

It is readily agreed that willingness to pay is an inappropriate remedy for resources restoration.[164] A better solution is to make resources *restoration* schemes take future generations into consideration as a latent function. Undoubtedly, the instrument of restoration, or alternatively, replacement cost, is appropriate.

7.2.6 *Restoration of coastal resources: an illustration*

We are weighing one remedial possibility that links personal liability to restoration for harm done. One feasible connection between customary law and sustainable development, therefore, entails a system of restoration. Let us illustrate the restoration policy with an example from the coastal fisheries. The issues at stake when dealing with the public property rights of fisheries, the public trust,[165] involve nuisance, liability and legal protection. Do self-governing, open access systems reach their sustainable development goal by acquiring legal protection against losses and damages? There seems to be some positive correlation here. In fact, the Norwegian courts have already adopted this principle.

On the one hand, the Norwegian Supreme Court has rejected the market value of fisheries concessions, holding that the Fisheries Agencies termination of licenses without compensation to the license-holder does not constitute a taking.[166] Iceland's Supreme Court rejected a similar claim involving the closed-entry scheme of Iceland.[167] This indicates that courts *still recognize fisheries as a common pool*, regardless of the Ministry of Fisheries limited-entry provisions.

At present, courts have provided legal protection to fishermen against competing uses of the sea that have damaged the fishery resources.[168] With the courts having taken that position, fishermen supposedly also enjoy legal protection against competing fishermen if the latter are overexploiting the stocks. If sustainable development were recognized by international law, this would be a possible outcome under domestic adjudication. States as well as individual fishermen have a responsibility not to overexploit fishery resources. If they breach this duty, the most commonsensical remedy is restitution or restoration. The trespassers could make up for the overexploitation by "re-injecting" farmed fish to increase the stocks or by having their following year's quota reduced in proportion to their over-fishing. As a result, the local self-governing units managing the commons by means of customs or local customary law seem very successful.

Although private property is currently the dominant cultural position, the competing institution of public property rights has not been extinguished. Despite strong trends toward privatizing whatever common goods (*res communes omnium* and *res nullius*, which are part of the *res sacrae*, those things consecrated to the greater good)[169] exist, customary-law-based public property rights regimes remain. Accordingly, under transaction-cost ideology,[170] these institutions must be economically efficient; otherwise, they would already have been converted into private property rights.

It is our ambition to reveal the main principles managing the commons, and to see which customary law system might be successful (see especially Chapter 6). Supposedly it is wise to "search for regularities,"[171] that is, regularities that qualify as customs or customary law. In fact, it is a widely accepted belief that "individuals cannot organize themselves and always need to be organized by external authorities."[172] In the words of Elinor Ostrom, one might be led to believe that without an adequate theory of self-organized collective action, one could not predict when local societies would be incapable of solving common problems through self-organization alone. The road ahead is through a customary law institution constructed so that the necessary resiliency is attained. Resiliency is presumptively influenced by the capacity to restore, which must garner a vital place under the customary law scheme.

Legal protection provided to the beneficiaries of public property rights (i.e. the *res communes omnium*, the free items of the world, like fish or derelict goods) and the "public trust," by means of procedural rights like *class action suits*, is vital in a customary system of viable resources management. A system of *restoration* duties to counterbalance the excessive exploitation of resources seems to be necessary. Individuals have the responsibility to refrain from overexploiting natural resources. If their personal conduct causes damage, they are the ones to blame, and the compensation scheme should then be measured on the scale of restoration remedies.

To summarize the present findings, it follows that customary law is instrumentally important in qualifying the precautionary principle. The developed normative structures occur in a collective plurality decision arena. The deficits of the *economic man* are not empirically demonstrated, at least under Norwegian fisheries law. The customary law system must make room for restoration mechanisms. Breaching resources regulations, environmental law or other sustainability provisions should lead to legal liability for reconstructing resources. *De lege lata* American and Norwegian cases already subscribe to restoration solutions.

Customary laws may reach important sustainability objectives. Since public regulation and private markets may also lead to that end, these alternatives should be examined. Which one amongst public regulation, markets, or customary law would best achieve that objective?

7.3 The public control and command

Does *statutory law* work more efficiently to cure the problems of overexploitation? If so, the customary law scheme will clearly play a subordinate role in sustainable development. Many would probably say that some norm is needed, but whether that norm is statutory or customary law is not the "big thing." The traditional point of view is that the substance and structure of environmental laws are political and should be decided by the legislature. The court is to apply environmental law that coordinates the conflicts between resource exploitation and utilization. Cass R. Sunstein said:

> These various problems – collective action problems, lack of coordination, lack of expertise, and democratic failures – suggest that a common law system will be both inefficient and undemocratic. This was the basic insight that led to the substitution of regulatory machinery for the common law in the environmental area.[173]

Many jurists agree with the above statement. Regulation by public laws is considered necessary to achieve sustainable development. It is further believed that both common law and customary law are insufficient to cope with environmental objectives. Despite this rather widely held understanding, customary law has played a key role in local, self-governing sustainable societal development. As Henry Sumner Maine stated: "The preservation, during a number of centuries which it would be vain to calculate, of this great body of unwritten custom, differing locally in detail, but connected by common general features, is a phenomenon which the jurist must not pass over."[174] Even so, statutory law may play an even bigger role. Whether statutory law is an indispensable instrument for sustainability remains to be considered. Our first task is to figure out whether the importance of statutory law is overstated. Then we will share some thoughts on the need for customary law solutions despite the alleged insurmountable stronghold of statutory law.

Is statutory law really as good as claimed? When considering the well-established system of governmental command and control ("the public solution," also called the visible hand),[175] a question that arises is why not just consider direct public regulation? Why take alternative legal mechanisms into consideration in the first place? Of course, the customary law perspective based on individualist legal protection certainly reflects a skepticism toward public regulation mechanisms. This skepticism is shared, however, with economists like Ronald Coase who observed: "It is my belief that economists, and policy-makers generally, have tended to over-estimate the advantages which come from governmental regulation."[176] Lawyers in civil law countries are part of that positivist hypothesis.

Let us first look into some fisheries law observations of 1982. They conclude that fisheries agencies often deviate from the intended public goals through misinterpretation. Despite the clear objective of the public trust fisheries, agencies have *de facto* introduced private ITQ (Individual Transferable Quota) solutions allowing for private sales of licenses along with the vessel. Fisheries agencies have upheld this practice even though it is contrary to positive legislation.[177] The "outcome" of the bureaucratic implementation does not mirror the "input" of policy intentions. These unintended, adverse consequences now dominate the scene.[178] The fallout from this distortion pervades the regulatory regime today.[179]

Historic events serve to document how "governmental control and command" is adverse to achieving political goals. Executive changes through the mechanics of law, is in many instances a task of Sisyphus.

> The modernization process, even relatively sedate, always contains elements of suspenseful confrontation. In few cases, however, has it been quite so dramatic as in the attempted modernization of Central Asia under Soviet auspices . . . Soviet law tended to be . . . dysfunctional to the extent that the local traditional milieu was alienated . . . It was at a disadvantage . . . in that (a) it lacked the sacred qualities and personalities of the antecedent system; (b) it tended to be abstract, rigid, and impersonal; (c) it could not easily gain access to traditional communities either because the latter were physically distant, or nomadic-pastoral (hence elusive), or because they were governed by a combination of religious and customary law, and could thus be independent of, and elusive to, formal legal structures.[180]

The Soviet State confronted the same difficulties as the Tsar had encountered a century earlier when the Russians codified, for themselves, a purely German legal system.[181] While Russian and Soviet leaders seemed unconcerned by the social consequences of a strict, non-sensible centralized legislative policy, Maine noted the opposite reaction by British rulers in India during and after the 1857 riot:

> A nervous fear of altering native customs has, ever since the terrible events of 1857, taken possession of Indian administrators . . . What an oriental is really attached to is his local custom"[182] . . . [T]here exist in India several – and it may even be said, many – considerable bodies of customary law, sufficiently alike to raise a strong presumption that they either had a common origin or sprang from a common social necessity.[183]

Thus statutory laws that ignore mainstream social norms ("der Volksgeist") are condemned to failure. Maine admitted that customary law should be included in the *status quo* of popular conduct. Because this *status quo* can be defined as conduct engaged in from generation to generation, aspects of customary law have reflected significant degrees of inequality in legal status. Social context, such as Christianity's passion for the downtrodden and its emphasis on the brotherhood of man, as well as the modern reliance on an increasing degree of division of labor, have all contributed to a shift from the *status quo* construct to an *inter partes* covenant model of customary law. Trade-offs and face-to-face bargains are component parts of the decision-making system under the *inter partes* covenant model. This explanation is the best way to conceptualize the shift from ancient law to modern law. The paradigmatic shift to a contract model did not terminate the bottom-up model of self-governing and self-organizing municipalities. The continued existence of the bottom-up model may result in a gradually increased element of freedom in society. For its part, the contract model will ensure that the popularly based production of law prevails.

Customary law has been criticized for not reacting to democratic exigencies. Of course, democratic deliberation is beautiful. However, legal issues are initiated or decided upon in the political sphere. Also, bureaucrats have influence. Besides, mistakes are made. A judicial review of democratic failures is appropriate. "Consequently, [there] ought to be some kind of judicial review based upon democratic failures."[184]

First and foremost, legal conflicts evolve whether or not legislators have considered the issue. Since legal conflicts merit a legal solution, the courts have no choice; decisions must be made! Common or customary law does close legal loopholes. Hopefully, some practice exists that fulfills the customary law prerequisites. If not, we have to rely on general presumptions, such as the freedom of trade, speech and religion. As a result of the strict prerequisites for customary law, the popular, unanimous element is clearly necessary. The parties involved must have the overwhelming impression that the actual norm is generally adhered to.

The dearth of court decisions reflects the fact that statutes or other written law have handled relatively few fisheries rights conflicts. From a realistic perspective, it seems that modern day conflicts involving fisheries are mostly subsumed under unwritten property law. In addition, under the current trend of market liberalism, private law instruments, i.e. markets, contracts and quasi-organ-produced customs, are held near and dear. The democratic deliberation argued by Cass R. Sunstein, is not available, simply due to lack of public regulation. Consequently, we are searching for extra-governmental private law solutions, which may promote sustainable development. For instance, the "public trust doctrine," the institution of public property rights and customary law are all mechanisms to achieve sustainable development. These legal institutions ought to be construed so that conflict-solving organs like courts encourage easy transitions while balancing competing multiple uses of common pool resources, i.e. the open access trades.

An important function of resource management systems is "preventing the destabilizing disappointment of expectations held in common but without formal recognition such as title."[185] Some examples include the legal protection of public property rights, and the customary property system of "subtle signs of management in traditional societies."[186]

The dynamics of social and technological change are an obvious threat to popular expectations. One cannot simply copy last year's analysis and normative solutions. One could argue that public authorities may wind up destabilizing a social equilibrium found at long last. Customary law combined with the remedy of public trust doctrine is a viable instrument for protecting public property rights that are put under governmental pressure. "Happily, it [the public trust doctrine] was available when needed to protect the public's rights in navigable waters against supposed legislative protectors."[187]

If agencies fail to respect basic rights, litigation is the last resort. However, unwritten legal solutions are in many ways unsatisfactory. Individual litigants push for maximum liability, nuisance damages and compensation. Litigating these claims may turn out to be contradictory to what a democratic legislature might prescribe. As Cass R. Sunstein said: "If you like the current law of products liability, then you would love common law approaches to environmental protection, where the problems will probably be even worse."[188] However, the basic response is that one must move to customary law, like it or not, since this field of law is, under all circumstances, completely unregulated by statutes. Private law solutions are mostly unwritten, customary based law. Seemingly, the public environmental remedies have obtained the characteristics of a "democratic approach" to environmental protection, while private remedies have been labeled "free market environmentalism."[189] To positivists, the customary private law solutions are not, therefore, by any definition of the word, "democratic" (but see Section 5.2).

In closing, one might comment that an overly favorable attitude toward public control and command seems to result from people ignoring the fact that bureaucracies repeatedly deviate from indisputable legislation. Perhaps a self-governing form of republicanism is the answer? One possible solution is the free cities of a commonwealth[190] or free states in a federation (the classical ideal of the *civitas libera*). Do societies that leave the popular activities to their citizens, who are free to pursue their own ends, have any chance to succeed in sustainable development efforts? Is customary law the "invisible hand" that directs local community members toward political ends?[191] Are local community members, through experience, educated to pursue the right direction toward resources management?[192]

7.4 Private markets

As indicated, a connection between customary law and sustainable development exists. Perhaps that solution is only second best? At issue is the school of neoclassic economists who fight the "tragedy of the commons" paradigm[193] by introducing closed entry schemes.[194] Why escape to customary law if the perfect solution is buried in Individual Tradable Quotas (ITQs)?[195] The resource value of this system is equivalent to the market's willingness to pay for quotas of herring, cod and other species. Anthony D. Scott[196] describes the march toward the quota and license-based fisheries. In many countries the right to fish is transferred by means of licenses and quotas.[197] Similarly, the right to manipulate common, clean air might be privatized and made tradable by the means of Emission Reduction Credits.[198] According to some spokesmen, ignoring privatization will result in overexploitation and the breakdown of resources. However, is it necessarily so? Is the attainment of sustainable yields, by means of distributive plurality decisions within the framework of the free market, possible *without* the exclusion of access that occurs when transforming public rights into private property rights?

The answer is simply not that easy. A tremendous opposition to the privatization scheme has been mobilized during the last twenty years. The market, instead of being the salvation of sustainability, is defined as one of the causes of non-viability. "[T]he market is accountable and responsible for its actions, and the market is not and cannot become an equal partner with the state in the enterprise of sustainable development."[199] Presumably Larson and Bromley are right when stating:

> Based on a clear understanding of the nature of property and the axiomatic foundations of private and common property analysis, we show that the two premises upon which received doctrine now rests are inconsistent with both theoretical results and empirical observations. The literature review also shows that resource degradation can be an optimal response to economic and environmental circumstances under a much wider range of property regimes than conventionally accepted . . . Based upon a clear understanding of common property arrangements we show that the household's time-rate-of-use problem does not imply that a resource will be depleted more severely under common than property.[200]

The "commons closing up" program has been judged a "misleading if not harmful" theoretical model.[201] We are challenging the "classical belief" here that the establishment of private property rights will terminate the inefficiencies of resource use under open access.[202] Obviously pure economic efficiency is not the one and only goal. Clearly equality and justice are vital ends.[203] Other objectives include "the maintenance of viable natural systems."[204] The customary public property allocation mechanism avoids the unjust and unequal distribution that is the result of privatizing the commons. Consequently, under this mechanism, people are not deprived of their open access resources rights.[205] Satisfying the aspirations of distributive justice does not, however, simultaneously equate with a sustainable development scheme. How should common pool societies be organized to obtain long-lasting viable solutions?

7.5 Arguments in favor of customary law

An important reason for considering self-governing strategies of local societies is the lack of success of the public control and command systems, and the often unjust results arising from the market mechanism. Even the poorest of the poor and the least assertive individuals have a voice under the customs regime. "Custom surrounds the law and lives within it; corporate self-regulation, shared expectations and special local and ethnic practices, are as likely if not more likely to prevent or resolve disputes or disorder than the centralized bureaucratic and highly expensive legal administration."[206]

The task I have proposed is that we investigate the conditions of advantageous autonomous decisions in the distributive plurality, under the auspices of the unorganized public. The legal justice system allows informal organizations ("quasi-organs") to establish legal rules. Parliaments and other governmental organizations do not enjoy exclusive law-making authority. The capability of open access participants to organize some normative system coordinating the distributive plurality decisions is imperative. Obviously:

> custom may be an informal technique for managing a commons . . . The managed and organized aspect of customary rights, then, casts new light on the public rights in roads and waterways. Like the customary rights of traditional communities, travel and commercial transport occur where even the public-at-large can manage itself and prevent waste of a resource; the "unorganized public" begins to seem more like a civilized and self-policing group. Custom, in short, can tame and moderate the dreaded rule of capture that supposedly tends to turn every commons into a waste.[207]

Mandatory solutions developed by informal organizations, which may be initiated by the few, but accepted by the many, serve as the spark that ignites and creates new legislation and legal rights. The success of such a self-governing informal organization relies on its law-producing capacity amongst members and against aliens, i.e. the competence of producing customary law. Customary law is *not* self-viable or sustainable in and of itself. Customary law is the product of prolonged trial and error. Indeed, many bad experiences have laid the ground for what we now consider good resource law practices. Obviously customary law may be harmful to sustainable development if not correctly construed. The key issue is to investigate under which conditions customary law may effectively work.

Under traditional economic theory, the question is whether public or common property management systems satisfy the private property "composition and authority axioms," i.e. that the property right is vested in a well-defined group, that acts with a unified purpose, for socially efficient use. The lack of such well-defined groups is the ultimate cause of the tragedy of the commons.[208] To many economists, composition and authority elements are inherent to private property regimes. According to their theory, private property owners constitute the requisite well-defined group. These same economists do not consider informal, loose-knit public property user groups to be "well defined." No such group of private property owners is to be found among open access utilization systems.

However, there may be other ways to circumvent the lack of group-identity. Can the solution be found in a restoration scheme policy?[209] We are in the midst of typical collective action problems here. These collective action problems can be described as the connection between resource degradation and different forms of management systems. A response is to force trespassers to take externalities into consideration. Since the degradation of common pool resources is a result of externalities, a workable strategy is to construct legal systems for externality eradication. A viable customary law solution must internalize the externalities. Restoration schemes make this possible.

Obviously, sustainable development is easier to achieve when resources are increasingly abundant. Situations of scarce resources cry out for careful consideration. Modern technology is challenging traditional resources extraction. The question is how to conserve the open access regime under efficient technology. Are the customary law strategies of the ancient self-governing societies still possible?

A viable resource management system must be constructed so that it is workable even though unfaithful servants invade it. What are the conditions for making self-governing conservation regimes work? Perhaps the answer lies with "self-government." Victoria Curzon-Price reasons that if "the right of private individuals to clean air, water, etc. were recognized by the courts, permitted and appropriate damages awarded against polluters, one would not even need Emission Reduction Credits (ERCs) to guarantee cleanliness."[210] Here Curzon-Price crystallizes the point we wish to make for fisheries. If future fisheries possibilities were given legal protection, the fisherman would then be liable to lose his fisheries rights if he fished hazardously or overexploited the stocks. Once he has over-fished his quota, for instance, a fisherman should be held legally responsible either to have his next year's quota reduced by the amounts over-fished, or to actively replace the lost bio-mass fish-farming. This is the case for restoration or reparation.

It is important to investigate the legal recognition of public property rights.[211] Has the evolving customary tort law finally made public property rights visible? The possibility of achieving sustainable yields through free play of the market depends on whether public property rights enjoy legal protection. Assuming that decisions having environmental consequences are withdrawn from governmental, political control, and if private decision-makers are obligated to take public property rights into consideration when deciding on environmental and resource management issues, then sustainability is the ultimate result. Considering further the "economic man" and the self-interest of individuals, such a position is still within reach if trespassers are liable for damages to public property rights. In strict economic terms, the remaining challenge is how to integrate the "full social cost of pollution . . . into all private costs."[212]

The more general problem is the transition of externalities. The evolving market system, as a basic resource distribution mechanism, and the shrinking of the state intervention system in the United States of America, Norway and most other western societies, necessitate the rethinking of the market decision framework. My task is to determine the fisherman's legal protection for his present and future public property fisheries rights, and to assess the degree to which today's system is prepared for sustainable development. This starting point necessitates my investigating two paths toward the goal of sustainability. The first is the status of fisheries participation rights, hereunder the legal protection of public property fisheries rights. The second involves establishing the positions of customary law. How does "the third solution" of public property rights improve the legal status of fisheries? Is the restoration principle the answer to the "living-fabric-of-life challenge," transporting us safely from one era to another?

Even if a market value could be found, the "willingness to pay" method[213] seems legally invalid.[214] This method is unsatisfactory according to Cass R. Sunstein.[215] However, one should not be blind to alternatives like restoration and "willingness to accept payment." Both would *de lege ferenda* give better solutions, but neither one of these theories seems to have sufficient support.[216] It is really time to discuss whether willingness to accept payment deserves a better reception. For instance, in *State of Ohio v. United States Department of the Interior*, the court found:

> DOI [Department of the Interior], in the face of critical comments, "recognize[d] that the application of willingness-to-accept," formerly a factor in option and existence valuation, "can lead to more technical difficulties and uncertainties than willingness-to-pay." Final Rule, supra note 70, 51 Fed.Reg. at 27,721. The conclusion was reached that, as studies indicated, use of willingness-to-accept – meaning an individual is to be paid to forfeit his interest in a resource, as opposed to the individual himself paying to preserve that interest – yielded disproportionally high dollar assessments. For example, one study showed that actual payments for goose hunting licenses were $880,000 while willingness-to-sell was $1,411,000, and willingness-to-pay was only $293,000.[217]

It seems that neither willingness to pay nor willingness to accept payment is appropriate. *De lege lata* restoration or reparation costs, however, do seem like appropriate damage assessment models for the impairment of natural resources. Since both instruments are customary lawbased and developed, one may make the claim that at present the customary law system seems promising.

Endnotes

1. Alexis de Tocqueville, *Democracy in America* (HarperPerennial, New York, 1987), p. 238.
2. See T. M. Franck, *The Power of Legitimacy Among Nations* (Oxford University Press, Oxford, 1990).
3. As cited in Ben Chigara, *Legitimacy Deficits in Custom* (Ashgate, Dartmouth, 2001), p. 105.
4. Paul Janet, *Alexis de Tocqueville et la science politique au XIXe siècle. Revue des deux mondes* (transl. by J. P. Mayer, Paris, 1861), p. 110. Alexis de Tocqueville, *A Biographical Study in Political Science* (Harper, New York, 1960), pp. 105–106.
5. Pierre Bourdieu, *Distinction. A Social Critique of the Judgement of Taste* (Harvard University Press, Cambridge MA, 1984).
6. In taking up the bottom-up democratic agenda, we, like the "Legal Culturalism" to which this book subscribes, seek to prove that the top-down democracy of Scandinavian Legal Realism does not fully capture the self-determination core of genuine democracies (see Chapter 1 note 21, with further reference to note 1 of same chapter).
7. Jon Elster, "Arguing and Bargaining in the Federal Convention and the Assemblée Constituante," in Raino Malnes and Arild Underdal (eds.), *Rationality and Institutions. Essays in Honour of Knut Midgaard* (Scandinavian University Press, Oslo, Bergen, Tromsø, 1991), pp. 25–26.
8. UK High Court Judge Lord Lloyd of Hampstead – Citation is from Torstein Eckhoff and Nils Kristian Sundby, *Rettssystemer* [*Legal Systems*] (Universitetsforlaget, Oslo, 1991), p. 1.
9. See Fikret Berkes, *Sacred Ecology. Traditional Ecological Knowledge and Resource Management* (Taylor & Francis, Philadelphia PA, 1999) with further references.
10. See Jon Elster, "Weakness of the Will and the Free-Rider Problem" (1985) 1 *Economics and Philosophy* 231–265, cf. the transition from "distributive decisions" to "collective plurality decisions."
11. Cass R. Sunstein, *Designing Democracy. What Constitutions Do* (Oxford University Press, Oxford, 2001), p. 98.
12. *Ibid.*
13. As for Canada, see Brian Slattery, "The Land Rights of Indigenous Canadian Peoples, as Affected by the Crown's Acquisition of their Territories" (Unpublished D.Phil. thesis, Oxford, 1979).

14. As for common law countries, see Kent McNeil, *Common Law Aborigional Title* (Clarendon Press, Oxford, 1989), p. 162, with further references.
15. J. G. A. Pocock, *The Ancient Constitution and the Feudal Law. English Historical Thought in the Seventeenth Century* (Norton, New York, 1967), p. 46.
16. *Ibid.*, at p. 48.
17. J. W. Gough, *Fundamental Law in English Constitutional History* (Oxford, 1955).
18. John Henry Thomas and John Farquhar Fraser (eds.), *Sir Edward Coke: Reports* (Original edn., London, 1826, new print, Lawbook Exchange Ltd, 2003), vol. IV, p. 6.
19. A. E. Dick Howard, *Magna Carta. Text and Commentary* (The University Press of Virginia, Charlottesville VA, 1964), p. 45.
20. *Martin v. Waddell*, 41 U.S. 367, 410 (1842). In the same way that basic customary inalienable rights, such as those confirmed by the Magna Carta, have a bearing in Anglo-American law, customary "checks and balances" also frame Norwegian legislation and adjudication (see Chapter 2). In the areas of traditional fisheries that managed without state participatory intervention until 1990, customary law has had a tremendous impact over the years.
21. Bourdieu, *Distinction.*
22. Gough, *Fundamental Law in English Constitutional History.*
23. Thomas and Fraser (eds.), *Sir Edward Coke*, vol. IV, p. 6.
24. See as illustration Josiah Ober, *The Athenian Revolution. Essays on Ancient Greek Democracy and Political Theory* (Princeton University Press, Princeton NJ, 1996), p. 108.
25. Vincent Ostrom, *The Meaning of Democracy and the Vulnerability of Democracies. A Response to Tocqueville's Challenge* (Michigan University Press, Ann Arbor, 1997), p. 4.
26. John Rawls, *A Theory of Justice* (Oxford University Press, Oxford, 1973), p. 288.
27. Sunstein, *Designing Democracy*, p. 143.
28. *Ibid.*, at p. 137.
29. Peter Ørebech, "Public, Common or Private Property Rights: Legal and Political Aspects," in S. Arnfred and H. Petersen (eds.), *Legal Change in North/South Perspective* (Occasional Paper No. 18, Roskilde University, 1996) p. 48.
30. Robert Michels, *Political Parties: A Sociological Study of the Oligarchical Tendencies of Modern Democracy* (Free Press, New York, 1962).
31. John Milton "Eikonoklastes," in *Complete Prose Works of John Milton* (ed. by Merrit Y. Hughes, Yale University Press, New Haven Conn., 1962), vol. III, p. 458.
32. See Quentin Skinner, *Liberty before Liberalism* (Cambridge University Press, Cambridge, 1998), pp. 50–58.
33. In the Norwegian arena, the extreme discrepancy between law in books and law in action is set forth in Peter Ørebech, "Om torskeresolusjonen av 1989. Den skjulte agenda og ranet av fiskeriallmenningen" ["On the 1989 Cod Resolution. The Hidden Agenda and the Robbery of the Commons"] 2002

Report to the Norwegian Power and Democracy Commission 1998–2003 (Unipub as, Oslo).

34. Hans Kelsen, *Vom Wesen und Wert der Demokratie* (Mohr, Tübingen 1929).
35. Ostrom, *The Meaning of Democracy*, p. 4.
36. Kelsen, *Vom Wesen und Wert der Demokratie*, p. 5.
37. Leon Sheleff, *The Future of Tradition. Customary Law, Common Law and Legal Pluralism* (Frank Cass, London and Portland, Oregon, 2000), p. 381.
38. 426 U.S. 668, 678–679 (1976).
39. Peter Ørebech, "Om rettslige og rettspolitiske sider ved den norske grunnlovs mindretallsgarantier, særlig om avgivelse av suverenitet ved folkeavstemning i forbindelse med tilslutning til EF" ["On Legal and Political Aspects of Norwegian Constitutional Minority Guarantees, with a Special Emphasis on Depletion of Sovereignty by Referendum, by Accession to the European Union"] (1993) *Retfaerd* [*Justice*], vol. 62, pp. 77–88.
40. See Ober, *The Athenian Revolution*, p. 108.
41. Skinner, *Liberty before Liberalism*, p. 26.
42. J. Ely, *Democracy and Distrust: A Theory of Judical Review* (Harvard University Press, Boston, 1980).
43. Alexis de Tocqueville, *Democracy in America* (Mentor Books, New York and Ontario, 1956), pp. 114 ff.
44. James L. Huffman, "A Fish Out of Water: The Public Trust Doctrine in a Constitutional Democracy" (1989) 19 *Environmental Law* 527, 571.
45. See Nuclear Weapons Advisory Opinion, 1996 I.C.J. 226, 279–80 (July 8).
46. Sunstein, *Designing Democracy*, p. 146.
47. Case 68/86 *United Kingdom v. Council*, 1988 ECR 855 para. 24.
48. Ørebech, *Om Torskeresolusjonen av 1989.*
49. See G. Pagès, *The Thirty Years War 1618–1648* (Harper & Row, New York, 1970), p. 228, cf. Chapter IX.
50. Gough, *Fundamental Law in English Constitutional History.*
51. John Austin, *The Province of Jurisprudence Determined* (Weidenfeld & Nicolson, London, 1954), p. 18.
52. *Ibid.*, at p. 31.
53. Huffman, "A Fish Out of Water," p. 527.
54. Jeremy Bentham, *Observations on the Restrictive and Prohibitory Commercial System* (ed. by John Bowring, E. Wilson, London, 1821), vol. IX, p. 100.
55. For law and economics topics, see Karl Renner, *The Institutions of Private Law and their Social Functions* (1904 reprint, Routledge, London, 1949).
56. See Sheleff, *The Future of Tradition*, p. 486 with further references.
57. Janet, *Alexis de Tocqueville et la science politique*, p. 110, Tocqueville, *Biographical Study in Political Science*, pp. 105–106.

58. See, e.g., Henry Sumner Maine, *The Nature of Democracy in Popular Government* (Routledge and Kegan Paul, London, 1886), p. 98.
59. Pocock, *Ancient Constitution and the Feudal Law*, p. 46.
60. Chigara, *Legitimacy Deficits in Custom*, see esp. pp. 302 ff. The difficulties set forth by Ben Chigara are basically prompted by the fact that the International Court of Justice – in the criticized instances – did not clarify its legal position. It simply found for customary laws without documenting why notification, visibility, vital firmness of mind, unity and harmony, all of which are supposedly part of the legitimacy requirement, were satisfied in the cases presented to the court. Clearly, if basic legitimacy concerns fail, the court should not find for customary law. See also *ibid* at p. 136 ("blind spots").
61. Thomas Hill Green, *Lectures on the Principles of Political Obligation* (Longman, London, 1895), p. 97.
62. James Harrington, *The Commonwealth of Oceania and a System of Politics* (ed. J. G. A. Pocock, Cambridge University Press, Cambridge, 1992), p. 166.
63. Marchamont Nedham, *The Excellencie of a Free State* (ed. by Richard Baron, London, 1767), p. xv.
64. Austin, *The Province of Jurisprudence Determined.*
65. Cass R. Sunstein, "Public versus Private Environmental Regulation" (1994) *Ecology Law Quarterly*, vol. 21, pp. 455, 456.
66. Jeremy Bentham, *The Principles of Morals and Legislation* (Prometheus Books, New York, 1988), p. xv.
67. Immanuel Kant, "Zum Ewigen Frieden" (1795) in Karl Vorländer (ed.), *Kleinere Schriften zur Geschichtsphilosophie Ethik und Politik, Philosophische Bibliothek* (Meiner, Hamburg, 1913), vol. I, p. 129.
68. Friedrich Carl von Savigny, *Von Beruf unserer Zeit für Gesetzgebung und Rechtswissenshaft* (Heidelberg, 1814).
69. Jeremy Bentham, *The Limits of Jurisprudence Defined* (Columbia University Press, New York, 1945), p. 274.
70. Sheleff, *The Future of Tradition*, p. 55.
71. H. L. A. Hart, *The Concept of Law* (Oxford University Press, Oxford, 1961).
72. Peter Goodrich, *Reading the Law: A Critical Introduction* (Basil Blackwell, London, 1986), pp. 63–64.
73. John Salmond, *Jurisprudence* (Sweet & Maxwell 1924), p. 229.
74. James L. Huffman, "A Fish Out of Water," pp. 527, 530.
75. J. Story, "A Report of the Commissioners Appointed to Consider and Report Upon the Practicability and Expediency of Reducing to a Written and Systematic Code the Common Law of Massachusetts, or any Part thereof; made to His Exellency the Governor," January 1837 (in *The Miscellaneous Writing of Joseph Story* (1951), p. 707).
76. *Ibid.*

77. *Ibid.*, at p. 711.
78. *Ibid.*, at p. 712.
79. See as an illustration; the Quebecoise offer to negotiate a new social contract with Native Nations, Bjarne Melkevik, "The First Nations and Québec: Identity and Law, Self-Affirmation and Self-Determination at the Crossroads," in José Serguinot Barbosa (ed.), *Globalization in America: A Geographical Approach* (Université Laval, Quebec, 1998).
80. See Ober, *The Athenian Revolution*, p. 4.
81. Jon Elster, "Arguing and Bargaining," pp. 24–25.
82. Kelsen, *Vom Wesen und Wert der Demokratie*, p. 30.
83. Elster, "Arguing and Bargaining," p. 22.
84. Terence Ranger, "The Invention of Tradition in Colonial Africa," in Eric Hobsbawm and Terence Ranger (eds.), *The Invention of Tradition* (Cambridge University Press, Cambridge, 1983), p. 254.
85. Jeremy Bentham, *Plan of Parliamentary Reform*, in *The Works of Jeremy Bentham* (II vols., W. Tait, Edinburgh, 1838–1843), vol. III, p. 515.
86. H. L. A. Hart, *Essays on Bentham. Studies in Jurisprudence and Political Theory* (Clarendon Press, Oxford, 1982), p. 83.
87. See the opposition to the Swedish School of Legal Realism by Norwegian legal scientist Nils Kristian Sundby. "Legal Right in Scandinavian Analyses," Natural Law Forum 1969. Notre Dame University s. 72.
88. Bentham, *The Book of Fallacies*, in *The Works*, vol. II, p. 379.
89. For a presentation of the natural rights theories, see Stephen Buckle, *Natural Law and the Theory of Property. Grotius to Hume* (Clarendon Press, Oxford, 1991).
90. Bentham, *Plan of Parliamentary Reform*, p. 212.
91. See Peter Ørebech, "Hva kom, først høna eller egget" [("What came first, the egg or the hen?,"] in Nils Christie (ed.), *Festschrift to Professor Anders Bratholm* (Universitetsforlaget, Oslo, 1990).
92. Some argue that natural law is the only basis for customary law. Unfortunately the term "natural law" is confusing. The confusion was caused by the text of *Gaius Institutes* which stated that "*jus gentium*" is that which "*naturalis ratio inter omnes homines constituit.*" Hugo Grotius, *The Freedom of the Seas* (transl. by Magoffin, Oxford University Press, Oxford, 1916). Here, natural laws refer to general principles among men. Thus Grotius relied on rationally experienced norms that emerged *de facto*. The hostility toward natural law among positivists is based upon a concept of predetermined norms that Grotius himself opposed.
93. Jeremy Bentham, *Letter to the Citizens of the United States*, in *The Works*, vol. IV, pp. 479, 504.
94. Bentham, *Principles of Morals and Legislation*, p. 330.
95. *Ibid.*, at xv.

96. Bentham, *The Limits of Jurisprudence Defined*, p. 274. Maine was critical of some aspects of Bentham and Austin's denunciation of customary law: "Now without the most violent forcing of language, it is impossible to apply these terms, *command, sovereign, obligation, sanction, right*, to the customary law under which the Indian village-communities have lived for centuries . . . And hence, under the system of Bentham and Austin, the customary law of India would have to be called morality – an inversion of language which scarcely requires to be formally protested against." As regards Austin's position, see Jes Bjarup's contribution in Chapter 3 and the Preface.
97. Pocock, *The Ancient Constitution and the Feudal Law*, p. 35.
98. Thomas and Fraser (eds.), *Sir Edward Coke*, vol. IV, p. 6.
99. Skinner, *Liberty before Liberalism*, p. 105.
100. An opinion expressed by the Norwegian Supreme Court Judge, Mr. Skatteböl, at a judicial conference in the 1920s. None of the other six judges in attendance reacted against this opinion.
101. Henry Sumner Maine, *Village Communities in the East and West* (John Murray, London, 1876), p. xxx.
102. Jean-Jacques Rousseau, *The Social Contract* (Prometheus Books, New York, 1988). Green, *Lectures on the Principles of Political Obligation*, p. 97.
103. Several property law codes state that statutory law is valid if not otherwise decided by customary law.
104. NOU [Norwegian Public Studies] 1988:16 *Eigedomsgrenser og administrative inndelingsgrenser* [*Possessory and Administrative Borders*], s. 56 sp. 2.
105. Niklas Luhman, *A Sociological Theory of Law* (Routledge, London, 1985), p. 160.
106. Maine, *Village-Communities in the East and West*, p. xxx.
107. Sunstein, "Public versus Private Environmental Regulation," pp. 455, 456.
108. Sheleff, *The Future of Tradition*, p. 83.
109. Ostrom, *The Meaning of Democracy*, p. 4.
110. Huffman, "A Fish Out of Water," pp. 527, 549.
111. Karl Marx and Friedrich Engels, *The German Ideology* (London, 1974), p. 109.
112. Henry Sumner Maine, *Dissertations on Early Law and Custom* (Henry Holt & Company, New York, 1883), pp. 174–175.
113. See Martin Chanock in Chapter 8.
114. Renner, *Institutions of Private Law*.
115. Hans Kelsen, *General Theory of Law and State*, p. 135 (1945).
116. Maine, *Village Communities in the East and West*, p. 75.
117. Story, "Report of the Commissioners," p. 721.
118. *Ibid.*, at p. 723.
119. Ørebech, "Public, Common or Private Property Rights," p. 48.
120. See Ragnhild Övrelid, *Demokrati eller rettssikkerhet?* [*Democracy or Rule of Law?*] (Universitetsforlaget, Oslo, 1984).

121. O. W. Holmes, *The Common Law* (Little, Brown & Co., Boston, 1881), vol. 1.
122. This is the question Svein Jentoft is posing in his book, *Dangling Lines. The Fisheries Crisis and the Future of Coastal Communities: The Norwegian Experience* (ISER – Institut of Social and Economic Research St. Johns, Newfoundland, 1993), pp. 117 ff.
123. *Ibid.*, at p. 131.
124. *Ibid.*, at pp. 137–42.
125. Sveinung Eikeland, "Flexibility in the Fishing Commons," in Svein Jentoft (ed.), *Commons in a Cold Climate. Coastal Fisheries and Reindeer Pastoralism in North Norway: The Co-Management Approach* (Man and the Biosphere Series No. 22, Parthenon, New York, 1998), p. 99.
126. Some economists also do; see Bruce A. Larson and Daniel W. Bromley, "Property Rights, Externalities, and Resource Degradation. Locating the Tragedy" (1990) *Journal of Development Economics*, vol. 33, p. 235.
127. Garrett Hardin, "The Tragedy of the Commons" *Science* (1962), vol. 162, pp. 1242–1248.
128. Garrett Hardin, "The Tragedy of the Unmanaged Commons" (1994) *Trends in Ecology and Environment*, vol. 9, no. 5, p. 199.
129. As regards the autonomy of Tribal Courts, see Mark D. Rosen, "Multiple Authoritative Interpreters of Quasi-Constitutional Federal Law: Of Tribal Courts and the Indian Civil Rights Act" (November, 2000) 69 *Fordham Law Review* 479.
130. NOU 1988:16 *Eigedomsgrenser og administrative inndelingsgrenser*, p. 56.
131. F. Marina D'Engelbronner-Kolff, *Justice in a Legally Pluralistic Society: A Court Tale from Sambyu. In Human Rights and Democracy in Southern Africa* (New Namibia Books, Windhoek, 1998), p. 195.
132. See the famous Emperor Justinian's ban on interpreting the "Institutiones" (the Roman Empire Codex).
133. Arne Naess, *Økologi og filosofi* [*Ecology and Philosophy*] (Universitetsforlaget, Oslo, 1972).
134. Robert Axelrod, *The Evolution of Cooperation* (Basic Books, New York, 1984).
135. R. Fisher and W. Ury, *Getting to Yes* (Houghton Mifflin, Boston, 1981).
136. This is John Nash's solution, see William Poundstone, *Prisoner's Dilemma* (Anchor Books, New York, 1993).
137. Robert Friedheim, "Fostering a Negotiated Outcome in the IWC" (Reykjavik, March 1, 1997) *Political and Economic Perspectives* 6.
138. Article 20(2) of the Pacific Ocean Highly Migratory Fish Stock Convention of September 9, 2002 illustrates this point.
139. Poundstone, *Prisoner's Dilemma.*
140. See Axelrod, *The Evolution of Cooperation.*

141. See *Continental Shelf* (*Tunis v. Libya*), 1982 I.C.J. at 45–47.
142. Hardin, "The Tragedy of the Unmanaged Commons," vol. 9, no. 5, p. 199.
143. P. Ørebech, K. Sigurjonsson and Ted L. McDorman, "The 1995 United Nations Straddling and Highly Migratory Fish Stocks Agreement: Management, Enforcement and Dispute Settlement" (May 1998) *The International Journal of Marine and Coastal Law*, no. 2.
144. John F. Nash, *Essays on Game Theory* (Edward Elgar, Cheltenham, 1996).
145. Nash, *Essays on Game Theory.*
146. Jon Elster, *The Cement of Society* (Cambridge University Press, Cambridge, 1989), p. 272.
147. Nash, *Essays on Game Theory.*
148. Jon Elster, *Nuts and Bolts for the Social Sciences* (Cambridge University Press, Cambridge, 1989), p. 22.
149. Nash, *Essays on Game Theory.*
150. In general, see Elster, "Weakness of the Will and the Free-Rider Problem," pp. 231–265), cf. the transition from "distributive decisions" to "collective plurality decisions."
151. Hardin, "Tragedy of the Commons," pp. 1242–1248.
152. P. Ørebech, "The Repetitive Players Game illustrated by the Regional Fisheries Organization of the North East Atlantic Convention (NEAFC)," in T. Bjørndal, G. Munro and R. Arnason (eds.), *Proceedings from the Conference on the Management of Straddling Fish Stocks and Highly Migratory Fish Stocks*, and the UN Agreement (Norwegian School of Business Administration, Bergen, 1999).
153. Skinner, *Liberty before Liberalism*, pp. 28, 34. The example is originally from Harrington, *Commonwealth of Oceania*, p. 22.
154. As implemented by Nobel prize winner Amartya Sen, *Poverty and Famine: An Essay on Entitlement and Deprivation* (Clarendon Press, Oxford, 1982).
155. Minna Gillberg, *From Green Image to Green Practice. Normative Actions and Self-Regulation* (University of Lund, Lund, 1999).
156. Scott Gordon. See also Partha S. Dasgupta, *The Control of Resources* (Harvard University Press, Cambridge MA, 1982) with further references.
157. Ernst Fehr and Klaus M. Schmidt, *A Theory of Fairness, Competition, and Cooperation* (University of Zürich/University of Münich, Zürich and Münich, 1998), p. 1.
158. Arthur M. Okun, *Equality and Efficiency: The Big Tradeoff* (The Brookings Institution, Washington, 1975).
159. This story was told by the leader of the action, Mr. Dagfinn Alisøy, to the author.
160. R. H. Coase, "The Problem of Social Cost" (1960) *Journal of Law and Economics*, vol. 3, p. 1.

161. Robert C. Ellickson, *Order Without Law: How Neighbours Settle Disputes* (Harvard University Press, Cambridge MA, 1991).
162. Robert C. Ellickson, "A Hypothesis of Wealth-Maximizing Norms: Evidence from the Whaling Industry" (1989) *Journal of Law, Economics & Organization*, vol. 5, no. 1, pp. 83, 84.
163. Sunstein, "Public versus Private Environmental Regulation," p. 455.
164. *State of Idaho v. Southern Refrigerated Transport Inc. et al.* 1991 U.S. Dist. LEXIS 1869. See also *State of Ohio v. United States Department of the Interior* 880 F.2d 432 (1989), regarding the Department of the Interior's regulations governing the recovery of money damages from those responsible for the despoilment of natural resources. The court held that the DOI's "lesser of" regulation, which limited damages to the lesser of the cost of restoring or replacing the equivalent injured resource, or the lost use value of the resource, was directly contrary to the intent of Congress as expressed in the Comprehensive Environmental Response, Compensation, and Liability Act (CERCLA). Therefore, the court held the regulation invalid.
165. Peter Ørebech *Om allemannsrettigheter. Særlig med henblikk på rettsvernet for fiske ved igangsetting og utøving av petroleumsvirksomhet* [Public Property Rights. With a Special Emphasis on the Conflict between the Petroleum and Fishing Industries] (Osmundsson, Oslo, 1991).
166. Norsk Retstidende (Rt.) 1993 p. 272 *The Berghorn Case.*
167. See Court Decision of 3 December 1998. Case no 145/1998 *Valdimar Johannesson v. Islenska Rikinu.*
168. See RG (Rettens Gang – High Court Decisions) 1967 p. 351. *The Waste Dumping Case.*
169. Maine, *Dissertations on Early Law and Custom*, p. 66.
170. R. H. Coase, "The Problem of Social Cost" (1960) *Journal of Law and Economics*, vol. 3, p. 1.
171. Elinor Ostrom, *Governing the Commons. The Evolution of Institutions for Collective Action* (Cambridge University Press, Cambridge, 1990), p. 24.
172. *Ibid.*, at p. 25.
173. Sunstein, "Public versus Private Environmental Regulation," pp. 455, 456.
174. Maine, *Village Communities in the East and West*, p. 193. See also Henry Sumner Maine, *The Native of Democracy in Popular Government*, pp. 138 ff.
175. The Economist, *A Survey of the World Economy* (Annex to *The Economist*, September 20, 1997).
176. See Coase, "The Problem of Social Cost," vol. 3, pp. 1, 18.
177. Peter Ørebech, "Norsk fiskerirett; lovverk, hodeverk eller legitimering av markedsstyrt makt?" ["Norwegian Fisheries Law; Legal Rules, Headache or the Legitimization of Markets?"] (1982) *Lov og Rett* [*Norwegian Journal of Law & Right*] s. 67.

178. For a more detailed presentation of the "salvation theory," see Peter Ørebech, "Public, Common or Private Property Rights," p. 48.
179. This is documented in Ørebech, "Tvers igjennom lov til seier!".
180. G. J. Massell, "Law as an Instrument of Revolutionary Change in a Traditional Milieu – The Case of Soviet Central Asia" (1968) *Law & Society Review*, vol. 2, pp. 182–226.
181. See Paolo Grossi, *An Alternative to Private Property* (University of Chicago Press, Chicago, 1981), p. 115, referring to Maksim M. Kovalevski: "Etudes sur le droit coutumier russe" (1890) *Nouvelle revue historique de droit français et étranger.*
182. Maine, *Village Communities in the East and West*, pp. 38–39.
183. *Ibid.*, at p. 65.
184. Ely, *Democracy and Distrust.*
185. Joseph L. Sax, "Liberating the Public Trust Doctrine from Its Historical Shackles" (1980) *University of California Davis Law Review*, vol. 14, pp. 185, 191.
186. Hardin, "The Tragedy of the Unmanaged Commons," vol. 9, no. 5, p. 199.
187. Jan S. Stevens, "The Public Trust: A Sovereign's Ancient Prerogative Becomes the People's Environmental Right" (1980) *University of California Davis Law Review*, vol. 14, pp. 195, 210.
188. Sunstein, "Public versus Private Environmental Regulation," pp. 455, 456.
189. *Ibid.*, at p. 455.
190. John Milton, "The Readie and Easie Way to Establish a Free Commonwealth," in *Complete Prose Works of John Milton* (ed. by Robert W. Ayers, Yale University Press, New Haven, Conn. 1980), vol. VII, pp. 458–459.
191. Hardin, "The Tragedy of the Unmanaged Commons," vol. 9, no. 5, p. 199.
192. The answer of Charles E. Larmore, *Patterns of Moral Complexity* (Cambridge University Press, Cambridge, 1987), p. 8 would tend to say yes, on the basis that "moral examples . . . exemplify the exercise of moral judgment."
193. Hardin, "The Tragedy of the Commons," pp. 1242–1248, dealing with pasture. In relation to fishery, see A. Scott: "The Fishery: The Objectives of Sole Ownership" (1955) *Journal of Political Economy*, vol. 63, pp. 116–124 and H. S. Gordon, "The Economic Theory of a Common Property Resource: The Fishery" (1954) *Journal of Political Economy*, vol. 62, pp. 124–142.
194. See R. Quentin Grafton, Dale Squires and Kevin J. Fox, "Private Property and Economic Efficiency: A Study of a Common-Pool Resource" (2000) *Journal of Law & Economics*, vol. 43, p. 679.
195. Harold Demsetz, "Toward a Theory of Property Rights" (1967) *American Economics Review*, vol. 57, pp. 347, 347–359.
196. Anthony D. Scott, "Conceptual Origins of Right Based Fishing," in Philip A. Neher, Ragnar Arnason and Nina Mollett (eds.), *Rights-Based Fishing* (Kluwer Academic Publishers, Dordrecht, 1989), p. 11.

197. Ragnvaldur Hannesson, "Markedsmekanismens positive egenskaper," in H. Jervan (ed.), *Fra forhandling til marked* (Gruppen for ressursstudier, Oslo, 1984).
198. See, e.g., Hege Westskog, *Market Power in a System of Tradable CO_2 Quotas* (SUM, Oslo, 1996).
199. Michael Decleris, "The Coming Systematised State of the 21st Century" in *Tercera Escuela de Sistemas* (Valencia, 1995), p. 47.
200. Bruce A. Larson and Daniel W. Bromley, "Property Rights, Externalities, and Resource Degradation. Locating the Tragedy" (1990) *Journal Development Economics*, vol. 33, pp. 236–237.
201. Bonnie McCay, *Oyster Wars and the Public Trust. Property, Law, and Ecology in New Jersey History* (The University of Arizona Press, Tucson AZ, 1998), p. 189.
202. As stated by Demsetz, "Toward a Theory of Property Rights," pp. 347, 347–359, and rejected by Larson and Bromley, "Property Rights, Externalities, and Resource Degradation," pp. 235, 239.
203. Nobel prize winner Amartya Sen, *Poverty and Famine.*
204. Sax, "Limits of Private Rights in Public Waters," pp. 473, 476.
205. These arguments are investigated in P. Ørebech, "What Restoration Schemes Can Do? Or Getting It All Right Without Fisheries Transferable Quotas," *Ocean Development and International Law*, vol. 36, pp. 159–178.
206. Goodrich, *Reading the Law*, p. 64.
207. Carol Rose, "The Comedy of the Commons: Custom, Commerce, and Inherently Public Property" (1986) *University of Chicago Law Review*, vol. 53, pp. 711, 744–46.
208. Larson and Bromley, "Property Rights, Externalities, and Resource Degradation, p. 235.
209. First presented in Peter Ørebech, *Om allemannsrettigheter.* See also Peter Ørebech, "Sustainable Development by Means of Market Distribution Mechanism," in Andrea Baranzini and Fabrizio Carlevaro (eds.), *Econometrics of Environment and Transdisciplinarity* (AEA List, International Conference, Lisbon, 1996), p. 906.
210. Victoria Curzon Price, "Treating Protection as a Pollution Problem or How to Prevent GATT's Retreat from Multilateralism," in Thomas Oppermann and Josef Molsberger (eds.), *A New GATT for the Nineties and Europe '92* (Nomos, Baden-Baden, 1991), p. 28.
211. For an investigation into public property rights as recognized under the Norwegian legal system, see Ørebech, *Om allemannsrettigheter.*
212. Price, "Treating Protection as a Pollution Problem," p. 26.
213. Ronald Dworkin, *Law's Empire* (Fontana, London, 1986), p. 277.
214. US District Court in *State of Idaho v. Southern Refrigerated Transport Inc. et al.* (1991 U.S. Dist. LEXIS 1869). In this case concerning compensatory damages for defendant's having polluted the river and killed the fish, the court relied

on the value of the fish market, and rejected the fishermen's willingness to pay as a valid method of calculating damages.

215. Sunstein, "Public versus Private Environmental Regulation," p. 455, claiming that what you end up with is, "at best, aggregating private willingness to pay."

216. Richard C. Bishop and Thomas A. Heberlein, "Measuring Values of Extra Market Goods: Are Indirect Measures Biased?" (1979) *American Journal of Agricultural Economics*, vol. 61.

217. 880 F.2d 432, 477, n. 82 (1989).

8

Customary law, sustainable development and the failing state

MARTIN CHANOCK

8.1 Beyond Blackstone, Maine and Weber

The argument in this chapter is that in order to understand the possible uses of a customary law in the third world, where many of the looming environmental crises are, we need an account of the development of the idea of customary law there, and that this will be one that differs from custom as law in European states and European jurisprudence. In particular the historical trajectory, and a new jurisprudence of customary law, will have to encompass not only the role of custom tolerated on the fringes of powerful state legal systems, but its role where states are inadequate or incapacitated. Furthermore, it will need to take into account, which the jurisprudence of custom in European state and legal systems has historically not done, of the growing role of international organizations as participants in governance, and of international law in validating customary laws.

The narrative of the customary law in this chapter is not situated within European nation-states, and does not revolve around the jurisprudential issues which arose, historically, out of the increasing centralization of these states and the claim of the centre to control, and to make, law. This chapter is concerned with imperialism and its continuing aftermath. In the European Empires the laws of the colonized were displaced and became, in relation to the laws of the colonial state, similarly placed to customary law in Europe. Indigenous law in the colonies lived on the fringes of legal respectability, tolerated under certain strict conditions. Even after the end of formal Empire, and period of legal unification by the successor states, indigenous laws have never quite returned to the legal centre.

In, roughly, the first two decades after the end of empire, a period of emphasis on economic development through statist expansion and control, customary law was marginalized even further, being identified with obstinate opposition to developmental objectives and the nation-state and its nation-building priorities. But the spectacular failures of the development states and the collapse both of their economic models and their bureaucratic structures, have re-opened the field for the displaced law known as customary law. Simultaneously there is an increased tendency to look to the market for solutions to the problems of resource distribution and management. The issue here is different from that of finding a place for regional and local ways of doing things within the ordered and functioning states of the "North." Where states do not function, custom competes not with "law" or with "market" but with corruption, anarchy and resource expropriation by uncontrollable non-state actors. Custom contends not with "law" or "market," but with organized kleptocracy, with collapsing states, and bandit economies.

As the title suggests, the discussion that follows seeks to re-situate the prevailing jurisprudential paradigms. It suggests that the Blackstonian view of customary law as immemorial practice was never relevant to the colonial and post-colonial worlds; that the Weberian model of law in the legal rational state is not useful in a world of state decline, corruption and contending sources of power; and that for customary law to be useful in the new environment Maine's distinction between status and contract must be laid to rest.

8.2 Customary law and empire

I shall begin with an account of how the idea of customary law was developed and deployed in the creation of colonial states, my primary frame of reference being Britain, and its African Empire.[1] The starting point must be with "custom" as an idea that simultaneously embodies two contradictory stances. One is that it refers to practices that have a high degree of permanence and stability: but it also refers to practices that have considerable scope for fluidity and adaptability. The tension between these two faces of custom are always present in discussion, jurisprudential and otherwise. With this tension in mind, we must, when the notion of custom, or the world of the customary, is invoked, think about the circumstances in which each of these stances are being reflected or deployed. For lawyers the concept of custom is usually deployed in a specific context – that of law and legality. (Non-lawyers are more likely to be talking about "culture" – a point to which I shall return.) When lawyers use the terms custom or customary law it is within the context of a relationship with state law. Both facets of custom, its rigidity and its fluidity, exist within this relationship.

In a jurisprudential frame the defining markers of the difference between the ideas of custom and law are their relationship with the state. This relationship can only be explicated historically. The meaning accreted by both words – custom and law – is a part of the history of the growth of the European state: of increasing centralization of power; and of the decline in the autonomy of localities and regions and minorities. The centralization involved the claims of the King's Courts to determine the basis of entitlements, the power to settle disputes and to determine rules. The making of modern law is a part of this story of centralization – the triumph of the Crown over local powers. But the triumph was not easy or complete. It involved forms of negotiation with and recognition of other powers in the forming states. The role given to custom and the ways it was defined in relation to the state's law therefore depended on the completeness and the effectiveness of centralization.

It depended also on the philosophy underlying the state's law. My remarks here relate basically to the English common law situation. In English common law both custom and the common law (that was to become the law of the King's Courts) were (and are) based on the notion of law as something that has been long practiced and built up by accretion over long periods. The centralizing courts of the King, in developing the English common law for the kingdom as a whole, purported simply to find what the law was. They did not claim to make it. While in practice their version of the common law became the commands of the sovereign, in theory they were explicating the already existing rights, entitlements and practices of the kingdom. Any local variation had to fit into this concept of law. Local differences could not come directly into conflict with centralized sovereignty, and thus legal variations could not lay claim to recognition on the basis that it was, say, the edict of a local Baron, of a sovereignty rival to that of the Crown's. But it could insert a claim that was philosophically aligned with that of the common law, that it was an inherent practice of long standing. Likewise recognition could be conceded where necessary to practices as long as they could be presented as law-like – certainty, longevity etc. – while it could not be conceded to practices that were newly made as this would constitute a direct challenge to centralized sovereignty. This is what I mean when I say that the concept of custom derived its meaning from a relationship with that of law. The effect was that, rather than being a more flexible version of law (as was a common understanding), it had to be a harder, less flexible, unchanging and unchangeable kind of law before it would be recognized by the state. Nonetheless the fact that the centralizing state would only recognize local forms of regulation that were very law-like (longstanding and certain) did not mean that what was successful in becoming recognized was always really longstanding and certain. What was crucial was that this was how it had to be presented and acknowledged.

This becomes even clearer when we move to the period of the establishing of the European empires, where a different, yet strangely similar, process of legal centralization and claims of centralized sovereignty took place within a different configuration of power. In Britain the power of the state was incomplete: recognition of custom, of canon law, and the privileges and autonomies of a variety of local corporations were concessions. Though localities had lost autonomy they could still defend some limited interests. In colonies the central government was more implacably sovereign in the legal sense, yielding nothing to the "liberties" of those conquered by violence. The colonial states were politically autocratic yet limited in their administrative capacity (both features that were bequeathed to their successor states). But recognition of custom was a part of colonial governance because for small administrations with limited military and police forces it was sometimes politically necessary; and because it was often politically desirable to secure the compliance of local rulers by incorporating both them and their modes of governance into the colonial state apparatus. As before the meaning given to custom derived from its relationship with state law, not from any intrinsic features, though the relationship was not the same as it was in Britain.

We can contrast the construction of the realm of the customary in Africa with the recognition of the laws of the conquered in, for example, India. In the Indian empire the laws of both Hindu and Muslim were recognizable – as written sources – and were acknowledged by leading British jurists to be systematic regulation by "great" religions. They fitted easily into the general British idea of governing the Empire through the recognition of the law of the subordinated people (subject to the principle of repugnancy). In Africa the situation was different. "Laws" did not appear to be present in the Indian sense to be recognized. What was there was something lesser which was called "customary law." But there was an essential difference between the way this customary law was understood, and the way "custom" was seen in Britain. In Britain all were subjects of the Crown and of the common law of the realm – part of the same state, nation and legal system. Local customs were limited variations: they did not conflict with the basic premises of the common law, and they were not practiced by, or valid for, people of a different cultural or political identity. In Africa it was different. African subjects "retained" in theory legal systems that did not share a common community with the common law, or with different "ethnic" communities within the colonial state. Indeed it was a vital part of the colonizing project ideologically that colonizers and colonized were different, that each had laws suitable to their place on an evolutionary scale. This difference, this exclusion, is fundamental to the different relationship between law and custom in the colonial state and that in the metropole.

What developed was the construction of a new realm of law that was not common law, nor custom, nor statute. It was "customary law" – a law of and for subordinates – racially and culturally, which was seen as suitable to their state of evolution. It was recognized specifically because of their cultural difference; the need to emphasize that difference; the requirements of governance; and the incapacity of the colonial state, which was too weak to extend a common law to all and, by the second half of the nineteenth century not inclined to do so until its subjects were "civilized." This "customary law" was not something that was seen as belonging to geographical localities, as "custom" in Britain did, but to cultural groups.

How could this new type of law be fitted into the jurisprudential schema that Europe had developed? It was unwritten. And it had not been developed in a series of precedents by Courts of Record. Nor was it changeable by edict. So how was it to be known and its content controlled? The state had to have a way of knowing it once it became a means of governance. Ideas about it were, as I have indicated, heavily influenced by the racist ideas about evolution of civilizations. African customary law was comprehensible to, and observable by, Europeans only within an evolutionary framework. In this framework the laws Africans deserved were seen to be those appropriate to the infancy of mankind, in that way similar to European laws of very long before. Analogies were often drawn between early "tribal" Europe and contemporary Africa. Thus while the customs of localities in Britain had to have longevity and be static in order to prevail over the King's law, those of Africa were characterized as having longevity, and being static, because of a cultural judgement that was made about African societies, which were seen as having failed to be "progressive," as being trapped forever in a state of perpetual infancy. Thus the living and changing systems of law, which had governed Africans prior to the establishment of colonial states, were re-conceptualized to fit into a racist ranking of legal development, as well as into the understood relationship that the colonizers already had of "custom" that it was longstanding and beyond living memory. I would stress the enormous influence of this European jurisprudential idea that custom had to be static and fixed in order to have legal force combined with the idea that non-European societies were static in nature, i.e. that their culture was one of stasis as opposed to the Western one of progressive movement.

This framework for characterizing and understanding the realm of the customary had profoundly important effects. The western jurisprudential notions were applied not simply to a small part of a national legal system, but to the whole law of colonized peoples, which was, suddenly, in the eyes of the state, frozen forever, incapable of legitimate development and change. However new behaviors, and new customary law that was evolving, were necessitated by economic change, loss of land, the impact of the market and the money economy, and migrant labour. All these factors necessarily revolutionized relationships between genders and generations; and strangers and kin. But these changed relationships were considered illegitimate according to the static notion of custom.

As I have already said, the colonial state had to know custom in order to use it and thus great new power was given to the interlocutors, those who became the repositories of the "real" customary law. In a view of custom that legitimized stasis and longevity, and quite specifically de-legitimized change, only the old, or those directly informed by the old, could know the true law, and distinguish it from the claims that were all the time being falsely asserted as "customary law." As basic economic relationships and behaviors changed, it was vital to colonized communities to try to establish new ground-rules for themselves. But they had no influence over the making of colonial law at all: the only language they were permitted to speak was the language of custom. Because colonized people cannot demand change effectively (without rebellion), they had to find ways of inserting their claims into a system that the colonial state would hear as legitimate. So the language had to be that of "custom," but whose voice could legitimately speak? Colonized communities were not unified. They were divided not only ethnically and culturally but each such group was increasingly divided on class lines between those who were managing to do well in the new colonial economy and those who were not; on gender lines; and, most importantly, on generational lines, between those who were able to assert legitimately their hold on resources (land, women, the control of the labor of dependents) and those who could not. So, in the representation of customary law, which was a new formulation of the colonial state, embodying its view of age and stasis, and which masked a necessary world of conflict and change, considerable power was given to a particular class of the colonized.[2] (Also, not to be forgotten here, was the power given to "experts," the administrators and anthropologists, whose interests were served by the continuing reinforcement of the notion of irreducible difference between the "native" and the "modern," and who themselves played an important part in the development of the customary legal regime.)

8.3 The post-colonial states

The place of the customary law has changed since the end of Empire. We may identify two phases: an initial one of the growth and consolidation of the successor states during which they were characterized by an attempt to establish national unity out of fragmented and ethnically plural polities, and an aggressive involvement in economic development. This has been followed by institutional decay and the decline of state-led economic development. In one way the successor states were more like the old states of Europe, at least in their ambition to be single sovereignties with one legal system created from the centre. The new governments were unhappy with the idea of a dual legal system – one suitable for the "modern" sector and people and another for the "backward" – or, at best, different. For reasons of state, as well as cultural pride, the aim after colonialism was to unify the legal system of the ex-colonial state. The first logical step appeared to be to make the customary law into state law by codifying it and writing it down, or "re-stating" it in legal terms, and then to incorporate it as state law into a national system. This ambition altered the nature of the customary law by drawing it into the centralized realm of sovereignty. But these were heterogeneous states, not culturally uniform. To an extent the colonial government's creation of the customary law had been an ideal way of dealing with cultural heterogeneity, at least in relation to legal regimes. For it could encompass variety legitimately, as being the customary law of whichever group asserted it. But this mechanism was not open to the new states that sought to build national identity and specifically saw a unified law was one way of doing this. They thereby lost an essential mechanism for dealing with cultural difference. And there was another destabilizing feature. Once customary law was drawn into the realm of state law, its disguise as something old and static had to be dropped. Thus, while the new states were losing the colonial state's way of dealing with cultural and local differences through the customary law, they still faced ever more insistent assertions of new interests that were cast as customary legal claims. Partly this was because such assertions were by now a familiar political metaphor in these states, and partly because the new states, like the old ones had been, were authoritarian and undemocratic, and other forms of political assertion were strictly limited.

In addition these states were to become ever increasingly linked into an international (now globalized) world of economic transactions and definitions of economic rights in land and resources. Growing populations, ever more rapid urbanization, massive migrations within and across borders, and drastic changes in the terms of trade, altered the conditions of economic and social life. This was a gradual process, not a sudden happening, but it was one that accelerated in the development era and that challenged local assertions of rights to control resources. Development created new pressures to define rights of ownership in a range of resources that could now be "developed" for an international market. This definition necessarily involved an allocation of legal rights, and therefore of wealth, from some to others.

In these circumstances how were the successor states to renegotiate their relationship with the realm of the customary? At this point we can return to where I started and recall the other attributes of custom – its fluidity and adaptability. This is, as it were, the "real" (as opposed to the idealized or "jurisprudentialized") aspect of customary practices. It is what prevails when custom is not forced into the relationship with a centralizing law that I have described. Throughout the developing world, massive changes affected the lives and practices of communities in relation to the areas that the legal systems had largely "regulated" by "custom" like land tenure, labour obligations and kinship. In essence these relationships were everywhere corroded and renegotiated as the capitalist money economy spread. Custom was anything but stable in these circumstances. It was fluid and adaptable, sometimes defensively (nearly always defensively in terms of self-presentation) but basically pragmatic.

Large gaps had opened between what was represented as "customary" (i.e. the old ways) and what had in fact become customary practices. Different sets of behaviors and values were accorded legitimacy by the state (and its interlocutors) and by communities. Commercial dealings in land (sale, lease etc.) and control of marriage and descendants were perhaps the most crucial areas. State-sanctioned custom continued to recognize rights and concepts that had barely retained symbolic meaning and had effectively been abandoned. And, as I have indicated, the language of custom continued to carry a freight of ethnic politics making it both a dangerous and a necessary part of political communication. Weak states had to deal with diverse political constituencies that were under the most severe economic stress. Ethnic variety and the concomitant cultural politics threatened state survival. But these were polities within which assertions in the name of custom and culture had become a primary part of the language of the law and state.

We have come to the point at which we are dealing with custom as fluid in two contexts in the post-colonial state. The first is in the context of the cultural politics of fragmenting multi-ethnic states in which custom (even when it is in the form of claims about the fundamentals of past practices) is now a vital political language, a way of talking about identity and asserting interests rather than a jurisprudential category or a type of law. To say this is to stress that there have been important changes in the nature of custom as a discursive strategy since the colonial period. At first the colonial state confined its subjects to a backward world of custom. Now custom represents a claim not just to practices, but to identity, and therefore to autonomy and self-determination. The second is in the context of economic development where challenges to local communities and their attempts to define and protect their interests are often most severe and where, again, custom is a language which involves not just a claim of legal right, but again a claim to autonomy and control. The use of the language of custom within the disputes about development is more often than not highly misleading, most especially when it is linked to the language of "culture." But it is used mainly because of the failure of the democratic processes and civic cultures in the societies affected. And it is also a language to talk against the language of globalization.

8.4 Imagined worlds: the state and the customary

Under what circumstances, then, will custom be the naturalized language in which localities, and minorities, speak to sovereignty, and represent their political and economic claims and inherently embedded, cultural practices? What kind of state do they speak to in this language? Specifically in colonial and post-colonial situations it has been a state that has played a primary role in destroying the viability of local communities, and in which continuing state regulation reduces the capacity for self-management. If we are to make any sense of this state we must abandon the Weberian image of its bureaucratic neutrality. The states involved in these processes have commonly been predatory and corrupt; at best they represent, as do states everywhere, the interests and politics of elites.

We might begin our situating of the place of custom as a language in these states by considering Ferguson's account of how development institutions generate their own discourse, which constructs large parts of the world as particular kinds of objects of knowledge and "creates a structure of knowledge" around them.[3] In particular, as he says, the "structure of knowledge" has effects "which include the expansion and entrenchment of bureaucratic state power, side by side with the projection of a representation of economic and social life which denies 'politics' and, to the extent that it is successful, suspends its effects." The development apparatus is "an 'anti-politics machine,' depoliticising everything it touches, everywhere whisking political realities out of sight, all the while performing, almost unnoticed, its own pre-eminently political operation of expanding bureaucratic state power."[4] We shall need to understand the use of "customary law," its language and its legitimating devices, in this light. For invoking such language is pre-eminently a way of making political demands in a non-political medium, another "anti-politics machine." Furthermore, Ferguson notes, development discourse differs from academic discourse in that its purpose is to "target" a particular kind of intervention.[5] In particular development discourse emphasizes the contrast between a backward/traditional and a developed condition. In the case of Lesotho, the subject of his book, he writes that development discourse constructs Lesotho as a nation without history, classes, rulers or politics. The modern "capitalist" nature of the society is "systematically understated or concealed."[6] Emphasizing the obstinate persistence of a world of the customary, rather than displaying the political and economic complexity of developing economies that have been evolving over more than a century of capitalism, is an essential strategic mechanism of "development discourse." (Sustainable development discourse incorporating the use of indigenous structure of governance, we may observe, is now the restructured "package"[7] of development agencies, to be applied to "problems without politics."[8]) In this, as before, one of the most important development premises is that the target must be "aboriginal, not yet incorporated into the modern world."[9] Yet, as Ferguson notes, "If the cultural rules . . . persist, it is because they are made to persist; continuity as much as change must be created and fought for. These rules may be 'traditional', and they may be resistant to change, but they are not inert; they are perpetually challenged and always at issue, and there is always something at stake."[10]

Throughout the third world, Ferguson writes, one finds the same "development" institutions, "often a common discourse and the same way of defining 'problems,' a common pool of 'experts,' and a common stock of expertise."[11] These discourses, as we have seen, are now ready to expand to incorporate the languages of custom, but whether this language will then serve the intentions of those who first spoke it, is moot. The relative powerlessness of those whose language "custom" is might lead one to the conclusion that "custom" will become part of the discourse of sustainable development, and, like customary law in the colonial situation, be expropriated from its original users, something that will appear to be based on indigenous inputs, yet still subject these to larger external ends. Development projects, Ferguson writes, expand the power of the state and depoliticize poverty: "alongside the institutional effect of expanding bureaucratic state power is the conceptual or ideological effect of depoliticising both poverty and the state."[12] The links between the "old" style of development and the expansion of third world state power seems to be clear. What is less clear is how "development" will adapt to the reduction (or the changes) in the power of the state, but it may be that a new de-politicizing discourse is a part of the process.

There are further features of development discourse that might usefully be noted now. One has been to oppose "customary" and "market" behavior even though it is futile to base a notion of the customary on non-market behavior after, for all but the most isolated, more than a century of intense market involvement. It has no doubt been the case that the long period of market pressures has eroded the exchange relationships of communities in which there were (also) other forms of exchange. But these markets, and the monetisation of exchange relationships, are the bedrock of societies that can simultaneously maintain lively "customary" discourse. The existence of this discourse should, however, not lead to the conclusion that, in communities that live in markets, a customary discourse that contains elements of a non-market ethos, reflects a timeless cultural essence and way of life. Secondly, and this follows from the depiction of the market as divisive, and non-market relationships as unifying, there is the strategy of idealizing a lack of conflict in traditional or indigenous communities. Yet as McCay and Jentoft write, "Communities are not always well integrated, homogeneous, co-operative or equitable in their management of resources."[13] But this image is nonetheless vital to "symbolic construction." Another is the discursive construction of the realm of indigenous practical wisdom in the new discourse of sustainable development in which certain strategies are, again, de-politicized. In this discourse, traditional communities are idealized and naturalized as part of the ecology and environment and their cultures are essentialized as inherently conservationist and ecologically wise.

Hardin's "tragedy of the commons" thesis, and the numerous responses to it are well treated elsewhere in this book and I shall not recover that ground.[14] During the 1970s and 1980s many development initiatives were influenced by Hardin's thesis. The problems of environmental degradation, for example in areas of pastoralism, were to be remedied by privatization of ranges, commercialization of ranching and sedentarization.[15] However, a counter view has since emerged that stresses that the "tragedy" is not an inevitable result of the absence of the regulation which property rights would bring, but a "failure of community," which occurs when customary tenure rules were not operating.[16] Bromley and Cirnea rejected Hardin's view that commons regimes involved "open access" to the resource. They were, they said, "structured ownership arrangements" with developed management rules; known and enforced group size; and incentives and sanctions to ensure compliance. Resource degradation, they said, inverting the Hardin thesis, "actually originates in the dissolution of local-level institutional arrangements whose very purpose was to give rise to resource use patterns that were sustainable."[17] From this they drew the conclusion that "Interventions aimed at sustainable agricultural development must explicitly address the social arrangements among the people as they interact with each other and with the natural resource base and help build up forms of social organisation conducive to sustainable productive use of natural resources."[18]

The state of play now is not whether resource users can manage the resource (which Hardin said they inevitably could not) but how – using what tools and concepts – and how these concepts may be recognized by an overarching state? The emphasis now is on the social and moral aspects of user behavior, not simply their presumed and modeled economic behavior. "Users form communities. Natural resource extraction is guided by social rules and norms, many of them non-contractual . . ."[19] They go on to say that "community in its moral and experiential" and "social" meanings is critical to the evolution of viable "commons" institutions, and that it is community which provides the "normative guidelines" for these. Furthermore, they note, communities are not simply geographical nor only sets of transactional relationships, but are "symbolically constructed."[20] It is in relation to this that the role of what is presented as customary is important. In particular we may want to pay attention to the circumstances under which communities are shattered, and the symbolic resources that may be used in their reconstruction.

The post-Hardin analyses place the emphasis not simply on destructive user behavior, but on the prior loss of control by local communities over economic resources, and their governance. McCay and Jentoft argue that the State and the Market are the "two most powerful causes of community failure. The tragic irony is that these are also the best known policy prescriptions for Tragedies of the Commons."[21] The "tragedy of the commons" thesis, Bromley and Cernea write, is about "market failure," but these situations need to be approached through the analysis of "community failure," by which they mean ". . . the social conditions required for tragedies of the commons may result from situations where resource users find themselves without the social bonds that connect them to each other and to their communities and where responsibilities and tools for resource management are absent." Bureaucratic regulation, they suggest, involves people in relations with a state machinery and personnel, rather than with each other.[22] This paradigm of "community failure" highlights the possibility of the use of the realm of the "customary." The shift away from the "tragedy of the commons" thesis also involves, therefore, a move away from simple ideas about the exercise of state power over local communities to a view of governance by incorporating local communities, local authorities and local normative structures into the machinery of control. (It was almost as if Indirect Rule had been reinvented, but with a discourse that emphasized local democracy rather than chieftainship.) In this context the stage is set for a revival in the role of "custom." But it has to be emphasized that the transitions between the deployment of this realm in the processes of the symbolic construction, maintenance and reconstruction of communities and the specifications of specific allocatory rights and rules, are not simple.

In this context it is important to situate a "customary" law of property. Rose notes that the standard paradigm in property law, which she finds inadequate, is that property is either private or public.[23] However, a closer look at property rights in systems of customary law is necessary especially because such an analysis opens up areas in which customary law is now highly contested and is something that divides rather than unites communities. The thinking about customary property rights in the context of environmental management has focused on issues surrounding land tenure, and associated claims to resources (marine tenure; forestry etc.). But this is, of course, but a small part of customary law relating to property rights. Western legal classifications tend to get in the way here, and prevent western lawyers from seeing clearly that areas that they might classify as family law or labor law involve what are often core property rights in customary systems. These are not only the conventional and easily seen matters of inheritance and dowry, but also include the claims to the labour of women and the younger generation generally, and the claims to support. These crucial resources in the labor of others are vital to the ways that people manage their economic lives, and their more easily seen western-defined resources. Indeed it is these claims to support that keep the language of customary law alive under circumstances in which it might otherwise be becoming redundant, such as the increasingly rapid urbanization of populations and their divorce from dependence on land and other customary resources. This is now as vital a part of the core of customary law of property as land tenure systems, but it is the latter which is the focus of those who would use a revivified "custom" in environmental management. Yet the claims to support by others are a part of customary systems based on clear inequalities between genders and generations, which are not validated by, and are under assault from, international human rights discourses. Is it possible to imagine the revival and use of custom in the resource management area, while at the same time it is under attack in others?

In Rose's classical paradigm, markets are based on private rights. If they fail, state management is resorted to. As she notes, this appears to exclude other regimes. But is a customary form of, say, land tenure, another kind of regime? Certainly the idealized view tends to treat customary tenurial regimes as if they were somehow more in the public realm than the private. But claims to customary rights in land, when advanced by those making them amongst each other, are not claims to "public" rights. They are really more part of the law of private property, being claims brought on behalf of and for the benefit of specific people. It is only when customary claims are made on or to an authority beyond the group concerned, when they have to be validated by a superior authority, that they take on a public character, and they appear to be a way of establishing prior property rights by a means that involved neither the market nor the state. The "public" or "communal" aspects of customary land tenure were developed to defend communities against expropriation by outsiders.[24]

In the post-colonial world there is a problem for people in states in which the formal legal system continued to recognize "customary" tenures that were not adequately defined and defensible in law. As we shall see below, this issue has been highlighted where, as in Australia and post-apartheid South Africa, states now want to recognize customary tenure but are experiencing great difficulties in defining its content in terms that are satisfactory both to the state's law and the people whose rights are at stake. In some cases customary tenures are threatened as outside investors seek to control a resource, in others by the increase in the numbers of people seeking a living from already marginal resources. Control of "common property" like grazing lands, marine resources or forests thus needs to be maintained under changed political and economic conditions: different state structures; different economies and economic policies; different laws; and different population numbers and changing definitions of group membership. The customary law that regulated access to a resource in the past has now to be adapted to a changed political environment, as well as a new developmental ethos in which state governments focus on the maximization of national product, and the institutionalization of the market.

The processes of creating a customary law by negotiation between states and communities that I described for the colonial period remain in the post-colonial world. Customary law remains as a relationship between state and localities. It remains a particularly important political language for the localities because these characteristically live within non-democratic states in which there is little popular participation in policy-making, and, even if there is, economic policies are dominated by state-focused development projects and a process of quasi-legitimate or corrupt extension of control over resources. As with any analysis of the use of a language we must be concerned with issues of audience in the use of the language. Here the crucial issue is whether the language is being spoken inside the community, or to outsiders who threaten it. In representing local interests against a hostile state, as I have suggested, a language of unity and community will be spoken, which is less evident when there are disputes within the community about customary rights. In the colonial period customary law was mobilized to advance and defend gendered interests in property resources and its use to protect sectional interests remains an important part of its rationale. In periods of "development," as new economic opportunities present themselves, wide differences of interest have typically developed between those customary claimants who wish to maximize their access to resources for commercial and entrepreneurial reasons, and those whose strategy is simply to defend the access they have. Many of the difficulties in understanding customary law are caused by the conflation of the search for ways of using customary law as a mode of regulation with the ideological search for alternatives to private property and the market. The "other" becomes the source of the communal, but it is a western model of the "communal" that is being found.

There are other reasons why the idiom of custom is so important and these relate, as I have said, to the fragmenting communities under severe economic pressure, in which issues of identity and belonging are crucial both materially and symbolically. The issues of belonging are made complex by the huge increases in the pace of urbanization, and the growth of new forms of labour migrancy, both under conditions of severe economic disadvantage. Home is both a welfare safety net and a symbol, and is simultaneously lived away from and lived with. The departed are both separated from and attached to community. What is the role of these non-traditional people in the formulation of "customary" defences of the unshared traditional way of life of "their" people? Absence does make the heart grow fonder of symbols and symbolic discourses. In this sense urbanization, the major feature of the economies within which the threatened resources are embedded, has intensified rather than weakened the grip of custom-based discourses. Issues of group membership and group governance are crucial to the success of any custom-based regime of resource management but they cannot be simply solved or clearly defined as long as they derive their ultimate legitimacy from a vision of cultural membership, because this would include those "absent" members who do not use the resource. As I shall suggest at the end of this chapter contractual arrangements may be a more practical way of limiting the group to actual resource users.

In considering the use of customary law as a policy resource in the construction of working systems of sustainable development, there are, therefore, a number of things to bear in mind. One is that one should not overestimate the depth of the "customary" element in terms of age and embedded cultural practices. Secondly, one should nevertheless not underestimate the legitimacy of the language of the customary in the tactics of representation of local interests. Likewise, while one should not overestimate "custom" as representative of the interests of all involved in a group or locality, one should not underestimate its necessary role in defending localities against state and private predation in the mobilization for development. In considering alternative statutory/bureaucratic or contractual regimes for resource use one needs to maintain in the forefront the impurity of the administrative machinery of the states, and the reasons for the lack of both cultural legitimacy and current faith in the security and equity of contract. It may be possible to overcome these factors by the construction of local self-management structures to administer consensus-based regimes but these will be unlikely to work unless set within the structure of a democratic and incorrupt state. Without that custom will continue to appear to be, (and to be) the most secure way of salvaging what can be of local control.

Western-inspired environmentalism has had a large and increasing impact on the most recent phase of development policies followed by the governments of the colonial successor states. In the context of increasing populations; the demand for the maximization of gross national product and exports to service the needs of growing urban populations; and rising demands and increasing debts; these states had embarked upon an era of aggressive economic development. However, it eventually came to be understood that the overexploitation of vulnerable economic resources placed their sustainability at risk and also endangered the existence of peoples who depended on them. This has led to a position in which people and environments were conflated and the preservation of a "way of life" became a part of the environmental mission (which is clearly justifiable in situations of forest, marine resource and range destruction). Environmental ideology could in these circumstances easily slide towards social preservationism – i.e. towards a stance that placed value on the preservation of cultures and the customs that were perceived to be necessary parts of cultures. The issues of the sustainability of resources and the protection of the people who depended on them has thus been conceptually linked to the issue of the preservation of the "cultures" of those people, and this stance would clearly favor the use of the "customary" as the primary instrument for the regulation of the use of those resources. A customary wisdom (rather than the quite different material, technological and political circumstances of the past) is held to have protected the resources in the past and to be best adapted to the future. However, one should note also that the idea of "sustainability" is new, and not a part of old wisdoms, because it has arisen in conditions of new pressures on depleting resources due to intense overexploitation. What "sustainability" requires are types of regulation, of care and control, which were unnecessary in "customary" times, and that will be new measures with old justifications.

Changing state strategies in economic development have also produced new divisions in local communities. State policies may open up the way to newly legitimized ways of claiming exclusive control over resources, and new responses, using the language of custom, will seek to utilize or to contest new opportunities. However, development policies may also facilitate the introduction of outsiders, just as, in any case, the integration of localities into new nation-states has done. The invocation of the customary to resist this will emphasize traditional conditions of group membership and will invoke solidarity and unity. Among the challenges to custom in the era of development is that new economic policies, opportunities and activities produce not only challenges to the definition of who is entitled to a resource but also profound challenges to the established norms of resource use. One of the enduring problems for local entrepreneurs who throughout the colonial period and beyond, have sought to enter new markets has been to reconcile new behaviors in relation to buying and selling land, labour and goods with economic and cultural expectations developed in another economy.[25] These processes have intensified and continue to create severe social divisions. The construction of states inevitably changed the parameters – the boundaries and membership – of the "communities" that could claim access to resources. Internal migration takes place within states as people, often losers of claims to land in their own localities, seek to use what appear to be unexpropriated resources. The issue that arises within any state is on what legal and ethical basis to exclude such members of the national community from the local community that has a customary claim to the resource, where that customary claim is not validated by the national laws of property. But in the realm of the customary, in order to speak legitimately, one cannot reflect division without fragmenting the cultural identity on which the legitimacy of custom rests. Thus custom cannot be "descriptive," or be a language of pragmatism, and this creates serious difficulties for its use as a pragmatic and legalized basis for economic and social relationships.

If custom is not a language of description and is one that is used to mask sectional interest and advantage, how then can it legitimate itself in cultural terms and become an alternative discourse of justification? To answer this it is necessary to consider which alternative normative visions it draws on, and which notions of community it echoes. To be usable as a basis upon which the legal claims to the resources that support life can be made, not only must these visions be powerful, but they must be able to be linked in real ways to both the preservation and revitalization of divided and threatened communities. And they must be utilizable against alternatively justifiable "national" demands to benefit from resource use that will resist efforts to encapsulate and protect for local benefit.

Within the context of state structures there are other difficulties in using custom. States will try to write custom, especially when it founds a claim to resource ownership and use. The most powerful in local communities will usually benefit from the placing of custom partly within the state's realm, as this will sustain their claims both externally and internally. Those less powerful may hope to sustain custom without incorporation and to ground it in culture and identity rather than the state. The outcome can be different worlds of custom, both speaking the same language, but less than congruent in both content and justification, especially where, as is frequently the case, the state itself uses, partially, the language of custom within its bureaucratic project.

Even if it is accepted that customary law changes as circumstances change, the underlying ethos and rationale of the customary law of rural populations who are being stressfully incorporated in market systems remains linked to pre-capitalist economic and social practices. But the circumstances with which the new customary law has to deal are those of intensified capitalist exploitation of resources that have been absorbed into wider state and global economies. The capacity of the discourses and values of custom to cope alone with this disjuncture must be doubted. The century of integration into world commodity markets does not make these discourses false in a cultural sense, for they are clearly a part of the processes of adaptation. But law, which is concerned (particularly in the realm of property) with clear definitions of rights, is interested in the issue of truth and falsity in a way in which interpreters of culture are not. Custom-based claims in the realm of property involve some people benefiting at the expense of others. In legally validating the underwriting of these advantages a broad sociological view of custom as validly changeable is not really helpful and can function to mask real inequalities that have developed in the processes of economic change.

8.5 After the state; beyond Weber

State control over the realm of the customary may well be quite different where the state is weaker.[26] Okoth-Ogendo has written of the "totally inadequate conception of law and its relationship to power in Africa."[27] We must, therefore, depart from the Weberian model of the state, of law and of bureaucracy. Law, Okoth-Ogendo says, is not based in these states on determinate rules that provide bases for predicting or evaluating authoritative decisions. He identifies two features of both the colonial and post-colonial state in Africa – bureaucracy and coercion. Bureaucracy, he writes, is completely dominant in a context in which there is no such thing as civil service neutrality. Ghai confirms that in developing countries "general norms play a secondary role." Both socialist and capitalist economies in developing countries, he writes, "are essentially administered economies, where the license in king and discretion is the norm . . . As the state is the primary instrument of accumulation, corruption is endemic, woven into the very fabric of the apparatus of the state."[28] Clientelism, sustained by regular favors, is the basis of political support; public control and accountability are absent. In this State there is no scope for social autonomy, or rights of association. Thus within them the remedies for misuse of resources, like the locally controlled and governed institutions, which are set out in the theoretical literature (see above), were and are politically impossible, except where the state became so weakened that people were able to withdraw from its domain and evade its laws. Hutchful describes the process as one of "shrinkage in the competence, credibility, and probity of the state," "state decline" and "political decomposition."[29] And he observes a deflation and reallocation of state power, a "dispersion of social, economic and political life away from the state and towards more enclosed, self-reliant local and horizontal entities."[30] All this amounts to a "severe erosion of the de facto reality of the state in many African countries," a condition of "state debilitation." Devisch's analysis of a post-colonial state collapse notes a revival of "villagization" as state law and justice disappear; institutions and realms of security shrink; and the focus of the "collective" returns from state to local communities.[31] This raises the wider question of whether a state-ordered "legality" was ever really constructed by the colonial successor states. It is, de Boeck says, difficult to determine where the state begins and where it ends and what "precisely legality and illegality or constitutional or unconstitutional in the African context means . . . In varying degrees, one could say that, paradoxically, unlawfulness, arrogant arbitrariness and illegality are the only elements that put an increasingly fictional 'state' in evidence and continue to make it visible."[32]

It is tempting to seize upon these developments as opening a new space for customary law and local self-management. As the era of statist developmentalism in the hands of a predatory form of state recedes, can a new custom-based normative order be the basis for a working legality? Will this be helped by the international developments described below, which have made the major institutional and discursive partners no longer the post-independence states but NGOs, the World Bank, international organizations, and aid donors? Ideally the answer would be that the collapse of predatory states, or even just of the development states whose destructive vision Scott describes in *Seeing Like a State*,[33] creates an environment for the development of a customary law linked to sustainable development practices. Seeing like an NGO, even seeing like a Bank, might be less dangerous to local communities than seeing like a state. But state illegality and state implosion can lead to the uncontrollable exploitation of resources by new forms of organized violence (as in the cases of diamonds in parts of Africa) or by virtually "lawless" states that can use the language of conservation to exclude competitors and ensure the profits of corrupt elites (for example game "conservation" policies in Kenya, Zaire and apartheid South Africa). Once again any account of relationship between sustainable development and customary law must take account of not only the world of jurisprudence and the Rechtstaat, but the realities of the successfully corrupt states, and of imploding and collapsed states.

One of the problems related to law in the post-colonial world, which bears on the possible development of customary law, is that of language. One of the major reasons for the ineffectiveness of state law has been that it is usually written in, and conducted largely in, certainly at the higher levels, the language of the former colonizer. This in itself makes it inaccessible to most of the population of these states. A return to customary law in much of the world implies what it did not in the European states from which the jurisprudence of custom is derived, a returning of the law to local linguistic communities. In countries characterized by linguistic plurality this has obvious implications. For a customary law to be real within its community it must be in the language of its users, not that of the colonial language used by the state's elites and the state's law (and not in the more distant language of international legal discourse). Fragmentation is inherent in this process of linguistic pluralism, which would take states in a direction opposite to that of legal unification, which was the lawyers' and the national elites' goal after independence. But this ambition has failed. As Ake writes, "The state is in effect privatised: it remains an enormous force but no longer a public force; no longer a re-assuring guaranteeing the rule of law but a formidable threat to all except the few who control it, actually encouraging lawlessness and with little capacity to mediate conflicts in society."[34]

The model of development that reigned in Africa in the decades following independence depended not only on what Ake describes as the "rising tide of statism," which proliferated bureaucratic apparatuses and an associated parasitical class, but also on the associated development theory, which regarded political authoritarianism in a positive light and pluralist democracy as an obstacle to development.[35] Customary law, which implies a degree of local participation, had little place in this paradigm. Its challenge is to see whether it can be part of the new paradigm of democratic participation in the state, and in development, and it is within this political framework that any program to make use of customary law must ultimately be considered. Ake suggests that there is a cultural basis in Africa for a law that does not treat people as social atoms and legal subjects but that rests on a sense of cultural identity derived from kinship and shared cultural experiences, a law for those who are not part of a "general public" but a "primordial public in their communities of origin." The "lawless governance" of the post-colonial states, he suggests, violates the sense of a rule of law in communal societies; "rules which encompass values, norms, customs . . . which encapsulate the society's total experience (and) apply not to abstract persons but to real human beings. In the end, the logic of Africa's communal tradition and values is one for which the modern state is simply incompatible."[36] All of this suggests that a political and legal strategy that aims at increasing the role of customary law in the development process, even if it focuses only on the management of common resources, must be a part of re-imagining the state and its relations with its subjects in communities. Once again we return to the customary law as part, not simply of local communal societies, but of the relationship between these and the state.

The recognition of the customary certainly raises fears among lawyers about the challenge it appears to present to the legal sovereignty of the state, and it does make inroads into the state paradigm at a time when rule-of-law-based constitutionalism guaranteed by a fundamental law of the state has become globally virtually unchallengeable as the basis for legitimate politics. But constitutionalism, and the idea of a constitution, was not always tied obviously to this kind of model. As Rose puts it "Constitutionalism in the model of the ancient constitution was a vision of a fundamental law deriving from long-standing ways of doing things, justified either by the sheer antiquity of the practice or by the wisdom and subtleness that antiquity signifies."[37] From this point of view the customary law is not a challenge to the African state but a part of its constitutionalist fabric, embodying its fundamental law far more effectively than the written constitutions so cynically ignored by rulers. As Rose continues, the term constitutionalism "could be understood to apply to a great range of practices so long as they were seen as fundamental law." In the "broader sense . . . the ancient constitution encompassed all kinds of long established laws . . . practices, customs and local privileges . . . that were thought to be constitutive of a given political realm . . ." It was from this set of established practices that the body politic derived its proper identity.[38] African legal systems constituted in this manner could form the basis of the different kind of state that Ake envisages.

While there may be justification, from the point of view of western jurisprudence in functioning political democracies, in the objection that the legal validation of "new custom" subverts the political process by subjecting people to binding legal obligations in a manner not envisaged in the constitutional processes, this is not an objection that can realistically be made in states with irregular and corrupt legal and political processes. The state model within which the western concept of custom was formed does not exist in large parts of the world. Indeed it is precisely the absence of a working state, of political democracy, and of a sense of national community, that makes "custom" such an important part of the political language of many polities. This language is not necessarily connected to an ongoing world of customary practices or system of customary rights. In these circumstances a continually evolving customary law is a necessary feature of new states that have failed to construct the kinds of legal system that were envisaged at the time of decolonization.

It follows from my emphasis on the various forms of state incapacity and collapse, which forms the institutional framework in much of the third world and which now provides the institutional setting for a use of customary law, that we should investigate the other forms of governance of development in this period. In recent years there has been an enormous increase in the role of NGOs in the conceptualizing, planning, delivery and administration of development and it can be argued that the administrative bureaucracies of recipient states are no longer at the core of development administration. Thus these processes are already to a high degree in the hands of non-state actors, which are not catered for in the usual legal paradigms. It is not simply the large northern-based NGOs that I have in mind here but the "voluntary activism" of tens of thousands of grass-roots agencies that are at the heart of the sustainable development movement. Fisher writes that "a non-governmental revolution is already sweeping the Third World" challenging the scope of top-down decision making.[39] At the 1992 United Nations Conference on Environment and Development in Rio, 20,000 participants representing 9,000 organizations attended the parallel Global Forum.[40] This expansion of the NGO sector is an essential part of the governance of sustainable development and is, rather than the weak and compromised state institutions, the crucial environment into which use of customary law should be injected. It is also probably the most responsive precisely because so many grass-roots NGOs are locally based and work through empowerment of and responsiveness to those "below," and because, unlike states, they are specific vectors of the practice of sustainable development. As NGOs mobilize forms of increased participation of far larger numbers of people in what has previously been thought of as "development administration" – a place for experts – so one could expect a far larger tingeing of all the processes with customary ideas and practices, which will come from the bottom up and be a part of the process of participatory development. The relation of these developments to states and their processes will depend on the nature of the polity but it is clear that new forms of mobilization are competing with and sometimes taking over governmental functions in the development area. The power and the strategies of the large NGOs may be illustrated by Oxfam's statement on land rights in Africa. It describes the current situation as a form of ". . . land grab reminiscent of the original scramble for Africa . . . involving mining investors, tourist speculators, ruling elites and corrupt chiefs." States are clearly not seen as the appropriate defenders of the rights of their own inhabitants. In the face of the states' "resource and capacity constraints" and "lack of political will," Oxfam assumes the role of "helping communities to become more aware of their rights" and "determining how best to demand and defend them," as well as the external diplomatic role of "vigorously" lobbying powerful donors.[41]

It is through the NGOs, therefore, that the international norms relating to customary sustainable development are now being developed,[42] both because of the NGOs' initiatives, and because local people now seek linkages to the international world through NGOs, often to bypass the nation-state. Theorization of the role of customary law in relation to third world states cannot be done in the framework of western state models and western jurisprudence, but must come to terms with the realities of the current state forms, and their interaction with NGOs that often have greater financial and persuasive resources than states. These unaccountable and largely external agencies can now play a role in the development and validation of "customary" regimes, which may augment or bypass state and community. We need, therefore, to consider the extent of NGO influence on the development of sustainable development norms both locally and internationally and the tremendous growth of environmental NGOs as an integral part of environmental politics and governance. Our analysis must have a perspective that not only understands the diminishing states as they are, but one that integrates the internationalized non-state role into governance of localities. A top-down analysis of states and law underestimates the ways in which NGO and grass-roots movements are developing a partly local and partly internationalized set of ways – discourses, approaches to institutions – in dealing with sustainable development issues. This may not be "customary law" in some long-term culturally embedded, or time immemorial practice sense, but it is the extra-state normativity that we must consider.

The activism of the NGO sector does raise new questions about the discursive construction of customary law, and the way in which it can become divorced from customary practices and become the work of environmentalists and development agencies. In a landmark article Zerner[43] has examined the "historical changes in the discursive construction" of customary law in an area of Indonesia. He notes that the intention of early codification of custom in the late nineteenth century was the regulation of access to commercially exploitable resources and was the result of collaboration between colonial officials and local elites. In recent decades there has been what he calls a "second era of inscription." Legal and environmental scholars "promoted and produced *sasi* customary law as a living armature for the construction of biological diversity, sustainable development and social equity in village communities..." Colonial texts have been deployed, he writes, "as if they reflected social realities rather than colonial refractions of social facts."[44] Quite specifically he sees a recently reconstructed *sasi* being set up as a legal counter-culture. The reconstruction of *sasi* is "deployed in the service of support of local community autonomy in the face of perceived private sector and central government control of local resources." This is a process that he sees as going on throughout the developing world. In this process, information and imagery flow in a variety of directions. "Cosmopolitan groups . . . represent themselves as speaking for local communities, and they situate marginalised groups within powerful international discourses on human rights, indigenous communities, conservation and environmental sustainability . . ." In the other direction indigenous leaders "are learning to speak the environmental discourses spoken and legitimated by international development and conservation agencies."[45] This contemporary re-mapping of custom and community employs new terms of social equity and community resource management "as if communities were spatially and temporally stable." As Zerner says, acts of documenting customary law are not transparent representation but a form of advocacy. From the perspective of the "national environmental elite," local "conservation practices" have to be invented if not found, because the construction of customary law in this way makes it a legitimate site for "progressive interventions."[46] But the customary laws were never the "coherent products of a purely local community . . . Rather, these practices and their textual embodiments were and continue to be hybrid creations shaped by a multiplicity of authors . . ."

And he also emphasizes the role of "non-governmental activists for social and environmental justice" on creative deployment of customary law.[47] This reinforces the points made earlier: administration captured and used the language of custom in both colonial and post-colonial situations, so while it may start off as local communities, or elites, talking to the state, custom became an idiom in which the state talks to the communities. And as state dialect dominated, so it regularized practices, which is the only way of seeing them administratively. In the new phase a new international dialect has become a part of the language of custom, and a new dialogue between local communities and international partners supplements, and may be replacing, that between communities and the state that had been the locus of formation of customary law.

To understand the relationship between sustainable development and customary law and the possible uses of customary law one must, therefore, understand the ways in which the discourses and practices of customary law have been evolving along with the now related discourses of sustainable development and human rights, because these are now interlocked and interleaved discourses. Current versions of customary law, as Zerner's study suggests, represent resources for the major strategic players in policy processes and discursive construction. In these policy processes the construction of customary regimes as democratic and egalitarian is a prime step in construction of environmentally sensitive customary law regimes. Zerner writes, "By projecting a conservationist past onto current *sasi* practices, these interpretations authorize supportive actions by important central governmental and non-governmental actors . . ." These interpretations, he continues, are "enabling fictions. They create discursive links between past and present, channeling meanings and energies, projects and potential financial flows of powerful, cosmopolitan centers to singularly remote locations . . ."[48] However there is often a cleavage between the new discourses and the actual local practices because of connection of the new "green" version of custom with government authority and controls. And this increase in control over resource use is associated with opportunity for corruption and diversion of profits.[49] All of this points to the difficulties of making "allocational" decisions (even when cast in the language of local customary law) in circumstances of administrative corruption and degradation, lack of democracy in political cultures, and huge differences in power between central and local agents.

The non-localness of the revived custom pointed to by Zerner is underlined by the sale of newly defined customary rights to outside entrepreneurs. The existence of markets make any closed customary community very hard to sustain. If, as Ostrom says, the keys to governance of the commons are the participation of the appropriators in creating and maintaining the regime, and ability to restrict use of the resource, the existence of markets all too often means that local users do not have these keys. Zerner's discussion indicates the links between the use of customary law and national endorsement, and that it is endorsed on the state's terms. It is the state that deals directly with international and national corporations in granting of concessions for resource use – e.g. timber – and the state that may or may not invoke a regime of customary law to manage the resource. It is vital that we note the connection between the rise of the new custom-based discourses and the intensified resource destruction, and in so noting that we do not assume that customary words will control the practices. In the 1990s, Zerner writes, "NGOs continue to search, through time, and through Indonesia's vast coastal and forested territories, for local institutions and practices, and values that may be deployed in the struggle to effect changes in inequitable, even oppressive, relationships between central national government and capital intensive private sector . . . and local communities . . ." This resuscitation of community-based management, "part of a much wider move in the strategic politics of the environmental movement . . ."[50] can also be a part of the strategy of the state. The discovery of customary law is used because there is no other discourse that legitimates either local self-regulation, or property rights acquired and governed by non-market and non-state means. All of this, it should be emphasized, is taking place not in the context of peaceful discussion between jurist, anthropologists and administrators, but of widespread violent resistance, even where the state has not imploded, to the destruction of resources by outsiders. State "recognition" of customary law is in this context a part of a process of mediating the violence of opposition by using a differently focused vocabulary in which to speak about the processes.

In this context we should also consider Keebet van Benda-Beckmann's important and insightful discussion of the interaction between NGOs, indigenous peoples and the new discourses and, practices of environmental protection programs at the grass roots. She observes the ways in which indigenous peoples have been constructed as keepers of the environment, a "static and idealistic image." As she points out the "indiscriminate emphasis" on the ecological role of some indigenous people, and the "static approach underlying the assertion that people have lived the same way for time immemorial" might place "severe restrictions" on their lives. There are, as she points out, "very few indigenous peoples who manage to develop a sustainable lifestyle" once technological inventions and new social and economic opportunities become available to them. Indeed there is "ample evidence" that given new technologies indigenous peoples, far from demonstrating inherently superior environmental wisdom, exploit their environment beyond sustainability. One should not assume therefore, she writes, that customary knowledge and practices will provide directly applicable solutions to rapidly changing environments.[51]

It is the NGOs, she points out, which now serve as the interlocutors between indigenous communities and states and international donors, and as vital players in the implementation of environmental protection programs at the grass roots. It is often through NGO-implemented programs that the concrete practices of sustainability will be developed. However, the NGOs' world of "black and white stories and colored photographs"[52] is given to the creation of stereotypes to generate public support. These, she says, could ultimately threaten those peoples who fail to meet stereotypical expectations. The tension between the worlds of complexity and change and that of public stereotypes is dangerous and the reliance on NGOs as intermediaries encourages a homogeneity of perception of indigenous peoples and threatens their ability to manage their own processes of change.[53] The NGOs, in other words, not only take on state functions, but (see below) "see like states." NGOs, in taking over state roles and functions in the development process, will govern rather than represent the indigenous people. And, in doing so, they will be infused with a stereotypical environmentalism popular with western donors. Only those customary practices that fit this model will have a chance of being legitimized as customary law.

8.6 Custom and democracy: the need for a new jurisprudence of custom

I have discussed the contexts and pressures under which groups seek to frame and validate notions of rights by attachment to the past practices and visions of community, rather than by adaptation and change on the basis of democracy. Peter Ørebech points to the conflict between customary law and democracy, and to him a major problem in validating claims based on custom is that they are produced outside of legitimate parliamentary democratic processes. He asks by whose right a minority customary practice is transformed into a law: "the purely formal notion of democracy excludes custom from the formulation of law." However, while this may be a problem for certain states in the West, in many parts of the world not only are democratic processes not the source of state law, but the western Weberian rule-governed, bureaucratic model state and its legal rational law are also absent. Instead of thinking only of the conditions for incorporating custom into state law, we need to think in terms of going beyond the state as it has been constituted in the last decades. The legitimacy of a customary law has long been a challenge to the jurisprudence of the West, dominated as it came to be by the idea that law was an expression of state-organized sovereignty and was produced by courts, kings or legislatures. The lawyers' attachment to state sovereignty, centralization and unity overwhelmed analyses that situated law in community practice, or in *Volksgeist*. The latter were worlds of legal darkness. Even Henry Maine, the most attuned to the world of the customary of all the English jurists, thought that early peoples were "enslaved to custom" and that overcoming this was the aim of "scientific jurisprudence." Bentham's view of customary law captured the positivist approach: "here is no rule established, no measure to discern by, no standard to appeal to: all is uncertainty, darkness and confusion."[54] Yet this jurisprudential framework of the relationship of positive law to custom, a part of the history of the rise of effectively bureaucratized, centralized states is irrelevant and inappropriate to new needs. The western jurisprudence of law and custom is meaningless in most of the world. Not only is the model of the state inappropriate, but so is the model of customary law that was developed to fit the claims and demands of this state. For in that model customary law had essentially to be a passive acceptance of a deep structure, ancient and unchanging: a reflection of a *Volksgeist* – as Maine put it, "the customary law under which Indian village communities had lived for centuries."[55] Only the sovereign could make and change laws, and the idea that the realm of the customary involved a changeable world of agreed mutual activities could have no place in a statist jurisprudence because of the challenge to sovereignty that this involved. It is here that we must turn away from positivism towards both the realist and pluralist paradigms because both of these emphasize the limited role that state law has, not only in the normative universe, but also in its use as a means of settling disputes. State law is only a part of the normative universe of those who live in the West, and state courts settle remarkably few disputes. Even the "shadow" in which it has been rightly said, people "bargain," is often cast by norms other than state law. In any case in the collapsed or collapsing states in parts of the third world it seems irrelevant to be debating the precise nature of the difference between law and other rules.

A new jurisprudence of custom will transcend the opposition between the ideas of the "customary" and the "modern," which underlies much of the western lawyers' understanding of customary law. This is vital if using customary law is to become a part of environmental management. It is not simply a matter of acknowledging that customary law is not fixed and unchanging but can be used as an instrument of flexible adaptation to environmental crises. Before it can be so used, it must not be mistaken as representing pre-market forms of social organization. Communities that now draw on customary law and its concepts have been involved in the market for over a century. Like societies in the West, some members seek to modify or resist the logic of the market, others seek to turn this logic to their advantage. Both can use the language of custom. The discourse of ecology and its particular construction of "custom" often appears to validate the inherent rationality of "pre-development" or "pre-capitalist" economic activities. But we need now to use the idea of customary law in the new situations of population increase, globalizing markets, resource degradation/exhaustion, state taxation and predation and technological change. Custom in the sense of past usages is clearly irrelevant (except as a source of symbols). Custom must now be seen as new "community" based responses to these pressures, and implies no inherent "non-market" response. Much of the study of and comment on the realms of traditional and indigenous has been largely in the hands of those who are hostile to "markets" and "globalizing" and neo-modernity and could well tend to underestimate the responses, and to mistake the direction, to new circumstances that can be made within the idiom of indigeneity. Indigenous peoples' readiness to advertise using cultural symbols and to place their art and stories, among the most intimate symbols of their cultures, in the market place, and to profit from them, is illustrative of this.

8.7 The post-development paradigm

Current international requirements of what the post-colonial states should be pose new challenges for the utilization of the customary law as a tool for sustainable resource use. The model of the top-heavy *dirigiste* state, directing and controlling the economy, has now been replaced (at least conceptually), with a leaner state, providing the framework of effective government, a rule of law, and an economic "level playing field," as a framework for private sector development. The possibility of an expanded utilization of customary law must also be placed in the context of the view now taken by the World Bank (and more broadly within the "Washington consensus") of the role of law in development. The Bank's 1997 report says that,

> The legal framework of a country is as vital for economic development as for political and social development. Creating wealth through the cumulative commitment of human, technological and capital resources depends greatly on a set of rules securing property rights, governing commercial and civil behavior, and limiting the power of the state ... The legal framework also ... has become an important dimension in strategies for poverty alleviation.[56]

One may wonder whether the "rule of law" requirements for the developing states and economies is helpful or antithetical to the new version of "creative" custom. It is not simply a matter of a new universalist constitutionalism that emphasizes versions of rights such as gender equality that may challenge customary regimes anew. There are other ways in which the new international language of rights and a "rule of law" can pose challenges to custom-based legal particularisms. One is that they provide a language in which opposition to custom can be articulated in terms of an overarching language of a more universal rights-based equity and this will challenge the image of custom as a language of resistance. A second is that to validate legally claims to resources that are made on the basis of new and changeable customs is not compatible with the "rule of law" certainty that the new economic environment requires, and indeed is closer to the world of bureaucratic discretion that the new globalization seeks to replace. It could be that contractual regimes, while they may lack the resonances of customary ones, hold more promise for local control of resources in the new international economic environment. James Scott has written of the ways in which the state attempts to make a society "legible"; of its need to know its subjects and its resources; of its "rationalizing and standardizing."[57] "Seeing like a state" has involved "the imperial or hegemonic planning activity that excludes the necessary role of local knowledge and know-how."[58] He concludes that "Just as the buzzing complexity and plasticity of customary land tenure practices cannot be satisfactorily represented in the straitjacket of modern freehold law, so the complex motives and goals of cultivators . . . cannot be effectively portrayed by the standardization of scientific agriculture."[59] While one need not completely subscribe to his polarized models of state-inspired, destructive scientific agriculture on the one hand, and peasant farmer localities that practice conservationist agriculture on the other, his analysis of the different visions of state and local communities in relation to development is important to the consideration of the possible uses of the customary in sustainable development. Would a revival of the customary involve the reversal of the process of rationalizing and standardizing that has, as Scott says, so greatly enhanced state capacity? Or will it be a customary law that is used by the state in its hegemonic projects? As Scott shows, the sad Tanzanian experience suggests that however much communal and customary images are invoked by the state, its conscriptive ambitions will destroy the customary.

Scott's discussion dramatizes the ways in which development is a state project. And we might also think about it in more routine ways, as a matter of administration. Indeed much of the business of the state's structures in the developing world has been the *administration* of development projects. Perhaps it could be said that the sustainable development literature that is based on property rights starts with the wrong end of the problem. Paradoxically there is a tendency among lawyers to forget government as a process, even while remembering the state as the source of law and rights. The development story, Diwedi writes, has been one of failure. After four United Nations Development Decades the North's remedies have had many failures; squalor, despotism and poverty have increased, and an environmental crisis looms.[60] So we might think about the processes of development administration: first with Ferguson's paradigm in mind, of the specialized discourse, the suppression of the political, and the discursive opposing of the customary and the modern; and secondly in the light of the crisis of corruption and collapse of state capacity. To take the first point, the huge emphasis on "modernization" (perceived as value-free and culturally neutral) not only of technology, but of values, relegated the entire customary realm simply to something that would be superseded.[61] In relation to the second, the western system of development administration was based on a dichotomy between politics and administration and premised on public service neutrality.[62] The trope of the customary in the discourse of development administration is one in which the customary, as a mode of governance, is "corrupt," or at least pre-Weberian, in attitudes to administration: a world in which personal favors and kinship connections, rather than rules, form the basis of administrators' actions. The modernization and development of government is seen as a process that will replace personal favors with rules. However, as is now apparent, a Weberian model of administration has not developed in most third world states, and in this sense, there is little to choose between the portrayal of a "corrupt" customary past, and the states of the present. Two questions arise: one is if the state has failed, what are the alternatives? The second is how far the version of governance attributed to the "customary" world is really dramatically opposed to what could be acceptable within the current global vision of what the state should be, and the ever-tightening weave of international treaties and law. Diwedi writes that the administrative culture of the third world is the product of colonial heritage and post-independence modernization "plus a smattering of indigenous . . . ways of doing things" and that the resultant administrative style "appears to combine the worst of these three influences." The basic feature of these administrations was the dominance of the culture of central planning in which bureaucratic administration and expertise was seen as the essential mechanism for attainment of development goals.[63] This perspective gave the key role in development, in the project of nation building, and planning, to the bureaucracy that was focused on the development of the public sector.

This paradigm has been severely damaged by the policies of the World Bank since 1987 and by the collapse of the communist regimes. State-run planning is no longer seen as the model for successful development administration. Conditions relating to the freeing of markets, and to human rights, have been attached to development aid. In the last decades we have had weakened states working, at least nominally, within a rights and market-oriented framework. We must therefore ask, specifically, what the implications of these developments (in combination in many places with an environmental crisis) are for the "customary" sector. Long constructed as an opposite to "modernization" and an obstacle to state administration in achieving that goal, is there now a new role for the customary in administering development in weakened states working nominally within a rights and market framework? What are the implications for the customary in the weakening of big government and the governance of development by "experts"? Will a new form of environmental expertise, working within the sustainable development paradigm, take the place of the expertise in bureaucratic modernization? It does seem to be the case that in the world of development administration there is a renewed interest in the ways in which some of the pathologies of development might be solved locally with the resources of local cultures, and an interest in indigenizing development administration in order to harness local traditions, culture and governance styles. This new style of development administration has been enhanced by the downsizing of modernist bureaucracies, and by a change in the size and focus of development projects. The sustainable development paradigm is one of smaller scale development, focusing on the poor, closer to their localities, concerns and knowledge. Diwedi writes that "The alternatives to traditional Weberian hierarchy are considerable:

participatory 'bureaucratic populism' types and community based decentralised structures offer numerous options."[64] Acknowledging that the Weberian model of administration has been a fantasy in many developing countries does not in itself efface the problems associated with its opposite, and the issues of officials' preference towards tribe, kin, neighbourhood and village. Whether a non-Weberian state, guided by "customary" values, can develop an administrative culture acceptable to all its constituents, must be a part of the consideration of the use of customary law for sustainable development by developing states, because any such project will depend on the successful organization of the tasks of government, not simply on the designation of rules.

The new development paradigm is based on the empowerment of people in localities instead of the bureaucracy of a development state. But the problem of the relationship between the "experts" and the people remains. Empowered local people will not necessarily kowtow to western environmental fashions. They may instead found their claims to self-management in their "customs" and these will not necessarily meld with environmental wisdom. As Hanne Petersen suggests in Chapter 2, "culture" and "custom" can be invoked (in this case in a hunting and fishing culture) to defend non-sustainable practices, especially where these are important markers not only of cultural identity, but of gender identity within a culture. The destruction of resources is not the exclusive activity of the rich, or of outsiders. And, while in relation to agricultural schemes, Scott is persuasive in presenting the limitations of "scientific" knowledge, as opposed to cultivators' knowledge, in hunting and fishing cultures, the local knowledge, precisely because it is local, is unlikely to be able to encompass a broader picture of resource decline. Given that there is a need for local cooperation to make sustainable development schemes work, there will be a need to validate indigenous politics and concepts. But more difficulties arise when outsiders look to pick and choose usable pieces of customary behavior to validate, treating the customary world view as a "useful scrapbook," because this undermines some of the potency of the legitimacy of the customary. Any scheme of sustainable development based on the empowerment and customs of local user groups would have to come to grips with the fact that it is usually the local groups who are overusing the resource, though sometimes with dramatic and lop-sided competition from new users with new technologies (e.g. in fishing and logging). Customary law is made for small groups of repeat players, but can this work when rapacious outsiders pressure the resource? It may be that the incorporation of customary law is not the best way to validate the local users and their indigenous practices in resource management. It is customary processes rather than customary rules that could be the basis for sustainable development resource management. Indigenous systems of management embody adaptive responses, not stable traditions with long unchanging histories. Indeed, as I have emphasized. most of what is customary now has little in the way of time span as circumstances have changed so dramatically everywhere. In customary systems, as all the anthropological studies have shown, flexibility rather than the dead hand of time immemorial underpins pragmatic learning processes.

Once the emphasis is on process, the importance of customary law could be its participatory nature. It enables an escape from the assumption that law and settlement of legal disputes must be in the hands of legal professionals, which would not be the best way of constructing a sustainable development regime managed by users. Where notions of community are rooted in popular culture a customary system cannot be one administered by professionals from outside a community.

8.8 Indigenous law in "first world states": a different problem

There has been a successful revival of the realm of the "customary" in centralized legal systems in the former colonies of settlement where minority indigenous communities survive amidst a democracy of a racially different majority. In so-called first world states, where there is a functioning legal and administrative system, issues relating to indigenous customary law can be approached differently. Political assertions within these polities can be effectively made through the creation of a neo-indigeneity and the use of the language of custom, and they do not endanger the central sovereignty in these "strong" states. But here also, the relevance of the state as the only validator of law has been called into question by the development of an international law that has become an alternate validator of indigenous laws. While in a realist analysis it has to be said that the decision to recognize indigenous law in Canada and Australia derives from the state, the legal position is that indigenous legal rights are not granted by the state, but derive from rights that existed prior to establishment of the colonizing states. That is, both rights to native title to land, and also, by extension, the customary law, are grounded in an order prior to state law. Both jurisdictions recognize, however, the right of the state, now sovereign, to prevail over indigenous law. And both use the complex apparatus of western legal concepts and reasoning not just to protect but also to define native title and customary law. But this state authority over, and discursive reconstruction of, indigenous law, now takes place within a framework of international law that we must consider if we are to understand another context in which customary law may develop, far from its localities, and unhinged from both state and communities. (See Chapter 10, p. 405.)

The temper of the legalistic reconstruction of indigenous law in Canada can be gleaned from the criteria listed by Lamer CJ in *R v. Van Der Peet* 1996 (137) DLR 289. In the determination of aboriginal rights, he said, the court must take into account the precise nature of the claim; the continuity of the practice; whether it is of "central significance"; whether the practice is "distinctive"; whether it is a "custom, practice or tradition" of a group; and he added also at the end of his list, heavily influenced as it clearly was by the Blackstonian tradition, the "perspectives" of Aboriginal people. Other judges focused in a less Blackstonian fashion on a broad notion of Aboriginal rights rather than on specific practices: that rights would be recognized if they were sufficiently significant to culture and social organization and also conceded that indigenous custom might change and that the court should recognize the potential evolution of Aboriginal practices. It was argued that as Aboriginal economies and cultures were not static prior to conquest, they should not be required to be so afterwards. Nonetheless, it seems that custom still has to be regular rather than episodic, and community rather than individual behavior.[65] Other "first world" legal systems, like Australia's, also struggle to fit customary law's categories and concepts into those of western law. Sometimes it is a question of definition arising from the problems of reconciling the highly defined forms of written law with a customary law that was built around processes rather than rules. The accommodations made by judges in the dominant state system are always going to be grudging and confining, as they are concerned with protecting the integrity of the common law. From this one might conclude that, even where legal rights prior to colonial conquest are recognized, as now in Canada and Australia, a broader role for customary law could only follow if forms of institutional autonomy were established, as customary law cannot be adequately understood and expounded by the state's courts. Canada's Royal Commission on Aboriginal Peoples, which reported in 1996, said that First Nations peoples' right to self-government is inherent, not derived from the Canadian Government, and that the resources they have jurisdiction over include land, water, trapping and fishing.[66] But ultimately it will be the courts of the Canadian State that preside over the way in which the customary law is developed.

Where, in first world states like Australia, indigenous customary title to land has been recognized, it has been necessary to create legal structures of a non-customary kind to allow for the management and control of lands held under customary tenure in a way that will allow linkage with the state's law. In Australia sections 55 to 60 of the Native Title Act require that a prescribed body corporate be designated to hold title as trustee for Aboriginal land holders recognized by common law holders. We can see a process similar to that of Canada's in the difficulties that first world legal systems have in accommodating different legal concepts into a highly systematized law. Initially it was anticipated that these bodies could be corporate devices that would reflect the customary nature of the rights. Introducing the Aboriginal Councils and Associations Act 1976 to Parliament, the Minister said that the law would "recognise cultural differences between Aboriginal and non-Aboriginal societies and enable Aboriginal communities to develop legally recognisable bodies which reflect their own culture and do not require them to subjugate this culture to overriding Western legal concepts." This aspiration has "largely been disappointed by the relentless process of law reform which has replicated . . . the structures of the Corporations Law."[67]

As Mantziaris points out the Registrar has model rules for such Aboriginal corporations that are not derived from any customary background; that there has been a process of tightening up of financial reporting; that the "very centrepiece of the governance system," the ability of the corporate constitution to be based on "Aboriginal custom," has also been subverted by the systemic need to produce certainty.[68] Because there is no defined pure customary law there has been no development of the idea of an indigenous corporation, for example, one in which membership is based on kinship, or connection with the land, though there would be problems here with dormant and non-consensual members.[69] Complaints relating to fraud and mismanagement in Aboriginal corporations have been rife, leading to cases in the courts and a government response that has increased control over financial management. The argument that different cultural roles and expectations should be taken into account in interpreting the moral duties of office holders is unconvincing in the context of a global struggle against corruption and for accountability. One answer has been to say that issues of internal accountability should be left to custom, but the Australian experience suggests that custom will be contested, that communities are not united and that people seek the protection of the state's laws. Mantziaris suggests that consensus is typically found in smaller extended family units rather than at the level of aggregation of units formed by indigenous corporations. Another suggestion he canvasses is that corporations could simply incorporate customary law into their rules. He writes:

> This opens up a spectrum of possibilities. At one end, the wholesale adoption of "customary laws" into the corporate constitution raises the spectre of the complete "juridification" of social relationships between the members of the corporation. At the other end, low rule specificity runs the risk of unchecked power within organisational structures. Between these two poles lies the possibility of individual actors using the juridical character of intra-corporate relations electively and strategically to advance individual ends or minority conceptions of the collective good.[70]

All this suggests that it will be difficult in states with a "first world" legal system to separate the indigenous customary law categories and the state's legal categories, and that the latter will tend to redefine the former in state law terminologies. Because of this the customary law is not necessarily the best way to secure customary interests within such a state law system. It may be more effective to harness the forms of the state's law and its rights provisions, especially where these are effectively supported by international law and obligations. But the situation may well be quite different where there is no functioning state legal system of this kind.

This search for a means of governance of land held by its "traditional" owners has also been a feature of the attempts to restructure land tenure regimes in post-apartheid South Africa. There the customary law, which gave substantial powers of governance to traditional chiefs, has lost some of the discursive battle in a legal arena now oriented towards democratic participation and constitutionally entrenched rights. What could be put in its place if, as has been the case, privatization of rights has been rejected as an overall solution? The Community Property Associations Act of 1996 illustrates, as does the Australian experience, the difficulties involved in harnessing a customary law to a state system, especially within a framework of rights protection. The new statute created ways in which indigenous "customary" communities can construct themselves in order to receive returned and redistributed land. In other words the "community" for this purpose is the product of the statute and is bound by the state's legal principles in its self-administration, its decision-making processes, accountability mechanisms and dispute resolution procedures. The land is to be governed procedurally by a self-governing association structured entirely by western legal concepts – a sort of statutorily imposed contract. It is evident that the ways in which communities can constitute and run themselves, nominally according to their own customary law, is now constrained and influenced by a range of national and internally inspired legal factors. Among the thorny problems of defining the membership of the group and households, of gender issues, of inheritance, entry and exit, and daily governance, the customary law evaporates before the state's new processes. Self-management of the commons can not now escape western administrative and property law where there is a working state (as in South Africa) even where it purports to embody a customary approach to property law. Broadening the role of indigenous law can also create other problems. In South Africa, where the transition from white to majority rule might be expected to enhance the role of African law, the new constitution both encourages and inhibits this process. While the constitution gives support to customary law, its Bill of Rights, which protects gender equality, threatens to undermine a core feature of this law. This same issue has been the subject of conflict elsewhere in Africa.

8.9 Beyond Maine

The context for this consideration of customary law and sustainable development has been the increasing intensity of pressures for economic growth in a globalizing economy. The concept of sustainability lives in the shadow of the drive to maximize production, while that of localized custom is in the shadows of both the state, and of the new legal universalism. The new international requirements of state organization were spelled out by the World Bank recently:

> . . . the objectives of stability, predictability and elimination of governmental arbitrariness . . . are pre-conditions to economic development . . . (R)eform of the judiciary and the establishment and strengthening of arbitral and other dispute settlement mechanisms which help achieve efficient and expedient enforcement of agreements between private parties, resolutions of disputes and enforcement of laws and regulations is intrinsically tied to economic progress.[71]

The link made is between law and governance and the development of a market economy. Reducing state controls, supporting private property rights are central to the program, while state accountability, and the establishment of the rule of law are seen as important mechanisms of achieving these goals.

This concept of the kind of law that is relevant to the new development process may not be one into which a renewed emphasis on custom can easily be inserted. As McAuslan notes the new international aid environment is one in which donors place "a greater reliance on legal forms and a legal culture similar to that of the West."[72] But to be successful the promotion of customary law would have to fit within the new good governance, rule of law paradigm. In many parts of the world, while there is ground for some skepticism about the effectiveness of changes in formal law, there is nonetheless a state mechanism that is developing the capacity to carry through the kinds of reform suggested and in those circumstances claims based on the efficacy of the customary would seem to be taking the process backwards, potentially threatening as they are to stability, predictability and the securing of property rights in a market system. But where state capacities are severely compromised, and where there is a strong indigenous law, as, for example, in land tenure arrangements, a revitalization of customary law may well fit the paradigm, especially as there is a long record of lack of success in substituting imported ideas of tenure for indigenous ones, which, it should be emphasized, are not necessarily opposed to the clear definition of property rights. Furthermore, if improving dispute settlement mechanisms is taken to extend to the population as a whole, then the claim of the customary law for an enhanced role is very strong. While anthropologists established over the years the vitality of local non-state judicial institutions, these have been downplayed by a state-focused law and development paradigm. Such local judicial processes challenged the state, which sought to replace or incorporate them, but state incapacity now suggests that their relationship with central government could change.[73] But if the role of customary law is seen as defending communities against the market it will struggle for acceptance within current paradigms of development. As McAuslan writes, aid providers focus on the part of the economy that can be integrated into the global economy and therefore focus on "market facilitating law reform. Governance is seen as being that form and process of government which facilitates the operation of the market." And, as he says, "the rule of law . . . is being re-defined to emphasise its role in facilitating the enforcement of private contracts so that law reform to advance the rule of law is the same as law reform to advance the private economy."[74]

All of this provides a new context in which to consider the role of customary law as it develops in response to new political and economic pressures. The customary law has always been defined, as I have said, by its relationship with the state. As the state changes and as other loci of power emerge, the customary law will be defined within relationships with different partners and different ideational categories of law, which will affect both its content and its role. It is not simply the phenomenon of state collapse that is affecting the coherence of the model of a state-based law. Many of the post-colonial states have to cope with a legal pluralism brought about by ethnic and religious difference and the sharpening trends in communal demands for the recognition of special systems of law. At the same time, as Thome writes, "the global economy is producing a push toward supra-national law and judicial review. In the process, as Merryman puts it, 'The state is losing power in both directions,' as we are witnessing a 'redistribution of sovereignty.'"[75]

The chapters in this book have canvassed three possibilities for the governance of common property – state control, customary law and privatization. Development-minded states, captured by international and local elite economic interests and frequently undemocratic, corrupt and committed to a form of development that aims at a maximization of gross national product, have not proved themselves to be ideal custodians of common resources. The fluidity of customary law renders it an imperfect instrument for the definition of property rights, most especially because, while it has spoken a language of inclusiveness, it has not necessarily prevented the concentration of advantage. This may leave us with contract, the mode of autonomous choice, by which people can agree on the conditions of their use of the commons. It is important to stress that the abstract freedom, consensuality and rationality of contract exists only in the world of ideal types. The possibilities of contract do not exist outside of the cultures in which they are made. Not only do people bring cultural assumptions to any contractual regime, but all societies and legal systems place limits on what can and cannot be contracted. A contractual regime for resource management need not be, therefore, diametrically opposed to a customary one. It can and must be a regime that endorses and includes the language of new custom, and that takes customary ideas into account in prescribing the limits of the possibilities of contract. In such a regime, legal rights will rest not on customary claims, but on contractual arrangements. But the contractual regimes will themselves be based on current customary ideas and practices, themselves informed by older symbolic discourses. The considerations of who forms the community relevant to the sustainable management of a resource and what rights and duties they may contract for can be constrained by "new custom." Institutional arrangements that can combine both contract and custom, rather than "new custom" alone can provide both an individual basis for consent and responsibility and a cultural basis for the acceptability of measures to deal with new situations.

We have never, in spite of the numberless disavowals of an evolutionary paradigm, really superseded Maine's eurocentric evolutionary paradigm of the movement from "status" to "contract." This must be the final step in the development of a new jurisprudence of custom. If custom is, as has been said, expectations held in common, it is also this that ideally underlies all contracting. Societally defined notions of equity inform any contract law. Custom, once we concede that it is constantly being newly made, is a form of contract, not its obverse side. A new jurisprudence of custom must transcend Maine, as well as Blackstone and Weber, if it is to provide a framework for the place of customary law now. Custom as contract rather than custom versus contract may form the basis of a jurisprudential paradigm within which to develop successfully the role of customary law for sustainable development. A turn towards contract may appear to be a privatizing of inherently public issues. Can contract, informed by customary equity, serve as an instrument of justice in the governance of public resources? Both markets and contracts require the security provided by state regulation, and if the reducing capacity of many states leads one to look to contract (i.e. localized and private practices and regulation) rather than the state for solutions, the discovery will probably soon be made that this too will be disabled by state weakness.

It is important to stress, in concluding what I have said above, that customary law is a language in which claims are made, and images of equity invoked, rather than a set of rules belonging to and observed by a community. Cousins has rightly turned our attention towards both the absence of common goals in relation to the commons, and to the widespread misapprehensions in the literature about the relationships between rules and behaviors. He notes that there are contradictory twin pressures on the African rural commons (and the same could be said of fishing and forest resources elsewhere in the world) of "increasing use of subsistence and increasing commoditisation" that involve quite different users of the resources with radically different aims and interests.[76] As he says, "institutionally regulated patterns of resource use in small, stable, relatively homogeneous units is becoming rarer." Tension, conflict and "unruly behavior" are produced not only by the fluidity and ambiguity of common pool resource rights, but by the weakness of states producing a situation in which "neither states nor traditional authorities can be relied on for effective conflict resolution." In addition to the radical divergence of interests among users of the commons, he notes the weakness of the post-Hardin models of resource governance, which overemphasize the role of rules and rule observance. Endorsement of customary rule systems, themselves comprising ever-contested practices, does not bridge the gaps between rules and observance. The oscillating debates about market, state and customary regulation, produced by the growing contestation for the commons, must not be allowed to obscure the potential for violence inherent in the struggles to appropriate, or to preserve a share of, scarce resources. No kind of "law" – state, customary or international – provides a solution to violence and a collapsing social compromise. Nor is the answer simply to be found in the restoration of the authority of those states whose capacity is now in question. Yet it is against the ethos of this volume to end on a note of contradiction and despair. I have noted the continuing vitality of customary discourses, if not behaviors. The symbolic language of customary equities, which is called upon in relation to disputes in the areas of market, politics and law, may be the most fruitful resource for both struggling states and struggling communities.

Endnotes

1. For full accounts see M. Chanock, *Law, Custom and Social Order* (Cambridge University Press, Cambridge, 1985), P. Fitzpatrick, *Law and State in Papua New Guinea* (Academic Press, London, 1980), F. Snyder, *Capitalism and Legal Change* (Academic Press, New York, 1981).
2. See, in general, Chanock, *Law, Custom and Social Order.*
3. J. Ferguson, *The Anti-Politics Machine* (Cambridge University Press, Cambridge, 1990), p. xiv.
4. *Ibid.*, xv.
5. *Ibid.*, 28.
6. *Ibid.*, 66.
7. *Ibid.*, 70.
8. *Ibid.*, 71.
9. *Ibid.*, 71.
10. *Ibid.*, 166.
11. *Ibid.*, 8.
12. *Ibid.*, 256.
13. B. J. McCay and S. Jentoft, *Market or Community Failure. Critical Perspectives on Common Property Research*, p. 27.
14. See Chapter 1, pages 23–27.
15. P. Fratkin, "Pastoralism: Governance and Development Issues" (1997) *Annual Review of Anthropology*, p. 236.
16. *Ibid.*, 242.
17. Bromley and Cernea, *The Management of Common Property Resources* (World Bank Discussion Papers, Washington DC, 1989), pp. 57, iii.
18. *Ibid.*, iv.
19. McCay and Jentoft, *Market or Community Failure*, p. 22.
20. *Ibid.*, 23.
21. *Ibid.*, 25.

22. Bromley and Cernea, *Management of Common Property Resources*, p. 26.
23. Carol Rose, *Property and Persuasion: Essays on the History, Theory and Rhetoric of Ownership* (Westview Press, Boulder, 1994).
24. M Chanock, "Paradigms, Policies and Property: A Review of the Customary Law of Land Tenure," in K. Mann and R. Roberts (eds.) *Law in Colonial Africa* (Heinemann, Portsmouth NH, 1991).
25. M. Chanock, "A Peculiar Sharpness: An Essay on Property in the History of Customary Law in Colonial Africa" (1991) *Journal of African History* 31.
26. While I have drawn largely, though not entirely, on African examples, the "failing state," to which the Weberian ideal type of legal-rational law and bureaucracy is inapplicable as a model for understanding, is in differing ways common across the former colonial world.
27. H. Okoth-Ogendo, "Constitutions without Constitutionalism: Reflections on an African Political Paradox," in D. Greenberg and S. Katz (eds.), *Constitutionalism and Democracy* (Oxford University Press, Oxford, 1993).
28. Y. Ghai, "The Theory of the State in the Third World and the Problematics of Constitutionalism," in Greenberg and Katz (eds.), *Constitutionalism and Democracy*, pp. 192–193.
29. E. Hutchful, "Reconstructing Political Space: Militarism and Constitutionalism in Africa," in D. Greenberg and S. Katz (eds.), *Constitutionalism and Democracy*, p. 221.
30. N. Chazan quoted in ibid at 221.
31. R. Devisch, "Colonial State Building in the Congo and its Dismantling" (1998) 42 *Journal of Legal Pluralism* 221–224.
32. F. De Boeck, "Democracy and the State-Society Paradigm" (1998) 42 *Journal of Legal Pluralism* 89–93.
33. J. Scott, *Seeing Like a State* (Yale University Press, New Haven, 1998). See below.
34. C. Ake, "The Democratisation of Disempowerment in Africa," in J. Hippler (ed.), *The Democratisation of Disempowerment* (Pluto Press, London, 1995), p. 73.
35. *Ibid.*, 74–77.
36. *Ibid.*, 88–89.
37. Rose, *Property and Persuasion*, p. 73.
38. *Ibid.*, 74.
39. J. Fisher, *The Road from Rio. Sustainable Development and the Nongovernmental Movement in the Third World* (Praeger, Westport, Conn., 1993), p. xi.
40. *Ibid.*, 3.
41. See www.oxfam.org.uk/landrights/intro.htm (last accessed 22/3/00).
42. T. Princen and M. Finger, *Environmental NGOs in World Politics* (Routledge, London, 1994), p. 40.
43. C. Zerner, "Through a Green Lens; the Construction of Customary Environmental Law and Community in Indonesia's Maluku Islands" (1994) *Law and Society Review*, vol. 28, p. 1080.

44. *Ibid.*, 1080–1081.
45. *Ibid.*, 1081.
46. *Ibid.*, 1082–1083.
47. *Ibid.*, 1088.
48. *Ibid.*, 1105.
49. *Ibid.*, 1109.
50. *Ibid.*, 1114–1115.
51. K. von Benda-Beckman, "The Environmental Protection and Human Rights of Indigenous Peoples: a Tricky Alliance," in F. and K. von Benda-Beckman (ed.), *Natural Resources, Environment and Legal Pluralism. Legal Anthropology* (Martinus Nijhoff, The Hague, 1992), pp. 302–304.
52. *Ibid.*, 307.
53. *Ibid.*, 314.
54. 1876. Quoted by Peter Ørebech in Chapter 7.
55. *Ibid.*
56. Quoted in P. McAuslan "Law, Governance and the Development of the Market: Practical Problems and Possible Solutions," in J. Faundez (ed.), *Good Government and Law. Legal and Institutional Reform in Developing Countries* (Macmillan, Basingstoke, 1997), p. 25.
57. Scott, *Seeing Like a State*, pp. 2–3.
58. *Ibid.*, 6.
59. *Ibid.*, 300.
60. O. P. Diwedi, *Development Administration. From Underdevelopment to Sustainable Development* (St Martin's Press, New York, 1994), p. xi.
61. *Ibid.*, 7.
62. *Ibid.*, 15.
63. *Ibid.*, xii; 5.
64. *Ibid.*, 27, 29, 30.
65. G. D. Meyers, "Environmental and Natural Resources Management by Indigenous Peoples in North America: Inherent Rights of Self-government, Part 2. Defining the Content of Aboriginal Rights in Canada." *Governance Structures for Indigenous Australians On and Off Native Title Lands.* Austlii Reconciliation and Social Justice Library. See www.austlii.edu.au/special/rsjproject/rsjlibrary/arcerp/dp5/htm.
66. See *Ibid.*
67. C. Mantziasris, "Beyond the Aboriginal Councils and Associations Act Part 2" (1997) *Indigenous Law Bulletin*, vol. 4, p. 19.
68. *Ibid.*, 22.
69. *Ibid.*, 27.
70. *Ibid.*, 9.
71. World Bank, *Sub Saharan Africa: From Crisis to Sustainable Growth* (1989), p. 28.

72. P. McAuslan, "Making Law Work: Re-structuring Land Relations in Africa" (1998) *Development and Change* 526.
73. J. Faundez (ed.), *Good Government and Law. Legal and Institutional Reform in Developing Countries* (Macmillan, Basingstoke, 1997), p. 19.
74. P. McAuslan, "Law, Governance and the Development of the Market: Practical Problems and Possible Solutions," in J. Faundez (ed.), *Good Government and Law*, pp. 41, 42.
75. Quoted by Faundez, *Good Government and Law*, p. 49.
76. B. Cousins, "Tenure and Common Property Resources in Africa," in C. Toulmin and J. Quan (eds.), *Evolving Land Rights, Policy and Tenure in Africa* (DFID/IIED/NRI, London, 2000), p. 168.

9

Towards sustainability: the basis in international law

PETER ØREBECH AND MARTIN CHANOCK

Having considered the theoretical and legislative pros and cons of customary law, we change direction toward sustainability as principle developed under international law. We are interested in both how sustainability develops as principle at the international level (see Sections 9.1 to 9.5) and how this top-down pressure may involve domestic local or native customs (see Sections 9.6 and 9.7). This chapter describes the connection between international law and domestic customs in a world of expanding universality, and explores the position of general principles of sustainability and precaution as instruments of law and legal sources. The first issue is whether international law – by its building of legal principles like sustainability and precaution, opens up for wide range recognition of local customs proven valid to viable resources management. Secondly, our task is to investigate whether the arena of international law is unshackling indigenous customary law from its national state constraints.

We believe that the "ultimate test of a concept intended to have legal force and profound social and economic consequences is whether it changes behavior at both the individual and institutional levels."[1] This chapter reveals that the general principles of law and international custom as important sources of the International Court of Justice (ICJ),[2] evolve legal principles of precaution and thus also sustainability out of purely political ideas. Members of the international society of states have mostly embraced these principles, and international courts, in cases they have adjudicated, solve legal disputes based on the precautionary principle. If precaution or sustainability have become a *jus cogens* principle, it is – under the sociologically-oriented school of "objectivism" that these authors apply – peremptorily binding upon all national states. We will see that the precautionary principle has, for areas outside of cornerstone treaties such as, for instance, the WTO Agreement provisions on Sanitary and Psytosanitary Measures (see Section 9.5.3), gained a stronghold under ICJ general, non-convention-based environmental adjudication.

Thus, unless otherwise decided under treaty law, the case law basis of precautionary principle is valid.

This chapter further shows how international law considers local or native customs in the context of the protection of the rights of indigenous peoples. Both the Rio Declaration of 1992 and the Johannesburg Summit of 2002 call upon states to provide indigenous peoples with "effective participation in the achievement of sustainable development" based on their "knowledge and traditional practices."[3] Canada and Australia have been world leaders in recognizing the importance of validating the customary laws of indigenous peoples.[4] It remains to be seen whether other countries will take significant actions in response to this mandate.[5]

9.1 The customary law of the international society of states

Although customary law exists as a concept in both domestic and international law, its utterances vary in the different legal arenas. Customary law at the international level differs substantially from the criteria for domestic customary law (see Chapters 4 and 5) in at least four important respects.

First, while domestic law customs are norms developed bottom-up in competition with, and sometimes even contrary to, state legislation, customs among nation-states do not challenge higher ranked legal structures. It is the privilege of state subjects to decline from any conventional law position.[6] The superiority of parliamentary legislation over popular practice makes domestic customary law more vulnerable and less easy to develop. An international norm, on the other hand, may be transformed into customary law through essentially universal adherence, widespread participation or support, and frequent application. A Swedish international law scholar described customary international law as follows: "International customary law is clearly not static. On the contrary, it is dynamic and ever changing. A state intervention contrary to past practice which at first seems to express a breach of international law is simply the initial step into a brand new rule of law."[7] [Translation by this author.]

Second, no preference for ancient usage exists at the international level. As the ICJ held in the *North Sea Continental Shelf Case*, "a passage of only a short period of time is not necessarily, or of itself, a bar to the formation of a new rule of customary international law."[8]

A third factor distinguishing domestic from international customary law relates to geographically limited custom, that is, a custom having a distinct outer boundary. Domestic legal systems seem to accept geographically bound customs. In international law, however, the question is whether customary law may accommodate a regional or local custom *at all*. Two ICJ decisions support the view that it can. The *Asylum Case*[9] applied the particular customary law of refugees to the northern part of South America, and the *Indian Passage Rights Case*[10] operated with a "constant and continual practice between two nations" (India and the Portuguese colony of Dão).

The fourth and final distinction turns on law production. As international law mainly addresses nation-states, the law production role is shared with non- or inter-governmental organizations. Regional Fisheries Organizations (RFO), for instance, play a very important role in developing new resource management standards. Quasi-governmental entities such as these help develop customary international law, which is, in turn, binding upon all nation-states.

Science has also recognized the relevance and accuracy of knowledge obtained through widespread practice and derived outside the traditional scientific procedures and methods. Marine biologists stated their views clearly, as follows: "We conclude that fishermen can answer the question of local spawning and that science may use these data despite the fact that they are not gained using traditional biological methods."[11]

The question now is whether international law can legalize the potential that exists in local knowledge for viable living in local societies?

9.2 The incorporation of extra-legal rules

As a starting point we can see that current court practices are based on the following assumption: no social situation escapes rule of law. If written rules are impossible to discover, customary law or general principles of law may be developed by moral, ethical or equitable rules. The 1992 Rio Declaration (*Agenda 21*)[12] introduced the term "sustainable development" (Principle 8) along with the notion of "precautionary principle" (Principle 15). Ten years later, in connection with the 2002 Johannesburg Summit, Secretary General Kofi Annan said that:

> The major outcome document, the Plan of Implementation, contains targets and timetables to spur action on a wide range of issues, including halving the proportion of people who lack access to clean water or proper sanitation by 2015, restoring depleted fisheries by 2015, reducing biodiversity loss by 2010, and, by 2020, using and producing chemicals in ways that do not harm human health and the environment.

In addition, for the first time countries committed to increase the use of renewable energy "with a sense of urgency," although a proposed target for this was not adopted.

Moreover, rather than concluding with mere words, the Summit has gone on to establish concrete partnership initiatives by and between governments, citizen groups and businesses. These partnerships, in turn, contribute additional resources and expertise to attain significant results where they matter: in communities across the globe. "The Summit represents a major leap forward in the development of partnerships," Mr. Annan said, "with the UN, Governments, business and civil society coming together to increase the pool of resources to tackle global problems on a global scale."

As a result of the Summit, governments agreed on a series of commitments in five priority areas. Each commitment was then backed up by specific government announcements on programs, and by partnership initiatives. More than 220 partnerships, representing $235 million in resources, were formed during the Summit process to complement the government commitments, and many more were announced outside of the formal Summit proceedings. "The true test of what the Johannesburg Summit achieves," Mr. Annan said, "are the actions that are taken afterward. We have to go out and take action. This is not the end. It's the beginning."[13]

Although a report was prepared, no binding resolutions were adopted at or pursuant to the Johannesburg Summit. Consequently, the Johannesburg principles are no more legally binding than the 2002 ILA New Delhi Declaration on Principles of International Law Relating to Sustainable Development (the "2002 ILA Principles"). As Mr. Annan stated, the critical check is the actions taken in the years to come. Unfortunately, the two draft resolutions implementing sustainable development issues are still pending.[14]

Clearly, at the present time no broad and general principle of sustainable development is *codified* international law, whether by way of UN resolutions or under conventional law. The next question is whether these extra legal principles have been transformed into international law through case law?

Such political, moral, ethical and other extra-legal rules may become international law if generally observed and adhered to over a long period of time. As one important undertaking, the court should verify established rule of law or legal principles originally of extra-legal character. The *Barcelona Traction Case* stated that the courts' task is "to confirm and endorse the most elementary principles of morality."[15] An extra-legal principle that courts lay down through the process of adjudication is by definition "law." See the Statute of International Court of Justice, Article 38(1)(b): "The Court, whose function is to decide in accordance with international law such disputes as are submitted to it, shall apply . . . international custom, as evidence of a general practice accepted as law." The court identifies customs that qualify as sources of international law. Since recognized international customary law is binding upon all national states, it is irrelevant, for purposes of their domestic law, whether states expressively adhere to these general principles of law. Both monistic and dualistic states are bound by these principles.

These principles are binding upon all states whether or not they have contributed to the development of a specific practice. Advocates of the school of "voluntarism" refute this view, but since the *Lotus Case* is the only legal source for their position, it is without strong support. It is clearly stated that "the rules of law binding upon States . . . emanate from their own free will as expressed in conventions *or* by usages generally accepted as expressing principles of law."[16] The word "or" seems to indicate that the qualifying phrase, "from their own free will" modifies only the first alternative – conventions. Otherwise, the court would have used the conjunction "and."[17]

Customary law is often considered a legal source that fills the gaps of law. Since customary law and general principles of law actually exist, however, in principle there are no legal lacunae or gaps. As Judge Higgins has stated: "the judge's role is . . . to decide which of two . . . norms is applicable . . . As these rules indubitably exist [the validity or illegality of atmospheric nuclear testing], there can be no question of judicial legislation."[18] Because of legislative deficiency in foreseeing all possible future conflicts, customary law solutions may provide solutions for conflicts not covered by conventional texts.

Thus customary law, *a priori* of court adjudication, binds all members of the international society of states. The question for further elaboration is which customary laws may contribute most significantly to viable resources management.

9.3 Sustainability and precaution as legal rules

Clearly, treaty-based (international positive law) and customary law have been converging. Environmental concerns have been a topic for the international society of states for a considerable time. Take, for instance, the

1969 International Convention on Civil Liability for Oil Pollution Damage requiring Member States to install "preventive measures" (Article II). While the main concern under this early class of environmental agreements was the legally recognized restoration of private property losses, excluding pure economic loss, later agreements such as the 1972 Convention for the Prevention of Marine Pollution by Dumping from Ships and Aircraft target more widespread liability (for general property damages). "Ecological equilibrium" is put forth as a *political* goal in the 1972 Convention.[19] Sustainability issues are incorporated into these texts. Our main interest is the possible transformation of the political norms of sustainability and precaution into legal rules.

Sustainable development[20] is a top-down, internationally developed norm of social justice.[21] The 1992 UN Rio Declaration *(Agenda 21)*, confirmed it.[22] The 2002 Johannesburg Summit, whose principles have been adapted as national strategy by a large number of states,[23] as well as the International Law Association (ILA), further validated it. Customary law, for its part, is a bottom-up legal concept developed within internal legal systems. Our first task is to determine the legal status of sustainability, especially the precautionary principle. At issue is whether that principle paradigm has converted into valid law.[24]

Over the years several legal instruments have introduced the concept of sustainability. The Draft Convention on State Responsibility, Article 19(3), of the ILC, proposed that a breach of sustainable resource management qualify as a "crime by a state" toward the international community of states. Under the draft convention, sustainable resource management was defined as a peremptory norm (i.e., *jus cogens*; a universal, non-derogable obligation) whose infringement would constitute "a serious breach of an international obligation of essential importance for safeguarding the preservation of the human environment, such as those prohibiting massive pollution of the atmosphere or of the seas."[25] Even though some states were sympathetic to the notion of promoting environmental protection, the specific *jus cogens* proposal was rejected by a considerable number of states.[26] The opposition stemmed from the fine-grained nature of the proposal, however. No state opposed the principle of sustainable development as such. In this *lacuna* lies a possibility for evolving customary laws.

The *political* principle of *precaution* was first laid out in the 1982 UN General Assembly World Charter for Nature. The 1992 UN Rio Declaration subsequently recognized the precautionary principle. These international instruments encourage every state in the world to protect the environment by promoting "the precautionary approach." This means that when states are faced with "threats of serious or irreversible damage, lack of full scientific certainty shall not be used as reason for postponing cost-effective measures to prevent environmental degradation" (Article 15). The precautionary principle was confirmed in the 1994 Protocol to the 1979 Convention on Long-Range Transboundary Air Pollution on further Reduction of Sulphur Emissions (Preamble). The last brick in this wall is the 2000 Cartagena Protocol on Biosafety to the Convention on Biological Diversity. Annex III, Paragraph 1 of the Protocol provides detailed rules on how to "identify and evaluate the potential adverse effects of living modified organisms on the conservation and sustainable use of biological diversity."[27]

Today the drive for evolving international law of sustainable development is reflected in the 2002 Johannesburg Summit and the 2002 ILA Principles. The ILA declared that "States are under a duty to manage natural resources . . . in a rational, sustainable and safe way so as to contribute to the development of their peoples, with a particular regard for the rights of indigenous peoples, and to the conservation and sustainable use of natural resources and the protection of the environment, including ecosystems."[28] Like the ILA, the 2002 Johannesburg Summit enjoys political support, but its provisions are not legally enforceable. The ILA is an NGO, a quasi-governmental entity capable of developing customary international law (see Section 9.1 above). The United Nations convened the 2002 Johannesburg Summit. The UN General Assembly never got past the draft provisions, however.[29] Thus, the standards proposed in these instruments are still political in character and do not embody legal rules at this time.[30]

In specialized fields of law, the principle of precaution is now a legal one. Its legal status has been declared both in legal texts and in court decisions. The early signs of its legalization appeared in 1987. In 1990 two Ministerial conferences on pollution from ships (MARPOL 73/78) corroborated and validated its position as a legal norm.[31] Under MARPOL, member states must bring vessel-source pollution to a halt without regard to scientific evidence.[32] Since then, the precautionary principle has been set forth in other marine conventions.

9.4 Fisheries management under the precautionary perspective

Today precautionary measures have a place in most environmental agreements. The precautionary principle has a solid grip on fisheries management systems, which we will demonstrate and develop in the next section. Marine legal systems are based on sustainable resources management. Articles 63, 68 and 118 of the 1982 UN Law of the Sea Convention establish "maximum sustainable yields," which are a "system for sustainable development."[33] The concept of the precautionary approach set forth in the 1995 UN Straddling Fish Stock Agreement, Article 6 (cf. Annex II) further develops the concept of viability. Member states have a duty to adopt precautionary measures even when information is uncertain, unreliable or inadequate:

1. A precautionary reference point is an estimated value derived through an agreed scientific procedure, which corresponds to the state of the resource and of the fishery, and which can be used as a guide for fisheries management.
2. Two types of precautionary reference points should be used: conservation, or limit, reference points and management, or target, reference points. Limit reference points set boundaries that are intended to constrain harvesting within safe biological limits within which stocks can produce maximum sustainable yield.
3. Precautionary reference points should be stock-specific to account, *inter alia*, for the reproductive capacity, the resilience of each stock and the characteristics of fisheries exploiting the stock, as well as other sources of mortality and major sources of uncertainty.
4. Management strategies shall seek to maintain or restore populations of harvested stocks, and where necessary associated or dependent species, at levels consistent with previously agreed precautionary reference points. Such reference points shall be used to trigger pre-agreed conservation and management action. Management strategies shall include measures that can be implemented when precautionary reference points are approached.
5. Fishery management strategies shall ensure that the risk of exceeding limit reference points is very low. If a stock falls below a limit reference point or is at risk of falling below such a reference point, conservation and management action should be initiated to facilitate stock recovery. Fishery management strategies shall ensure that target reference points are not exceeded on average.
6. When information for determining reference points for a fishery is poor or absent, provisional reference points shall be set. Provisional reference points may be established by analogy to similar and better-known stocks. In such situations, the fishery shall be subject to enhanced

monitoring so as to enable revision of provisional reference points as improved information becomes available.

7. The fishing mortality rate that generates maximum sustainable yield should be regarded as a minimum standard for limit reference points. For stocks that are not over-fished, fishery management strategies shall ensure that fishing mortality does not exceed that which corresponds to maximum sustainable yield, and that the biomass does not fall below a predefined threshold. For over-fished stocks, the biomass that would produce maximum sustainable yield can serve as a rebuilding target.

We see that member states have a duty to implement management strategies and measures so as not to violate precautionary reference points. These features form the basis for creating legal institutions. In this framework, customary law may have the qualities necessary to become a *technique to reduce risks and uncertainties.* Instead of random "second guessing," one should "rely on past experiences."[34]

The Brundtland Report specifies the following ocean management imperatives: (1) "the unity of oceans claim effective global management regimes"; and (2) "the shared resource characteristics of many seas, makes forms of regional fisheries agencies mandatory."[35] These rather *vague, mostly political* norms become increasingly more precise through the implementation of the 1995 UN Straddling Fish Stocks Agreement.[36]

Under this 1995 agreement, legal obligations are *set in stone*, and legislative-administrative institutions (RFO) are thereby created.[37] The RFO are management organs, which, under their own foundation statutes,[38] have the power to initiate, apply and even enforce conservation and management measures on fishing stocks. They are entitled to develop principles of sustainable resources management. How far each RFO may go depends upon its own founding instrument. For instance, the Highly Migratory Fish Stock Convention (MHLC) of September 9, 2000, provides its Commission (RFO) with decision-making power. The commission (Article 5, cf. Article 34 MHLC) enjoys international legal personality. This commission must live up to the following political goals: sustainable use, precautionary approach, optimal utilization, cooperation and long-term conservation (Article 2 MHLC) throughout the entire range of stocks (Article 3(3) MHLC) within its entire distribution area.

Using its *prescription power*, the commission shall adopt conserving and management provisions based on the best scientific evidence available and assess the impact of fishing, using the precautionary approach to obtain sustainability (Article 5 MHLC). The commission shall also make its own provisions (Article 8 MHLC) compatible with the applied management measures within EEZ (UNCLOS Article 61) regarding how to minimize waste and deal with discards, lost or abandoned gear, pollution, bycatch. The commission should also eliminate excess fishing capacity (Article 5(f) MHLC) and collect data on fishing activities (Article 5 (i) MHLC). According to Annex III, the commission may determine the terms and conditions for fishing (Article 6 MHLC). The commission may also provide non-discriminatory trade measures to prohibit shipment of illegal catches. The interests of artisan and subsistence fishermen shall be taken into consideration (Article 5 (h) MHLC), as well as the needs of small states (Article 10(d) MHLC). Under Article 7 of the MHLC Agreement, those coastal states that are members of the MHLC must apply the provisions of Article 5 of the EEZ when implementing the agreement in their domestic law.

The decision-making procedure is interesting. Some decisions fall under a non-derogative consensus agenda (Article 10 (4) MHLC), which means that you may not opt out of the decision by means of reservation. TAC, allocation, and exclusion of vessel types come under this category. Other decisions are within the derogative consensus type. Article 20(2) cases, where all efforts to reach a decision must first be exhausted, belong to this category. A third category is the simple majority vote, which includes procedural cases, e.g. Article 26, on boarding and inspection. A fourth category requires decisions to be taken under qualified majority vote for questions of substance. A three-fourths majority vote is required to determine TAC under this fourth category, for instance. Finally, some sets of conservation measures and management systems require unanimous agreement by all member states.

The RFO enforcement competency is limited to taking measures to prevent and eliminate over-fishing and to ensuring that fishing levels do not exceed TAC (Article 5(g) MHLC). The commission must implement and enforce conservation measures and management systems through effective monitoring, control and surveillance (Article 5(j) MHLC). However, according to Part VI of the agreement, the commission's power is only subsidiary. As a starting point, the flag state has exclusive power over its own ships. Nonetheless, member states may deter ships of other member states (Article 25.11). Duly authorized RFO inspectors (Article 26) may board and inspect ships of other member states.

Finally, the RFO may also adjudicate disputes between member states. According to Article 20(6), the RFO has two avenues of review. It may appeal decisions to which it objects, and it may also appeal decisions made by panel (cf. Annex II). It may also opt for the system of special arbitration under Article 2 of the 1982 UN Law of the Sea Convention, Annex VIII. Alternatively, the commission may mediate or negotiate under Part VIII of the Straddling Fish Stock Agreement (SFSA), which applies to any dispute between members. Any remaining disputes are either within the domain of politics or under the jurisdiction of either the International Court of Justice or the International Tribunal of the Law of the Seas (Part IX).

The RFOs present a fully institutionalized system of sustainable fisheries management. The institutional disconnect that severely hampers domestic law is in place here as well. Of course, RFO decisions only bind member states. For as long as the principles of precaution and sustainability are not part of international customary law, no obligations may be imposed upon non-member states, who cannot be bound by any RFO decisions.[39] Thus, states flying flags of convenience are not bound to sustainable development obligations.

The provisions in Annex II of the 1995 SFSA obviously convey legal norms. The precise textual formulation under Annex II clearly dispels any uncertainty as to whether these provisions might be mere political norms. When a state becomes a member, the substance of sustainability is laid out in detail. Reliable scientific data are not required. States shall under all circumstances apply the precautionary principle to conservation, management and exploitation of straddling fish stocks and highly migratory fish stocks in order to protect the living marine resources and preserve the marine environment (Article 6(1) SFSA). The next paragraph (Article 6(2) SFSA) clarifies the meaning of "precautionary approach." Lacking scientific evidence, having only uncertain, unreliable or inadequate information is no excuse for states to postpone or fail to take conservation and management measures. Moreover, when implementing the principle of precaution, states shall apply the guidelines set out in Annex II. So-called "reference points" must be established. There are two possible kinds of reference points. "Limit" reference points set boundaries for safe biological harvesting within which stocks can produce maximum sustainable yields. The "Target" type refer to management objectives.

Customary law may serve as a procedural rule of the precautionary principle. According to Article 6(3) of the 1995 Straddling Fish Stock Agreement, the member states shall "improve decision making for fishery resource conservation and management by obtaining and sharing the best scientific information available *and improved techniques for dealing with risk and uncertainty*" (italics added). The most advanced risk assessment system found in international treaties is the Recommendations by the International Office of Epizootics (OIE – 1928 World Organization of Animal Health).

The "Guidelines for Risk Assessment" in Chapter 1.4.2 are also implemented by the World Trade Organization (WTO), see Agreement on the Application of Sanitary and Phytosanitary Measures Article 3.3. The Agreement on the Application of Sanitary and Phytosanitary Measures (SPS Agreement) recognizes the OIE as the relevant international organization responsible for the development and promotion of international animal health standards, guidelines and recommendations affecting trade in live animals and animal products, whether aquatic or terrestrial in origin. The SPS Agreement encourages governments to increase their use of risk analysis. WTO Members shall undertake an assessment as appropriate to the circumstances of the actual risk involved. The risk assessment method of the OIE has become the standard. See the extensive provisions now valid under the 2000 Cartagena Protocol on Biosafety to the Convention on Biological Diversity, Articles 15 and 16, cf. Annex III.

While the sustainability measures are based on safe scientific evidence, the need for quick action – which states are obliged to pursue under the precautionary approach, points to other forms of risk assessment. *Is customary law one such "improved technique" that the international society of states is searching for?* An experienced solution that is acknowledged by and safely anchored in customary law is incredibly better than risk assessment based on pure guesswork. User-group experiences manifestly founded in customary law represent just such an improved technique requirement. "Reliance on past experiences" is an important factor advocated by the British Inter-Departmental Liaison Group on Risk Assessment (ILGRA).[40]

When the 1995 Agreement recently entered into force,[41] an international law of sustainable fisheries management evolved, signifying the beginning of a new era in marine environmental responsibility. Resource management concerns are considered to be appropriate subject-matter jurisdiction by international courts. The *Southern Bluefin Tuna Case* added momentum to the precautionary principle. "*Considering* that, although the Tribunal cannot conclusively assess the scientific evidence presented by the parties, it finds that measures should be taken as a matter of urgency to preserve the rights of the parties and to avert further deterioration of the southern bluefin tuna stock."[42]

According to the Statutes of the International Court of Justice, the court's decision should be based upon written and unwritten sources of international law as well as international principles. The court's adjudications originate from *law*, not extra-legal principles. See Article 38(1): "The Court, whose function is to decide in accordance with international law such disputes as are submitted to it, shall apply . . . (c) the general principles of law as recognized by civilized nations." Because the task of international courts is "to confirm and endorse the most elementary principles of morality,"[43] one could say that the *Southern Bluefin Tuna Case* premises validate the *legal* principle of precaution. As opposed to former harvesting practices, one may argue that the recommended technique of reducing risk through assessment evaluations is now customary law. Through this judicial approval, extra-legal norms are *converted into bona fide* legal norms. The as-yet extra-legal principles that the court finds relevant are combined with the moral understanding of the justices and become "the law in action."[44] A principle that *has been acknowledged* by the court is by definition "legal." Whether it has obtained the position of marine customary law, *in casu jus cogens* (non-derogative peremptory norms), or *jus dispositivum* (customary law that can be derogated from) is debatable (see Section 9.3). Thus far it is sufficient to say that customary law is building sustainable management systems.

Since the *Gabcikovo Nagymaros Case*,[45] the precautionary principle has been recognized in general international law. The customary law of precaution is valid international environmental customary law, and not just an isolated principle under the 1995 UN Agreement. How should we track the instrument of customary law into the realm of sustainable development? Legislative action is not the only route. Legal dogma will take you there as well.

Basic to all trade-related environmental regulations is the scientific evidence requirement. Because of the often urgent need for action, environmental disasters might occur if *precautionary principle* based decisions could be dispensed with. Article 6 of the 1995 UN Straddling Fish Stock Agreement, however, requires states to take the precautionary principle into consideration and strongly encourages them to pursue "improved techniques" for dealing with "risk and uncertainty" (see Article 6(3) SFSA; cf. Annex II). Precautionary measures are such a technique when information is uncertain, unreliable or inadequate. This principle is promoted by the International Tribunal of the Law of the Sea in the *Southern Bluefin Tuna Cases.*[46] Because the 1995 Agreement is now in effect, the precautionary principle now has legal scope under the Law of the Sea, and is no longer just a loosely implied political principle. If replacing random solutions based on "second guessing," customary law represents an improved technique that by *de facto* functionality has documented its strength. This assessment is only possible on a precautionary basis. The customary approach produced a viable harvesting practice in the past, and may prove to be successful once more.

9.5 More illustrations

9.5.1 EU fisheries law

The year 2003 marks what was supposed to be the European Union's first year following the transitional period to a common fisheries policy. After more than three decades of resources degradation, the EU made enormous strides toward implementing sustainable exploitation strategies in a single year. This turnaround is not limited to the EU fisheries policy,[47] nor does it exist solely at the treaty level (see EC Treaty Articles 6 and 174). Instead, the EU seems to be headed quickly in the direction of institutionalizing both the precautionary principle and sustainable exploitation strategies. The Council Regulations are grounded in basic environmental law principles.[48] While there are several provisions that move toward the sustainable development goal, we shall limit ourselves here to the important provision of 20 December 2002:

> (3) Given that many fish stocks continue to decline, the Common Fisheries Policy should be improved to ensure the long-term viability of the fisheries sector through sustainable exploitation of living aquatic resources based on sound scientific advice and on the precautionary approach, which is based on the same considerations as the precautionary principle referred to in Article 174 of the [EC] Treaty.[49]

These bare ideas illustrate the important message of Dan Tarlock: ideas of sustainability need institutions to survive.[50] The organizational "takeover" of sustainable exploitation has clearly occurred, just as it has for the implementing measures. See in that same regulation, the preamble:

> (23) The Commission should be able to take immediate preventive measures if there is evidence of a risk that fishing activities could lead to a serious threat to conservation of living aquatic resources.
>
> (24) The Commission should be provided with appropriate powers to carry out its obligation to control and evaluate the implementation of the Common Fisheries Policy by the Member States.
>
> (25) It is necessary to intensify cooperation and coordination between all relevant authorities in order to achieve compliance with the rules of the

Common Fisheries Policy, in particular through the exchange of national inspectors, by requiring Member States to treat inspection reports drawn up by Community inspectors, inspectors of another Member State or Commission inspectors equally to their own inspection reports for the purpose of establishing the facts.

This evidence of risk, not specified here, provides the Commission with strong implementing powers. The competency of:

(26) The measures necessary for the implementation of this Regulation should be adopted in accordance with Council Decision 1999/468/EC of 28 June 1999 laying down the procedures for the exercise of implementing powers conferred on the Commission(7).

(27) To contribute to the achievement of the objectives of the Common Fisheries Policy, Regional Advisory Councils should be established to enable the Common Fisheries Policy to benefit from the knowledge and experience of the fishermen concerned and of other stakeholders and to take into account the diverse conditions throughout Community waters.

The Regional Advisory Council, Fisheries Inspectors, and the Directorate of Fisheries (DG XIV) are organizing a checkpoint and surveillance system. These entities will operate to implement and enforce the precautionary principle and sustainable development as specified in the EC regulations governing the management schemes.

9.5.2 Non-marine international law agreements

The precautionary principle developed within marine agreements and regulations is the model used in international law agreements. It appears in non-marine covenants such as the 1990 Bamako Convention on the Ban of the Import into Africa and the Control of Transboundary Movement and Management of Hazardous Wastes within Africa (Article 4 (3) (f)).[51]

Each Party shall strive to adopt and implement the preventive, precautionary approach to pollution problems which entails, inter-alia, preventing the release into the environment of substances which may cause harm to humans or the environment without waiting for scientific proof regarding such harm. The Parties shall co-operate with each other in taking the appropriate measures to implement the precautionary principle to pollution prevention through the application of clean production methods, rather than the pursuit of a permissible emissions approach based on assimilative capacity assumptions.

In Article 3(3) of the UN Framework Convention on Climate Change, to which the 1997 Kyoto Emission Control Provisions are a Protocol, all Member States agreed that:

> The Parties should take precautionary measures to anticipate, prevent or minimize the causes of climate change and mitigate its adverse effects. Where there are threats of serious or irreversible damage, lack of full scientific certainty should not be used as a reason for postponing such measures, taking into account that policies and measures to deal with climate change should be cost-effective so as to ensure global benefits at the lowest possible cost. To achieve this, such policies and measures should take into account different socio-economic contexts, be comprehensive, cover all relevant sources, sinks and reservoirs of greenhouse gases and adaptation, and comprise all economic sectors. Efforts to address climate change may be carried out cooperatively by interested Parties.[52]

Under Article 14(2) of the Convention all parties acknowledge – "as compulsory *ipso facto*" – the competency of the ICJ or an arbitration court set up by the parties to the agreement. The institutionalization step, so important to legalizing the sustainable development principle, has taken place here. The "institutional disconnect" so widespread in domestic legal systems,[53] is coming to an end internationally.

The precautionary principle has gained support not only in environmental law arenas, but also in international trade law. Article 5(7) of the important WTO Agreement on the Application of Sanitary and Phytosanitary Measures, applies the precautionary principle idea indirectly:

> In cases where relevant scientific evidence is insufficient, a Member may provisionally adopt sanitary or phytosanitary measures on the basis of available pertinent information, including that from the relevant international organizations as well as from sanitary or phytosanitary measures applied by other Members. In such circumstances, Members shall seek to obtain the additional information necessary for a more objective assessment of risk and review the sanitary or phytosanitary measure accordingly within a reasonable period of time.

As stated in the *Gabcikovo Nagymaros Case*, the precautionary principle is a casuistic illustration of a universal principle of precaution under *general international law* valid for the protection of transboundary resources. "Article 2 § 5(a) of the Convention on the Protection and Use of Transboundary Watercourses . . . provides support for the obligation in general international law to apply the precautionary principle to protect a transboundary resource."[54] Clearly the conventional texts are only codified illustrations of a customary law principle of precaution.

From this platform, international agencies may, under their discretionary power, develop customary laws of sustainability in greater detail. Since international customary law is binding upon all nation-states, the precautionary principle is a buttress supporting more extensive and expansive rules. For instance, under the 1995 UN Straddling Fish Stock Agreement, the RFO has the discretion to decide whether "top-down" or "bottom up" resources allocation should be considered.[55] The subsequent practice of international agencies is *proposed* customary law that may become *manifest* customary law over time.[56]

Further favorable developments are emerging from international law. As explained in Sections 9.7 and 9.8, international law is advocating indigenous tradition-based knowledge of sustainability. Does international law sanction the superiority of local customary laws to "the law of the land"?

The reader should keep in mind the underlying understanding of

> *indigenous knowledge* on nature . . . [as] a sort of non-scientific "authentic" knowledge rooted in premodern, precolonial culture and tradition. Ethnographers have documented medical, ecological and agricultural knowledge from different parts of the non-industrialized world and the potential of such knowledge for environmentally sound management of natural resources and sustainable development has been underlined, for instance by the 1992 UN Conference on the Environment and Development in Rio de Janeiro.[57]

9.5.3 WTO and sustainable development[58]

A difficult question – that relates to a variety of international agreements – is the scientific justification requirement. Accepting the precautionary principle is identical to rejecting scientific justification. Under the GATT Agreement Article XX (b) – the food security clause – trade embargo is valid if not causing "unjustifiable discrimination" or represents "a disguised restriction on international trade." Does the WTO encourage nations to take advantage of the precautionary principle as a basis for domestic restrictions on international trade? As mentioned in Section 9.4, the WTO Members[59] shall undertake an assessment as appropriate to the circumstances of the actual risk involved. The SPS Agreement recognizes the OIE as responsible for the development and promotion of international animal health standards, guidelines, and recommendations affecting trade in live animals and animal products, whether aquatic or terrestrial in origin. Thus the risk assessment method of the OIE has in different regards, become the standard. The WTO Agreement[60] strongly emphasizes the high contracting parties' responsibility for "sustainable development," but gives no opening for the precautionary principle. The preamble reads as follows:

> *The Parties* to this Agreement, *Recognizing* that raising standards of living, ensuring full employment and a large and steadily growing volume of real income and effective demand, and expanding the production of and trade in goods and services, while allowing for the optimal use of the world's resources in accordance with the objective of sustainable development seeking both to protect and preserve the environment and to enhance the means for doing so in a manner consistent with their respective needs and concerns at different levels of economic development . . . *Agree* as follows: . . .

Sustainable development is among the basic WTO objectives of strengthened attention in the interpretation of the WTO agreements. The indiscriminate free trade objective should be balanced against the objective of sustainable development. Important in the matter of illustrating the scientific justification claim of risk assessment is whether national trade restrictions are in accordance with WTO Article XX(b) or (g) and SPS Agreement Article 2.2. "Members shall ensure that any sanitary or phytosanitary measure is applied only to the extent necessary to protect human, animal or plant life or health, is based on scientific principles and is not maintained without sufficient scientific evidence, except as provided for in paragraph 7 of Article 5." Justification requires that a ban is "necessary" in order to protect animal life and health. Narrowly defined, nothing but scientific evidence is sufficient. Just what should qualify as scientific evidence is debatable, however. For instance, in the *Japan-apple Case*, Japan insisted that knowledge derived from "good sense" based upon "historical facts," was sufficient:

> In contrast, Japan argues, Japan's assessment of the risk reflects the historical facts of trans-oceanic spread of the bacteria, the rapid growth of international trade, and the lack of knowledge on the pathways of transmission of fire blight. Japan contends that the Panel should not have discarded Japan's approach to risk assessment, which was "reasonable as well as scientific" and derived from "prudence and precaution."[61] Therefore, according to Japan, the Panel's improper analysis of the scientific evidence

> underlying Japan's measure, failed to recognize the discretion conferred on an importing Member by [SPS Agreement] Article 2.2.[62]

By upholding the Panel's findings the Appellate Body rejected the Japanese point of view, which was "that Japan's phytosanitary measure at issue is maintained 'without sufficient scientific evidence' within the meaning of Article 2.2 of the *SPS Agreement.*"[63] Thus common-sense, discretionary understanding of risks, is insufficient to build a full-blown scientific justification case.

9.6 Conclusion: the extra-conventional principle of precaution

Summing up, the International Court of Justice confirmed, in the *Gabcikovo Nagymaros Case*, that "general international law . . . appl[ies] the precautionary principle to protect a transboundary resource."[64] The European Union declares: "Hence this principle has been progressively consolidated in international environmental law, and so it has become a full-fledged and general principle of international law."[65] While the precautionary approach is a general principle of environmental law for resources that are distributed across borders, we have no indication that the precautionary principle has been generally accepted. The international society of states seems to have adapted to this fact.

Thus the reach of precautionary principle under international environmental law is limited to areas of law not otherwise regulated under conventional law. One such area of codified law is the food safety clause under GATT Article XX.

9.7 Saami native rights under the international law perspective

As clarified in Chapter 2, the customary law in Norway is rooted in an order that pre-dates statutory law. Interestingly enough, despite this strong claim, the Norwegian public agencies responsible for Saami affairs have failed to give customary law its deserved place when promulgating their rules. Self-management of the commons must be recognized by public agencies. Therefore, even though the Saami claim has clear support in municipal customary law, we will have to determine the obligations imposed upon Norway by international law. Could this be the turning point for the indigenous people of Northern Norway?

This section addresses two issues. The first is whether native rights are protected under international cultural and economic obligations towards minorities. The second question relates to the human rights perspective.

The Chairman of the Saami Law Committee, former Chief Justice of the Norwegian Supreme Court, Mr. Carsten Smith, raised the first issue in a 1990 Report to the Ministry of Fisheries.[66] In a cogent argument, he stresses the Norwegian authorities' international law obligations not only to take Saami interests into consideration when implementing their policies, but also to *positively* discriminate *for the benefit of* Saami fishing. Professor Smith claims that Norway is legally bound to the 1989 International Labor Organization (ILO) Convention No. 169 and to Article 27 of the 1966 International Covenant on Civil and Political Rights, which states: "[P]ersons belonging to such minorities shall not be denied the right, in community with the other members of their group, to enjoy their own culture..." This provision protects not only the cultural mores of the Saami minority, but also *the economic basis* for traditional Saami trades. Consequently, this element of economic concern should have a place in the economic decision-making models with which fisheries agencies are entrusted these days. In complete contrast, the present Norwegian position promotes close-up operations, which *severely* limit the Saami fishing possibilities.

More than a decade has passed since these international legal obligations were enacted and since former Chief Justice Smith informed the Norwegian fisheries authorities of them. Nevertheless, Norway remains ignorant of it all. Thus, the traditional knowledge of viable fishing has still not been recognized by executive fisheries officers (see the resiliency perspective in Chapter 6). This continues today when only "few requests from fjord fishermen have received positive treatment from the Finnmark Committee."[67] Thus, elements which appear natural to fjord fishing households, but irrational to the bureaucracy, can be elucidated through a Chayanov[68] kind of economic dynamics.[69] There is a structural explanation for this: fisheries bureaucrats are glued to their *cost-benefit economic models.* Powerful interests pushing the corporate channel are efficiently blocking any influence from small-scale fishermen in general and Saami fishermen in particular. Both traditional knowledge and legal perspectives are excluded from decision-making processes in a physical as well as a technical sense.[70] Since the economic models of the bureaucratic policy-makers of central fishery agencies are macro-level oriented, the fine-grained nuances of local economics have no place in them. Resiliency adaptation (see Fred Bosselman in Chapter 6) is simply kept off the record. Policy-makers do not adjust their decision-making procedures to take local knowledge or legal perspectives into consideration. Presumably this structural barricade must come down before customary-law-based, viable resource management solutions can once again occupy the arena.

The second issue involves the 1950 European Convention on Human Rights (EHRC). The questions addressed in the EHRC belong to a non-ethnic or minority-based framework, but may fuel Saami arguments as well. As the Icelandic Supreme Court held on December 4, 1998, in a fisheries case reversing the Icelandic ITQ system that had been in place since 1988, an aspect of the "robbery of the commons" *is* affected by the EHRC. This convention provides relevant protection measures for small-scale fishermen, including the Saami.[71] Norwegian authorities have not taken either one of these international law obligations into consideration. Since the presumption rules the interpretation of Norwegian law (requiring that it be interpreted in accordance with international human rights), international law is obviously one of the background contexts for the customary law discussions. Fisheries agencies need to consider the following.

Just like the economic models of "privatizing the commons" cannot be separated from poverty and famine,[72] international law obligations cannot be isolated from the actions taken and the regulations promulgated by the Norwegian Fisheries Agencies. These international legal obligations *matter*. Does the 1950 European Convention on Human Rights force nation-states to keep a high social policy profile? The first question is whether member states to this convention are obliged to carry out certain kinds of social policies. Obviously, the EHRC as such does not impose any specific policy obligations upon its member states. Not surprisingly, the European Human Rights Court is reluctant to jettison the validly initiated and determined policy of a democratic state.[73] Specific international legal obligations, however, do set some limits on domestic policy implementation. Article 1 of the 1952 First Additional Protocol (FAP) to the EHRC guarantees the protection of "possessions." Whether the deprivation of public property fisheries rights constitutes expropriation may be disputed. A claim can be made that common property rights – and not just private property rights – come under Article 1 "possessions" protection.

Any "possessions deprivation" should be motivated by and based upon "the public interest." The decision should be anchored in a concrete need for public action that necessitates expropriation. To put it another way: "the compulsory transfer of property from one individual to another may . . . constitute a legitimate means for promoting the public interest."[74] Obviously the adjudication made by the actual nation state is determinative. This holding clearly shows that there is a considerable "margin of appreciation" in relation to the substantive content of the concept of "public interest." The sole possible reason for disregarding the judgment would be if it were found "manifestly without reasonable foundation."[75]

None of these issues have been addressed by the Norwegian Fisheries Agencies. Their lack of interest in international law in general and human rights in particular reflects the clout of powerful shipping interests and other decision-making instruments of *cost-benefit economic modeling*, which allows no room for externalities like international law.

9.8 International support for indigenous law

Any expanded role for indigenous law must be considered not simply within the context of nation-states, but also set in the wider realm of international law and international human rights law. International law is now moving toward supporting the effective participation of indigenous peoples in decisions affecting environmental protection and sustainable development. In 1997 the United Nations Committee on the Elimination of Racial Discrimination issued General Recommendations regarding the interpretation of its draft Convention in relation to Indigenous Peoples. The recommendations called on states to "provide indigenous peoples with conditions allowing for sustainable economic and social development compatible with their cultural characteristics."[76] Principle 22 of the Rio Declaration on Environment and Development of 1992 acknowledges the "vital role" indigenous and local communities have in these matters and says that "States should recognise and duly support their identity, culture and interests and enable their effective participation in the achievement of sustainable development" based on their "knowledge and traditional practices." The 1992 Conference also issued Agenda 21: Program of Action for Sustainable Development. Chapter 26 of this agenda relates to "Recognizing and Strengthening the Role of Indigenous People and their Communities" and reads: "In view of the interrelationship between the natural environment and its sustainable development and the cultural, social, economic and physical well-being of indigenous people, national and international efforts to implement environmentally sound and sustainable development should recognize, accommodate, promote and strengthen the role of indigenous people and their communities." States are called on to establish processes to "empower" indigenous peoples; recognize indigenous knowledge and "resource management practices"; recognize the importance to cultures to have access to renewable resources; and enhance the capacity building of indigenous communities. Similarly, the 1995 Copenhagen World Summit for Social Development addressed the matter of empowering indigenous peoples and "building on traditional communal practices" in resource management.

These approaches are set forth in the UN Draft Declaration on the Rights of Indigenous Peoples. Article 4 states that Indigenous Peoples have the "right to maintain their distinct political, economic, social and cultural characteristics." Article 12 acknowledges the "rights to practice and revitalize their traditions and customs." Article 21 further acknowledges the right to "maintain and develop their political, economic and social systems, and to be secure in the enjoyment of their own means of subsistence and development." In pursuit of these objectives, Article 26 establishes the "right to the full recognition of their laws, traditions and customs, land tenure systems and institutions for the development and management of resources . . ." Finally, Articles 32 and 33 acknowledge the "right to determine the structures and select the membership of their institutions in accordance with their own procedures . . ." and the "right to promote, develop and maintain their distinctive juridical customs, traditions, procedures and practices, in accordance with internationally recognized human rights standards."

9.9 Concluding remarks

We can see that if we are looking for recognition of the place of customary law in relation to sustainable development, we are more likely to find it in developing international law than in the national legal systems of the first or third worlds. We have argued above that the jurisprudence of customary law needs to be reconsidered in light of the diminished capacity of many states, and because governmental functions have been taken over by international non-governmental organizations. Likewise, the jurisprudence of customary law must be re-cast in light of international law's willingness to validate it, a trend in apparent contrast to nation-state legal systems.

Endnotes

1. See A. Dan Tarlock, "Ideas Without Institutions: The Paradox of Sustainable Development" (2001) *Indiana Journal of Global Legal Studies*, vol. 9, p. 35, at p. 37 – with further references.
2. The 1945 Statute of the International Court of Justice Article 38.
3. See Rio Declaration on Environment and Development 1992, Principle 22 (1992).

4. See Chapter 8 at pages 372–375.
5. While indigenous rights in Anglo-American jurisdictions arenas seem to carry weight, the Norwegian Saami are hampered by the extremely rigid cost-benefit-economics modeling of fisheries agencies which have entirely abandoned rule-oriented decision-making, as discussed in Chapter 10.
6. See Conference on Security and Co-operation in Europe, Final Act (Helsinki Accords), 14 ILM. 1292 (1975). Under Chapter 1 of the Declaration on Principles Guiding Relations between Participating States, states "also have the right to belong or not to belong to international organizations, to be or not to be a party to bilateral or multilateral treaties."
7. Torsten Gihl, "Aktuella problem inom folkrätt och allmän rättslära" ["Contemporary Challenges of International Law and Theory of Law"] (1953) *Svensk juristtidning* [*Swedish Journal of Jurisprudence*] 366.
8. ICJ 1969 3.
9. ICJ 1950 266.
10. ICJ 1960 6.
11. Anita Maurstad and Jan H. Sundet, "The Invisible Cod – Fishermen's and Scientists' Knowledge," in Svein Jentoft (ed.), *Commons in a Cold Climate. Coastal Fisheries and Reindeer Pastoralism in North Norway: The Co-Management Approach* (Man and the Biosphere Series No. 22, Parthenon, New York, 1998), p. 179.
12. A/CONF.151/26 (Vol.I), 12 August 1992. Signed by every state of the world.
13. Sustainable Development Summit Concludes in Johannesburg: UN Secretary-General Kofi Annan Says It's Just the Beginning, at http://www.johannesburgsummit.org/html/whats_new/feature_story39.htm#top.
14. Environment and Sustainable Development. Implementation of Agenda 21 and the program for further implementation of Agenda 21. Report from the Second Committee (UN General Assembly, A 57/532/Add.1).
15. ICJ Rep. 1970 p. 23. Supportive practice is found in the *Lotus Case* PCIL 1927 Ser. A # 10 and the *Nicaragua Case* ICJ 1986 p. 135.
16. PCIL 1927 Ser. A # 10, at 21.
17. This is further demonstrated by a close and comparative reading of the sub-paragraphs of Article 38(1) of the Statute of the International Court of Justice (59 Stat. 1055, T.S. 993, 3 Bevans 1179). Whereas Article 38(1(a)) describes the required recognition of the parties to the dispute, Article 38(1(b)) focuses on the general evidence of practice without regard to the origin of or the participation by the legal subjects. Article 38(1(c)) has the same focus as (b) and stresses the need for recognition by "civilized nations," rather than just that of the states parties to the conflict. We therefore adhere to the "objectivist" direction of legal thought, and not to the school of "voluntarism."
18. ICJ 96/583, 592 – *the Nuclear Test Case.*
19. See the preamble, second indent.

20. World Commission on Environment and Development, *Our Common Future.* (United Nations and Oxford University Press, New York, 1987). Adopted by the General Assembly Resolution 44/228 of 22 December 1989.
21. Michael Decleris, "The Coming Systematised State of the 21st Century" in *Tercera Escuela de Sistemas* (Valencia, 1995).
22. A/CONF.151/26 (Vol. I), 12 August 1992.
23. See, e.g., US President's Council on Sustainable Development ("PCSD") established on June 29, 1993 by Executive Order 12852 (58 FR 35841). The PCSD endorsed the Brundtland Commission's definition of sustainable development in 1996.
24. See G. Noland, "Ocean Frontiers: 'Initiatives in the 21st Century'," in S. Y. Hong, E. Miles and C-H. Park (eds.), *The Role of the Oceans in the 21st Century* (Law of the Sea Institute, Honolulu, 1995), pp. 218–220.
25. UN Doc.1976/A/31/10 p. 226.
26. UN Docs. A/C.6/31/SR.13–33.
27. Cartagena Protocol on Biosafety to the Convention on Biological Diversity, 39 ILM. 1027 (2000). This instrument entered into force ninety days after the reception of the 50th ratification, acceptence approval or accession. See Article 37, in casu 11th September 2003. As of this writing, a hundred states have acceded. Available at: http://www.biodiv.org/biosafety/default.aspx.
28. ILA, Resolution 3/2002, Annex paragraph 1.2, New Delhi 2002.
29. Environment and Sustainable Development. Implementation of Agenda 21 and the program for further implementation of Agenda 21. Report from the Second Committee (UN General Assembly, A 57/532/Add.1).
30. As recognized by ILA, Resolution 3/2002, Annex, preamble p. 1.
31. 1973 International Convention for the Prevention of Pollution from Ships, 12 International Legal Material 1319. For the 1978 protocol, see 17 ILM 546.
32. For further details see Peter Ørebech, "The Northern Sea Route. Conditions for Sailing according to European Community Legislation" (Insrop Working Paper No. 20, 1995, Oslo, St. Petersburg, Tokyo). Also published in (1996) *European Transport Law, Journal of Law and Economics*, vol. XXXI, No. 3, p. 313.
33. Protection & Preservation of the Marine Environment: Report of the Secretary General Doc. A/44/461 (UN, 18 September 1989), paras. 10–13.
34. ILGRA; Interdepartmental Liaison Group on Risk Assessment, "The Precautionary Principle: Policy and Application" (30 September 2002), Annex 3, p. 16.
35. The World Commission on Environment and Development, *Our Common Future.*
36. In force as of 21 November 2001. According to Article 40(1), the Agreement entered into force 30 days after the date of deposit of the thirtieth instrument of ratification or accession.
37. See Peter Ørebech, Ketill Sigurjonsson and Ted L. McDorman, "The 1995 United Nations Straddling and Highly Migratory Fish Stocks Agreement:

Management, Enforcement and Dispute Settlement" (1998) *The International Journal of Marine and Coastal Law*, p. 119, esp. pp. 121–124.

38. For instance, the 1980 North East Atlantic Fisheries Convention (NEAFC); the 2000 Convention on the Conservation and Management of Fisheries Resources in the South-East Atlantic Ocean (CCAMFR); or the 2000 Convention on Conservation & Management of Highly Migratory Fish Stock in the Western & Central Pacific (MHLC).
39. See Peter Ørebech, "Hva gjør Norge med sine 'piratfiskere'? – En rettslig og rettspolitisk gjennomgang av norsk domisilstatsjurisdiksjon p det pne hav" ["What is the Answer to the Fishing Pirates? A Legal and Legislative Analysis of Norwegian Domicile Jurisdiction on the High Seas"] (2001) *Retfaerd Nordic Legal Journal* 67, 82.
40. ILGRA, "The Precautionary Principle: Policy and Application" (30 September 2002), Annex 3, p. 16.
41. On December 13, 2001.
42. *New Zealand v. Japan; Australia v. Japan*, ITLOS, 27 August 1999, paragraph 80.
43. *Barcelona Traction* 1951 ICJ 23.
44. Roscoe Pound, *Law and Morals* (Chapel Hill, 1926), p. 80.
45. 1997 ICJ 7 § 31.
46. *New Zealand v. Japan*; *Australia v. Japan*, ITLOS, 27 August 1999.
47. Commission of the European Communities, Green paper on the future of the common fisheries policy COM (2001) 135, p. 4.
48. See esp. Council Regulation (EC) No 2371/2002 of 20 December 2002 on the conservation and sustainable exploitation of fisheries resources under the Common Fisheries Policy, Official Journal L 358, 31/12/2002 p. 0059–0080.
49. *Ibid.*
50. Tarlock, "Ideas Without Institutions," 35, 39.
51. Adopted 30 January 1991 and entered into force 22 April 1998.
52. Entered into force on 21 March 1994. As of 6 November 2002, 188 states were members.
53. Tarlock, "Ideas Without Institutions," pp. 35, 39.
54. 1997 ICJ 7 § 31.
55. Ørebech, Sigurjonsson and McDorman, "The 1995 United Nations Straddling and Highly Migratory Fish Stocks Agreement."
56. Ørebech, "The Repetitive Players Game."
57. Einar Eythorson, "Voices of the Weak – Relational Aspects of Local Knowledge in the Fisheries," in Svein Jentoft (ed.), *Commons in a Cold Climate. Coastal Fisheries and Reindeer Pastoralism in North Norway: The Co-Management Approach* (Man and the Biosphere Series No. 22, Parthenon, New York, 1998), pp. 197–198.
58. For a more comprehensive analysis see Ole Kristian Fauchald, *Environmental Taxes and Trade Discrimination* (Kluwer Law, London, The Hague, Boston, 1998), at pp. 345 ff.

59. As of June 17, 2004 the number of member states are 147. See http://www.wto.org/english/thewto_e/whatis_e/tif_e/org6_e.htm.
60. Signed by 111 states on April 14, 1994.
61. Japan's appellant's submission, paras. 81–82.
62. Japan – Measures affecting the important of apples, AB-2003–4. WT/DS245/AB/R, p. 288.
63. *Ibid.*, p. 91.
64. 1997 ICJ 7 § 31.
65. Commission of the European Communities COM(2000) 1 final, Brussels, 2.2.2000: Communication from the Commission on the precautionary principle p. 10. This was endorsed as the "European Resolution on the Precautionary Principle" (paragraph 5) by Heads of Government at the General Affairs Council in Nice in December 2000.
66. Carsten Smith, "Rettslige forpliktelser myndighetene er bundet av overfor den Saamiske befolkningen ved regulering av fiske." *Legal Report for the Ministry of Fisheries*, 1990 ["The Governmental Agencies' Legal Obligations Toward the Saami under the Fisheries Regulations"].
67. Eythorson, "Voices of the Weak," pp. 197–198.
68. A. V. Chayanov, *The Theory of Peasant Economy* (Irwin, Illinois, 1966).
69. Tor Arne Lillevoll, "Open Common for Fjord Fishery in Coast Saami Areas," in Svein Jentoft (ed.), *Commons in a Cold Climate. Coastal Fisheries and Reindeer Pastoralism in North Norway: The Co-Management Approach* (Man and the Biosphere Series No. 22, Parthenon, New York, 1998), p. 134.
70. This is one of the main conclusions of a recently finished project for the Power and Democracy Commission designated by the Norwegian Prime Minister in 1998: Peter Ørebech, Om torskeresolusjonen av 1989, Den skjulte agenda og ranet av fiskeriallmenningen" ["On the 1989 Cod-Resolution, the Hidden Agenda and the Robbery of the Commons"], p. 146.
71. See Peter Ørebech, "Do Fishery Rights Enjoy Human Rights Protection?" – draft paper under preparation.
72. Amartya Sen, *Poverty and Famines. An Essay on Entitlement and Deprivation* (Clarendon Press, Oxford, 1982): "Starvation is the characteristic of some people not *having* enough food to eat. It is not the characteristic of there *being* not enough food to eat."
73. Lars Adam Rehof and Tyge Trier, *Menneskerett* [*Human Rights*] (Jurist–og Økonomforbundets forlag, Copenhagen, 1990), p. 384.
74. *James v. U.K.* EHCR February 21th 1986, Series A, Vol. 98, para. 40.
75. *Ibid.* at para. 46.
76. G. Nettheim, *Governance Structures for Indigenous Australians On and Off Native Title Lands*, Austlii Reconciliation and Social Justice Library, www.austlii.edu.au/special/rsjproject/rsjlibrary/arcerp/dp5/htm4.

10

The case studies revisited

FRED BOSSELMAN, HANNE PETERSEN AND PETER ØREBECH

These issues suggest that we need to study carefully the technical and procedural details by which customary law systems operate to identify systems that are likely to promote sustainable development. With this objective in mind, we return to the examples of customary law in Hawaii, Northern Norway and Greenland. To what extent is the customary law in these areas exhibiting the characteristics needed to maintain sustainable resources management?

10.1 Hawaii: symbolism over substance

Native Hawaiians have acted to protect their customary rights to gather and hunt on privately owned property through the Hawaiian court system. Their efforts have achieved notable success in the form of the Hawaii Supreme Court's recognition of a state-wide right of native Hawaiians to hunt, fish and gather on all property other than property that has been developed for private residential use.[1] These successes have undoubtedly strengthened the self-image of the largest indigenous group living in the United States.[2] However, the victories of the native Hawaiians have proven to be more symbolic than substantive.

The ability of native Hawaiians to maintain their ethnic identity has been threatened by a decision of the United States Supreme Court in *Rice v. Cayetano*.[3] The court invalidated a Hawaii statute that allowed only descendants of the races inhabiting the Hawaiian Islands before 1778 to vote for trustees of the Office of Hawaiian Affairs. The Court found that the statute violated the Fifteenth Amendment of the United States Constitution, which states: "The right of citizens of the United States to vote shall not be denied or abridged by the United States or by any state on account of race, color, or previous condition of servitude."[4]

The court rejected the argument that native Hawaiians should have the same status as American Indians, who are treated as having a special trust relationship with the federal government that allows the government to grant Indians "political preferences" that will be deemed not to be based on race and thus not in violation of the Fifteenth Amendment.[5]

The *Rice* decision has been widely criticized because, as Professor Cheryl Harris puts it, "Applying a rule of symmetrical treatment to conditions, which are fundamentally unequal actually reproduces inequality."[6] The court's decision casts doubt on the validity of a number of other state and federal programs designed to provide special benefits for native Hawaiians, including educational benefits, small business loans, health care and homestead land.[7] Although the effectiveness of these programs has often been criticized,[8] they have been of some significant benefit to native Hawaiians.[9]

Native Hawaiians have responded by seeking relief from Congress, so far without success.[10] Some native Hawaiians have gone further, seeking independence from the United States.[11] They recently sought international recognition of the continuing sovereignty of the Hawaiian Kingdom that was deposed by the United States' government in 1893.[12] The Permanent Court of Arbitration Tribunal declined to hear the merits of the case on procedural grounds.[13]

Whether the Supreme Court's vision of a colorblind constitution might eventually overturn the state courts' use of Hawaiian customary law remains to be seen. But in the long run, it seem likely to be a matter of little consequence because the native Hawaiians' exercise of their customary rights seems to be more of an annoyance to their neighbors than a substantive benefit to the native Hawaiians themselves.[14]

The "ohana principles" that form the basis of native Hawaiian substantive law suggest a recognition of a need to conserve natural resources.[15] But native Hawaiians are not claiming any exclusive right to hunt, fish or harvest these resources, nor are they accepting any responsibility for the management of those resources. The native Hawaiians' success in court does not appear to have had any effect on the sustainability of natural resource management in Hawaii,[16] because the most serious risk to Hawaii's natural resources is not from the utilization of the resources but from competition by "unnatural" resources.

Natural resources in Hawaii are being overwhelmed by a process begun by the ancestors of the native Hawaiians themselves and accelerated by later generations of immigrants – the importation of exotic plants and animals.[17] The Hawaiian Islands grew from volcanoes rising out of the ocean over 2,000 miles from any continent or other islands of substantial size. Because plants and animals had to reach the islands after traversing huge expanses of open water, many kinds of plants and animals, such as reptiles and conifers, never reached the islands in pre-human times.[18]

The relatively small number of species that succeeded in reaching the islands found ways of adapting to the wide range of niches that evolved as the volcanic activity subsided and the environment became more hospitable.[19] Through "adaptive radiation," the original arrivals evolved into a wide range of plants and animals uniquely adapted to ecological systems specific to Hawaii.[20]

When the Polynesians became the first human occupants of Hawaii they brought pigs, dogs, chickens, rats and lizards; later, European sea captains brought cattle, goats, sheep and horses; the mongoose was subsequently introduced, as were more than 130 species of birds.[21] In addition, non-native plants were brought into the islands in great numbers. There were some 900 species of plants at the time Captain Cook landed. Since that time, another 870 non-native species of plants have become established and are reproducing in the wild. Many of these species are highly invasive, such as the Banana poka, lantana and blackberry, and are crowding out native vegetation.[22]

Today, many of the native plants and animals of Hawaii have become extinct or are gravely threatened; for example, at least 77 endemic species of birds have become extinct since the arrival of the Polynesians.[23] The "ohana rules" that discourage overexploitation of resources[24] will have little relevance if the native resources disappear under an onslaught of exotic invaders.

Much more active management of the native Hawaiian resources is essential if the resources are to remain plentiful. The most serious issue facing native ecological systems in Hawaii is the need for active removal of invasive exotic species of plants and animals.[25] This is a constant and difficult undertaking for which appropriations have been difficult to find.[26]

Would Hawaiian customary law have provided a basis for sustainable resource management in the absence of the wholesale invasion by non-native species? We'll never know. Today, the State of Hawaii recognizes the need to protect its native resources and closely controls any further importation of exotic flora and fauna.[27] But feral pigs, some of which are undoubtedly descendants of those brought by the original Polynesians, outwit the scientists and hunters that seek to control their expanding populations.[28]

10.2 Northern Norway: the Saami Ædnan

In an inaugural ceremony at the University of Tromsö's Faculty of Law,[29] Professor Carsten Smith, the former Chief Justice of Norway's Supreme Court, said that the future of the Saami people is irrevocably tied to the institution of Saami legal rights.[30] Although an ethnically based customary Saami law of fisheries does not exist,[31] this does not suggest that only universal common law applies to Saami legal rights. Rather, at issue is whether Saami practices have contributed to a customary law related to Saami "nuclear-areas." According to Professor Smith, "the inner life of Saami societies is anchored in ancient customs, some of which possibly enjoy the status of customary law."[32] The main point is whether fisheries practice actually qualifies as customary law. In order to determine this, the nuclear-area fisheries of the coastal Saami must be compared with the customary law prerequisites. Only persistent, high intensity practice qualifies as customary law. Do Saami fisheries participation rights qualify?

Since the early 1990s the open access main Saami cod fishery has been closed. Fishing rights in "Saami nuclear-areas" have been reduced and lots of small-scale fishermen have been forced out of business due to fisheries agencies' decisions. The question is whether the customary laws under which Saami fishermen have participated in the fisheries should prohibit administrative agencies from terminating the commons in the absence of specific legislative authority.

Unlike the native Hawaiians, and contrary to Saami living in the inland parts of the Nordic countries, the Saami people of the Norwegian coastal areas have not maintained their exclusive ethnic identity. While coastal Saami do not engage in any Saami-specific trade of their own and have intermarried with other Norwegians,[33] inland Saami have maintained their ethnic identity by the means of their exclusive right to reindeer pasture.[34] Coastal Saami now seek to establish legal protection for coastal fishing. They do not seek exclusive fishing rights based on their ethnic identity, however. Instead, the coastal Saami base their claim on ancient common pool practices, and hope to establish coastal fishing rights for all residents of the coast, not just for themselves.

Saami fishing tools and practices are identical to those of the Norse. The Saami claim no areas of their own – no Saami "land" or fishing grounds. This makes identification and classification of Saami fishing practices rather complicated. The Saami position differs from the Indians of North America who typically used special Indian fishing traps that differed from the "white man's" fishing equipment.[35] In the United States, land-based treaties between the Indians and the Federal government regulate the right of fishing.[36] In contrast, Norwegian legislation dictates that all Saami land is public land, and states that all people on the public land of the northernmost county of Finnmark are equally entitled to rights.[37]

There is no place for special Saami treatment under Norwegian codified law. So, if special treatment for Saami is to be granted, it must rely on Saami customary law. The underlying norms of Saami resources management protected Saami fisheries in a manner that never threatened the stock. Customary law provided seasonal protection by harvesting only well-grown fish, and not the juveniles. Cod live seven years before breeding. In the past, they could breed at least once. This is in sharp contrast with what happens today. Currently high sea fisheries trawlers harvest almost 70 percent of the stock, and focus their fishing efforts upon two to three year old fish that never will come back to the coasts of Norway to breed. The return to traditional fishing gear and practices would presumably bring back the ancient viable resource management.

As documented in interviews with the Saami,[38] the Saami social norms included a relaxed attitude towards fellow fishermen, whether local or from more distant spots. The social systems of the local fishermen never included the "ideology of grabbing"[39] or exclusion. The Saami principle of open access simply does not go along with the kind of thinking that reserves the maximum possible for one's own self.

In keeping with their own history, the coastal Saami have chosen not to demand fishing rights based on their ethnicity. Instead, the Saami ask that residence in the "Saami Ædnan" – the land of the Saami – be used to define the right to participate in the fishery, regardless of ethnicity. They seek open access to the coastal waters of Finnmark for all Finnmark residents according to ancient customary law. By emphasizing localism rather than ethnicity, the Saami strategy differs not only from that of the native Hawaiians but also from the strategies of the indigenous groups of Australia and North America.

Norway recognizes non-confirmed customs as valid property law as long as people themselves unanimously adhere to the custom (see Chapter 5.5). Most of the Norwegian court decisions relate to terrestrial use, which is characterized by multiple users and the conflict between the public as users and private owners. Since there are no private owners involved in these maritime issues, the potential for conflict is reduced. As shown in Chapter 5.5, some important off-shore and in-lake court decisions contribute significantly to the understanding of fisheries customary rights.

As the British case of *Blount v. Layard* illustrates, usage may be permitted through indulgence or owing to the carelessness or goodwill or good nature of those who actually hold title to the soil. In no case, however, is there a public right to fish there. Acceptance of the usage, however, should not qualify as granted rights. (See the opinion in *Graham v. Walker*, holding that "this right was not assumed to arise from a grant by an owner of land or an easement in it."[40]) To avoid confusion, the beneficiary should be notified that recognition is a kind gesture only. The justification of passivity is time balanced; the longer the period the stronger the reason to react against improper usage. Through the lack of protest, a *precario usage* may convert into legal rights.

Recognition conflicts are illustrated by the continuous development of new fishing techniques. Clearly Saami protests did not have any effect on these alien fishing practices. Instead of bringing foreign fishing disputes to the courts, the Saami appealed to the central government to legislate exclusive rights for specially reserved areas. This makes it evident that the Saami did not believe that *existing* exclusive gill net, hand line or long-line fishing rights could close fishing fields. The establishment of closed-entry regimes appeals to the political arena. Consequently, one cannot say that coastal Saami envisioned an open access rule as incorporating traditional fishing gears only. *If* there is a customary law rule on open access fisheries, these rights belong to all fishermen, regardless of their fishing gear.

Norway enjoys exclusive autonomy over all parts of the realm, including the Saami nuclear-areas of Finnmark. Undoubtedly, the supremacy of the Norwegian legal order includes the power to terminate improper customary laws, but the legislative body has never taken such an action.

In Norway, local customary law may prevail over otherwise generally applicable rules of law, as has happened in the County of Finnmark. For instance, in an 1854 Supreme Court judgment, the court upheld the local custom, where individuals who picked unidentified timber got an ownership right in that timber. This holding was contrary to the widely held Norwegian law solution, which provided the original owner with the right of vindication. Those on the coasts of Finnmark who retrieve drifting timber enjoy possessors' rights according to ancient custom.[41] Consequently, local customary law may supplant – and even contradict – the general law of the land unless national legislation puts an end to the local customary law.

Accordingly, there is a place in the Norwegian legal system for those specific Saami customary laws that are proven valid. The tests for proof of customary law in Norway are set out in Section 5.5.[42] The Saami must show: (1) that the policy of open access was perceived as a legal obligation (*opinio juris necessitatis*); (2) that the policy was in place for a long time; (3) that it was uninterrupted; (4) that it was free from dispute; and (5) that it was reasonable. If a policy of open access is to be perceived as an obligation, it cannot be merely tolerated (*precario*) usage.

Undoubtedly, after the 1830 Fisheries Act, an open access fisheries policy was implemented without respect to ethnicity or area. Two questions deserve consideration in determining whether that unanimous open access practice has become customary law. First of all, do Saami practices in the great fjords qualify as customary law, or have they merely been tolerated by the state, as owner of the sea?[43] Secondly, have the Saami initiated or practiced any kind of exclusion policy during the last 150 to 200 years, in which case fishing by foreigners may be nothing but tolerated usage?

In answer to the first question, according to principles laid down in the 1983 fisheries case of Lake Vansjö,[44] one could not possibly claim that use of outer common fishery results from the owner's generosity. The concept of King's Stream (the King's regale) never influenced the outer commons fisheries of North Norway after 1107 when the King's Gift (Rettarbot) transmitted the "regale," or fishing rights of the outer commons, to the joint ownership of the coastal population.[45] Later the 1604 King Christian IV Norwegian Codex and then the King's Resolution of May 27, 1775 codified the outer commons. Since the Norwegian State enjoyed no ownership rights in Saami fishing, no Saami *precario* usage applies.

Secondly, if the local Saami population actually had the power to exclude foreign fishermen whenever appropriate, then open access of foreigners is not the rule, but is only a factual consequence of implicit approval based on Saami generosity. Before the 1830 Act, such a conclusion might have been appropriate, but not today. The suitability of the *precario* usage concept depends upon whether the group of fishermen in question enjoyed the right to restrict other fishermen from fishing whenever they chose, whether or not the others' fishing actually harmed them. Considering the 1995 *Balsfjord Grazing Case* principle of *precario* usage, no groups of fishermen – under the same principle – enjoy this right of exclusivity. It is quite clear that no fisherman has ever succeeded in expelling other fishermen from any fishing field in the fjords or along the coast of Finnmark. Given this finding, *precario* usage does not apply here.

Saami fishing customs also meet the requirement of longevity. Duration of time is important to ensure that parties engage in conduct over sufficiently long periods to determine if the adopted conduct is widely accepted as just.[46] The long-time usage shows two things. First, it demonstrates that the actual usage or practice is not simply fleeting or transient. Secondly, long-time usage proves that the practice is recognized as a legal category. Additionally, it confirms that the usage has been followed by generations of fishermen, and not just by a random group who supposedly fished in that particular area. To fulfill the longevity requirement, it is sufficient that user-groups have reflected upon the legality and validity of the normative solution. That perhaps explains why no court has mandated a specific length of time as a minimum requirement, unlike the case of prescriptive rights.

Blackstone's characterization of long lasting custom, "that the memory of man runneth not to the contrary," describes the ancient claim requirement well. As illustrated by the 1888 *Trondheimfjord Mussels Case*[47] and the 1963 *River Herring Case*[48] the span of "time immemorial" is related to the memory of the living generations. With regards to the period of time, the 1995 *Balsfjord Case* states that a period of approximately 150 years will satisfy the ancient time requirement.[49] "The 1962 *Jessheim Case* of common pasturage states that 100 years is sufficient."[50] Some of the Saami fishermen interviewed who were born around 1900 provided first-hand information dating back to 1910 that fishermen enjoyed the right of open access. As a general rule, therefore, we may surmise that the 1830 breakdown of the special Saami exclusive fishing areas of the fjord bottoms initiated public property fisheries rights. Some information about the Varangerfjord fisheries seems to indicate special fisheries rights ("sæteiere"), but these rights were terminated around 1890.[51] Therefore, it seems that all fjord areas more than one hundred years old have passed under the hegemony of open access rights. Consequently, the ancient practice prerequisite is satisfied.

The Norwegian "firm practice requirement" is identical to the Anglo-American "non-interruption criterion." The firm practice criterion relates to actual practice and not to a belief or understanding held by the customary law right beneficiaries. Cf. the 1995 *Balsfjord Case*.[52] "Decisive is whether the firm and repeated usage is sufficient to confirm joint grazing fields."[53] The necessary continuing practice relates to an intense, customary practice that forms a perennial, uniform and non-fortuitous social pattern. In other words, the practice has to be stable. Just how stable is judged by the multiple uses of the sea, and the potential conflict between native and foreign fishermen. If the intended customary law is verified, lack of potential conflict obviously results in a reduced stability claim.

A shorter period of unanimous practice may then satisfy the firm practice requirement. Cf. the 1888 *Trondheimfjord Mussels Case*[54] and the 1963 *River Herring Case.*[55] Therefore, it is important that the constant usage fishery requirement was satisfied in these two cases. If these requirements are satisfied, one can justifiably conclude that conduct so firmly established should not be altered. Further fishery activity should be perennial or engaged in repeatedly. This differs from the antiquity requirement or "a number of years" or any other diachronic requirements. Instead, it relates to the strong effort behind the conduct at issue. The 1995 *Balsfjord Case*[56] is relevant in this regard because it emphasizes the importance of topographic conditions and the plenitude of nature. The hard, brute facts of nature substantiate that the firm practice engaged in is natural and logical. Lacking the practical remedy of fencing off intruders from fjord fishing grounds, the topography requires a system of joint fisheries. The fishermen of Finnmark have repeatedly confirmed a steadfast joint usage. The fishermen of Finnmark have participated annually and thereby satisfied the condition of firm practice. The common pool fisheries activity was not interrupted at any time. Therefore, the two basic customary law requirements of ancient and firm practice have been satisfied.[57]

In order to become customary law, a practice should be *peaceable* and *free from dispute.* If it is, the justification for or popular ruling in favor of the practice is found in good faith. This faith must be based on an understanding that the practice is legal. A unilateral understanding of legality is insufficient. Both parties engaging in or affected by the practice must recognize it as the law. The necessary undisputed understanding of usage or custom as the outcome of a legal principle does not exist if its lawfulness is disputed. The successful open access fisheries that did not enforce restrictions upon fishermen from remote locales reflects the awareness shared by Norse and Saami that "oceans are free" and that no village possesses or adheres to exclusion schemes. The interviewees' unanimous answer to the question of closed fishing fields clearly acknowledges the regional support for the principle of open access fisheries rights.

In judging reasonableness, the most critical question for Saami districts is whether the customary law solution lacks the economic efficiency that was cited in the 1995 *Balsfjord Case.* "The joint exploitation of the pasture . . . is of utmost importance for the farming industry."[58] The argument in support of an acknowledged customary law development is stronger if the practice is also economically rational. In the 1963 *Lake Vansjö Case,* economic efficiency is mentioned as an element to be considered when evaluating a proposed customary law. Even though recreational fishing is not economically efficient, the prior statement indicates that it would still qualify as *precario* usage more easily than professional fishing. Like farming, fishing needs a safe, predictable and reasonable framework. Given its tremendous economic importance for Finnmark, a *precario* usage solution is as unworkable in the fishing industry as it is in the farming industry.

The method of proving a custom among indigenous people is a question of evidence. What is the documentation required for recognizing customary law? We clearly need to distinguish between the *social facts* behind behavioral attitudes and the *institutional facts* that constitute the informal structures of law.[59] What people actually do may be different from what they should do.[60] Studies of practices provide insight into "ways of living," not "norms of life." The objective of the investigation should be to determine people's sense of justice. The "hidden institution" of customary law is significantly subtler than mere human practices. This explains the difficulties the Saami-Law Commissions faced in finding customary law.[61] Under the customary laws of the Saami, special witnesses play no decisive role. This differs from the Hawaiian system of proof by the "kamaaina witnesses," meaning persons "familiar from childhood with any locality," ancient tradition, custom, practice and usage, *in casu* the delineation of boundaries between private and public land (along the shores).[62] As Hawaiian Supreme Court Chief Justice Richardson held in *In re Ashford*: "The method of locating the seaward boundaries was by reputation evidence from kamaainas and the custom and practice of the government's survey office . . . In this jurisdiction, it has long been the rule, based on necessity, to allow reputation evidence by kamaaina witnesses in land disputes."[63]

The legal situation of the coastal Saami does not parallel that of North American native tribes, either. No Saami-specific fishery generates genuine Saami legal rules similar to Indian salmon trap fisheries of North America.[64] Contrary to the US situation, Norway has not recognized special evidentiary positions for indigenous people, so the Saami must prove their customs by ordinary evidence through oral and documentary presentations to the court. In the *Fluberg Pasture Case*,[65] the court based its decision upon the legal statements of eighty persons inhabiting the area. Interviews with fishermen in Finnmark indicate that should they be called as witnesses, they would support the position that the customary law prerequisites have been satisfied. Therefore, because those areas inhabited by the coastal Saami are subject to the customary law of open access fisheries, a fact which prompted formal legislation, those fisheries rights should only be terminated through formal legislation as well. Only the Storting may close the commons.

Can customary law based on locality function more or less effectively than customary law based on ethnicity? A comparison with Australian experience may be helpful.[66] The case of *Mabo v. Queensland* (*1992*)[67] and the 1998 *Croker Island Case*, (*Mary Yarmirr v. The Northern Territory of Australia*)[68] were important breakthroughs for the Aboriginal people of Australia. In the *Croker Island Case*, the trial court ruled that native title rights "in accordance with and subject to their [the clans] traditional laws and customs [gave] free access to the sea and the seabed."[69] The court held that each clan on Croker Island was responsible for an area of the sea, and could prevent other clans from entering that area.[70] The court further held, however, that this exclusive traditional right under Aboriginal law applied only to Aboriginal people, not to non-Aboriginal people.[71] The trial court decided that non-Aboriginal people could ignore Aboriginal law,[72] and the Australian Supreme Court affirmed.[73] This case illustrates a potential weakness of customary law based on ethnicity.

The objective of the Saami strategy is to assure the right to fish in the Northern fjords to all people living in the area who use relatively small-scale fishing technology. The Saami have succeeded in having the large trawlers excluded from the northern fjords and coastal areas,[74] but they have not yet managed to persuade the Ministry to reopen the common pool and again allow new local entrants into the fishing industry. Will the Saami strategy reinvigorate the northern fishing economy and provide for sustainable management of coastal fisheries? In view of the sorry state of many North Atlantic fisheries, it seems likely that any reduction in the use of large-scale fishing technology would contribute to the re-growth of viable fish populations. Given the difficulties associated with life and work in the Arctic, it seems unlikely that newcomers would overrun Saami Ædnan seeking the right to participate in the local fishing rights using small-scale equipment. Interviews among local high school students show that only one out of twenty would really settle down as a professional fisherman in North Norway.[75]

In the days when the local Saami fisheries were open, the resources of the sea were far more plentiful than today. The regulations promulgated by the Ministry of Fisheries, excluding the smaller boats used by coastal Saami fisheries, have not improved fisheries resources, which remain at a constant, historic, low level. The hi-tech fishing fleet, which has increased its activity during the same period as the Saami have ceased theirs, is the basic explanation for the crisis.

Norwegian fisheries biologists have proposed measuring total allowable catch in terms of the number of fish caught, rather than in tons. This would increase stocks and give strong priority to those who use selective equipment, such as the Saami. With this step Norway would adapt to the traditional knowledge of Saami fisheries and place longlines exclusively on fields occupied by more mature fish. Of course, current decimation of fish resources is occurring on a global scale far more extensive than simply the coast of Northern Norway.[76] Whether localization of fishing rights in this region could make a dent in the worldwide problem remains to be seen, but it would seem to be a logical step in the right direction.

10.3 Greenland: custom, adaptation and myth

The residents of Greenland exhibit far more ambivalent attitudes about their ancient customs than do either the native Hawaiians or the Saami. Greenlanders make up 85 percent of the population of their island, so that they are the governing majority under their home rule system. Unlike their counterparts, they have the authority to implement legislation enforcing customary rules, but for the most part have failed to do so.

In comparison to tropical Hawaii and even to the coast of Norway, Greenland is not an easy place to make a living. An icecap covers the bulk of the island, so that although Greenland covers some two million square kilometers, less than 400,000 square kilometers are free from the permanent icecap.[77] Only the coastal areas are habitable.[78] The landscape is largely treeless and not suitable for agriculture. Fish, seals and caribou are available, but not without hard work under very cold conditions.[79]

By custom, traditional hunting was a cooperative effort by extended families in which various rituals were observed.[80] Adult men dominated the hunting process, while young men and women assisted and all women prepared and shared the food and performed such redolent tasks as cleaning sealskins.[81] In the north, where the coldest and least populated parts of Greenland remain less affected by modern ways, there remain some settlements in which the old ways persist, but in the more populated areas of southwestern Greenland the lifestyle of the hunter is seen to be anachronistic.[82]

As discussed in Chapter 2, when opportunities arose for the export of seal products and for larger scale fish processing, many of the women of Greenland were easily persuaded that wage labor in a fish processing plant or sealskin factory was more appealing than their traditional occupation.

As in many traditional societies, the availability of paid jobs for women meant that the male's lead role in the economic process evolved into a more equal responsibility among men and women for the maintenance of the household. Women also began to play a more important role in the political process as they left home and participated in the market economy. And with improved education, the young people of both sexes became less inclined to play the subsidiary roles expected of them in the highly structured communal hunting processes that had developed through customary law.[83]

With the advent of home rule, the people of Greenland increasingly developed a national consciousness that was often inconsistent with the geographic localism that characterized hunting customs. "Establishing Greenland as a self-governing nation has given the national identification prominence at the expense of the local as well as the ethnic affiliation."[84] Former Greenlandic premier Lars Emil Johansen has emphasized two main aspects of the Greenlandic society which seem paradoxical: (1) In the short run the country is dependent on an optimal use of the natural resources to maintain the standard of living; and (2) in the long run it is important to regulate the use of the resources to ensure that future generations are able to make use of them. He saw the need for Greenland to diversify its economic base:

> Thus for Greenland a reduction in the catch level, or in the demand for fish products, affects the society severely. This emphasizes our dependence on natural resources – a dependence which is much larger than in a large economy with many export products . . .
>
> As we have seen, the main problem for Greenland when we talk about sustainable development, is our dependence on natural living resources. It is important for us to continuously maintain and develop the level of welfare. If we are going to succeed, it is vital that we become less dependent on the natural living resources. This process will, of course, affect the society at all levels, but it does not have to be so fundamental a change that it affects the society, the environment and the people in a negative way."[85]

What the former premier underlines here is that national and economic interests have become dominant over older values of caring about nature. To be overly dependent upon nature is something to be avoided. But his caution also reflects earlier Greenland traditions. As Dahl notes, "a hunter must have access to a large variety of resources and he must have the choice to behave in a flexible way . . . Hunting is based on the incorporation of new opportunities, rather than selecting one opportunity or one strategy as the only one to be followed."[86] The Greenlanders have "revitalized and reinvented ancient traditions in response to new realities."[87] Their resilient customary practices made them realize the need for diversification as a way of adapting to changing conditions.

During a meeting in Denmark at the beginning of 2002, then premier Jonathan Motzfeldt spoke about a change of mentality in Greenland. Previously it had been the general opinion that *everybody* had a right to go hunting. Now an important distinction is made between commercial hunters and leisure hunters. The basis for earlier customs, and thus also for earlier direct dependency upon and respect for nature as a means for survival and resource for food, has been transformed during the greater part of the twentieth century. Although Greenlanders are proud of their ability to have developed customs that allowed them to maintain a sustainable economy in a demanding and sometimes hostile environment, most modern Greenlanders prefer to treat their customs as a resource rather than as a limitation.

In the twenty-first century, the road may be paved for future hybrid norms and organizations that may draw upon both myths, traditions and customs in the regulation and organization of future interrelationships between humans and nature, and that may consider a diversity of both old and new values. The external image of Greenland and of many indigenous peoples has become an image of people who have a continuing tradition and practice of respecting nature and taking good care of it. This image is today important for the economic viability of an export industry based on marine resources.

Although earlier attitudes of dependence on nature may not rank high in government policy, they remain alive in a form that may be as important as law – myth. There is a myth heard again and again in contemporary Greenland when relations between humans and nature are discussed. It is also a myth that concerns gender relations. The myth is often called the "Myth of the Sea Mother." In the 1990s, two South Greenlandic female artists retold it in a children's book.[88] This myth is still a source of inspiration and contemplation in contemporary Greenland.[89]

NERRIVIK[90]

A bird once wished to marry a woman. He got himself a fine sealskin coat, and having weak eyes, made spectacles out of a walrus tusk, for, he was greatly set upon looking as nice as possible. Then he set off, in the shape of a man and coming to a village, took a wife, and brought her home.

Now he began to go out catching fish, which he called seal, and brought home to his wife.

> Once it happened that he lost his spectacles, and his wife, seeing his bad eyes, burst out weeping, because he was so ugly.
>
> But her husband only laughed. "Oho, so you saw my eyes? Hahaha!" And he put on his spectacles again.
>
> Then her brothers, who longed for their sister, came out one day to visit her. And her husband being out hunting, they took her away with them. The husband was greatly distressed when he came home and found her gone, and thinking someone must have carried her off, he set out in pursuit. He swung his wings with mighty force, and raised a violent storm, for he was a great wizard.
>
> When the storm came up, the boat began to take in water, and the wind grew fiercer, as he doubled the beating of his wings. The waves rose white with foam, and the boat was near turning over. And when those in the boat began to suspect that the woman was the cause of the storm, they took her up and cast her into the sea. She tried to grasp the side of the boat, but then her grandfather sprang up and cut off her hand.
>
> And so she was drowned. But at the bottom of the sea, she became Nerrivik, the ruler over all the creatures in the sea. And when men catch no seal, then the wizards go down to Nerrivik. Having but one hand, she cannot comb her hair, and this they do for her, and she, by way of thanks, sends seal and other creatures forth to men.

This is the tale of the ruler of the sea. Men call her Nerrivik[91] because she gives them food.[92]

In his book *The Wisdom of the Mythtellers*, Sean Kane writes that the intertia of social habit cannot be overestimated. "Myths are embodied in the customs of a people, and the customs replicate the essential patterns of a mythology with each of its aspects a sign pointing to another sign in an endless circularity."[93] The well-known scholar of religion, Mircea Eliade, writes that in many societies myth "supplies models for human behaviour and, by that very fact, gives meaning and value to life."[94] He continues:

> Myths are the most general and effective means of awakening and maintaining consciousness of another world, a beyond, whether it be the divine world or the world of ancestors. This "other world" represents a superhuman "transcendent" plane, the plane of absolute realities. It is the experience of the sacred – that is, an encounter with a trans-human reality – which gives birth to the idea that something really exists, that hence there are absolute *values*, capable of guiding man, and giving a meaning to human existence. It is then, through the experience of the sacred that the ideas of reality, truth and significance first dawn, to be later elaborated and systematized by metaphysical speculation.[95]

Myths are thus embodied in customs, and myths are about values, which are capable of guiding humans and giving meaning to human existence. During the last decade there has been a lot of discussion about ethics and law, and of the values underlying western legal thought. The discussion about sustainability is in part a discussion about the necessity of broadening the value base of western and international rule-making. Sustainability may also be seen as a standard for decision-making, but standards are often also related to values, which are capable of guiding people in situations of insecurity and uncertainty. The Myth of the Sea Mother actually presents and represents quite a long list of values:

- marriage (relationship between humans and humans and nature);
- beauty;
- vision (good/beautiful eyes/eyesight);
- maintenance;
- food, seal, marine animals;
- family relationship and love;
- visits;
- joy;
- power and (supernatural) strength;
- survival;
- intuition;
- sacrifice;
- gratitude;
- helpfulness; and
- generosity.

This rather long list – of at least fifteen different values – indicates the complexity of values that may have been underlying relationships between humans and nature in earlier Greenland. These values overlap and are mixed and combined, and the way they are celebrated and cultivated is ambiguous. For example, a custom of meat gifts existed in earlier Greenland, where the generous giving of meat gifts was a necessity for survival in a society without welfare state regulation. It survives in watered-down versions in contemporary Greenland but mostly in family relations. It is still an expression of the need for maintenance, helpfulness and generosity. But it may be of less importance in teaching the values of respect and care for animal life.

The Myth of the Sea Mother is also a story about metamorphosis of humans and animals, about relations between humans and animals – as relations of both love and dependence, and about violent sacrifice of humans to nature for the purpose of both peaceful conditions and survival. Sacrifice, from the Latin *sacrificare*, means to make holy. The woman in the story, who has married an animal with supernatural force, is sacrificed – made holy – in order to establish a proper relationship with nature – mediated through shamanic visits. In the contemporary versions of the myth this is understood as a need to respect nature. If humans do not treat marine animals well, and if they pollute their living conditions, then the Sea Mother will withhold the animals until practices have changed.

Myths with similar values are found throughout the Inuit people. Murray Sinclair, an aboriginal judge from Manitoba, describes characteristics of aboriginal belief systems, world views and life philosophies as being so fundamentally different from those of the dominant Euro-Canadian society that they are inherently in conflict. He says that many Euro-Canadian institutions are incompatible with the moral and ethical value systems of Aboriginal Canadians.

> The Aboriginal world view holds that human beings are the least powerful and least important element in creation. They cannot influence events, and are disrespectful if they try. Human interests are not to be placed above those of any other part of creation. Regarding the relative hierarchy and importance of beings in creation therefore, Aboriginal and Western traditions are diametrically opposed.[96]
>
> . . .
>
> Most Aboriginal societies value the interrelated principles of individual autonomy and freedom, so long as their exercise is consistent with the preservation of relationships and community harmony. Other values include respect for other human (and non-human) beings, reluctance to criticize and interfere with others, and avoidance of confrontation.[97]

A book entitled *A Farewell to Greenland's Wildlife*, written by Danish environmentalist journalist, Kjeld Hansen,[98] and translated into Greenlandic, has sparked a considerable debate about the unsustainable ways of hunting in Greenland. Sustainability is, of course, seen and understood through the lens of the sustainability-friendly Danish in this work. In August 2002 a meeting was held in the Zoological Garden in Copenhagen to discuss problems relating to protection and administration of nature in Greenland. A new NGO concerned with nature conservation in Greenland, Uppik, was also introduced at this meeting. The meeting materials warned that "The atmosphere is changing: regulations must be observed." Obviously, given this language, adherence to regulations was not the norm. This demonstrates both the continuing power of custom and the fact that it is not always possible for people to observe imitated and imported regulations such as the marine environmental protection regulations at issue. Regulations such as these have rarely taken into account the huge distances and scarce populations that define arctic conditions.

What seems to work, and what seems to have an impact on Greenlandic politics and regulation are market pressure and a threat to the national image that could negatively impact export income. We should not overestimate the role and importance of either custom or regulation as a form for achieving sustainability. The interest in customs by people who are also interested in furthering a sustainable society on both the local and global levels is probably inspired by the impression or experience of a broader range of values than those that underly many local customs.

On a state level as well as on an international level, there is little doubt that it has been very difficult to include the diversity of customary values. Nevertheless, customs and customary law will very likely become more important in a globalized world, as will standards such as sustainability. Danish national law may not gain hegemony in Greenland, but the importance of the world market and market regulation will probably mean that the old local customs will come under very strong internal and external pressure. We must hope that some of the earlier sustainability-rewarding values survive in the future legal landscape, and that the Inuit of Greenland continue to be adept at selecting new cultural items and absorbing them into their culture in a non-disruptive way. As Mark Nuttall noted a decade ago,

> What is striking about Inuit is a willingness to see potential and possibility in all things; not only in commodities, but in people, kinship, animals and the environment, in imported belief systems and in modern technology. In being re-shaped and modified, new cultural items take on new meanings and, rather than being necessarily disruptive, can actually go some way to convey, express and strengthen fundamental tenets of local unity.[99]

Endnotes

1. *State of Hawai' i v. Hanapi*, 970 P.2d 485 (1998). See Section 2.1. See also Ka Pa'akai.
2. Statement of Eni F. H. Faleomaraega, hearing before the United States Senate Committee on Indian Affairs, September 14, 2000. The 2000 census allowed

people to report one or more races. A total of 141,000 respondents reported Native Hawaiian only and an additional 261,000 reported Native Hawaiian and another race. US Census Bureau, the Native Hawaiian and other Pacific Islander Population: 2000, p. 8 (December 2001).

3. 528 U.S. 495 (2000).
4. US Constitution Amend XV, section 1.
5. *Morton v. Mancari*, 417 U.S. 535 (1974).
6. Cheryl I. Harris, "Equal Treatment and the Reproduction of Inequality" (2001) 69 *Fordham Law Review*, 1753.
7. Becky T. Chestnut, "Matters of Trust: Unanswered Questions after Rice v. Cayetano" (2000) *Hawaii Law Review*, vol. 23, pp. 363, 386–387. See United States Senate Committee on Appropriations, Special Hearing of Federally Funded Native Hawaiian Programs, August 16, 1999 (106th Congress, 1st Session).
8. See Hawaii Advisory Committee to the United States Commission on Civil Rights "A Broken Trust: The Hawaiian Homelands Program: Seventy Years of Failure of the Federal and State Governments to Protect the Civil Rights of Native Hawaiians" (1991).
9. See US Department of the Interior and Department of Justice, "From Mauka to Makai: The River of Justice Must Flow Freely: Report of the Reconciliation Process between the Federal Government and Native Hawaiians" (2000), pp. 30–35, 45–48. See generally the website of the state's Office of Hawaiian Affairs, www.oha.org/index3.html and the Department of Hawaiian Home Lands, www.state.hi.us/dhhl/.
10. S. 1783, A Bill expressing the policy of the United States relationship with Native Hawaiians and to provide for a process for the recognition by the United States of the Native Hawaiian governing entity, and for other purposes. 107th Congress, 1st session (2001). See Annmarie M. Liermann, "Seeking Sovereignty: The Akaka Bill and the Case for the Inclusion of Hawaiians in Federal Native American Policy" (2001) *Santa Clara Law Review*, vol. 41, p. 509.
11. See Eric Steven O'Malley, "Irreconcilable Rights and the Question of Hawaiian Statehood" (2001) *Georgetown Law Journal*, vol. 89, p. 501.
12. *Larsen v. The Hawaiian Kingdom*, www.pca-cpa.org.
13. See David J. Bederman and Kurt R. Hilbert, "International Decision: Lance Paul Larsen v. The Hawaiian Kingdom" (2001) *American Journal of International Law*, vol. 95, pp. 927, 929–930.
14. See Greg Barrett, "Custom in Hawaii: Hawaiians Thundering Protest Shakes Private Property Debate" (April 29, 1997) *Christian Science Monitor* 3.
15. See Section 2.1, pp. 45–46.
16. A high percentage of land in Hawaii is publicly owned. For a description of the process of public land management in Hawaii, see David L. Callies, *Regulating Paradise: Land Use Controls in Hawaii* (University of Hawaii Press, Honolulu, 1984), pp. 153–162.

17. Lloyd L. Loope and Dieter Mueller-Dombois, "Characteristics of Invaded Islands, with Special Reference to Hawaii," in J. A. Drake (ed.), *Biological Invasions: A Global Perspective* (SCOPE/ICSU, John Wiley, Chichester and New York, 1989), pp. 257, 260–263.
18. Sherwin Carlquist, *Hawaii: A Natural History* (Natural History Press, Garden City NY, 1970), p. 82. See also Christina Heliker, "The Volcanic Origin of the Hawaiian Islands," in Charles P. Stone and Danielle B. Stone (eds.), *Conservation Biology in Hawai'i.*
19. Leonard A. Freed, "Extinction and Endangerment of Hawaiian Honeycreepers: A Comparative Approach," in Laura A. Landweber and Andrew P. Dobson (eds.), *Genetics and the Extinction of Species* (Princeton University Press, Princeton NJ, 1999), pp. 137, 155–156; Robert J. Whittaker, *Island Biogeography: Ecology, Evolution, and Conservation* (Oxford University Press, Oxford, 1998), pp. 93–104.
20. Bruce A. Stein et al., "A Remarkable Array: Species Diversity in the United States," in Bruce A. Stein et al. (eds.), *Precious Heritage: The Status of Biodiversity in the United States* (Oxford University Press, New York, 2000), pp. 55, 89–92. See generally Dolph Schluter, *The Ecology of Adaptive Radiation* (Oxford University Press, Oxford, 2000).
21. Charles P. Stone, "Non-Native Land Vertebrates," in Stone and Stone (eds.) *Conservation Biology in Hawai'i*, pp. 88–91.
22. Clifford W. Smith, "Non-Native Plants," in Stone and Stone (eds.), *Conservation Biology in Hawai'i*, p. 60.
23. National Research Council, *Science and the Endangered Species Act* (National Academy Press, Washington DC, 1995), pp. 31–32. Other estimates range from about sixty to over a hundred species of birds lost in Hawaii. Whittaker, *Island Biogeography*, p. 236.
24. See Section 2.1.
25. Freed, "Extinction and Endangerment of Hawaiian Honeycreepers," pp. 137, 151–155.
26. Faith Campbell, "The Appropriations History," in Kathryn A. Kohm (ed.), *Balancing on the Brink of Extinction* (Island Press, Washington DC, 1991), pp. 134, 139, 142–143.
27. Lloyd L. Loope, "Hawaii and the Pacific Islands," in *United States Geological Survey, Status and Trends of the Nation's Biological Resources* (accessed December 4, 2001).
28. Kenneth Brower, "The Pig War," in Frank Stewart (ed.), *A World Between the Waves* (Island Press, Washington DC, 1992), p. 71.
29. March 25, 1987.
30. Carsten Smith, *Samerett – gamle rettskilder og ny rettsdisiplin* [*Saami Law – Ancient Courses of Law and a New Legal Discipline*] No. 1 (Institutt for rettsvitenskap skriftserie, Tromsö, 1987) p. 1.

31. See Section 2.2.
32. Smith, *Samerett*, p. 2.
33. Hurst Hannum, *Autonomy, Sovereignty, and Self-Determination: The Accommodation of Conflicting Rights* (University of Pennsylvania Press, 1990), p. 248.
34. Hugh Beach, "The Saami of Lapland," in Mark Nuttall (ed.) *Polar Peoples: Self-Determination and Development* (Minority Rights Group, London, 1994), pp. 152–155.
35. See Hilary Stewart, *Indian Fishing. Early Methods on the Northwest Coast* (Douglas & McIntyre, Vancouver, 1982), pp. 99 ff.
36. See pages 61–62.
37. Resolution of 27 May 1775 § 6 and Act of 12 March 1965 on State Possession to Unregistered Land of Finnmark.
38. Some of which is presented in Chapter 2.
39. Trygve Haavelmo, *A Study in the Theory of Economic Evolution. Section 19: Strategies of Grabbing, Protection and Cooperation* (North Holland Publishing Company, Amsterdam, 1954).
40. 61 A. 98 (1905).
41. Rt. 1854 s. 412.
42. See pages 233–240 above.
43. The King's Streams of the Middle Ages, see Arnold Rœstad, *Kongens Strømme. Historiske og folkerettslige undersøkelser angaaende sjøterritoriet* [*Kings' Streams. Historical and International Law Investigations regarding Territorial Sea*] (Kristiania, 1912).
44. Rt. 1983 s. 569.
45. Peter Ørebech, *Om allemannsrettigheter. Særlig med henblikk på rettsvernet for fiske ved igangsetting og utøving av petroleumsvirksomhet* [*Public Property Rights. With a Special Emphasis on the Conflict between the Fishing and Petroleum Industries*] (Osmundsson, Oslo, 1991), Chapter 6.
46. Oscar Platou, *Forelæsninger over Retskildernes Theori* [*Lectures in the Theory of Legal Sources*] (T. O. Brøgger, Kristiania 1915), p. 56.
47. Rt. 1888 s. 682.
48. Rt. 1963 s. 370.
49. Rt. 1995 s. 644.
50. RG 1962 p. 261, at s. 265–266.
51. NOU 1994:21, *Bruk av land og vann i Finnmark i historisk perspektiv* [*The Use of Land and Lakes in Finnmark in Historical Perspective*], Norges offentlige utredninger [Norwegian Public Reports] (Statens forvaltningstjeneste, Oslo, 1994), p. 88.
52. Rt. 1995 s. 644.
53. *Ibid.*
54. Rt. 1888 s. 682.
55. Rt. 1963 s. 370.

56. Rt. 1995 s. 644.
57. Some attempts were made to privatize fisheries south of Magerøya (the Municipality of Nordkapp), during the 1950s. Some fishermen, either Saami fishermen or others, said that lack of access was the result of unorganized private attempts to close them up.
58. Rt. 1995 at s. 648.
59. See especially Hans Kelsen, *Pure Theory of Law* (University of California Press, Berkley, CA, 1967); and Neil MacCormick, "Law as Institutional Fact" (1974) *Law Quarterly Review*, vol. 90, p. 102.
60. Hans Kelsen, *Allegemeine Staatslehre* (Julis Springer, Berlin, 1925), pp. 16–21.
61. Paul Vinogradoff presents the following illustration during British rule in India: "It would be the grossest travesty of justice if English judges in considering the customs were guided solely by European conceptions of right and wrong. The jurisprudence of the Medical Committee of the Privy Council affords many signal instances of a respectful treatment of foreign popular customs. In a case of 1906 – *Musammat Lali v. Murli Dhar* – the question at issue was one of disputed succession. The respondent claimed the property under a will in a wajib-ul-arz, which was legal evidence which an English Court was *bound* to consider." Paul Vinogradoff, *Common Sense in Law* (Oxford University Press, London, 1959).
62. *In re Boundaries of Pulehunui*, 4 Haw. 239, 245 (1879).
63. 440 P.2d 76.
64. See Hilary Stewart, *Indian Fishing. Early Methods on the Northwest Coast*, pp. 99 ff.
65. Rt. 1959 s. 1321.
66. As to why comparative law studies are important, see Gordon R. Woodman, "Customary Laws and Customary Legal Rights: A Comparative Consideration of Their Nature and of the Relationship Between Laws" (11–12 February 1999) *Saami Customary Law Seminar* 1–2.
67. (1992) 175 CLR 1.
68. 1998 Aust Fed Ct Lexis 500 (Aust Fed Ct, 1998).
69. *Ibid.*
70. *Ibid.*
71. *Ibid.*
72. *Ibid.*
73. 2001 Aust High Ct Lexis 48 (Aust High Ct, 2001).
74. See Section 2.2.
75. Norwegian Coastal Fishermen Organization, Inquiry among high school students of November 2001.
76. "The trend toward over-capitalization, over-fishing, and threatened depletion" has been almost universal. Christopher J. Carr and Harry N. Scheiber, "Dealing with a Resource Crisis: Regulatory Regimes for Managing the World's Marine

Fisheries" (2002) *Stanford Environmental Law Journal*, vol. 21, p. 77. Recent studies suggest that the FAO has been grossly overestimating fish populations because of over-reporting by certain countries. Reg Watson and Daniel Pauly, "Systematic Distortions in World Fisheries Catch Trends" (2001) *Nature*, vol. 414, p. 534.

77. Axel Kjær Sørensen, "Greenland: From Colony to Home Rule," in Sven Tägil (ed.), *Ethnicity and Nation Building in the Nordic World* (University of Southern Illinois Press, Carbondale, Ill., 1995), p. 85.
78. Elizabeth Kolbert, "Ice Memory" (January 7, 2002) *The New Yorker* 30.
79. For a recent description of a California native's perception of life in Northern Greenland, see Gretel Ehrlich, *This Cold Heaven. Seven Seasons in Greenland* (Pantheon Books, New York, 2001).
80. I. Kleivan and B. Sonne, *Eskimos Greenland and Canada* (E. J. Brill, Leiden, 1985), pp. 19–21.
81. See generally the discussion in Chapter 2.
82. Mark Nuttall, *Arctic Homeland: Kinship, Community and Development in Northwest Greenland* (University of Toronto Press, Toronto, Buffalo, 1992), at pp. 22–23, 156–157.
83. See below.
84. Jens Dahl, *Saqqaq: An Inuit Hunting Community in the Modern World* (University of Toronto Press, Toronto, Buffalo, 2000), at p. 254.
85. Lars Emil Johansen, "Autonomy, Dependency, Sustainability: A Greenland Perspective," in Hanne Petersen and Birger Poppel (eds.), *Autonomy, Dependency, Sustainability in the Arctic* (Ashgate, Aldershot, UK, 1999), pp. 13, 14–15.
86. Dahl, *Saqqaq*, p. 10.
87. Richard A. Caulfield, *Greenlanders, Whales, and Whaling: Sustainability and Self-determination in the Arctic* (University Press of New England, 1997).
88. The writer, Maliâraq Vebæk, is one of the oldest and best known women writers in Greenland. The illustrator is her younger colleague, Aka Høegh, who is a painter and sculptor as well. Aka Høegh's mother was the court magistrate in her hometown, Julianehaab, or Qaqortoq, for many years.
89. You will also find an illustration of the Mother of the Sea on this year's Greenlandic telephone book. The East Greenlandic artist, Buuti, created it. Inside the telephone book, below a miniature version of the front page, the artist writes "without limits (borders) to communication we may come far. We must not forget to communicate, also not with our past – perhaps we should try to communicate with the Sea Mother? By communicating without borders we might learn more about ourselves?"
90. This is a very short version of the Myth of the Sea Mother taken from Knud Rasmussen's collections of myths and legends from Greenland. This specific myth is printed in the third volume, which contains myths from the Cape York district and from Northern Greenland. Knud Rasmussen, *Myter og Sagn fra*

Grønland (Gyldendalske Boghhandel, Nordisk Forlag, 1925). The translation is taken from "Eskimo Folk-tales" collected by Knud Rasmussen and selected and translated by W. Worster (Gyldendal, Copenhagen and Christiania, 1921).
91. Lit., "Meat. Dish."
92. Rasmussen records the myth as "Told by Aisivik from Agpat."
93. Sean Kane, *Wisdom of the Mythtellers* (Broadview Press, Toronto, 1994), p. 194.
94. Mircea Eliade, *Myth and Reality* (Harper Torchbooks, New York, 1974), p. 2.
95. Eliade, *Myth and Reality*, p. 139.
96. Murray Sinclair, "Aboriginal Peoples and Euro-Canadians: Two World Views," in John Hylton (ed.), *Aboriginal Self-Government in Canada. Current Trends and Issues* (Purich Publishing, Saskatoon, 1994), p. 23.
97. *Ibid.*, p. 25.
98. Kjeld Hansen, *A Farewell to Greenland's Wildlife* (Gads Forlag, Copenhagen, 2002).
99. Mark Nuttall, *Arctic Homeland: Kinship, Community and Development in North-west Greenland* (University of Toronto Press, Toronto Buffalo, 1992), at p. 179.

11

The choice of customary law

FRED BOSSELMAN

People choose to use customary law for a wide variety of reasons. Some choose to maximize ethnic identity, some local solidarity, and some adaptation to modern conditions. Customary law provides an important element in all of these situations, whether as a symbol to be treasured, an ideal to be regained, or a tradition to be honored in the adaptation.[1] To blindly assume that customary law will produce sustainable development is naïve. Michael Soulé suggests that the myth of moral superiority of non-western traditions "has led guilt-ridden Westerners to glorify the environmental ethics of non-western traditions . . . Some indigenous people can provide excellent guidance, some not."[2]

Customary law in its original form may be a vulnerable instrument wholly dependent upon popular recognition, but it is also a valuable source that should be studied in the never-ending search for ways to accommodate to an environment that has been and will remain constantly changing. The growing volume of case studies of customary systems is evidence of a growing recognition that such systems may be a source of wise resource policies.

11.1 Reasons to choose customary law

Why might policy-makers choose to implement customary law systems? A review of the literature suggests that the following are some of the arguments most commonly heard in favor of customary law systems.

11.1.1 Empowerment

Giving a group's customs legal stature may reinforce a group's sense of responsibility that comes with law-making power.[3] Resource user groups themselves often see their traditional customs as a source of potential power for their group.[4] As the anthropologist Shepard Krech points out, native Americans have fostered the image of the "ecological Indian" through efforts to obtain legal backing for their traditional customs.[5]

Indigenous people in Canada and Australia have also used the sustainability of their customs as a way of building power and solidarity.[6] The desire for empowerment is not limited to indigenous people; many occupational groups engaged in fishing, grazing or other forms of resource utilization also seek the power that comes with the authority to interpret customs.[7] In many cases, attaching power to indigenous knowledge is the only incentive that is able to keep indigenous knowledge alive.[8]

11.1.2 Cooperation

In other cases, the desire to incorporate user customs into resource management systems comes from resource managers who see a need (perhaps reflecting political pressure, tribal influence or simply dissatisfaction with results of the current system) to obtain local cooperation in order to make their management systems work. For example, protection of the threatened dugong in the Torres Straits between Australia and New Guinea will be impossible without the support of the Torres Islanders, given the remote and lightly populated character of the area.[9]

Consultants have often found that if they can promote conservation projects that build on existing indigenous practices they are more likely to become successful.[10] Such results are due to the fact that solutions are familiar and legitimate. Madhav Gadgil suggests that sustainable management can be achieved when local people perceive that the resource is scarce, that substitution is difficult, and that their own control over the resource base is extensive.[11]

11.1.3 Innovation

Other resource managers view systems of customary law more like scrapbooks that might contain useful knowledge that could be incorporated into management systems.[12] "The use of traditional ecological knowledge in an experimental way to learn from management interventions, with subsequent policy changes, makes it a potential tool for Adaptive Management . . ."[13] The fact that local groups have worked through difficult resource management problems by trial and error suggests that the study of their conclusions may illustrate not only what worked but also what did not.[14] Customary management systems are not "final solutions" but "evolving knowledge systems" that should be evaluated impartially through trial and error and careful and comprehensive analysis.[15]

For example, the custom of many indigenous people to rely on a wide variety of food sources to ameliorate disastrous effects of storms, droughts and similar problems has stimulated the development and retention of innovative ways of coping with the natural environment.[16] Relying on traditional ecological knowledge and institutions for implementing conservation may contribute to the rediscovery of new principles for more sustainable uses of the natural environment that can be used in developed countries as well.[17]

11.1.4 Data collection

Some observers focus on the advantage of being able to use the empirically derived local knowledge that user groups typically possess. "Adaptive management can be seen as a rediscovery of dynamic practices and institutions already existing in some traditional systems of knowledge and management, and to some extent in contemporary local communities."[18] Milton Freeman concluded, in his study of the Alaskan Eskimo Whaling Commission, that the whalers' beliefs about the migration patterns of bowhead whales proved to be more accurate than those of the scientists.[19] A steadily upcoming claim in Norway is that fishermen's advice should be taken into account when catch limits are being determined.[20] A recent study of clam harvesting in Maine found that

> A unique aspect of Maine's soft shell clam fishery is the integration of informal local knowledge with locally generated formal scientific information... The state regulatory regime explicitly recognizes the value of local knowledge in providing for clam conservation plans. Community residents work in conjunction with state biologists to develop plans and conduct resource surveys in a co-operative production of scientific knowledge.[21]

Giving weight to popular knowledge and data collection, bottom-up knowledge will influence the decisions made, which make the outcome legitimate to local user groups.

On the other hand, some user groups are reluctant to share their locally derived knowledge. Australian aborigines, for example, have balked at full disclosure of their fire management policies because they fear loss of control of their intellectual property.[22] Other observers, however, suggest that user groups already exercise too much influence over resource management and are typically predisposed to overutilization of the resource, so that their information may be suspect.[23] And the ability to effectively collect and distribute indigenous data out of the context of local surroundings has been called into question.[24]

11.2 Reasons to be cautious about endorsing customary law

The precautionary principle should apply to decisions to endorse customary law in the same way as it applies to other policy-making decisions. Some arguments made on behalf of customary law should be approached with a great deal of caution.

11.2.1 Nostalgia

As James Gleick has pointed out in his recent book *Faster*, the world seems to be moving at a more rapid pace every year.[25] Many people wish they could return to an earlier era – one in which life was simpler and changes happened less often. In the United States, this yearning is often expressed in the form of admiration of the way of life of the American Indians that occupied North America before the European settlement.[26] Shepard Krech's book *The Ecological Indian* chronicles many examples of nostalgic reverence for Indian customs by today's descendants of the Europeans who settled America. Many of these judgements are based on uninformed assumptions that do not withstand analysis. Some Indian customs of resource management were sustainable and some were not.[27]

Hawaii also faces pressure to reactivate ancient Polynesian customs. While much of this pressure comes from the understandable desire of native Hawaiians to regain their identity, much of the support for it reflects an emotional rebellion against modern lifestyles without analysis of the real consequences. Although it is easy to sympathize with sentimental emotions such as nostalgia, the prospect that society would forego the comfort, convenience and productivity of modern technology is remote. If we wish to advocate the return to specific customary practices of an earlier time, we should do so based on an analysis of the adaptability of the practice to current and prospective future conditions, not because of some untested assumption that old ways must have been better.

11.2.2 Privatization

The privatization drive that arises out of the dislike of government is pointing in two directions, atomized market decisions and customary law. The collapse of centralized economic planning has given strong support to a desire to reduce the role of the government in people's affairs. The complexity of modern governmental systems aggravates the hostility that many people have to government in general. This has given rise to increasing scholarly analysis of customary law systems by people eager to find less bureaucratic ways of organizing society. Many of these studies have produced excellent products that have thrown new light on the operation of particular customary law systems.[28] And the motivation of replacing complex "top-down" structures with "bottom-up" systems is quite logical.

Nevertheless, like nostalgia, privatization should be subject to rational analysis, not allowed to become an ideology. Empirical studies suggest that non-governmental entities can sometimes manage resources sustainably using customary systems, but failure is also common. The extensive studies of resources management systems at the University of Indiana have led Elinor Ostrom and her colleagues to warn against the assumption that market-led privatization is automatically the cure for resource management problems.[29] We should approach privatization instrumentally and find those situations in which it works.

11.2.3 Domination

Some observers of customary law systems have noted conflicts between the sexes or among age groups. In Hanne Petersen's study of Greenland she found that women and younger people were often ambivalent about customary systems that allowed older males to interpret and administer the rules.[30] Similar issues have surfaced in other case studies.[31]

Post-colonial societies are particularly subject to concern over the use of customary systems as a means of dominating groups perceived by the rulers to be "inferior." Martin Chanock has examined the unfortunate legacy for Africa of the colonial powers' use of customary law to marginalize indigenous populations. Other studies have found similar concerns.[32]

Advocates of the use of any particular customary law system need to be alert for issues of equity in the system's operation. But these issues arise in any legal system, and there seems to be no reason to believe that customary law systems are more prone to domination by particular groups than written law systems.[33] An emotional fear of domination should not become translated into an ideological rejection of custom.

11.2.4 Exclusion

Resentment by ethnic groups against what they perceive as the invasion of their territory by other ethnic groups remains a frequent cause of bloodshed throughout the world, in places as disparate in background as Yugoslavia, Indonesia, Fiji and Liberia. International institutions spend much of their time on attempts to avert such violent encounters. In some cases, customary law systems have become a vehicle for debate about the exclusion of outsiders.

In other instances, outsiders who have access to more capital and newer technology effectively exclude traditional users of a resource. The story of the Saami people of Northern Scandinavia shows how a people that originally welcomed outsiders can feel victimized when large-scale fishing interests refuse to follow local customs and drive the Saami people out of trade through overexploitation and the intruders' subsequent claim on common pool closure. But in other cases, local people have been successful in enforcing local customs that make it difficult for outsiders to share in the use of local resources, as the Hawaiian case study shows.

In the third world, the post-colonial construction of states inevitably changed the boundaries and membership of the "communities" that could claim access to resources. Internal migration takes place within states as people, often losers of claims to land in their own localities, seek to use what appear to be unexpropriated resources. The issue that arises within any state is the legal and ethical basis for excluding any members of the national community from the local community that has a customary claim to the resource, unless that customary claim is validated by the property law of the nation-state.[34] But can one speak legitimately about such issues without fragmenting the cultural identity on which the legitimacy of custom rests? This creates serious difficulties for the use of custom as a pragmatic and legalized basis for economic and social relationships.

Equity issues between old and new residents can be found in any system of resource management, whether customary or not. It should be noted, however, that the exclusion of outsiders is the practical result of most attempts to avoid the tragedy of the commons. Elinor Ostrom suggests that users "who interact with each other in many situations other than the sharing of their common-pool resources are apt to develop strong norms of acceptable behavior and to convey their mutual expectations to one another in many reinforcing encounters."[35] The opposite side of the coin, of course, is that a mobile and multi-ethnic society may have difficulty in maintaining this type of local cohesiveness without enforcing it by legal or extra-legal sanctions designed to exclude outsiders.[36] If such exclusion is designed to hoard available resources to a degree far beyond the needs of those to whom the entitlement is reserved, it is rightly subject to charges of antidemocratic bias.[37] But reasonable restrictions on potential new users are an inevitable element of any policy to promote sustainable resource use, and even powerfully motivated land reform programs have hesitated to throw out the principle of first possession for fear of the chaos that might follow.[38]

Sympathy for excluded groups must be balanced against the fact that most resources have a carrying capacity that must not be exceeded if sustainable use of the resource is to be achieved. An emotional reaction against exclusionary attitudes must not be used as an excuse for over-exploitation.

We hope that the reader of this book will come away from it with a greater respect for customary law as one possible way to promote the objective of sustainable development in particular situations, but with a recognition that each customary law system needs to be evaluated fairly on its merits.

Endnotes

1. See Hanne Petersen, "The Lion King and the Lady and the Unicorn. Jurisprudential Considerations on Visual Normativity," in Alberto Febbrajo, David Nelken and Vittorio Olgiati (eds.), *European Yearbook in the Sociology of Law. Social Processes and Patterns of Legal Control* (Giuffré Publisher, Milan, 2000).
2. Michael E Soulé, "The Social Siege of Nature," in Michael E. Soulé and Gary Lease (eds.), *Responses to Postmodern Destruction* (1995), at pp. 160–161.
3. Carol M. Rose, "Common Property, Regulatory Property, and Environmental Protection: Comparing Common Pool Resources to Tradable Environmental Allowances," paper prepared for delivery at the International Association for the Study of Common Property Resources (Bloomington, Indiana, May–June, 2000), p. 23.
4. See, e.g., Luciano Minerbi, "Indigenous Management Models and Protection of the Ahupua'a" (1999) *Social Process in Hawaii*, vol. 39, p. 208 (native Hawaiian groups promote their sustainable agriculture strategies as a vehicle for empowerment); Mark V. Prystupa, "Barriers and Strategies to the Development of Co-Management Regimes in New Zealand: The Case of Te-Waihora" (1998) *Human Organization*, vol. 57, no. 2, p. 134 (Maoris base claim for co-management of lake on traditional fishing rights).
5. Shepard Krech, *The Ecological Indian* (W. W. Norton & Co., New York, 1999), pp. 213–215.
6. See generally Edwin M. Wilmsen (ed.), *We Are Here: Politics of Aboriginal Land Tenure* (University of California Press, Berkley CA, 1989).
7. A. Dan Tarlock, "Can Cowboys Become Indians: Protecting Western Communities as Endangered Cultural Remnants" (1999) *Arizona State Law Journal*, vol. 31, p. 539; Robert C. Ellickson, "Of Coase and Cattle: Dispute Resolution Among Neighbors in Shasta County" (1986) *Stanford Law Review*, vol. 38, p. 623.

8. Arun Agrawal, "Dismantling the Divide between Indigenous and Scientific Knowledge" (1995) *Development and Change*, vol. 26, pp. 413, 431–32.
9. H. Marsh et al., "The Sustainability of the Indigenous Dugong Fishery in Torres Strait, Australia/Papua New Guinea" (1997) 11 *Conservation Biology* 1375. As Carol Rose puts it, "It has now become very fashionable to enlist local populations in wildlife or forest preservation." Carol M. Rose, "The Several Futures of Property: Of Cyberspace and Folk Tales, Emission Trades and Ecosystems" (1998) *Minnesota Law Review*, vol. 83, pp. 129, 168.
10. T. Anderson White and Jon L. Jickling, "Peasants, Experts, and Land Use in Haiti: Lessons from Indigenous and Project Technology" (1995) *Soil and Water Conservation* 7, 13.
11. Madhav Gadgil, "Prudence and Profligacy: A Human Ecological Perspective," in Timothy M. Swanson (ed.), *The Economics and Ecology of Biodiversity Decline: The Forces Driving Global Change* (Cambridge University Press, Cambridge, 1995), p. 101.
12. See, e.g., Arpad C. Kalotas, "Recording and Applying Aboriginal Botanical Knowledge in Western Australia: Some recent examples and future prospects," in Nancy M. Williams and Graham Baines (eds.), *Traditional Ecological Knowledge: Wisdom for Sustainable Development* (Australian National University Centre for Resource and Environmental Studies, Canberra, 1993), p. 94.
13. Fikret Berkes, *Sacred Ecology: Traditional Ecological Knowledge and Resource Management* (Taylor & Francis, Philadelphia PA, 1999), p. 30.
14. E. N. Anderson, *Ecologies of the Heart: Emotion, Belief, and the Environment* (Oxford University Press, Oxford, 1996), p. 151. Of course, some customs of indigenous groups may be the antithesis of sustainable policy. See, e.g., Holly McEldowney, "Lime Collection and its Effects on Coral Reefs," in Williams and Baines (eds.), *Traditional Ecological Knowledge*, p. 150.
15. Eugene Hunn, "What is Traditional Ecological Knowledge?" in Williams and Baines (eds.), *Traditional Ecological Knowledge*, pp. 13, 15.
16. See, e.g., S. Olusegun Apantaku, "Indigenous Technical Knowledge and Use of Forest Plant Products for Sustainable Control of Crop Pests in Ogun State, Nigeria" (1999) *Journal of Sustainable Agriculture*, vol. 14, pp. 5, 8–12 (local information about natural insecticides is widely used); Ricardo Godoy et al., "Strategies of Rain-forest Dwellers against Misfortunes: the Tsimane' Indians of Bolivia" (1998) *Ethnology*, vol. 37, p. 55 (measuring extent to which reliance on rain forest is used as insurance mechanism); Pierre Montagne, "Contributions of Indigenous Silviculture to Forestry Development in Rural Areas: Examples from Niger and Mali" (1985) *Rural Africana*, vol. 23–24, pp. 61, 63–64 (local entrepreneurs develop nurseries of trees known to have beneficial effects).
17. Edward B. Barbier et al., *Paradise Lost: The Ecological Economics of Biodiversity* (Earthscan Publications, London, 1994), p. 217.

18. Carl Folke, Fikret Berkes and Johan Colding, "Ecological Practices and Social Mechanisms for Building Resilience and Sustainability," in Fikret Berkes and Carl Folke (eds.), *Linking Social and Ecological Systems: Management Practices and Social Mechanisms for Building Resilience* (Cambridge University Press, Cambridge, 1998), pp. 414, 431.
19. Milton M. R. Freeman, "The Alaska Eskimo Whaling Commission: Successful Co-management under Extreme Conditions," in Evelyn Pinkerton (ed.), *Co-operative Management of Local Fisheries* (University of British Columbia Press, Vancouver, 1989), pp. 140–141. See also Milton M. R. Freeman, "Traditional Land Users as a Legitimate Source of Environmental Expertise," in Williams and Baines (ed.), *Traditional Ecological Knowledge*, pp. 153, 158–159 (finding similar superiority of local knowledge in regard to musk ox).
20. Fisheries Directorate have since the 1950s used fishermen as data collectors, under a program called "Forsøksfiske" – Experimental fishing. These experiences are the basis for agencies' decisions on opening a fishing field, a fishery, usage of special fishing gears etc.
21. Susan S. Hanna, "Managing for Human and Ecological Content in the Maine Soft Shell Clam Fishery," in Berkes and Folke (eds.), *Linking Social and Ecological Systems*, pp. 190, 195–196.
22. Rosemary Hill et al., "Aborigines and Fire in the Wet Tropics of Queensland, Australia: Ecosystem Management Across Cultures" (1999) *Society and Natural Resources*, vol. 12, p. 205.
23. David A. Dana, "Overcoming the Political Tragedy of the Commons: Lessons Learned from the Reauthorization of the Magnuson Act" (1997) *Ecology Law Quarterly*, vol. 24, p. 833.
24. Agrawal, "Dismantling the Divide between Indigenous and Scientific Knowledge," pp. 413, 425–427.
25. James Gleick, *Faster: The Acceleration of Just About Everything* (Pantheon Books, New York, 1999).
26. See, e.g., Arthur Versluis, *Sacred Earth: The Spiritual Landscape of Native America* (Inner Traditions International, Rochester VT, 1992).
27. Shepard Krech, *The Ecological Indian* (W. W. Norton & Co., New York, 1999).
28. See, e.g., Robert C. Ellickson, *Order Without Law: How Neighbors Settle Disputes* (Harvard University Press, Cambridge MA, 1991); Robert D. Cooter, "Structural Adjudication and the New Law Merchant: A Model of Decentralized Law" (1994) *International Review of Law and Economics*, vol. 14, p. 215.
29. C. Dustin Becker and Elinor Ostrom, "Human Ecology and Resource Sustainability: The Importance of Institutional Diversity" (1995) *Annual Review of Ecological Systems*, vol. 26, pp. 113, 122. This research group is, however, much more friendly towards bottom-up customary-law-based management.
30. See pages 422–423 above.

31. Pages 255–256 above. See also Deborah Bird Rose, "Reflections on ecologies for the twenty-first century," in Williams and Baines (eds.), *Traditional Ecological Knowledge*, pp. 115, 117; Graham Baines and Edvard Hviding, "Traditional Environmental Knowledge for Resource Management in Marovo, Solomon Islands," in Williams and Baines (eds.), *Traditional Ecological Knowledge*, pp. 56, 60.
32. See, e.g., Jesse C. Ribot, "Representation and Accountability in Decentralized Sahelian Forestry: Legal Instruments of Political-Administrative Control" (2000) *Georgetown International Environmental Law Review*, vol. 12, p. 447.
33. This is made clear by Peter Ørebech, *Om torskeresolusjonen av 1989. Den skjulte agenda og ranet av fiskeriallmenningen* [*On the 1989 Cod Resolution. The Hidden Agenda and the Robbery of the Commons*] 2002 Report to the Norwegian Power and Democracy Commission 1998–2003 (Unipub as, Oslo).
34. This puzzle was solved by the total capitulation of ethnic customs in favor of locally based customs in Saami land, see Section 2.2.
35. Elinor Ostrom, *Governing the Commons: The Evolution of Institutions for Collective Action* (Cambridge University Press, Cambridge, 1990), p. 206.
36. See, e.g., Arthur F. McEvoy, *The Fisherman's Problem: Ecology and Law in the California Fisheries, 1850–1980* (1986), pp. 65–90; Ellickson, *Order Without Law*, p. 2884; Bonnie J. McCay, "The Culture of the Commoners: Historical Observations on Old and New World Fisheries," in Bonnie J. McCay and James M. Acheson (eds.), *The Question of the Commons* (University of Arizona Press, Tucson AZ, 1987).
37. For a recent commentary on the underlying issue, see Richard Thompson Ford, "The Boundaries of Race: Political Geography in Legal Analysis" (1994) *Harvard Law Review*, vol. 107, pp. 1841, 1910–13. See generally Richard J. Lazarus, "Pursuing 'Environmental Justice': The Distributional Effects of Environmental Protection" (1993) *Northwestern University Law Review*, vol. 87, p. 787; A. Dan Tarlock, "Environmental Protection: The Potential Misfit Between Equity and Efficiency" (1992) *Colorado Law Review*, vol. 63, p. 871; Carol Rose, "Rethinking Environmental Controls: Management Strategies for Common Resources" (1991) *Duke Law Journal* 1. The same issue is posed by local growth management regulation. A. Dan Tarlock, "City Versus Countryside: Environmental Equity in Context" (1994) *Fordham Urban Law Journal*, vol. 21, p. 461; Fred P. Bosselman, "Can the Town of Ramapo Pass a Law to Bind the Rights of the Whole World?" (1973) *Florida State University Law Review*, vol. 1, p. 234. Cf. Richard F. Babcock and Fred P. Bosselman, "Suburban Zoning and the Apartment Boom" (1963) *University of Pennsylvania Law Review*, vol. 111, pp. 1040, 1080–83 (1963).
38. See generally, Charles C. Geisler and Frank J. Popper, *Land Reform, American Style* (Rowman and Littlefield Publishers Inc., Lanham, Maryland, 1984). See also Elinor Ostrom, *Governing the Commons*, pp. 88–89.

12

Conclusion: customary law in a globalizing culture

FRED BOSSELMAN AND PETER ØREBECH

In this book we have tried to demonstrate the important role that customary law plays in modern, western society. We have explored the importance of sustainability and the search for legal systems that can provide cautious avenues for achieving sustainable objectives. And we have looked at the growing importance of international law's recognition of both sustainablility and custom. We have explained that customary law is an alternative to "governmental control and command."[1]

12.1 The importance of customary law

In order to understand the role of customary law today, we need to reemphasize some basic philosophical principles. We must acknowledge that humans have the capacity to formulate rules to guide cooperative behavior relating to each other and to their surrounding environment. We need to emphasize that customs are not simply reflex responses to outside stimuli, but are developed intuitively by humans who seek to benefit by cooperation.

Enlightenment philosophers argued that this rationalist capacity distinguished humans from the other animals. Although modern science may blur the lines between humans and animals, and between rational and instinctive behavior, it remains unquestioned that humans surpass all other species in the extent of their ability to use rational processes to establish customary rules.

Customary law exists whenever people act as if they were legally bound to observe customary rules. No endorsement by any legislative, judicial or administrative body is needed to create customary law if people accept rules as the law. Customary law is pervasive in modern societies. Even in nations with complex and efficient governmental structures, customary law is the guiding force in many areas. And in the world's many "failing states," customary law plays a key role as a process for establishing claims and resolving disputes.

Customary law also finds its way into more formal legal formats. Courts look to the customs of the community in defining many kinds of permissible behavior. Administrative agencies learn the customs of "stakeholders" in the process of formulating regulations. And legislators often incorporate or defer to custom in enacting laws. In this way, customary law directs important parts of property and environmental law.

Not every social norm deserves customary law status. Of course members of special trades and local societies may, explicitly or tacitly, agree upon legal solutions, but when doubt and tension arise, the final word belongs to third party institutions. Where people dispute the binding nature of a particular custom, the courts have established procedural rules for establishing whether it is customary law. These rules, many of which are based on the pre-nineteenth century English court decisions analyzed by William Blackstone, apply common-sense tests to determining whether the rules reasonably reflect the actual practices of a local community.

Some observers have assumed that the Blackstonian rules apply only to quaint customs of ancient lineage and dubious relevance. But an analysis of the application of these rules shows that they endorse many flexible customs that continue to have important modern applications. Such customs often provide an underlying regime of equity that is used as a basis for key contractual relationships.

But even where particular customary rules have been abandoned in the light of changing conditions, the values that underlay the customary rules may still serve an important function. These values can serve to guide the adoption of new rules or the creation of new rule-making processes. In this sense, customary law is a continually ongoing process by which people seek to improve their interpersonal relations, as the Scottish philosopher Thomas Reid pointed out over two centuries ago. Custom, he said, includes the process by which the people actively engage in the common pursuit of applying reason, experience, instinct and the views of others to the regulation of human conduct in relation to each other and the environment. We the people, today as before, possess the capacity to agree upon laws to govern our own behavior.

12.2 The importance of sustainable development

As recently as fifty years ago, our ability to determine whether natural resource development strategies were sustainable was quite limited. We kept good records of a few key commodities and environmental conditions, but these records existed for relatively short time periods. Our ability to observe the environment was quite limited in both space and time, and the complexity of the environment precluded any ability to predict long-range future conditions.

Today, computers and satellites are only the most obvious examples of how technology has improved our ability to study and predict the impact of our activities on the world around us. We understand far better how past practices led to unsustainable resources, and we can model the future well enough to worry about the effects of our current activities on future generations. While the complexity of ecological systems makes the predictive value of many such models somewhat speculative, the modeling allows scientists to think in expanded ways that were not feasible for an earlier generation.

Our increasing scientific capabilities have gradually influenced our policy-making processes. This is apparent not only at the national level but at the international level, where our capacity to see the interrelationship of the world's natural resources is most apparent. Even those nations that are reluctant to exercise the self-restraint necessary to achieve sustainable resource development themselves are beginning to recognize the seriousness of the issue. Internationally adopted aspirations of sustainability have become well accepted, and are gradually being implemented with binding commitments to sustainable behavior.

Better science has also made us aware of the difficulty of predicting the behavior of complex systems. We are more aware of the rapidity with which epidemics, ecological collapse and sudden climate change have affected human lifestyles in disastrous ways. Our improved knowledge has led us to be cautious taking possible non scientifically justified risks into consideration, not only in introducing changes in the natural environment, but in reasoning that no change is needed. A precautionary principle has become an inherent part of many natural resource management processes, and has been incorporated in a number of important international agreements.

12.3 The search for sustainable legal systems

Today the law of natural resource management is the subject of much soul searching. Science has awakened us to the complexity of the ecological, technological, social and economic issues that managers most address, but has not produced a consensus about ways to resolve the complexity. Some people argue that strictly enforced regulatory measures are the best way to manage natural resources sustainably. They believe that the human propensity to greed will defeat any system other than one buttressed by tight regulations. Others argue that efficient natural resource management must simulate the conditions of a private market. By letting the price of natural resources vary with scarcity, the invisible hand of the market will channel demand toward those resources that are most sustainable. The government's role is simply to ensure that fair market-making institutions exist.

Can customary role play a role in this polarized argument between regulations and markets? In this book we have looked at examples of how customary law can be used as input into both regulatory and market systems. For example, in regulatory systems of natural resource management customary rules may be incorporated into administrative regulations if the administrators appreciate the local knowledge and experience on which the customs are based. In some instances statutory rules are identical to customary. In others, statutes are purely complementary – applying only when customary law does not offer viable solutions. Another use for customary law in regulatory systems is to provide a process through which institutions representing local user groups can participate in both the formation and implementation of administrative rules. Sometimes this takes the form of cooperation between local groups and government agencies, but in other cases the customary law provides a vehicle through which local groups can make claims and achieve negotiated agreements.

Similar examples are found in market-based management systems. Such systems need ways to weigh those non-economic values that are not quantified in ordinary market transactions. Customary rules and institutions can point the way to values held by local people that the market may be missing. Moreover, the processes by which customary law systems weigh and honor various values may suggest the extent of the weight that people would be comfortable with placing on such values.

We have also looked at situations in which customary law has been allowed to stand on its own, rather than as just one component of a market or regulatory system. Because producing sustainable regulatory or market mechanisms of resource management requires long and patient effort and significant expense, in some situations governments have simply concluded that the most efficient solution is to turn certain sectors of management over to customary law institutions, relieving the taxpayers of oversight responsibilities.

The delegation of resource management to customary institutions or rules by no means guarantees sustainable development. If the users of customary law fail to defend norms under attack, replacement takes place and new norms may emerge. Despite their superior quality, sustainable practices face no better odds of survival than any other resource management practice. Consequently, the survival of an ancient practice may indicate its superiority in *inter partes* conflicts over resource harvesting and allocation, but its survival does not warrant that practice is sustainable, since it may happen that customary changes takes place long after resource decline has taken place.

Nevertheless, there are enough success stories that the authors of this book believe that case studies of natural resource management should attempt to identify those situations in which customary law is either a help or hindrance to sustainable development. It is often argued that customary wisdom protected the resources in the past, and is therefore best adapted to the future. In practice, although the use of the term "sustainability" is rather new, an awareness of the economics of sparse resources is often part of old wisdom, because it has always been necessary to consider the future viability of resources in the face of potential overexploitation. Good customs and practices deserve long life.

12.4 The role of international law

The evolving codification of environmental principles in international law may help to reawaken knowledge of sustainability buried in ancient traditions. As stated in the 1995 Straddling Fish Stock Agreement, Article 6(3)(a) "States shall apply the precautionary approach widely to conservation, management and exploitation . . . In implementing the precautionary approach, States shall . . . improve decision-making . . . implementing improved techniques for dealing with risk and uncertainty." The hunter-gatherer-fisher's practical insights that have served well over the centuries shall again become the main focus in building a new society based upon precautionary findings. The precautionary principle suggests the need to search continually for improved techniques for dealing with risk and uncertainty. The synthesis of knowledge gained by experience in customary laws may make precautionary decisions more predictable.

But because many ancient indigenous societies were more static than modern societies, the hopes that have been vested in customary arrangements for promoting sustainability – not least those of indigenous peoples – should not be exaggerated. Sustainability as a value is probably not linked to just one legal instrument or form. Sustainable lifestyles may result from custom, legislative regulation or other cultural norms, and from many other influences which change the legal consciousness in a community or society.

Lawyers and others interested in sustainability should perhaps focus less on legal *forms* as such and more on how to gain support for the protection of sustainability. Both old and new emerging customs and advanced forms of practice may contribute to this aim, as may other types of norms. There is no guarantee that modern state law or international regulation will lead to a state of sustainability. There is no guarantee either, that a return to, or conservation of, earlier forms of customs is a better avenue. These former customs may be sustainable, but under conditions such as gender divisions of labor that are based on values no longer considered attractive.

In order to be able to survive in the world society and market, most people do not want to be locked up in ancient customs. Nevertheless, those customs may still represent a resource capable of inspiring innovation and legitimizing practical activities in the process of administering living resources and adapting to changing circumstances in a changing world. We see signs of return to customary practices in the cry for a precautionary approach to resource management and hope that this and other studies will encourage more research into the various ways by which sustainable customs may be incorporated into modern legal systems.

Endnote

1. Which is an alternative solution to the one of Duncan A. French, "The Role of the State and International Organizations in Reconciling Sustainable Development and Globalization" (2002) *International Environmental Agreements: Politics, Law, and Economics* 135.

REFERENCES

Abercrombie, Michael et al. (eds.), *The New Penguin Dictionary of Biology* (8th edn., Penguin Books, New York, 1990).

Adaptive Management Practitioners' Network at http://www.iatp.org/AEAM/index.html (accessed March 13, 2002).

Adolphsen, Jes and Tom Greiffenberg, "Social Democratism and the Development of Greenland," in Hanne Petersen and Birger Poppel (eds.), *Dependency, Autonomy, Sustainability in the Arctic* (Ashgate, Burlington, 1999).

Agrawal, Arun:

1999 *Greener Pastures: Politics, Markets, and Community among a Migrant Pastoral People* (Duke University Press, Durham NC).

1995 "Dismantling the Divide Between Indigenous and Scientific Knowledge" *Development and Change*, vol. 26, p. 413.

Ake, C., "The Democratisation of Disempowerment in Africa," in J. Hippler (ed.), *The Democratisation of Disempowerment* (Pluto Press, London, 1995).

Akimichi, Tomoya, "Indigenous Resource Management and Sustainable Development: Case Studies from Papua New Guinea and Indonesia" (1995) *Anthropological Science*, vol. 103, p. 321 (Anthropological Society of Nippon).

Allen, Robert C., "The Efficiency and Distributional Consequences of Eighteenth Century Enclosures" (1982) *The Economics Journal*, vol. 92, p. 937.

Allen, Timothy F. H. and Thomas W. Hoekstra, *Toward a Unified Ecology* (Columbia University Press, New York, 1992).

Anderson, E. N., *Ecologies of the Heart: Emotion, Belief, and the Environment* (Oxford University Press, Oxford, 1996).

Arnold, J. E. M., "Management of Forest Resources as Common Property" (1993) *Commonwealth Forestry Review*, vol. 72, p. 157.

Arnold-Baker, Charles, *Local Council Administration* (4th edn., Butterworths, London, 1994).

Arrow, Kenneth et al., "Economic Growth, Carrying Capacity, and the Environment" (April 28, 1995) *Science*, vol. 268, p. 520.

Augdahl, Per, *Rettskilder* [*Sources of Law*] (Aschehoug, Oslo, 1973).

Austin, J. L., *How to do Things with Words* (ed. by J. O. Urmson, Oxford University Press, Oxford, 1962).

Austin, John:

1996 *Lectures on Jurisprudence or the Philosophy of Positive Law* (4th edn, ed. by Robert Campbell, Thoemmes Press, Reprint Bristol).

1954 *The Province of Jurisprudence Determined* (Weidenfeld & Nicolson, London, 1954).

Axelrod, Robert, *The Evolution of Cooperation* (Basic Books, New York, 1984).

Ayensu, Edward et al., "International Ecosystem Assessment" (October 22, 1999) *Science*, vol. 286, p. 685.

Baack, Bennett, "Testing the Impact of Exclusive Property Rights: The Case of Enclosing Common Fields," in Roger L. Ransom, Richard Sutch and Gary M. Walton (eds.), *Explorations in the New Economic History: Essays in Honor of Douglass C. North* (Academic Press, New York, 1982).

Babcock, Richard F. and Fred P. Bosselman, "Suburban Zoning and the Apartment Boom" (1963) *University of Pennsylvania Law Review*, vol. 111, p. 1040.

Bacon, Francis, *Essays* (ed. by Michael J. Hawkins, K. M. Dent & Sons Ltd, London, 1972).

Baines, Graham and Edvard Hviding, "Traditional Environmental Knowledge for Resource Management in Marovo, Solomon Islands," in Nancy M. Williams and Graham Baines (eds.), *Traditional Ecological Knowledge: Wisdom for Sustainable Development* (Australian National University Centre for Resource and Environmental Studies, Canberra, 1993).

Baker, Richard, "Traditional Aboriginal Land Use in the Borroloola Region," in Nancy M. Williams and Graham Baines (eds.), *Traditional Ecological Knowledge: Wisdom for Sustainable Development* (Australian National University Centre for Resource and Environmental Studies, Canberra, 1993).

Barbier, Edward B., et al., *Paradise Lost: The Ecological Economics of Biodiversity* (Earthscan Publications, London, 1994).

Barrett, Greg, "Custom in Hawaii: Hawaiians' Thundering Protest Shakes Private Property Debate" (April 29, 1997) *Christian Science Monitor 3*.

Baskerville, Gordon L., "The Forestry Problem: Adaptive Lurches of Renewal," in Lance H. Gunderson et al. (eds.), *Barriers and Bridges to the Renewal of Ecosystems and Institutions* (Columbia University Press, New York, 1995).

Bateson, Mary (ed.):

1972 *Borough Customs* (2 vols., Seldon Society, Professional Books Ltd, 1972).

1972 *Seldon Society Volumes* (Multivolume, Seldon Society, 1972).

Beach, Hugh, "The Saami of Lapland," in *Polar Peoples: Self-Determination and Development* (Minority Rights Group, London, 1994).

Bean, J., "A Policy Perspective on Biodiversity Protection and Ecosystem Management," in Steward Pickett et al., (eds.), *The Ecological Basis of Conservation: Heterogeneity, Ecosystems, and Biodiversity* (1997).

Becker, C. Dustin and Elinor Ostrom, "Human Ecology and Resource Sustainability: The Importance of Institutional Diversity" (1995) *Annual Review of Ecological Systems*, vol. 26, p. 113.

Bederman, David J., "The Curious Resurrection of Custom: Beach Access and Judicial Takings" *Columbia Law Review*, vol. 96, p. 1375.

Bederman, David J., and Kurt R. Hilbert, "International Decision: Lance Paul Larsen v. The Hawaiian Kingdom" (2001), *American Journal of International Law*, vol. 95, p. 927.

Bellon, Mauricio R., "Farmers' Knowledge and Sustainable Agrosystem Management: An Operational Definition and an Example from Chiapas, Mexico" (1995), *Human Organization*, vol. 54, p. 263.

Benda-Beckman, K. von, "The Environmental Protection and Human Rights of Indigenous Peoples: A Tricky Alliance," in F. and K. von Benda-Beckman (ed.), *Natural Resources, Environment and Legal Pluralism. Legal Anthropology* (Martinus Nijhoff, The Hague, 1992).

Bengtsson, Bertil, "Epilog," in Birgitta Jahreskog (ed.), *The Saami National Minority in Sweden* (Rättsfonder [The Legal Rights Foundation], Stockholm, 1982), p. 250.

Bentham, Jeremy:

1988 *The Principles of Morals and Legislation* (Prometheus Books, New York), p. 330.

1977 *A Comment of the Commentaries and a Fragment of Government* (ed. by J. H. Burns and H. L. A. Hart, The Athlone Press, London).

1970 *Of laws in General* (ed. by H. L. A. Hart, The Athlone Press, London).

1945 *The Limits of Jurisprudence Defined* (Columbia University Press, New York).

1838–1843 *Letter to the Citizens of the United States*, in *The Works of Jeremy Bentham* (11 vols., W. Tait, Edinburgh), vol. IV.

1838–1843 *Plan of Parliamentary Reform*, in *The Works of Jeremy Bentham* (11 vols., W. Tait, Edinburgh), vol. III.

1838–1843 *The Book of Fallacies*, in *The Works of Jeremy Bentham* (11 vols., W. Tait, Edinburgh), vol. II.

1821 *Restrictive and Prohibitory Commercial System*, vol. IX.

Bentzon, Agnete Weis:

1968 *Familiens økonomiske administration og ejendelenes tilhørsforhold i de Vestgrønlandske samfund* (Nyt fra Samfundsvidenskaberne no. 11, Copenhagen).

1968 *Familiens organisation i de grønlandske samfund* (Nyt fra Samfundsvidenskaberne no. 10, Copenhagen).

Berkes, Fikret, *Sacred Ecology: Traditional Ecological Knowledge and Resource Management* (Taylor & Francis, Philadelphia PA, 1999).

Berkes, Fikret, et al.:

2000 "Rediscovery of Traditional Ecological Knowledge as Adaptive Management" *Ecological Applications*, vol. 10, p. 1251.

1999 "Role and Significance of 'Tradition' in Indigenous Knowledge" *Indigenous Knowledge and Development Monitor*, vol. 7, p. 19.

1999 *Sacred Ecology: Traditional Ecological Knowledge and Resource Management* (Taylor & Francis, Philadelphia PA).

1989 "The Benefits of the Commons" *Nature*, vol. 340, p. 91.

Bernt, Jan Fridthjof and David R. Doublet:

1998 *Vitenskapsfilosofi for jurister – en innføring* [*Philosophy of Science for Lawyers – An Introduction*] (Ad Notam Gyldendal, Bergen).

1996 *Juss, Samfunn og Rettsanvendelse* (Ad Notam Gyldendal, Oslo).

Binger, Brian R. and Elizabeth Hoffman, "Institutional Persistence and Change: The Question of Efficiency" (1989) *Journal of Institutional and Theoretical Economics*, vol. 145, p. 67.

Bishop, Richard C. and Thomas A. Heberlein, "Measuring Values of Extra Market Goods: Are Indirect Measures Biased?" (1979) *American Journal of Agricultural Economics*, vol. 61, p. 926.

Bjarup, Jes "Authority and Roles," in Werner Krawietz, Robert S. Summers, Ota Weinberger, Georg Henrik von Wright (eds.), *The Reasonable as Rational? Festschrift for Aulius Aarnio* (Dunker & Humblot, Berlin, 2000).

Blackstone, Sir William:

1857 *Commentaries on the Laws of England* (John Murray, London), vol. 1.

1765–69 *Commentaries on the Laws of England* (1st edn., The Avalon Project at Yale Law School, at www.yale.edu/lawweb/avalon/blackstox), vol. 1.

Blaikie, Piers and Harold Brookfield, *Land Degradation and Society* (Methuen, New York, 1987).

Blomquist, William, *Dividing the Waters, Governing Groundwater in Southern California* (1992).

Blume and Ketscher (eds.), *Ret og skønsomhed i en overgangstid. Festskrift til Agnete Weis Bentzon* (Akademisk Forlag, Copenhagen, 1998).

Bordewick, Fergus, *Killing the White Man's Indian: Reinventing Native Americans at the End of the Twentieth Century* (Doubleday, New York, 1996).

Bosselman, Fred P.:

1997 "The Statutory and Constitutional Mandate for a No Surprises Policy" *Ecology Law Quarterly*, vol. 24, p. 707.

1996 "Limitations Inherent in the Title to Wetlands at Common Law" *Stanford Environmental Law Journal*, vol. 15, p. 247.

1973 "Can the Town of Ramapo Pass a Law to Bind the Rights of the Whole World?" *Florida State University Law Review*, vol. 1, p. 234.

Bourdieu, Pierre, *Distinction. A Social Critique of the Judgement of Taste* (Harvard University Press, Cambridge MA, 1984).

Brækhus, S. and A. Hærem, *Norsk Tingsrett* [*Norwegian Property Law*] (Universitetsforlaget, Oslo, 1964).

Brandt, Frederic, *Tingsretten fremstillet efter den norske Lovgivning* [*Property Law as displayed in Norwegian Provisions*] (Kristiania, 1867).

Bridwell, Randall and Ralph Whitten, *The Constitution and Common Law.* (Lexington Books, Lexington, Mass., 1977), p. 17.

Brightman, Robert A., "Conservation and Resource Depletion: The Case of the Boreal Algonquins," in Bonnie J. McCay and James M. Acheson (eds.), *The*

Question of the Commons: The Culture and Ecology of Communal Resources (University of Arizona Press, Tucson AZ, 1987).

Brøgger, Kr. Fr., *Lov og Rett* [*Law and Right*] (Aschehough, Oslo, 1951).

Bromley, David and Michael Cernea, *The Management of Common Property Resources* (World Bank Discussion Papers, Washington DC, 1989).

Brower, Kenneth, "The Pig War," in Frank Stewart (ed.), *A World Between the Waves* (Island Press, Washington DC, 1992).

Buckle, Stephen, *Natural Law and the Theory of Property. Grotius to Hume* (Clarendon Press, Oxford, 1991).

Callies, David L.:

2000 "Custom and the Public Trust" *Environmental Law Reporter*, vol. 30, p. 10003.

1999 "Regulatory Takings and the Supreme Court: How Perspectives on Property Rights Have Changed From Penn Central to Dolan, and What State and Federal Courts Are Doing About It" *Stetson Law Review*, vol. 28, p. 523.

1984 *Regulating Paradise: Land Use Controls in Hawaii* (University of Hawaii Press, Honolulu).

Campbell, Bruce and Ricardo A. Godoy, *Commonfield Agriculture: The Andes and Medieval England Compared* (Proceedings of the Conference on Common Property Resource Management, National Resource Council, 1986).

Campbell, Faith, "The Appropriations History," in Kathryn A. Kohm (ed.), *Balancing on the Brink of Extinction* (Island Press, Washington DC, 1991).

Care, Jennifer Corrin and Jean G. Zorn, "Statutory Developments in Melanesian Customary Law" (2001) *Journal of Legal Pluralism* 46–50.

Carlquist, Sherwin, *Hawaii: A Natural History* (Natural History Press, Garden City NY, 1970).

Carlsson, Lars, "Management, Resilience and the Strategy of the Commons," paper prepared for delivery at the International Association for the Study of Common Property conference (Bloomington, Indiana, May–June, 2000).

Carr, Christopher J. and Harry N. Scheiber, "Dealing with a Resource Crisis: Regulatory Regimes for Managing the World's Marine Fisheries" (2002) *Stanford Environmental Law Journal*, vol. 21, p. 77.

Caulfield, Richard A., *Greenlanders, Whales, and Whaling: Sustainability and Self-determination in the Arctic* (University Press of New England, 1997).

Chandler, Paul, "Adaptive Ecology of Traditionally Derived Agroforestry in China" (1994) *Human Ecology*, vol. 22, p. 415.

Chanock, M.:

1991 "Paradigms, Policies and Property: A Review of the Customary Law of Land Tenure," in K. Mann and R. Roberts (eds.), *Law in Colonial Africa* (Heinemann, Portsmouth NH).

1991 "A Peculiar Sharpness: An Essay on Property in the History of Customary Law in Colonial Africa" *Journal of African History* 31.

1985 *Law, Custom and Social Order* (Cambridge University Press, Cambridge).

Chayanov, A. V., *The Theory of Peasant Economy* (Irwin, Illinois, 1966).

Chestnut, Becky T., "Matters of Trust: Unanswered Questions after Rice v. Cayetano" (2000) *Hawaii Law Review*, vol. 23, p. 363.

Chigara, Ben, *Legitimacy Deficits in Custom* (Ashgate, Dartmouth, 2001).

Christensen, Norman L. et al., "The Report of the Ecological Society of America Committee on the Scientific Basis for Ecosystem Management" (1996) *Ecological Applications*, vol. 6, p. 665.

Ciriacy-Wantrup, S. V. and Richard C. Bishop, "'Common Property' as a Concept in Natural Resources Policy" (1975) *Natural Resources Journal*, vol. 15, p. 713.

Clanchy, Michael T., *From Memory to Written Record* (Edward Arnold, London, 1979).

Clark, William C., "Sustainable Science for a Sustainable Environment: A Transition Toward Sustainability" (2001) *Ecology Law Quarterly*, vol. 27, p. 1021.

Coady, C. A. J., *Testimony. A Philosophical Study* (Clarendon Press, Oxford, 1992).

Coase, R. H., "The Problem of Social Cost" (1960) *Journal of Law and Economics*, vol. 3, p. 18.

Colding, Johan and Carl Folke, "The Taboo System: Lessons Learned About Informal Institutions for Nature Management" (2000) *Georgetown International Environmental Law Review*, vol. 12, p. 413.

Commission of the European Communities, Green paper on the future of the common fisheries policy COM(2001) 135.

Commission of the European Communities (COM(2000)) 1 final, Brussels, 2.2.2000: Communication from the Commission on the precautionary principle. This was endorsed as the "European Resolution on the Precautionary Principle" (paragraph 5) by Heads of Government at the General Affairs Council in Nice in December, 2000.

Coomes, O. T. and G. J. Burt, "Indigenous market-oriented agroforestry: dissecting local diversity in western Amazonia" (1997), *Agroforestry Systems*, vol. 37, p. 27.

Cooter, Robert D., "Structural Adjudication and the New Law Merchant: A Model of Decentralized Law" (1994) *International Review of Law and Economics*, vol. 14, p. 215.

Cortner, Hanna J. and Margaret A. Moote, *The Politics of Ecosystem Management* (Island Press, Washington DC, 1999).

Costanza, Robert and Carl Folke, "The Structure and Function of Ecological Systems in Relation to Property Rights Regimes," in Susan S. Hanna et al. (eds.), *Rights to Nature: Ecological, Economic, Cultural, and Political Principles of Institutions for the Environment* (1996).

Court Rolls of the Manor of Dernford Sawston in the County of Cambridge for the Years 1336–1360, as expanded and translated by T. F. Tevesham, B.Sc., from the original rolls at Sawston Hall, Sawston, 1965, copy given to the author by David Hall, solicitor and partner, Linklaters and Paynes, London, and Lord of the Manor of Littleport in June, 1999.

Cousins, B., "Tenure and Common Property Resources in Africa," in C. Toulmin and J. Quan (eds.), *Evolving Land Rights, Policy and Tenure in Africa* (DFID/IIED/NRI, London, 2000).

Cox, Susan J. B., "No Tragedy on the Commons" (1985) *Envl Ethics*, vol. 7, p. 49.

Craig, Edward, *The Mind of God and the Works of Man* (Clarendon Press, Oxford, 1987).

Cutter, Susan L. et al., *Exploitation, Conservation, Preservation: A Geographic Perspective on Natural Resource Use* (2nd edn., J. Wiley, New York, 1991).

D'Engelbronner-Kolff, F. Marina, *Justice in a Legally Pluralistic Society: A Court Tale from Sambyu. In Human Rights and Democracy in Southern Africa* (New Namibia Books, Windhoel, 1998).

Dahl Jens:

2000 *Saqqaq. An Inuit Hunting Community in the Modern World* (University of Toronto Press: Toronto, Buffalo, London).

"Arktisk selvstyre. København, Akademisk Forlag, and Greenland: Political Structure of Self-government" *Arctic Anthropology*, vol. 23(1–2), p. 315.

Dahlman, Carl J., *The Open Field System and Beyond: A Property Rights Analysis of an Economic Institution* (Cambridge University Press, Cambridge and New York, 1980).

Dana, David A., "Overcoming the Political Tragedy of the Commons: Lessons Learned from the Reauthorization of the Magnuson Act" (1997) *Ecology Law Quarterly*, vol. 24, p. 833.

Dasgupta, Partha S., *The Control of Resources* (Harvard University Press, Cambridge MA, 1982).

Davidson, Julie L., "Sustainable Development: Business as Usual or a New Way of Living?" (2000), *Environmental Ethics*, vol. 22, p. 25.

Davidson-Hunt, Iain J. and Fikret Berkes, "Environment and Society through the Lens of Resilience: Toward a Human-in-Ecosystem Perspective," paper prepared for delivery at the International Association for the Study of Common Property Conference (Bloomington, Indiana, May–June, 2000).

De Boeck, F., "Democracy and the State-Society Paradigm" (1998) *Journal of Legal Pluralism* 42, 89–93.

De Leo, Giulio A. and Simon Levin, "The Multifaceted Aspects of Ecosystem Integrity" (1997) *Conservation Ecology*, vol. 1 (online journal).

Decleris, Michael, "The Coming Systematised State of the 21st Century" in *Tercera Escuela de Sistemas* (Valencia, 1995).

Dei, George, "Indigenous African Knowledge Systems: Local Traditions of Sustainable Forestry" (1993) *Singapore Journal of Tropical Geography*, vol. 14, p. 28.

Demsetz, Harold, "Toward a Theory of Property Rights" (1967) *American Economics Review*, vol. 57, p. 347.

Dernbach, John C. "Sustainable Development as a Framework for National Governance" (1998) *Case W. Res. L. Rev.*, vol. 49, p. 1.

Devisch, R., "Colonial State Building in the Congo and its Dismantling" (1998) *Journal of Legal Pluralism*, vol. 42, p. 221.

Dewey, John, *The Public and Its Problems* (Henry Holt & Co, New York, 1927).

Diwedi, O. P., *Development Administration. From Underdevelopment to Sustainable Development* (St Martin's Press, New York, 1994).

Doremus, Holly:

2001 "Adaptive Management, the Endangered Species Act, and the Institutional Challenges of 'New Age' Environmental Protection" *Washburn Law Journal*, vol. 41, p. 50.

1991 "Patching the Ark: Improving Legal Protection of Biological Diversity" *Ecology Law Quarterly*, vol. 18, p. 265.

Dworkin, Ronald, *Law's Empire* (Fontana, London, 1986).

Dyer, Christopher L. and James R. McGoodwin (eds.), *Folk Management in the World's Fisheries* (University Press of Colorado, Niwot CO, 1994).

Eckhoff, Torstein, *Rettskildeläre* [Sources of Law] (ed. by Jan Helgesen, 5th edn, Universitetsforlaget, Oslo, 2001).

Eckhoff, Torstein and Nils Kristian Sundby, *Rettssystemer* ([*Legal Systems*] Universitetsforlaget, Oslo, 1991).

The Economist, *A Survey of the World Economy* (Annex to *The Economist* September 20, 1997).

Edwards, Victoria M. and Basil M. H. Sharp, "Institutional Arrangements for Conservation on Private Land in New Zealand" (1990) *Journal of Environmental Management*, vol. 31, p. 313.

Ehrlich, Eugen, *Fundamental Principles of the Sociology of Law* (Harvard University Press, Cambridge, MA, 1936).

Ehrlich, Gretel, *This Cold Heaven. Seven Seasons in Greenland* (Pantheon Books, New York, 2001).

Eikeland, Sveinung, "Flexibility in the Fishing Commons," in Svein Jentoft (ed.), *Commons in a Cold Climate. Coastal Fisheries and Reindeer Pastoralism in North Norway: The Co-Management Approach* (Man and the Biosphere Series No. 22, Parthenon, New York, 1998).

Eisenhardt, Kathleen M., "Making Fast Strategic Decisions in High-Velocity Environments" (1989) *Academy of Management Journal*, vol. 32, p. 543.

Ekelöf, Per-Olof, *Är den juridiska doktrinen en teknik eller en vetenskap?* [*Is Legal Dogmatism a Matter of Mechanics, or a Science?*] (Gleerup, Lund, 1951).

Eliade, Mircea, *Myth and Reality* (Harper Torchbooks, New York, 1974).

Ellen, R. F., "Patterns of Indigenous Timber Extraction from Moluccan Rain Forest Fringes" (1985) *Journal of Biogeography*, vol. 12, p. 559.

Ellickson, Robert C.:
1991 *Order Without Law: How Neighbours Settle Disputes* (Harvard University Press, Cambridge, MA).
1989 "A Hypothesis of Wealth-Maximizing Norms: Evidence from the Whaling Industry" *Journal of Law, Economics and Organization*, vol. 5, no. 1, p. 83.
1986 "Of Coase and Cattle: Dispute Resolution Among Neighbors in Shasta County" *Stanford Law Review*, vol. 38, p. 623.

Elmqvist, Thomas, "Indigenous Institutions, Resilience and Failure of Co-management of Rain Forest Preserves in Samoa," paper delivered at the International Association for the Study of Common Property Conference (Indiana University, May–June, 2000).

Elster, Jon:
1991 "Arguing and Bargaining in the Federal Convention and the Assemblée Constituante," in Raino Malnes and Arild Underdal (eds.), *Rationality and Institutions. Essays in Honour of Knut Midgaard* (Scandinavian University Press, Oslo, Bergen, Tromsø).
1989 *The Cement of Society: A Study of Social Order* (Cambridge University Press, Cambridge).
1989 *Nuts and Bolts for the Social Sciences* (Cambridge University Press, Cambridge).
1985 "Weakness of the Will and the Free-Rider Problem" (1985) *Economics and Philosophy*, vol. 1, p. 231.

Ely, J., *Democracy and Distrust: A Theory of Judicial Review* (Harvard University Press, Boston, 1980).

Environmental Law Institute:
1995 *Brazil's Extractive Reserves: Fundamental Aspects of Their Implementation* (Environmental Law Institute, Washington DC).
1999 *Sustainability in Practice* (Environmental Law Institute, Washington DC).

Epstein, Richard A., *Takings: Private Property and the Power of Eminent Domain* (Harvard University Press, Cambridge MA, 1985).

Ewald, Jens, *Retskilderne og den juridiske metode* (2nd edn., Jurist-og Økonomforbundets Forlag, Copenhagen, 2000).

Eythorson, Einar, "Voices of the Weak – Relational Aspects of Local Knowledge in the Fisheries," in Svein Jentoft (ed.), *Commons in a Cold Climate. Coastal Fisheries and Reindeer Pastoralism in North Norway: The Co-Management Approach* (Man and the Biosphere Series No. 22, Parthenon, New York, 1998).

Eythorson, Einar and Stein R. Mathisen, "Changing Understandings of Coastal Saami Local Knowledge," in Svein Jentoft (ed.), *Commons in a Cold Climate Coastal Fisheries and Reindeer Pastoralism in North Norway: The Co-Management Approach* (Man and the Biosphere Series No. 22, Parthenon, New York).

Falck, N., *Juridische Encyclopädie* (Kiel, 1821).

Farber, Daniel A., *Eco-pragmatism: Making Sensible Decisions in an Uncertain World* (University of Chicago Press, Chicago, 1999).

Fauchald, Ole Kristian, *Environmental Taxes and Trade Discrimination* (Kluwer Law, London, The Hague, Boston, 1998).

Faundez, J. (ed.), *Good Government and Law. Legal and Institutional Reform in Developing Countries* (Macmillan, Basingstoke, 1997).

Federspiel, Holger, *Romerske Retskilder* (Nyt Nordisk forlag, Copenhagen, 1930).

Fehr, Ernst and Klaus M. Schmidt, *A Theory of Fairness, Competition, and Cooperation* (University of Zürich/University of Münich, Zürich and Münich, 1998).

Fenger, Ole, *Romerret i Norden* [*Roman Law in the Nordic Countries*]. (Berlingske forlag, Copenhagen, 1977).

Ferguson, J., *The Anti-Politics Machine* (Cambridge University Press, Cambridge, 1990).

Finnmark Dagblad newspaper, 27. Februari 1993 with Dagny Larsen, the last Saame-woman in Porsanger municipality to participate in the traditional coastal Saami trade for a living.

Fisher, J., *The Road from Rio. Sustainable Development and the Nongovernmental Movement in the Third World* (Praeger, Westport Conn, 1993).

Fisher, R. and W. Ury, *Getting to Yes* (Houghton Mifflin, Boston, 1981).

Fitzpatrick, P., *Law and State in Papua New Guinea* (Academic Press, London, 1980).

Fleischer, C. A., *Petroleumsrett* [*Petroleum law*] (Universitetsf orlaget, Oslo, 1983).

Folke, Carl, Fikret Berkes and Johan Colding, "Ecological Practices and Social Mechanisms for Building Resilience and Sustainability," in Fikret Berkes and Carl Folke (eds.), *Linking Social and Ecological Systems: Management Practices and Social Mechanisms for Building Resilience* (Cambridge University Press, Cambridge, 1998).

Ford, Richard Thompson, "The Boundaries of Race: Political Geography in Legal Analysis" (1994) *Harvard Law Review*, vol. 107, p. 1841.

Forman, Richard T. T., *Land Mosaics: The Ecology of Landscapes and Regions* (Cambridge University Press, Cambridge, 1995).

Foster, M. B.:

1936 "Christian Theology and Modern Science of Nature" *Mind*, vol. 45, p. 1.

1934 "The Christian Doctrine of Creation and the Rise of Modern Natural Science" *Mind*, vol. 43, p. 446.

Franck, T. M., *The Power of Legitimacy Among Nations* (Oxford University Press, Oxford, 1990).

Franz, R. Sharpe, *Two Custumals of the Manor of Cockerham 1326 and 1483*, a translation of the Lancaster and Cheshire Antiquaries Society, (1954), vol. 64.

Fratkin, P., "Pastoralism: Governance and Development Issues" (1997) *Annual Review of Anthropology* 236.

Freed, Leonard A., "Extinction and Endangerment of Hawaiian Honeycreepers: A Comparative Approach," in Laura A. Landweber and Andrew P.

Dobson (eds.), *Genetics and the Extinction of Species* (Princeton University Press, Princeton NJ, 1999).

Freeman, Milton M. R.:

1993 "Traditional Land Users as a Legitimate Source of Environmental Expertise," in Nancy M. Williams and Graham Baines (eds.), *Traditional Ecological Knowledge Wisdom for Sustainable Development* (Australian National University Centre for Resource and Environmental Studies, Canberra).

1989 "The Alaska Eskimo Whaling Commission: successful Co-management under Extreme Conditions," in Evelyn Pinkerton (ed.), *Co-operative Management of Local Fisheries* (University of British Columbia Press, Vancouver).

Freese, Curtis H., *Wild Species as Commodities: Managing Markets and Ecosystems for Sustainability* (Island Press, Washington DC, 1998).

French, Duncan A., *The Role of the State and International Organizations in Reconciling Sustainable Development and Globalization. International Environmental Agreements: Politics, Law, and Economics* (2002), p. 135.

Friedheim, Robert, "Fostering a Negotiated Outcome in the IWC" (Reykjavik, March 1, 1997) *Political and Economic Perspectives* 6.

Fukuyama, Francis, *Trust: The Social Virtues and the Creation of Prosperity* (The Free Press, New York, 1995).

Fuller, Lon L., "Human Interaction and the Law" (1969) *American Journal of Jurisprudence*, vol. 14, p. 1.

Gadgil, Madhav, "Prudence and Profligacy: A Human Ecological Perspective," in Timothy M. Swanson (ed.), *The Economics and Ecology of Biodiversity Decline: The Forces Driving Global Change* (Cambridge University Press, Cambridge 1995).

Gaines, Sanford E., "Rethinking Environmental Protection, Competitiveness and International Trade" (1997) *University of Chicago Legal Forum* 231–232.

Ganter, Elizabeth, "Indigenous Participation in Coastal Management in the Northern Territory Australia: Issues and Options" (1996) *Ocean and Coastal Management*, vol. 33, p. 193.

Geisler, Charles C. and Frank J. Popper, *Land Reform, American Style* (Rowman & Littlefield Publishers Inc., Lanham, Maryland, 1984).

Ghai, Y, "The Theory of the State in the Third World and the Problematics of Constitutionalism" in D. Greenberg and S. Katz (eds.), *Constitutionalism and Democracy* (Oxford University Press: Oxford, 1993).

Gihl, Torsten, "Aktuella problem inom folkrätt och allmän rättslära" ["Contemporary Challenges of International Law and Theory of Law"] (1953) *Svensk juristtidning* [*Swedish Journal of Jurisprudence*] 356.

Gill, Duane A., "Environmental Disaster and Fishery Co-management in a Natural Resource Community: Impact of the Exxon Valdez Oil Spill," in Christopher L. Dyer and James R. McGoodwin (eds.), *Folk Management in the World's Fisheries* (University Press of Colorado, Niwot CO, 1994).

Gillberg, Minna, *From Green Image to Green Practice. Normative Actions and Self-Regulation* (University of Lund, Lund, 1999).

Gillette, Clayton P., "Rules and Reversibility" (1997) *Notre Dame Law Review*, vol. 72, p. 1415.

Gleick, James, *Faster: The Acceleration of Just About Everything* (Pantheon Books, New York, 1999).

Gobster, Paul H. and R. Bruce Hull (eds.), *Restoring Nature: Perspectives from the Social Sciences and Humanities* (Island Press, Washington DC, 2000).

Godoy, Ricardo, et al., "Strategies of Rain-forest Dwellers against Misfortunes: the Tsimane' Indians of Bolivia" (1998), *Ethnology*, vol. 37, p. 55.

Goodhart, A. L. (ed.) *Jurisprudence and Legal Essays* (London, 1961).

Goodrich, Peter, *Reading the Law: A Critical Introduction* (Basil Blackwell, London, 1986).

Gordon, H. S., "The Economic Theory of a Common Property Resource: The Fishery" (1954) *Journal of Political Economy*, vol. 62, p. 124.

Gordon, John and Jane Coppock, "Ecosystem Management and Economic Development," in Marion R. Chertow and Daniel C. Esty (eds.), *Thinking Ecologically: The Next Generation of Environmental Policy* (Yale University Press, New Haven CT, 1997).

Gough, J. W., *Fundamental Law in English Constitutional History* (Oxford University Press, Oxford, 1955).

Grafton, R. Quentin, Dale Squires and Kevin J. Fox, "Private Property and Economic Efficiency: A Study of a Common-Pool Resource" (2000) *Journal of Law & Economics*, vol. 43, p. 679.

Green, Thomas Hill, *Lectures on the Principles of Political Obligation* (Longman, London, 1895).

Greenland, Statistical Yearbook (Greenland, 1997).

Grossi, Paolo, *An Alternative to Private Property* (University of Chicago Press, Chicago, 1981).

Grotius, Hugo, *The Freedom of the Seas* (transl. by Magoffin, Oxford University Press, Oxford, 1916).

Guy, Richard K., "The Strong Law of Small Number" *American Mathematical Monthly*, vol. 95, p. 697.

Haavelmo, Trygve, *A Study in the Theory of Economic Evolution. Section 19: Strategies of Grabbing, Protection and Cooperation* (North Holland Publishing Company, Amsterdam, 1954).

Hacker, P. M. S., "Davidson on First-Person Authority" (1997) *The Philosophical Quarterly*, vol. 47, p. 285.

Haeckel, Stephan H., *Adaptive Enterprise: Creating and Leading Sense-and-Respond Organizations* (Harvard Business School Press, Cambridge MA, 1999).

Hägerström, Axel, "Begreppet viljeförklaring på privaträttens område" (1935) *Theoria*, vol. 1, pp. 32 ff.

Hagerup, Francis, *Retsencyclopædi* (Aschehoug, Kristiania, 1919).
Halsbury's Laws of England (4th edn. reissue, Butterworths, London, 1998), vol. 12(1), paragraph by J. H. Baker, Fellow of St. Catherine's College, Cambridge University.
Hamilton, Walton H., "Property – according to Locke" (1931) *Yale Law Journal*, vol. 41, p. 864.
Hanna, Susan S., "Managing for Human and Ecological Content in the Maine Soft Shell Clam Fishery," in Fikret Berkes and Carl Folke (eds.), *Linking Social and Ecological Systems: Management Practices and Social Mechanisms for Building Resilience* (Cambridge University Press, Cambridge 1998), pp. 190, 195–196, 204–206.
Hanna, Susan S. et al. (eds.), *Rights to Nature: Ecological, Economic, Cultural, and Political Principles of Institutions for the Environment* (Island Press, Washington DC, 1996).
Hanna, Susan and Svein Jentoft, "Human Use of the Natural Environment: An Overview of Social and Economic Dimensions," in Susan S. Hanna et al. (eds.), *Rights to Nature: Ecological, Economic, Cultural, and Political Principles of Institutions for the Environment* (Island Press, Washington DC, 1996).
Hannesson, Ragnvaldur, "Markedsmekanismens positive egenskaper," in H. Jervan (ed.), *Fra forhandling til marked* (Gruppen for ressursstudier, Oslo, 1984).
Hannum, Hurst, *Autonomy, Sovereignty, and Self-Determination* (University of Pennsylvania Press, Philadelphia PA, 1990).
Hansen, Kjeld, *A Farewell to Greenland's Wildlife* (Gads Forlag, Copenhagen, 2002).
Hardin, Garrett:
1999 "The Tragedy of the Commons Revisited" *Environment*, vol. 41, issue 2.
1994 "The Tragedy of the Unmanaged Commons" *Trends in Ecology and Evolution*, vol. 9, no. 5, p. 199.
1968 "The Tragedies of the Commons" *Science*, vol. 162, p. 1242.
Harrington, James, *The Commonwealth of Oceania and a System of Politics* ed. by J.G.A. Pocock (Cambridge University Press, Cambridge, 1992).
Harris, Cheryl I., "Equal Treatment and the Reproduction of Inequality" (2001) *Fordham Law Review*, vol. 69, p. 1753.
Hart, H. L. A.:
1994 *The Concept of Law* (2nd edn., Oxford University Press, Oxford).
1982 *Essays on Bentham. Studies in Jurisprudence and Political Theory* (Clarendon Press, Oxford).
1961 *The Concept of Law* (Oxford University Press, Oxford).
Hawken, Paul, *The Ecology of Commerce: A Declaration of Sustainability* (Harper Collins Business, New York, 1994).
Hawkins, Michael J. (ed.), Francis Bacon, *Essays* (London, 1972).
Hawaii, State of: Office of Hawaiian Affairs, www.oha.org/index3.html and the Department of Hawaiian Home Lands, www.state.hi.us/dhhl/.

Healey, Chris and Eugene Hunn, "The Current Status of TEK: Papua New Guinea and North America," in Nancy M. Williams and Graham Baines (eds.), *Traditional Ecological Knowledge: Wisdom for Sustainable Development* (Australian National University Centre for Resource and Environmental Studies, Canberra, 1993).

Heilmann, Parnûna, "Sælskindet – spændt ud af dilemmaer." Final thesis for MA at Ilisimatusarfik (unpublished, 1997).

Helberg, Bjørn Hebba, *Fiskeriteknologi som uttrykk for sosial tilhørighet. En studie av nordnorsk fiske i perioden 400–1700 e.Kr [Social Membership as Expressed by Fishery Technology. A North-Norwegian Fishery Study from the Period of 400–1700 AD] Stensilsierie B nr. 38* (University of Tromsø, Tromsø, 1993).

Heliker, Christina, "The Volcanic Origin of the Hawaiian Islands, in Conservation Biology," in Charles P. Stone and Danielle B. Stone (eds.), *Hawai'i* (1989).

Heller, Michael A., "The Boundaries of Private Property" (1999) *Yale Law Journal*, vol. 108, p. 1163.

Hellner, Jan, *Rättsteori* (2nd edn., Juristförlaget, Stackholm, 1994).

Hertz, Ole, *Økologi og levevilkår i Arktis. Uummannamiut* (Christian Ejlers Forlag, Mellemfolkeligt Samvirke, 1995).

Hill, Rosemary et al., "Aborigines and Fire in the Wet Tropics of Queensland, Australia: Ecosystem Management Across Cultures" (1999) *Society and Natural Resources*, vol. 12, p. 205.

Hinz, Manfred O., "The Conflict between the Constitution and Customary Law – Conflicts between System and Concepts," in Karin Fischer-Buden (ed.), *Human Rights and Democracy in Southern Africa* (New Namibia Books, Windhoek, 1998).

Hobbes, Thomas, *Leviathan, or The Matter, Forme, & Power of a Commonwealth, Ecclesiasticall and Civill* (ed. by Richard Tuck, Cambridge University Press, Cambridge, 1991).

Holdsworth, Sir William Searle, *A History of English Law* (3rd edn. Methuenale, London, 1923), vol. II.

Holland, T. E., *The Elements of Jurisprudence* (9th edn. London, 1900).

Holling, C. S.:

1996 "Engineering Resilience versus Ecological Resilience," in Peter C. Schulze (ed.), *Engineering Within Ecological Constraints* (National Academy Press, Washington DC).

1994 "New Science and New Investments for a Sustainable Biosphere," in AnnMari Jansson et al. (eds.), *Investing in Natural Capital: The Ecological Economics Approach to Sustainability* (Island Press, Washington DC).

Holling, C. S. (ed.), *Adaptive Environmental Assessment and Management* (John Wiley and Sons, Washington DC, 1978).

Holling, Crawford S. and Steven Sanderson, "Dynamics of (Dis)harmony in Ecological and Social Systems," in Susan S. Hanna et al. (eds.), *Rights to Nature:*

Ecological, Economic, Cultural, and Political Principles of Institutions for the Environment (Island Press, Washington DC, 1996).

Holloway, William, *The History of Romney Marsh* (John Russell Smith, London, 1849).

Holmes Jr., Oliver W.:

1897 "The Path of Law" *Harvard Law Review*, vol. 10, p. 457.

1881 *The Common Law* (Little, Brown & Company, Boston) vol. 1.

Houck, Oliver A., "On the Law of Biodiversity and Ecosystem Management" (1997) *Minnesota Law Review*, vol. 81, p. 869.

Hovelsrud-Broda, Grete, "Sharing of local produce – sharing of imports and cash. A study of differential distribution patterns." Paper presented at the 11th Inuit Studies Conference, September 1998, Nuuk.

Howard, A. E. Dick, *Magna Carta: Text and Commentary* (The University Press of Virginia, Charlottesville VA, 1964).

Huffman, James L., "A Fish Out of Water: The Public Trust Doctrine in a Constitutional Democracy" (1989), *Environmental Law*, vol. 19, p. 527.

Hume, David:

1978 *A Treatise of Human Nature: Being an Attempt to Introduce the Experimental Method of Reasoning into Moral Subjects* (ed. by P. H. Nidditch, 2nd edn., including "an abstract of a Book," Clarendon Press, Oxford).

1975 *Enquiries Concerning Human Understanding and concerning the Principles of Morals* (ed. by P. H. Nidditch, 3rd edn., Clarendon Press Oxford).

Hunn, Eugene:

1993 "The Ethnobiological Foundation for Traditional Ecological," in Nancy M. Williams and Graham Baines (eds.), *Traditional Ecological Knowledge: Wisdom For Sustainable Development* (Australian National University Centre for Resource and Environmental Studies, Canberra, 1993).

1993 "What is Traditional Ecological Knowledge?" in Nancy M. Williams and Graham Baines (eds.), *Traditional Ecological Knowledge: Wisdom for Sustainable Development* (Australian National University Centre for Resource and Environmental Studies, Canberra, 1993).

Hunt, Colin, "Cooperative Approaches to Marine Resource Management in the South Pacific," in Peter Larmour (ed.), *The Governance of Common Property in the Pacific Region* (National Centre for Development Studies, Pacific Policy Paper 19, The Australian National University, Canberra, 1997).

Hutchful, E., "Reconstructing Political Space: militarism and constitutionalism in Africa," in D. Greenberg and S. Katz (eds.), *Constitutionalism and Democracy* (Oxford University Press, Oxford, 1993).

Ihering, Rudolf, *Geist des römischen Rechts, auf den verchiedenen Stufen seiner Entwichlung* (Leipzig, 1871).

Inter-Departmental Liaison Group on Risk Assessment (ILGRA), "The Precautionary Principle: Policy and Application" (30 September 2002).

International Institute for Sustainable Development, Assessing Sustainable Development (International Institute for Sustainable Development, Winnipeg, 1997).

International Law Association (ILA), Resolution 3/2002 (New Delhi 2002).

Jahreskog, Birgitta (ed.), *The Saami National Minority in Sweden* (Stockholm, 1982).

Janet, Paul, *Alexis de Tocqueville et la science politique au XIXe siècle. Revue des deux mondes* (transl. by J. P. Mayer Paris, 1861), p. 110.

Jansson, AnnMari, et al. (eds.), *Investing in Natural Capital: The Ecological Economics Approach to Sustainability* (Island Press, Washington DC, 1994).

Jentoft, Svein, *Dangling Lines – The Fisheries Crisis and the Future of Coastal Communities: The Norwegian Experience* (ISER – Institut of Social and Economic Research, St. Johns, Newfoundland, 1993).

Jentoft, Svein (ed.), *Commons in a Cold Climate. Coastal Fisheries and Reindeer Pastoralism in North Norway: The Co-Management Approach* (Man and the Biosphere Series No. 22, Parthenon, New York, 1998).

Johannes, R. E. and Henry T. Lewis, "The Importance of Researchers' Expertise in Environmental Subjects," in Nancy M. Williams and Graham Baines (eds.), *Traditional Ecological Knowledge: Wisdom for Sustainable Development* (Australian National University Centre for Resource and Environmental Studies, Canberra, 1993).

Johansen, Lars Emil, "Autonomy, Dependency, Sustainability: A Greenland Perspective," in Hanne Petersen and Birger Poppel (eds.), *Autonomy, Dependency, Sustainability in the Arctic* (Ashgate, Aldershot, UK, 1999).

Jordan, Danny, "Negotiating Salmon Management on the Klamath River," in Evelyn Pinkerton (ed.), *Co-operative Management of Local Fisheries* (University of British Columbia Press, Vancouver, 1989).

Juergensmeyer, Julian C. and James B. Wadley, "The Common Lands Concept: A 'Commons' Solution to a Common Environmental Problem" (1974), *National Resources Journal*, vol. 14, p. 362.

Justinian:

1904 *The Digest of Justinian* (transl. by Charles Henry Monro, Cambridge University Press, Cambridge) D. 1.3.32.21.

1987 *Justinian's Institutes* (transl. and intro. by Peter Birks and Grant McLeod, Duckworth, London).

Kalotas, Arpad C., "Recording and Applying Aboriginal Botanical Knowledge," in Nancy M. Williams and Graham Baines (eds.), *Western Australia: Some Recent Examples and Future Prospects, in Traditional Ecological Knowledge: Wisdom for Sustainable Development* (Australian National University Centre for Resource and Environmental Studies, Canberra, 1993).

Kane, Sean, *Wisdom of the Mythtellers* (Broadview Press, Toronto, 1994).

Kant, Immanual:

1997 *Critique of Pure Reason* (transl. and ed. by Paul, Guyer and Allen W. Wood, Cambridge University Press, Cambridge.

1996 *Practical Philosophy* (transl. and ed. by Mary J. Gregor, Cambridge University Press, Cambridge, 1996).

1996 *What Does it Mean to Orient Oneself in Thinking, in Religion and Rational Theology* (transl. and ed. by Allen W. Wood and George di Giovanni, Cambridge University Press, Cambridge.

1913 "Zum Ewigen Frieden" (1795) in Karl Vorländer (ed.), *Kleinere Schriften zur Geschichtsphilosophie, Ethik und Politik, Philosophiche Bibliothek* (Meiner, Hamburg), vol. I.

Karsten, Peter, *Between Law and Custom* (Cambridge University Press, Cambridge 2002).

Keiter, Robert B., "Beyond the Boundary Line: Constructing a Law of Ecosystem Management" (1994) *University of Colorado Law Review*, vol. 65, p. 293.

Kelsen, Hans:

1966 "On the Pure Theory of Law" *Israel Law Review*, vol. 1, p. 2.

1960 *Pure Theory of Law* (University of California Press, Berkley, CA).

1945 *General Theory of Law and State*, p. 135.

1929 *Vom Wesen und Wert der Demokratie* (Mohr, Tübingen).

1925 *Allegemeine Staatslehre* (Julis Springer, Berlin).

The Keystone Center, *The Keystone National Policy Dialogue on Ecosystem Management: Final Report* (The Keystone Center, Washington DC, 1996).

Khaleque, Kibriaul and Michael A. Gold, "Pineapple Agroforestry: An Indigenous System Among the Garo Community of Bangladesh" (1993), *Society and Natural Resources*, vol. 6, p. 71.

King, Anthony W., "Hierarchy Theory: A Guide to System Structure for Wildlife Biologists," in John A. Bissonette (ed.), *Wildlife and Landscape Ecology: Effects of Pattern and Scale* (Springer, New York, 1997).

King Christian IV, 1604 General Codex, available at http://www.hf.uio.no/PNH/chr4web/chr4innhold.html.

King Christian V, 1687 General Codex, available at http://www.hf.uio.no/PNH/chr5web/chr5fortale.html.

Kiralfy, Albert, "Custom in Medieval English Law" (1988) *Journal of Legal History*, vol. 9, p. 26.

Klami, Hannu Tapani, "Om rättsdogmatisk forskning" ["About the Science of Legal Dogmatism"] (transl. by Peter Ørebech) (Åboakademi, 1984).

Kleivan, I. and B. Sonne, *Eskimos Greenland and Canada* (E. J. Brill, Leiden, 1985).

Kolbert, Elizabeth, "Ice Memory" (January 7, 2002) *The New Yorker*, 30.

Kolsrud, Knut, *Sjøfinnane i Rognsund* [*The Coastal Saami People of Rognsund*] (Studia Septentrionalia, Oslo, 1955), vol. 6.

Kovalesvski, Maxim M., "Le passage historique de la propriété collective à la propriété individuelle," in *Annales de l'institut international de sociologie* (Paris, 1986), vol. 2, p. 207.

Krech, Shepard, *The Ecological Indian: Myth and History* (W. W. Norton & Co., New York, 1999), pp. 212–215.

Lal, P. et al., "The Adaptive Decision-Making Process as a Tool for Integrated Natural Resource Management: Focus, Attitudes, and Approach" (2001) *Conservation Ecology*, vol. 5(2). [online at http://www.consecol.org/vol5/iss2/art11]

Lambert, E., *Etudes de droit législatif ou de droit civil comparé, I Série, B. 1. La fonction de droit civil compare* (Paris, 1903).

Lambert, Edouard, "Codified law and Case-law: Their Part in Shaping the Policies of Justice," in *Science of Legal Method. Selected Essays by Various Authors* (transl. by Ernest Bruncken and Layton B. Register, The Macmillan Company, New York, 1921).

Larmore, Charles E., *Patterns of Moral Complexity* (Cambridge University Press, Cambridge, 1987).

Larmour, Peter (ed.), *The Governance of Common Property in the Pacific* (Region National Centre for Development Studies, Pacific Policy Paper 19, The Australian National University, Canberra, 1997).

Larson, Bruce A. and Daniel W. Bromley, "Property Rights, Externalities, and Resource Degradation: Locating the Tragedy" (1990) *Journal of Development Economics*, vol. 33, p. 235.

Lazarus, Richard J., "Pursuing 'Environmental Justice': The Distributional Effects of Environmental Protection" (1993) *Northwestern University Law Review*, vol. 87, p. 787.

Lele, S., *Sustainable Development: A Critical Review* (World Development, Montreal, 1996).

Lennert, Lise, *Kvinder i Grønland – sammen og hver for sig* (Atuakkiorfik, Nuuk, 1991).

Liermann, Annmarie M., "Seeking Sovereignty: The Akaka Bill and the Case for the Inclusion of Hawaiians in Federal Native American Policy" (2001) *Santa Clara Law Review*, vol. 41, p. 509.

Light, Stephen S. et al., "The Everglades: Evolution of Management in a Turbulent Ecosystem," in Lance H. Gunderson, et al. (eds.), *Barriers and Bridges to the Renewal of Ecosystems and Institutions* (Columbia University Press, New York, 1995).

Lillevoll, Tor Arne:

1998 "Open Common for Fjord Fishery in Coast Saami Areas," in Svein Jentoft (ed.), *Commons in a Cold Climate. Coastal Fisheries and Reindeer Pastoralism in North Norway: The Co-Management Approach* (Man and the Biosphere Series No. 22, Parthenon, 1998).

1998 Åpenallmeming for fjordfiske i Sjøsamiske områder?" ["A Still Open Outer Common For the Fishermen in the Coastal Saami Areas"?], in Bjørn Sagdahl (ed.), *Fjordressursen og Reguleringspolitikk* (Kommuneforlaget, Oslo, 1998).

Lloyd, Dennis, *The Idea of Law* (Penguin Books, London, 1991).

Locke, John:

1963 *Two Treatises of Government* (ed. by Peter Lasslett, The New American Library, London).

1956 *Second Treatise of Civil Government* (Basil Blackwell, Oxford).
Loope, Lloyd L., "Hawaii and the Pacific Islands," in *United States Geological Survey, Status and Trends of the Nation's Biological Resources* (accessed December 4, 2001).
Loope, Lloyd L. and Dieter Mueller-Dombois, "Characteristics of Invaded Islands, with Special Reference to Hawaii," in J. A. Drake (ed.), *Biological Invasions: A Global Perspective* (SCOPE/ICSU, John Wiley, Chichester and New York, 1989).
Luhman, Niklas, *A Sociological Theory of Law* (Routledge, London, 1985).
Lundstedt, A. V., *Grundlinjer i skadesståndsretten, senare delen bd II:2* [*Basic Structures in Tort Law*] (Almquist & Wiksell, Uppsala, 1953).
Lynge, Finn:
1998 "Nature Management: Kill and Care. Reflections on the Origins of a Controversy," in Hanne Petersen and Birger Poppel (eds.), *Dependency, Autonomy, Sustainability in the Arctic* (Ashgate, Aldershot, Brookfield USA, Singapore, Sydney).
1992 *Arctic Wars. Animal Rights, Endangered Peoples* (Dartmouth, New England).
MacCallum, Raymond, "The Community-Based Management of Fisheries in Atlantic Canada: A Legislative Proposal" (1998) *Dalhousie Law Journal*, vol. 21, p. 49.
MacCormick, Neil, "Law as Institutional Fact" (1974) *Law Quarterly Review*, vol. 90, p. 102.
Machiavelli, Niccolò, *The Prince* (Harvey C. Mansfield, Jr., trans., University of Chicago Press, Chicago, 1985).
Maine, Henry Sumner:
1996 *Ancient Law: Its Connection with the Early History of Society, and its Relation to Modern Ideas* (London 1861, Theommes Press, reprint Bristol).
1897 *Lectures on the Early History of Institutions* (7th edn., John Murray, London).
1886 *The Nature of Democracy in Popular Government* (Routledge and Kegan Paul, London).
1883 *Dissertations on Early Law and Custom* (John Murray, London).
1876 *Village Communities in the East and West* (John Murray, London).
Maitland, Frederick William and William Paley Baildon (eds.), (Seldon Society, Bernard Quaritch, London, 1890), vol. IV. *The Court Baron.*
Mantziasris, C., "Beyond the Aboriginal Councils and Associations Act Part 2" (1997) *Indigenous Law Bulletin*, vol. 4, p. 9.
Marsh, H., et al., "The Sustainability of the Indigenous Dugong Fishery in Torres Strait, Australia/Papua New Guinea" (1997) *Conservation Biology*, vol. 11, p. 1375.
Marshall, Alfred, *Principles of Economics* (Macmillan, London, 1890).
Marx, Karl and Friedrich Engels, *The German Ideology* (London, 1974).

Massell, G. J., "Law as an Instrument of Revolutionary Change in a Traditional Milieu – The Case of Soviet Central Asia" (1968) *Law & Society Review*, vol. 2, p. 182.

Maurstad, Anita, *Sjarkfiske og ressursforvaltning* [*Law-tech Fishery and Resources Management*] (University of Tromsø, Tromsø, 1997).

Maurstad, Anita and Jan H. Sundet, "The Invisible Cod – Fishermen's and Scientists' Knowledge," in Svein Jentoft (ed.), *Commons in a Cold Climate. Coastal Fisheries and Reindeer Pastoralism in North Norway: The Co-Management Approach* (Man and the Biosphere Series No. 22, Parthenon, New York, 1998).

McAuslan, P.:

1998 "Making Law Work: Re-structuring Land Relations in Africa" *Development and Change* 526.

1997 "Law, Governance and the Development of the Market: Practical Problems and Possible Solutions," in J. Faundez (ed.), *Good Government and Law. Legal and Institutional Reform in Developing Countries* (Macmillan, Basingstoke).

McC. Netting, Robert:

1993 *Smallholders, Householders, Farm Families and the Ecology of Intensive, Sustainable Agriculture* (Stanford University Press, Stanford, CA).

1981 *Balancing on an Alp: Ecological Change and Continuity in a Swiss Mountain Community* (Cambridge University Press, Cambridge).

McCay, Bonnie J.:

1998 *Oyster Wars and the Public Trust: Property, Law and Ecology in New Jersey History* (University of Arizona Press, Tucson AZ).

1987 "The Culture of the Commoners: Historical Observations on Old and New World Fisheries," in Bonnie J. McCay and James M. Acheson (eds.), *The Question of the Commons* (University of Arizona Press, Tucson AZ).

McCay, B. J. and S. Jentoft, *Market or Community Failure. Critical Perspectives on Common Property Research* 1998 Human Organization V. 57.

McDonald, Miriam, Lucassie Arragutainaq and Zack Novalinga, *Voices from the Bay. Traditional Ecological Knowledge of Inuit and Cree in the Hudson Bay Bioregion.* Canadian Arctic Resources Committee (Environmental Committee of Municipality of Sanikiluaq, 1997).

McEldowney, Holly, "Lime Collection and its Effects on Coral Reefs," in Nancy M. Williams and Graham Baines (eds.), *Traditional Ecological Knowledge: Wisdom for Sustainable Development* (Australian National University Centre for Resource and Environmental Studies, Canberra, 1993).

McEvoy, Arthur F., *The Fisherman's Problem: Ecology and Law in the California Fisheries, 1850–1980* (n.p., 1986).

McGregor, D. Masters Thesis on File, University of Hawaii.

McKean, Margaret A. "Common-Property Regimes as a Solution to Problems of Scale and Linkage," in Susan S. Hanna et al. (eds.), *Rights to Nature: Ecological,*

Economic, Cultural, and Political Principles of Institutions for the Environment (Island Press, Washington DC, 1996).

McKenzie, Melody Kapilialoha *Native Hawaiian Rights Handbook* (Native Hawaiian Legal Corp., Honolulu, 1991).

McNeely, Jeffrey A., "Common Property Resource Management or Government Ownership: Improving the Conservation of Biological Resources" (1991) *International Relations*, vol. 10, p. 211.

McNeil, Kent, *Common Law Aboriginal Title* (Clarendon Press, Oxford, 1989).

Megard, Bjørn Olav, "Om å forstå 'de lite samevennlige' i Finnmark og om forslaget til 'Samisk grunnforvaltning'" ["To Understand the 'Saami Critical' Inhabitants of Finnmark and the Saami Land Resources Management Scheme"] *Kritisk Juss* (Oslo, 1999).

Meine, Curt, *Aldo Leopold: His Life and Works* (University of Wisconsin Press, Madison WI, 1988).

Melkevik, Bjarne, "The First Nations and Québec: Identity and Law, Self-Affirmation and Self-Determination at the Crossroads," in José Serguinot Barbosa (ed.), *Globalization in America: A Geographical Approach* (Université Laval, Quebec, 1998).

Messerschmidt, Donald A., "Indigenous Environmental Management and Adaptation: An Introduction to Four Case Studies from Nepal" (1990) *Mountain Research and Development*, vol. 10, p. 3.

Meyer, Judy L.:

1997 "Conserving Ecosystem Function," in Steward Pickett et al. (eds.), *The Ecological Basis of Conservation: Heterogeneity, Ecosystems, and Biodiversity* (Chapman & Hall, New York).

1994 "The Dance of Nature: New Concepts in Ecology" *Chicago-Kent Law Review*, vol. 69, p. 875.

Meyers, G. D., "Environmental and Natural Resources Management by Indigenous Peoples in North America: Inherent Rights of Self-government, Part 2. Defining the Content of Aboriginal Rights in Canada" *Governance Structures for Indigenous Australians On and Off Native Title Lands.* Austlii Reconciliation and Social Justice Library. See www.austlii.edu.au/special/rsjproject/rsjlibrary/arcerp/dp5/htm.

Michels, Robert, *Political Parties: A Sociological Study of the Oligarchical Tendencies of Modern Democracy* (Free Press, New York, 1962).

Mill, John Stuart, *Utilitarianism* (Prometheus Books, New York, 1987).

Milton, John:

1980 "The Readie and Easie Way to Establish a Free Commonwealth," in *Complete Prose Works of John Milton* (ed. by Robert W. Ayers, Yale University Press, New Haven, Conn.), vol. VII.

1962 "Eikonoklastes," in *Complete Prose Works of John Milton* (ed. by Merrit Y. Hughes, Yale University Press, New Haven, Conn.) vol. III.

Minerbi, Luciano, "Indigenous Management Models and Protection of the Ahupua'a" (1999) *Social Process in Hawaii* 39, 208.

Montagne, Pierre, "Contributions of Indigenous Silviculture to Forestry Development in Rural Areas: Examples from Niger and Mali" (1985) *Rural Africana* 23–24, 61, 63–64.

Mushala, H. M., "Soil Erosion and Indigenous Land Management: Some Socio-economic Considerations" (1997) *Soil Technology*, vol. 11, p. 301.

Naess, Arne, *Økologi og filosofi* ["*Ecology and Philosophy*"] (Universitetsforlaget, Oslo, 1972).

Nance, Dale, *Law & Justice* (1st edn., Carolina Academic Press, Durham, 1994).

Nash, John F., *Essays on Game Theory* (Edward Elgar, Cheltenham, 1996).

National Resource Council:

1999 *The Community Development Quota Program in Alaska* (National Academy Press, Washington DC).

1999 *Sharing the Fish, Toward a National Policy on Individual Fishing Quotas* (National Academy Press, Washington DC).

1995 *Science and the Endangered Species Act* (National Academy Press, Washington DC).

1986 Proceedings of the Conference on Common Property Resource Management.

Nedham, Marchamont, *The Excellencie of a Free State* (ed. by Richard Baron, London, 1967).

Neeson, J. M., *Commoners: Common Right, Enclosure and Social Change in England 1700–1820* (Academic Press, New York, 1993).

Nettheim, G., *Governance Structures for Indigenous Australians On and Off Native Title Lands*, Austlii Reconciliation and Social Justice Library, <www.austlii.edu.au/special/rsjproject/rsjlibrary/arcerp/dp5/htm 4.>

Niemi, Einar, *Vadsøs histori* (Universitetsforlaget, Oslo, 1983), bd. I.

Nolan, Associate Justice Joseph R., *Black's Law Dictionary* (6th edn., West Publishing Co., St. Paul MN).

Noland, G., "Ocean Frontiers: 'Initiatives in the 21st Century'" in S. Y. Hong, E. Miles and C-H. Park (eds.), *The Role of the Oceans in the 21st Century* (Law of the Sea Institute, Honolulu, 1995).

Norwegian Coastal Fishermen Organization, Inquiry among high school students of November 2001.

Norwegian Storting [the parliament]: Innst. O.nr.38 1998–1999 *Innstilling fr naeringskomiteen om lov om retten til å delta i fiske og fangst (deltakerloven) s. 5 sp. 1* [*Proposal on a New Act of Fishery Participation Rights*], confirmed Innst.O.nr. 73 (2000–01).

Norton, Bryan, "Change, Constancy and Creativity: The New Ecology and Some Old Problems" (1996) 7 *Duke Environmental Law and Policy Forum*, vol. 49, p. 58.

NOU:

2001 Peter Ørebech, *Sedvanerett i fisket. Sjøsamene i Finnmark* [*Fisheries Customary Law. The Coastal Saami*] (Statens Forvaltningstjeneste, Oslo).

1997 Gudmund Sandvik, *Om oppfatningar av retten til og broken av land og vatn i Finnmark fram mot lutten av 1960-ara* [*About the legal opinions regarding Finnmark onshore and offshore utilization during the period up to the end of the 1960s*]. (Statens Forvaltningstjeneste, Oslo).

1994: 21 *Bruk av land og vann i Finnmark i historisk perspektiv* [*The Use of Land and Lakes in Finnmark in Historical Perspective*], Norges offentlige utredninger [Norwegian Public Reports] (Statens Forvaltningstjeneste, Oslo, 1994), p. 88.

1988: 16 *Eigedomsgrenser og administrative inndelingsgrenser* [*Possessory and Administrative Borders*], s. 56 sp. 2 (Statens Forvaltningstjeneste, Oslo).

1985: 32 *Revisjon av allmenningslovgivningen* [*Moderation of the Commons Legislation*] (Statens Forvaltningstjeneste, Oslo).

1984: 18 *Om samenes rettstilling* [*About the Saami Rights and Obligations*] (Statens Forvaltningstjeneste, Oslo).

Nuttall, Mark, *Arctic Homeland: Kinship, Community and Development in Northwest Greenland* (University of Toronto Press, Toronto, Buffalo, 1992).

Oakley, Francis:

1997 "Locke, Natural Law and God – Again" *History of Political Thought*, vol. 18, p. 624.

1961 "Christian Theology and the Newtonian Science: The Rise of the Concept of the Laws of Nature" *Church History*, vol. 30, p. 433.

Ober, Josiah, *The Athenian Revolution. Essays on Ancient Greek Democracy and Political Theory* (Princeton University Press, Princeton NJ, 1996).

O'Connor, Pam, *Indigenous Policy, Native Title and the Rule of Law* (Australian National University, 1998) *Agenda* vol. 5, p. 501.

Odner, Knut, *The Varanger Saami* (Scandinavian University Press, Oslo, 1992).

Okoth-Ogendo, H., "Constitutions without Constitutionalism: Reflections on an African Political Paradox," in D. Greenberg and S. Katz (eds.), *Constitutionalism and Democracy* (Oxford University Press, Oxford, 1993).

Okun, Arthur M., *Equality and Efficiency: The Big Tradeoff* (The Brookings Institution, Washington, 1975).

Olivecrona, Karl, *Law as Fact* (Stevens, London, 1939).

Olusegun, S., "Apantaku, Indigenous Technical Knowledge and Use of Forest Plant Products for Sustainable Control of Crop Pests in Ogun State, Nigeria" (1999) *Journal of Sustainable Agriculture*, vol. 14, p. 5.

O'Malley, Eric Steven, "Irreconcilable Rights and the Question of Hawaiian Statehood" (2001) *Georgetown Law Journal*, vol. 89, p. 501.

Ørebech, Peter:

2005 "What Restoration Schemes Can Do? Or, Getting It Right Without Fisheries Transferable Quotas," *Ocean Development and International Law*, vol. 36, p. 159.

2003 "Overruling the Law." *Report to the Power and Democracy Studies* (Oslo).

2003 *Om torskeresolusjonen av 1989. Den skjulte agenda og ranet av fiskeriallmenningen* [On the 1989 Cod Resolution. The Hidden Agenda and the Robbery of the Commons] 2002 Report to the Norwegian Power and Democracy Commission 1998–2003 (Unipub as, Oslo).

2002 "Tvers igjennom lov til seier!" in *Om torskeresolusjonen av 1989, den skjulte agenda og ranet av Fiskeriallmenningen* ["Overruling the Law!" in *On the Cod Resolution of 1989. The Hidden Agenda and the Robbery of the Commons*] 2002 Report to the Norwegian Power and Democracy Commission (Unipub as, Oslo).

2001 "Hva gjør Norge med sine 'piratfiskere'? – En rettslig og rettspolitisk gjennomgang av norsk domisilstatsjurisdiksjon på det åpne hav" ["What is the Answer to the Fishing Pirates? A Legal and Legislative Analysis of Norwegian Domicile Jurisdiction on the High Seas"], *Retfaerd Nordic Legal Journal* 67, 82.

1999 "The Repetitive Players Game illustrated by the Regional Fisheries Organization of the North East Atlantic Convention (NEAFC)," in T. Bjørndal, G. Munro and R. Arnason (eds.), *Proceedings from the Conference on the Management of Straddling Fish Stocks and Highly Migratory Fish Stocks, and the UN Agreement* (Norwegian School of Business Administration, Bergen).

1998 "Sedvanereet som grunnlag for bærekraftig forvaltning av fiske i de 'ytre almenninger'" ["Customary Law as a Foundation for Sustainable Fishing Management"] in Bjørn Sagdahl (ed.), *Fjordressurser og Reguleringspolitikk* (Kommuneforlaget, Oslo).

1996 "Public, Common or Private Property Rights: Legal and Political Aspects," in S. Arnfred and H. Petersen (eds.), *Legal Change in North/South Perspective* (Occasional Paper No. 18, Roskilde University).

1996 "Sustainable Development by Means of Market Distribution Mechanism," in Andrea Baranzini and Fabrizio Carlevaro (eds.), *Econometrics of Environment and Transdisciplinarity* (AEA List, International Conference, Lisbon).

1995 "The Northern Sea Route. Conditions for Sailing according to European Community Legislation" (Insrop Working Paper No. 20, Oslo, St. Petersburg, Tokyo).

1993 *Norwegian Fisheries Regulations in Historical Retrospect* (Paper presented to the Man & Biosphere UNESCO conference in Svolvaer, Norway).

1993 "Om rettslige og rettspolitiske sider ved den norske grunnlovs mindretallsgarantier, særlig om avgivelse av suverenitet ved folkeavstemning i forbindelse med tilslutning til EF" ["On Legal and Political Aspects of Norwegian Constitutional Minority Guarantees, with a Special Emphasis on Depletion of Sovereignty by Referendum, by Accession to the European Union"] *Retfaerd* [*Justice*], vol. 62, p. 77.

1991 *Om allemannsrettigheter. Særlig med henblikk på rettsvernet for fiske ved igangsetting og utøving av petroleumsvirksomhet* [*Public Property Rights. With a Special Emphasis on the Conflict between the Fishing and Petroleum Industries*] (Osmundsson, Oslo).

1990 "Hva kom, først høna eller egget," ["What came first, the egg or the hen?"] in Nils Christie (ed.), *Festschrift to Professor Anders Bratholm* (Universitetsforlaget, Oslo).

1986 *Reguleringer i Fisket* [*Fisheries Regulations*] (Marinjuss, Tromsø).

1984 *Norsk havbruksrett* [*Norwegian Ocean Ranching Law*] (Grøndahl, Oslo).

1982 *Konsesjoner i fisket* [*Fisheries Licencing System*]. (TANO, Oslo).

1982 "Norsk fiskerirett; lovverk, hodeverk eller legitimering av markedsstyrt makt?" [Norwegian Fisheries Law; Legal Rules, Headache or the Legitimization of Markets?] *Lov og Rett* [Norwegian Journal of Law & Right] s. 67.

Ørebech, Peter, "Do Fishery Rights Enjoy Human Rights Protection?" (draft paper under Preparation).

Ørebech, Peter, K. Sigurjonsson and Ted L. McDorman, "The 1995 United Nations Straddling and Highly Migratory Fish Stocks Agreement: Management, Enforcement and Dispute Settlement" (May 1998) *The International Journal of Marine and Coastal Law*, No. 2, p. 119.

Osherenko, Gail, "Indigenous Political and Property Rights and Economic/ Environmental Reform in Northwest Siberia" (1995) *Post-Soviet Geography*, vol. 36, p. 225.

Ostrom, Elinor:

2001 "Reformulating the Commons," in Joanna Burger et al. (eds.), *Protecting the Commons: A Framework for Resource Management in the Americas* (Island Press, Washington DC).

1992 *Crafting Institutions for Self-Governing Irrigation Systems* (ICS Press, San Francisco, CA).

1990 *Governing the Commons: The Evolution of Institutions for Collective Action* (Cambridge University Press, Cambridge), pp. 24, 88–89, 206.

Ostrom, Elinor, et al., *Rules Games and Common-Pool Resources* (University of Michigan Press, Ann Arbor, 1994).

Ostrom, Elinor, Thomas Dietz, Nives Dolsak, Paul C. Stern, Susan Stonich and Elke U. Weber (eds.), *The Drama of the Commons Committee on the Human Dimensions of Global Change* (National Research Council, National Academy Press, Washington DC, 2002).

Ostrom, Vincent, *The Meaning of Democracy and the Vulnerability of Democracies. A Response to Tocqueville's Challenge* (Michigan University Press, Ann Arbor, 1997).

Övrelid, Ragnhild, *Demokrati eller rettssikkerhet?* [*Democracy or Rule of Law?*] (Universitetsforlaget, Oslo, 1984).

Oxfam GB, div. of Oxfam International, Ltd., at www.oxfam.org.uk/landrights/intro.htm. (22 March 2000).

Pagès, G., *The Thirty Years War* 1618–1648 (Harper & Row, New York, 1970).

Paine, Robert, *Herds of the Tundra* (Smithsonian Institution Press, London, 1994).

Parker, V. T. and S. T. A. Pickett, "Restoration as an Ecosystem Process: Implications of the Modern Ecological Paradigm," in Krystyna M. Urbanska et al. (eds.), *Restoration Ecology and Sustainable Development* (Cambridge University Press, Cambridge, 1997).

Pawluk, Roman R., "The Role of Indigenous Soil Knowledge in Agricultural Development" (1992) *Soil and Water Conservation*, vol. 47, p. 298.

Payoyo, Peter Bautista, "Cries of the Sea," in Payoyo, *World Inequality, Sustainable Development and the Common Heritage of Humanity* (Martinus Nijhoff, Dordrecht, Boston, Lancaster, 1997).

Pearce, D. W., et al., *Blueprint for a Green Economy* (Earthscan, London, 1989).

Petersen, Hanne

2000 "The Lion King and the Lady and the Unicorn. Jurisprudential Considerations on Visual Normativity," in Alberto Febbrajo, David Nelken and Vittorio Olgiati (eds.), *European Yearbook in the Sociology of Law. Social Processes and Patterns of Legal Control* (Giuffré Publisher, Milan).

1998 "50 år efter Den Juridiske Ekspedition – Spredte refleksioner over kolonier, køn og ret," in Blume and Ketscher (eds.), *Ret og skønsomhed i en overgangstid). Festskrift til Agnete Weis Bentzon* (Akademisk Forlag, Copenhagen).

1998 "'The Best of Two Worlds' – Pluralism or Ambivalence in Norms and Values." (Paper presented for the 11th Inuit Studies Conference, September 1998, Nuuk (unpublished).)

Petersen, Hanne and Birger Poppel (eds.), *Dependency, Autonomy, Sustainability in the Arctic* (Ashgate, Burlington, 1999).

Petersen, Hanne and Jacob Janussen (eds.), *Retsforhold og samfund i Grønland.* (Atuagkat, Nuuk, 1998).

Pinkerton, Evelyn, "Attaining Better Fisheries Management through Co-management – Prospects, Problems, and Propositions," in Evelyn Pinkerton (ed.), *Co-operative Management of Local Fisheries* (University of British Columbia Press, Vancouver, 1989).

Platou, Oscar, *Forelæsninger over Retskildernes Theori* [*Lectures in the Theory of Legal Sources*] (T. O. Brøgger, Kristiana, 1915).

Plucknett, Theodore F. T., *A Concise History of the Common Law* (5th edn., Little Brown, Boston, 1956).

Pocock, J. G. A., *The Ancient Constitution and the Feudal Law. English Historical Thought in the Seventeenth Century* (Norton, New York, 1967).

Pollock, Sir Frederick, "The Science of Case Law (Essays in Jurisprudence and Ethics, 1882)," in A. L. Goodhart (ed.), *Jurisprudence and Legal Essays* (London, 1961).

Poos, L. R. and Lloyd Bonfield (eds.), *Selected Cases in Manorial Courts 1250–1550* (Seldon Society, London, 1998).

Postema, Gerald J., *Bentham and The Common Law Tradition* (Clarendon Press, Oxford, 1986).

Potts, Rick, *Humanity's Descent: The Consequences of Ecological Instability* (William Marrow and Company, New York, 1996).

Pound, Roscoe, *Law and Morals* (Chapel Hill, 1926).

Poundstone, William, *Prisoner's Dilemma* (Anchor Books, New York, 1993).

U.S. President's Council for Sustainable Development (PCSD) established on June 29, 1993 by Executive Order 12852 that in 1996 endorsed the Brundtland Commission's definition.

Price, Richard, *Two Tracts on Civil Liberty in Political Writings* (ed. by D. O. Thomas, Cambridge University Press, Cambridge, 1991).

Price, Victoria Curzon, "Treating Protection as a Pollution Problem or How to Prevent GATT's Retreat from Multilateralism," in Thomas Oppermann and Josef Molsberger (eds.), *A New GATT for the Nineties and Europe '92* (Nomos, Baden-Baden, 1991).

Princen, T. and M. Finger, *Environmental NGOs in World Politics* (Routledge, London, 1994).

Prugh, Thomas, *Natural Capital and Human Economic Survival* (2nd edn., ISEE Press, Solomon MD, 1999).

Prystupa, Mark V., "Barriers and Strategies to the Development of Co-Management Regimes in New Zealand: The Case of Te-Waihora" *Human Organization*, vol. 57, no. 2, p. 134.

Ræstad, Arnold:

1913 *Om gyldigheten av lokal sedvanerett efter norsk ret* [*About the Validity of Local Customary Law according to Norwegian Law*].

1912 *Kongens Strømme. Historiske og folkerettslige undersøkelser angaaende sjøterritoriet* [*Kings' Streams. Historical and International Law Investigations Regarding the Territorial Sea*] (Doctoral thesis, Kristiana).

Random House Dictionary of the American Language, Unabridged (2nd edn., New York, 1987).

Ranger, Terence "The Invention of Tradition in Colonial Africa," in Eric Hobsbawm and Terence Ranger (eds.), *The Invention of Tradition* (Cambridge University Press, Cambridge, 1983).

Rappaport, Roy, *Pigs for the Ancestors* (2nd edn., Yale University Press, New Haven CT, 1984).

Rasmussen, Knud, *Myter og Sagn fra Grønland* (Gyldendalske Boghhandel, Nordisk Forlag, 1925). The translation is taken from "Eskimo Folk-tales" collected by Knud Rasmussen and selected and translated by W. Worster (Gyldendal, Copenhagen and Christiania, 1921).

Rawls, John, *A Theory of Justice* (Oxford University Press, Oxford, 1973).

Rehof, Lars Adam and Tyge Trier, *Menneskerett* [*Human Rights*] (Jurist-og, Økonomforbundets forlag, Copenhagen, 1990).

Reid, Thomas:

1990 *Practical Ethics* (ed. by Knud Haakonssen, Princeton University Press, Princeton).

1983 *The Works of Thomas Reid* (ed. by Sir William Hamilton, reprint with intro. by Harry M. Bracken, Georg Olms Verlag, Hildeshein, 1983). *The Works* include:

– *Inquiry into the Human Mind.*

– *Essays on the Intellectual Powers of Man.*

– *Essays on the Active Powers of Man.*

Rieser, Allison:

1999 "Prescriptions for the Commons: Environmental Scholarship and the Fishing Quotas Debate" *Harvard Environmental Law Review*, vol. 23, p. 393.

1997 "Property Rights and Ecosystem Management in U.S. Fisheries: Contracting for the Commons?" *Law Quarterly*, vol. 24, p. 813.

Renner, Karl, *The Institutions of Private Law and their Social Functions* (1904 reprint, Routledge, London, 1949).

Renouf, M. A. P., *Prehistoric Coastal Economy in Varangerfjord, North Norway* (University of Cambridge, 1981).

Ribot, Jesse C., "Representation and Accountability in Decentralized Sahelian Forestry: Legal Instruments of Political-Administrative Control" (2000), *Georgetown International Environmental Law Review*, vol. 12, p. 447.

Ricoeur, Paul, "The Plurality of Sources of Law" (1994) *Ratio Juris* vol. 7 no. 3, p. 272.

Rieser, Alison, "Ecological Preservation as a Property Right: An Emerging Doctrine in Search of a Theory" (1991) *Harvard Environmental Law Review*, vol. 15, p. 393.

Rink, Henrik, *Tales and Traditions of the Eskimo* (C. Hurst & Company: London. Arnold Busck International Booksellers, Copenhagen, 1875/1974).

Rode, Fredrik, *Optegnelser fra Finmarken, samlede i Aarene 1826–1834: og senere udgivne som et Bidrag til Finmarkens Statistik* [*Notes from Finmarken assembled in the Years 1826–1834*] (Skien, 1842).

Rodgers Jr., William H.:

1994 "Adaptation of Environmental Law to the Ecologists' Discovery of Disequilibria" (1994) *Chicago-Kent Law Review*, vol. 69, p. 887.

1994 *Environmental Law* (2nd edn., West Publishing Co., St. Paul MN).

Roepstorff, Andreas, "Sustainability, Knowledge and Knowing What to Do" in Hanne Petersen and Birger Poppel (eds.), *Dependency, Autonomy, and Sustainability in the Arctic* (Ashgate Publishers, Aldershot and Burlington, 1999).

Rose, Carol M.:

2000 "Common Property, Regulatory Property, and Environmental Protection: Comparing Common Pool Resources to Tradable Environmental

Allowances." Paper prepared for delivery at the International Association for the Study of Common Property Resources (Bloomington, Indiana, May–June).

1999 "From Local to Global Commons: Private Property, Common Property, and Hybrid Property Regimes: Expanding the Choices for the Global Commons" *Duke Environmental Law and Policy Forum* vol. 10, p. 45.

1998 "The Several Futures of Property: Of Cyberspace and Folk Tales, Emission Trades and Ecosystems" *Minnesota Law Review*, vol. 83, p. 129.

1994 *Property & Persuasion: Essays on the History, Theory and Rhetoric of Ownership* (Westview Press, Boulder).

1991 "Rethinking Environmental Controls: Management Strategies for Common Resources" *Duke Law Journal* 1.

1986 "The Comedy of the Commons: Custom, Commerce, and Inherently Public Property" *University of Chicago Law Review*, vol. 53, p. 711.

Rose, Deborah Bird:

1997 "Common Property Regimes in Aboriginal Australia: Totemism Revisited," in Peter Larmour (ed.), *The Governance of Common Property in the Pacific Region.* (National Centre for Development Studies, Pacific Policy Paper 19, The Australian National University).

1993 "Reflections on Ecologies for the Twenty-first Century" in Nancy M. Williams and Graham Baines (eds.), *Traditional Ecological Knowledge: Wisdom for Sustainable Development* (Centre for Resource and Environmental Studies, Australian National University).

Rosen, Mark D., "Multiple Authoritative Interpreters of Quasi-Constitutional Federal Law: Of Tribal Courts and the Indian Civil Rights Act" (November, 2000) *Fordham Law Review*, vol. 69, p. 479.

Ross, Alf:

1959 *On Law and Justice* (University of California Press, Berkley, CA).

1958 *On Law and Justice* (Steven and Sons Ltd., London).

1966 *Dansk Statsforfatningsret* [*Danish Constitutional Law*] (Nyt Nordisk forlag, Copenhagen), vol. 1.

1953 *Om Ret og Retfärdighed* (Nyt Nordiskforlag Arnold Busck, Copenhagen).

Rousseau, Jean Jacques:

(1913) *A Discourse on the Origin of Equality* (transl. by G. D. H. Cole, J. M. Dent & Sons Ltd, London).

1988 *The Social Contract* (Prometheus Books, New York, 1988).

Ruddle, Kenneth, "Local Knowledge in the Folk Management of Fisheries and Coastal Marine Environments," in Christopher L. Dyer and James R. McGoodwin (eds.), *Folk Management in the World's Fisheries: Lessons for Modern Fisheries Management* (University Press of Colorado, Niwot CO, 1994).

Ruhl, J. B., "Thinking of Environmental Law as a Complex Adaptive System: How to Clean up the Environment by Making a Mess of Environmental Law" (1997) *Houston Law Review*, vol. 34, p. 933.

Rumelt, Richard P., Dan E. Schendel and David J. Teece, "Fundamental Issues in Strategy," in *Fundamental Issues in Strategy: A Research Agenda* (Harvard Business School Press, Cambridge MA, 1994).

Runge, Carlisle Ford, "Common Property Externalities: Isolation, Assurance, and Resource Depletion in a Traditional Grazing Context" (1981) *American Journal of Agricultural Economics*, vol. 63, p. 595.

Ruong, Israel, "Saami Usage and Customs," in Birgitta Jahrestrog (ed.), The Saami National Minority in Sweden (The Legal Rights Foundation, Stockholm, 1982).

Rynning, Lorents, *Allemandsret og særret. Belyst ved forskjellige arter av raadighet over fremmed grund, som ikke gaar ind under de almindelige bruksrettigheter* [*Public Property Right and Possessory Rights*] (Oslo, 1928).

Safina, Carl, *Song for the Blue Ocean* (Henry Holt & Co, New York, 1997).

Sagdahl, Bjørn, *Fjordressurser og Reguleringspolitikk* [*Fjord-resources and Regulation Policies*]. Specifically Peter Ørebech, "Sedvanerett som grunnlag for bærekraftig forvaltning av fiske i de "ytre almenninger" [Customary Law as a Foundation for Sustainable Fishing Management]. (Kommuneforlaget, Oslo, 1998).

Salmond, John:

1924 *Jurisprudence* (Sweet & Maxwell, London).

1957 *Jurisprudence* (11th edn., Sweet & Maxwell, London).

Salwasser, Hal, "Ecosystem Management: A New Perspective for National Forests and Grasslands," in Jennifer Aley et al. (eds.), *Ecosystem Management: Adaptive Strategies for Natural Resources Organizations in the Twenty-First Century* (Taylor & Francis, Philadelphia PA, 1999).

von Savigny, Carl Friedrich:

1834 *Geschichte des Römischen Rechts im Mittelalter* (J. C. B. Mohr, Heidelberg, 1834).

1840 *System des heutigen Römischen Recht* (Weit und Comp., Berlin, 1840) transl. by W. Holloway, as *System of Modern Roman Law* (J. Higginbottom, Madras, 1867).

1814 *Von Beruf unserer Zeit für Gesetzgebung und Rechtswissenschaft* (Heidelberg, 1814), transl. by Abram Hayward, *Of the Vocation of our Age for Legislation and Jurisprudence* (Littlewood & Co., London 1831).

Sax, Joseph L.:

1989 "The Limits of Private Rights in Public Waters." *Environmental Law*, vol. 19.

1980 "Liberating the Public Trust Doctrine from Its Historical Shackles" *University of California Davia Law Review*, vol. 14, p. 185.

Schlicht, Ekkehart, *On Custom in the Economy* (Clarendon Press, Oxford, 1998).

Schluter, Dolph, *The Ecology of Adaptive Radiation* (Oxford University Press, Oxford, 2000).

Scott, A., "The Fishery: The Objectives of Sole Ownership" (1955) *Journal of Political Economy*, vol. 63, p. 116.

Scott, Anthony D., "Conceptual Origins of Rights-Based Fishing," in Philip A. Neher, Ragnar Arnason and Nina Mollet (eds.), *Rights-Based Fishing* (Kluwer Academic Publishers, Dordrecht, 1989).

Scott, J., *Seeing Like a State* (Yale University Press, New Haven, 1998).

Searle, John R., "Contemporary Philosophy in the United States" in Nicholas Bunnin and E. P. Tsui-James (eds.), *The Blackwell Companion to Philosophy* (Blackwells, Oxford, 1996).

Sedjo, Roger A. and David Simpson, "Property Rights, Externalities and Biodiversity," in Timothy M. Swanson (ed.), *The Economics and Ecology of Biodiversity Decline: The Forces Driving Global Change* (Cambridge University Press, Cambridge, 1995).

Segalla, Paolo, "The Oil Palms of Southern Benin: Indigenous Knowledge and Agroforestry Developments" (1999) *Agroforestry Today*, vol. 11, p. 5.

Seligman, Edwin R. A. (ed.), *Encyclopaedia of the Social Sciences* (Macmillan Company, New York, 1930), vol. 4.

Sen, Amartya, *Poverty and Famine: An Essay on Entitlement and Deprivation* (Clarendon Press, Oxford, 1982).

Shafer, Craig L., "Terrestrial Nature Reserve Design at the Urban/Rural Interface," in Mark W. Schwartz (ed.), *Conservation in Highly Fragmented Landscapes* (n.p., 1997).

Sheleff, Leon, *The Future of Tradition. Customary Law, Common Law, and Legal Pluralism* (Frank Cass, London and Portland, Oregon 2000).

Siegel, Sharon R., "Applying the Habitat Conservation Model to Fisheries Management: A Proposal for a Modified Fisheries Planning Requirement" (2000), *Columbia Journal of Environmental Law*, vol. 32, p. 141.

Simberloff, Daniel, "Flagships, Umbrellas, and Keystones: Is Single-Species Management Passé in the Landscape Era" (1998) *Biological Conservation*, vol. 83, p. 247.

Simpson, Brian, *The Common Law and Legal Theory* (ed. by William Twining, Basil Blackwell, Oxford, 1986).

Sinclair, Murray, "Aboriginal Peoples and Euro-Canadians: Two World Views," in John Hylton (ed.), *Aboriginal Self-Government in Canada. Current Trends and Issues* (Purich Publishing, Saskatoon, 1994).

Skinner, Quentin, *Liberty before Liberalism* (Cambridge University Press, Cambridge, 1998).

Slattery, Brian, "The Land Rights of Indigenous Canadian Peoples, as Affected by the Crown's Acquisition of their Territories" (Unpublished D.Phil. thesis, Oxford, 1979).

Smellie, K. B., "Sir Henry Maine" *Economica*, vol. 8, p. 64.

Smith, Carsten:

1990 "Rettslige forpliktelser myndighetene er bundet av overfor den Sammiske befolkningen ved regulering av fiske" ["The Governmental Agencies' Legal Obligations toward Saami Fisheries Rights"] *Legal Report for Ministry of Fisheries.*

1987 *Samerett – gamle rettskilder og ny rettsdisiplin* [*Saami Law – Ancient Courses of Law and a New Legal Discipline*] No. 1 (Institutt for rettsvitenskap skriftserie, Tromsö).

Smith, Clifford W., "Non-Native Plants, in Conservation Biology" in Charles P. Stone and Danielle B. Stone (eds.), *Hawai'i* (1989), 60.

Snyder, F., *Capitalism and Legal Change* (Academic Press, New York, 1981).

Solem, Erik, *Lappiske rettsstudier [Saami Legal Studies].* (Universitetsforlaget, Oslo, 1970).

Solnørdal, O., *Den trønderske almenningsretten i gamalnorsk tid.* [*The Ancient Trøndelag (law district of Mid Norway) Common Pool Legislation*] TfR (1933).

Sørensen, Axel Kjær, "Greenland: From Colony to Home Rule," in Sven Tägil (ed.), *Ethnicity and Nation Building in the Nordic World* (University of Southern Illinois Press, Carbondale, Ill., 1995).

Soulé, Michael E., "The Social Siege of Nature," in Michael E. Soulé and Gary Lease, (eds.), *Responses to Postmodern Destruction* (n.p., 1995).

Spender, J. C., *Industry Recipes: An Enquiry into the Nature and Sources of Managerial Judgement* (Basil Blackwell, Oxford and New York, 1989).

Spiertz, H. L. J., "The Transformation of Traditional Law: A Tale of People's Participation in Irrigation Management on Bali" (1991) *Landscape and Urban Planning*, vol. 20, p. 189.

Stein, Bruce A. et al., "A Remarkable Array: Species Diversity in the United States," in Bruce A. Stein et al. (eds.), *Precious Heritage: The Status of Biodiversity in the United States* (Oxford University Press, Oxford, 2000).

Stevens, Jan S., "The Public Trust: A Sovereign's Ancient Prerogative Becomes the People's Environmental Right" (1980) *University of California Davis Law Review*, vol. 14, p. 195.

Stevenson, Leslie, "Why Believe What People Say?" (1993) *Synthese*, vol. 94, p. 429.

Stewart, Hilary *Indian Fishing. Early Methods on the Northwest Coast* (Douglas & McIntyre, Vancouver, 1982).

Stewart, Julie, "Untying the Gordian Knot! *Murisa v. Murisa* S–41–92, a Little More Than a Case Note" (1992) *Legal Forum*, vol. 4, p. 92.

Stoffle, Brent W. et al., "Folk Management and Conservation Ethics Among Small-Scale fishers of Buen Hombre, Dominican Republic," in Christopher L. Dyer and James R. McGoodwin (eds.), *Folk Management in the World's Fisheries* (University Press of Colorado, Niwot, CO, 1994).

Stone, Charles P., "Non-Native Land Vertebrates," in Charles P. Stone and Danielle B. Stone (eds.), *Conservation Biology in Hawai'i* (1989).

Story, J., "A Report of the Commissioners Appointed to Consider and Report Upon the Practicability and Expediency of Reducing to a Written and Systematic Code the Common Law of Massachusetts, or any Part thereof; made to His Excellency the Governor," January 1837, in *The Miscellaneous Writing of Joseph Story* (1951).

Strömholm, Stig, *Rätt, Rättskällor och Rättstillämpning* (Stockholm, 1996).

Sullivan, Paul, "Customary Revolutions: The Law of Custom and the Conflict of Traditions in Hawaii" (1999) *University of Hawaii Law Review*, vol. 20, p. 99.

Sundby, Nils Kristian:

1976 *Om normer* [*On norms*] (Universitetsforlaget, Oslo).

1969 "Legal Right in Scandinavian Analyses" *Natural Law Forum* (Notre Dame University).

Sunstein, Cass R.:

2001 *Designing Democracy. What Constitutions Do* (Oxford University Press, Oxford).

1994 "Public versus Private Environmental Regulation" *Ecology Law Quarterly*, vol. 21, p. 455.

Sustainable Development Summit Concludes in Johannesburg: UN Secretary-General Kofi Annan Says It's Just the Beginning, at http://www.johannesburgsummit.org/html/whats_new/feature_story39.htm#top.

Svensson, Tom G.:

1976 *Ethnicity and Mobilization in Saami Politics* (Stockholm Studies in Social Anthropology, Stockholm).

1982 "Local Communities in the South Saami Region," in Birgitta Jahreskog (ed.), The Saami National Minority in Sweden (The Legal Rights Foundation, Stockholm, 1982).

Takahashi, Nobuo, *Design of Adaptive Organizations* (Springer-Verlag, New York, 1987).

Tang, Shui Yan, *Institutions and Collective Action: Self-Governance in Irrigation* (n.p., 1992).

Tarlock, A. Dan:

2002 "Who Owns Science?" *Pennsylvania State Environmental Review*, vol. 10, p. 135.

2001 "Ideas Without Institutions: The Paradox of Sustainable Development" *Indiana Journal of Global Legal Studies*, vol. 9, Fall, p. 35.

1999 "Can Cowboys Become Indians: Protecting Western Communities as Endangered Cultural Remnants" *Arizona State Law Journal*, vol. 31, p. 539.

1996 "Environmental Law: Ethics or Science" *Duke Environmental Law & Policy Forum* vol. 7, p. 193.

1994 "City Versus Countryside: Environmental Equity in Context" *Fordham Urban Law Journal*, vol. 21, p. 461.

1994 "The Nonequilibrium Paradigm in Ecology and the Partial Unraveling of Environmental Law" *Loyola of Los Angeles Law Review*, vol. 27, p. 1121.

1992 "Environmental Protection: The Potential Misfit Between Equity and Efficiency" *Colorado Law Review*, vol. 63, p. 871.

Tevesham, T. F. (trans.), Court Rolls of the Manor of Dernford Sawston in the County of Cambridge for the Years 1336–1360, B.Sc., from the original rolls at Sawston Hall, Sawston, 1965, copy provided to the author by David Hall, solicitor and partner (Linklaters and Paynes, London, and Lord of the Manor of Littleport, June 1999).

Thayer, James Bradley, *A Preliminary Treatise of Evidence* (Little, Brown & Co., Boston, 1896).

Thomas John Henry and John Farquahar Fraser (eds.), *Sir Edward Coke: Reports* (Original edn., London 1826, new print, Lawbook Exchange Ltd, 2003, vol. iv).

Thompson Jr., Barton H., "People or Prairie Chickens: The Uncertain Search for Optimal Biodiversity" (1999) *Stanford Law Review*, vol. 51, p. 1127.

Thuen, Trond, *Quest for Equity. Norway and the Saami Challenge* (ISER 1995).

Tietenberg, Tom, "The Tradable Permits Approach to Protecting the Commons: What Have We Learned?" Paper prepared for delivery at the International Association for the Study of Common Property conference (Bloomington, Indiana, May–June, 2000).

de Tocqueville, Alexis:

1987 *Democracy in America* (HarperPerennial, New York).

1960 *A Biographical Study in Political Science* (Harper, New York).

1956 *Democracy in America* (Mentor Books, New York and Ontario), 114 ff.

Tønneson, Sverre, *Retten til jorden i Finnmark. Rettsreglene om den såkalte "statens umatrikulerte grunn" – en undersøkelse med særlig sikte på sameness rettigheter* [*The Possessory Right to Finnmark. The Rules of the Public Land – with the emphasis on Saami Legal Rights*] (Universitetsforlaget, Oslo, 1979).

Tubbs, J. W., "Custom, Time and Reason: Early Seventeenth-Century Conceptions of the Common Law," (1998) *History of Political Thought*, vol. 19, pp. 363 ff.

Tuck, Richard, *The Rights of War and Peace. Political Thought and the Internatinal Order from Grotius to Kant* (Oxford University Press, Oxford, 1999).

Udenrigspolitisk Redegørelse fra Grønlands (Landsstyre, 1993).

Ullman, Walter:

1946 *The Medieval Idea of Law as Presented by Lucas de Pena. A Study in Fourteenth-Century Legal Scholarship* (London).

1940 "Bartolus on Customary Law", *The Juridical Review*, vol. 52, p. 265.

United Nations:

Protection & Preservation of the Marine Environment: Report of the Secretary General Doc. A/44/461 (18 September 1989).

UN Doc.1976/A/31/10 p. 226. Environment and Sustainable Development. Implementation of Agenda 21 and the program for further implementation of Agenda 21.

UN Docs. A/C.6/31/SR.13-33. Article 37, in casu 11th September 2003. To date 100 states have acceded. See http://www.biodiv.org/biosafety/default.aspx

UN General Assembly, A 57/532/Add.1.

UN Straddling Fish Stocks Agreement (1995) In force as of 21 November 2001. According to Article 40(1), the Agreement entered into force 30 days after the date of deposit of the 30th instrument of ratification or accession.

US Census Bureau, the Native Hawaiian and other Pacific Islander Population: 2000 (December, 2001).

United States Commission on Civil Rights: Hawaii Advisory Committee. "A Broken Trust: The Hawaiian Homelands Program: Seventy Years of Failure of the Federal and State Governments to Protect the Civil Rights of Native Hawaiians" (1991).

United States Congress: S. 1783, A Bill expressing the policy of the United States' relationship with Native Hawaiians and to provide for a process for the recognition by the United States of the Native Hawaiian governing entity, and for other purposes. (107th Congress, 1st session, 2001).

United States Department of the Interior and Department of Justice, "From Mauka to Makai: The River of Justice Must Flow Freely: Report of the Reconciliation Process between the Federal Government and Native Hawaiians" (2000).

United States Senate Committee on Appropriations, Special Hearing of Federally Funded Native Hawaiian Programs, August 16, 1999 (106th Congress, 1st Session).

United States Senate Committee on Indian Affairs, Statement of Eni F. H. Faleomaraega, hearing (September 14, 2000).

Urbanska, Krystyna M. et al. (eds.), *Restoration Ecology and Sustainable Development* in V. T. Parker and S. T. A. Pickett, "Restoration as an ecosystem process: implications of the modern ecological paradigm" (Cambridge University Press, 1997).

Ussing, Henry, *Aftaler* [*Agreements*] (G. E. C. Gads, Copenhagen, 1955).

Verheggen, Claudine, "Davidson's Second Person" (1997) *The Philosophical Quarterly*, vol. 47, p. 361.

Versluis, Arthur, *Sacred Earth: The Spiritual Landscape of Native America* (Inner Traditions International, Rochester VT, 1992).

Vinogradoff, Paul, *Common Sense in Law* (Oxford University Press, London, 1959).

Waldman, Theodore, "Origins of the Legal Doctrine of Reasonable Doubt" (1959) *Journal of the History of Ideas*, vol. 20, p. 299.

Walsøe, Per, "Grønlands kredsretter," in Blume and Ketscher (eds.), *Ret og skønsomhed i en overgangstid. Festskrift til Agnete Weis Bentzon* (Akademisk Forlag, Copenhagen, 1998).

Walsøe, Per and Kirsten Trolle, "Det grønlandske retsvæsen indsigter og udsigter," in Hanne Petersen and Jacob Janussen (eds.), *Retsforhold og samfund i Grønland* (Atuagkat, Nuuk, 1998).

Walters, Carl, *Adaptive Management of Renewable Resources* (Macmillan, 1986).

Ward, R. Gerald, "Changing forms of communal tenure," in Peter Larmour (ed.), *The Governance of Common Property in the Pacific Region* (Australian National University National Centre for Development Studies, Canberra, 1997).

Ward, William and Priscilla Weeks, "Resource Managers and Resource Users: Field Biologists and Stewardship," in Christopher L. Dyer and James R. McGoodwin (eds.), *Folk Management in the World's Fisheries* (University Press of Colorado, Niwot CO, 1994).

Watson, Reg and Daniel Pauly, "Systematic Distortions in World Fisheries Catch Trends" (2001) *Nature*, vol. 414, p. 534.

Watson, Robert T. et al., *Annual Review of Environment Matters at the World Bank* (World Bank Report No. 20104, 1999).

Westerlund, Steffan, *Rätt och miljö [Law and Environment]* (Carlssons, Stockholm, 1988).

Westley, Frances, "Governing Design: The Management of Social Systems and Ecosystem Management," in Lance H. Gunderson, et al. (eds.), *Barriers and Bridges to the Renewal of Ecosystems and Institutions* (Columbia University Press, New York, 1995).

Westskog, Hege, *Market Power in a System of Tradable CO_2 Quotas* (SUM Oslo, 1996).

Wetterstein, Peter, "Damage from International Disasters in the Light of Tort and Insurance Law," General Reports to the 8 World Congress on Insurance Law, The World Commission on Environment and Development, *Our Common Future 1987* (United Nations, 1990).

Wharton, Francis, *Commentaries on Law* (Kay & Brother, Philadelphia, 1884).

White, Neville and Betty Meehan, "Traditional Ecological Knowledge: A Lens on Time," in Nancy M. Williams and Graham Baines (eds.), *Traditional Ecological Knowledge: Wisdom for Sustainable Development* (Centre for Resource and Environmental Studies, Australian National University, Canberra, 1993).

White, T. Anderson and Jon L. Jickling, "Peasants, experts, and land use in Haiti: Lessons from indigenous and project technology" (1995) *Soil and Water Conservation*, 7, 13.

Whitney, Gordon G., *From Coastal Wilderness to Fruited Plain: A History of Environmental Change in Temperate North America 1500 to the Present* (Cambridge University Press, Cambridge, 1994), pp. 98–120.

Whittaker, Robert J., *Island Biogeography: Ecology, Evolution, and Conservation* (Oxford University Press, Oxford, 1998).

Wilkins, David P., "Linguistic Evidence in Support of a Holistic Approach to Traditional Ecological Knowledge," in Nancy M. Williams and Graham Baines (eds.), *Traditional Ecological Knowledge: Wisdom for Sustainable Development* (Australian National University Centre for Resource and Environmental Studies, Canberra, 1993).

5 Willistone, *Law of Contracts* (7–11), (Jaeger 3rd. edn. 1961), p. 649.

Wilmsen, Edwin M. (ed.), *We Are Here: Politics of Aboriginal Land Tenure* (University of California Press, Berkley, Calif., 1989).

Wilson, James A. et al., "Chaos, Complexity and Community Management of Fisheries" (1994) *Marine Policy*, vol. 18, p. 291.

Women's Party Site at www. arnat.gl.

Woodman, Gordon R., "Customary Laws and Customary Legal Rights: A Comparative Consideration of Their Nature and of the Relationship Between Laws" (11–12 February 1999) *Saami Customary Law Seminar*.

Woozley, A. D., "The Existence of Rules" (1967) *Nous*, vol. 1, p. 63.

World Bank:

1994 The World Bank and Participation (Operations Policy Department, World Bank, September 1994).

1996 World Bank Participation Source Book (Environment Department, World Bank, February 1996).

1989 World Bank, *Sub Saharan Africa: From Crisis to Sustainable Growth* (1989).

World Commission on Environment and Development, *Our Common Future.* (United Nations and Oxford University Press, New York, 1987). Adopted by the General Assembly Resolution 44/228 of 22 December 1989.

World Trade Organization (WTO) June 17th 2004 the number of Member States are 147, at http://www.wto.org/english/thewto_e/whatis_e/tif_e/org6_e.htm.

World Trade Organization, Sanitary and Phytosanitary Agreement.

Yelling, J. A., *Common Field and Enclosure in England 1450–1850* (Archon Books, Hamden, Conn., 1977).

Yolton, John, "Action: Metaphysics and Modality" (1973) *American Philosophical Quarterly*, vol. 10, p. 71.

Zahle, Henrik, *Dansk statsforfatningsret* [*Danish Constitutional Law*] (Christian Ejler's Forlag, Copenhagen, 1989), vol. 1.

Zavaleta, Erika, "The Emergence of Waterfowl Conservation Among Yup'ik Hunters in the Yukon-Kuskokwim Delta, Alaska" (1999) *Human Ecology*, vol. 27, p. 231.

Zerner, Charles:
1994 "Through a Green Lens; the Construction of Customary Environmental Law and Community in Indonesia's Maluku Islands" *Law and Society Review*, vol. 28, p. 1080.
1994 "Tracking Sasi: the Transformation of a Central Moluccan Reef Management Institution in Indonesia," in Alan T. White et al. (eds.), *Collaborative and Community-Based Management of Coral Reefs: Lessons from Experience* (Kumarian Press, West Hartford CT).

INDEX

AUTHORS INDEX